THE GERMAN EMPIRE
1867—1914
AND THE UNITY MOVEMENT

THE MACMILLAN COMPANY
NEW YORK · BOSTON · CHICAGO · DALLAS
ATLANTA · SAN FRANCISCO

MACMILLAN & CO., LIMITED
LONDON · BOMBAY · CALCUTTA
MELBOURNE

THE MACMILLAN CO. OF CANADA, LTD.
TORONTO

THE
GERMAN EMPIRE
1867—1914
AND THE UNITY MOVEMENT

BY

WILLIAM HARBUTT DAWSON *1860 -*

Author of "The Evolution of Modern Germany," "Germany
and the Germans," "Municipal Life and Government
in Germany," etc., etc.

IN TWO VOLUMES

VOLUME II

New York
THE MACMILLAN COMPANY
1919

COPYRIGHT, 1919

BY THE MACMILLAN COMPANY

Set up and electrotyped.   Published, May, 1919

CONTENTS OF CHAPTERS

CHAPTER XIII

(1879–1887)

PROTECTION AND FISCAL REFORM

Protection a National Tradition, 1 — The Customs Union, 2 — The Free Trade Movement, 3 — Causes of the Return to Protection, 6 — The Bubble Company Era, 7 — Industrial Depression in the 'Seventies, 9 — Bismarck's Fiscal Theories, 10 — Changes in the Government, 11 — The Imperial Taxation System, 15 — Formation of the Free Economic Union, 18 — Introduction of the Tariff Bill, 20 — Attitude of the National Liberals, 22 — Counter-action of the Clericals, 22 — The Franckenstein Compromise, 24 — Entrance of Hamburg and Bremen into the Customs Union, 28 — The Tariff Amended, 31 — The Railway Nationalization Movement, 32.

CHAPTER XIV

(1871–1890)

SOCIAL ADJUSTMENTS

Commercial Development after the War of 1870–1, 35 — Discovery of the Social Question, 38 — Bismarck and Social Reform, 39 — His Attitude towards Questions of Work and Wages, 40 — The Social Insurance Laws, 42 — Attitude of the Radicals and Socialists, 45 — Labour Law Reforms, 46 — The Organization of the Imperial Province (Alsace-Lorraine), 47 — The Party of Protest, 51 — Grant of Modified Autonomy, 52 — Failure to Conciliate the Population, 54 — The Polish Question, 55 — The Danish Question in North Schleswig, 58 — Moltke's Plea for a Strong Army, 60 — The Peace Strength re-fixed on a Septennial Basis, 63 — German Sea Power after 1871, 66 — Imperial Expenditure, Debt, and Taxation, 68 — The Beer, Tobacco, and Brandy Taxes, 69, 70 — Tobacco and Brandy Monopoly Projects Defeated, 72 — Stagnation of Political Life, 73 — The (Ministerial) Substitute Law of 1878, 74 — Bismarck Misses the Support of the National Liberals, 75 — Herr von Puttkamer and the Manipulation of Elections, 76 — Attack upon the Independence of State Officials, 77 — Retirement of Herr von Bennigsen, 78 — The Lasker Condolence Resolution, 79.

CHAPTER XV

(1871–1887)

FOREIGN RELATIONS — (i) FRANCE

Count Beust on the Events of 1866 and 1870, 81 — Attitude of the Powers towards France, 81 — M. Thiers on French Policy, 82 — Bismarck's

Fear of Isolation, 83 — German Relations with Russia, 84 — Overtures to Austria-Hungary, 86 — Count Beust succeeded by Count Andrassy, 86 — The *Drei-Kaiser-Bund,* 87 — Italy joins in a Quadruple Entente, 90 — The Recovery of France, 91 — Count Harry Arnim, 91 — Bismarck's Policy towards France, 91 — M. Thiers gives place to Marshal MacMahon, 94 — Activity of the French Clericals, 94 — Quarrel between Bismarck and Arnim, 95 — Arnim's Dismissal and Humiliation, 97 — Prince Hohenlohe succeeds to the Paris Embassy, 98 — Germany and the Carlist Excesses, 99 — French Military Measures, 100 — The " Is War in Sight? " Scare, 102 — Bismarck's Complicity Discussed, 103 — Intervention of the Czar and Gortchakoff, 104 —" *Maintenant la paix est assurée,*" 105 — Bismarck Proposes to Resign, 107 — Relations between Germany, France, and England, 108 — French Colonial Enterprises, 110 — Proclamation of a Protectorate in Tunis, 112 — Attitude of the British Government, 112 — A Franco-German *Entente,* 113 — General Boulanger, 114 — Dangerous War Agitation in France, 114 — The German Army Bill of 1886-7, 115 — Subsidence of the Unrest in France, 117.

CHAPTER XVI

(1875–1885)

FOREIGN RELATIONS — (ii) THE EASTERN QUESTION

Lord Aberdeen's Prediction of the Effects of the Crimean War, 119 — Changes in the Balkans, 119 — Revival of the Eastern Question, 120 —" The German Way of Looking at Things," 120 — Revolt of Herzegovina and Bosnia in 1875, 121 — The Andrassy Note, 122 — Spread of the Revolt, 122 — The Berlin Memorandum of May, 1876, 122 — Disraeli, his Characteristics, 123 — The Anti-Russian Movement in England, 125 — The Bulgarian Atrocities, 126 — Russia and " British Interests," 127 — Outbreak of the Russo-Turkish War, 129 — Division of Opinion in England, 130 — Treaty of San Stefano, 131 — The Anglo-Russian and Anglo-Turkish Secret Treaties, 131, 132 — The Berlin Congress and Treaty, 132 — Territorial Changes Effected by the Treaty, 133 — Bismarck's Part in the Berlin Congress: the " Honest Broker," 136 — Era of German Influence in Turkey begins, 139 — Signs of Russian Estrangement from Germany, 140 — Bismarck and Count Schouvaloff, 141 — Conclusion of the Dual Alliance (Germany and Austria-Hungary) of 1879, 143,— Conversion into the Triple Alliance by the Addition of Italy, 146 — Approaches to Russia, 149 — The Skiernievice Agreements, 150 — Anglo-Russian Frictions in the Far East, 152 — Unsettlement of Bulgaria, 154 — The Egyptian Question, 156 — The Financial Collapse, 157 — Military Mutinies and Arabi's Rebellion, 159 — Bismarck wants Great Britain and France to Settle Egypt alone, 160 — Bombardment of Alexandria, 161 — Bismarck's Attitude towards England Changes, 163 — The Anglo-German Colonial Rivalries, 166 — Did Bismarck advise England to Annex Egypt? 167 — The Mahdi Insurrection and Pacification of the Soudan, 170.

CHAPTER XVII

(1880–1890)

THE COLONIAL ERA

Early Migration of Germanic Tribes, 173 — The Hanseatic League, 174 — Colonial Enterprises of the Great Elector of Brandenburg, 174 — Earliest Emigration to North America, 176 — German Exploration in Africa, 176 — Formation of Societies for Emigration and Colonization, 178 — Schemes of Colonization in the Middle of Last Century, 179 — Bismarck's Attitude towards Colonization in 1866, 1870, and 1873, 180 — Growing Popularity of the Movement, 181 — German Designs in South Africa, 183 — The First Practical Colonial Endeavours, 186 — The Acquisition of Angra Pequena, 188 — Diplomatic Dispute with the British Government, 190 — Invitation to cede Heligoland, 192 — Further Acquisitions in West Africa, 197 — Annexations in the Western Pacific, 199 — The Congo Conference, 204 — The British Attitude towards German Colonial Ambitions, 208 — Annexations in East Africa, 214 — Early Administrative Difficulties, 221.

CHAPTER XVIII

(1888–1890)

BISMARCK — THE LAST PHASE

Death of Emperor William I, 223 — His Character, 224 — Emperor Frederick's Reign of Three Months, 226 — Accession of William II, 231 — A Round of Foreign Visits, 233 — Renewed Conservative Intrigues against Bismarck, 235 — First Signs of Tension between Emperor and Chancellor, 239 — Disagreement over the Socialist Law and the Labour Conference Proposal, 242 — The Prussian Cabinet Order of September 8, 1852, 244 — Bismarck's Despotic Power Broken, 246 — His Forced Resignation, 248 — The Nation takes the ex-Chancellor's Side, 251 — European Opinion of Bismarck's Fall, 252 — Estimate of Bismarck's Character, Political Methods, and Policies, 255 — His Successes and Failures, 268 — Bismarck " a postulate in himself," 270.

CHAPTER XIX

(1890–1900)

EMPEROR WILLIAM II. DOMESTIC AFFAIRS — (i)
THE NEW COURSE

Chancellorship of General von Caprivi, 272 — The Africa-Heligoland Convention of 1890, 272 — Effect of Bismarck's Disappearance, 274 — A New Social Spirit Abroad, 275 — Labour Legislation, 276 — The Caprivi Régime in the Polish Provinces and Alsace-Lorraine, 277 — The Socialists Unreconciled, 279 — Characteristics of the Emperor, 282 — A Reactionary Prussian Education Bill, 284 — Tariff Policy and the Caprivi Treaties, 286 — Rise of the Agrarian League, 289 — Legislation in Favour of Agriculture, 290 — Anti-Semitic Agitation, 292 — Army Bill and Taxation Reforms, 294 — Resignation of Caprivi, 299 — Appointment of Prince Hohenlohe as Chancellor: his

Character, 299 — The Anti-Revolution Bill, 302 — Domestic Legislation, 302 — Defeat of the Penal Servitude Bill, 305 — Naval Expansion, 305 — Resignation of Hohenlohe, 313.

CHAPTER XX

(1900–1914)

EMPEROR WILLIAM II. DOMESTIC AFFAIRS — (ii)
THE REACTION

Chancellorship of Count von Bülow, 316 — His Surrender to the Agrarians,
317 — The Revised Customs Tariff of 1902, 318 — Canal Construction in Prussia, 320 — Expansion of German Transport Facilities,
322 — Development of Industry and Commerce, 323 — Labour Legislation, 324 — A Retrograde Prussian Education Law, 326 — Payment of Members, 326 — The Colonial Empire and Abuses in Administration, 329 — The Herero Insurrection, 330 — The Government
Defeated by a Combination of Clericals and Social Democrats, 331
— A New Diet and the Conservative-Liberal *Bloc*, 333 — Formation
of a Colonial Office, with Dr. Dernburg as First Colonial Secretary,
334 — Progress of the Socialist Movement, 338 — The Personal
Régime, 339 — The Emperor "his own Chancellor," 340 — Slackening of Party Discipline, 343 — The Emperor's Interferences in
Politics, 345 — The *Daily Telegraph* Interview, 346 — Finance and
Taxation Reform, 349 — Resignation of Bülow, 352 — Characteristics,
353 — Growth of the Syndicates, 354 — Land Legislation for the
Prussian Polish Provinces, 355 — Effect of Repressive Measures,
357 — Chancellorship of Herr von Bethmann-Hollweg, 359 — Fric-
tion with the Vatican, 359 — Prussian Electoral Reform Bill
Wrecked, 361 — A Constitution for Alsace-Lorraine, 362 — Military
Excesses at Zabern (Saverne), 365 — Social Legislation, 366 —
Social Democracy and the Revisionist Movement, 367 — Death of
Herr Bebel, 370 — Party Characteristics and Relations, 372 — New
Army Bills, 378 — The Large-Navy Movement, 380 — Reply of the
British Government, 381 — Finance and Taxation, 385.

CHAPTER XXI

(1890–1904)

FOREIGN RELATIONS — (i) *WELTPOLITIK*

Bismarck's Policy of Consolidation, 388 — His Attitude towards Russia,
389 — Abandonment by Caprivi of the Reinsurance Treaty with
Russia, 390 — Bismarck's Policy towards Austria and Russia, 391 —
Formation of the Franco-Russian Alliance, 394 — Bismarck Discloses
the Reinsurance Treaty, 395 — The Era of *Weltpolitik*, 396 — Germany as a "Saturated State," 397 — The Emperor's Views of Foreign Policy, 398 — Origin of the Pan-German Movement and League,
398 — The Emperor's Telegram to President Krüger, 400 — Anglo-
German African Convention of 1898, 402 — The First Peace Conference of The Hague, 403 — Attitude of Germany in the Boer War,
404 — Acquisition of Kiauchau, 406 — The Boxer Rising in China, 406
— Germany's Attitude in the Russo-Japanese War, 408 — The Manilla
Incident, 410 — Purchase of the Caroline Islands from Spain, 410 —
Relations with the United States, 410 — The Emperor's Visit to Con-

stantinople and Palestine, 412 — The Bagdad Railway Concessions, 412 — German Commercial Penetration of the Turkish Empire, 415 — Great Britain's "Splendid Isolation" and the Policy of *Ententes*, 418 — The Anglo-French Conventions of April, 1904, 419.

CHAPTER XXII

(1904–1906)

FOREIGN RELATIONS — (ii) MOROCCO

Lord Salisbury's Premonition of Danger in Morocco (1891), 422 — Traditional British Policy in Morocco, 422 — The Convention of Madrid, 423 — Increase of French Influence in the Country, 425 — French Partition Proposals Rejected by Spain, 425 — The Anglo-French and Franco-Spanish Conventions of 1904, 426 — The Secret Articles, 427 — Reception of the Anglo-French Convention in England, 430 — Attitude of the German Chancellor, 434 — German Interests in Morocco, 438 — Reports of French Aggression, 440 — Visit of the German Emperor to Tangier, 441 — Secret Treaty concluded at Björkö between Germany and Russia, 443 — Tension between Germany and France, 444 — Resignation of M. Delcassé, 445 — The Algeciras Conference, 446.

CHAPTER XXIII

(1906–1913)

FOREIGN RELATIONS — (iii) THE TRIPLE ENTENTE

Reorientation of European Powers, 450 — British Relations with Russia, 450 — The Anglo-Russian Convention of 1907, 451 — The Triple Entente, 452 — Relations between France and Italy, 453 — Italy's Claim to Tripoli, 454 — Crispi and the Triple Alliance, 455 — The Weakness of *Weltpolitik,* 458 — Departure from Bismarck's Principles, 459 — The Alleged Policy of Encirclement, 461 — Further French Intervention in Morocco, 462 — The Franco-German Agreement of 1909, 464 — Disturbances in Morocco and French Armed Intervention, 464 — The German Gunboat *Panther* lands at Agadir, 466 — Compensation Negotiations between Germany and France, 467 — The British Government's Warning to Germany, 467 — The Final Morocco Settlement, 469 — Opposition of German Public Opinion, 470 — Anglo-French Relations and the Character of the *Entente Cordiale,* 474 — The Suspicions Entertained in Germany, 480 — War Incitements, 481 — The Theory of "Preventive Warfare," 482 — Lord Haldane's visit to Berlin and his Negotiations with the German Government, 484 — Attempts at a Naval Agreement, 486 — The Bagdad Railway Project, 490 — Results of the Berlin Conversations, 494 — British Naval Measures, 497 — A frustrated Colonial Convention, 498.

CHAPTER XXIV

(1913–1914)

FOREIGN RELATIONS — (iv) THE LATTER DAYS

Signs of Political Unrest in Europe, 501 — The Clouds in the East, 501 — Balkan Developments after 1878, 502 — Growth of Serbian Influence,

CONTENTS OF CHAPTERS

503 — Policies of Count Goluchowski and Baron von Aehrenthal, 503, 504 — Austrian Annexation of Bosnia and Herzegovina, 506 — Germany's Warning to Russia, 507 — Austrian Pleas of Justification, 507 — The Young Turk Movement, 509 — Italy's Claim to Tripoli and War with Turkey, 509 — The Balkan League and the First Balkan War, 510 — The London Conferences, 510 — The Second Balkan War, and the Treaty of Bucharest, 511 — German Support of Austria in the Balkans, 513 — Teutonism *versus* Slavism, 513 — William I's abandonment of Bismarck's Oriental Policy, 514 — Serbian Intrigue against Austria, 517 — The Tragedy of Serajevo, 517 — Outbreak of the European War, 520 — Breakdown of the Triple Alliance, 523.

APPENDIX A 525

APPENDIX B 527

INDEX 529

THE GERMAN EMPIRE

CHAPTER XIII

(1879–1887)

PROTECTION AND FISCAL REFORM

SATISFIED that he had put the Socialists in their right place in relation to public law and decorum, Bismarck proceeded to restore order in another part of the national house. The year which followed the passing of the anti-Socialist Law saw the reform of the fiscal system, a task still greater, calling for statesmanship of a more delicate kind and charged with consequences at least as far-reaching, though in other directions.

To regard this episode, as is often done, as an abrupt and violent new departure is to misunderstand and undervalue its significance. The introduction of protective legislation in 1879 was in reality the revival of a national tradition. This tradition had been based on the example of Prussia, where the protection of trade, industry, and agriculture had been the careful aim of public policy from the time of Frederick the Great. Not only did that ruler erect fiscal barriers upon his frontiers for the purpose of restricting imports, but his edicts went so far as to forbid the introduction of every class of goods which could be produced at home, even if less cheaply and of inferior quality. On the other hand, the exportation of raw material was forbidden in the interest of cheap production. By subsidies he established new industries, and encouraged old industries which languished. If the foreigner's goods were not desired, the foreigner himself was welcomed, provided only that he brought with him manufacturing skill and knowledge. The State was ever ready with liberal gifts or temporary loans for the purchase of raw materials, and it was quick to recognize the value of technical training, introducing for the purpose foreign teachers. Agriculture was likewise supported in every suitable way. The

1

great landowners were checked with a firm hand; the small peasant proprietors were encouraged to ways of enterprise and thrift; and the condition of the serfs was ameliorated in the rough spirit of an age to which the ideas of liberty, equality, and fraternity were still alien.

If the material prosperity of the Prussian monarchy was checked between the death of this benevolent autocrat in 1786 and the issue of the Emancipatory Edicts of Stein and Hardenberg, the decline must be attributed in part to the political troubles of the time, but in a larger degree to the untoward fate which placed the destinies of the country for eleven fateful years in the hands of perhaps the weakest member of the Hohenzollern race, Frederick William II, years which saw the abandonment by the Crown of the ardent and unwearying solicitude for the nation's economic welfare which was so important a feature of the earlier strong, if arbitrary, rule.

It has been shown in earlier pages how Prussia, from the second decade of last century forward, after sweeping away the fiscal barriers which prevented the free exchange of commodities within her own territories, won the secondary and minor German States, one by one, for a Customs Union which was intended ultimately to comprehend the whole of Germany proper. By the middle of the century this movement towards fiscal unity had made such progress that of the States comprised in the Germanic Federation only the Mecklenburgs and the Hanseatic Cities, with Austria, remained outside. Without becoming an integral part of the Union, however, Austria concluded a twelve years' treaty with it in February, 1853, on the principle of reciprocal preferential treatment. Within the Union customs duties were levied on the common account, and divided amongst the treaty States according to population.

The Customs Union treaty was renewed for the last time in 1865. No sooner had it been done, however, than it lapsed owing to the succeeding internecine war and the consequent formation of the North German Confederation. In the following year, by treaty between the Confederation and the South German States, a new Union was formed, again for twelve years, with a Customs Parliament consisting of the North German Diet enlarged for customs questions only by the addition of deputies from the South. Four years later the laws and regulations of the Customs Union, as then modified, passed into the legislation of the German Empire, which had just been established, and became substantially the basis of the fiscal system which lasted until 1879. Only the Free Cities of Hamburg and Bremen were now excluded in virtue of the option, secured to them by the constitution, of remaining outside the customs area until they were disposed to seek admission of their own accord.

Throughout the history of the Customs Union there had been a steady tendency favourable to freer commercial intercourse with foreign countries, and this tendency found expression in lower duties. England adopted Free Trade in 1846, and the example of the first mercantile and industrial country of the world had great influence upon German statesmen and public opinion. Several years later the textile manufacturers of Saxony were won over to the new doctrine, and in 1848 even the agricultural societies of that kingdom petitioned the Frankfort Parliament against customs duties of all kinds. The iron manufacturers of the West and South, however, still continued predominantly Protectionist.

Amongst publicists and in academic circles there had in the meantime grown up a vigorous Liberalistic school, whose leaders included John Prince Smith, an Englishman by birth, who settled in Germany, and was later elected both to the Prussian and Imperial Diets; W. A. Lette, a Prussian State official; Max Wirth, honourably associated with the Trade Union movement; Otto Michaelis, an able economic writer, who ended his career as Prussian Minister of Finance; Schulze-Delitzsch, already named as the founder of co-operation in Germany; and Julius Faucher, for some years a leader of the Progressive party in the Prussian Diet. At the instigation of Prince Smith and Faucher, a Free Trade party was organized in Berlin, and its influence gradually extended from North Germany to other parts of the country. Prince Smith especially was unwearied in the agitation which he carried on both by speech and writing on behalf of the economic theories which had just won so signal a triumph in England. He travelled over a large part of the country as an apostle of the Free Trade gospel, imparting everywhere some at least of his own enthusiasm and conviction, organizing societies, encouraging the establishment of literary sheets in the service of the new faith, and successfully identifying economic with political and Parliamentary Liberalism. He contended for the immediate introduction of complete Free Trade, without half measures or compromise of any kind. To those who, only partially convinced of the unwisdom of a protective policy, pleaded for slow and cautious progress in the new direction, he replied that any dallying with Protection was a mere protraction of economic injury. It was, he said, like docking a dog's tail an inch a day, just to spare its feelings. So far did his temporary influence go, that at the beginning of the 'sixties he was able to convince some of the agricultural societies of West and East Prussia — later a hot-bed of extreme Protectionism and agrarianism — that their truest interest was to be sought in a policy of free imports.

Free Trade principles also found expression in the Economic Congress formed in 1858 by Lette, Wirth, Victor Böhmert, and Pickford, another Englishman, which first met at Gotha, and in the German Commercial Diet, or national federation of the Chambers of Commerce and Industry.

The economic life of the country underwent a powerful development at this time. During a long period of peace, bought at the cost of much political humiliation at Austria's hands, industry had prospered and trade expanded both at home and abroad. The factory system was rapidly coming in; the great inventions which had revolutionized manufacturing processes in the staple industries of England had been welcomed from abroad;[1] English capital, brains, and initiative were busily engaged in creating in Germany industries which were at a later date to prove a sore trial of endurance and capacity at home. At the world exhibitions held in London in 1851 and in Paris four years later German goods were prominently and creditably represented. Yet up to that time English manufacturers viewed with curiosity rather than alarm the rise of the young competitor whose ambitions were still too modest to justify his being regarded as a serious rival.

So great had become the demand of the factories and workshops for labour that agriculture for a time ran short, in spite of the growth of population, though it still maintained quite one-half of the population. For agriculture, too, had likewise moved with the times. In Prussia particularly a new generation had come into possession of the soil since the emancipation of the peasantry, and its energies were stimulated and fructified by the consciousness of freedom and by the enlarging influence of

[1] Werner Sombart writes in his *Deutsche Volkswirthschaft im neunzehnten Jahrhundert* (p. 154): "I do not propose to enumerate the various inventions which have created the modern machine industry during the nineteenth century, and there is the less cause for doing so since for the most part they did not originate with Germans."

education, long compulsory throughout the monarchy and now nominally free. The peasant had become a new man, with larger hopes and a wider outlook, while the knowledge that he worked now for himself, his family, and the future encouraged him to greater enterprise. The number of small proprietors and holders increased greatly, except in the East, where the large landowners continued supreme. Year after year a larger area was brought under cultivation and the land cultivated gave a larger yield.

A more decided step towards Free Trade was taken when by the commercial treaty of February, 1853, Prussia and Austria agreed to levy corn duties no longer against each other. In 1856 the Customs Union tariff was further reduced, but it was the conclusion by Prussia in 1862 of a commercial treaty with France — following one concluded by England with the same country two years before — which came into operation throughout the whole area of the Union in 1865, that gave the greatest practical stimulus to the new movement.[1] Bismarck found the treaty ready drawn up when he became Minister-President in the autumn of 1862, but it fell to him to carry it through Parliament, and while it is true that the treaty belonged to the period of his official life when, as he frequently said in after years, his economic conscience was in the keeping of others, the reasons which influenced him in accepting it were in the main political. When the episode was later mentioned during a discussion in the Diet (February 21, 1879) in proof of changed convictions, he retorted that convictions had nothing to do with the matter; the treaty, he said, was meant to be a weapon for use against Austria. Whatever the immediate purpose of the French treaty, it unquestionably committed Germany to further progress on Free Trade lines, while its effects upon her foreign trade were very marked. The tariff was again revised, and now in a decidedly liberal spirit. The duties on corn and flour, for example, were repealed altogether, while other duties were greatly reduced.

When the Empire was established in 1871, therefore, little was wanting to complete the transition to freedom of trade. The corn duties had gone, such of the industrial duties as remained were now nominal in amount, and the protective aspect of the tariff had given place to the purely financial. Then in

[1] See Chapter IV., vol. i., pp. 157-9.

1873 the duties on iron and steel goods were reduced to rates varying from 1s. to 2s. 6d. a cwt., and two years later the Diet was persuaded to adopt a resolution approving of their total abolition as from the first day of 1877. The final abandonment of Protection was the work of three Prussian Ministers, Rudolf Delbrück, Otto von Camphausen and August von der Heydt, of whom the first two still remained in office.

German politics is so much an affair of the Government, so little one of the nation and of public opinion, that Bismarck, immersed in foreign affairs, and bearing upon his shoulders the entire burden of their complex and manifold problems, had failed to notice that this gradual rupture of the old tradition had aroused widespread dissatisfaction. The year which was to have seen the disappearance of the last vestige of Protection witnessed instead a vigorous reaction against Free Trade. During 1876 the iron and steel industries organized themselves for mutual defence, and urgently petitioned the Government to refrain from putting into effect the impending repeal of the iron duties. Delbrück's influence was still at that time paramount upon economic issues, and the petition was rejected, but this victory of Liberalism in the Ministry was its last. The agrarians also moved in sympathy. Hitherto they had raised no objection to the policy of open frontiers, and as late as 1876 had advocated the abolition of customs and duties of all kinds. Now they began to clamour for a return to the good old days of a closed market and steady and ample prices.

The strongest impulses behind the reaction originated in the severe commercial depression which set in directly the first wave of prosperity caused by the war of 1870 had exhausted itself. Industry had at first taken a great leap forward. To the political influences which favoured an awakening of economic life came the stimulus of the French milliards. Thanks to the wonderful elasticity of the conquered nation, the instalments were paid long before they were due, and they had to be expended far too precipitately for Germany's good. Prince Bismarck once spoke of the war indemnity as an acute embarrassment for the time being, and a German writer has said: " It broke over us like a water-spout, carrying great devastation everywhere, whereas if it had fallen gradually, and in small quantities, it might have been beneficial in an extraordinary degree."

Germany's position was that of a young and inexperienced

heir who has unexpectedly come into a large fortune. Thoughtful men had warned the nation of the dangers involved in the dispersal of so large a sum of money. When in 1872 negotiations were begun with France with a view to the acceleration of the payment of the indemnity, and the practical men of affairs who had the transaction in hand were rubbing their hands in glee over their shrewdness, it was a theorist, Dr. Ludwig Bamberger, who urged the risks of the course contemplated and predicted demoralizing national extravagance and ultimate financial catastrophe from the too rapid flow of wealth into new Germany. The money was paid, however, and it had to be spent. The millions of pounds which were expended by the various Governments on public works — fortifications, barracks, munitions, railways and their equipment, public buildings, dockyards and ships, mines and workshops — circulated in a thousand channels and fertilized industrial and commercial enterprise of every kind. From factory and workshop everywhere the cry rose for labour, and responding to it the rural population flocked to the towns. Thus it was that the era of industrial enterprise was also an era of town building. The inevitable effect of this abnormal activity was a sudden rise in values. Raw materials, both home and foreign, were needed in unexampled quantities, and because the want was great and urgent, every seller demanded high prices and every buyer was willing to pay them. Wages and salaries increased in response to the quickened demand for labour and service, and it was said that during the three years following the return of the victorious armies from France there was a greater advance in the general standard of life than in the whole of the preceding generation.

Unfortunately the garish structure of national prosperity proved to have been built upon unstable foundations. An economic development legitimate in origin, and beneficial so long as it followed healthy lines, culminated in excesses of a lamentable kind. Even to-day, after the lapse of over forty years, the great company frauds which fell to that time are vividly remembered in Germany as the national counterpart of the famous South Sea Bubble. Suddenly everybody seemed to have money to spare, and there was no lack of cunning rogues eager and able to take care of it. The promotion of companies reached unheard-of proportions. More blast furnaces, iron works, and machine works were established in Prussia during the years 1871 to 1874 than in all the preceding seventy years.

An ignoble scramble for illicit wealth arose. The Jews revelled in it, but the Christians were not slow to emulate them; and members of all grades of the aristocracy were as ready to clutch at dishonest gain as the professional sharper whose only capital were his wits. At that time of perverted morals, it even happened that State officials were proved guilty of granting concessions to railway adventurers under questionable circumstances, of aiding and abetting in the evasion of the company law, and of receiving commission for valuable services rendered to company promoters in an official capacity; while in one notorious case — that of Councillor of State Wagener, of earlier *Kreuzzeitung* fame — public opinion was only satisfied when the offender had been dismissed from his post. Other men of hitherto honoured name and reputation soiled the one and lost the other past recovery by complicity in transactions which only escaped punishment because of loopholes in the law. It was the merit of Dr. Lasker that at that time he exposed the facility with which fraud could be perpetrated under legal forms, and gave the impetus to a reform of criminal law which made it more difficult for dishonest men to thrive.

The people who chiefly benefited were the promoters, directors, bankers, middlemen, and, in many cases, their tools — the people whose undertakings were bought far beyond their value in order that they might be sold to the public at a further largely enhanced price. Many an unlettered peasant who had tilled his own land in the neighbourhood of Berlin and other large towns became suddenly wealthy, and was able to spend the rest of his days in enervating luxury, by selling his property to a land development company, which promptly resold it to the public at an unconscionable profit. From that time dated the building banks and estate and land development companies which have been the bane of German municipal life, since to their unprincipled speculation are due in large measure the bad housing and high rents common to so many large towns.

The crash came towards the end of 1873, and month after month the devastation increased until it overspread the whole country. Hundreds of large company undertakings which, if honestly financed and conducted, would have brought legitimate gain to their shareholders and profit to the community

— railways, mines, banks, manufactories, building enterprises — came to a sudden standstill, their employees being thrown upon the streets, and the savings of thousands of investors, large and small, squandered.   Nowhere did the gold fever and the subsequent disaster reach dimensions so great as in Berlin, yet there was hardly a large town in Germany which did not suffer.   Writing several years later, a historian of the period said: " Wherever we look, on all sides, the wounds caused by the cruel year 1873 still bleed.   Thousands of existences are broken, countless thousands are severely injured; suffering, care, want and despair knock at the doors and have become daily guests in hut and palace.   All of us have suffered more or less, whether we gambled with the promoters and bought their dear wares or not; for our daily necessities are dearer and our business lies low."   Side by side with evils of an economic character came the inevitable moral *sequelæ* of widespread social disturbance, and the records of fraud, violent crime, and suicide reflected the material pressure under which large sections of the population struggled.

From the industrial standpoint it was the hopeless condition of the iron and textile trades at that time which principally determined the return to Protection.   The iron and steel and allied industries had shared liberally in the distribution of the French milliards, but directly the abnormal expenditure on State and public works ceased stagnation began, and many industrialists found themselves in possession of works and plants which had been built or extended on an excessive scale in order to meet what had proved to be a temporary and transient spell of prosperity.   In 1873 over-production had reached such a limit in the iron trade that Lotz estimates that the smelting and rolling works of Germany were then producing iron enough to cover the demand of the entire world.   Prices sank ruinously; having reached their highest in 1873, they fell in the following year to one-half and later to one-third of the maximum figures.   On the other hand, the textile trade had suffered owing to the incorporation in the Empire of the large and progressive weaving and spinning industries of Alsace, whose production, hitherto sold to France, was now largely thrown upon the German market, so that the less efficient manufacturers of Saxony found themselves face to face with a new and severe competition.

Agriculture had benefited for the time by the increased

consuming capacity of the community, but the subsequent re-action involved it in the general misfortune. Prices fell, and with them land values, and where leases lapsed rents fell in sympathy. Up to 1874 both values and rent had steadily risen, but then came the climax, and after it the decline. Apart from the depression in home industry and trade, the corn-growers had to contend with severer competition from abroad, favoured by improved ocean transport and railway facilities. Germany was now steadily becoming less an ex-porting and more an importing country.

Such being the economic condition of Germany in the early 'seventies, and remembering that these years had marked a clear departure from Protection, nothing was more likely than that, reasoning *a priori*, the industries which had fallen on evil days should unite in casting the blame on the new-fangled policy of Free Trade.

It would not be strictly correct to say that in embarking upon a policy of fiscal reform Bismarck only sought for a jus-tification of that policy when he had already adopted it. It is nevertheless true that his ideas on the subject were at first vague and indefinite, and that he repeatedly changed his ground and modified his measures. He never concealed the fact that on political questions he was an opportunist. Con-temptuous of theories, and convinced that political action must be determined solely by interest, it was not difficult to detach himself from his earlier preconceptions and to revert to the old Prussian tradition.

He has said that the year 1877 marked for him a turning-point in German fiscal policy. It was his recognition of the prevailing acute depression, as evidenced by the stagnation of the staple industries, the wholesale damping down of blast fur-naces, and the impoverishment of the working classes, that led him to ask whether Free Trade was proving the national boon which it had been represented. Hitherto he had never given any thought to the merits of the question. " For the first fifteen years of my Ministerial life," he said, " I was ab-sorbed in foreign affairs and did not regard it as my business to trouble myself seriously about the domestic policy of the Empire, nor had I the time; I assumed also that it was in good hands. Afterwards, when the men whom I needed failed me, I was compelled to look at the matter myself, and . . . I formed the opinion that under the Free Trade system introduced in

1865 we fell into atrophy, which was only relieved for a time by the new blood that came with the French indemnity, and that it was necessary to apply a remedy." To the reproach that he had changed his mind, and was now disowning his earlier economic theories, especially as avowed in 1862, he replied: " I should be proud if I could say that I held any economic theories at all in those days, but I must confess to my shame that I had none."

Already in 1877 he had set his Press and Press agents to work, and all the other influences at the Government's command when " public opinion " had to be formed were being actively mobilized.   Prince Hohenlohe notes in his Diary that in the autumn of that year Jewish bankers in Berlin, taking a hint from above, were busily making propaganda for the coming economic departure.   Before anything could be done, however, it was evident that new Ministers would be needed.   Ever since 1867 Bismarck's right hand had been Rudolf Delbrück.   He became the first President of the Federal Chancellery Office in the Government of the North German Confederation in that year, and a Prussian Minister in 1868, and on the establishment of the Empire he retained both offices.   His influence in the Government was second only to that of Bismarck himself.   A Liberal and an individualist, he had throughout directed fiscal policy in Liberal channels.   Accepting now the necessity of financial reform, he nevertheless still clung to the idea of revenue taxes, and had no thought of abandoning the principles of Free Trade, to which he had only just succeeded in giving full play.   Up to 1875 Bismarck agreed with him; he was, indeed, already wishful to go further than his colleague in developing the indirect taxes, yet, up to this point, only with a view to revenue and not as a measure of protection.   It did not take Delbrück long, however, to discover that Bismarck and he were traversing paths which were certain to go more and more apart.   Bismarck, too, soon recognized that the difference between himself and his valued colleague was one of principle and therefore allowed of no compromise.

In June, 1876, Delbrück resigned office, and a little later secured election to the Imperial Diet, where he continued to oppose the new policy earnestly, yet with dignity.   Bismarck would have made great sacrifices rather than have lost the help of this trusted adviser and able administrator, and his resig-

nation was one of the few defections which, in the course of
his long Ministerial life, actually grieved him. He had been
so fully occupied with foreign questions that he was only too
glad to have at his side a Minister of Delbrück's marked ability, a man full of initiative, a fierce worker, and a comrade of
unflinching loyalty. Delbrück's jurisdiction and powers were
defined neither by laws nor regulations, and it was natural that
he came to exercise a sort of dictatorship within the sphere assigned to him. In fiscal questions in particular Bismarck neither agreed with nor differed from his colleague; he simply
accepted his opinions and acts as those of an oracle. " My
recognition of his authority was so great," he said on one occasion (December 1, 1881), " that, in view of the importance
and technical superiority of this colleague whom I had no
wish to lose, I immediately suppressed the grave doubts which
I began to entertain as to whether we were on the right path."
Even now no shadow of personal antipathy fell upon their
relationships.[1]

German economists of the Free Trade school have often contended that the departure from the old protectionist lines
was made too quickly and at last too completely. Albert
Schäffle held that both sides went to extremes, and that if a
moderate course had been taken not only in 1879 but earlier
the result might have been a wider Customs Union, embracing
Austria, on the basis of moderate protection, instead of the
succession of tariff wars which fell to later years. It is certain that when Delbrück resigned the extent of the contemplated change had not been settled, and Bismarck professed to
believe that his colleague had been unduly alarmed. It is conceivable that if Delbrück had remained the Protectionist party
might have been kept for a long time under check. Nevertheless, with his resignation Bismarck's principal motive for moderation disappeared, and he speedily came round to the view
that if protection was to be effective it must be thorough.

At this stage occurred an unexpected check, which, had
Bismarck been a weaker man, might have shaken his resolve
and deterred him altogether from making so momentous a departure. Harassed by ill-health and political perplexities, the
longing for rest again came over him early in 1877, and on
March 20th he tendered his resignation. This time he was
in earnest, and it was only the Emperor's emphatic " Never ! "

[1] Delbrück died in 1903.

— interpreting the alarm which the bare rumour of a change of Chancellor had created in the country — that put the idea out of his mind. Nevertheless, he was persuaded to pass the remainder of the year in retirement at Varzin. There he worked out the broad outlines of a large scheme of fiscal reform, and when he returned to Berlin in the following February he immediately threw himself with characteristic vigour into this new campaign. In the interval he had twice attempted to induce the National Liberal leader, Rudolf von Bennigsen, on the whole the most statesmanlike figure in the Diet, to take office as successor to Count Friedrich Eulenburg, whom he was prepared to supplant on the ground of his failing health. When the overtures were first made to him in July, Bennigsen had received them favourably, but had imposed the condition that he should take with him into the Cabinet two Liberal colleagues, Forckenbeck and Stauffenberg, the one as Minister of the Interior and the other as head of the Imperial Treasury. Such a leaven of Liberalism would have entailed a clear break with the past policy of the Government, and to that Bismarck was opposed. The negotiations, therefore, broke down. In December they were reopened, and now Eulenburg, displeased by the prospect of being sacrificed for Bismarck's convenience, disclosed them to the Emperor, who rebuked his Minister, in a letter of unusual asperity, for having dared to discuss behind his back a transaction of such importance. Highly mortified by the affront, Bismarck renewed his resignation, but a prompt letter of contrition from the same hand led to its withdrawal. As Bennigsen still declined to enter office alone, the incident had no further consequence.

One other serious obstacle remained in the way of advance, and it was his Liberal colleague and deputy in the presidency of the Prussian Ministry, Otto von Camphausen, who since 1873 had been Minister of Finance, and as such had been responsible for imperial finance. His was what Bismarck was wont to call " a subaltern nature," and it was his chief's special complaint against him that he deliberately hid his head in the sand, refused to face the accumulating difficulties of his department, and looked to the head of the Ministry to do his work. After he had long and vainly pressed Camphausen to produce some practical scheme of taxation reform, Bismarck determined at last to bring his policy of procrastination to an end. In a letter written from his Varzin retreat on December 21, 1877, he told his easy-going colleague: "It is a complete confusion of ideas that the Finance Minister should expect from the President a programme for his own Ministry, on the understanding that after examining it he will reserve criticism. On the contrary, the preparation of a programme for discussion is the duty of the Finance Minister himself. It is not my business as President of the Prussian Ministry either to invent or to advocate financial programmes; I am responsible only for seeing that the office of Minister of Finance is filled in a way agreeable to the general policy of the Ministry."

In face of so direct an injunction either to act himself or make room for some one who would, Camphausen set to work, and before many weeks had passed produced a series of measures which, if approved, might have relieved the Empire for a long time of its money difficulties. The principal proposal was the higher taxation of tobacco; but it was also hoped to obtain a much larger revenue by the taxation of lotteries, playing-cards, and Stock Exchange contracts. Unhappily for its author the plan completely miscarried. Of the several proposals made to it the Diet, to Bismarck's disgust, adopted only a trumpery tax on playing-cards. The measure upon which his principal expectations had been built, the increase of the tobacco duties, fared the worst; this was rejected by a large majority, which included the National Liberals and the Radicals, who had been frightened by the Chancellor's premature avowal that he was feeling his way towards a State monopoly in tobacco.

Although the taxation scheme failed, however, it had two important results: it led to the resignation of Camphausen, whose half-hearted interest in Bismarck's fiscal reform plans had encouraged the Opposition, and it made clear and unambiguous the attitude of political parties on the question. Bismarck expended no regrets over his vanished colleague. Referring to Camphausen's retirement several years later, he reproached him with obstinate adhesion to old ways and an unconquerable conviction that nothing in his system of ideas was capable of improvement; he was " as convinced as God Himself on the sixth day of the creation that everything was very good."

Camphausen having gone, and Bennigsen having failed him,

Bismarck in reconstructing the Ministry looked for colleagues who could be relied on to support the new policy without troubling him with scruples and reservations. Camphausen was succeeded by Arthur Hobrecht, who had been Chief Mayor of Berlin, and had hitherto sat in the Prussian Diet as a National Liberal, and Count Friedrich Eulenburg and Achenbach gave place to Count Botha Eulenburg and Count Stolberg, the latter becoming Vice-President of the Prussian Ministry and Vice-Chancellor.

Although Protection was now Bismarck's goal, his object was at first and for a long time purely fiscal; he wished to reform the system of imperial taxation in order to provide the Empire with a sufficient revenue, and so to make it independent of the States and their Legislatures. In the forefront of domestic needs he had for years placed fiscal reform in this sense. " The entire reform of taxation, inclusive of the customs duties — who does not wish it? " he said in the Diet on November 22, 1875, " but it is a Herculean work which one must have touched experimentally as a comparative layman in these matters, such as I am, in order to really comprehend its difficulties." The strongest of his convictions, in holding which he never wavered, was the superiority of indirect to direct taxation.

The Imperial constitution adopted in 1871 had provided that in so far as the expenditure of the Empire was not covered by revenues set apart for its special use — in the main, certain customs, excise, and stamp duties, and the profits of the Post Office — the deficiency should be made up by contributions from the Federal States, levied according to population. These were the " matricular contributions " known both to the Germanic Federation and the old Empire, and their aggregate amount was fixed in the budget each year. These contributions were not intended, originally, to be permanent, but merely to tide the Empire over the early days, until more suitable and more popular sources of revenue could be found. Nevertheless, for a long time they had occupied a far more prominent place in the budget than had been contemplated. Instead of being a stop-gap, they threatened to become a mainstay of imperial finance. Bismarck had always chafed under this system of State maintenance, which he regarded as undignified and as partaking of the character of charity. The Empire's position was that of the young man who on coming of age is bidden to remember the dignity of man's estate, but is still kept in pecuniary dependence — expected to cut a creditable figure in the world and to spend freely, yet not allowed to pay his own bills.

On the other hand, the States objected to the contributions because of the violent fluctuations to which they were exposed — a disadvantage doubly serious in those States whose budgets were fixed for several years at a time — and of the inequity of the principle upon which they were levied, which was the crude principle of population. With the latter objection in particular Bismarck fully sympathized. " It can hardly be denied," he said (November 22, 1875), " that the form of matricular assessment is one which does not fall on the States equitably, according to their capacity to pay. If, however, a tax is acknowledged to be unjust, it does not, from my standpoint as Imperial Chancellor, belong to the things which consolidate the Empire." He was still haunted by the dread of the " centrifugal elements " which did not share his own attachment to the Empire or his own conviction of its permanency. The spirit of particularism was not dead, and he desired to make the Empire as independent as possible by placing it in possession of ample and elastic resources. He did not want the citizens of the new Confederation to be perpetually asking themselves as they reckoned out the incidence of the matricular contributions, " What does the new Empire cost us, and is it worth the price? " The financial aspect of empire he therefore wished once for all to force into the background. He may also have been influenced by a wish to break the power of the Diet over finance, so that when he spoke of the desirability of the Empire being financially independent he meant by the Empire the Executive, and by independence freedom from parliamentary control. Certainly the popular parties favoured the retention of the matricular contributions just because they emphasized the Government's dependence upon the Diet for money, and hence preserved effectively the Diet's constitutional right to control the budget.

Attempts had already been made to dispense with these contributions by the introduction of new and the increase of existing taxes and duties, but never with lasting success, for sooner or later the ever-growing expenditure exhausted the new revenue, and the obnoxious poll-tax remained as before. Worse still, since 1876 there had been deficits, leading to borrowing, a practice to which, though no financier, Bismarck was opposed. A man who in all his dealings was thoroughgoing, he had no patience with the policy of covering up unpleasant facts. If the national revenue was not sufficient to meet the national needs, the only proper thing was to make it so, instead of hiding the deficiency and pretending that all was well. Down to 1878, however, Bismarck and the Federal Government did not seriously contemplate a measure of industrial and agricultural protection. The revision of the tariff was already determined on, but it was to be undertaken solely in the interest of revenue. In August the Finance Ministers of the various States met in conference at Heidelberg, and here likewise the same views were represented and the same intention adhered to. Their report merely recommended the increase of the imperial revenue by means of a tobacco duty and of revenue duties on certain suitable articles.

It was at this point that the question was taken out of Bismarck's hands, to be developed and settled in a way which hitherto he had not seriously anticipated. For the friends of reaction in the Diet had meantime been active. They recognized that the moment was propitious for a return to the policy discarded under Delbrück's influence, and thanks to the promptitude and vigour of their intervention, they were able to create the impetus which sent the Chancellor, while still wavering with open mind, clear across the border-line which divided fiscal from protective policy.

The composition of the Diet was favourable to such a course. The election which followed the two attempts made in 1878 upon the life of the Emperor William I placed the Liberal parties in a minority. The two Conservative groups numbered 78 in the House of 1877, but 116 in that of 1878; while the National Liberals fell from 128 to 99 and the Radicals and the Socialists from 51 to 36. The Ultramontane Centre controlled 93 votes. The outlook of Liberalism was therefore gloomy. It was clear that the Conservatives would have to form the backbone of the new Government majority; the only doubtful question was, who would be their partners, the National Liberals or the Clericals, for one of these groups would be necessary in order to create the requisite majority.

For a time the attitude of the National Liberals seemed uncertain. Accepted by Bismarck as a Ministerial party in 1867, they had become so accustomed to regard themselves as the main pillar of the State that the idea of taking a second place was unwelcome to them. They no longer held the leading position in the Diet, and now they were faced by the alternatives of retiring into the shades of opposition or accepting a policy with which, as a party, they did not agree. When the alliance with Bismarck was concluded twelve years before there were amongst them sturdy democrats who viewed co-operation with a reactionary Minister with suspicion, and these men had often chafed under a yoke which had committed them to a course of action in which there was far more Nationalism than Liberalism. Yet having already given up their political cloak, they were now invited to surrender their economic coat also.

While the National Liberals were still considering what their collective attitude should be, the constitution of the Ministerial majority which was to carry through the impending changes was decided by the formation of the Free Economic Union of the Diet, an association of 204 deputies, of whom 95 were Conservatives, 87 Clericals, 27 National Liberals, and the remainder members of minor fractions. This body on October 17th published a formal declaration pledging itself to the advocacy of fiscal reform on protectionist principles. The declaration was believed to have received the sanction, and it was certainly issued with the knowledge, of the Chancellor, whose position and resolve it greatly strengthened. Here was a majority which was to be had for the mere taking, for it had literally thrown itself at his feet; with 204 votes, at the least, at his disposal, he would be able to carry whatever reforms he pleased. Accordingly he let it be known that if the Conservatives and Clericals wished to work with him their assistance would be welcome.

Thus encouraged, Bismarck on November 12th formally proposed to the Federal Council that a commission of fifteen members should be appointed to revise the tariff by the aid of such advice as they chose to take, and when this had been done he laid before the Council an exhaustive memorial in which he discussed the question of fiscal reform in great detail and disclosed his proposals with the utmost frankness. Even in this memorial he repeated that financial reform was his special concern, and pointed out that what he desired was not heavier but juster taxation. " The financial reform whose realization the revision of the customs tariff is intended to help does not consist in the increase of the necessary burdens required by

the needs of the Empire and the States, but in the transference
of a larger part of these unavoidable burdens to the less
oppressive indirect taxes." There were to be more customs
duties, but as taxation was to be spread over a wider area, its
weight was to be felt less rather than more by the individual.
It was his intention " not only to impose higher duties upon
isolated articles which are specially suited thereto, but to return to the principle of taxing all objects imported over the
frontiers, as recognized by the Prussian customs legislation of
1818, and applied by the general entrance duties of the Customs Union tariff until 1865." The only exceptions were to
be raw materials indispensable for industry. The idea of giving special protection to particular industries was expressly
disowned. It was contemplated at that time that the duties
to be imposed should average 5 per cent., and that on this
basis an additional revenue of three and a half million pounds
would be raised without any appreciable increase in the costs
of collection.

The publication of this memorial at Christmas let loose the
floods of political controversy. If the Protectionists in Parliament, who had for years regarded with dismay the growing
abandonment of their principles by Delbrück, were jubilant,
the Free Traders were plunged into blank despair. They had
long seemed to be fighting a winning battle, and the very slow-
ness of the Government's acceptance of their views had made
them confident that once the conversion was complete it would
be permanent. Now, in the very moment of apparent triumph,
the fruits of all their patience and toil were to be snatched
from their hands.

Public opinion in the country was divided on the whole according to interest, imaginary or real. Perhaps the only class
of the community which was altogether won over to a policy
of Protection were the agrarians, comprising at that time not
only the large proprietors but the small owners and cultivators, for the fall in agricultural prices had injured all equally.
Of the industrial classes those warmly favoured Protection who
suffered from foreign competition, but those to whom cheap
raw materials from abroad were essential objected in the same
degree. The trading classes, the shipping interest, and the
banking interest were in general hostile, at least to the threatened corn duties, and the salaried and wage-earning classes
wished for no change. The attitude of the mercantile popu-

lation was reflected by the vigorous opposition offered by the seaport towns, particularly the free ports of Hamburg, Bremen, and Lübeck, and by a joint protest issued by a congress of fifty of the most important Chambers of Commerce.

Early in 1879 the Tariff Commission reported in favour of the introduction of a large number of new duties falling equally upon agricultural and industrial products, including corn and its derivatives, live stock, meat, timber, coal, textile goods and yarns, glass, iron and steel goods, and copper. The duty on wheat and oats was to be 10s. a ton, and on rye, barley, and maize 5s. a ton. The discussion of the customs tariff so revised occupied almost the whole of the session of the Diet, which opened on February 12th.

"I regard it as my duty," said the Emperor in his opening speech from the throne, " so to work that the German market shall be reserved for our national production, so far as may be consonant with our general interests, and that our customs legislation shall accordingly return to the proved principles on which the Customs Union prospered for nearly half a century, and which have to a large extent been abandoned by our commercial policy since 1865. I cannot admit that real success has attended the change."

This uncompromising declaration of war upon Liberalism in fiscal policy was accepted by the Opposition as a clear indication that, supported by a Diet so reactionary in composition, the Government would not stop at half-measures. Bismarck himself took charge of the Tariff Bill and piloted it through the Diet with unwearied energy, consummate tact, and unfailing resource. In the speeches made during the debates on the first reading in May, he said:

" The first motive which impels me to enter upon such a reform is the Empire's need of financial independence. This need was recognized when the imperial constitution was drawn up. The constitution presumes that the system of matricular contributions should be a temporary one, and should only last until imperial taxes were introduced. . . . Certainly it is undesirable that the Empire should be a burdensome boarder or a dunning creditor, while it might be a liberal contributor to the individual States if only proper use were made of the revenues which the constitution put in the Empire's way, yet which hitherto have been disregarded.

" A second reason why a change of the present system seems

necessary lies in the question, Does the burden which must necessarily be imposed in the interest of the State and the Empire take the form in which it can most easily be borne, or does it not? This question must, according to my conviction, be answered in the negative. . . . The Federal Governments are convinced that indirect taxes, a source of revenue so long neglected by the Customs Union, are the form in which the burden that we may have to bear will fall most lightly."

Turning to the question of protection for industry, he continued:

" It is a reproach to our existing legislation . . . that the incidence of our indirect taxes does not afford to our national labour and production the measure of protection which can be given to it without danger to the interests of the community. No one can expect Germany to remain permanently the dupe of an honest conviction. Hitherto the wide-opened gates of our imports have made us the dumping-place of all the over-production of foreign countries. . . . Let us close the doors and erect the somewhat higher barriers which are proposed, and see that we at any rate preserve the German market for German industry."

The bill left committee almost in the form proposed by the Government, whose difficulty was less to incite its followers to enthusiasm than to keep the duties within moderate limits. The agrarians did their best to increase the corn duties, but their only success was in persuading the Government to tax rye, like wheat, at 10s. instead of 5s. a ton. It was these duties which roused the strongest hostility, since they affected all classes equally, and their effect was most clearly understood. The deputy Lasker, in one of the passionate speeches with which he intervened in the debates, predicted a formal feud between town and country as a result of the new policy, which he described as one of preference for the propertied against the unpropertied classes, and as such a conspiracy against social peace.

In his eagerness to get to work upon the task which now absorbed him, Bismarck had not been deterred by the reflection that of the two parties upon which he would in the main have to depend one had not long ago deserted him at a critical moment in circumstances which pointed to personal even more than to political motives, while with the other he had been engaged in a long struggle marked on both sides by extreme bitterness and rancour. Now he had no compunction in throwing over the faithful allies who had been the shield and buttress of his majority since 1867. The National Liberals, unwilling to be identified with the parties of indiscriminate opposition, strove to the last to find some reasonable basis of accommodation. They were not all uncompromising free traders, like their near neighbours of the Left, and they were genuinely sympathetic towards fiscal reform. Hence they were willing to accept the purely "financial" duties, as the duties on petroleum, wine, coffee, and tea were called, as well as an increased tobacco duty, provided the Government would give guarantees against any weakening of the constitutional rights of the Diet in relation to the control of the budget. On the other hand, they held reservations on the subject of the protective duties, and were loath to give any binding undertaking regarding them. The demand for guarantees was the more reasonable since it was expected that with the operation of the revised tariff the needs of the Empire would be more than met without resort to matricular contributions, leaving the Government in command of a steadily increasing revenue. As, however, taxation once approved could only be altered by law, it followed that the Government would be placed in a position of dangerous independence, unless means were devised whereby certain of the new taxes would remain under the direct control of the Diet. To this problem Bennigsen, the National Liberal leader, applied himself, in the hope that by solving it he would simultaneously succeed in retaining for his party continued influence upon Ministerial policy.

The Clericals, on the other hand, were prepared to vote the protective duties without any reservation whatever, but in return for their support of the financial duties they demanded concessions in the domain of ecclesiastical legislation. Suddenly there had opened to this party prospects of influence and power which had never before been within its reach. The Ultramontanes had hitherto been pariah to the dominant castes, whether Conservative or Liberal; now fortune seemed to have thrown in their way the chance of playing a leading part in national politics. Happily for the party, it was still under the direction of one of the shrewdest of political leaders, a man of rare resource and of infinite patience, a man also who never made a tactical mistake. Windthorst saw his chances, and turned them to excellent use. His policy lay in outbidding the National Liberals in this competition for the privilege of official recognition, and he waited his time, knowing that he had more to offer than his rival; for to the National Liberals complete acceptance of the Government's programme was impossible, while the Centre, a party created for confessional purposes, was bound by no economic and hardly by any political ties. When, therefore, Bismarck asked the National Liberal party with Mephistopheles, "What hast thou, poor devil, to give?" the answer was apologetic and unsatisfying; without ceasing to count as a Liberal force, the party was able to concede little that was of value to a Government that wanted so much.

Before the die was cast Bismarck again offered Bennigsen a seat in the Cabinet, wishful to make sure of his co-operation and influence. The offer was declined, yet, still unwilling to see his party disowned and isolated, and also sincerely apprehensive of the fruits of a Conservative-Ultramontane coalition, Bennigsen suggested a new compromise. It was that, given guarantees for the maintenance of the Diet's effective control of the budget, his party should accept the financial duties as they stood, but that decision on the protective duties should be left to the free discretion of the House, on the clear understanding that in the final division the National Liberals would vote for the tariff in the form given to it by the Diet, an arrangement which, while it might not in the event give the Government all it wanted, would at least assure its scheme against total wreck.

Whatever chances of success this offer might have had if endorsed by a united party, the hopes built upon it were rudely dispelled by disagreement amongst the National Liberals themselves. The left wing of the party, led by Lasker, refused to accept any compromise upon the general principle of Free Trade. As Bennigsen was thus unable to carry his party with him on the major question, his proposed compromise on the minor one of constitutional guarantees did not ease the situation. His suggestion was that the Diet should fix each year the revenue to be derived by the Empire from the important taxes on salt and coffee, and that any excess should be divided amongst the States according to population, unless disposed of otherwise by special law. Of the other duties the Government would receive the complete proceeds. It was expected that this arrangement, by placing a largely increased revenue at the disposal of the Treasury, would have made matricular contributions unnecessary. Windthorst's colleague, Baron von Franckenstein, proposed an analogous guarantee, except that he was prepared to vote all the taxes once for all, while assigning to the Empire only the same revenue as hitherto from the customs and tobacco duties, the excess to be in future divided amongst the States. In other words, the matricular contributions would in this case still continue, but only for accounting purposes; they would be levied *pro formâ* in order to meet deficits which would be more or less fictitious, and the States would then receive back from the Imperial exchequer payments which would fall below or exceed these contributions according to circumstances.

Bismarck heartily disliked the Franckenstein proposal as still perpetuating the matricular contributions, and greatly preferred that of Bennigsen. At the eleventh hour, indeed, before the fate of the bill and the composition of the future Ministerial coalition had been decided beyond revocation, he tried once more to come to an arrangement with his old allies. The National Liberal party by this time, however, was hopelessly split, and the Free Trade section in particular was hostile to any form of compromise. Lasker, the fiery spirit of revolt, had gathered around him a following of resolute adherents, resolved to defend the party's Liberalism against its Nationalism at all hazards, and Bennigsen was now only able to count on the support of seventy members, a number quite insufficient to create with the two Conservative groups a majority of the House.

Working to a time limit, since the longer the choice between the two rival parties was deferred, the greater was the danger that he might lose the support of both, Bismarck now saw himself compelled to abandon the coalition which had served him so well for twelve years. The Conservatives and the Protectionist National Liberals together would have numbered at the outside 186, in an assembly of 397, while the Conservatives and the Ultramontanes controlled 210 votes, a number which would give him a majority and something to spare. Of the alternatives a coalition of the Conservatives and semi-Conservatives was the more natural, and in the event it might have succeeded in attracting many of the waverers who in German parliamentary life hang upon the fringe of the larger parties, but in such a crisis Bismarck was not disposed to take risks.

Looking to the future also he had to weigh the fact that while he might have to pay heavily for the support of the Conservative-Clerical combination, these two groups were the most homogeneous and best disciplined in the Diet, the groups freest from internal frictions, and therefore most likely to offer him a support upon which he would be able to count at all times, so long as he was himself willing to continue the compact and pay the price.

He therefore decided to accept the " Franckenstein clause," as it was called, and hence the Conservative-Clerical alliance which its acceptance implied.   This clause was in the end modified in one particular.   Instead of the condition that all revenue from the customs and tobacco duties beyond the amount hitherto received (108 million marks) should be divided between the States, as had been originally proposed, it was agreed that such a division should apply only to the excess beyond the sum of 130 million marks.   The Franckenstein clause was approved by the Diet on July 9th by 211 votes to 122, the majority being composed of the full strength of the Conservative and Clerical groups, while the National Liberals emphasized their resentment by voting solidly with the Opposition.

It was the last display of unity made by the National Liberal party.   Divided upon the principal issues of the day, paralysed by internal discords, antipathies, and rivalries, the party now rushed headlong into disaster.   A group of fifteen members of the right wing pronounced unreservedly for the Government and accepted the Tariff Bill without reservations, but the majority continued for a time unconvinced.   In the following year, after the immediate occasion of the rupture had passed away, those members of the party whose Liberalism was more than a name — among them Lasker, Bamberger, Rickert, and Forckenbeck — dissociated themselves from perverts and opportunists alike by seceding.   Declaring that " the National Liberal party is no longer actuated by that unity of political conviction upon which alone its justification and its influence depend," these members founded a group of their own, called the Liberal Union, which in 1881 entered the Diet twenty-one strong.

The Franckenstein clause was disliked by most of the thoughtful members of the Diet as perpetuating the evils of the matricular system, as a concession to particularism, and a humiliation to the Empire, which besides remaining dependent in finance as before now became a tax-collector for the federal States. Ever fertile in resource, Bismarck sought to justify his capitulation to the Centre by the tardy discovery that the question whether the Empire received its necessary revenues direct, or mediately from the States, was after all immaterial — a mere choice between *bonnet blanc* or *blanc bonnet.* His opponents did not allow him to forget, however, that a desire to abolish the matricular system of contributions altogether, with its arbitrary principle of assessment according to population, had been his principal object in revising the tariff, and that he was now perpetuating it in an even more objectionable form than before.

To his old associates, the National Liberals, Bismarck was far less than just. Their fault in his eyes was that they had dared for once to be independent; that they had shown themselves willing to go a long way in the desire to please him, even at the sacrifice of conviction, weighed as nothing in the scale against the fact that they had refused to sacrifice and stultify themselves entirely. While, therefore, they complained that he too lightly severed the old relationship, he persisted in regarding himself as the victim of base desertion, and his resentment against them was both bitter and permanent. Upon the question of separation itself reproaches were as unreasonable on the one side as the other. The alliance, for Bismarck at least, was one of political convenience, and when the allies were no longer able to see eye to eye it was open to either side to discontinue it. The manner of the separation was on Bismarck's part abrupt and ungracious, but if the disowned associates could not emulate him in the rancour of his upbraidings, they at least put into feeling all that he put into words. From this time may be dated the decay of the National Liberal party as an influential, and almost as a serious, factor in German parliamentary life.

Bismarck had attained his end; and the revised tariff was now secure, but already it was evident that the honours of the tourney would have to be shared with Windthorst and the Clericals. Although his party was making common cause with a Government which for some years had been relentlessly fighting the Roman Church and the Papacy, Windthorst made it clear that its motives were purely egoistical, and that there had been no bargaining. " What we are doing," he said, "we are doing for reasons which lie in the situation. We have promised nothing, and no promise has been made to us. I say that because it has been asserted that we shall eventually be duped. If we had made promises it would be objectively possible that we might be duped, but as we have neither given nor received them it is impossible, and, moreover, let me say that the man who intends to dupe me will have to get up early." Windthorst was resolved already that if any duping was to be done at all it should be done by himself; for the present it was enough to know that as no other Ministerial coalition was practicable, the fate of the Government, for the duration of one Parliament at least, was altogether in his hands.

The division which decided the fate of the Franckenstein clause decided the fate of the bill, which was adopted in the same sitting by a vote of 217 against 117. Seventeen National Liberals voted with the Conservatives and Clericals for Protection, but the great majority of the party voted with the Radicals and the Socialists against it. Before this the new Ministerial coalition had been cemented by a proceeding of unmistakable significance. Forckenbeck, the Liberal President of the Diet, and the first Vice-president having resigned their offices, the new allies promptly divided the vacant positions.

Part of the new tariff was to come into operation at once, part on October 1, 1879, and the remainder on January 1, 1880. Grateful for the success of a cherished scheme, the Emperor wrote a warm letter of congratulation to his victorious Chancellor (July 20th), in which he said: "You undertook to stir up a wasps' nest, and I sided with you from conviction, though I feared the result of your enterprise. It is rare that such a complete change of opinion has been achieved in so short a time."

The new tariff was now law, and in order that there might be no doubt that it was intended to be strictly enforced, Bismarck added to his offices of Imperial Chancellor and Foreign Minister that of Minister of Commerce in the Prussian Government. He was convinced that covert opposition and unwillingness to accept new departures were obstructing the transition to Protection. Accordingly he insisted upon some forcible removals in that somewhat hide-bound department, and for the rest appealed to the loyalty of his subordinates. Calling the higher officers together, he gave them to understand in his most affable manner that Free Trade was dead and buried, and that Germany's fiscal system had passed under the sovereignty of other ideas.[1] Let them be loyal to the new order, and all would be well.

One of the first direct results of the change of policy was a strong attempt to force the Hanseatic Free Cities into the Imperial Customs Union. Possibly the attempt might have succeeded at once had it been made in a different way. A year had not passed before the Chancellor addressed to the Federal Council (April 19, 1880) a memorial on the subject in which he complained that both Hamburg and Bremen " persist still in keeping outside the customs territory," and that they seemed to regard their position as free ports " no longer as a temporary one, as it was intended to be according to the treaty of July 8, 1867, and the intentions of the constitution, but as permanent." As regards Hamburg, therefore, he proposed on Prussia's behalf that the twin-seaport of Altona, situated in that kingdom, and the St. Pauli harbour quarter of Hamburg, adjacent to it, should cease to be outside the customs territory. A week later Hamburg replied with a counter-memorial declaring simply that any such interference with the treaty rights of the State without its consent was unpermissible, and inviting the Council to come to a decision upon this major question of law before discussing the Prussian proposal. The Federal Council had no intention to override the rights of one of the smaller States at Prussia's request, yet for reasons of policy it sought to evade the constitutional issue. The Diet, however, emphatically declared itself on the side of Hamburg and against the overbearing Chancellor in a declaration to which politicians now so alienated as Windthorst (Clerical), Lasker (National Liberal), and Richter (Radical) subscribed.

Bismarck, who never suffered opposition or accepted defeat tamely, promptly answered Hamburg's challenge by cancelling all the special facilities which the Prussian railways had hitherto afforded the port in connection with its live stock traffic. He had also in reserve another rod wherewith to punish the refractory State, should it be needful. This was a new Elbe navigation treaty with Austria, which had been concluded in March, 1880, and now awaited ratification by the Diet. One of the articles of this treaty provided that all goods, whether they entered Germany from the sea or from Bohemia, should

[1] H. von Poschinger, *Aus grosser Zeit*, p. 85.

" become liable to customs duty on crossing the customs boundary on the Elbe just in the same way as in crossing the customs boundary on land." As the fixing of the customs boundary on the Elbe was left to the Federal Council, it rested with that body, in which Prussia had so large an influence, to make the line either favourable or unfavourable for Hamburg. The Diet detected the possibilities of reprisals herein offered, however, and while unable to alter the wording of the treaty, approved it subject to the proviso that no new customs line should be fixed except in virtue of a special law. It was Delbrück who unkindly put this spoke in the Ministerial wheel.

The opposition of the Federal Council was overcome by Bismarck's proposal of a compromise to the effect that for the present only Altona and the Elbe from that town and Harburg (both in Prussia) to Cuxhaven should be incorporated in the Customs Union, leaving Hamburg in possession of all its treaty rights, but in splendid isolation. The proposal was warmly resented by the Free City, and led to another storm in the Diet. Feeling became doubly embittered when the Radical deputy Dr. Virchow read a letter in which the Chancellor candidly admitted that the removal of the customs boundary to Cuxhaven would compel Hamburg to seek admission into the union on pain of seeing the Elbe estuary converted into a Free Trade *mare clausum*, with neither ingress nor egress. There was, indeed, no disguise whatever as to Bismarck's intentions. He wanted to complete the economic unity of the Empire, and a Free Trade enclave in a Protectionist country was to him an intolerable incongruity.

The Diet was prorogued at the end of the year, and before it met again the financial provisions necessary to the proposed change had been prepared. In the meantime public opinion had come round to the view that the interests of the Empire were larger than those of its principal seaport, and that in clinging too tenaciously to its ancient rights Hamburg was placing itself in an unwise and untenable position. In the end a violent and impolitic controversy was settled by peaceful negotiation. In March it became known that the Senate of Hamburg and the Chancellor were in negotiation, and soon afterwards the Free City saw the wisdom of capitulation, convinced by reflection that it had been fighting for rights and privileges which, if lawful, were no longer expedient. By friendly agreement it was stipulated that with the exception of a small area, which should permanently remain a free harbour, unless Hamburg itself agreed to the contrary, the whole of the territory of the City State should from October 1, 1888, become part of the Imperial Customs territory. The law on the subject (February 16, 1882) stipulated that the Empire should contribute to the extent of two million pounds to the costs of the buildings, docks, equipment, and other arrangements necessary in the interests of traffic, as well as the expropriation proceedings incidental to the change. The costs to Hamburg itself were estimated at five million pounds. The incorporation of Bremen was not equally urgent, and it was only effected by a law of March 31, 1885. The cost to the Empire in this case was £600,000.

A further measure adopted at this time in pursuance of Bismarck's policy of protection for national trade recalled the early English Navigation Laws. A bill passed in 1881 provided that the German coasting trade might only be carried in German bottoms. Exceptions to the rule were to be allowed only in virtue of reciprocal international agreements. Upon the subject of navigation privileges in general Bismarck held strong opinions. When in November, 1879, Prussian ships navigating the Russian reaches of the Niemen, hitherto a free river, were required to pay dues, he promptly telegraphed from Varzin instructions that no Russian ships should be allowed to navigate the Prussian length of the river at all, dues or no dues, a counter-stroke which had the desired effect.

The operation of the new tariff was the signal for a strong wave of Protectionism which, first sweeping over the Continent, passed thence to the United States and the British Colonies. Russia, Austria, and France all increased their duties in 1881 and 1882, and it was not long before customs barriers rose on all hands to a height hitherto unknown. England alone retained her old faith in the policy of a free market. From the industrial standpoint Germany's first experiences of the new tariff were not in general encouraging, for the protection of one industry proved to the prejudice of another. Those who had known clearly what they wanted and had succeeded in obtaining it were well satisfied, but for a time discontent and disillusionment were common. The extent to which corn-growing benefited in the early years is uncertain; but there is general agreement that the small cultivators gained little or nothing, for the fall in corn prices which succeeded was not for a long time followed by a proportionate fall in rents, and this relief, when it came, proved to be of brief duration.

In 1884 Bismarck claimed that Protection had "freed the country from economic pressure," and that its prosperity was steadily increasing; imports and exports were both advancing, and there was in every port more shipping. Even yet, however, that drooping flower of the national garden, agriculture, had not lifted up its head. In 1885 the price of wheat was lower than for thirty years, and that of rye was far below the average. Before Protection was introduced there were far-seeing politicians who suspected that although agriculture was brought last into the scheme of fiscal reform it would end by taking the first place. Baron von Schorlemer-Alst predicted in 1876 that he "heard already the iron tread of the agrarians, with Bismarck as tambour-major at the head." Now the cry of need was again raised by this depressed industry; alike in the Imperial and State Legislatures there was urgent appeal to the all-powerful State to complete the good work of rescue which it began five years before. The Government did not hesitate to respond to the call. Early in 1885 a bill was introduced revising the tariff on both sides. The *exposé des motifs* which accompanied it claimed that by the law of 1879 the country's "economic development has been diverted from a false course into one which will enable energetic and discerning effort to compete successfully with other countries both in the home and foreign markets." It was held, however, that "a natural development and improvement" of the tariff was necessary to the better attainment of the goal desired. Bismarck once more stepped into the arena and championed the cause of Protection against its critics, boldly claiming that, in spite of the necessity for severer duties, the existing tariff had worked well according to its limitations.

The law as passed in May increased the corn duties all round — those on wheat and rye threefold, from 10s. to 30s. a ton — and also raised the duties on other farm produce and a few industrial articles. There was little serious opposition, and the Ministerial majority was composed as before of Conservatives, Clericals, and National Liberals. This second measure of Protection was passed in the special interest of agriculture, yet the new duties proved no more successful than the old in arresting the fall of prices, which continued during the following two years, and reached their lowest point in Germany in 1887. In that year the agricultural party once more reminded the Government of its obligations, and there was a further increase of the corn and live stock duties. In February there had been elected a Diet in which the Conservatives and National Liberals held a majority, and Bismarck, yielding to agrarian pressure, endeavoured to increase the duty upon wheat and rye from 30s. to 60s. per ton. The National Liberals, a hundred strong, held the balance, however, and their resistance led to a compromise, though the rate fixed, 50s., was then equalled in no other European country.

During the years which saw the reversal of Germany's Free Trade policy Bismarck carried out another project of great importance for the interests of commerce. This was the unification and nationalization of the railways of Prussia, a measure resorted to in default of a larger scheme, by which the entire railway system of Germany was to have been taken over by the Empire and worked as an imperial enterprise. The idea was not a new one. The constitution drawn up by the " Professors' Parliament " of Frankfort in 1848 proposed to give to the Empire then contemplated control over all existing railways and the right to construct and work new lines on its own account. A little later Bismarck himself, as a deputy in the first Prussian Diet, had advocated the closer connection of the State and the railways, with a view to the ultimate adoption of a large scheme of nationalization. It was in pursuance of this aim that he introduced in the constitution of the new Empire provisions giving to the Imperial Government power to build railways and also a large measure of control over the railway system generally.

In proposing the nationalization of the railways Bismarck did not ignore the consideration of revenue, yet the desire to reduce to order the existing chaos in railway administration and to develop the railways for the national advantage was the governing motive of his action. An incidental object which he had in view was the abolition of the illicit system of import premiums in vogue at that time. These premiums were offered in the form of preferential railway tariffs, under which corn from abroad was conveyed from the coast at low rates, to the benefit of the consumers, but to the great injury of the home producers.

Ever since 1871 the Prussian State had been competing more and more with private capital in railway enterprise. While some of the States applied to the reduction of their public debts so much of their share of the French indemnity as remained after other indispensable expenditure in the common interest had been covered, Prussia wisely allowed her moderate debt to remain, and invested the available money in railways and other productive undertakings. Several small railways were also bought by the State at the end of the bubble company period, when owing to exhausted resources their proprietors were unable to complete or work them, yet still for a long time private enterprise greatly predominated.

An impetus was given to the nationalization movement by the irregularities in connection with the promotion of Prussian railway companies which were unearthed by Dr. Lasker in 1873. These were debated in the Diet, with the result that the Government appointed a committee to investigate the whole question of railway construction, ownership, and administration. The result of this committee's report was the establishment in January, 1874, of a State Railway Council, one of whose duties was to exercise a continuous survey of the national railway system with a view to the construction of lines according to a considered plan. The Imperial Diet had already, by a law passed in 1873, created an Imperial Railway Board which was intended to act as a supervisory authority and as a court of complaints both for the Empire and the individual States. The Board entered upon its career amid high hopes, but from the first it had to encounter stubborn opposition on the part of the railway administrations, both State and private, with the result that its practical value proved small.

Faced by the refusal of the railway administrations of the various States to co-operate in introducing some degree of uniformity in the management of their lines, Bismarck tried in 1876 to win the Federal Council for a scheme under which all the important railways in the Empire would have become part of an imperial enterprise. As the head of the Government it was not difficult to persuade the Prussian Diet to lead the way by offering to hand over the whole of the State railways to the Empire on condition that the other States agreed to do the same. Many Radical deputies, jealous for the fetish of individualism, joined with the representatives of the private railway companies in opposing the bill on the subject, but there was a large majority in its favour. Prussia's willingness to be the *corpus vile* upon which this large experiment in railway nationalization was to be tried proved futile, however, for all the other States refused to fall in with the scheme. In part, their opposition was due to a natural desire to benefit still further by profitable undertakings which experience had shown to be a useful source of indirect taxation, but other reasons were the old jealousy of Prussian aggression and a fear that any new concessions made to the Empire would lead to yet further demands. Bismarck thereupon abandoned the idea of imperial railways, and it was never revived.

Nevertheless, failure to bring the States into line only strengthened the Prussian Government in its resolve not to rest until the entire railway system of the northern kingdom was either owned or administered by the State. Company after company was therefore bought out, particularly after 1879; where new lines were necessary the State constructed them; and within a few years the great majority of the railways, and all the important trunk lines, had passed into State ownership. The administration of the railways was also thoroughly reformed, and while greater consideration than before was given to the interests of commerce and agriculture, the lines were made to an increasing degree a source of revenue. While Prussia thus benefited, the effect of her vigorous railway policy was felt throughout the whole Empire, since it compelled the backward States to bring their own railway systems and administrations into a condition of greater efficiency. In the event the example and initiative of the major State brought about the very reforms which its allies had refused to accept under direct pressure.

CHAPTER XIV

(1871–1888)

SOCIAL ADJUSTMENTS

THE foremost episodes in the domestic history of Germany during the period of Bismarck's Chancellorship having been related in detail, other notable events and tendencies incidental to the new epoch may be reviewed more summarily. The dominant mark of this epoch was expansion, in the form of greater political influence abroad and in the development of the nation's material resources at home. The war of 1870–1871 had not been attended in Germany by any of the violent economic and social disturbances which had convulsed France. No German territory was invaded, no systematic blockade of the German coasts was attempted, and the temporary dislocation of labour, large though it was, caused no serious set-back to industry. The conclusion of a victorious peace was the signal for a great outburst of activity throughout the entire country, and the nation was carried forward on a wave of patriotic enthusiasm into new spheres of material enterprise and conquest. The foundations of German industrial and commercial prosperity had been laid long before; now the fabric itself sprang suddenly into sight, beneath the busy hands of her myriad builders.

Seldom has a nation so rapidly bridged the gulf between a position of relative poverty and one of positive well-being. For the first half of the century Germany still ranked as an impoverished country. Wages everywhere were low, being seldom much above and often below the subsistence level; local dearth was frequent; in many of the districts dependent upon home industries " hunger typhus " periodically decimated the population; the rising manufacturers of the factory towns had hardly begun to talk of fortunes; the successful business man was the man who had just enough, and he was usually well satisfied with that. Germans then lived frugally because they could not do otherwise. Until after the middle of the century about a quarter of all the wheat produced in the country was sold abroad, and the coarser rye was kept at home for food.

35

Yet even by this time the nation had given pledges of an assured economic future. Compulsory education had given to the artisan and labouring classes a high level of intelligence and aptitude, while compulsory military service had developed in them in a large degree the spirit of order, discipline, and co-operation. These advantages could not fail to prove of great effect in a material competition which was destined to be one of brains, science, and organization. There could be no hope of any marked advance, however, so long as the States closed their doors to each other, and the first definite commercial awakening may be dated from the time when the breaking down of internal customs barriers converted all Germany into one market. How important was this unification of the country for economic purposes will be understood when it is remembered that during the forty years following the middle of the century the population of the German customs territory increased from thirty-two to nearly fifty millions. The next necessary step was to introduce within the union of States greater uniformity in the media of commercial exchange and a common body of commercial law. Attempts to unify weights, measures, and coinage had been made since 1833, and they had partially succeeded; it was not until 1868, however, that this measure was carried out thoroughly for the States forming the North German Confederation; three years later it was applied to the Empire as it exists to-day. The metric system of weights and measures, first introduced optionally, became compulsory in 1872.

New forms of commercial enterprise, and especially the public company system, enlisted the resources of the community in the service of trade and industry upon a scale unknown and impossible hitherto. It is commonly supposed that Germany's first era of company promotion dated from the 'seventies, when the distribution of the French milliards gave an artificial impetus to enterprise and speculation. It really began twenty years before, in the flotation of large banks and other financial institutions, but it soon spread in other directions; in addition to railways, both State and private, many of the large mining, smelting, iron and steel, machinery, sugar manufacturing, steam shipping, and textile companies were established in the middle of the century. In those days were laid the foundations of many industrial undertakings which have since ranked with the most famous in the world, and of many princely fortunes which later enabled their owners to exchange the rank of commoner for that of the minor nobility. It was at this time also that the banks began to cultivate the relationship to industrial enterprise which became so intimate in later years. The idea of the co-operation of bank and industry had in 1852 given rise in France to the *Crédit Mobilier,* and German financiers were not slow to turn the idea to use. The German Bank for Trade and Industry was established in the following year at Darmstadt, and other banking institutions followed on the same lines. Only in the 'seventies did company promotion become for a time a mania; yet while it then led to many unhealthy developments, a large balance of solid advantage remained. Enterprise became more daring; many large new industries were established, and not a few old towns were recreated on industrial lines.

Now also Germany began to take a prominent place in foreign markets. The value of her foreign trade increased from 2,100 million marks in 1850 to 3,200 millions in 1860, 4,240 millions in 1870, and 5,980 millions in 1880. Later the progress was equally marked, and the increase in value during the following decade was to 7,470 millions. The export trade in particular received a powerful stimulus owing to the colonial movement which took practical shape in 1884 and 1885, with the concurrent introduction of mail steamship subsidies, by the aid of which regular communication by German vessels was established with East Asia, Australia, and parts of Africa. The years from 1880 onward were, as has been shown, a period of active emigration, and no fewer than 1,362,000 persons of German birth were lost to the Empire from this cause during the ten years 1880–1889 alone.[1] But the loss of population brought gain in other ways; if the emigrants did not make new Germanies over the seas, they made markets and consumers for German goods, and thus more work for the hands left at home.

The economic transition which was diverting the nation's energies in an increasing degree from agricultural into industrial and mercantile channels was illustrated by the growing aggregation of population in the towns. In the middle of the century one in four of the inhabitants of Prussia, one in five in Würtemberg, and one in seven in Bavaria lived in towns.

[1] It has been estimated that the number of Germans who emigrated from their native land during the nineteenth century was at least five millions. Fully a quarter of this emigration took place during the decade 1881 to 1890.

Thirty years later two out of five and at the end of the century one-half of all the inhabitants of Germany belonged to the urban class.

Notwithstanding these changes, so momentous in their influence, the years immediately preceding and following the establishment of the Empire were years of comparative barrenness in legislation for the welfare of the people. The third quarter of the century had passed before either the Government or the nation became conscious of the existence of a social question. As late as 1871 the Tübingen political economist, Gustav Schönberg, wrote deploring "how little we in Germany know about the real position of our working classes." It has been shown already that economic individualism had obtained a foothold in Germany. Copied from England, where it had from the first been embraced with passionate devotion by the hard-headed industrial pioneers of the North — *dura virum mater* — this austere faith had all the harshness and crudeness of copies, and it was under its unfavourable influence that the first great development of industrialism and the factory system took place. With the introduction of the constitutional era a strong revulsion against restraints of all kinds set in, and in sheer relief the middle-class parties welcomed liberty in any form and degree, little concerned about its effects.

When at the inaugural meeting of the Association for Social Policy, formed at Eisenach in 1872 to counteract the State policy of *laissez faire*, Gustav Schmoller claimed that the just desires and demands of the working classes should be emphasized with " moral pathos," the phrase was turned to a jest by the individualistic school of politicians, who replied that economic science had nothing to do with either morality or pathos. Nevertheless, from the Eisenach movement went forth beneficial influences which powerfully reacted upon the later development of the social question. From the first the leaders of the new movement — among whom were many well-known professors of political economy, including Schmoller and Adolf Wagner of Berlin, Conrad of Halle, Lujo Brentano of Munich, Schönberg of Tübingen, and Wilhelm Roscher of Leipzig — were called " Socialists of the Chair," a label more infelicitous than labels given in reproach usually are, since not one of them was identified, directly or indirectly, with either the party or the programme of Social Democracy. The name clung, however, and it has been used ever since with complete inconsequence to denote those university teachers and writers who, in their criticism of Socialism, have persisted in discriminating between the false doctrines and the true. So strongly entrenched was individualism in the Diets at that time that it was 1874 before factory inspection was introduced in Prussia, at first for Berlin and Silesia, and later for the whole kingdom; Saxony followed suit, but only in 1878 did it become obligatory — at least by statute — throughout the Empire. The most resolute opponents of this innovation were the Radicals, individualists almost to a man, who scoffed at it as a revival of the old police despotism.

When the question of social reform was taken up in earnest it was on the initiative of a Minister who hitherto had not touched and had barely looked at it. Bismarck had, indeed, already shown in his own crude way that he was not insensible to the sufferings of the poorer classes. Visiting England in 1862 he heard of the success of the co-operative movement, and on his return home he interested the King of Prussia in the movement. When a little later Lassalle came forward with his project of Productive Associations on a co-operative basis he persuaded the King to make a grant from his privy purse towards the cost of forming societies. Owing to his influence also the Silesian handloom weavers in 1865 received from the same source help in starting a co-operative manufactory. All this may have been laudable benevolence, but it was not social reform. Years were to pass before Bismarck realized that social conditions required ameliorative legislation. Busch, strong on the motives and origins of Bismarckian policies, says that he awakened to the recognition of a social question as early as 1871, when exchanging ideas with European Governments regarding the measures best suited to counteract the Internationalist movement. If he awakened, he did no more at that time, for it was his struggle with Socialism at home, which began seven years later, that really opened his eyes to the fact that all could not be well with the social system under which hundreds of thousands of the most patient people in the world were flocking to the banner inscribed " Proletarians of all countries, unite!"

Was Bismarck ever a social reformer by study and reasoned conviction? It is doing him no injustice to answer this question negatively. Upon this, as upon most questions, he was guided by intuition and instinct. He saw that things were wrong, and without troubling about scientific theories and sanctions, he tried, by heroic measures and straight cuts, to make them right. Yet his solicitude for the working classes was an acquired solicitude, and he arrived at it under the pressure of political difficulties. The whole bent of his mind was against any interference with the "natural" relations of capital and labour. When, as late as 1877, the Prussian Minister of Commerce prepared a bill which was intended to afford to the working classes greater protection in matters affecting their physical and moral welfare, Bismarck criticized it so severely that it had to be dropped. He regarded the labour question still as essentially one of more or less wages, of longer or shorter hours of employment, and he was far more concerned that employers should not be unduly crippled in their power to meet labour's just demands than that work should be done under ideal conditions. For traces of any genuine comprehension of social problems, or even of intimate knowledge of the working classes, Bismarck's speeches will be searched in vain. They abound in vivid intuitions of economic truth, in true and sagacious reflections upon social relations, and invaluable *dicta* of common sense and worldly wisdom, which even the best trained sociologist may still read with profit, but they reflect a mind influenced rather by expediency than deep conviction and impelling enthusiasm. He passed social laws because they were necessary; social reform was never to him a passion, but always a policy.

When, however, Bismarck had once decided to enter this untried path, progress was far easier for him than it was for the early reformers in England, where the prejudices and preconceptions to be overcome were so many and so deeply rooted. Individualism seemed to have conquered in Germany, but the truth was that the victory had merely been that of the handful of men who had for the time controlled fiscal and economic policy in the Ministries, and it lasted only so long as they lasted. Never did individualism obtain a firm hold upon national thought. The theory that the State had an unquestionable right to interfere in any direction in which the common good was endangered, and that it was the special duty of the Crown to hold the balance between conflicting interests, had for generations been a ruling tradition of Prussian statecraft. Now, in the conditions incidental to a time of transition, this tradition proved of immense value. It was not necessary to create precedents for State action; precedents existed in abundance, and all that was needed was to go back to the forsaken ways.

The student who compares the different lines followed by social movements, particularly as reflected in labour law reforms, in England and Germany will find an invaluable clue in the fact that these movements have relied for their chief impetus in one country upon self-help and in the other upon State initiative and furtherance. In England the tendency was to set labour free from fetters and then leave it to fight its own battles. Hence freedom to organize in trade unions was given to the English working classes as early as 1825. In Germany the tendency was the other way. There labour has never yet been free, and such liberty of action as it enjoys to-day was gained in England half a century ago. To Governments still steeped in the traditions of absolutism it seemed safer to admit a tacit obligation to do for labour what it was not able or allowed to do for itself. That labour has so seldom given proof of gratitude for the boons conferred upon it is chiefly due to the fact that the State has never seriously tried to view labour questions from the labour standpoint, and that reforms for its benefit have too often been carried out only under pressure. "While we laud and magnify the great deeds of the Imperial Government in social politics," writes a German historian of social movements, Dr. F. Naumann, "it must never be forgotten that many of these great deeds were only necessary because of the gigantic blunders of the same Government, and that all the laws for the protection of skilled workmen are a poor substitute for the free activity of the trade unions."

Inheriting these traditions, Bismarck decided before the Empire was ten years old to embark upon the largest and most original experiment in constructive social reform ever attempted, an experiment which threw into the shade the best that had been done by the heavy-handed but well-meaning patriarchalism of the past. Brushing on one side all questions of wages and hours of labour, as questions which the working classes should be left to settle with their employers, and ignoring all demands for the right of free organization and combination, as opening up a vista of dangerous possibilities at a time when Socialistic doctrines were making ominous headway, he proposed a great scheme of social insurance by which the workers were to be afforded care and provision in all the vicissitudes of industrial life — medical treatment and maintenance in sickness, generous compensation in the event of accident, support during periods of unemployment, and finally pensions in the time of old age and permanent disablement.

The germ of this idea of social providence was to be found in existing institutions, some with a long and honourable past. Ever since the time of Frederick the Great there had been miners' benefit societies in Prussia, affording help to members and their dependents in times of need, societies so admirable in purpose and organization that all the modern insurance legislation has left them still free to do their old work in their own way. Since the middle of the century also societies for the relief of sickness had been formed in large number by the working classes on the voluntary principle which had already been successfully developed in England; in many parts of the country the same purpose was served by the workshop clubs, often subsidized by the employers; and in South Germany the municipalities insured the labouring classes against sickness. In spite of all these agencies, however, the number of wage-earners for whom such provision existed was still far smaller than the number of those without it.

One of the first measures passed by the Imperial Diet in 1871 had been an Employers' Liability Law, applying to factories, mines and quarries. Not only was that legislation partial, but liability was contingent on proof of culpability, and even more than the corresponding law of England it proved a fruitful source of litigation, engendering much bitterness. Often the injured workman's only chance of obtaining redress lay in appeal to the law court, where he fought against hopeless odds and under conditions which gave him every inducement to accept a fraction of his rights rather than risk the loss of the whole. On the other hand, the law was onerous and inequitable from the standpoint of small employers, since it made no provision for distributing the risks, with the result that these men often were either unable to meet their liabilities or were crushed beneath the weight of them.

A beginning was therefore made with the improvement of the provision for injured workmen. Instead of tinkering the existing law, as was done later in England with deplorable results, Bismarck decided to legislate afresh upon the two principles of compulsory insurance and mutuality. The first Accident Insurance Bill was laid before the Diet in March,

1881. It was intended to apply only to some of the more dangerous industries and enterprises and to secure almost automatically to the workpeople employed therein pensions for injuries which destroyed or reduced their earning capacity, with pensions to their dependents in the event of fatality. The employers were to pay two-thirds and the workpeople one-third of the premiums, and the State was to make a contribution towards increasing the benefits. Insurance was to be effected through a State institution with a view to eliminating private gain. Bismarck at once resolutely took the field on behalf of this social crusade, and during the five years occupied in passing the early Insurance Laws he expounded and defended his proposals at every step.

The only parties which took up an unfriendly attitude were the Social Democrats and the Radicals, the former because nothing short of the immediate realization of the collectivist State would satisfy them, the latter because the proposals were in conflict with their cherished individualistic doctrines. The Diet struck out the proposals for a Central Insurance Board and for State subsidies, and Bismarck withdrew the bill for the purpose of reconsidering both it and the Diet, for new elections were due in the autumn. In the hope of rallying the working classes to the support of the bill he now promised that part of the proceeds of a State tobacco monopoly, which he proposed simultaneously, should be applied towards the cost of social reform, thus becoming a " patrimony for the disinherited." So confident was his belief in social reform as a political asset that he appealed to the country mainly upon this question. The issue was, however, complicated by the Protectionist controversy, and the part of the nation which supported him on that question was smaller than that which endorsed his social insurance policy. The result was that the Ministerial parties lost many seats, and that for his new majority Bismarck had to depend upon a coalition of Conservatives and Clericals.

The new Diet was opened on November 17th with a striking Imperial Message on the social question, since regarded as a classical declaration of State policy towards labour, and still spoken of to-day as the German charter of social reform. Emperor William I is commonly credited, if not with the authorship, at least with the inspiration of this memorable document. With neither authorship nor inspiration had he anything whatever to do, for while it is true that it received his cordial endorsement, as well as that of the Crown Prince, with whom Bismarck conferred before its final form was decided, the work itself, both in conception and composition, was his Chancellor's. The Imperial Message was the precursor of a larger scheme of social reform than had been contemplated hitherto; it was in effect a declaration that social reform could never again be regarded as a chapter of national life that could be completed by any specific measures at any specific time, but must rather be thought of as a running record of amelioration and progress, to which each generation and each decade must make its own due contribution.

It was not until June, 1884, that a law on accident insurance was passed. A larger group of trades and industries was embraced; the principle of mutuality was retained; but the entire cost was now placed upon the employers, who voluntarily renounced the offer of a State subsidy rather than submit to the large measure of Government interference which its acceptance would have entailed. The law came into force on October 1, 1885, and during the succeeding three years it was extended so as to include practically all the wage-earning classes.

In the meantime a sickness insurance scheme had been enacted on equally comprehensive lines. Introduced in the Diet in May, 1882, it was submitted to discussion and scrutiny for a whole year before it was deemed fit to leave the Legislature, so that when it became law in May, 1883 (with force as from December 1, 1884), it was a masterly piece of constructive legislation, so thoroughly and honestly wrought in every part that it was able to stand the test of practice for a generation without any alteration of its main principles. The contributions required to meet the cost of benefits were to be paid to the extent of two-thirds by the workers and one-third by the employers; a State subsidy was neither given nor asked for.

Bismarck did not carry measures of such magnitude without encountering a vast amount of prejudice and much vehement hostility. Only two parties in the Diet carried their opposition to extremes — the Radicals on the plea that his reforms went too far, the Social Democrats on the plea that they did not go far enough. When Dr. Bamberger crystallized the objections of the former party in the dogmatic utterance, " To carry on social policy is to commit the State to a series of Socialistic postulates," Bismarck answered that he was too old to be terrified by phrases; it was enough for him that the policy which underlay his proposals, let these be called by whatever name the Radicals wished, was the traditional policy of Prussia. To the Socialists he replied that what they really feared was that ameliorative legislation might promote social contentment, and that their mills might in consequence have to stand still.

Provision for old age and incapacity remained to be made, and this likewise took the form of insurance. Before a bill on the subject was introduced, an outline of the intended proposals was submitted to the Prussian Economic Cabinet at the end of 1887, and later was published for general discussion. Criticisms and suggestions were invited from public authorities, associations of employers and workpeople, social workers, and the Press, and only after this inquest of the thought of the nation had been made was a bill submitted in the Diet. Like the other two measures of social insurance, this likewise was compulsory, while the cost was equally divided between the workers and their employers, except that the State undertook to make a contribution to the pensions given. The bill was ultimately passed in May, 1889, though by a small majority — 185 against 165. The Conservatives and National Liberals voted solidly in its favour, but all the Clericals except thirteen, all the Radicals except one, and the whole of the Social Democrats voted against it.

The question of making provision for the unemployed, either in the form of insurance or assistance by work, was allowed to stand over, and meanwhile the municipal authorities were encouraged to regard this province of social providence as specially suited to local effort.

Of all the opposition offered to the social insurance laws that of the Socialists, the representatives of the class to be benefited, was the most incomprehensible. In later years the leaders of the party gave currency to the myth that they were the true friends of this beneficial legislation, and that without them it would not have come into existence. It is undoubtedly true that the Socialist agitation had directed public attention to social evils which had been ignored so long as they were borne by the victims patiently. Bismarck himself admitted that without that agitation social reform might have been indefinitely postponed. If, however, the Socialists entertained friendship for these laws, they showed it in remarkable ways. Most of their criticism was negative and barren, and their only positive action took the form of demands so extreme and

impracticable that their effect, if not their purpose, was purely
obstructive.

It was unfortunate that repression at this time went hand in
hand with attempts to conciliate the working classes by ameliorative legislation, for the effect was to cause the Government's
professions of good-will to be received with sullen ingratitude.
Hence as soon as social legislation was promised Bebel declared in the Diet (May 4, 1880), " To your positive measures
for their benefit the workers reply with ringing laughter,"
while the Dresden party congress of 1882 formally decided to
" reject State Socialism so long as it is inaugurated by Prince
Bismarck and is designed to support the Government system."
The party soon had reason to change its mind, however, for the
Copenhagen congress of 1883 decided to accept the proposed
reforms for what they were worth. In later years it might
truly be said that the blessings showered upon Bismarck's insurance legislation by the Social Democrats were more emphatic
than their earlier curses ; yet the fact remains that had the
leaders of the party had their way the social insurance laws
might not have been passed to the present day.

No sooner had social reform begun in one direction than
other labour problems were found to need attention. One related to Sunday labour. No one was more hostile at that
time to interference in the relations of capital and labour than
Bismarck. A prodigious worker himself, he refused to listen
to any proposal to regulate the hours of labour, either of men
or women, holding that upon such a question no general rules
could be laid down, and that the individual worker should be
allowed to fix for himself the limits of his endurance. Only
under great pressure was he persuaded to abandon his attitude
of non-intervention even in regard to Sunday labour. The Industrial Code of 1869 exempted workpeople from the obligation to work on Sunday except in industries which required un-
interrupted operations, but it did not forbid Sunday work, and
for many years it was common both in factories and workshops. In the industrial districts of the West there were employers who kept their workpeople at the wheel all the year
round except on the high festivals, with the curious result that
if prisoners were employed with them, as was often the case,
the forced workers rested every seventh day while the free men
toiled on. In 1882 Bismarck tardily capitulated in principle
upon this question, but it was only in 1886 that he moved seri-

ously in the matter by referring it to a commission of investigation. The report of this commission was a tragic document, particularly as throwing light upon the destruction of home life. The evidence of the employers showed great difference of opinion as to the need for Sunday work, some contending that industry could not exist without it, and others frankly admitting that in most cases it was due to greed of gain. The workpeople were almost unanimous in demanding at least one free day in the week. Nevertheless, five years more passed before the question was regulated by imperial legislation, as the result of an international labour conference held in Berlin.

Meanwhile, something was done to preserve the existence of the small tradesmen and handicraftsmen by weakening the provisions of the Industrial Code relating to freedom of occupation. That law was, as has been shown, the result of a Liberal awakening, and as such it was obnoxious to the feudal Conservatives and hardly less to the Clericals. Hence one of the first fruits of the coalition of these parties in 1879 was a successful attempt to replace certain trades and occupations under the old restrictions by means of a system of concessions and licences, some granted by the State, others by the local authorities. More important were the efforts made by the same parties to subject the trade guilds to far-going restrictions. After vainly trying in 1879 and 1880 to secure the passing of a rigorous bill on the subject, the Government produced one of its own. The Conservatives clamoured for compulsory guilds. Declining to go so far, the Government nevertheless gave to the guilds certain powers of pressure and even coercion in relation to handicraftsmen desirous of remaining outside. The law also created Chambers of Handicrafts, on the analogy of the Chambers of Commerce, of Industry, and of Agriculture, for the representation of the collective interests of the guilds of given areas, the exercise of general oversight over these organizations, the regulation of apprenticeship and the examination of masters and journeymen. Like some other hastily devised social legislation of that and a later time, the law relating to trade guilds has since undergone much amendment, chiefly in directions regarded by the Liberal parties as reactionary.

Not the least difficult of domestic problems was that of the government of the border populations which had been united to Germany against their will, and the last of the conquered peoples, the French of the *Reichsland* or Imperial Province, promised to give more trouble than the first, the Poles of the East of Prussia. Lorraine was almost wholly French, while Alsace, notwithstanding a strong survival of German traditions in the rural districts, had become strongly French in sentiment. To the difficulties thus created by race and language were added others due to religious antagonisms. For except in Lower Alsace the population of both territories was overwhelmingly Roman Catholic, and the alienation which thus existed from the first was deepened by the fact that soon after the annexation Germany entered upon her quarrel with Rome upon a question of dogma and faith. Nevertheless, if success was not achieved in the work of conciliation the causes did not all lay in the antecedent conditions. For a time Alsace-Lorraine was placed under absolute rule, like a vassal territory. Governed from Berlin by the Emperor, which meant the Imperial Chancellor, it was inevitable that the administration of the Province should from the first have fallen into Prussian hands. It was doubtless with the best intentions that the Prussian bureaucracy was specially chosen for the difficult task, and the choice made unquestionably for efficiency. It does not seem to have occurred to the statesmen in power in that day that efficiency might have waited until progress had been made with conciliation.

The obligation of military service had been introduced as soon as the Province passed into the new occupation, for though 47,000 Alsatian women petitioned Bismarck to defer the levying of recruits for several years, he refused to delay a measure which he professed to believe would hasten rather than retard attachment to the new citizenship. Next the French system of local government was superseded except in the towns, where it continued in part for many years. The Province was subdivided into districts and circles on the Prussian principle, and to all three administrative areas were assigned the customary representative assemblies. Local government was decidedly improved, for the officials introduced from the North were able and honest, if narrow. In a short time the laxity incidental to the French system disappeared, and unaccustomed activity reigned under the influence of men who had been taught that the business of governments, whether national or local, was to govern, and that laws were meant to be enforced. The municipal *maires* in particular were harassed in a way unknown so long as they were under the light and easy-going supervision of the French prefects, who had valued a good political record more highly than well-managed towns. Many important reforms were introduced; local finance was reorganized and taxation equalized; the economic resources of the Province were developed; the railways were improved and fares reduced; and the road system was extended. While, however, all these and other benefits were appreciated, they were outweighed, in the minds of the native population, by the fact that they came from hostile hands. Above all, the " dictator paragraph " of the law of December 30, 1871, which empowered the Chief President to proclaim martial law at his discretion was a source of vexation to a proud and sensitive people. This obnoxious emblem of what to the French was an alien Cæsarism lasted until 1902.

The first Chief President was Eduard von Möller, a bureaucrat of the best type, and he went to Strassburg with ardent hopes and generous intentions. In so far as he was free to follow his own wishes he leaned towards leniency, and it was not his fault if the Province showed itself as hostile to moral as to military conquest. Under his direction much was done for the social and intellectual welfare of the population, not without regard for its speedier Germanization. A university was re-established at Strassburg in May, 1872, at the cost of the Empire, and 300,000 volumes were presented to its library from all parts of the country. The value of the institution was admitted, but if the gift was appreciated there was little public sign of gratitude. At its opening Strassburg refused to decorate itself, and the only German flags displayed were those which floated over the cathedral and the public buildings. The first rector of the university, a local professor of theology, was for a time boycotted by his old colleagues as a renegade.

One of the first measures by which it was sought to combat French influence was the restriction of the use of the French language in the schools and in official intercourse. The educational changes in particular caused great friction, and this increased when school attendance was made compulsory. The Germans had found education largely in the hands of the Roman Catholic priests and nuns, and comparatively few of the teachers held diplomas. By the School Law of February 3, 1873, which was passed as a weapon in the struggle with

Rome, school inspection was transferred to the State, and henceforth only German teachers, who had capacity, if not always tact, were appointed.

Amongst the most difficult of the problems which had to be faced was that of the future citizenship of the old population of the Province, and here almost inevitably much bad blood was created. The inhabitants were given until October 1, 1872, to decide whether they would for the future be German or French subjects, and according to the Peace of Frankfort all who " optated " for France were required to leave the country within a specified period, failing which they were to be regarded and treated as German citizens, possessing all rights as such, but liable also to the corresponding duties, including that of military service. So hard were the conditions of choice found to be in practice that of 165,000 " optants " only 50,000 (12,000 being immigrant French people) were able to make their choice effective, by seeking a home and a livelihood across the frontier, and many of those who thus emigrated were compelled later to return and become German citizens against their will.

All these measures, with the rigour of their enforcement and the want of consideration shown by the minor bureaucracy, provoked deep resentment, which made unavailing the Chief President's personal urbanity. The most hopeless fact of all was the astonishment of Berlin that the French did not accept the new rule with joy and gratitude. When the elections to the district and circle diets took place in the summer of 1873 more than half the members returned refused to take the oath of allegiance to the Emperor, and as a consequence few of the diets were allowed to meet. In the same year the Strassburg Town Council was suspended because of a quarrel with the Government, and in April, 1874, it was dissolved, the affairs of the town being administered in commission for some time.

It was originally intended that the constitution of the Empire should be introduced into the Province at the beginning of 1873, and that until then the Emperor and his Chancellor should continue the autocracy, but the time was found to be too short for a transition so fundamental, and the date of the change was postponed for a year. From January, 1874, however, the Province was given direct representation in the Imperial Diet by fifteen deputies, eligible on the same franchise as the rest of the members. The first elections resulted

in the return of a compact body of " Protesters," not all
equally vehement in their anti-Germanism, but all bound by
mandate to declare solemnly against annexation in the Diet of
the Empire. Of the deputies two were bishops and five priests,
and nearly all were Roman Catholics, so forming a welcome
addition to the newly organized Centre party. The first act
of the " Protesters " in the Diet was to propose a resolution
declaring that " inasmuch as the population of the Province
had been incorporated in the German Empire without being consulted, the Government should at once take a vote upon the
question." The resolution received only twenty-one votes, and
on its rejection most of the " Protesters " left the assembly
and Berlin, and took no further part in the Diet's proceedings
during the session.

Later the deputies from Alsace-Lorraine divided into two
parties; the " Protesters " continued to protest, but there was
formed a group of Alsatians who would have been satisfied with
autonomy within the Empire. The action of this party at
home was directed towards the cultivation of local patriotism,
acceptance of the new situation, and the promotion of the
moral and material interests of the provinces; in the Diet it
worked for the amelioration of the dictatorship, the abolition
of restrictions upon civil freedom and the Press, and of the
rigour of the School Law, and the defence of the French language. The moderation shown by this party encouraged Bismarck to advance more quickly than he had intended upon the
path of devolution. An imperial decree of October 29, 1874,
created a Provincial Council of thirty members, co-opted from
members of the three district diets, whose function it was to
deliberate and advise upon measures and questions relating
to the Province — including the yearly budget — not falling
within the jurisdiction of the Imperial Diet, prior to legislation thereon. The Council met for the first time in April,
1875, and was opened by the Chief President in a conciliatory
speech, in which he expressed the hope that the Government
would soon entrust to the Province the entire management of
its affairs — a hope destined to be realized only thirty-six
years later. The Council was warmly welcomed, and it proved
at first so successful that in the following year Bismarck obtained the Imperial Diet's willing assent to a further concession
to autonomy in an arrangement providing that laws for Alsace-
Lorraine which had been approved by the Federal Council and

assented to by the Provincial Council might be promulgated
without any co-operation on the part of the Legislature.

When in the elections of 1877 the autonomists were further
strengthened, Bismarck, accepting the fact as a good omen,
increased the powers of the Provincial Council, which was now
allowed to pass laws and approve the budget, still subject to
control from Berlin. A more important step in the direction
of autonomy was taken in 1879. The deputies from Alsace in
the Diet had persistently called for an independent Government, free from interferences which were a constant reminder
to the population of its subordinate position. Willing to meet
them half-way, Bismarck now caused a constitution to be drawn
up empowering the Emperor to delegate the sovereignty in the
Province to a Governor, to be resident at Strassburg, who
should represent the Imperial Chancellor in the internal affairs
of the country. The Alsace-Lorraine department of the Imperial Chancellery and the office of Chief President of the Province were to be abolished, and in their place was to be created
a formal Ministry, under a Secretary of State, with several
departments, each directed by an Under-Secretary of State.
The Governor was to be assisted by a Council of State composed of officials (including the members of the Ministry) and a
number of notables of the Province chosen by the Emperor.
The Provincial Council was to continue, and its membership
to be increased to fifty-eight, and the Province was to be represented in the Federal Council by commissaries *ad hoc* when
matters concerning them had to be decided, yet without votes.
The Diet approved the scheme in July, and it came into operation in October.

It seemed likely for a time that the popular Crown Prince
Frederick would be sent to Strassburg as the first Governor or
Stadholder, but the proposal broke down. The next best choice
was made by the appointment of Field-Marshal von Manteuffel,
who retained the office until his death in June, 1885. He made
an honest attempt to win the confidence of the population,
respecting religious susceptibilities so far as his own influence
went, improving the educational system, and making the lot of
" optants " easier, even to the extent of allowing many emigrants to return to their native communes. His conciliatory
policy displeased the advocates of forcible Germanization, who
complained that for a Prussian official he was too friendly to
France, and called for stricter measures. Manteuffel himself

was disappointed when in the elections of 1881 the autonomists
disappeared and the " Protesters " swept the polls with 133,000
out of 166,000 votes. Now Bismarck lost patience. He
had hoped to reconcile the Province to the new rule by setting
over it clement administrators, and he saw that he had failed.
No longer disposed to waste sympathy and good-will upon people who refused to respond, he began in 1881 a new policy,
marked by rigorous measures, such as the suppression of anti-
German societies and newspapers, wholesale prosecutions, the
expulsion of French citizens and political agitators, and further
restrictions upon the use of the French language.

Manteuffel was succeeded in 1885 by Prince Chlodwig von
Hohenlohe, whose appointment was made the occasion of a determined effort by the reactionary party in Berlin, led by Herr
von Bötticher, Minister of the Interior, to persuade the Emperor and Bismarck to discard the new constitution and return
to the autocratic system of administration. The effort failed,
but the spirit which prompted it conquered. By way of compromise more power was given to the Governor, and in order
further to emphasize the change of system the Under-Secre-
taries of State were abolished. Severity on one side was answered by resentment on the other. When before the imperial
elections of February, 1887, on the Army Bill, Hohenlohe
lectured the inhabitants of the Province upon their duty to
their own land and the Empire, they replied by again returning a solid body of extremists, all pledged to oppose the Government. The result was more compulsion and more bitterness. Hohenlohe repelled French agitation with a rigorous
hand; he freely expelled French agents, weeded out of the public authorities all persons suspected of entertaining sentiments
that could be regarded as either actively French or passively
anti-German; he dissolved hostile organizations, banished
" optants " whom his predecessor had allowed to remain in the
country, proscribed the French language, prohibited the use
of the French currency, required all French residents in the
Province to take out registration papers, and in the hope of
making difficult intercourse with France introduced a rigid compulsory passport system which proved a prolific source of aggravation. Strictly speaking, the passport regulations were
contrary to the spirit, if not also the letter, of the Treaty of
Frankfort under which Alsace-Lorraine was ceded to Germany,
for article 11 of that convention stipulated that most-favoured-

nation treatment should be given reciprocally by the two countries in relation to " rights of ingress and egress, transit, customs formalities, and the admission and treatment of the subjects of the two nations as well as of their agents."

In this year there was again talk of the partition of the Province, Alsace going to Bavaria and Baden and the whole of German Lorraine, with its rich iron-ore mines, to Prussia, but Hohenlohe was against it, and it is not likely that the Diet would have approved it. On the other hand, Bismarck seriously considered the repeal of the Governorship Law of 1879, the transference of the seat of administration from Strassburg back to Berlin, and the conversion of the Province into a Crown colony. A bill was even drawn up with these objects in view, but at the last moment he was induced to change his mind. All the more determined was he, however, that the form of government it had should be made more rigorous for the discontented population. Hohenlohe's memoirs afford many glimpses of the iron hand in action. In August Bismarck hears that an Old German separatist party has been formed in Alsace, led by certain professors and schoolmasters at Strassburg and elsewhere, and he writes to the Governor that if this be the case " it must be the result of an inclination to subordinate State interests to personal feelings," and as " State officials have no right " to personal feelings, he orders them to be " sternly dealt with."

So the struggle between the races passed more and more completely into the vicious circle of provocation and retaliation, and when Hohenlohe laid down his office in 1894, after Alsace-Lorraine had for nearly a quarter of a century been under German rule, they seemed as far apart as at the beginning. Hohenlohe was not seen at his best as a local political administrator. With all his open-mindedness upon political questions in general, he shared the pedantry of the scholar, and was apt to make a fetish of logic and consistency. His unbending attitude towards the French, with whom in France he had been so much in sympathy, showed that in his urbane South German character there was yet a vein of Northern iron. Perhaps he was at the time too much under the influence of Bismarck, whose successor he hoped to be, to have cared to give frank conciliation a further chance. It is certain that he would have been the first to blame in another many of the hard measures which were carried out in the Province with his

own approval and authority. The only result achieved was to
create everywhere a deeper feeling of discomfort and irritation,
and to efface the memories of the milder *régime* which had pre-
ceded. When the third Emperor and Empress visited Strassburg and Metz in August, 1889, the welcome they received was
German and official; the great mass of the population looked
on coldly. Hence it was that Alsace-Lorraine remained at the
end of Bismarck's Chancellorship unpacified, sullen, discontented, no diadem in the imperial crown, but a thorn.

While the pacification of Alsace-Lorraine was an imperial
concern, Prussia had in two parts of the monarchy her own
race difficulties, in each case a similar legacy of conquest. In
the case of the Polish provinces the trouble went back a hundred years, to the time when Frederick the Great divided the
old Polish kingdom with Austria and Russia. After the recon-
stitution of Prussia by the Congress of Vienna in 1815, an
earnest attempt was made by Frederick William III to establish harmony in that part of his realm. He renewed in effect
the promise made to the Poles and broken by Frederick the
Great, and repeated in identical terms by Frederick William
II after the final partition of Poland in 1795, that he would
" confirm all and sundry in their possessions and rights, spiritual and temporal, protect the Roman Catholic faith, allow
every man to follow his religion freely and peaceably, and in
general so rule the land that the sensible and well-disposed inhabitants may be happy and contented and have no cause to
regret the change." For a time it seemed as though the good-
will of the population would really be won. So far did conciliation go that the Poles were allowed to have a Governor of
their own, sitting side by side with the Prussian Chief President. The only visible result, however, was a steady decline of
Prussian influence in the Polish districts. After the Polish
revolution in 1830, though there had been no active response
to it over the German frontier, the Government in Berlin decided that the policy of conciliation had been carried too far
for safety, and that it was time to assert again the strong hand
of authority.

Now began the exasperating device of colonization or settlement, first associated with the names of Chief President E. H.
Flottwell and General von Grolmann, which a generation later
was to be elevated into a settled policy of State. If the Poles
could not be Germanized, they might at least be supplanted by

Germans. Accordingly, efforts were made, by the purchase of estates in Polish ownership, to eject the untractable peasants and labourers from the soil, and to establish in their stead German immigrants from Protestant districts. The more the national spirit was repressed, however, the more it gained in strength and purpose. Coercion and persecution multiplied agitation a hundredfold. Political societies, secret and open, were formed in large numbers both in town and country; if the Germans boycotted the Poles, the Poles reciprocated with interest. During the reign of Frederick William IV repression was stayed, and altogether a milder *régime* continued until Bismarck came to power.

Bismarck repeatedly said that it was the activity of the priests in support of the Polish nationalist movement in Prussia which first convinced him in 1870 of the danger of capitulating to the claims of the Roman Catholic Church after the declaration of the Dogma of Infallibility, and led him early in the struggle with Rome to abolish the clerical inspectorship of schools. Perhaps his least excusable mistake in his dealings with the Poles was this decision to attack the Polish movement from the ecclesiastical and religious side, since by so doing he stirred up against himself and against Prussia the deepest resentment of a passionate people whose attachment to their faith was closely bound up with the chequered history and tragic memories of their dissolved kingdom. For the priests were the natural leaders of the people, and persecution only served to draw the two more closely together. Meanwhile, the Polish cause had gained the assistance of a compact party of about twenty members both in the Prussian and the Imperial Diet. Besides voicing the wrongs and claims of the Polish population, this party was always ready to swell a hostile demonstration against the Government and to work together with the Centre on questions of controversy between State and Church.

Side by side with repressive measures against the Prussian Poles, there began in 1885 a series of wholesale expulsions from the provinces of West Prussia and Posen of Poles of Russian and Austrian nationality, who had settled in these provinces in large numbers. These expulsions inflicted serious injury upon the victims and the communes in which they had lived, and also created a very unfavourable impression in Russia. In the Imperial Diet the episode led to a strong protest, in which the Poles were supported not only by the representatives of the other alien nationalities, the French of Alsace-Lorraine and the Danes of Schleswig, but by the combined strength of the Clerical, Radical, and Socialist groups. The protest having been addressed to the Federal Council in the form of a memorial (January 16, 1886), that body declined to consider it on the ground that the subject of complaint was one of Prussian internal politics, with which the Empire and its Executive had no concern, an attitude not less convenient than correct, but far from satisfactory to St. Petersburg.

In the meantime the Prussian Government had decided upon a measure of a more practical kind; it was a return to the abandoned colonization policy of Flottwell. The first Colonization Law of 1886 created a Land Commission for the Polish districts, and set aside the sum of five million pounds for use in the purchase of estates in Polish hands and their division into holdings of suitable size for occupation by German families. During the first four years of the operation of the law the Land Commission bought in this way some 110,000 acres of land. The effect of this resuscitated form of pressure was to draw the Poles more closely together and to lead them to pool their resources with a view to a united counter-movement. Land banks were established for the purpose of buying German estates in turn and parcelling them out amongst the families who had been displaced by the Government's action. So successful was this policy of retaliation that the land bought and settled by Poles soon far exceeded in extent that acquired by the German Land Commission, and the consequent rise in prices necessitated additional Government grants at intervals until the Land Commission's original capital had been increased fivefold. Great and undeserved hardship was done by the indiscriminate supplanting of thousands of Polish citizens, whose misfortune it was that they loved their nation and its great past not wisely but too well, yet the Poles as a whole gained rather than lost by the political pressure to which they were subjected. To this policy of expatriation, more than to any other cause, must be attributed the economic and social awakening of the Germanic branch of the Slavic race. Of the Poles displaced many flocked to the neighbouring towns, but a still larger number migrated to the mining and industrial districts of the West, there to create new enclaves in the midst of communities which hitherto had been solidly German.

In the extreme north-west of the kingdom, where in 1866

Prussia had annexed, together with German Holstein, the partially Danish territory of Schleswig, the same problem of the pacification of an alien people had to be faced. The Holsteiners had soon settled down under the new rule, disappointed that their duchy had not been fated to become part of an independent State under the Augustenburg family, yet not lamenting the break with Denmark, and relieved that the age-long dispute over the question of succession had been closed. The Germans of Schleswig were in general equally favourable to a change of government which gave them part and lot in a larger kingdom. Not so the Danes of the northern districts of the duchy, who held passionately to the displanted dynasty and the old political ties, and this all the more since by article 5 of the Treaty of Prague Prussia had given a promise that the population of these districts should be allowed to decide by *plébiscite* whether it would choose permanent union with the old or with the new kingdom. The pledge had been given on pressure from Louis Napoleon, and as it had not been redeemed by 1870, in spite of Napoleon's reminder, Bismarck had no intention of redeeming it now that the power of France was broken.

Almost from the beginning the administration of the Danish districts lacked sympathy and insight. After the French war spasmodic attempts at conciliation were made there as in Alsace-Lorraine, but they were only a prelude to a rigorous rule which was neither commended by intelligence nor justified by success. There, too, the Germanization movement took the form of aggravating attacks upon the Danish language, first in 1871 by the abolition of the Danish schools, accompanied by compulsion to attend German schools, then by restrictions upon the use of Danish in public instruction, until for practical purposes the language of a quarter of a million inhabitants was restricted to the home and private intercourse. Inasmuch as the Protestant churches became annexed to the State ecclesiastical system of Prussia, the Danes were likewise deprived of their religious independence until they had established free communities and built new places of worship of their own, conducted by ministers who had refused to take the oath to the new Sovereign. Like the other discontented races of the Empire, the Danes carried their grievances into parliamentary life. The Prussian constitution had been amended in 1867, so as to give to the new province nineteen representatives in the Lower House of the State Diet, and when the Empire was established in 1871 it became entitled to return ten deputies to the Imperial Parliament. In Holstein and the German portions of Schleswig the elections were from the first fought on normal party lines; in the Danish districts, on the other hand, the postponed *plébiscite* for years dominated all other questions, and in election after election a small Danish group was returned to both Diets in Berlin, there to protest against annexation to Prussia and to swell the anti-Ministerial vote.

There were short periods when, under the influence of a more clement administration, it almost seemed that the Danes would settle down and adapt themselves to the new conditions, but always there followed a sway of the pendulum; and with a return to harsher measures the old hopeless deadlock returned. Severity reached a climax under Herr von Köller, " the man with the iron hand," who became Chief President in 1898. He went to the province with the single determination to assert Prussia and Prussia's influence, and he stopped at no measure which seemed helpful to that end. The Danes who protested were expelled, and those who remained were put on their good behaviour. Relating his experience when recalled, he said: " I came here with a burning wish to promote Germanism with all the means at my command. The policy I followed was free from all sentimentality, and was based on the principle that Prussia had the right to be mistress in her own house. It was a policy that was apt to be hard and ruthless where necessary." He failed in his attempt to rule an alien people against its will, and like most despots who have essayed the same task with the same result, he never knew the reason why.

Much of the soreness of later years arose upon the question of " optation " for Danish citizenship. By the Treaty of Vienna the Danish inhabitants of Schleswig had been given six years in which to choose whether they would retain the old citizenship and in consequence cross the northern frontier. Tens of thousands of " optants " emigrated, settling for the most part in the northern kingdom. The great majority of the Danes, however, omitted to make their choice in due time, believing that the promised *plébiscite* would settle the matter automatically. The longer the choice was deferred, however, the more anomalous became their position, and when in 1878 Austria agreed to the annulment of the *plébiscite* pledge a new situation was created. Now the Government insisted that the " optants " who had chosen Danish citizenship must either leave the country or, if they wished to remain in Prussia, be treated as nationals and be prepared to meet the consequent liabilities. A rigid interpretation of the question of " opta- tion " was held to justify the expulsion of large numbers of Danes and people of Danish descent, though themselves Prus- sian by citizenship and residence, who, owing to Danish sym- pathies or other reasons, had become obnoxious to the authori- ties. Only after many years and long after Bismarck's death was an arrangement concluded with Denmark by which the position of the " optants " and their families resident in Schleswig was regularized and the worst of the legal hardships from which they had suffered were removed.

In North Schleswig, as in the Polish districts, endeavours were made at an early date to Germanize the population by the purchase of Danish estates and the settlement upon them of Prussian families. Like the Poles, however, the Danish sub- jects of Prussia have refused to be supplanted in this way, and by co-operative efforts, by the creation of credit agencies, and by the cultivation of national sentiment by means of a large network of political, literary, and other societies, they have so far succeeded in maintaining their position.

Army bills and other measures relating to national defence played from the first a prominent part in the proceedings of the Imperial Diet, for the Empire had been created by force and by force it had to be maintained. One dominating aim has been steadily followed by the organizers of the German military sys- tem ever since the institution of federal contingents or quotas, as provided for by the constitution of the old Germanic Federa- tion, was superseded by a unified national army. Germany was to have at command a force so large and efficient that she should be able at all times to keep the peace of Europe and, if need be, impose it upon her own terms. Moltke avowed this aim of German statesmanship as early as 1868 in a speech in the North German Diet (June 15th), wherein he said:

" What sensible man would not wish that the enormous ex- penditure incurred in Europe for military purposes should be directed towards peaceable objects? But international negotiations, such as have often been recommended, will never lead to that result. If this end is to be achieved I see only one possibility, and it is that in the heart of Europe there shall be created a Power which, without itself being one of conquest, shall be so strong that it will be able to forbid its neighbours to

enter upon war. Hence I believe that if this beneficent work
is ever to be achieved it will proceed from Germany. That,
however, will only come when Germany is sufficiently strong,
that is, when it is united. In order to attain this result in
spite of Europe's disfavour we need a navy as well as an
army."

When Sybel, the historian of modern Germany, spoke of
these words as " truly prophetic," in that they " drew for the
European world the picture of the future," he did Moltke something less than justice. For the military supremacy desired
by him continued to be a foremost object of successive German Governments ever since. The attainment of this ambition, however, entailed constant additions to Germany's fighting
forces, first the land and later the sea forces, and a corresponding growth of expenditure which kept the Empire in chronic
financial straits, and necessarily committed the other nations
of Europe, indisposed to submit to the military predominance
of any one Power, to similar prodigal outlay upon armaments.

From 1867 to 1875 the peace strength of the army was
fixed at 1 per cent. of the population according to the census
of 1867, giving a force of 402,000 men, and the expenditure
upon it at £33 15s. per man called up. How the money
should be spent was a matter for the Emperor — in practice
for the military administration — to decide, for the financial
competence of the Diet did not go beyond fixing the amount of
the votes. Hitherto both peace strength and expenditure had
been approved for definite periods. In 1874 the Government
sought to arrive at a permanent understanding with the Diet,
asking that both figures should be made permanent until a new
law to the contrary should be passed, the total duration of
service to remain at twelve years. The question created great
controversy, and only a compromise proposed by Herr von
Bennigsen, the National Liberal leader, averted a dissolution
and an appeal to the nation against legislators who seemed unwilling that the Empire should be allowed to defend with the
sword the conquests which the sword had won.

The Conservatives were the only party willing to pass the
bill as it stood. The other groups objected to the retention of
the peace strength at a figure which in 1871 had been regarded
as excessive and intended to meet abnormal conditions, and
they still more objected to its permanency. Bismarck was ill
and unable to appear in the Diet, and the defence of the bill fell

to Moltke and the Minister of War. In an alarmist speech Moltke prepared the nation for the duty of protecting the new Empire by arms for half a century. " Since our successful wars," he said, " we have everywhere won respect but nowhere love. On all sides we are confronted by the suspicion that Germany, having become great, may in future become an inconvenient neighbour." Moltke never spoke in the Diet except on military questions, and as a rule his utterances, which were rather urgent than eloquent, carried great force. On this occasion, however, he failed to convince; for whatever effect his plea for a larger army may have created was neutralized for the majority by his excessive emphasis of the need for strengthening the arm of the State. " Not the schoolmaster," he said, to the indignation of the deputies on the Liberal benches, not a few of whom were professors, teachers, and journalists, " but the State has won our battles, the State which has now for sixty years trained the nation to physical efficiency and intellectual vigour, to order and punctuality, fidelity and obedience, patriotism and manliness. You cannot dispense with the army, for it is the nation's educator."

This appeal for greater submission to the State was not likely to impress favourably the popular parties, and still less the Clericals, who were then in conflict with it over the question of papal authority, and when the bill was referred to committee the peace strength proposal of 402,000 was rejected almost unanimously, and alternative figures, 385,000 proposed by the Imperialists and 360,000 proposed by the National Liberals, likewise failed to obtain a majority. From his sick-bed Bismarck addressed an impressive appeal to parties to sink political differences in love for the fatherland, ending with the threat that as soon as he was able to take up a pen he should hand in his resignation. " Perhaps some one else will be found," he added, " who will be able to form a reliable majority in the Diet." The cry of "Wolf!" was at this time still new to the ears of the nervous nation, and the Chancellor's threat produced an immediate effect.

A short recess gave the deputies time to reflect and take counsel with their constituents, and before the Diet met again the National Liberal leader had produced a compromise which the Government and the generals were willing to accept. The peace strength was to be as the Government proposed, but it was to be fixed for seven years only, and the army estimates were to be voted yearly. So amended the bill was passed in April by a substantial majority — 224 against 146 — after Moltke had bidden the Diet take to heart the warlike preparations which were being made not only by France but by some of Germany's other neighbours. From the standpoint both of numbers and finance the military authorities in effect won a notable victory. Hitherto the fixed *per capita* grant had been insufficient, and the yearly levy of recruits had been reduced in order that the total army vote might not be exceeded. Now it was possible to call up the full authorized levy with a certainty that the needed votes would be forthcoming.

In 1881 the septennate agreement was renewed by the help of the Conservatives and National Liberals and the abstention of the Clericals, and now the peace strength was fixed at 1 per cent. of the population of 1875, giving an increase of 26,000 men. Before the second Septennial Act had expired, however, the Government in 1886 demanded its renewal on the basis of a peace strength equal to 1 per cent. of the population in 1885, giving a total of 468,000 men. This time the Diet refused to renounce financial control for seven years, but offered to bind itself for three. From the obdurate deputies, therefore, Bismarck promptly appealed to the nation. The elections of February, 1887, led to the formation of a " cartel " of parties, consisting of the two Conservative groups and the National Liberals, pledged to the support of the bill. Effectively assisted by the Government and the electioneering machinery at its disposal, as well as by the never-failing cry of " The fatherland in danger! " these parties between them captured sixty-three seats at the expense of the Radicals and the Social Democrats, with the result that they formed alone a substantial majority of the Diet. Not only was the Army Bill passed unaltered, but for three years Bismarck was able to legislate upon other questions with an ease and a freedom to which he had long been a stranger.

The history of the other branch of the defensive service, the navy, since the establishment of the Empire falls into two periods, the first a period of slow growth, during which shipbuilding followed no clearly defined plan and still less formed part of a considered foreign policy, and then a period of feverish activity, during which an endeavour was made to redeem in years the ground lost in generations. The earlier of these periods ended in 1890, when Bismarck retired from the Chancellorship.

Attempts to create a German navy had been made since the middle of the century. Before 1848 Prussia had a few ships of war of small size and capacity, but not an organized navy. The consequence was that in the war over the Danish succession in that year Denmark with its relatively large fleet was able to blockade the entire German coast, while Prussia was powerless to retaliate. In order to minimize the disadvantages from which Germany then suffered, a committee of naval enthusiasts was formed at Hamburg, and by means of voluntary funds it succeeded in forming a flotilla of small vessels. In the same year the Frankfort National Assembly voted nearly a million pounds to be spent on shipbuilding. The money was to have been contributed in due proportion by the various States of the Empire which had just been created on paper, but only half of it was paid. The Assembly went further, and formed a naval department of the new Imperial Ministry of Commerce; appointed a commission, with Prince Adalbert of Prussia as president, to prepare and carry out a shipbuilding programme suited to the Empire's needs; and in the meantime nominated Karl Bromme, who had seen service in the British and American navies, as the first admiral of the incipient fleet. With the dissolution of the Assembly in the following year naval enthusiasm evaporated, and in 1852 the fleet was dispersed, Prussia buying the two best vessels for £60,000, and the rest being sold by auction for about the same sum.

Prussia continued to make additions to her navy, but spasmodically and without settled plan. During the ten years 1854 to 1864 over three million pounds were expended on shipbuilding, and the work of creating a new naval port on the North Sea, on a site of land bought from Oldenburg, was in progress all this time. Already, too, Prussian naval experts had, with admirable foresight, planned a waterway which should connect the North Sea with the Baltic. The difficulties in the way were political rather than physical, and chiefly the fact that the canal would need to penetrate a territory subject to Danish sovereignty. Bismarck, an adept in discovering after the event motives which did not exist before it, said in later years that it was the recognition that the possession of

Schleswig-Holstein was an essential condition of German naval power that determined him to go to war with Denmark in 1864. Whatever may have been his intentions in dragging Austria into that enterprise, directly Prussia had come into joint occupation of the duchies he determined that Kiel harbour should not again pass out of her hands. Demanding of the Diet a grant for naval construction (June, 1865), he invited the deputies to make their sanction dependent upon the condition " No Kiel, no money! " and promised them that the money would be duly claimed. At that time, however, he was faced by an unfriendly Diet. The constitutional conflict was still in progress; the Government was carrying on the business of the country without a duly approved budget; and the popular parties were in a large majority. In these circumstances the Lower House, which otherwise might have been willing enough to assist in strengthening the navy, was not prepared to place more power in the hands of a usurping Executive, which was every day defying the rights of the Diet and making the constitution of no effect, and it refused the votes asked for.

Nothing further was done until the formation of the North German Confederation after the war of 1866, but in the meantime Prussia's annexation of Schleswig-Holstein made it possible for her to develop her fleet under more favourable conditions. Already its headquarters had been transferred to Kiel from Danzig, at the other end of the Baltic. The creation of the Confederation now gave to the question a larger aspect. In the second war with Denmark, in 1864, Prussia had again suffered severely owing to the inability of her fleet to take the offensive or even to cover her own coasts efficiently. Now it was necessary to create a navy capable of protecting the entire littoral of North Germany, including, in addition to some of Prussia's largest and richest provinces, the Hanseatic Cities, Oldenburg, and Mecklenburg. " Bismarck is very amusing with his baby fleet," wrote Earl Russell to Lord Clarendon at this time (1866). Little did the first naval nation in the world then dream how large were the developments that would spring from small beginnings. In forming the new Confederation, Prussia transferred to it all her ships of war, which now became the nucleus of a federal navy. The funds refused by the Prussian Diet in 1864 and 1865 were granted in 1867 by the North German Diet, one of whose first acts was to vote a yearly expenditure on shipbuilding and other naval works of nearly a million and a quarter pounds a year for ten years. Two years later the naval port of Wilhelmshaven, built at a cost of a million and a half pounds, was completed and opened by the King.

During the war of 1870 the vigilance of the German fleet was confined to the protection of the naval ports and the river mouths, and fortunately for Germany the difficulties which France had to meet on land discouraged her from undertaking any bold adventures by sea. A blockade of the Baltic coast was formally declared, but it was not practically enforced, and on both sides the naval operations in the war were of little account. The great numerical inferiority of the German fleet to that of France was, none the less, a reminder that however strong the victors might have shown themselves on land they were far from invulnerable on water. In order to remedy this weakness a carefully planned but still modest programme of shipbuilding was laid before the now Imperial Diet in 1873. The purpose of the enlarged fleet was to be limited in the main to coast defence and the patrol of the Baltic; though it was hoped that it would prove strong enough to maintain an open passage for German shipping through the Sound and the Belt, any idea of its playing an active part on the high seas either in peace or war was disclaimed. The programme exceeded that of 1867 in the number of vessels to be built, but fell below it in fighting strength. For the first time provision was made for a flotilla of torpedo boats. Important harbour and coastal fortification works were also part of the scheme, the execution of which was to be spread over ten years.

Other changes were made at this time in sign that Germany intended for the future to take her navy more seriously. The naval administration, such as it was, had hitherto been regarded as a department of the Ministry for War, and Roon, as the head of the army, had incidentally been responsible for the fleet. Now a separate Board of Admiralty was formed, with General von Stosch as its first head. At the beginning of the 'eighties when the programme had been completed, the naval estimates were still below two million pounds a year. The early additions to the imperial navy were made by the help of the French indemnity, but from 1875 forward that source of revenue was exhausted and loans had to be resorted to. Up to this point most of Germany's large war vessels had been built abroad, owing to the inability of her few private yards to undertake contracts of the kind. Now the work was kept at home, though shipbuilding material and machinery had still to be largely imported, particularly from Great Britain.

An event important for the later expansion of the navy was the resignation in 1883 of the first Minister of Marine, von Stosch, and the appointment of General von Caprivi as his successor. Up to this point little national enthusiasm for the navy had been awakened, and for this fact Bismarck's own lukewarmness — for which there was ample justification in the greatness of his other tasks and the necessity for caution in all matters affecting Germany's relations with other Powers — was to a large extent responsible. Already, however, there was a strong and restless naval party in official circles, and the experts had abandoned the idea of keeping the fleet within coastal waters and building only for home defence. In a memorial which he addressed to the Diet in 1883, Caprivi said: " A navy whose centre of gravity was on the land or off the coast would no longer be worthy of the name. The seas cease more and more to divide nations, and the course of history points to the fact that a State dare not withdraw from the sea if it intends to maintain beyond the immediate future a position in the world." It was also Caprivi who first seriously raised the question of the cession of Heligoland. His recognition of the importance for Germany of the possession of the Elbe island, as a cover for her navy, was shared by Bismarck, with the result that advances were made to the British Government on the subject in 1884.[1]

Nevertheless, Germany still continued to build her navy piecemeal, ship by ship, satisfied if only obsolete vessels were duly replaced and the relative strength of the navies of the second class, in which her own was reckoned, did not change to her disadvantage; there was no suggestion of a navy on large lines, and the idea of naval supremacy would have been repudiated at that time as preposterous. Between 1881 and 1891 the *personnel* of the navy only increased from eleven to sixteen thousand. Midway in this decade, in February, 1886, the Diet adopted a bill for the construction of the Kiel Canal and made the necessary grants.

Throughout the entire period of Bismarck's Chancellorship the Empire had to struggle under an ever-increasing load of expenditure, and ultimately of debt, and legislative propos-

[1] See Chapter XVII., pp. 192–4.

als, large or small, to amend the system of taxation in the interest of ampler revenue were almost of yearly occurrence. Most of the Government's attempts to escape from financial embarrassment were received with indifference or open hostility by the Diet, whose appreciation of the Empire was greater than its willingness to provide it with adequate resources. The choice lay between the development of the customs and excise duties which had been assigned to the Empire by the constitution and a new system of direct taxation. Bismarck himself was on principle favourable to the former, though quite prepared to accept the latter if the Diet compelled him. The Radicals pressed for the introduction of an imperial income tax as a solution of all difficulties, present and future. Out of consideration for the State Governments and the municipalities, both of which relied largely upon the income tax for their revenue, Bismarck did not favour this solution, yet after repeated attempts to reform the tobacco and beer duties and to introduce stamp duties had failed he had to threaten in 1877 that an income tax might be his next proposal.

The position became worse when the Empire began to fall into debt. Up to 1875 it had by painful effort paid its way, but then came the need to borrow, though the loans contracted in the early years were inconsiderable as compared with those of later date. Part of the money was used for remunerative undertakings, like the Imperial post and telegraph service, part for shipbuilding, fortifications, and other defensive purposes; but the time came when loans were contracted in order to pay off deficits.

The reform of the fiscal system which took place in 1879 was thought to have cleared the way and given the Empire a new start, as had been intended. Had the Imperial Treasury been allowed to retain the whole of the larger revenue derived from the revised customs and excise duties the relief would have been substantial, but the effect of the Franckenstein proviso, already explained, was to give with one hand and take away with the other. For a time it was possible to dispense with matricular contributions, which was a sentimental gain, but by limiting the Empire's share in the new revenue the Diet had defeated Bismarck's main purpose. An administrative change made at this time was of importance for the easier transaction of financial business. Until 1879 the Chancellor directly controlled the financial like every other branch of the imperial administration. In that year an informal Ministry of Finance with the name Imperial Treasury was created, with a Secretary of State at the head. The new director of finance continued to be subordinate in all matters to the Chancellor, and therein was unlike the Finance Minister of Prussia or that of Saxony, who in finance is independent of the rest of the Cabinet to which he belongs and in consequence is not bound by any resolution of the majority with which he may disagree.

A series of new taxation proposals, which for the most part failed to mature, at least for a time, began to appear in 1880. In that year a bill was introduced to extend the stamp duties. There were already duties on bills and playing-cards. Now it was proposed to charge similar duties on share certificates and bonds, promissory notes, lottery tickets, mortgage deeds, receipts, and other documents relating to credit transactions or traffic in goods. Only the Conservatives were in favour of the bill, and it failed to secure assent, though it was passed in a modified form in 1881, and four years later the Stock Exchange taxes were increased. Another novel tax proposed at this time was a national defence tax (*Wehrsteuer*), to be payable by or in respect of persons who, though liable to military service were not called up owing to physical incapacity or were put back owing to excess of recruits. Bavaria and Würtemberg already had a tax of the kind, and it existed also in Austria and Switzerland. Nevertheless, the proposal was not received favourably by the Diet, and still less by the country. To most people the idea of commuting the obligation of military service by a money payment seemed a degradation of a duty which had hitherto been regarded as one of the highest of citizenship. It was also feared that such a tax would work inequitably, since there could be no guarantee that a Government when in financial straits would not find ways of proving to the military authorities that men of means were more valuable to the country as taxpayers than as soldiers. Combated from various sides, the proposal of a national defence tax was stillborn. Hardly a speaker had a good word to say for it, and it was rejected by general consent. It was the first and last time that a poll-tax of the kind was proposed in the Diet.

Bismarck was not more successful with proposals to increase the taxation of beer. Here he had to encounter resolute opposition from many sides. There was first the jealousy of

the South German States, one of whose most important privileges was now threatened.　The constitution reserved to Bavaria, Würtemberg, and Baden the right to tax home-produced
beer and brandy according to the principles and on the scale
habitual in those States, while at the same time requiring them
to pay yearly to the Imperial Treasury a sum equal to the taxation which would fall upon them relatively to population on
the basis of the taxation raised at any given time from these.
sources in North Germany.　The same arrangement was continued in Alsace-Lorraine in regard to beer.　It was not until
1887 that this privilege was modified, and then only in the case
of brandy.　As the Southern States raised a large revenue for
their own purposes by the taxation of beer, of which the Bavarian, to whom it was a fifth element, drank four times as
much as the North German, any suggestion of a larger contribution to the Imperial Treasury from this source was
warmly opposed.　The North heartily supported the resistance of the South, since in the North German brewing area
beer had immemorially been taxed very lightly, and all parties
were united in the determination to defend this valued privilege.

After trying in vain to make both ends meet by the help
of small additions of revenue obtained in all sorts of ways, Bismarck at last decided that the time had come for abandoning
peddling measures and for making a bold departure from existing principles of taxation.　When specifying in 1869 the
articles which he regarded as most suited to high taxation he
had given prominence to tobacco and brandy.　With these
articles he now proposed that the State should experiment in
the untried capacity of monopolist.　He had made known his
intentions as early as 1878, when discussing a bill for increasing the tobacco duties.　In that year the Government appointed a commission to investigate the general subject of tobacco taxation, including the practicability of a *régie*, following the successful example of Austria, Italy, and especially
France, one of whose State tobacco manufactories, at Strassburg, had been carried on as an Imperial undertaking since
1871.　At that time the yield of the tobacco tax in Germany
was barely 4d. a head of the population as compared with 2s.
6d. in Italy, 3s. 8d. in Austria, 4s. 10d. in England, and 5s. 8d.
in France.　Bismarck could therefore claim ample justification
for his resolve that " Tobacco must bleed more than it has

hitherto done." The eleven members of the commission included eight State officials and three experts, the latter representing tobacco growers, manufacturers, and traders respectively. By eight votes to three — the three being all Government nominees — the commission reported against the principle of a monopoly, and in consequence the Government had for the present to be satisfied with a higher tax, which was approved in 1879. Though the question was postponed, however, it was not regarded as settled. Refusing to be discouraged, Bismarck next convened his trusty body-guard of economic counsellors, the Prussian Economic Council, and called for its blessing upon the proposal. To his surprise this body likewise failed him. Although of its seventy-five members thirty were nominated by the Government and the rest chosen by it from nominees presented by the Chambers of Commerce and Agriculture, the Economic Council reported almost unanimously against the institution of a monopoly.[1]

Notwithstanding these rebuffs, a monopoly project was foreshadowed in the Imperial Message of November 17, 1881, which laid down the lines of the future scheme of social insurance, and a bill was duly produced. The proposals would have given to the State control over the entire production, manufacture, and sale of tobacco in Germany, and consequently have interfered with the livelihood of over 159,000 tobacco cultivators, 15,000 manufacturers of the commodity, employing 141,000 workpeople, and 7,900 large and 359,000 small retailers. The vastness of the economic disturbance contemplated was illustrated by the fact that compensation to the aggregate amount of eleven and a half million pounds had to be provided for.

The Federal Council was hopelessly divided on the subject; in the country opinion was unfavourable; and the entire tobacco trade was bitterly hostile, growers, manufacturers, and retailers uniting in defence of their threatened interests. Of the parliamentary parties only the Conservatives were in favour of the bill, not because they approved of monopolies, but because they scented alternative forms of taxation likely to be more objectionable. The Government fought well, for the prize at stake, an estimated net revenue of over eight million pounds a year, was worth the effort, but the forces against it

[1] The Prussian Economic Council did not long survive Bismarck's Ministry; it was abolished in 1892.

were too strong. In the hope of allaying opposition Bismarck
proposed to give a social significance to the measure by undertaking that the proceeds of the monopoly beyond the amount
of the existing taxation of tobacco should be used in financing
his scheme of insurance and so form a " patrimony of the disinherited." As yet, however, neither the nation nor its parliament had been educated to the appreciation of grandiose
schemes of social reform, and the offer failed to impress them.
So much heat was imported into the parliamentary debates
that Bismarck at last began to apologize for his unpopular
bill. " No enmity, even if you do reject the monopoly," he
said; " you must not be vexed with us for having proposed it,
as though we had been guilty of high treason! " When the division took place in June the bill was rejected by 277 against
43, the latter all Conservatives.

In 1885 there was an increase of the import duties on corn,
meat, timber, and some other articles, but the larger revenue
afforded little relief to an ever-expanding budget. In urgent
want of money, Bismarck in the following year tried to win
over the Diet to another State monopoly project. This
time he wished to appropriate brandy, and for the same reason
as before, the inadequate revenue obtained on the existing principle of taxation from a commodity so well suited to be one of
the mainstays of national finance. Again the Radicals, weak
in numbers, but strong in convictions and in polemical resource,
led the opposition, and this project was likewise rejected.
The dissolution of the Diet on the military septennate question in 1887, as recorded above, gave the Government a majority which enabled it to increase the taxation of brandy and
sugar and to raise the corn duties, the latter professedly in
the interest of agriculture rather than revenue. To the existing duty on raw materials used in the production of alcohol
a duty on the manufactured article was added, though in the
interest of the large agricultural distilleries this duty was reduced upon a fixed quota of potable brandy, a privilege continued for many years and greatly resented by the popular
parties. Simultaneously the autonomy of the Southern States
in regard to the taxation of brandy was abolished. The effect
of the changes was to give the Government an increased revenue of between three and four million pounds. In the case
of sugar likewise the existing excise duty on raw material
(sugar beet) was supplemented by a duty on manufactured

sugar, and the export premiums were put on a new basis and reduced. Bismarck attempted no new monopoly schemes, however, though his belief in the equity and soundness of the principle remained unchanged to the last.

Owing to these various reforms in taxation, always for the purpose of higher revenue, the Empire enjoyed a short period of comparative financial prosperity after 1888, for while the average net yield of the customs and excise duties during the years 1872 to 1880 was about twelve and a half million pounds a year, that during the succeeding decade was twenty-two millions. Instead of having to call on the States for subsidies, therefore, the Imperial Treasury for some years was able to repay to them, in virtue of the Franckenstein provision, not only the full amount of the matricular contributions but a large sum in excess. During the five years 1888 to 1892 the sum so distributed as an imperial bonus was about twenty million pounds.

Only in political life, notwithstanding all the activity and movement visible in other directions, did Germany during these years stand still. There was much ferment all the time, and periods of apparent advance alternated with periods of more real reaction, but the practical gains to Liberalism and political progress were unsubstantial. During the earlier years Bismarck relied in the Diet upon the help of the National Liberal party, without which a Ministerial majority would have been impossible. After the war of 1866 the feudalist party in Prussia, holding that the time was ripe for abolishing a Diet which had served the country so ill over the question of army reform, and for returning to the less strenuous political conditions of twenty years before, clamoured for another bold *coup d'état*, but Bismarck refused to be tempted. Logical enough to recognize in the dethronement of crowned heads a violation of the sacred principle of legitimism, the Prussian Conservatives acquiesced only sullenly in the annexation of Hanover, Hesse, and Nassau, but they never forgave Bismarck for having sued the Diet for an indemnity when success in arms had placed not only Austria but the constitutional party at his mercy. Disappointment at what they regarded as an act of weakness and as unfaithfulness to principles which they had believed to be his own as well as theirs, created between them a coldness which drove him into the arms of the National Liberals and their allies. To the alliance thus formed was due the fact that the legislation of the North German Diet and of the Diet of the Empire in its early years followed lines which for Germany seemed progressive. Using their opportunities, the Liberal parties tried persistently, both in the Imperial and the Prussian Diet, to extend the principle of parliamentary control, but with no success.

A useful measure of devolution, known as the Substitute Law, was passed in 1878, with the object of relieving Bismarck of such work as did not need the dexterity of the master hand. This law empowered the Chancellor to appoint a deputy for his office or any part of it, and its result was the creation of Secretaries of State, for the direction of various branches of imperial administration, subject still to the Chancellor, who was entitled to resume at any time the delegated functions. In the interest of unity of policy the more important of these offices have since been filled by the Ministers holding the corresponding portfolios in the Prussian Cabinet. The Liberals demanded that the Imperial Chancellor, the only Minister known to the constitution, should be replaced by a collective Ministry, in which he should be only one member amongst many, and subject, like the rest, to the bidding of the legislative assembly, which meant in reality of the party or parties which might happen to form a majority. Bismarck had only overcome strong opposition to the bill in the Federal Council by giving the assurance that it was not intended to pave the way for an Imperial Cabinet and should not have that result. In the Diet he refused point-blank to consider such a degradation of his position, and referring his critics to the constitution, told them that though constitutional questions were for him questions of expediency, he was quite prepared to respect the *status quo* if the advocates of parliamentary government would agree to do the same.

Nevertheless, when the two attempts made upon the life of the Emperor in 1878 led to the election of a reactionary Diet, he did not fail to legislate accordingly. To that year and the years immediately following fell the law against Socialism, the return to Protection, a series of subtle attacks upon the constitutional right of free occupation, and severer restrictions of the right of assembly, combination, and free speech. In 1881 a general outcry arose over the Government's proposal that the duration of the legislative period should be increased from three to five years and the budgets be biennial. The urgency of such a change was not apparent, and few people believed that the reasons which influenced Bismarck in seeking it were those which he avowed, viz. to secure a more constant co-operation of the Diet in legislation and to prevent undue clashing between the sittings of the Imperial and State Diets. What was clearer and more certain was that the change would make the Government still more independent of parliamentary control than hitherto, and that if the budget needed approval only once in two years the Diet would hardly be wanted oftener. Although the Diet had done Bismarck's bidding so far, it rejected this proposal almost unanimously.

Already he was paying the penalty of the rupture of the alliance with the National Liberals, who had served him so well and so long. The Clericals had offered him their help in a critical emergency, and having become necessary to the continuance of a Ministerial majority, they were showing an increasing disposition to make an arbitrary use of their power. To Bismarck the new alliance had been attractive because the Clericals were organized and disciplined as no other part in the Diet. Before long he began to find their strength and cohesion inconvenient and their independence menacing to his position. In May, 1880, he bitterly reproached his uncertain allies with not doing their duty with sufficient ardour, forgetting that they had given no pledges, and then with curious disregard of his own responsibility for the break-up of the old Ministerial majority called upon the rest of the House and the Liberals in particular to join hands against the Centre as a common enemy. " If you cannot do that," he said, in an appeal to the National Liberals in which he emphasized the work still to be accomplished before German unity was firmly established, " then my prospects are dark; if you are able to do it, I will devote my last strength to the task." An appeal which only a short time before would have evoked enthusiastic response from the entire body of Bennigsen's followers now failed to move them. The rupture caused in their ranks first by the protectionist policy and then by Bismarck's ungrateful repudiation of them as a party directly they no longer served his purpose had left wounds which could not be healed by flattering words. The National Liberals suspected that Bismarck simply wanted to use them again as pawns in a party game, and they had no longer any liking for such a *rôle*.

At the beginning of the 'eighties Bismarck, still at the zenith

of his power, became increasingly despotic in home affairs.
In 1881 he made his relative by marriage, Herr von Puttkamer, Minister of the Interior, and as part of the duties of his
position Puttkamer had taken over the direction of the Press
and the manipulation of the elections. That meant a large
interference with the independence of civil servants. He virtually cancelled the civil rights of the bureaucracy, by requiring officials to abdicate all claim to act as free citizens, calling
upon them, as an act of duty, to support the Government
upon all occasions, and instructing them in elections to vote
and work for the candidates who bore the official *cachet.*
Criticized in the Diet for a gross violation both of the spirit
and letter of the constitution, he calmly replied that he " expected the officials in whose hands the political representation
of the Executive rested, in so far as they exercised their rights
as citizens at all, to support the Government," and he aggravated his offence by publicly thanking those officials who had
conspicuously helped the Government in the last elections, and
assuring them that they might count upon the Emperor's
gratitude as well. Dignified protests from moderate men of
the standing of Bennigsen had no effect upon the reactionary
Minister, who knew better than his critics how far he dared
to go. When flagrant attacks upon electoral rights published
by the semi-official *Provinzial-Korrespondenz,* which Puttkamer inspired and directed, were condemned in the Diet, the
journal's editor was promptly decorated with a royal order
in sign of approval both of master and man. Scores of elections in inconvenient constituencies were by Puttkamer's instructions manipulated in the interest of the Government, unwilling officials being terrorized into the commission of illegal
practices and the voters wantonly obstructed in the exercise
of their rights. When a Chief President of one of the provinces ventured to disapprove of such proceedings he was removed from office. In short, under Puttkamer the tone of political life was degraded as never before or since, and his name
was used to connote illicit political influence.

Bismarck discreetly kept away from the Diet while his relative was undergoing castigation at the hands of the politicians
who had the courage to condemn venality in high places.
That he approved of Puttkamer's acts was shown, however,
by the publication on January 4, 1882, of a decree declaring
it to be the will of the Emperor-King that " both in Prussia

and in the legislative bodies of the Empire there shall be no doubt as to my constitutional right, and that of my successors, to direct the policy of the Government personally. It is the duty of my Ministers to safeguard my constitutional rights against doubts and obscurity, and I expect the same thing from all officials who have taken the oath to me. It is far removed from my intention to interfere with the freedom of elections, but for those officials who are entrusted with the execution of my Governmental Acts, and therefore can be removed from their offices under the disciplinary laws, the duty imposed upon them by their oath includes the representation of my policy even in the elections."

The decree was a challenge to which the popular parties were not slow to respond. There were vehement debates in the Prussian Lower House, and the Radicals talked as though a new constitutional conflict was imminent. Bismarck did not improve matters when he declared the degree " was not intended to create a new law," for the implication that it simply reassured an old doctrine — that State officials possessed no right of personal opinion and never had possessed it — suggested to the constitutionalists that for over thirty years they had been living in a fools' paradise. Later he modified his words and tried to prove that the decree was really harmless. Officials, he said, had a perfect right to vote for whom they liked, even for Radicals, if they had no better taste; all that he meant was that they must to the best of their power combat misrepresentations of the Government's policy and aims. No one believed that this was the meaning of the King's decree or was his interpretation of it, but the National Liberals professed to be satisfied.

Liberalism had at that time to wage a severe uphill fight, and the struggle was all the more difficult because the two wings of the party refused to act together. Not so the Ministerial parties, now the Conservatives and the Clericals, the latter so largely augmented on critical occasions by Poles, Guelphs, and Alsatians that in the Prussian Lower House they formed in effect one-third of all the deputies. In anticipation of the Prussian elections Bennigsen in June, 1882, made a resolute attempt to unite all the Liberal forces both in the monarchy and the Empire in the hope of stemming the powerful reactionary currents which had been running since 1879. The attempt created much enthusiasm in the National Liberal

ranks, but it was wrecked owing to the irreconcilable attitude
of the Radicals, and particularly of their leader, Eugen Richter, who refused to listen to any suggestions of compromise,
obstinately, yet honestly, believing that the true secret of political progress was in the exclusive custody of his little party.
The immediate consequence of the rejection of Bennigsen's prudent counsels was that in the elections in the autumn the three
Liberal groups lost heavily.   Ten years before they had numbered 250 in a house of 432; that number had now fallen to
103.

Discouraged by his ill-success, despairing of the future, and
judging that his work was done, Bennigsen, alike to the surprise and dismay of his friends and the regret of his political
opponents, retired from the Imperial Diet and the Prussian
Lower House in the summer of the following year, and returned only four years later to an arena in which he had laboured for nearly two decades with clean hands and high
aims and accomplished for Germany and German unity a work
of inestimable value.   Forsaken now by the only conspicuous
statesman they ever had as a leader, the National Liberals
lost confidence, not for the first or the last time, in themselves
and their principles, and became more and more a nondescript
party, representing neither good Liberalism nor good Conservatism.   The Liberal Union formed of a body of seceders
in 1881 lived only until March, 1884, when it was merged, together with the Progressist groups, in the composite Radical
(*Freisinnige* or " Free-minded ") party then formed — a Cave
of Adullam in which a host of democrats of all shades at that
time sought refuge until the reaction was overpast.   The right
wing, made up for the most part of Liberals of wavering faith,
who ever since the Protectionist controversy had been longing
for the time when they might with decency return to the Ministerial fold, reorganized itself under Miquel and Marquardsen,
and at a conference held at Heidelberg in the same month of
1884 appealed to the country on a revised programme.   Accepting Protection as a closed issue, the party resolved to sink
all jealousies and differences and use its influence equally
against reactionary tendencies, as represented by feudal Conservatism and Clericalism, and extreme Radicalism, as represented by Social Democracy.   When in May the reorganization was confirmed at a national congress held in Berlin, Bennigsen was there to wish his old associates good-speed, but for

the present he refused to be drawn again into the ranks of active combatants. In the elections to the Imperial Diet in October the effect of purging the party of its more advanced members was seen. The Government removed the ban from which National Liberalism had suffered, and it was admitted to a share of the spoils of war in the form of a few seats. The lion's share fell, however, to the Conservative and Social Democratic groups, which gained heavily at the expense of the Radicals.

The Government's hopeless alienation from Liberal sentiment was illustrated by an incident which created painful comment both in Germany and the United States in 1884. On the death in America of Dr. Eduard Lasker, for a generation one of the foremost of German parliamentarians, the House of Deputies recorded its regret in a resolution which described Lasker as a " distinguished German statesman whose firm and consistent exposition of free and Liberal ideas, and whose devoted zeal for the same, have greatly promoted the social, political, and economic condition of his nation." The resolution, of which every word was true, was duly conveyed to the German ambassador in Washington, for communication to the Imperial Diet, but inasmuch as the implied compliment to Liberalism was contrary to Bismarck's mind, he refused to allow the message to be formally delivered. Eleven years later the Diet, then more Liberal in constitution, avenged itself by refusing to vote, at the Government's invitation, a message of congratulation to Bismarck, then living in retirement, on the attainment of his eightieth birthday.

In 1884 a further minor inroad was made upon the privileges of the Diet. Up to November of that year free railway passes had been issued to members during the session, allowing them to travel anywhere in Germany. Now the Government decided that free tickets should be issued only for journeys to and from their several constituencies and Berlin. That meant that members who lived in the capital or elsewhere than in their constituencies would be crippled in their electioneering campaigns. The Clericals and Radicals answered with a joint proposal for the payment of members, and it was carried by a large majority, after Bismarck had assured the House that the Federal Council would refuse to act upon it. In 1881, in order to emphasize his attitude, he instituted a prosecution against certain Progressist deputies for receiving maintenance allowances from their party's funds, though he had given an assurance when the constitution was under discussion that private assistance of the kind was not intended to come under prohibition.   The Supreme Court declared the party contributions to be illegal and forfeit to the State.   Four years later he came back to the question of quinquennial elections.   Encouraged by the election in February, 1887, of a tractable Diet, he renewed the proposal which had been rejected in 1881, and a law amending the constitution accordingly was passed on March 19th. A little later the same change was introduced in Prussia.

In sum, it may be said that all the changes made during Bismarck's Chancellorship modifying the relations of the Executive to either of the Diets with which he was concerned were in a reactionary direction.   Thus every attempt of the popular parties to secure a redistribution of seats, in view of the great disparities in representation which had been caused by the concentration of population in the towns and the industrial districts, failed in consequence of the opposition of the Government and the parties interested in the perpetuation of the existing anomalies.   The political life and institutions, and almost it might be said the political thought, of Germany remained in 1890 just where they were twenty years before.

CHAPTER XV

(1871–1887)

FOREIGN RELATIONS — (i) FRANCE

" The events of 1866 and 1870," writes Count Beust, who played a prominent part in some of the transformations of that period, " may be compared to volcanic eruptions. Where the fragments fall they lie, and it would be folly to wish to replace them in their former positions." [1] The Franco-German War in particular left the Great Powers of the Continent in new relations. These relations were not all created by the war, for some had been formed, or were forming, before the Peace of Frankfort, or even the decisive day of July, 1870, upon which Louis Napoleon made the gambler's throw that cost France and his dynasty so dearly. The Crimean War had seemed to shatter whatever had remained of the Holy Alliance, yet the three Eastern monarchies were now allies again in all but name. Prussia and Austria had already agreed to bury the hatchet, and the prospect of their reconciliation was for Russia a strong inducement to hold out to Austria likewise a friendly hand.

The attitude of the Powers towards France, on the other hand, seemed for the time to have changed for the worse. When the war broke out France had been cold-shouldered by all Europe as a mischievous disturber of the peace, and even now the sympathy which had been aroused by her misfortunes was tempered by a feeling that she was suffering only the results of her own folly. The countries from which France might have expected the greatest sympathy were those which gave her the least. Her relation to Austria, for a time so confidential, had become that of a negative diplomatic friendship. Austria had forgotten Napoleon's timely services in 1866, and for France Austria's halting response to the pressing advances made to her in 1869 and 1870 was a galling memory, difficult to efface. France seemed also to have entirely parted company from Italy. The new kingdom was not indif-

[1] *Memoirs* (English translation), vol. i., p. 286.

ferent to the services rendered by the fallen Empire to the cause of its unity, but of real gratitude the Italian nation retained only so much as was due for a patronage which had never been quite disinterested. What had been done by French arms at Magenta and Solferino, and by French diplomacy at Villafranca and again at Nikolsburg, might, indeed, have been done for the glory of Italy, but it was not done without a thought of the greater glory of Louis Napoleon. Even in the Emperor's devotion to his first love amongst the nations whom he sought to befriend the *pensée humanitaire* was not allowed to obscure the *pensée politique*. It was not forgotten that France had endeavoured to the last to keep Italy out of the holy place of nationalist aspirations, and that she was still in league with the Papacy.

It was clear that France's only hope of regaining the respect and confidence which had been forfeited lay in the pursuance of a policy which should prove to the world that though the crime of setting Europe aflame had been committed in her name it had not been committed on her responsibility. Thiers, in his presidential message to the first meeting of the National Assembly in December, 1871, proclaimed once again that the mission of France in the world was the sacred one of peace. " Our policy is that of peace," he said, " as far from despondency as defiance, proceeding from the conviction that a reorganized France will always be necessary for Europe, and that only such a France will be in a position to fulfil her duties to the other States as well as to herself. France wishes for peace; she declares this on her honour, and will not deviate from this her solemnly avowed word."

It was not only on the part of France, however, that discreet statesmanship was called for at that time, when old ties were broken and new ties had still to be formed. For Germany the need was even more urgent. From the moment of his return from Versailles Bismarck's one absorbing thought had been, How could the political forces of Europe be so organized and used as to ensure the permanency of the status created by three wars? His sole wish now was to consolidate Germany's strength and develop her resources in tranquillity. Could that boon be granted to her, he would have been willing that the new Empire should fall into the background of European politics. Yet while he wanted peace, he was too clearsighted not to recognize that he had created conditions which

made peace uncertain. He therefore feared the future more
than he had ever feared in the past, for since so much had been
gained there was now so much the more to lose. Already the
dread of isolation and the greater dread of a war on two
fronts, the West and the East, which were to be the pursuing
spectres of his later years, had cast a sombre shadow over his
spirit. Germany's success had made one half of Europe restless and the other half jealous. It became, therefore, his interest, as it was his hope, to prove that all suspicions of her
intentions were groundless, and that he, the war-maker, had
now no greater ambition than to be regarded as the preserver
of peace.

The idea, commonly attributed to Bismarck at that time
and later, that he was bent on adding the German districts of
Austria to the Empire and mediatizing the remaining smaller
German States — which could only have meant incorporating
them in Prusisa — may be dismissed as mere legend, and not
very credible legend.[1] Far from hankering for the partition
of Austria, he was too sagacious a statesman to have wished
to multiply the difficulties of the Empire and its Government,
to give to the Southern States an increase of strength, and to
modify the balance of confessional power in Germany, by
bringing in a large Roman Catholic population, and that at
a time when he was contending with Rome over the eternal
question of the provinces of State and Church. As for absorbing the smaller German States, it may be said frankly that
he never loved them, yet at no time would he have risked the
ruin of his handiwork by aggressive action against them; in
later years he even contrasted their willing acceptance of the
Empire with the persistent and stiff-necked particularism of
his own Prussia.

Bismarck's object was peace, peace almost at any price,

[1] Lord Odo Russell, the British ambassador in Berlin, entertained this
idea. "His policy, as you know," he wrote to Lord Lyons on February 20,
1874, with the excess of assurance which at times invalidated his judgments,
"is to mediatize the minor States of Germany and to annex the German
provinces of Austria, so as to make one great centralized Power of the Ger-
man-speaking portions of Europe." A year later Russell's confidence in his
forecast appears to have been weakened, for in repeating it in a letter to
Lord Derby (May 8, 1875) he was careful to add that it was only his opinion and that he "might be wrong." Wrong he undoubtedly was. Bismarck's disclaimer to Beust at Gastein in 1871 of any desire to acquire the
German provinces of Austria and his admission that "Vienna and the
Slavic and Catholic population would only cause embarrassment" simply
proved his common sense.

but he knew that this object could only be attained in proportion as Germany herself was made secure, and to this end it was necessary not merely to strengthen her armaments, but to win for her friends and to neutralize the influence of possible enemies. For many years Germany's foreign relations and policy were entirely determined by and subordinated to this single aim. In surveying this chapter of the Empire's early history it will be convenient to follow events rather in political than strictly chronological sequence, dealing first with Germany's relations with France, and in a later chapter with her relations with the Powers which were specially interested in the Oriental question.

But first Bismarck sought to draw closer the ties between Germany and her Eastern neighbour. Ever since their alliance at the beginning of the century the reigning houses of Prussia and Russia had continued in more or less close friendship, and this friendship had repeatedly translated itself into timely political action on both sides. Russia on the whole had unquestionably had the best of the bargain. Though her attitude towards Prussia in 1866 and towards Germany in 1870 had been specially cordial and helpful, on neither occasion were her motives altogether disinterested or the speculations behind them realized. In both wars Russia counted on a more determined and prolonged struggle and a less definite issue than actually occurred, and it was part of her calculations that sooner or later she might be called in to make peace between torn and exhausted combatants unable to agree without her aid. Now that France had disappointed Russia's expectations, just as Austria had done before, there was the greater reason for continuing on good terms with a Power which had proved its strength so unmistakably upon the battlefield. It was Bismarck's belief that Russia had not foreseen clearly that when the war with France was over she would " have so strong and consolidated a Germany as her neighbour."

It was to Russia, then, that Bismarck now looked, in the name of traditional dynastic attachments, for a relationship that should henceforth be something more than that of neighbourly good-will. With Gortchakoff, the Russian Chancellor, who had directed Russian foreign policy since 1856, he had been on terms of close intimacy ever since they were envoys together at the Diet of Frankfort and there laid down informally the basis of future co-operation. As ambassador to the

Russian Court from 1859 to 1862 he had succeeded in strengthening the tie of friendship and interest between the two States, and when he returned to Berlin, his mission completed, it was with the assurance that he brought with him " better traditions in regard to Russia." One of his first acts as Prussian Minister-President had been the conclusion of the convention of 1863 for the quelling of Polish revolutionary movements. Later, both in 1866 and 1870, he had been careful to make sure of benevolent neutrality on the Eastern frontier before seeking the arbitrament of arms. It was a due and grateful recognition of Russia's moral support in the late war that prompted the new German Emperor, as his first public act after the signing of the Preliminaries of Peace at Versailles on February 27, 1871, to thank the Czar for having done his part to restrict the area of conflict and to keep a fair ring for the combatants.

Even before this, however, Bismarck had been busily providing for the future. In September, 1870, when the issues of the struggle were still undecided, he had sounded not only Russia but Italy as to their willingness to enter into closer relations with Germany. The fear of any slackening in Russia's attachment was the one bitter drop in the cup of Bismarck's happiness when he returned home from Versailles in 1871, bringing as his trophies the French milliards, Alsace and Lorraine, and the new Empire. Great was his relief, therefore, and great the jubilation in Germany, when in June he was able to bring the two Emperors together in Berlin in friendly intercourse. In the following December a Prussian military delegation, headed by Prince Frederick Charles, the Emperor's nephew, with whom were Moltke and other generals, was entertained at the imperial festival of St. George in St. Petersburg, when high orders and cordial compliments were exchanged.

Russia at that time would have been better pleased if Germany had been contented with a dual friendship, but in his political attachments Bismarck was always polygamic. Ever since 1866 he had been endeavouring to bring Austria more definitely within the orbit of Germany's influence. Count Beust had resisted invitations and pressure as openly and as long as he dared. Whether or not it was Russia's restraining hand or Emperor Francis Joseph's unsentimental common sense that kept Austria entirely outside the complications of 1870, the defeat of France had nevertheless made it clear to

that monarch that for Austria the past was now a completed
chapter, and that the future required a new policy, new measures, and above all new men. In December, 1870, telegrams
had been exchanged between Bismarck and Beust through the
ambassadors of their respective countries, in which the one had
defined with due circumspection the new status in Germany
and the other had accepted it with apparent good grace. But
these purely decorous courtesies had not visibly advanced matters. More definite progress was made in the following August, when, after the visit of the Czar to Berlin, the German
and Austrian Emperors met at Salzburg, where just four
years before Louis Napoleon and Empress Eugénie had been
received with effusive cordiality by the Imperial family.

Bismarck was seeking health at Gastein. There Beust met
him, and before he left the two Emperors once more exchanged
assurances of friendship in the same place. It was significant
that Francis Joseph was attended not only by his Chancellor,
but by the Ministers-President of both halves of the Austrian-
Hungarian empire, an arrangement which enabled Bismarck
to come to closer quarters with Count Andrassy, already
marked out as the statesman who was to lead Austria to her
new day. Three months later Beust was invited to resign,
and he accepted the inevitable (November 8th), unwillingly,
but perhaps not too soon for his reputation. Later he became
ambassador in London and afterwards in Paris, where his career ended. Andrassy was installed in the vacant office, and
his first act was to address to the Austrian diplomatic representatives abroad a circular note announcing that the Emperor's policy would be " a policy of peace, decided, open, and
unshakable." The change of Chancellors was an open confession by one of the shrewdest and most calculating of modern rulers that Austria could not hope to thrive on the meagre
fare of hatred and resentment with which since 1866 Beust
had been stinting it, and that a total change of diet was necessary. Beust's disappearance now made the way clear for
the formal conciliation which both nations needed and for
which both were ready.

With mere declarations of platonic friendship, however, Bismarck was not satisfied. He aimed at a practical working
agreement — not necessarily a formal and documented alliance — under which the three empires, united by monarchical
traditions and by a common antagonism to violent political

changes, should serve as a breakwater against democratic tendencies and as a stay of European peace. He won the first signal victory of his foreign policy as Chancellor when the three Emperors met in Berlin from September 5 to 11, 1872, and their accompanying Chancellors were able to confer at leisure upon the basis of future co-operation in European affairs. Cautious and unwilling to commit himself to indefinite liabilities, William I wrote to his Minister at that time: " I shall agree to nothing binding." Nevertheless, before the imperial visitors left it was possible to announce that as a result of the meetings an understanding had been reached upon outstanding questions and upon the general aims towards which the foreign policy of the three Powers would in future be directed, though no formal agreement had been set down in writing. Above all, it was declared that the friendly deliberations of the three rulers might be accepted as a powerful proclamation in favour of peace.

The agreement thus arrived at is commonly known as the alliance of the three Emperors — the *Drei-Kaiser-Bund.* It was not, however, a Bund or alliance in the true meaning of the word, but rather an informal bond of amity; even if it be permissible to call it a union, it was only a union of good-will. Strictly speaking, it was no more than a friendly *rapport,* expressed in a mutual and verbal understanding that the Powers concerned should work together in matters of common interest as helpful associates.[1] Gortchakoff rejoiced that as a result of these meetings nothing had been reduced to paper.

For a time the so-called alliance secured to Europe the tranquillity which it needed and so much desired. Viewing it in the light of later events, however, it is easy to see how its purposes came to be regarded differently by its members. Germany had proposed it with her eyes specially turned upon France; on the other hand, neither Russia nor Austria had aught to fear from France, while they did not altogether trust each other. Nevertheless, of all the speculations built upon

[1] Defining its meaning at a later date (February 19, 1878), Bismarck said of the *Drei-Kaiser-Bund:* " The *rapport* (*Verhältnis*) of the three Emperors, as it may be termed, though it is usually called an alliance, does not rest at all on written obligations, and none of the Emperors is bound to allow himself to be outvoted by the other two. It rests on the personal sympathy between the three monarchs, on the personal confidence which they entertain towards each other, and on the relationships of the leading Ministers in all three empires, as based on long-standing personal intercourse."

the so-called alliance of the three Emperors those of Bismarck, its author, were destined to be the least fulfilled. He thought that he had now isolated France, and by isolating had permanently weakened her. On the contrary, in Russia he had admitted into the partnership a Power which had no interest whatever in seeing France doomed either to impotence or isolation. In the course of the two following years the Emperor William, accompanied by his Chancellor, paid return visits to St. Petersburg (May, 1873) and Vienna (October, 1874), and Europe then knew that the triple *entente* was complete.

But here Bismarck's schemes were not exhausted. The attitude of Italy towards the new concert of Powers remained to be defined. A closer relationship to her had been his aim ever since the Bohemian war. He wrote to Count Usedom in 1868: "Germany is the natural ally of Italy, since both States are surrounded by neighbours which wish to augment themselves at their cost. . . . Supremacy in the Mediterranean must be the constant thought of Italy and the aim of all her Ministers and their leading principle." Cavour had gone further, and said that an alliance between Prussia and Italy was "written in the book of history." Already Bismarck had, on behalf of the North German Government, given to that country a pledge of friendship by taking a financial interest in the construction of the St. Gothard Railway, a project which appealed to him and to Germany owing to the fact that it would establish communication with the peninsula without touching either French or Austrian soil. In asking the Diet in 1870 to agree to a contribution of ten million francs (£400,-000) towards the cost of the scheme he frankly admitted that political as well as commercial considerations weighed with him, adding: "It is a matter of paramount interest to us to possess a means of direct communication with Italy, a country friendly to us, and, as we believe, likely to remain so " (May 26th). The French Government was interpellated on the subject, but after taking time for reflection the Foreign Secretary, the Duc de Gramont, replied (June 20th) that it was not a matter that called for interference by France.

On the outbreak of the succeeding war Napoleon had tried in vain to win Victor Emmanuel as an ally. Garibaldi had, indeed, led a small band of volunteers against Prussia, with results somewhat inglorious. That expedition, however, was generally regarded in Germany as the chimerical enterprise of an ardent and impetuous patriot, to whom much was to be allowed and much forgiven, and for it no direct responsibility attached to the Italian Government. Bismarck was of opinion that the official protests against Garibaldi's enterprise might have been more vigorous, but victory had effaced any resentment which the incident caused at the time. Convinced that Italy would not choose to stand alone, and that unless she were brought into the new coalition she would end by falling again into the arms of France, concerned also to give to the monarchical principle in the peninsula the moral support of the three Empires, for the good of all, he lost no further time in approaching her. His advances found ready response. Since 1870 Italy had become increasingly conscious of the importance of either making peace with the Vatican or finding friends who were not leagued with it. But peace with the Pope was possible only on the Pope's terms, which implied the restoration to the Church of sovereignty in Rome, and France was ineligible either as ally or friend so long as her Governments were under Clerical influence. In the circumstances the friendship of Germany was not to be lightly rejected.

Here, again, the first advance took the form of complimentary visits. In February, 1872, Prince Frederick Charles, fresh from his successful mission to St. Petersburg, was despatched on a similar visit to Victor Emmanuel in Rome. In May of the same year the Italian Crown Prince (Humbert) and Princess were received as the Emperor's guests in Berlin, and in September, 1873, Victor Emmanuel visited both that capital and Vienna, accompanied by his Minister-President, Minghetti, and his Foreign Minister, Visconti-Venosta. It is said that the first words addressed to Emperor William by his guest when the two were alone were, " I must confess to your Majesty that I was just on the point of taking up arms against you in 1870," and that the Emperor met the frank confession with the affable rejoinder, " But I knew it." Cordial as had been the reception given to his son in Germany, the visit of the Italian King, the *galantuomo* around whose name so much romance had gathered, had a triple significance as royal guest, as political friend, and even more as the liberator who had won for his people the unity which Germany herself was now enjoying, and Berlin's tumultuous ovations voiced the sincere sentiments of the whole nation.

There was now no longer any reason why Italy should not

join the union of the three Emperors, and a quadruple *entente* was formed. In throwing in her lot with the allies Italy gained practical help in case of need. Writing to the German ambassador in Paris on January 18, 1874, Bismarck told him, for the better knowledge of the French Government, that if Italy were to be attacked by France, either for reasons which affected German interests or without justification, Germany would at once go to her assistance. It was not until the autumn of 1875 that the Emperor returned the visit of the Italian King. Out of regard for the feelings of the dethroned Holy Father no reigning prince had set foot in royal Rome since the expulsion therefrom of the papal Government, and the meeting took place in Milan. Bismarck was prevented by ill-health from accompanying the Emperor, but Moltke was there, in token that behind the alliance was the army as well as the Crown and the nation.

Although in the minds of three of the partners the agreement of the four Powers thus consummated was not intended to be a demonstration against France, its immediate effect, none the less, was to leave France without hope of allies, and as a consequence to throw her back upon her own strength and resources. All the time that he had been working to secure friends for Germany, and to strengthen her military position, Bismarck had been endeavouring to exert a restraining influence upon the relations of France with other countries. After the war France was for a time too demoralized to be a source of danger. The feelings of the French towards their conquerors were those of a proud nation which believed that humiliation had come accidentally and undeserved. The presence in the country of an army of occupation smarted like salt in a wound, yet France was helpless; at most she could give vent to her outraged feelings in paroxysms of impotent rage. Now and then public resentment found relief in indefensible acts, as when German soldiers were butchered in circumstances of gross cruelty and common juries refused to convict the murderers. Bismarck's self-restraint under such provocations was admirable. He might have retaliated with interest upon the vanquished foe, but he did not. " If crimes like premeditated murder go unredressed," he wrote to the German ambassador (December 7, 1871), " outraged feeling is apt to call for reprisals, since justice cannot be obtained. If it were possible for us to adopt the judicial attitude of Paris and Melun, the *jus talionis* would lead us to refuse to award punishment for the murder of Frenchmen did it occur within our jurisdiction. But the moral sense and the honourable respect of law which are peculiar to the German people make such a course impossible." Not often in his later dealings with weaker enemies did Bismarck make allowances so magnanimously.

In the meantime, Thiers, the old man eloquent — he was then well over seventy-four — applied himself with glowing patriotism and indomitable energy to the work of reconstruction. The first and most pressing task was the rehabilitation of the army. The war had left the army still more inferior to that of Germany, both in numbers and *moral*, than before, and to redress the inequality was a necessity of self-preservation. The nation warmly applauded the successive measures by which it was sought to make good the losses caused and the deficiencies brought to light by the war, and the needed money was voted readily by the legislature. For ten laborious years France was to work and live for the reorganization and strengthening of her defensive forces, until the time came when she should be able again to look out upon the world with confidence, conscious that her frontiers were secure and her homes safe against attack. To that end her manhood was trained and disciplined in arms and her wealth poured out with a prodigal hand. Universal service took the place of the old system of conscription, the exemptions were restricted, and the liability to serve with the colours for five years, and thereafter in the reserves for fifteen years, became the duty of all.

Germany was represented in Paris during the early years after the war by Count Harry Arnim, who had been Prussia's envoy to the Vatican and had helped Bismarck in all but the final negotiations leading to the Treaty of Frankfort. Arnim was a man of great, almost of brilliant, abilities, yet of somewhat erratic judgment, full of self-confidence, readier to give than to receive advice, and ever eager to play the leading *rôle* in his own corner of the diplomatic stage. Bismarck accepted him as the Empire's representative in France on the strength of his past service and the excessive valuation of his friends; he was conscious of Arnim's failings, however, and knew that he would prove difficult to control. From the first he left Arnim in no uncertainty as to the attitude which he would be expected to hold and the aims which he would be required to pursue. He desired to see France regain strength, without becoming so strong as to become a menace to her late conqueror. Hence she was to be politically boycotted — to be excluded from the respectable society of the monarchies of of the Continent, and by this policy of isolation to be made incapable of mischief. In order to ensure her isolation the republican form of government was to be maintained, for Bismarck argued that so long as France continued to be a republic she would be unable to conclude alliances with monarchical Powers. " Our need," he wrote to Arnim in one of many despatches in which this standpoint was pressed upon him, " is to be left in quiet by France and to prevent France from having allies in case she does not intend to keep the peace." It was Arnim's duty, therefore, while endeavouring to cultivate relationships of confidence and cordiality with France, though in the possibility of these Bismarck only half believed, to watch carefully and counteract any steps which the French Government might take to form close friendships with other Powers. There was another reason for Bismarck's determination to resist a monarchical revival, and it was the fact that the French monarchists were closely allied to the Ultramontanes, with whom in Germany he was now at war.

Bismarck soon found, to his annoyance, that he did not receive from the versatile ambassador in Paris the compliance and support which he expected. Arnim's mind ran on altogether different lines from his own. An aristocrat *pur sang*, and a monarchist by deep conviction, he believed that the principle of monarchism was one and indivisible, and that republics, especially when created by violence, existed only in order to be overturned. His ideas on the subject of legitimism, democratic government, and the " solidarity of Conservative interests," were those, in fact, of feudal Toryism, characteristic of the Pomeranian soil upon which he had been raised, and once formed were not to be moved. Unhappily for Arnim, as it proved, he had a sympathetic ally in the Emperor, whose strong convictions on the subject of the divine rights of Sovereigns, as opposed to sovereign peoples, prevented him from endorsing his Chancellor's preference for republican institutions in France. Honestly sharing the Emperor's legitimist views, Arnim made the mistake of parading to the point of importunacy his warm sympathies with the Bonapartist movement. Not only did he persistently press his ideas upon Bismarck, but he urged him to commend them to the Emperor,

of course without success. " As long as France has no allies,"
Bismarck again wrote to him (December, 1872), " she will not
be dangerous to us, and as long as the great European monarchies hold together, no Republic will be dangerous to them.
On the other hand, a French Republic will not readily find a
monarchical ally against us. This being my conviction, it is
impossible that I should advise his Majesty the King to encourage the French Monarchical Right, a proceeding which
would involve the strengthening of an Ultramontane element
which is hostile to us."

Undeterred by repeated rebuffs, and still as convinced as
ever that he, the man on the spot, knew better than his chief
in Berlin what was good both for France and Germany, Arnim
did not hesitate to go behind Bismarck's back in his determination to discredit with the Emperor the official policy of which
he was supposed to be the mouthpiece and to win approval for
his own policy of sentiment. From that time Bismarck's attitude towards him changed from that of vigilant distrust to
one of active antagonism.

The fact that Chancellor and ambassador were thus at variance did not improve the relationships between the two Governments. In France especially there grew a steady under-
current of suspicion that Germany's attitude was purposely
hostile and that she contemplated another attack. Early in
1873 this apprehension led M. Thiers to challenge Arnim on
the subject. " Is it true," he asked, " that your Government
seeks another war with France as soon as we have paid the indemnity? I am sure you will tell me the truth." Arnim gave
the assurance " as a man of honour " that neither the Emperor nor his advisers nor the German nation " planned, intended, or desired war." With this assurance M. Thiers was
satisfied, declaring for his part that France sincerely wanted
" la paix, la paix, et toujours la paix." Just before this Bismarck had written to the ambassador, in reply to a despatch
of January 22nd: " We do not want war, but we are ready
to wage it again at any time if new presumption on the part of
France makes it necessary. Oderint dum metuant."

The outlook of France became clouded at this time by events
at home. The Monarchists and Clericals, making common
cause, had worked with growing boldness for a double restoration, of monarchy at home and of the papal power in Rome.
The death of Napoleon at Chislehurst, in Kent (January 9,

1873), had further raised their hopes, and there were critical
moments when the stability of the republic seemed to be seriously endangered.   In May the coalition proved strong enough
to overthrow the sagacious and peace-loving burgher-Presi-
dent, M. Thiers, and to give to France in his place a military
head in the person of Marshal MacMahon.   Arnim at first welcomed the change as an important stage on the way towards
the monarchical restoration for which he wished and had secretly been working.   To Bismarck, on the other hand, the
apparent shock to the republic was a severe blow, and in his
disappointment he was disposed to attribute to the unruly ambassador more blame than was his just due.   Arnim's sin in
Bismarck's eyes was not that he mixed in French politics, for
that was meant to be part of his business, but that he did it in
the wrong way.   Moreover, bearing in mind the ambassador's
undisguised and successful attempts to influence the Emperor
against the Government's policy, he regarded the incident as
the first-fruits of a deliberate conspiracy to challenge his own
position.   Arnim seemed to have won the first round in what
was now a personal contest, at once of skill and strength, but
he was determined that it should be the last.

MacMahon, exercising the presidential prerogative, called
the Duc de Broglie, a noble of the old order and an adherent
of the Monarchical-Clerical party, to form a Cabinet.   Under
the new *régime* the relationship between the two countries at
once changed for the worse.   Thanks to Thiers's untiring efforts, the last instalment of the indemnity was paid in September, 1873, and with the money went the last remnant of the
force of occupation.   The payment was made on the 3rd of
the month, and five days later not a German soldier remained
on French soil.   France was again free to go her own way
and follow her own devices without restraint.   The national
elation aroused by this relief stimulated anew the desire for
revenge, and the reactionary parties did not fail to turn it to
their own purposes.

Bismarck's suspicion that the Clericals were the special danger of France seemed to be justified at that time.   They were
behind the intrigues for the subversion of the republic; they
were perpetually conspiring with Rome; and they kindled warlike passions with incredible levity.   Several of the bishops
whose sees adjoined the frontier, enraged by the bitter confessional conflict now in progress across the Rhine, where the

repressive laws associated with the name of Dr. Falk had already been proposed, made themselves conspicuous by the vehemence with which they preached a crusade of vengeance and called down fire from Heaven upon a Power which had desecrated France and was now laying violent hands upon Holy Church. These outbursts passed unrebuked by the authorities, and even Arnim ignored them officially until a despatch from Berlin recalled him to a sense of duty as the guardian of his country's dignity. Yielding to Bismarck's insistence that such incitements to lawlessness must cease, the Government early in January severely reprimanded the fire-eating bishops and suppressed one of the foremost of the Clerical newspapers, while the Foreign Minister, the Duc Décazes, offered to Germany a formal and sincere apology. So threatening were the portents, that Bismarck addressed to Germany's diplomatic representatives abroad a letter in which he declared that while Germany was actuated by peaceful sentiments towards France, " nevertheless, should it be placed beyond doubt that a collision was unavoidable, the German Government would not face before its conscience and the nation the responsibility of awaiting the time that might be most convenient for France."

However great may have been the guilt of the Clericals for the disorder into which France was thrown at that time, the nation was still more to blame. A mood of lassitude, restlessness, and discontent, with a deepening impatience of its warring parties, had come over it, and in its unreasonable disappointment at Ministries which were neither worse nor better than itself it seemed to be in two minds, uncertain whether to hold fast to the new form of government or to revert to the old, and willing to be convinced either way by vehement rhetoric or specious promises.

Arnim himself had now begun to recognize that under Thiers the republic had been more friendly towards Germany and a stronger safeguard for European peace than under a President who owed his elevation to a revolutionary coalition, and he so reported to Bismarck, only to be told with cutting sarcasm that his discovery was no discovery for Berlin and that for himself it had come too late. Before the year 1873 was out Bismarck had come to the conclusion that matters would not improve between Germany and France so long as Arnim continued in Paris. The two were still pulling against each other, and Arnim so far had seemed to be gaining ground; he had the ear of the Court, and a small body of influential Conservatives were conspiring to place him in the Chancellor's seat. There was also a black mark of another kind against him, for his banker, one Hansemann, had disclosed to Bismarck the fact that he had been speculating over the French war loans in conjunction with a Paris financier named Hirsch, and had made handsome gains thereby. Against his will the restless diplomatist was recalled from Paris in February, 1874, and was offered the embassy at Constantinople, to take or leave as he willed, while Prince Hohenlohe, changing the service of his native Bavaria, was nominated to Paris in his stead.

Arnim's later career has no direct interest for these pages, and may be summarized in a few sentences. His suspension from office was a fatal blow to his pride and, unfortunately, to his composure. Like many another man, before and after him, fatally endowed with excess of temperament, he lost self-control under affront, and having once slipped his moorings his course ended, as it was bound to do, in disaster. Arnim had never endorsed Bismarck's policy towards the Roman Catholic Church, or abandoned his belief that if his advice had been taken at the beginning there would have been no confessional conflict. In April there appeared in a Vienna newspaper a *pro-memoria* of Arnim's on the Infallibility question, together with letters addressed by him to Bishop Hefele and Dr. Döllinger in 1870, while he was envoy in Rome, and these were followed by communications to Berlin and Breslau newspapers on the same subject. The obvious purpose of the publication of these documents was to create the impression that Bismarck had wofully blundered over the *Kulturkampf*, and that had a wiser man been in charge of affairs the nation would have been spared an unspeakable misfortune. Arnim's action in stirring up domestic strife in this way — for he had himself supplied the documents to the Press, although on being challenged by the Chancellor he at first denied it — was an unpardonable breach of official etiquette, and was treated as such. Bismarck answered first by publishing his reasons for rejecting Arnim's too easy solution of the Infallibility problem, and therewith a report of the ambassador's in which he was shown as throwing doubt upon the propriety of his own proposals, then by calling upon the indiscreet diplomat to explain the origin of the Vienna newspaper's disclosures. As Arnim was unable to clear himself, his appointment to Constantinople was cancelled and he was relieved of further service.

What followed was creditable neither to Arnim nor Bismarck. Hohenlohe on succeeding to the Paris embassy found that certain documents which should have been in the archives had been abstracted. Required to account for their disappearance, Arnim returned some but retained others on the plea that they were his private property. Without bandying words with the man who had tried and failed to humiliate him and undermine his position, Bismarck caused Arnim to be arrested in his own house on the charge of theft. Tried in Berlin, the fallen ambassador was acquitted of charges of purloining documents and of official misdemeanour, but was found guilty of conduct injurious to public order and was awarded three months' imprisonment. Both sides appealed against the sentence, which was eventually increased to nine months' imprisonment, though the penalty was never paid, since Arnim took refuge abroad. Beaten in a contest with an antagonist for whom he was no match, he now resorted to pamphlet-writing of a kind only to be excused by the deep sense of wrong under which he was suffering. For this he was prosecuted on a charge of high treason and sentenced to five years' imprisonment with hard labour, a penalty of which he again cheated his persecutors by refusing to leave foreign soil. Discredited in the law courts by compromising accusations, to which he made no reply, he was now dismissed from the service of the State and deprived of his pension, and he died in 1881, an outlaw, broken and embittered. The public verdict upon the Arnim episode and its issue belied August von Platen's words:

> But small regard has human pain,
> And wounded men unheeded fall;
> A sick man's suffering ne'er was known
> To hurt a healthy man at all.

There was general agreement that Bismarck's treatment of the ambassador was harsh and vindictive, and his later ingenious plea, that his motive was not personal revenge but rather " bureaucratic dogmatism on the part of a superior official whose authority had been disregarded," did not carry conviction.

To the new ambassador in Paris were given the same marching orders which his predecessor had received but had disobeyed. " As to France," so Hohenlohe noted in his Diary at the time (May 2nd), " the chief point of interest for us was to see that she should not become so powerful internally and of so much weight externally as to secure for herself allies. A republic and internal dissensions were the best guarantee of peace." Bismarck went so far as to urge for the first time that France should be encouraged to entangle herself in Tunis, which was then attracting the attention of the French colonial party. " That," he said, " would be a good thing for us, as France would then busy herself in that quarter and would be held fast there." Hohenlohe pondered these things, but did not fail to note that the Emperor refused to endorse this too obvious policy of deliberately working for France's weakness. A certain antagonism of moral standards in statecraft is revealed by Hohenlohe in a report of a conversation of a few days later in which the Emperor criticized his Chancellor's policy. " He desired me," the new ambassador records, " to keep on the best terms possible with France. Bismarck specially emphasizes the point that France should not be too strong and desirable as an ally. That was all right. Yet it was neither proper nor possible that we should ourselves work for the destruction and demoralization of France."

Already, however, the Emperor had relinquished the substance of authority, and only the shadow remained in his hands. Bismarck was never more conscious and at the same time more jealous of his power than now. He managed foreign policy as if not the Emperor but he were Germany's ruler; he spoke to the Diet as a Coriolanus might have spoken to the assembly of the *plebs;* he was not only the head of the Government but the Government itself, and all his colleagues were but servitors overshadowed by his personality and ministering to his will. Prince Hohenlohe wrote of the old Emperor in his Diary on September 7, 1873: " He no longer has energy to oppose Bismarck or to decide on anything without first consulting him. All hopes of this must be entirely given up. Personally I abandoned hope long ago." Not long afterwards the Crown Prince confessed to Sir Robert Morier that both the Emperor and he were " powerless before Bismarck." It is doubtful whether the Emperor, who was now seventy-seven years old, was fully conscious of the extent to which his will had been broken and the servant had taken the master's place.

Nevertheless, the relations between the two continued unclouded, and on the Chancellor's side were those of deep and even tender attachment, for he loved the old Emperor the more, the more he succeeded in bringing him under control.

During 1873 events occurred calling for the exercise of masterful intervention in a part of Europe with which Germany had hitherto had little to do, and the action taken called the attention of the Powers in a dramatic manner to the significance of Germany's changed position in international affairs. Spain was again in the throes of insurrection. A republic had been set up in February, and in spite of the divisions and discords by which the nation was distracted, the Government, whose head was Marshal Serrano, had done well. There were two rival political parties, which seriously contended with the republicans for mastery in the much-disturbed country, and both represented members of the Bourbon dynasty. One of these parties sided with Don Alfonso, the young son of Isabel II, and the other with his cousin, Don Juan de Bourbon. The Alfonsists were indisposed to violent measures, convinced that if the republic were left alone it would sooner or later seal its own doom. The rival faction called itself after the name of Don Juan's son, Don Carlos, who vigorously prosecuted the family claim, which his father eventually renounced in his favour. The Carlists, who had behind them the Roman Catholic clergy, with all the influence which it was able to exert in the rural districts, raised a formidable force of irregulars, which, working from France, kept the northern frontier districts in disorder and alarm, and in the summer of 1873 forcibly occupied large parts of the North.

In the course of one of the engagements fought in the following year a retired Prussian captain of artillery named Schmidt, who had gone to Spain in the capacity of military correspondent for the German Press, was captured, and, though his papers attested his person and occupation, he was summarily shot as a spy after undergoing the farce of a court-martial trial. The news of the murder roused an angry feeling in Germany, and no one was more incensed than the Chancellor, who promptly ordered a German squadron, then anchoring before the Isle of Wight, to steam to the north coast of Spain. It was not clear what the ships would be able to do when they arrived there, since the Government of the country was still republican and friendly to all the enemies of the Carlists, but the act gave great satisfaction in Germany as a sign that the nation's interests were in strong hands.

In a speech made in the Diet later in the year (December 4th) Bismarck described the impression which the murder of Schmidt had made upon him. " My feeling," he said, " was this — that if he had been an English, an American, a Russian, or a French correspondent, the murder would not have occurred. I recalled all the old humiliations which Germany was formerly compelled to bear owing to her divisions, and I said to myself: ' It is time to accustom foreign countries to the idea that Germans, too, cannot be murdered with impunity.' " In August he went further, for with a view to strengthening the hands of the Government in power in its contest with Carlism and disorder, he formally recognized the republic and persuaded some of the other European Powers to do the same. Russia declined, however, to the satisfaction of France, which professed to see in her abstention a first rift in the lute of the quadruple *entente*. None the less, Bismarck now succeeded — where Serrano had failed — in inducing the French Government to check the abuse of hospitality of which the Carlists had been guilty in making the neutral territory north of the Pyranees a base for their lawless incursions into the neighbouring friendly State. Carlism itself was not destroyed by these reprisals, but the endeavours of the pretender were made doubly difficult, and no more German subjects were put to a violent death.

It was the relations with France which, more than any other consideration, determined the scope of the Army Bill which the Government brought forward in February, 1874, when the time came for revising the temporary arrangements sanctioned by the Diet in 1871.[1] The bill, which as passed continued the peace strength at 402,000 men as before, could not fairly be regarded as a challenge by France, whose military preparations had been so accelerated that she now commanded a fighting force twice as large as that which she had been able to put into the field in 1870; if figures represented realities, she would now have been able to mobilize nearly a million and a quarter men for service in the active army and over a million men in the territorial army. Nevertheless, the French army estimates for 1875 were fixed at 485 million francs and the peace strength

[1] See Chapter XIV., pp. 60–63.

at 461,000, figures both larger than the corresponding figures for Germany.

The feverish haste with which France was increasing her forces led Germany in 1874 to address to the French Government a formal protest and to the Great Powers collectively a letter of warning. Had France at the time been surer of her position, the affront might have led to complications. As it was, the remonstrance was answered with a disclaimer and a counter-accusation that Germany herself was the real menace to peace. It is doubtful whether any sane person seriously believed that France either desired or was prepared for war, since both her internal troubles and the still incomplete reorganization of her army would have made the risk too great. Nevertheless, all through the year 1874 Europe was disturbed by persistent rumours of impending evil. In the beginning of March Moltke said to the British ambassador in Berlin that " the idea of war was popular in Germany," that war was inevitable sooner or later, and that from his standpoint as a soldier it would be better that it should not be delayed too long. To the Belgian ambassador he was even more explicit. " He did not see," he told him on April 30th, " how Germany could avoid war next year, unless the Great Powers combined to persuade France to reduce her armaments to a reasonable peace establishment." About the same time also, Bismarck admitted to Hohenlohe his fear that the portents were unpropitious. " We want to keep peace with France," he said, " but if France goes on arming so that she may be ready in five years, and is bent on war at that time, then we will declare war in three years."

On the other hand, many of the friends of France suspected that the aggravation came from Bismarck's side, and that war was his aim. Hohenlohe relates that in October the Emperor objected to a reference to foreign affairs which his Chancellor proposed to put in a speech from the throne, as being " open to the construction that we were prepared to make war again upon France." " That was out of the question," he added; " he was too old to begin another war, and he feared that Prince Bismarck was trying to drag him little by little into fresh hostilities." Hohenlohe tried to remove these doubts, but without success. " I shall fall out with Prince Bismarck again over this matter," the Emperor said, " and it would gratify me if you would put it before him once more from my point of view "— a frank confession that Bismarck and not he was now the true ruler of Germany.

When a statesman who has deliberately schemed three wars, and has only recently been accused of planning another, suddenly begins to protest the transparency of his motives and the innocence of his intentions, there is room for a suspicion that he is again meditating deeply on stratagems and spoils; let no such man be trusted! Defending his foreign policy in the Diet in the last month of 1874, Bismarck said: " In our foreign relations we have perfectly clean linen, and there is nothing whatever to conceal." Events occurred early in 1875 which cast grave doubts upon this confident assumption of virtue. Within four months Europe had come perilously near to a repetition of the catastrophe of 1870.

On April 5th the semi-official *Cologne Gazette* created unrest by a declaration that the increase of the French army was only to be explained on the assumption that it was a preparation for a war of revenge, and three days later the Berlin *Post* published an alarmist article with the title " Is war in sight? " The writer reviewed the European political situation, took measure of the various conditions and tendencies making for disturbance or tranquillity, weighed the possibility of Continental alliances, and without answering his question affirmatively came to the conclusion that the outlook was gloomy. " There are people," the article concluded, " who take the view that if the roof of a house is burning and a good fire brigade is in sight there is no need to awaken the sleepers in the stories below. We are not disposed to act thus towards the German nation. We do not regard it as desirable to disturb people's minds and call them to arms, but we do not think it expedient to conceal from the nation the realities of the situation and the dangers which confront its statesmen."

The origin of this article was never authoritatively established. Referring to it at a later date, Bismarck disowned paternity. Both in structure and tone, however, the article was one which he might either have prompted or written, and with the knowledge which we possess — and for which we are indebted to Bismarck himself — of his intimate relations with the Press, and of the band of skilled journalistic mercenaries which he kept in his service, it is difficult to resist the belief that the inspiration of the article, if no more, originated in his calculating brain. That he was bent on war is very unlikely, but he was certainly willing to accept it if France were so disposed, and the most charitable view is that the article was intended to take stock of the situation with a view to making it either better or worse.

The immediate effect of the " Is war in sight? " article was to throw not only France but all Europe into perturbation. Distant though she was from the nerve-centre of the Continent, as Berlin might be regarded at that time, England experienced the unfamiliar sensation of panic. Sober men, insusceptible to alarm, were carried away by the prevailing apprehension. Sir Robert Morier, whose opinion of Bismarck's political morality was of the lowest, thought the danger of war at that time so real that he addressed an eloquent appeal to the German Crown Prince beseeching him to use his influence in staying the malign forces which seemed to be leading Europe towards an abyss. Bismarck had few friends in the Courts of Europe, and two crowned heads at least suspected his hand in the prevailing turmoil. Queen Victoria expostulated with the Emperor, and entreated by her to intervene the Czar made urgent remonstrances in the same quarter. The British Government also, in a despatch addressed to the ambassador in Berlin, offered its services as friendly mediator with France, and also in the same indirect way invited the Governments of other leading Powers to use their influence in the cause of peace. Bismarck professed to welcome these well-intended overtures and to regard them as a token of good-will, but in fact he resented them deeply. So ill did he take the Queen's intervention that he returned to the subject in September in correspondence with the Emperor, and believing by that time that he was really far more innocent than he had claimed to be, complained bitterly of her " unfriendly proceeding."

This time the Emperor was firm; he was determined that there should be no war, and his Chancellor was told so.[1] No sooner did it appear that the scare had miscarried than Bismarck tried to turn the scales against the critics who had ac-

[1] The episode is noteworthy as fixing the date at which the modern revival of the German doctrine of what is called, by a gross misuse of language, " preventive war " (i.e. war waged for the purpose of anticipating a hostile State's assumed preparations), received formal military endorsement. Disquieted by some remarks made by Moltke in advocacy of such a war, the Emperor wrote to Bismarck on August 6th: " No one is more convinced than I that the man who would provoke a European war would have against him universal public opinion, and thus would have neither allies nor benevolent neutrals, but only enemies."

cused him to his master. The real conspirators, he said, were in Paris, London, St. Petersburg, anywhere save in Berlin, and he, the reputed author of mischief, was the real warden of the Continent's peace. The variety of Bismarck's explanations of the war scare showed great ingenuity, but also an uneasy conscience. In private correspondence he admitted that both Moltke and Count Münster might have spoken to the Government "theoretically of the utility of a timely attack on France," though he professed to know nothing definite as to what may have been in their minds.[1] To Lord Odo Russell he complained that the trouble arose owing to the influential German Press being so much in the hands of the Jews. The theory reserved for the Emperor's special satisfaction was that the scare was due to the Stock Exchange speculations of the French Foreign Minister, the Duc Décazes. In later years he was accustomed to say that Gortchakoff was at the bottom of the mischief.

That the crisis passed over without greater danger was due to the personal influence of the Czar more than any other cause. Not only was the Czar resolved that peace should not be broken, but he was equally resolved that if France were to be involved against her will she should not stand alone. "My word will be sufficient to ensure peace to France," he had said to the French ambassador in St. Petersburg, General Leflô, in the middle of April, and he added that if Germany were to begin war without provocation and rightful cause she would not find herself in the same position as in 1870, for all Europe would be against her. "She would," he said, "go to war at her peril." Gortchakoff added his own assurances, and gave to the ambassador the parting counsel, "I have only one thing to say to you; see that you are strong." The relief felt by France when the danger was over and her gratitude to the friends of peace were a convincing proof that a desire for hostilities could not be laid to her account. When the war-clouds had passed away, the French Foreign Minister wrote to St. Petersburg (April 28th), declaring that "the attitude of the Russian Court has averted from us an imminent dan-

[1] "It is quite possible," he wrote to the Emperor on August 13th, "that he (Count Münster), like Count Moltke, may have spoken theoretically of the utility of a timely attack on France, though I am not aware of it, and he never received any such instructions. It may, indeed, be said that it is not conducive to peace if France were to have the assurance that she will not be attacked in any circumstances, whatever she may do" (*Reflections and Reminiscences*, vol. ii., p. 192).

ger," and acclaiming the Czar as " the arbiter of the world's peace." " I am ready to give the Czar," he added, " every guarantee he may wish that we have no thought of disturbing the peace of the world." Great Britain also earned France's good-will for her useful intervention.

The restoration of tranquillity was confirmed by a visit of the Czar to Berlin, accompanied by his Chancellor, in the second week of May. On that occasion Gortchakoff succeeded in inflicting upon Bismarck an indignity which was never forgiven or forgotten. After several days of conversations between the Emperors and the Chancellors, Gortchakoff addressed to the Russian legations throughout Europe a despatch in which he used the words, " Now peace is assured (*maintenant la paix est assurée*): a conviction of its necessity has been brought home." The implication that before the conferences peace had been endangered, and that Berlin was the centre of disturbance, was too obvious to be ignored. Bismarck accepted the suggestion as a personal attack, and according to his own story he accused Gortchakoff to his face of having sought to pose as the apostle of peace out of pure vanity, adding the reminder that he was " a good friend to friends but a good enemy to enemies." The bitterness and mordant sarcasm of many of his later references to his Russian rival showed how keenly the affront had been felt. The episode had also important political consequences. For some time he had chafed under the Russian Chancellor's proneness to take Germany too cheaply: " You do not treat us as a friendly Power," he had told him, " *mais comme un domestique qui ne monte par assez vite quand on a sonné.*" The new exhibition of arrogance warned him that Gortchakoff could no longer be counted with confidence upon the list of Germany's friends.

Gortchakoff was vain enough, and apt to magnify himself and his performances, and he may have welcomed the opportunity of humiliating a statesman whom he used to regard as his pupil, but was now no longer able to patronize as of old, yet his attitude on this occasion was more than a pose. In his intercourse with the diplomats and generals of Berlin he had formed the conviction that the recent alarm had a genuine foundation, and that the expediency of an attack upon France had really been considered.[1] The Czar himself was convinced

[1] That this is so may fairly be concluded from a passage in Bismarck's *Memoirs,* where he says: " According to the views of our military men it was probable that in 1875 we should have conquered France, but it was not

that the scare had been created purposely by Bismarck in order to relieve the pressure of domestic troubles, yet that it was not intended to be more than a scare. In the following January he said to the German ambassador in St. Petersburg that while he personally had no doubt whatever as to the sincerity of Bismarck's protestations of pacific intentions, " the ambassador must not be offended if he said that this view was not generally held."

Conscious of the danger through which the Empire had passed while the federal Governments had been kept in ignorance that mischief was brewing, the Würtemberg Minister-President wrote tactfully to Bismarck suggesting that for the future the special committee for foreign affairs created by the constitution should be taken into confidence and counsel in critical times. Bismarck took the implied reproach in good part, and promised to act upon the Minister's suggestion.

In later years Bismarck was wont to date from Gortchakoff's irritating telegram the coolness which sprang up in the relations between Russia and Germany. It would be truer to say that it was the episode in which the telegram was but a minor incident that tried the strength of the *entente* between these Powers. We have seen that in joining the two neighbouring empires Russia gave no pledge and no sign of hostility to France ; rather that her act was intended to prevent the very isolation of the Republic which was the real purpose of Bismarck's astute diplomacy. The events of April and May were to the Czar a clear proof that Germany was bent upon pressing France too hard. Such a policy was bound to modify Russia's attitude, and it did, in fact, cause her to turn henceforth friendlier glances towards the far West of Europe. Two years before this, Thiers, ever sanguine on the subject of alliances, had suggested to Lord Lyons the advisability of an *entente* between France, Russia, and Great Britain, and although warned by the British Foreign Secretary that the idea was premature, he had let it be known in St. Petersburg that France was ready to give or receive serious overtures. Now it seemed as though the first steps towards the realization of his

so probable that the other Powers would have remained neutral." So the military men had evidently speculated upon the matter from all standpoints. Moreover, two years after the crisis (October 30, 1877), in a letter written through his son to Gambetta in Paris, Bismarck said that there was still a military party which clamoured for a war while France was weak — a party which " has a hearing, it is true, but no power."

dream were to be taken. It was certain that if Germany and Russia fell out France would not be slow to seize her chance of making good the misfortune of 1870.

As yet, however, there was no outward change in the relations between Russia and Germany, and years were to pass before any positive strain became visible. Bismarck, seeing in Gortchakoff the fountain and origin of mischief, comforted himself by the thought that his rival had passed his prime and was losing favour and influence with the Czar. Just as, when it became clear that Beust's power was waning, he had made court to Count Andrassy, so now, foreseeing the eclipse of Gortchakoff, he turned his eyes to the new star now rising in the East, M. de Giers, who became Gortchakoff's assistant at the Foreign Office in 1875 and was already marked as his successor there.

In the story of the dark intrigue of the spring of 1875 the conduct of the aged Emperor stands out in bright relief. He had hated the idea of war, and no sooner was the scare over than he hastened to undo the mischief which it had caused in France. A week after the Czar had returned home he sent his ambassador back to Paris (May 18th) with a conciliatory message. Hohenlohe relates how, after the Emperor had spoken of " the friction between himself and Prince Bismarck," he added: " Give my compliments to Marshal MacMahon, and say to him that you are not the only messenger of peace, but that the real messenger of peace stands here."

Soon after the " Is war in sight? " incident the chagrins even more than the cares of office led Bismarck seriously to contemplate retirement. In a pressing letter to the Emperor (May 4th), in which he pleaded that owing to bad health his power to serve the State was exhausted, he begged for his discharge on the pension to which his service entitled him. A man of humours and of many nerves, Bismarck's wish to escape from harness appears this time to have been genuine. In conversation with Lord Odo Russell in the previous November he had explained how his life had fallen into periods of twelve years, and being then " sixty and worn out with the responsibilities and anxieties of office," he said it was his intention to begin the sixth span by retiring into private life. Convinced of his own and the country's need of the weary Chancellor, the Emperor agreed to a long rest, but refused to allow him to resign, and bade him keep his design secret. Bismarck accordingly remained in rural retreat for some months, consulted only by the Emperor on matters of exceptional moment, but before the end of the year he was able to return to Berlin and duty.

The war scare of the spring seemed to clear the air, and for a time the relations between the German and French Governments became uncommonly friendly. Developments in the internal affairs of France helped in this direction. The most notable of these was the rising storm of opposition to crozier rule. Under MacMahon the Clericals showed their colours openly as enemies of the Republic and plotters for the restoration of monarchy and through it of ecclesiastical domination. Hence the struggle in France for all parties which professed, under whatever name, to sympathize with the ideas of Liberalism and liberty became a struggle with the immutable Church. " Le cléricalisme, voilà l'ennemi," was the battle-cry with which, in a speech at Romans in September, 1878, the fiery Gambetta rallied the forces of political and intellectual progress for the resumption of " the struggle between the agents of the theocracy of Rome and the sons of 1789." The elections of October resulted in the defeat of the Government and brought in the Cabinet of M. Dufaure, in which M. Waddington, a Protestant in whose veins ran English blood, and who had also been educated in England, was the Foreign Minister.

The relations between Germany, France, and Great Britain at this time were peculiar, for while the first two were throwing friendly glances across the Channel, Bismarck was doing his best to establish influence over France. He was now building expectations upon Gambetta, both as a passionate champion of the Republic and a bitter antagonist of the Papacy. In 1877 he had allowed Count Henckel von Donnersmarck, a Silesian colliery proprietor who dabbled in politics, to open confidential negotiations with him in Paris in the hope of winning him for his campaign against the Jesuits and Rome. He had long wanted to meet Gambetta, who was himself willing, yet he had refrained from proposing a meeting from a belief that it might compromise the French tribune and so incapacitate him from doing Germany service. Gambetta, for his part, was then wishful for a *rapprochement* between the two countries, and the assurance which had been conveyed to him that the best way of promoting one was " a determined attitude against Rome " was entirely to his mind. Nevertheless, attracted though he was to Bismarck on personal grounds, and highly susceptible to the attentions which had been bestowed upon him, he was clear-sighted enough to recognize that the interests of France called still more for a good understanding with Russia and Great Britain, and this he furthered. In a conversation with the Prince of Wales in Paris in July, 1878, he even proposed a formal Anglo-French alliance, and possibly he meant it sincerely, though his emotions were notoriously uncertain and ephemeral. During Dufaure's Government a beginning was made with the anti-clerical legislation which was later to acquire so great a prominence in French political life.

In January, 1879, MacMahon, who had resisted repeated incitements to subvert the constitution and restore the monarchy in the person of the Comte de Chambord, resigned on a question of military policy, and the National Assembly, refusing another soldier-President, though one offered himself in the person of General Chanzy, elected M. Grévy, then President of the Chamber. The change seemed to indicate that a soberer appreciation of facts prevailed in France, and that the nation was seriously bent upon the maintenance of peace both at home and abroad. It fell to M. Waddington to form the next Cabinet, while Gambetta became President of the Chamber, waiting his turn at the helm. Within a year M. Waddington had resigned, and the Freycinet Ministry, of which M. Ferry was the best-known member, followed. Gambetta's partiality for Bismarck had in the meantime been rudely shaken by the Austro-German alliance of October, 1879,[1] which he regarded as aimed directly at France, on which account he tried to establish more intimate ties with Great Britain. For such endeavours, however, the times were now unpropitious. Causes of friction had arisen between the two countries in different parts of the world, and above all there was setting in the Egyptian darkness which was for many years to obscure their relations as custodians of the interests of Europe on the Nile.

Bismarck was not slow to turn the altered situation to advantage, and when in September, 1880, Freycinet was succeeded by M. Ferry, France and Germany began seriously to make reciprocal advances. The elections took place in August of the following year, and showed France to be still in a steady

[1] See Chapter XVI., pp. 142-4.

mood. Against 57 Bonapartists and 41 Monarchists, 459 Republicans were returned.

This powerful confirmation of the Republic was largely the work of Gambetta, who, on Ferry's resignation in November, became Premier and Foreign Minister. His administration proved of too short duration to produce great changes either abroad or at home, and when on the last day of 1882 he died, at the age of forty-four, from misadventure, German influence seemed still to be in the ascendant and the budding Franco-Russian *entente* to be a thing of the past. After three other Ministries had rapidly run their course, M. Ferry was again called to form a Cabinet in February, 1883, and with his second return to power France and Germany for a time worked together in unaccustomed harmony.

In spite of the bitterness of party passion, which gave to the Republic eighteen administrations in little over twenty years, the work of national reorganization and reconstruction, the common task and interest of all parties alike, had made further progress since 1875. After prodigious exertions and sacrifices it could be claimed that the fabric of national security, which had been so sorely battered in the great war, was at last renewed, and that France had regained all her lost strength and confidence. The nation seemed to have finally settled down to the new form of government; Louis Napoleon had died in exile; his only son, the Prince Imperial, had fallen on the battlefield in Zululand in England's service (June, 1879); and though the Princes of the royal houses still intrigued according to their ability, many of the foremost of their adherents in public life had in course of time deserted the cause of restoration as impolitic and hopeless. "We need a powerful France," Gortchakoff had said to the British ambassador in Berlin. "Be strong!" was the advice which he gave to French ambassadors and War Ministers on every possible occasion and in every gradation of urgency. It seemed that the strong France had arrived, dangerous as an enemy yet no less desirable as friend and ally.

The decade which had just opened saw France committed to a new era of colonial enterprise, and here Germany readily gave her a helping hand. Prussia founded the pillars of her later strength, the army and the national system of education, in the darkest hour of her humiliation in the nineteenth century — the seven years which came between Jena and Leipzig.

For France, too, the first task to be faced after the disaster of 1870 had been the rebuilding of the army which, trusted not wisely but too well, had failed in the time of supreme trial. Yet even in the early years of despondency there were Frenchmen who turned their gaze again outward, following upon fields of imperialistic adventure the eternal quest of glory and prestige for their country's sake.   France had long turned envious eyes towards Tunis, the annexation of which she had seriously contemplated and might have carried out as early as 1868 had not Bismarck at that time put in a speculative claim on Prussia's behalf.   During the Berlin Congress of 1878 Bismarck changed his mind and reminded M. Waddington, the French plenipotentiary, of the attractions of that still unappropriated territory.   Two years later, in 1880, the German Government openly encouraged France to establish herself in Morocco. In November of that year Bismarck authorized Prince Hohenlohe, still ambassador in Paris, to tell the French Premier that so far as Germany was concerned France might annex where she could — in North Africa, West Africa, or the East — and fight, if she wished, by land or sea, so long as no glances were turned to Strassburg or Metz.   Still later, at the end of 1882, he told Hohenlohe, " If the French want the English to give them a free hand in Syria, it does not matter to us.   The French are to be allowed to do what they like everywhere, so long as they keep away from the Rhine."

In May, 1881, with Germany's support and regardless of British protests, France proclaimed a protectorate in Tunis, to the deep mortification of Italy, which had likewise cherished the hope of gaining, with the assent of the Powers, this outpost of the ancient Roman Empire.   Almost the French may be said to have been pushed into the country by Bismarck, who was only too pleased to see Germany's restless neighbour dissipate her political interests and military resources in foreign enterprises.   The official attitude of Great Britain in the matter had been inconsistent and contradictory.   At the Berlin Congress Lord Salisbury, her second plenipotentiary, had, like Bismarck, encouraged France to annex the country.   In a letter of that time (August 7, 1878) to M. Waddington, then Foreign Secretary, he had given the assurance that the British Government would not " view with distrust the legitimate and increasing influence of France " in that region, and hinting that " even the fall of the Bey's Government, were it to come

about, would in no way change the attitude of England, who
has no interests of her own there." [1]   Later attempts made by
Lord Salisbury to weaken the effect of these encouragements
were received by his countrymen as a confession that he had
gone farther than prudence warranted. Constantly pressed
by the French Government to declare himself openly in favour
of annexation, he nevertheless declined to go to the length of a
public approval, though he was always prepared, as he told
Lord Lyons, to view such action by France without remonstrance. His successor at the Foreign Office, Lord Granville,
maintained a severer attitude. " The French," he wrote to
Lord Lyons on April 5, 1881, " cannot be allowed to seize
Tunis without the consent of Turkey and communication with
the rest of Europe." Yet the French did seize Tunis, and
that with the connivance of Germany only, the rest of Europe
not being consulted. The day after Lord Granville thus wrote
the French Government assured Lord Lyons that it had no
intention to annex the country, and that such a step would be
for France " a mistake and a misfortune," and this assurance
was duly conveyed to the Italian ambassador in London in
complete confidence. Nevertheless, fortified by the knowledge
of Bismarck's acquiescence, France concluded the Treaty of
Kassar Said on May 12th, by which Tunis passed under her
protection, as a prelude to formal appropriation at a more
convenient season.

Honestly indignant at the irregular proceeding, the British
Government now put its foot down, and warned the French
imperialists that though Tunis had been taken against its protests it would not look on quietly if the same tactics were repeated in regard to Tripoli. A fit of righteousness had come
over the British Cabinet, and it might have done more had it
been able, but Lord Salisbury's action and the appropriation
of Cyprus three years before made England at the time a weak
advocate of the integrity of the Sultan's empire.[2] The warning drew a virtuous disclaimer of any designs in that quarter. In the previous year, indeed, M. Freycinet, in conversation with the Italian ambassador in Paris (July 25, 1880),

---

[1] Published in *The Times* of April 11, 1881.
[2] " A Cabinet about Tunis," Lord Granville wrote to Mr. (later Lord)
Goschen, on May 13, 1881. " As to that question, we think Cyprus and the
language of Lord Salisbury leaves little ground under our feet to take a
strong attitude. We only insist on our treaty rights, and proper treatment of foreign subjects, creditors, and trade " (*Life of Lord Goschen*, by
the Hon. A. D. Elliot, vol. i., pp. 237-8).

had advised Italy not to make French designs upon Tunis a grievance, but to prepare for the acquisition of Tripoli. From that time may be dated France's formal recognition of that Turkish province as falling within the Italian sphere of influence.   On May 11, 1884, M. Ferry honoured his predecessor's bond when he assured the Italian ambassador, " privately, in the strictest confidence," that if Italy wished to occupy Tripoli France would offer no opposition.

Two years after Tunis was thus definitely marked out for French occupation, Madagascar likewise became virtually a French possession, though the transaction was only regularized by international treaty seven years later.   Between 1884 and 1886 Annam and Tonquin also came under French rule. While all these acquisitions were being made Bismarck looked on approvingly.   The arrangement was, in fact, equally advantageous for both sides.   If Germany gave her support to France in her enterprises in North-West Africa and elsewhere, as well as in the serious controversies which had arisen in Egypt, she could count upon timely French help in her colonial difficulties with Great Britain, and particularly in the West African (Congo) conference of 1884–1885.[1]   France seemed all at once to have forgotten the enmities born of humiliation in 1870, and to have put interest in the place of pride.   The statesman had played his cards well who could draw from the Paris *Temps* in 1884 a frank admission of the cordiality of Franco-German relations and the flattering tribute, " It is remarkable that we have come so far as to ask whether our country is not about to enter, at least tacitly, the concert of the Powers which has been formed around the Prusso-Austrian alliance, and whether Bismarck will not succeed in drawing us into the ambit of German policy and ranging us in a system whose true name is German hegemony."

But now the dream of a truce to the old feuds was to be dispelled.   Before a year had passed a sequence of events began which proved that a Franco-German *entente* was unnatural, and that in seeking it the Ferry Cabinet had not represented the nation's true feeling.   The bare prospect of a formal peace with the victors of 1870 revived passions which had slowly been subsiding, and once more the Monarchists and Clericals, seeing their chance, renewed the old agitations and intrigues.   Ferry fell early in 1885, discredited by the dis-

[1] See Chapter XVII., pp. 203–205.

aster which befel French arms in Tonquin, and for France the next three years were the most dangerous since 1871. The persistent leaning to Cæsarism, the desire to be mastered and ruled by a strong man — that paradoxical trait in a national character essentially democratic and individualistic — once more asserted itself. It seemed as though the days of the Republic were numbered, and that the nation might easily have been won back to the monarchy if only a strong dictator had been ready to lead the way. General de Galliffet was thought for a time to be the Monk who would usher in the restoration, but later, and as it appeared with greater reason, the monarchists fixed their hopes upon General Boulanger.

Ferry gave place to Brisson, and after several months (January, 1886) Freycinet formed his third Cabinet. In this Cabinet Boulanger was the Minister of War. Now began between France and Germany a feverish rivalry in military measures which seemed to be a crowning preparation for the second struggle which had been so long deferred. Boulanger wanted both a larger and a better trained army; the peace strength was to be increased to over half a million. Bismarck promptly answered with an Army Bill increasing Germany's peace strength from 427,000 to 468,000, once more for seven years. While, however, the German Chancellor, though aided by all the influence of the generals, failed to move the Diet, the French War Minister for a time seemed to carry all before him. Freycinet resigned, indeed, in December, and was followed by M. Goblet, but Boulanger remained in office, the " strong man " of the Cabinet, the favourite of the Chamber, and the idol of the nation. Never since the time when Gambetta had seared upon the soul of France, with the branding-iron of his fiery eloquence, the adjuration " Think always of revenge, but speak of it never! " had a man arisen who seemed to interpret so faithfully the ever-present longing of a proud people to retrieve defeat and restore its shattered self-esteem. From being the Minister of a party Boulanger became the head of a party himself, and a Boulanger cultus began. Renewed intrigues by the Comte de Paris, encouraged by the disturbed state of public opinion, led to the expulsion of the Princes as a measure of national safety, while all the time the true danger of the Republic was its own infatuation for a military adventurer who was only too ready to lead it to ruin. At the end of 1886 Boulanger had a majority of the Chamber on his side, and signs were not wanting that France was prepared to welcome him as a dictator.

Bismarck watched the events in France with apprehension, yet the Diet refused to share his anxiety. Internal dissensions handicapped him at a time when national security required that parties should present a united front. He had now surrendered to the Papacy on most points, yet the Centre party, which held the balance of power, remained as implacable as before; the Socialists were exasperated by the repressive measures from which they were suffering; and the Liberal parties had been strengthened both in numbers and resolve by the policy of Protection which had been forced upon the country against its will. Bismarck asked support for his Army Bill on the ground of imperious necessity, but it was evident from the beginning that its fate would be decided by other considerations than the needs of national defence. Replying to the suggestion that if the Government were placed beyond Parliamentary control in military matters for seven years it would raise taxes wherewith to go to war at its convenience, so repeating the illegality of 1864, he said: " We have no needs that must be satisfied by war. Germany belongs to the ' saturated States ' of which Prince Metternich spoke. Under no circumstances shall we attack France. The stronger we are, the more improbable will be war. But if France has any reason to believe that she is more powerful than we, war is assured." This one-sided argument did not convince the majority of the Diet. In speech after speech he appealed, warned, and admonished by turn, but in vain.

Moltke likewise stepped into the breach, but again his weighty words lost their spell. " I believe," said the old soldier, " that no Sovereign will willingly take upon himself the responsibility of throwing a torch into the combustible material which is more or less accumulated in all countries. Strong Governments are a pledge of peace. But popular passions, the ambitions of party leaders, a public opinion misguided by word and writing — all these are elements which may prove stronger than the will of the Governments. Such a position might occur if this bill, whose purpose is the maintenance of peace, were rejected. Then I believe that we should certainly have war." Even this pointed reference to Boulanger and the danger of a military dictatorship in France failed to convince. The Conservatives and National Liberals were

heartily for the bill, but the Clericals, Radicals, and Social
Democrats were working in co-operation, and they held a majority. No sooner had the Opposition negatived the first
clause of the bill, increasing the peace strength, than without
waiting for further rebuffs the Chancellor produced from his
pocket an imperial message dissolving the Diet.

In the hope of dividing his opponents Bismarck had approached the Pope with a request that he would instruct his
advocates in the Diet to support the Government. There were
conditions to be complied with before this could be done —
more capitulations on the ecclesiastical question — but these
having been satisfied, Cardinal Antonelli, the Secretary of
State, in January, 1887, wrote to the papal nuncio in Munich
a letter notifying him that inasmuch as the Prussian Government had given "formal assurances" that the exceptional
laws against the clergy were about to be revised the Pope
wished the Centre party to support the bill. For once the
leaders of the party were wanting in respect for the Holy
See. This letter was communicated to Baron von Franckenstein, Dr. Windthorst, and several other deputies in the inner
councils of the party, but it went no farther. Only after the
Centre had voted in a body against the bill were the rank and
file informed of what had taken place.

Now began a bad time for Germany — one of those periodical panics into which nations which lack the steadying influence of a sound and well-informed public opinion are ever prone
to fall. The nation's infinite capacity for taking alarm was
illustrated as seldom before, and the Government spared no
effort to turn to advantage the scare which it had created.
Thanks to much stampeding of volatile emotions, more creditable to the heart than the head, a large section of the nation
seriously believed that the fatherland was really in danger,
and the belief called forth a wave of patriotic enthusiasm which
swept the opponents of the Septennate into discredit and
oblivion. Leaving nothing to chance, however, Bismarck induced the Pope to repeat with emphasis his disregarded wish
that the Centre party should support the Government. This
time the papal admonition was published independently of the
leaders of the party, making suppression impossible.

The elections took place towards the end of February.
Bismarck had relied on, and had skilfully schemed, a combination or Cartel consisting of the two Conservative groups and

the National Liberals, and the result exceeded his expectations, for the allied parties gained seventy seats, giving them a majority of twenty. On the other hand, the Radicals and Socialists were reduced by more than one-half, the People's Party disappeared, and even the Centre lost ground. The defeated parties were not slow to take their lesson to heart. When the Diet met in March the Army Bill was reproduced and passed in two days almost without alteration. In its favour there voted 223 deputies and against it only 23; the Clericals for the most part abstained. It was during the parliamentary debates on this bill that Bismarck informed France that if she made an unprovoked attack upon Germany she would be " bled to death."

Three years before this (1882) Bismarck had been successful in concluding the Triple Alliance of Germany, Austria-Hungary, and Italy.[1] He had now the satisfaction of seeing its renewal for five years, though this satisfaction was dulled by the knowledge that feelers were being put forward in various directions testing the possibility of a closer approach between Russia and France. An endeavour made to draw Spain into the alliance, though forwarded by the Government then in power, failed, but only narrowly.

For France the enthusiastic response of Germany to the call of her Chancellor was at once sobering. Even the hot spirits who had been clamouring for revenge were persuaded by this clear warning that the " watch upon the Rhine " was no mere poetic fiction, and that another war, if it came, would, in Bismarck's phrase, be " mere child's play " as compared with the last. M. Grévy pronounced a blessing upon peace and all peace-makers, and strove to win the Republic back to quiet ways. Yet still the pixies of mischief continued to make trouble. An untoward frontier incident occurred in April in Alsace, where a French police commissary, by name Schnaebele, wanted by the German authorities, was first enticed upon hostile soil and then arrested. The Paris Press protested vigorously, but the prompt release of the prisoner, by Bismarck's orders, baulked betimes what threatened to become a critical *affaire*. Prompt amends were similarly made later in the year, when a German soldier shot a French workman who had crossed the frontier, in the belief that he was a poacher. Before the French Government had had time to demand recom-

[1] See Chapter XVI., pp. 142–47.

pense Bismarck sent an offer of £2,500, the acceptance of which satisfactorily closed the incident.

In May Boulanger fell with the Goblet Cabinet, never to rise more, and in December of the same year the weak President Grévy resigned in consequence of a relative's misdemeanour, in which he was wholly unconcerned. For nearly three years Boulanger continued to be a disturbing element in French and European politics. Over Paris he had thrown an unaccountable spell. There he received the homages which are usually reserved for Kings; even the Socialists, who refused to pay tribute to worth, bowed down to this pinchbeck hero, and in January, 1889, returned him to the Chamber by a triumphant majority, willing to accept him either as comrade or dictator. Three months later Boulanger fled the country rather than face a trial on a charge of treason to its laws, and France knew him no more, for he died abroad. Acclaimed and idolized for a time as few of the new men of modern France had been, he proved, after all, to be a creature of very common clay, and his bubble reputation shared the fate of all phantoms of the air, and sooner than most. He came into prominence for the first time in 1885, and in 1889 he was forgotten. Yet for France and Germany equally the years during which he seemed to have his country's fate altogether in his hands were a time of intense suspense and anxiety. The private letters written during 1887–1888 by Moltke, who was not unduly nervous where war was concerned, show that he was all that time *en vedette*, ready for any sudden summons to produce his battle plans.

CHAPTER XVI

(1875–1885)

FOREIGN RELATIONS —(ii) THE EASTERN QUESTION

THE year 1875, which saw the shadow of war fall again upon Europe, brought into new prominence the perennial problem of Ottoman rule. Lord Aberdeen had predicted that the Crimean War might for twenty-five years protect the peace of Europe from disturbance through the Eastern question. He was too hopeful; before that time had passed Russia was again at war with her old enemy. Turkish misgovernment had become worse instead of better, and the Christian populations upon whom its harshest rigours fell still cried in vain for relief. Roumania had been formed in 1861 out of the Danubian provinces of Moldavia and Wallachia, and with the choice, five years later, of Prince Charles of Hohenzollern as ruler had entered upon a career of peace and prosperity. The spirit of independence had become stronger in the other Balkan territories, and particularly in Bulgaria and Serbia, yet there had been no corresponding weakening of the Porte's effective sovereignty. The government of its subject races was now, as before, that of a despotism varied on the one side by massacre, on the other by revolt. At intervals the Powers conferred and made proposals of reform, but without any serious intention of reopening a question which was complicated by many and perilous difficulties.

Bismarck had said in 1867: "The Orient lies so far away that I do not even read the reports of our ambassador in Constantinople." That attitude of comfortable detachment could not last indefinitely. Since then the Orient had been brought appreciably nearer to the consciences of the Powers by the hopeless, unchanging monotony of Ottoman misrule. Bismarck tried as long as possible to prevent the question from becoming so acute as to compel diplomatic measures, but the more the Turk paraded his incapacity or unwillingness to reform himself, the more urgent became the need for external pressure.

The Eastern question meant more, however, than Turkish misrule; behind it were the old British jealousy of Muscovite aggression, the problem of the Slavic races in the Balkans, and above all the rival ambitions in that corner of Europe of Russia and Austria. It was one of the settled purposes of Bismarck's foreign policy to prevent the entrance into the line of political vision of any question that might lead to difficulty between these two Powers, with both of which it was of vital importance that Germany should work harmoniously. Not without reason, therefore, was he conscious of the need for walking warily upon a path so thorny and treacherous.

No sooner was the Franco-German War at an end than an ominous stirring occurred at the opposite end of the Continent. Early in 1871 Serbia asked if it would be untimely to suggest the cession to her of Bosnia and Herzegovina, still under direct Turkish government. Russia and Austria both opposed the idea, and it was not pressed. It was publicly said at that time that Bismarck supported the Serbian claim, but the *Official Gazette* contradicted the suggestion; neither by word, sign, nor inference, it said, had he favoured an act so unfriendly to Austria. To Russia the disclaimer seemed unnecessarily emphatic, for it suggested that if the time ever came for Bismarck to take sides on the Oriental question it would be in support of Austrian rather than Russian interests. All the more necessary, therefore, did it appear to Russia that she should make clear her claim to be regarded as the protector of Serbs, as of the other Slavic races under Turkish rule. When in the following autumn, after the cordial meetings of the German and Austrian Emperors at Salzburg and Gastein, the Czar received Prince Milan of Serbia at Livadia, it was with the flattering greeting, "I receive your Highness as my own child."

Thus the *entente* of the three Emperors had scarcely been completed before Bismarck had begun to experience the disappointment of the man who tries to be on friendly terms with two rivals whose interests seem fated to go apart. In his difficult position he resolved to observe still more scrupulously a strict attitude of impartiality. In July, 1872, just before the imperial meeting in Berlin, he had declared: "I am not carrying on a Russian and still less a West European or an Austrian policy. Diplomacy must accustom itself to my German way of looking at things." At that time the "German way of

looking at things " was to turn a blind eye to all inconvenient
problems of Eastern politics, and so long as he was able it
was upon this principle that Bismarck continued to act. It
was the spectre of the Eastern question, growing ever larger
and clearer, which drew from him the remark, when he received
the freedom of the city of Berlin on September 10th of the
same year, that he would not object if after the great events
of 1870 and 1871 world-history would for a time, like Joshua's
sun, stand still. When, two years later, he sent Prince Hohenlohe to Paris in the place of the rejected Arnim, he still
harped on the necessity of letting the sleeping dogs of the
East lie. " As to the Eastern question," Hohenlohe records,
" I must always bear in mind that we have no direct interest
in it. We could only look on sympathetically, and see that
Russia and Austria maintain good relations, and support their
mutual interests." An easy saying, for if Governments and
nations pursued only mutual interests most of the tasks and
anxieties of statecraft in foreign affairs would disappear.

No sooner had the war scare of April, 1875, been dissipated
than the Eastern question came to the front in a form that
could not be ignored. Spurred into desperation, the hard-
living people of mountainous Herzegovina rose in revolt in
the early summer, and Bosnia soon joined them in sympathy.
It was in vain that Bismarck spoke in impatient tones of
" petty Herzegovina," and declared that the peace of Europe
should not be endangered on its account; in vain also that he
warned Gortchakoff of the rashness of reopening a Pandora's
casket whose contents it were so much better not to know. If
Germany had not been willing to move, Russia would have done
so on her own account. Now, however, an event occurred
which forced Bismarck's hand against his will. This was the
brutal murder by fanatical Mohammedans of the German consul at Salonica, together with his French colleague. The an-
ger which had caused him to call vengeance upon the Carlists
for a similar crime only the year before again flared up in him.
The German ambassador at the Porte was instructed to demand ample reparation, including the condign punishment of
the murderers and of the local officials who could not keep their
criminals in check, and a squadron was despatched to Turkish
waters in order to insist upon prompt compliance. The Sultan was easily persuaded to put the ringleaders in the Salonica
riots to death; less readily he punished and cashiered the lax

authorities of the port; but only on direct threat of punitive measures did he agree to pay a suitable money compensation to the relatives of the murdered officials.

Meanwhile, as the revolt threatened to spread until it involved the whole of the Balkan provinces, the Chancellors of the three Empires agreed to address to the Powers which were parties to the last general settlement of Turkish affairs, the Treaty of Paris of 1856, a Note, drawn up by Count Andrassy and dated December 30, 1875, calling on them to join in requiring the Sultan to fulfil his disregarded pledges of better government. The French and Italian Governments at once accepted the proposal. Great Britain stood out for a time, but eventually came in likewise. Lord Derby, the Foreign Secretary, admitted that interference implied some restriction of the Sultan's independence, but " a Sovereign who can neither keep the peace at home nor pay his debts must expect to submit to some disagreeable consequences." The Sultan excelled himself in masterly inactivity; while readily promising to do everything that was asked of him, in the event he did nothing.

In 1876 the flames of revolt burst out more fiercely, and now Bosnia, Herzegovina, Serbia, Montenegro, and Bulgaria all united in a desperate effort to throw off the oppressor's yoke. Once again misrule triumphed; the insurrection was suppressed with a rigorous hand, in Bulgaria in circumstances of special ferocity. It was the atrocities committed by Turkey at this time that drew from Mr. Gladstone some of the most vehement yet warmly human of his political speeches and writings, with the reiteration of an earlier British statesman's wish to see Turkish rule ejected from Europe " bag and baggage." [1]

On the occasion of a visit of passage made by the Czar to Berlin in May the three Chancellors again conferred, and this time adopted a series of proposals known as the Berlin Memorandum. Bismarck was still opposed to armed intervention, and when urged to part Turkey and her rebellious tributaries he declared: " Before they have hacked each other interference will be useless; when one has lost a leg and the other an eye the

---

[1] Sir Stratford Canning wrote to Mr. Canning on September 29, 1821: " As a matter of humanity I wish with all my soul that the Greeks were put in possession of their whole patrimony, and that the Sultan were driven, bag and baggage, into the heart of Asia, or, as a provisional measure, that the divided empire which existed four centuries ago could be restored " (*Life of Stratford Canning, Viscount Stratford de Redcliffe*, by Stanley Lane Poole, vol. i., p. 307).

task will be easier." Constrained at last to assent to active measures, he agreed to endorse any arrangement, not affecting Germany's interests, which might be acceptable to the other Empires, on the clear understanding that if hostilities followed Germany should be allowed to remain passive. The proposals agreed upon were that there should be an armistice for two months, and that meanwhile negotiations should be opened with a view to a settled peace and the introduction in the disturbed territories of serious reforms, to be carried out under the supervision of all the Powers. This time Turkey was not merely to be bidden to reform herself; the work was to be done for her, and if necessary against her will. Submitted to the Western Powers, France and Italy agreed to the Memorandum, but the British Government refused assent.

The second Disraeli administration (February, 1874) had entered its third year, and Disraeli was nearing the summit of his political fame. Under his masterful leadership England was, for good or ill, reviving in foreign affairs the vigorous traditions of Palmerston and Russell. Born in comparative obscurity, he had compelled the recognition of his talents and genius by hard work and a dominating will which offered defiance to all obstacles, until he saw himself acclaimed as leader by the very political party which at that time represented most rigidly the spirit of caste and social exclusiveness.

A Jew of undiluted blood, this remarkable man typified at once the qualities and the defects of his race. Pre-eminent amongst his characteristics were an outward brilliancy unbalanced by inner depth or by any trace of reverence, a singular agility and subtlety of intellect which made easy sophistry and equivocation, a boundless ambition uncorrected by that instinct of conduct which so strikingly marked his great rival Gladstone, a passion for power unaccompanied by any deep sense of responsibility, a high opinion of success combined with a low opinion of men in general, and an altogether inadequate appreciation of moral values.

An Oriental in every fibre of his being, Disraeli sought to orientalize English political thought. He introduced into controversy a violence and also a flippancy of language which jarred on the feelings of the older generation, accustomed to severer standards of taste; brought a too fertile imagination to the treatment of questions calling for exactitude of statement and calmness of judgment; and exhibited in matters of public principle novel elasticities which shocked old-fashioned politicians, trained in the healthy belief that the rules which govern private should apply also to public dealings, and that any tampering with an ethical code which had given to England her high place amongst the nations was not likely to be an improvement.

Still more this master of political wizardry was bent upon orientalizing British foreign policy, and here his success was greater. A man whose geographical knowledge of the world was, by all accounts, singularly meagre, he yet conceived of a British sway vaster than Cæsar ever knew. It was here that his orientalism was most conspicuously displayed, for the British empire of his ambition was an empire over eastern peoples. Long before this he had spoken (1866) of England as an Asiatic rather than a European Power. For the colonies and colonial politics at that time he cared little.[1]

The British Empire has been ruled by greater statesmen, but no modern Minister succeeded as he did in kindling the imperialistic idea and in bringing the Empire home to the imagination of Englishmen, though less perhaps — for the time at least — as an object of affection and sober pride than as one of ambition and boastfulness. He had delighted the nation whose love of the bold throw he knew so well, and was only too ready to humour, when in November, 1875, following the prompting of the Foreign Secretary, Lord Derby, he bought the shares of the Khedive of Egypt in the Suez Canal for four million pounds, a transaction which made England almost half-owner of the waterway along which lay the nearest and quickest approach to her Indian Empire.[2] Early in 1876

[1] In 1852 Disraeli wrote to Lord Malmesbury that "these wretched colonies will all be independent in a few years," and that they were "a millstone round our necks," while fourteen years later he wrote to Lord Derby (September 30, 1866): "It can never be our pretence or our policy to defend the Canadian frontier against the United States. . . . Power and influence we should exercise in Asia; consequently in Eastern Europe, consequently also in Western Europe; but what is the use of these colonial deadweights which we do not govern? Leave the Canadians to defend themselves; recall the African squadron; give up the settlement on the West Coast of Africa; and we shall make a saving which will, at the same time, enable us to build ships and have a good Budget" (*Life of Benjamin Disraeli, Earl of Beaconsfield,* by G. E. Buckle, vol. iv., p. 476).

[2] Disraeli had stated in the House of Commons seventeen years before (1858) that "his own opinion was that the project of executing a canal across the isthmus of Suez was a most futile idea, totally impossible to be carried out. It would be attended with a lavish expenditure of money, for which there would be no return; even if successfully carried out in the first

he startled the country again by making Queen Victoria Empress of India, though to a considerable section of public opinion, even on his own side, the surprise was this time greater than the pleasure.

Most of all Disraeli appealed to British sentiment and prejudice as the interpreter of the traditional suspicion of Russia which the tragic fiasco of the Crimean War had failed to exorcize. After that war, Gortchakoff had said of his country: "La Russie ne boude pas, elle se recueille." A nation which defies the strokes of adversity, and in the time of defeat refuses to paralyse its will by dreams of revenge or to blur its sight by futile passion, but quietly resumes the broken course, is sure to arrive safely at its journey's end sooner or later, by fair ways or other. Russia had been arriving in the East ever since, by slow and unostentatious movements, always consciously directed, always concentrated upon the one unchanging goal.

The certificate which Gortchakoff, in a message to Lord Derby, gave to his own candour, " Je suis comme Adam — tout nu ; je ne cache rien," may not always have applied, but it is impossible to doubt his sincerity of purpose in 1876. " Fiat lux!" was his ready rejoinder to Loftus when the ambassador sought his sanction to the publication of a certain despatch in a forthcoming British Blue Book. The Russian Chancellor and still more the Czar honestly wished to see the Sultan coerced in the interest of the Christian populations, and in their concern that the six Great Powers should act together, from a belief that such concerted pressure, and it alone, would achieve that end. Disraeli refused to be convinced, however, to the disappointment of the other Powers. For forty years, and more than ever since the Crimean War, Great Britain had constituted herself the Sultan's special patron, France not unwilling to concede to her the honour and the onus, and her influence had been pledged to the maintenance of Turkish sovereignty against menace from any side. The cause which now enlisted Russia's sympathies aroused the suspicions of the British Government and its supporters, and it was left to the Opposition and to private citizens to respond to the calls from the East for help in the name of humanity and a common religion.

instance, the operation of nature would in a short time defeat the ingenuity of man."

Disraeli's attitude has been variously judged, often harshly, seldom indulgently. Mr. Gladstone, in a fit of righteous indignation, roundly accused his Jewish rival of sheer indifference to the sufferings of Christian populations: more than ever convinced that Disraeli's " crypto-Judaism has had to do with his (Turkish) policy," he wrote: " What he hates is Christian liberty and reconstruction." However that may be, it is certain that Disraeli honestly objected to the partition of the Ottoman Empire, and with it the weakening of what to him was a bulwark against Russian aggression, for it was suspected that by the arrangement proposed in Berlin Bulgaria would come under the direct influence of Russia and Bosnia under that of Austria. He even declared that those who were agitating against the Turk and for his victims were as flagitious as the perpetrators of the Bulgarian atrocities themselves. The weakness of his position — and for it the Foreign Secretary was equally responsible — was that it represented a policy of negation and inaction; for once in her history England left to other countries the championship of the oppressed.

The effect of her refusal to co-operate with the Powers was that the Berlin Memorandum was still-born, and that rebellion and the enormities wreaked upon the insurgent peoples in the name of law and order continued throughout the Balkan territories as before. Poetic justice was satisfied by the fact that the revolutionary fires were kindled in Constantinople itself, and that within several months two Sultans, Abdul Aziz and Abdul Murad V, were dethroned. Under their successor, Abdul Hamid II, the insurrection in Bulgaria was suppressed with a ferocity the like of which had hitherto been unparalleled in modern European annals, and quiet was at last restored — the " quiet of the graveyard."

Almost at any moment during the autumn of 1876 war between England and Russia might have seemed probable. In her attitude England had little sympathy and no support in Europe. Thiers in France feared lest Disraeli's stubbornness and provocation should " trop tracasser la Russie," and in Germany a temperate statesman like Hohenlohe warned Sir Robert Morier, for the benefit of his Government, of the danger of England using her favourable position inconsiderately, with the object of humiliating her rival.

The reports of the barbarities committed upon the Bulgarians, which Disraeli first scoffed at as " coffee-house babble," sent a wave of indignation throughout Europe, and the struggles of the oppressed nationalities now excited enthusiasm where such endeavours had usually been regarded with apathy and impatience. England alone held back, for to Disraeli and his followers the abominations of Turkish rule were a lesser evil than Russian aggression. Disraeli knew, as no other man, the weak points in the national character, as Palmerston in his time knew the strong ones. Both men appealed, with equal conviction and equal success, to the empire instincts of the race, but while in addition Palmerston was not above exploiting its magnanimity and humanitarianism in the interest of a foreign policy which was not always virtuous and often was rash and dangerous, Disraeli enlisted in the same service the less noble characteristics of prejudice, suspicion, and credulity. Hence it was that the political catch-cry of the day, " British interests in danger! " rallied to his side all the nervous and inflammable elements in the population. " Now what are those British interests which are so suddenly springing up and producing this alarm? " Gortchakoff later demanded of Lord Augustus Loftus, the British ambassador in St. Petersburg. " Name them to us, and we shall then know what is their nature, their value, and how they can best be safeguarded." Loftus answered evasively that " Every country must be the judge of its own interests, and must claim to protect them itself," an answer which, if diplomatic, was not brilliantly so, for it threw no light upon the question at issue.

It was in vain that the Czar had assured the British Government (November 2nd) that he had no idea of acquiring Constantinople, and that all he asked was that it should not fall into the hands of any other Power; that he purposed no encroachment in India; that the famous " Will of Peter the Great," which was believed to impose upon succeeding Czars boundless schemes of conquest, did not exist; and that even if, in his resolve to protect the Christians, he entered Turkish territory, he would withdraw as soon as his humane object had been attained. A large part of the nation — and it was not confined to one party — had allowed itself to be convinced, by the constant iteration of sounding phrases, that Russia was England's irreconcilable enemy, and it honestly believed that her concern for the oppressed Christians was only a pretext for a well-devised policy of aggression by which she was to plant herself on the Bosphorus, destroy the Ottoman Empire, and so menace and ultimately subvert British influence and prestige in the Near East as a preparation for a larger scheme of conquest in Far Asia.

Germany was now wholly on Russia's side. Only a year before Queen Victoria and her Government had arraigned the Chancellor on suspicion of a desire for war with France. Referring to that episode, Lord Odo Russell wrote at the time that, though professing good-will to England, and satisfaction that that country's relationships with Russia were friendly, " behind our backs Bismarck raves like a maniac, and swears he will take his revenge." Now he was able to turn the tables neatly. Not only did the Empress write to the Queen of England, urging her to put restraint upon her bellicose Ministers, but the German ambassador in London, Count Münster, was bidden to use a pacifying influence in the same quarter. Bismarck, owing to ill-health, was living in retirement at the time, and Count Münster received his instructions on the subject direct from the Emperor. With a malicious satisfaction the Minister added the injunction (July 6th) that in offering pacific counsels " you could keep closely to the text of the English circular to us in the spring of 1875." Bismarck was, indeed, bent on two objects — to make Russia's path smooth in the East and to keep her on good terms with Austria. As a realist politician he saw that it was to Germany's interest that Russia should be encouraged to extend her eastern sphere of influence as far as possible, so as to hold England fully occupied in India, for pressure there would always mean relief in Europe.

A threat to Russia, which was not even veiled, was conveyed by Disraeli (now Lord Beaconsfield) at the Lord Mayor's banquet in November. " If," he said, " England were to go to war in a righteous cause, her resources would prove inexhaustible. She is not a country that, when she enters into a campaign, has to ask herself whether she can support a second or a third campaign. If she enters a campaign she will not terminate it until right is done." On the day following this challenge (though not in reply to it, since it had not yet come to his knowledge) the Czar declared that unless Turkey would cease warring against her subjects and reform herself at the command of the Powers he would compel her on his own account. In the meantime the Russian and Austrian Emperors had met at Reichstadt (July, 1876), and there had come to the agreement that the two Empires should for the present refrain from interference, but that in the event of intervention becoming necessary all the Powers should be invited to act together with a view to restricting the area of disturbance. A formal convention followed early in 1877, securing the neutrality of Austria in the event of war between Russia and Turkey, and preparing the way for the reacquisition by Russia of Bessarabia and for the extension of Austrian influence in Bosnia and Herzegovina.

Feeling at last that Russia was being pressed unduly by England, Bismarck came forward with an emphatic declaration that Germany would stand by her. Addressing himself to the leaders of the Opposition in the Imperial Diet, who had criticized his attitude as being too subservient to Russia and too little sympathetic to the oppressed Christians, he said (December 5th): "As long as I stand upon this floor they shall not succeed in breaking up our good, intimate, and healthy relations with Russia." Then followed the memorable words, often to be recalled in later years: "I shall not advise Germany's active participation in any way so long as there is involved no German interest which would be worth the bones of a single Pomeranian grenadier."

A conference of the ambassadors of the Powers, called at Constantinople on the proposal of the Czar, sat from the end of December until the end of January, and drew up, for presentation to the Porte, a manifesto containing eleven proposals in the nature of recommendations, but all in vain. All the Powers were now agreed as to what Turkey should do, but they could not induce her to do it. As Lord Salisbury said, the Porte would give promises but no guarantees.[1] So events dragged on, the Powers pressing, the Porte prevaricating, until on April 24, 1877, Russia brought matters to an issue by

[1] That Lord Salisbury ever shared to the full Disraeli's anti-Russian and pro-Turkish bias may fairly be doubted. As early as 1878 he had protested against the idea that his country should be expected to buttress Turkish rule at all costs. "The great blunder of the Sultan and of his sympathizers and subjects," he said, "was that they put too high a price upon themselves. They considered that Turkey was so important that England would do and bear everything rather than let her existence be endangered" (*Rambling Recollections*, by Sir H. D. Wolff, vol. ii., p. 233).

a formal declaration of war. To the last Gortchakoff had
tried to keep the Powers together, and so successfully that
their last concerted act was the acceptance of a Russian protocol urging on Turkey, in substance, the demands of the ambassadors' conference, though with less appearance of pressure. This invitation to listen to reason had been refused like
its predecessors.

It was June before the campaign began in earnest, and for a
time it seemed to go in Turkey's favour. Larger numbers and
improved generalship told on Russia's side in the end, however, and in spite of several brilliant stands Turkey was beaten
after five months of hard fighting. By January, 1878, the
Russian army had occupied Adrianople. There was a fear in
England that the advance would be pushed as far as Constantinople, and when protests seemed to be ignored Lord Beaconsfield sent a fleet to the Dardanelles and called a large draft
of Indian troops to Malta. It was not the fault of the Czar
that Constantinople was not occupied, for he had taken the
bit into his mouth and against the advice of Gortchakoff had
given orders to that effect to the Commander-in-Chief of his
forces, the Grand Duke Nicholas, at the very time that a British squadron entered the Dardanelles. Happily for the peace
of Europe the orders were not obeyed, the Grand Duke pleading that they arrived too late.[1] A veritable war fever took
possession of the anti-Russian part of the British nation, and
it was probably the larger part. Seldom had public opinion
in England been so hopelessly confused and divided as at that
time: on the one hand, there was a widespread abhorrence of
Turkish misrule; on the other, an ineradicable suspicion that
Russia's aims in championing the oppressed nationalities were
only a cloak for a scheme of spoliation. So disunited was
even the Liberal party on the subject that when the Prime
Minister was on the point of plunging the country into war in
the winter of 1877-8 Lord Hartington was prepared to resign
the leadership of the parliamentary party rather than oppose
him. Nevertheless, Beaconsfield had now no longer a united
Cabinet behind him; the Colonial Secretary (Lord Carnarvon)
had resigned in January and the Foreign Secretary (Lord

[1] *Memoirs* (unpublished) *of M. Sabouroff* (*Nineteenth Century* for January, 1918).

Derby) in February, both in protest against his warlike policy.

In the meantime Russia had in March concluded with the beaten foe the Treaty of San Stefano, stipulating the conditions of peace and defining the future relations between Turkey and her subject peoples. Submitted to the Powers, England promptly refused assent, and demanded that an agreement which superseded the settlements embodied in the Treaty of Paris of 1856 must be deliberately ratified by all the States which were parties to that treaty, meeting in formal congress. The demand was reasonable, and Gortchakoff did not seriously seek to evade it. The only question now was, How could it be met in a manner at once satisfying to Great Britain yet sufficiently regardful of Russia's *amour-propre?* Would some benevolent Power suggest an acceptable formula? All through the months of April and May the peace-bringing formula was anxiously sought. Bismarck all the time acted as intermediary between the Governments of St. Petersburg and London, honestly endeavouring to facilitate an understanding, and early in June he was able to issue invitations to the Powers for a congress to be held in Berlin. Nevertheless, for some time longer there seemed a possibility that England would enter the war on Turkey's side, and the gravity of the outlook was now brought home to the public mind by persistent rumours of more Cabinet dissensions.

Then occurred one of those surprises that occasionally remind the parliamentary politician, quite as much as the " man-in-the-street," how small is his actual share in the government of his country and how little he knows about the questions which he discusses most freely. Suddenly tragedy turned to farce with the disclosure that all the time that the British nation, incited by the Prime Minister, was clamouring for war the hostile Governments, represented by Lord Salisbury and Count Schouvaloff, had been quietly negotiating a secret treaty for the disposal of part of the " Sick Man's " heritage. The motive for the agreement, which was signed on May 30th, was simple enough and not necessarily discreditable. Before Bismarck promised to act on Russia's suggestion and call the Powers together he had wisely insisted upon some general guarantee that such a meeting would achieve a serious purpose. This would only be possible if Russia were prepared to agree in advance upon a *modus vivendi* with England, her principal opponent.   Failing that, he saw that a Congress of the Powers would be little more than a bear-garden, and would probably do more harm than good.

The result of this stipulation of caution was the secret compact which gave rise to so much controversy in England at the time, and which was criticized in unreasonable terms as something intrinsically immoral; whereas its only objectionable feature was the fact that the terms of the treaty were entirely inconsistent with the demand made by Lord Derby, as a condition of British acceptance of a congress, that the negotiations thereat should be subject to no sort of restrictions, and that no arrangement which might have been already agreed upon should prejudice the full and free discussion of every question involved.   By this agreement the two Powers which just before had seemed at daggers drawn agreed upon the main provisions of the Treaty of San Stefano and upon the general attitude which they were to take in the coming congress; the objects of the congress, in fact, were virtually decided before it came together.

European opinion was more justifiably confused by Lord Beaconsfield's denial of the existence of the treaty when as a fact it had been signed, and by the later announcement that Great Britain had also concluded a secret treaty with Turkey (June 4th) under which she undertook to defend the Ottoman Empire in Asia against attack, while the Porte in return agreed to cede to England the island of Cyprus.[1]

The Congress of Berlin met from June 13 to July 12, 1878. Each of the Powers invited, except Turkey, was represented by three plenipotentiaries; the best known of these were Bismarck and Prince Hohenlohe, representing Germany; Lord Beaconsfield, Lord Salisbury, and Lord Odo Russell, representing Great Britain; Prince Gortchakoff and Count Schouvaloff, representing Russia; Counts Andrassy and Karolyi and Baron Haymerlé, who succeeded Andrassy in the following October, representing Austria; M. Waddington, representing France; the Counts Corti and de Launay, representing Italy,

[1] Disraeli makes one of the characters in his novel *Tancred* say: " The English want Cyprus, and they will take it as compensation. . . . The English will not do the business of the Turks again for nothing." In the same novel the creation of an Empress of India in the person of Queen Victoria is adumbrated.

and Sadoullah Bey, representing Turkey. Bismarck presided over the Congress, and his personality more than any other dominated it; he might defer now to Russia, now to England, but in the end it was he who struck the balance whenever conflicting claims had to be weighed and decided. Before the Congress met he had stated that it was his intention to act the part of the " honest broker " who had no interests of his own to serve, and he faithfully kept his word.

The resolutions of the Congress were embodied in the Treaty of Berlin of July 13th. Their effect was to introduce a large measure of autonomy in the Balkan territories. Roumania, Serbia, and Montenegro were made independent of Turkey, Montenegro being also given access to the sea; Northern Bulgaria was made an independent principality, and Southern Bulgaria, with the name Eastern Roumania, was given autonomy under a Christian governor; but Macedonia, like Armenia, remained under direct Turkish rule. Greece was promised a rectification of frontier. As to Bulgaria in particular, it was stipulated that while it was still to be a tributary State, it was, like Roumania and Serbia, to have its own prince, who was to be chosen by the people with the approval of the Powers, but was not to be a member of any of the greater reigning houses of Europe. Altogether, by the operation of the treaty, eleven millions of Christians obtained political liberation.

Few of the Powers which went to Berlin returned empty-handed. Russia had to forgo some of the spoil upon which she had counted, but she retained the essential gains of her victory. Practically the effect of the treaty was to undo the humiliation inflicted upon her by the Treaty of Paris after the Crimean War. The portion of Bessarabia then taken from her was regained from Roumania, which received part of the Dobrudja in exchange. The Black Sea had already been freed to her ships of war; now she obtained there the port of Batoum, which was to be a free port, and Kars and Ardahan, also in Asia Minor, fell to her. On the other hand, Austria received the right to occupy and administer Bosnia and Herzegovina, but not to annex them outright, though there were plenipotentiaries who believed at the time that this would be the effect. After the meeting of the Congress at which this momentous decision was taken, Count Corti addressed Count

Andrassy with, " But, my dear Count, your occupation of
Bosnia and Herzegovina is nothing but annexation badly disguised," upon which Andrassy replied: " Very badly disguised." Yet the disguise was not quite thrown off until thirty
years later. Austria was also given the right to administer
the Sanjak of Novi-Bazar, the neck of land lying between Serbia and Montenegro, and in September of the following year
she claimed jurisdiction in this territory, thus obtaining, as
Andrassy said, " a broad road into the Balkans."

Judged in the light of later events, the refusal of the Congress to countenance the nascent aspirations of the Slavic
peoples in the Balkans after unity seems incomprehensible. It
was the absence of any enthusiasm for these aspirations that
Mr. Gladstone made a principal reproach against the Government which spoke for Great Britain at the Congress, and
led him to say in the House of Commons soon afterwards
(July 30th): " I do not mean that the British Government
ought to have gone to the Congress determined to insist upon
the unqualified prevalence of what I may call British ideas.
They were bound to act in consonance with the general ideas
of Europe. But within the limits of fair differences of opinion, which will always be found to exist on such occasions, I do
affirm that it was their part to take the side of liberty, and I do
also affirm that as a matter of fact they took the side of servitude." Jealousy for the integrity of Turkish rule was still,
however, the corner-stone of British policy in the East. " A
chain of Slavic States stretching across the peninsula of the
Balkans," Lord Salisbury said, " would without doubt be more
dangerous to the independence of the Porte than any other
combination." Hence it was that Lord Beaconsfield did his
utmost to strengthen Austria's position in the Balkans. It
was his wish to see her become a sort of warden of the Orient,
so imposing an insuperable obstacle against Russian designs
upon Constantinople.

For the rest, England's direct gain in the territorial adjustments made at that time was confined to the formal confirmation of her occupation of Cyprus. Italy might probably have
had Albania if she had pressed for and been satisfied with it.
The year before the Congress, meeting for the first time Signor
Crispi, who was already angling for an alliance with Germany,

Bismarck had urged him to make sure of that little territory, whereupon Crispi had replied that Italy "would not know what to do with a province on the other side of the Adriatic." Asking now for compensation from Austria, in the form of the Trentino and Istria, she met with a refusal, and in the end received nothing at all. There was no part of the "Sick Man's" European heritage of special interest to France, but from Bismarck and Lord Salisbury she received a hint that Tunis was an eligible prize, and that if she cared to look that way Germany and England would not object. Germany neither obtained nor sought territorial advantage; the "honest broker" was content to take his commission in the form of the moral reward of a good conscience. Not often in his career did Bismarck play a large part so virtuously and so magnanimously as that which he voluntarily assumed at the Berlin Congress.

In diplomatic negotiations wise men, while striving for the best, are usually satisfied with something far short of it, and a bargain must be very bad indeed if it is so admitted. It was a tribute to the general spirit of accommodation which prevailed at Berlin, and above all to the ability and resource of Bismarck, the organizer and manager of the Congress, that if of the Powers represented none went away with full hands so few were sent empty away. Everything that was ceded was at Turkey's expense, of course, yet even Turkey, assisted by England's influence, fared better than she had hoped. As for the two principal rivals, Alexander II declared in a public manifesto that the treaty had given Russia "all that she wished to attain by force of arms," while Lord Beaconsfield took back to London "peace with honour." [1] On the other hand, Gortchakoff carried away with him from Berlin the feeling that Bismarck had overtrumped him in his own game of diplomacy. Sensitive to a degree where his vanity was concerned, he henceforth harboured a grievance which was personal as well as national. Neither in Russia nor in England was national opinion altogether satisfied with the settlement; while in the former

---

[1] Sir Henry Layard, the British ambassador at Constantinople, who had negotiated the Anglo-Turkish agreement of June 4th, predicted darkly of the Treaty of Berlin at the time: "I see in it the elements of future wars and disorders without number, and an upsetting of all the principles of justice and right which have hitherto governed the relations of and intercourse of States." Wars and disorders and further violations of Turkey's rights did, indeed, follow, though not because of the treaty.

country Germany and Bismarck were accused of proving false friends, in the latter the pro-Turkish enthusiasm had now exhausted itself, and in the succeeding general election Lord Beaconsfield's Eastern policy was strongly repudiated by the nation.

From Germany's standpoint the Treaty of Berlin was undoubtedly a mistake, since it led to that clearer definition of aims and attitudes which had hitherto been avoided by the *entente* of the three Emperors, and had made their co-operation possible. Russia and Austria entered the Congress as indifferent friends, but they left it as certain rivals for influence in the East, and Germany's task as mediator between them became one of increasing difficulty.[1]

In later years Bismarck gave two versions of the part which he tried to play in that fight of the diplomatic giants at Berlin. We have seen that before the Congress opened he had declared that it was his desire to act the part of the " honest broker," who is concerned to negotiate business on straightforward principles, in such a way that his clients will be satisfied and come to him again. When the Congress was over he protested that he had done his best to hold the balance fairly between the chief contestants — England, as representing Turkey, and Russia, as representing the Balkan territories and herself. Speaking in the Imperial Diet ten years later (February 6, 1888), and in altered circumstances, he changed his ground, and pretended that he had all through acted as Russia's advocate. " During the Congress," he said, " I can candidly say that so far as was possible without prejudice to our own interests or those of our friends (Austria only could have been meant here) I regarded my part as that of a fourth Russian plenipotentiary. Throughout the entire proceedings of the Congress not a single Russian proposal came to my knowledge which I could not have supported, ay, and carried through." [2]

Bismarck's first judgment upon his efforts was truer and

[1] In a letter of November 4, 1880, to Sir H. Drummond Wolff, Lord Beaconsfield said: " Next to making a tolerable settlement for the Porte, our great object was to break up and permanently prevent the alliance of the three Empires, and I maintain there never was a great diplomatic result more completely effected " (*Random Recollections*, vol. ii., p. 265).

[2] Compare also his remarks in his *Reminiscences and Reflections,* vol. ii., p. 117.

fairer to himself than his second.   For he did honestly strive for an equitable settlement.   If it proved comparatively easy to make peace between the disputants and to allow Russia to go away convinced that she had gained all that was worth fighting for, the reason was that the issue of the Congress was for practical purposes decided before the delegates met.[1]   It is certain also that during the Congress negotiations he formed the opinion that in Beaconsfield he had found his equal, and with the magnanimity of a great man he drew satisfaction from the discovery.   It may almost be said that at that time Prince Bismarck and Lord Beaconsfield divided the attention of the Continent.   Gortchakoff, long ageing, was overlooked, greatly to his chagrin.

The Turkish Empire had once more been consolidated by a process of excision.   Seventy years before (1809) Stratford Canning wrote of Turkey: " Destruction will not come upon this empire either from the North or from the South; it is rotten at the heart; the seat of corruption is in the Government itself."   Yet still Ottoman sovereignty and Ottoman misrule continued.   Perhaps no patient at any time defied nature, time, and his doctors as bravely as the Sick Man of Europe,

[1] Here the " honest broker " might have been left to history, in the full enjoyment of the fruits of virtuous self-abnegation, had he not at a later date revealed yet another aspect of his mind.   After the outbreak of hostilities between Russia and Japan in 1904, Dr. Chrysander, Bismarck's last private secretary, recalling his recollections of Friedrichsruh, told in the *Bergedorfer Zeitung* (February 11, 1904) how the ex-Chancellor said to him on one occasion: " The greatest folly of my political life was the Berlin Congress.   I should have let Russia and England fight and gnaw each other, like the two lions in the forest, of which only the tails were left. Then we should to-day have had greater influence, quiet, and less danger. But I then carried on politics like a town councillor."   Dr. Chrysander quoted these words as an illustration of Bismarck's rough humour, but Prince Herbert, as the guardian of his father's reputation, thought it necessary to write to the Press to remove the unfavourable effect of an indiscreet disclosure.

Nevertheless, in this revised judgment upon his attitude at the Congress, Bismarck was confirmed by the famous chief of the Political Department of the Foreign Office, Herr von Holstein, who once confided to Hohenlohe the opinion that Bismarck's endeavour at the Congress to conciliate Russia and Great Britain must be counted as one of the blunders of his political life.   Perhaps a greater influence upon German foreign policy than is justifiable has been attributed to this notable political wire-puller, yet it cannot be doubted that from Bismarck's retirement until his own Herr von Holstein was a great power behind the scenes.   Without being a Minister, he had more than a Minister's power.   As is the fate of such men, while every one in political life courted him, no one entirely trusted him.

who never seemed better and surer of life than after a surgical operation. Nevertheless, the relief from the pressure and worry of the Eastern question which Conservative statesmen in England ardently hoped for was denied them. Baulked for the present in the south-east of Europe, Russia turned her attention with increased eagerness to Far Asia, and there the rivals who had parted sullen and defiant at the gates of Constantinople were destined soon to meet again, still unconciliated. Before that time, however, a new administration had come into power, with the result that Mr. Gladstone, who had so resolutely opposed Lord Beaconsfield's policy, had his turn at the Eastern problem. His Cabinet came in, with Lord Granville at the Foreign Office, in April, 1880, just in time, as Lord Dufferin said, to prevent England from coming into conflict with all the world. The dethroned dictator of the Tory party died in tragic loneliness in April of the following year, never having truly understood England, which he nevertheless served devotedly according to his lights, and regarded to the last by most Englishmen as a baffling enigma, a man of wonder and mystery, brilliant but impenetrable, and alien to them in thought, feeling, and character — like an orchid amongst the roses of their gardens, a gorgeous exotic. With his death the party of militant imperialism suffered a temporary eclipse.[1]

An agreement over Turkey having been arrived at, Bismarck was determined that, as far as his influence went, it should be final. All his efforts, therefore, were directed towards securing compliance with the treaty of 1878, and preventing any reopening of the Eastern question. He said at that time (December 5, 1879) that he was not prepared to sacrifice " the sound bones of a single Pomeranian grenadier " for the sake of the Balkan wranglings. Soon he had an opportunity for the exercise both of pressure and restraint. In constituting Montenegro an independent principality the treaty gave to it new and enlarged frontiers. Further, by its 13th protocol the Congress also " invited " Turkey — whose plenipotentiaries as-

[1] Sir H. Drummond Wolff relates that to a follower who thought to console him for his fall with the remark, " It will turn out all right some day," Beaconsfield replied, " It is all very well for you to consider this quite lightly, but with me it is the end of my career " (Random Recollections, vol. ii., p. 248).

sented — to rectify the frontiers of Thessaly and Epirus in favour of Greece, and article 24 of the treaty provided that in the event of the Porte and Greece failing to come to an understanding on the subject the Powers should offer their mediation. In neither case did the Porte show any disposition to respect its obligations, the one legal and the other moral, and after waiting for nearly two years the States whose expectations were thus thwarted decided to take the matter into their own hands and seek to obtain by force the rights which were not to be gained by peaceable means.

With a view to the adjustment of Montenegro's claims England proposed a conference, to be held in Berlin, and the other Powers agreeing, it was duly called from London and met in June, 1880. The arrangement proposed was the cession to Montenegro of the port of Dulcigno and part of the adjacent coast. To this Turkey objected, and it was only after a demonstration before Dulcigno made by a united fleet, to which all the signatory Powers contributed, and further protracted parleying, that she yielded. In this naval demonstration Germany joined unwillingly, and only on the understanding that no shot should be fired and no troops be landed from the German vessels. Germany was also the first Power to call off her ships and order them to leave Turkish waters. The claims of Greece were settled in the following year, after renewed threats of hostilities and a further conference, this time held in Constantinople, in which Bismarck successfully played the part of conciliator, and thereby won Turkey's lasting gratitude.[1]

Hitherto the interest of Germany in the Eastern question and in the controversies over this question which divided the other Powers had been indirect and derivative, but the Berlin Congress incidentally marked the opening of a new era in the relationships of that country with the Turkish Empire. There her attitude as the passive onlooker changed to that of

[1] Mr. (later Lord) Goschen, who, as the British special envoy at Constantinople, took an important part in these negotiations, tells how in February, 1881, he proposed to the Cabinet at home the retrocession to Turkey of Cyprus, annexed to the British Crown only three years before, by way of appeasing Turkey. In reply, Lord Granville wrote that he " did not think it amiss," but that on referring the proposal to " certain of the cooler heads of the Cabinet " it had been rejected (*Life of Lord Goschen*, vol. i., pp. 221-2).

the sympathetic adviser, and gradually Berlin began to cultivate ties of close friendship with the ostracized Government of
the Porte.   Russia wanted territory, England influence, but
Germany was satisfied to begin that policy of peaceful penetration which served her so well in later years both there and
in more distant parts of the world.   At the Sultan's request
a German military mission was sent to Turkey in 1882, and
her army was reorganized on German principles by General
von der Goltz and Rustow Pasha, while many Turkish officers
entered the German army.   German officials were also lent to
Turkey for the reform of her administration and finance.
Where the diplomat, the soldier, and the bureaucrat went, the
trader was not slow to follow.   Manufacturers, bankers, engineers, and merchants invaded the hitherto neglected country
and its Asiatic possessions — wherever, in fact, there seemed
promise of reward to energy and enterprise — and the foundations were thus laid of the later economic conquest of Turkey which proved so sore a grievance to the displanted nations.

Although Bismarck could fairly claim that he had rendered
to Russia reasonable service at the Berlin Congress, the Czar's
professed satisfaction was not of long duration.   Signs of irritation were shown when in 1879 Bismarck was slow to give to
Russia the support she expected in connection with the measures necessary to the execution of the decisions of the Powers.
Speaking later of the friction thus caused, Bismarck said that
the opinion seemed to prevail in St. Petersburg that in all
these measures it was Germany's duty to fall in with the
Russian demands without counting the cost to her other
friendships.   Such a one-sided arrangement was totally opposed to his principle of *Do ut des*, and this he told Gortchakoff and, through him, the Czar.   This hesitation to do Russia's bidding brought the Emperor William a pointed letter
from the Czar in which occurred the words, " Your Majesty's
Chancellor has forgotten the promises of 1870 " — a reference to the effusive greeting sent to St. Petersburg from Versailles on the conclusion of the Preliminaries of Peace with
France.   Bismarck even spoke of the " written threats "
which were received in Berlin from the same quarter at this
time.   Coolness was only prevented from developing into misunderstanding when the Emperor paid a visit of conciliation
— a sort of Canossa pilgrimage — to his imperial nephew at

Alexandrovno on September 3rd. The visit was made on the advice of Field-Marshal Manteuffel and against that of the Chancellor, who was of opinion that the debt to Russia had been liquidated.

Later, Bismarck spoke of these incidents as affording a " lightning-like illumination of a situation which in recent years I had often been compelled to anticipate." The reminder of how unsubstantial were the foundations upon which the friendship with Russia rested was one of the bitterest disappointments of his official life. He had honestly done his best to strengthen the fabric of amity, as he believed with success. On Gortchakoff's good-will he had long ago ceased to count, and foreseeing the old Chancellor's early retirement, he had cultivated confidences with other Russian statesmen. One of his new friends was Count Schouvaloff, Gortchakoff's colleague at the Berlin Congress, who had returned his advances with the enthusiasm of a novice in great affairs. How heavily the thought of a possible rupture of cordial ties weighed upon him appears from a letter which he wrote to Count Schouvaloff on February 15, 1877. In this he spoke of the Russo-German friendship as " a work that will perhaps be easier to destroy than it was to create, especially if it happens that my successors do not show the same patience as I in cultivating traditions the experience of which they lack. . . . It will perhaps be easier to lead astray the Chancellors who will come after me by giving them a glimpse of the facility with which on your part a coalition could be built upon a basis of revenge. The calmness with which I regard this eventuality I shall not be able to bequeath to my successors."

During the Congress the correspondents had repeatedly discussed the relations between the two countries. To Count Schouvaloff's remark, " Vous avez le cauchemar des coalitions," Bismarck had assented, whereupon the younger man asked why Germany and Russia should not conclude a defensive and offensive alliance, so providing against any possible combination dangerous to either of them. Bismarck's chief objection was that while on the German side such an alliance would carry the entire sympathy and support of the reigning house and Government, it would rest in Russia solely on the good-will of the Czar personally, and that, his good-will withdrawn, no guarantee of its security would remain. From the standpoint of material force he even yet held an alliance with Russia to be preferable to one with Austria — and no third Power came into consideration — provided only that it offered equal promise of permanence.

It is probable that Bismarck's mind had dwelt on the idea of a more intimate advance to Austria ever since Gortchakoff had submitted him to humiliation in 1875. Disappointment at seeing his efforts at the Berlin Congress so ill requited by the Czar whom he had done his best to serve gave the final turn to his decision. One of the most momentous resolutions of his life was taken when he decided that the time had come to make the great choice, so long deferred, between Germany's Southern and Eastern neighbours. It was the choice between a complete alliance and an equivocal relationship which checked cordial advances on all sides, yet in now declaring for Austria wholly and solely he was fully conscious of the great risks involved. Nor did he forget that he was reversing Prussia's traditional policy as established by Frederick the Great, who in his " *Exposé du gouvernement Prussien* " laid down the maxim, " One of the first political principles is to endeavour to become an ally of the one neighbour who may become most dangerous to the State. For that reason we have an alliance with Russia, and thus we have our back free as long as it lasts."

That Austria was ready for a closer relationship had been shown in the year of the Congress by her willing acceptance of a treaty, concluded on October 11th and published the following February, by which article 5 of the Treaty of Prague was revoked without conditions. This article stipulated that the population of the northern districts of Schleswig should revert to Denmark if by free vote it expressed a wish to that effect. Bismarck had taken no steps to give effect to this provision, and may never have intended to do so. Now Austria agreed to its repeal as an act of friendship and a token of a " desire to draw closer the friendly tie between the two Powers." The treaty chiefly interested Denmark and the Danes who were no longer to have the hope of reunion with the mother country, but to Russia it was an unwelcome indication that the temperature of the Austro-German *entente* was rising.

Just before the Emperor William met the Czar at Alexandrovno Bismarck had met Count Andrassy at Gastein (August

27th and 28th) and discussed with him the conclusion of an Austro-German defensive alliance.   Prince Hohenlohe had also been summoned there for a conference on " grave matters," and he relates that when Andrassy heard of the project he " jumped right up to the ceiling with joy."   Hohenlohe at first disapproved, not entirely trusting Austria, nor convinced that Russia was seriously hostile, and apprehensive that an alliance with Austria would result in one between Russia and France, which was, in fact, the sequel.   Bismarck argued that Austria could not remain isolated in face of " the menace of Russia." She would sooner or later look about for an ally, and if that ally were Russia or France, Germany would be exposed to the danger of isolation.   He knew that if Russia and Austria ever came to blows Germany would be unable to remain neutral, since interest would require her to take the Austrian side. Were Austria vanquished, or even weakened, Russia would become a deadly menace to Germany; on the other hand, with Austria protected and preserved, Russia could be held in check. Moreover, the Czar's unexpected outburst had convinced him that Germany was depending upon a support which might fail her in any critical moment, and hence that it would be folly to neglect precautions.   " If one," he said to Hohenlohe, " had to go through a wood with a dear friend who had suddenly exhibited signs of madness, it would be well to put a revolver in one's pocket, but one might be very friendly all the same." Hohenlohe needed no more convincing, and the conferences left the treaty-makers of one mind.

Up to this point Bismarck had not breathed a word to the Emperor about the intended and virtually concluded alliance. He knew that the proposal would mean a severe struggle in that quarter, and with that prospect in view he fortified himself by taking into his confidence the King of Bavaria.   In a long letter written from Gastein he pictured to that monarch the political situation which Germany had now to face, and developed the argument for the proposed compact, receiving in reply a gratifying assurance of complete sympathy and approval.

The task of persuading the Emperor, now at Baden-Baden, proved even more difficult than had been expected.   Fresh from a friendly meeting with his nephew and M. Giers, the proposal to desert Russia suggested to his straightforward mind duplicity and deceit, and at first he refused point-blank to discuss it. Bombarded by letter after letter, he still remained unconvinced; all his Chancellor's appeals on the ground of political necessity were unavailing against the call of personal loyalty. To Andrassy, Bismarck wrote from Gastein on September 3rd that, although he had supported his proposal by an explanatory memorandum of sixty folio pages, " in spite of all my care I have not succeeded in completely obviating the misunderstanding that there must be some idea of an aggressive tendency behind our peaceful plan. This idea is, of course, very uncongenial to an old man of over eighty-two years, but I hope to be able to remove it completely, even if it should cost me a fairly long postscript to the said sixty pages."

From Gastein Bismarck had gone to Vienna, greeted everywhere on the way by popular ovations, which in the capital reached a torrid heat. There he had the satisfaction of receiving the assurance of Francis Joseph that the alliance was altogether welcome to him. Thus encouraged, he now resorted to a device too hazardous to be employed save on the most critical occasions. First winning over his colleagues in the Government, he made the question one of confidence, and presented to the Emperor an ultimatum in the words — acquiescence or resignations all round. Already he had told Hohenlohe that for himself it would be the treaty or retirement into private life. Then the Emperor surrendered, though even now, as Bismarck records, only because he was averse to Ministerial changes and not because he had been convinced by arguments of policy. Hohenlohe relates that the Emperor at the time confessed to him his suspicions that Bismarck was endeavouring to unite Germany, Austria, France, and Great Britain in a coalition against Russia.

Drawn up in Vienna in September, the German-Austrian treaty of alliance was formally concluded on October 7th, though its terms were only made known to the world in February, 1888. The preamble declared that " cordial co-operation between Germany and Austria-Hungary can menace no one, but is calculated to strengthen the European peace created by the Treaty of Berlin," and affirmed the promise of the two Sovereigns " never to give to their purely defensive agreement an aggressive tendency in any direction." The allies undertook to support each other with their entire military resources in the event of attack on either by Russia, and only to conclude peace jointly and in agreement, and in the event of either of them being attacked by another Power (France being here meant) the other promised to preserve an attitude of benevolent neutrality towards its ally. Should such second Power, however, be supported by Russia, the allies would make common cause as in the first case. It was characteristic of the mentality of the two men that while the Emperor insisted that the Czar should be informed confidentially that an attack made by him upon either Germany or Austria would be repelled by both, Bismarck deemed such frankness unnecessary.

German opinion was on the whole cordially favourable to the new alliance, the Conservatives because of their traditional leanings to Austria, though they more than any other party regretted that a choice had been necessary; the Ultramontanes from natural sympathy with a Power predominantly Roman Catholic and now the mainstay of the Papacy; the Liberal groups because, though political conditions were as backward in Austria as in Germany herself, they were still more backward in Russia. In England the alliance was equally well received, though there interested motives came into play. Lord Salisbury, regarding a strong and secure Austria as the best guarantee of " the peace of Europe and the independence of nations," welcomed the first news of the conclusion of the treaty as " good tidings of great joy."

Bismarck had lamented, " If only Russia would not compel us to choose between her and Austria!" If a choice was necessary at all, it cannot be doubted that, from Germany's standpoint at that time it was wisely made, and, indeed, that the alternative was impossible. An alliance with Russia would have been, alike as to the risks to be covered and the responsibilities to be incurred by the two Powers, an alliance on unequal terms. If far stronger than Austria as an ally, Russia would have been immeasurably less safe and reliable, and every advantage to be gained from union with her would have been neutralized by equal or greater disadvantages. Worst of all, such an alliance would have left Russia free to extend her policy of aggression from the Near to the Far East, and so to involve Germany, indirectly and perhaps in the end di-

rectly, in complications in which she had no conceivable interest.

The effect of the Vienna treaty was that henceforth Germany gave to Russia a finger only, but to Austria her whole
hand; yet though there could no longer be the old intimate
cordiality, there was no suggestion of a breach between Berlin and St. Petersburg. Nothing was further from Bismarck's mind than the idea of " cutting the wire to St. Petersburg." The Emperor William had also come to attach an almost superstitious importance to the triple *entente* as the only
reliable safeguard against the democratic movements which
were making headway in Western Europe. His idea was that
the three Empires should form a new Holy Alliance against
democracy, for with increasing years his deeply-rooted prejudices against Liberalism in any form and his reluctance to
make any concession to popular ideas, an attitude assiduously
fostered by his Chancellor, had been strengthened to the point
of obstinacy. He admitted to Hohenlohe his genuine fear that
the franchise legislation proposed in England a little later
might be the signal for a general wave of republicanism.

It would have been unlike Bismarck had he failed to use a
change in the international outlook for political purposes. In
February, 1880, there appeared in the *North German Gazette*
an article representing the attitude of Russia and France as
aggressive and menacing, and German public opinion — the
most nervous and highly-strung in Europe — was thrown into
panic. Hohenlohe relates how on the 22nd he looked in at the
Diet and was impressed by the alarm of the politicians there.
" Afterwards," he adds, " I learned at the Chancellor's that
he had only written the article to produce an effect on the
deputies, so that they might vote for the Army Bill. He
laughed when I told him of the result."

Three years after the conclusion of the Treaty of Vienna,
Italy joined hands with the two Empires, and the Triple Alliance was formed which was to last for over thirty years. In
thus extending the basis of Germany's security Bismarck
showed again, as in 1872, a preference for that system of " *accord à trois* " which he regarded as the only safe form of insurance in Continental dealings.[1] The *entente* of the three

[1] M. Sabouroff, the Russian diplomat, has recorded that Bismarck said

Emperors which Italy joined in 1874 was at most a diplomatic arrangement intended to ensure unity of action between the associated Powers in matters of common interest.   Bismarck drew closer the ties between the Courts of Berlin and Rome when in October of the following year he induced William I to visit Victor Emmanuel in Milan (following a visit by the Austrian Emperor to Venice in the preceding April), where he was rewarded by a reception impressive in its cordiality. " Our meeting," the Emperor telegraphed to the King from Bozen on regaining German soil, " was an event of historical importance, for we have both been called by Providence to the heads of nations which have won their unity after long struggle."   The friendship thus strengthened, though recorded in no written agreement, continued unimpaired until Victor Emmanuel's death (January 9, 1878).

Italy's decision to join the alliance was at last precipitated by the French appropriation (May, 1881) of Tunis, a territory which she had regarded as historically coming within her special sphere of influence.   Little did the Italian Government divine that just before Bismarck had told General Pittié, chief of the French President's Military Cabinet, that " the French were to go ahead in Tunis and not to trouble about the Italians."   The decisive step was taken by the Ministry of Signor Depretis in May, 1882, though it was only announced in the following year.   Signor Crispi, then a private deputy, assailed Depretis at the time with the reproach, " You have made yourself Germany's *gendarme!* "   Several years later he became a Minister, and after he had met Bismarck at Friedrichsruh (September, 1887) there was no more ardent adherent of the Triple Alliance than he.   Italy became a member of the Alliance in virtue of a treaty containing stipulations which bound her and Austria to maintain the *status quo* in the East of Europe and in no case to propose any change there without previous agreement.   The treaty was concluded for a first term of five years.   A year later Austria concluded with

to him in 1880: " You too often lose sight of the importance of being *trois* on the European chessboard.   This is the invariable objective of all the Cabinets, and of mine above all; nobody wishes to be in a minority.   All politics reduces itself to this formula: try to be *à trois* as long as the world is governed by the unstable equilibrium of five Great Powers " (quoted by Professor J. Y. Simpson from *The* (unpublished) *Sabouroff Memoirs, Nineteenth Century,* December, 1917).

Roumania, a kingdom since 1881, a treaty of alliance providing for reciprocal help in the event of unprovoked attack. Later both Germany and Italy accepted this treaty, which for Austria was in effect one of reinsurance against Russia.

Bismarck's cup of elation was filling, but not full. He had made Moab his washpot, and over Edom he had cast out his shoe; it remained to be seen whether his diplomacy would prove equal to the task of still holding Russian Philistia by chains of interest, if not of affection. For though Germany's relations with Russia continued to be cordial, he saw clearly the danger of a breach with her, and it became now his foremost object to prevent such a disaster, or at least to postpone it as long as possible. Germany henceforth lived, as it were, beneath an avalanche, which might be held back for five years or fifty, but was one day sure to fall. Diplomatic safeguards were therefore supplemented by measures of military and naval defence. Extensive works were undertaken for the protection of the Baltic coast and the eastern frontier districts; seaports were fortified and strategical railways built; larger garrisons were set up on the eastern marshes, and the navy was strengthened, not as yet against England.

For a time the tendency to alienation had been checked by a change in the Russian Chancellorship. Gortchakoff was over eighty years old, and his capacity for good work, though not his confidence in himself, had long been exhausted. Towards the end he had held the name of office without its full responsibilities. In 1876, on the occasion of the meeting of the Czar and the Austrian Emperor at Reichstadt, he had anticipated his retirement, and with characteristic vanity had declared that his reputation required that he should disappear with grace and dignity: " je ne veux pas m'éteindre comme une lampe qui file," he said, " je veux me coucher comme un astre." The formal close of his Ministerial career was to come only with his death, but upon the stage which had witnessed so many of his diplomatic successes during the larger part of a quarter-century an understudy had already appeared in the person of M. de Giers, and under the Czar it was he rather than Gortchakoff who now determined Russia's attitude to the neighbouring empire. An exchange of letters between the two Sovereigns when in February, 1880, the Czar celebrated the twenty-fifth anniversary of his reign, and again on the German Emperor's eighty-third birthday in the following month, seemed to recall the ardours of 1870.

A year later (March 13, 1881) Alexander II fell to the blow of the assassins who had shadowed him for years, and had already made five organized attempts upon his life. Gortchakoff also died in the same month, full of years and honour. In a letter addressed to the Russian diplomatic representatives abroad, notifying the new reign, M. de Giers gave the quieting assurance, " Russia has attained her full development. Feelings of envy and discontent are far removed from her. All she desires is to assure her position, to protect herself abroad, and to develop her powers, wealth, and welfare. The foreign policy of the Emperor will be altogether pacific. Russia will remain true to her friends, she will maintain unchanged her traditional sympathies, yet at the same time reciprocate the friendly attitude of all States." The German Crown Prince attended the funeral of the murdered Czar, and in the following September the Emperor, accompanied by the Crown Prince and Bismarck, journeyed to Danzig to meet Alexander III, with whom were his brothers, the Grand Dukes Vladimir and Alexei, and M. de Giers. All these exchanges of courtesies, conferences, and ratifications of friendship were reported to be as successful as the proverbial surgeons' operations; but they did not answer the question, What would happen when the reaction came?

When the reciprocal felicitations of the Emperors were over, their Chancellors took up the tale. At the end of 1883 Giers visited Bismarck at Varzin, and a year later he was at Friedrichsruh. It seemed as though Gortchakoff's influence had been altogether repudiated, and the two Governments were about to revive the cordiality of long-past days. There was one portent which boded no good, however, and it was the fact that the feeling of the Russian people in general continued distinctly hostile to Germany. At the very time that the Sovereigns and their chief Ministers seemed in full accord the Pan-Slavist leaders and Press in St. Petersburg were carrying on a bitter agitation against the neighbouring empires and nations. In January, 1882, General Skobeleff, who had proved himself a brilliant general in the war with Turkey, made a vehement attack first upon Austria and then upon Germany, for whose scientifically trained army, he said, that of Russia would at any

time prove a match. The irate soldier was given a period of
enforced leisure as a punishment for his indiscretion, whereupon he went to Paris and there repeated his offence in an
acuter form. Depreciation and defiance of Germany was as
music in French ears, and coming from Russia it was doubly
welcome.

At this time there were signs of an unmistakable advance
in the relations between Russia and France. The action taken
by the Czar and his Chancellor at the time of the war scare
of 1875 showed that Russia's political engagements towards
the neighbouring empires had not weakened her sympathy for
France, to whose culture she owed so much. In France, too,
there were many statesmen, like Thiers, who held that French
interests pointed to the wisdom of an alliance with the Eastern
empire which had lately served her so well, and who believed
that Germany's ascendant position in Europe would sooner or
later lead to a new grouping of the Powers.

Before the Triple Alliance was two years old Bismarck's fear
of Germany's isolation had given place to a worse fear of what
would happen if Russia were left in the same undesirable position. It was his brooding over the possibilities of his own diplomacy which led him in September, 1884, to conclude a supplementary treaty with Russia behind the back of Germany's
allies. In that month, at William I's suggestion, all the three
Emperors met at Skiernievice, Bismarck, Giers, and Kalnoky
being present, to confer upon what to him appeared an alarming spread of democratic ideas in Western Europe. Early in
the year Bismarck had drawn up a memorandum on the subject
for the Emperor's consideration, and it was not difficult to
convince him that the true way of safety lay in the cordial co-
operation of the Empires as representing the monarchical principle in its least attenuated form. The result of the meeting
was an agreement by which the Emperors entered into a sort
of Holy Alliance which was to do for monarchy what its pro-
totype of 1815 was intended to do for religion and the peace
of Europe.

A second and far more important secret agreement, however,
resulted from the Skiernievice meeting. It was a defensive
treaty between Germany and Russia, on the lines of the Austro-
German treaty of 1879, by which each Power undertook to pre-

serve an attitude of " benevolent neutrality " in the event of
the other being attacked. If not notified to the Austrian and
Italian Governments, the treaty soon came to their knowledge,
though the world at large remained in the dark until Bismarck
himself made it public in 1896. This reinsurance policy, which
seemed to ensure for Germany, in so far as treaty engagements
could do it, a favourable position in any contingency humanly
conceivable, was concluded first for six years. In his eagerness
to retain the friendship of Russia, Bismarck was willing at that
time to strain Germany's liabilities towards Austria to the utmost, not always to the satisfaction of that Power. " A war
with Russia in which we had to side with Austria," he said to
Hohenlohe, " would be a misfortune for us, for we could gain
nothing — not even our expenses." The full significance of
the treaty was to come to light only a few years later. The
alliance with Austria was barely five years old, yet its
author already seemed doubtful both of its wisdom and its permanence.

It cannot be doubted that Russia interpreted the secret
treaty of 1884 as giving her a free hand, so far as German
influence went, not only in the Near but the Far East, and that
Bismarck, at least for a time, tolerated, even if he did not encourage, that view. Long before this he had ceased to be disturbed by the prospect of Russia established on the Bosphorus.
To the Russian diplomatist M. Sabouroff he boasted that he
was the first of European statesmen " to break with the old
tradition, with which the Westerners inoculated all the Cabinets, that Constantinople in the hands of Russia would be a
danger to Europe. I consider that idea false, and I do not see
why an English interest ought to become a European interest."
When in September, 1886, the Crown Prince ventured to suggest to him that the Balkan States should combine against
Russia, he disagreed and said that he would prefer to see Russia take Constantinople, and the Balkan peninsula as well, " for
then she would be weakened."

There was a special reason for Bismarck's indisposition to
ease Great Britain's relations with Russia at that time, for in
the colonial enterprises upon which he had just entered he was
finding his progress obstructed at every turn by British claims
and objections. Hence when the rival Asiatic Powers again

came into collision he was content for some time to let matters take their course. Persistent Russian aggression had brought the dominions of the Czar and the Empress-Queen into perilous neighbourhood: for only Afghanistan now divided them, and even this neutral territory was a source of contention. Lord Granville had declared long before that while he could conceive of the Russians " pining for Constantinople," he could not understand " why they should push on to the extreme East." During his tenure of the Foreign Office he had shown every desire to be friendly and accommodating to Russia — some critics even said that he went too far in that direction — yet he had failed to check her forward march towards a goal which had never been satisfactorily defined, and which, for that reason, was assumed to be India. Early in 1884 Russian troops occupied Merv, though only two years before the St. Petersburg Government had disclaimed the bare idea of approaching it. Would Herat be the next objective, first to be disclaimed and then appropriated?

For England it had now become a question of " Thus far and no farther." [1] As early as 1867 Lord Clarendon had suggested to Gortchakoff that the two countries should agree to observe a neutral zone in the Far East — the original of the " buffer State "— and Russia appeared to favour the idea. Assuring Clarendon that the Czar regarded Afghanistan as " completely outside the sphere within which Russia may be called upon to exercise her influence," the Russian Chancellor a little later proposed that that State should so serve, subject to England acting as pledge for the Ameer's friendly attitude. Upon this condition the proposal was at the time wrecked. Now it was renewed with greater seriousness. But first it was necessary to fix upon the " scientific frontier " of which Disraeli (as Lord Beaconsfield) had preached the need after 1878, and over this question much valuable time was lost at a juncture when delay was fraught with danger to peace.

A frontier commission had been agreed upon, but for months

[1] Lord Clarendon wrote to Sir Andrew Buchanan on March 27, 1869, that in his view it was certain that Russia would be driven to acts of aggression, just as India had been. " There was always some frontier to be improved, some broken engagement to be repaired, some faithless ally to be punished, and plausible reasons were seldom wanting for the acquisition of territory. . . . Such in the main had caused the extension of our Indian Empire, and there was reason to apprehend that such was the course into which Russia, however unwillingly, was about to be drawn."

the British members waited in vain for their Russian colleagues, and there seemed ground for the suspicion that there was a desire in that quarter to obstruct this sensible settlement. In any negotiations capable of taking a serious turn Russia was at an advantage at the time, and she knew it. " If the Russians mean to advance on the Afghan frontier," wrote Lord Derby to Lord Granville on January 5, 1885, " now is their time, while we have Egypt on our hands and an army locked up in Africa." For a time forces of Russians and Afghans confronted each other in defiant restraint, as though ready to fly at each other's throats, and waiting only for the signal. On March 29th there was a slight collision, which happily led to no worse mischief, yet the war clouds still hung over the East, and a month later Mr. Gladstone asked the House of Commons for an emergency credit for eleven million pounds, and promptly received it, while a British fleet occupied Port Hamilton, off the Korea. Then peaceful counsels had their way, and the danger passed over. The frontier commissioners got to work, and the boundaries were fixed, Russia being awarded Pendjeh and Afghanistan the Zulfikar Pass. With the ratification of the agreement the relations between Russia and England passed into a new and more hopeful phase. Bismarck received the credit — and probably deserved it — of having encouraged Russia to resistance until war was probable, and only then of having used his influence in favour of conciliation. The secret treaty of the previous year was sufficient to explain his concern that the dispute should not end in hostilities. Now, as always, he was concerned to prevent the Oriental pot from boiling over.

His determination that questions in which Russia was concerned should not prove a source of friction nearer home was shown by his refusal to be involved in the affairs of Bulgaria during the first years of her troubles as an infant principality. Bulgaria had played an important part in the deliberations of the Congress of Berlin, and the first twenty-two articles of the Treaty of Berlin dealt exclusively with her future organization and government. One of these articles expressly placed the new principality under a Russian commissioner, supported by a Russian army of occupation, until its permanent government should have been organized. Prince Alexander of Battenberg was elected Prince of Bulgaria on April 29, 1879, and the election was duly confirmed by the Powers. Established in his little realm, the ruler found himself surrounded by Russian generals, officers, and Ministers, an arrangement which lasted for several years. All this time there was growing in the two halves of the old kingdom an agitation for reunion, and Russia seemed to favour the idea. Then in September, 1883, the Prince suddenly dismissed his foreign Ministers, on the suspicion of plotting to depose him and place the country under a direct Russian protectorate, though the military advisers still remained.

Two years later the Greater Bulgarian movement in Eastern Roumelia culminated in the capture of the Turkish pasha who represented the sovereignty of the Porte and an invitation to Prince Alexander to assume full sovereignty. The Prince accepted the invitation, which appears to have been endorsed both by the Christian and Mohammedan populations. Turkey protested against the act; the Powers also condemned it as an infraction of treaties, and solemnly warned the disturbers of the peace that they would be held responsible for the consequences, but did no more. Germany in particular refused to move in the matter, fearing to bring Russia and Austria into open antagonism. Battenberg, who had proved himself a capable administrator and a man of courage, thereupon entered upon his enlarged sovereignty, and Europe settled down as if nothing had happened.

All might have gone well with Bulgaria under the reunion had the people and their ruler been willing to place themselves under Russian protection more than in the past, but this they were not disposed to do. In September all the Russian officers in the Bulgarian army resigned by order of the Czar, and in November Serbia, incited by Russia, declared war upon the sister principality, only to be signally defeated within a fortnight.[1] Prince Alexander led the Bulgarian army and achieved feats of arms which excited general admiration, and nowhere more heartily than in his native Germany, where a princess of the imperial house was willing to share his throne, and take the risk of its stability. After peace had been concluded in the following February, the Porte formally acknowledged the

[1] King Milan told his Minister, Count Chedomille Mijatovich, in 1886 that his object in beginning the war was "neither the balance of power nor compensation, (but) to provoke war between Russia and Austria" (*Memoirs of a Balkan Diplomatist*, p. 53).

Prince as Governor of Eastern Roumelia. Then were illustrated anew the insecurity and lawlessness which had been en-
gendered in territories long ruled by force and fraud. In
August Prince Alexander was kidnapped in his palace by a
band of rebel officers, compelled, under threat of death, to abdicate, and carried away to Rahowa, on the Danube, and thence
shipped to Keni Russi, in Bessarabia. Set free on Russian soil,
he returned to Germany, whence he telegraphed to the Czar:
" Since Russia gave to me my crown, I am prepared to renounce it into the hands of Russia's ruler." The Czar's answer came promptly, warning the Prince against returning to
Bulgaria on pain of his patron's displeasure. Nevertheless, he
returned to Philippopolis at the beginning of September and
was enthusiastically welcomed by the population. His position at Sofia, however, had been compromised by his recognition of Russia instead of Turkey as the suzerain of the principality, and several days later he formally abdicated and left
the country for the last time.

From first to last Bismarck had refused to allow Germany
to interfere in the Bulgarian embroglio, and his action was
much criticized at home, as lacking the firmness and decision
which had invariably marked his foreign policy. Again, as in
1864, the democratic parties — this time aided by the Clericals
— would have driven him into war against his will had that
been possible. Yet his action, if not heroic, was perfectly consistent. He was still as determined as ever to prevent a breach
between Russia and Austria, and faced by a risk so serious he
declined to move. Addressing the Opposition benches, he
roundly asserted that the real disturbers of the peace of
Europe were the Radical and Clerical newspapers of Berlin,
which were inciting Germany to provocative acts against Russia, regardless of the Treaty of Berlin, and reproaching him
with cowardice and indifference to German prestige simply because he would not go to war for " the *beaux yeux* of Prince
Alexander."

" Are these incitements to war or are they not? " he asked
in the Diet, after reading (January 13, 1887) a choice selec-
tion of newspaper extracts breathing out fire and slaughter.
" Can it be concluded that the ' statesmen ' who are behind
these articles entertained the wish to embroil us in a war with
Russia? " Yet the politicians who were now working such

mischief were the same who had refused the Military Septennate Law just before! " Bulgaria, the little country between
the Danube and Balkan," he said later (February 6th), " is
not an object of such impressive importance that it should be
made the occasion for plunging Europe, from Moscow to the
Pyrenees and from the North Sea to Palermo, into a war the
result of which no one would be able to foresee, and at the end
of which it would be impossible to say why it had been waged
at all." It was solely owing to Bismarck's restraining influence at that time that Austria, loyally accepting, in spirit as
well as in letter, the provisions of the Treaty of Berlin which
gave to Russia a predominant influence in Bulgaria, supported,
or at least did not oppose, the Russian attitude on the Bulgarian question.

After a stormy *interregnum,* during which many rival candidates for the vacant throne were put forward or offered
themselves, the national Sobranje in July, 1887, ignoring Russia's favourite, elected Prince Ferdinand of Coburg, who accepted the invitation against the protests of Turkey and the
Powers. Fortune favoured him, however, and he maintained
his ground; the time came when he even made peace with the
Czar on condition of a revival of Russian influence in the principality.

As time passed it became increasingly obvious that the relations between Germany and Russia could not remain as they
were before 1879, and that the reinsurance treaty of 1884
was, from the standpoint of both countries, an inconclusive
compromise. Germany could not now desert Austria, while
Russia could not indefinitely remain without an ally of her
own. The later formal estrangement, leading to a new and
ominous grouping of the Great Powers, did not come, indeed,
in Bismarck's time, but the conditions which made it inevitable
were already in existence. In 1887 France supplied half a
million rifles to Russia on the condition that they should never
be used against Frenchmen. In the following year the first
Russian loan was placed on the French market.

From Turkey in Europe it is now necessary to turn to the
relations of the European Powers to another part of the Ottoman Empire, the land of the Pharaohs and the fellaheen. In
the developments which the internal affairs of Egypt have undergone Germany has taken little direct, though an important

indirect, part. That is to say, although the Egyptian question has never possessed for Germany the importance, either politically or commercially, which it has had for Great Britain and France, it has constantly proved a convenient occasion for political negotiations and bargaining over other matters in which she was more immediately concerned. In its modern aspects the Egyptian question may for convenience be dated from the *coup d'état* of the Khedive Ismail Pasha in 1879. Embarrassed by debts, due to wasteful public expenditure and personal extravagance, and unable to contract new loans, the spendthrift Ismail in April of that year decided that the only hope of evading his difficulties and beginning again lay in the violent rupture of all financial restraints. Accordingly, he dismissed his European Ministers and the advisers who had been deputed by the Powers to reorganize Egyptian finance, and proposed to liquidate his debts upon a scheme of his own, in which no one save himself had any confidence, and which, if put into execution, would have made the financial position of the country and the prospects of its creditors still more desperate.

Such a course of illegality and anarchy as the Khedive had chosen to adopt could not be passively tolerated by the Powers, and least of all by France and Great Britain, whose interests in Egypt were greater than those of the rest, and whose influence and prestige were specially involved in the maintenance of the financial administration which they had but recently organized. Nevertheless, it was Germany, who had less at stake in Egypt than any of the other Powers, who first protested against Ismail's acts of folly and turpitude. Two years before, when the Khedive was setting at defiance judgments of the law courts obtained by his creditors, the German Government had similarly protested, and had proposed to Lord Derby, Foreign Secretary in Disraeli's Cabinet, that the Powers should jointly bring pressure to bear upon him, " if only to avoid the possibility of separate action on the part of some of them."

The Khedive had notified his repudiation of the existing arrangements in a Decree of April 22nd. Germany waited in vain until May 18th for the other Powers to move, and then through her Consul-General in Cairo served on the Khedive a formal protest, declaring that " the Imperial Government sees in the Decree of April 22nd, by which the regulation of the debt is to be determined by the Egyptian Government alone, and existing recognized rights are to be abolished, an open and direct violation of the international obligations contracted with the judicial reforms; it declares the Decree to be without legally binding effect upon the competency of the Mixed Courts and the rights of subjects of the Empire; and it holds the Viceroy responsible for all the consequences of his illegal proceeding."

With the publication of this declaration European opinion received a mild shock, but all the Powers endorsed Germany's action. The *Journal des Débats* paid Bismarck the compliment of saying that " German diplomacy appears to act in the East, as everywhere else, with a capacity, emphasis, and opportuneness which are often lacking in the diplomacies of other countries." To this the *North German Gazette* replied that " The times are past when Germans abroad could be abandoned defenceless to high-handed treatment." Perhaps it was more to the point that this was an aspect of the Eastern question which concerned Russia only remotely, so that Germany was free to act with impunity. The Powers called for Ismail's abdication, and this promptly took effect; even the Sultan, when appealed to by the discredited Regent, refused to help him, and instead telegraphed his formal deposition (June 26th). His son Mohamed Tewfik was set up in his place, and the old system of Dual Control was re-established, a board of English and French commissioners being appointed to manage national finance, an arrangement which continued until the close of 1882. Germany's part in this arrangement was on the whole passive, for Bismarck was satisfied that intervention in Egypt should be left to the discretion of two Powers, to one of which Germany then stood in a cordial relationship and to the other in a relationship which was at least harmonious. " Germany," he said, " does not want to throw any stones into the Egyptian garden."

Following M. de Freycinet, Gambetta had become the French Premier and Foreign Minister in November, 1881, and from the moment of his entering into office he had endeavoured to obtain for France a predominant voice in Egyptian affairs, yet without hostility to Great Britain. The new British Government which had come into power in April of the preceding year, with Mr. Gladstone at its head, had pledged itself to the maintenance of the *status quo*, had disclaimed any designs upon the independence of Egypt or any sympathy with active interven-

tion, except in the event of anarchy occurring, and had let it
be understood that if such action became necessary it would
favour only the use of Turkish troops. Gambetta, on the
other hand, was eager to find a pretext for direct intervention,
and was determined that if it could be brought about France
and Great Britain should enter Egypt together, and they
alone. With no very clear idea of his own as to how an extreme situation would have to be met, Lord Granville, the
British Foreign Secretary, was induced to adopt a French
Note of January 6, 1882, in which the Khedive was assured
that the two Governments would be behind him in his efforts to
keep at bay the forces of disorder, and was bidden to " draw
confidence and strength " from the fact. Lord Granville did,
indeed, stipulate that his Government reserved decision as to
the form which the support of the Khedive should take in given
circumstances, but the Joint Note was none the less a pledge
which sooner or later was bound to materialize in active intervention. In all the measures hitherto proposed for the settlement of the country Great Britain and France had loyally endeavoured to meet Germany's views, but they were not disappointed that Bismarck, while approving, had declined to join
in enforcing them.

Egypt's troubles thickened when a spirit of revolt appeared
in the army. There had been minor mutinies in 1879 and 1881,
and on each occasion the Government had been compelled to
capitulate. This success had taught the soldiery that in order to gain their way it was only necessary to demonstrate
and threaten. Now the mutineers, chief among whom were
many active officers, not only demanded the removal of grievances, but claimed to dictate to the Khedive and the Executive.
Nor was discontent allayed when, in obedience to their will, the
Khedive dismissed an unpopular War Minister and in February, 1882, put in his place the nominee of the disaffected officers, Ahmed Arabi, a colonel of humble origin. Arabi described himself as " l'étoile qui se lève sur la Mer Rouge."
For Egypt he proved a very unpropitious star indeed. With
his rise to influence the country passed under a military despotism, and for a time the Khedive had to do the bidding of
his masters under threat of deposition and death.

The crisis came in June, when rebellion, accompanied by the
massacre of Europeans, occurred in Alexandria. The despatch of British and French squadrons to the port exasper-

ated rather than restrained the mutinous soldiery, and now Arabi, placing himself at the head of a combined military and nationalist party, proclaimed war against all outside interference in Egyptian affairs.[1] The reign of terror spread to Cairo and elsewhere, and the time for justifiable intervention which had been contemplated by the British Government seven months before seemed to have arrived. Now, however, it was France which held back, for at the end of January Gambetta had been overthrown, Freycinet had again come to power, and he promptly reversed his predecessor's aggressive policy. At the invitation of Great Britain the Powers, in the persons of their ambassadors, met in conference at Constantinople at the end of June, hampered, however, by the refusal of the Porte to send a representative to their meetings. While all the Powers were agreed that order must be restored, and that it could only be done by force, they were far from united upon the methods to be pursued. Germany, supported by Austria-Hungary, urged the formation of a Ministry acceptable to the military party as a whole, and even France wanted an arrangement with Arabi; but Great Britain favoured the unconditional overthrow of the arch-intriguer. On the question of intervention there was greater agreement, for most of the Governments supported the proposal that the Sultan should be invited to despatch troops to the disturbed province. That, however, would have meant indefinite delay, and meanwhile the condition of Egypt was fast passing from disorder into chaos. Great Britain now invited the Powers to join her in bombarding Alexandria, which Arabi was busily fortifying.

Bismarck still had no desire to interfere in any way. " Let the Powers interested settle it as they please," he wrote of the Egyptian embroglio in July, " but do not ask me how, for I neither know nor care." He wanted England and France to undertake the settlement of Egypt alone. France refused to co-operate, however, and Italy did the same, influenced by her treaty relations with Germany. The abstention of France

[1] Of the Arabi revolt one of the most competent of authorities writes: " It was more than a mere military mutiny. It partook in some degree of the nature of a *bona fide* national movement. It was not solely, or indeed mainly, directed against Europeans and European interference in Egyptian affairs, although native European prejudice exercised a considerable influence on the minds of the leaders of the movement. It was in a great degree a movement of the Egyptians against Turkish rule " (the Earl of Cromer, in *Modern Egypt*, vol. i., p. 324).

created surprise, yet there were strong practical reasons for it. The principal one was a fear lest by taking part she might find herself committed to indefinite responsibilities — a fear justified by the event — and to that extent handicapped in Europe, to the satisfaction and advantage of Germany. M. Clemenceau led the opposition to the proposal of joint intervention because he saw in it the hand of Bismarck. On the other hand, many politicians of note who did not share this suspicion of a German ruse were influenced in favour of abstention by the fact that the occupation of Tunis had not proved the easy task which it was expected to be and that France was occupied by enterprises in yet other parts of the world.

All such considerations would not have deterred Gambetta from adding Egypt to his country's existing responsibilities, and jealous as much for the prestige of France as for the success of her war policy, he urgently besought the Government not to abandon co-operation with Great Britain. Freycinet was, indeed, prepared to co-operate in defending the Suez Canal, but on July 29th the Chamber refused credits even for this purely precautionary measure. He resigned in consequence, and his Cabinet was succeeded by that of M. Duclerc, who on taking office gave a pledge to the Chamber that in the Egyptian affair he would act in loyal conformity with its vote. Thus it was that France virtually expelled herself from Egypt. One of those fateful moments in history which never return had passed unimproved by a nation whose statesmen have seldom failed to combine great foresight with quickness of decision.

With the withdrawal of the French fleet from Alexandria on the last day of July England was left isolated, but not greatly grieved over her isolation, which she had honestly done her best to prevent. In the events which immediately followed Bismarck gave England all the encouragement desired. Through the German ambassadors, both in London and Constantinople, he let Lord Granville understand that while he would not go so far as to give England a formal mandate to go to Egypt he would support her, if she went there, in any action which she might deem to be necessary, and instructions were, in fact, sent to the German Consul-General in Alexandria bidding him, in effect, to confine his functions to looking on.

Alexandria was bombarded on July 11th, and its forts having been reduced, troops were landed and took possession of the town. Arabi was now dismissed from office by the Khedive and declared a rebel by the Sultan. Following the Egyptian army, which was still in his hands, into the interior, a British expeditionary force under General Wolseley inflicted upon it signal defeat at Tel-el-Kebir on September 13th.

From this single-handed intervention, resorted to unwillingly, followed now step by step the assertion of British supremacy in Egypt, which, though still remaining under the nominal sway of the Khedive, was henceforth governed not from Constantinople but from London. Lord Palmerston once declared that rather than join France in schemes of aggression in North Africa he would sacrifice England's alliance with that Power, greatly though he valued it. "We don't want to have Egypt," he wrote. "What we wish about Egypt is that it should continue attached to the Turkish Empire, which is a security against its belonging to any other European Power.[1] That had been the policy of successive British Governments. In quite recent years Lord Salisbury and Lord Derby had declared on every suitable occasion that England would never annex Egypt, and that those who would not believe her word to that effect were incredulous only because of their own crooked ways. Mr. Gladstone, Lord Granville, and the Government to which they belonged were still of the same mind. They meant to retire, wished to retire, and probably would have retired had not events proved too strong for them. It is one of the romances of British history that a momentous step in the expansion of empire, from which even an aggressive imperialist like Palmerston shrunk less than a generation before, was taken by an administration of professed non-interventionists and friends of peace, to whom their opponents had hitherto denied the courage to say boo to a goose.

With the victory of Tel-el-Kebir, upon which Bismarck promptly sent to London his hearty congratulations, the first rebellion was at an end. The native army was disbanded, and Arabi and the other ringleaders were put on trial and exiled, greatly to their surprise, for with true Oriental fatalism and an equally true knowledge of their deserts they had expected death. Now it remained for the new rulers to take in hand the work of internal reorganization and undo the evil effects of centuries of misgovernment. Approaching the Powers with a

[1] Letter to Lord Clarendon, March 1, 1857.

request for a mandate, or rather for the endorsement of a mandate which she claimed in view of past sacrifices and present occupation, Great Britain stipulated for a free hand in internal affairs, subject to consultation with the Powers on questions of common concern, but gave the undertaking that British troops would remain in the country only so long as might be necessary to the re-establishment of authority, order, and security.

Bismarck's influence was still used in England's favour. He did his best to persuade not only the Sultan but the Powers to concur in such measures as the British Government might propose to adopt, content that Germany should continue to remain, as before, a more or less passive spectator, whose voice should be heard only when necessary. Not so France, who now began to regret her refusal to accept any share of the responsibility of tranquillizing the country, and unreasonably to demand that though she had left England all the duties she should now share in the corresponding rights. With the commencement of the British occupation the Dual Control disappeared, greatly to the chagrin of France. When now a British adviser was appointed to superintend finance, she protested, and her protests being unregarded, she claimed full liberty of action. In the further measures adopted by the British Government France constantly figured as the importunate petitioner knocking for admission at a door which she had deliberately closed to herself. In the Egyptian house England now settled down for good, not as visitor or lodger, but as leaseholder on an indeterminate tenure, and having installed in her establishment a brand-new equipment of London furniture, in the shape of an efficient administrative system, she did her best to feel at home.

The time came, however, when Germany, so long the patient well-wisher, ceased to be patient with England or to wish her well in the task which she had undertaken, and made of the Egyptian question a lever wherewith to advance her own special interests elsewhere. She wished for nothing in Egypt, had staked nothing, and had sacrificed nothing, yet to Bismarck that was no reason why she should not turn to advantage her position there as a Great Power.

It was the colonial question, which Bismarck first took up in 1884, and the difficulties with England which immediately arose out of it, which directed his mind to Egypt as a legitimate means of relieving English pressure in other parts of the world. Reserving the colonial episode for later and more detailed treatment, all that is necessary here is to refer to the effects upon the general relations of the two countries of the untoward colonial controversies of that time. For some years Bismarck had been not only willing but genuinely desirous to be on good terms with England, and had a formal alliance been possible under the English parliamentary system, he would probably have welcomed it. That he then or at any time entertained cordial feelings towards England or the English may be doubted. There were certain things in English political life in particular with which he was entirely out of sympathy — the democratic tendencies of legislation, the amazing vitality of Free Trade doctrines, and the generous toleration extended to the Roman Catholic Church — since England's practice in relation to them was in conflict with, and a condemnation of, the policy which was now being pursued in Germany. Yet difference upon such domestic matters was no just bar to agreement and co-operation in foreign affairs, and it was one of his fixed principles of public action that personal likes and dislikes should never be allowed to obtrude themselves in practical politics.[1]

Early in the 'eighties the barometer of Bismarck's relations towards England was marked "marked fair," and was still rising. He had indulged in bitter words when in March, 1880, during his agitation over the Eastern question, Mr. Gladstone had in a passionate electioneering speech attacked Austria, Germany's ally, as a Power which nowhere in Europe had ever exerted an influence for good; but when on coming into office the following month the fervent orator repented of his exuberance and explained to Vienna that his words had been based on inaccurate evidence, the incident was not allowed to prejudice the relations between the two countries, much as Beaconsfield's disappearance was lamented in Berlin. Lord Granville, as we

[1] " I regard England," Bismarck said, almost at the end of his Ministerial career (January 26, 1889), " as the old traditional ally between whom and ourselves there are no contentious interests: but when I speak of an ally the word must not be understood in a diplomatic sense, for we have no treaties with England: I wish to preserve the *rapport* (*Fühlung*) which we have had with England for at least a hundred and fifty years, on colonial questions as on others. And if it could be shown that we were losing it, I should be cautious and seek to prevent its loss."

have seen, was Foreign Secretary in the new administration, and to him Lord Odo Russell was able to write from Berlin on May 1st: " I think you will find Prince Bismarck all you can wish, anxious for the most friendly relations with England and willing to act in concert with her Majesty's Government when asked to do so," while later in the same month he told how Bismarck had confided to him his inability to understand " why England should not be on terms as intimate and cordial with Germany as with France." [1]

Bismarck was then at the height of his power, the arbiter of the policies of half the States of Europe. There was no Chancellery which did not believe, even if it did not admit, that nothing could be done in European affairs without his assent. Nervous Governments feared when he spoke and feared still more when he was silent. The friendship of such a man was deemed to be a flattery, his disregard a misfortune, his hostility a disaster.

It might have seemed that Bismarck was only waiting for England to claim him as a willing ally. It has been shown that when the Egyptian difficulties arose he wished England to undertake the work of disentanglement and to do it, if she pleased, without France. He spoke, indeed, of Egypt at that time as the Schleswig-Holstein which would lead to a rupture between the two Powers if they attempted the dualism which had resulted so disastrously in the case of the Elbe duchies. There is no reason to doubt the sincerity of that avowal, though with Bismarck the visible motive was not always that which chiefly determined his action. Bismarck wanted England and France to be friends, though perhaps not too cordial friends. He, indeed, wanted no nations to fight each other; if he was no pacifist, he was also no firebrand. His policy aimed rather at maintaining between the Powers just that suggestion of tension, that " minor state " of friction, which made it possible for him to intervene at any time, always in Germany's interest, as the impartial adviser and friend, either with the soothing word of conciliation, the encouraging word of sympathy, or, if need be, the stern word of caution, as circumstances dictated. For his desire to see England and France, in particular, on at least tolerable terms there was a particular reason, for so long as that relationship existed it was un-

[1] *Life of the Second Lord Granville,* vol. ii., p. 211.

likely that France would need to seek a friend in the East of
Europe.

In the spring of 1882 Bismarck showed further his wish for
good relations with England by sending his eldest son, Count
Herbert, now a rising Councillor in the Foreign Office, to London, nominally in order to study English politics at first hand,
in view of the diplomatic career which awaited him, but also,
and perhaps mainly, in the hope that the progress of the desired *entente*, of which the German ambassador, Count Münster, did not seem to realize the full importance, might be expedited by this more visible token of good-will.   Count Herbert
had been given, both in town and country, a " good time," and
Bismarck, always susceptible to personal attentions, had been
deeply touched by the kindness shown to him not only by the
political world but by London society generally.   The mission
was prolonged, on Lord Granville's suggestion, and the friendly
assurances which the envoy extraordinary gave to the Foreign
Office in London were confirmed in Berlin by Bismarck himself
in intercourse with the British ambassador.   " The key to Bismarck's policy," Lord Ampthill (Lord Odo Russell) wrote on
January 20, 1883, " is to be sought in the true interests of
Germany, and those interests require the maintenance of the
Anglo-French alliance and of intimate relations between England and Germany."   All this time, as we have seen, Bismarck
was giving England consistent, timely, and invaluable support
in Egypt.   He had backed up her action in going there, and
now (March, 1883), in conversation with the same ambassador,
he advised that British troops should not be withdrawn from
the country " before safety and stability could be guaranteed
by England to Europe."   Bismarck seems to have known better than the British Government that such advice would defer
withdrawal to the Greek Kalends.

The progress of friendly relations, begun in circumstances
so favourable, was rudely disturbed by the frictions to which
Germany's earliest colonial adventures gave rise in 1884 and
1885.   The unhappy story is told in its proper place — a
story of masterful energy, dogged persistence, and finally of
arrogant defiance on one side, and of weakness, prevarication,
and, until too late, want of magnanimity on the other; above
all, of clashing interests, mutual jealousies, and conflicting
aims, the outcome of which was that the harmony and unity,
upon the attainment of which so much effort had been ex-

pended, were suddenly dissipated like sunlight by a storm. It is questionable whether British statesmen, accustomed to a Ptolemaic view of their country's relations to the rest of the world, not given to speculation upon cause and effect, and seldom disposed to look far ahead, took the rupture so tragically as it was taken in Germany. Bismarck's resentment at what he regarded as inconsiderate treatment, however, was profound, and proportionate to the pains which he had taken to come nearer to the cold island nation which was so coy to woo and so hard to win, and the hopes which he had built upon an understanding with Governments which, as he scoffingly said, changed every fortnight.

He had warned the Foreign Office at an early stage in the colonial movement, when he saw that if Germany was to make headway it would be against British opposition, that unless a more friendly spirit were shown he would make advances to France, and cease to give to England the support in Egypt which she had hitherto received and now rewarded, as he thought, so ungratefully. When Lord Granville in the House of Lords (February 27, 1885) said that Bismarck had advised him, and Beaconsfield before him, that England should " take Egypt," the Chancellor flatly contradicted him. In a wrathful speech made in the Imperial Diet on March 2nd, in which he recited a formidable list of the wrongs — some real, others trivial, others fabricated — done to himself and Germany by England in the course of a short twelve months, he declared that though British Ministers had deliberately gone to him for advice on the question of annexation, he had refused to think and decide for them.[1]

" I have never," he said, " given any advice to the British Government as to the treatment of Egypt. I have certainly been asked for it on different occasions, and in every case the question addressed to me was whether I should be prepared to give the English Government ' an advice or a hint ' as to what they should really do in Egypt and what would have our approval. To that question I have always answered that in my capacity as the Foreign Minister of the German Empire I must refrain from advising on English policy, since such ad-

[1] " I have not the slightest right," Lord Granville said, " to complain of Prince Bismarck — of his expressing an unfavourable view of our Egyptian policy — for the simple reason that the policy of the Government has never yet been in accord with the advice with regard to Egypt which he gave to the late Government and to ourselves, namely, to take it."

vice, given in an official capacity, would carry a certain responsibility towards other Cabinets and also responsibility for the consequences which might result. I was then asked whether I would not express an opinion as to what might happen in Egypt. To this I replied that I could imagine that if I were the English Minister I should not at the present moment advise the annexation of Egypt, but that I recognized that it might be for England a necessity to have a certain secure position in this connecting link between its European and Asiatic dominions. Short of coming into collision with treaties, however, England could only obtain this position through the Sultan. I said, therefore, that if I were the English Minister I should seek the Sultan's mediation in order to obtain through him such a position as would safeguard English interests."

All this sounds just like what Bismarck might have said, had he not said something different. What did he really say? Later passages in the same speech seem to indicate that Lord Granville had not misrepresented him. After further talking round the subject he ended by admitting that he had advised England that she should seek to become a " leaseholder " in Egypt, and that he even went so far as to say that " If England should prefer to annex Egypt, we should not regard it as our duty to prevent it. The friendship of England would be for us more important than the future fate of Egypt." Again, however, he denied that he positively advised annexation. Lord Granville's reply in the House of Lords to this direct imputation of misstatement did not lack dignity. It was in effect that if Bismarck did not give the advice which had been attributed to him, he did not, and there, with a thousand apologies, was an end of the matter; he had simply been misunderstood. This courteous acceptance of Bismarck's disclaimer, in the English gentleman's way, was received in Germany, by people without sufficient *finesse* of judgment to recognize that not to contradict an opponent's statements does not necessarily mean to accept them, as a humiliating confession of misrepresentation. Certainly, if Lord Granville was wrong he was wrong with many others, able to know the facts quite as well as he. Lord Odo Russell spoke as early as 1877 [1] of Bismarck's constant incitements to Great Britain to take Egypt and to do it at once, before France should be strong enough

[1] Conversation with Mr. W. E. Forster, September 11, 1877, *Life*, by T. W. Reid, vol. ii., p. 178.

to prevent it, though he was careful to add that the motive of Bismarck's generosity was a desire to make an Anglo-French alliance impossible. The only fact which emerged clearly from the controversy was that British Ministers had more than once taken counsel with the German Chancellor as to how they should conduct foreign affairs. They were not, however, the only Englishmen who appeared to forget at that time what was due to their country. Leaders of the Opposition thought it seemly to belittle the Queen's advisers by quoting against them the depreciatory estimates of the same statesman.

The rent in the Anglo-German friendship was now closed up, but with a patch; the new relationship was never again as sound and whole as the old, and for a long time England's position in Egypt suffered in consequence.

So menaced and uncertain did British tenure there appear in 1884 that in June Lord Granville concluded with M. Waddington, the French ambassador in London, a provisional agreement under which England was to withdraw from Egypt at the beginning of 1888, to neutralize the country on the principle of Belgium, to internationalize the highroad to the Indian Empire, the Suez Canal — of which England was now a principal proprietor — and, in Egyptian finance, to replace the control by many Powers for that of France and herself. In effect the agreement was a capitulation to France upon all points which to her were of importance, and a sacrifice of every interest which England had so painfully established in the khediviate. The agreement gave satisfaction in France, and just in the same proportion created indignation at home. It hung, however, upon an uncertain contingency; its provisions were only to have effect in the event of the successful issue of a conference of the Powers to be held in London to consider the reform of Egyptian finance. This conference duly met at the end of June and quarrelled until the beginning of August, without arriving at an understanding. The Anglo-French agreement, therefore, fell to the ground.

The principal result of the abortive conference was to convince the British Government that it could no longer rely on the good-will of the Powers, and that whatever England did must be done on her own responsibility and at her own risk. Upon the financial question, however, Lord Granville in the spring of 1885 addressed to the Powers new proposals. Germany and Austria replied that whatever satisfied France would be acceptable to them, and in the end it was in the main the proposals of France which were adopted. In the meantime (January, 1885), France, Austria, and Italy had supported a request of Germany and Russia that they should be allowed to nominate each one member of the Debt Commission, and the Egyptian Government agreed. The effect was to strengthen international control and to perpetuate the attendant frictions in an acuter form than before. In relation to all the measures proposed in 1885 by the British Government for the reorganization of Egyptian finances and their administration Germany found opportunities for obstructive reservations or counter-proposals, usually with support from France, Austria, or Russia, or all together.

Matters might have taken a still more serious turn had not Germany's good relations with France been disturbed by the fall of M. Ferry's Cabinet in March of that year. Allowing for temporary revulsions, due to resentment and pique, Bismarck must be given full credit for understanding the value to Germany of a good understanding with England. Recalled now by the uncertain situation in France to self-control and a due appreciation of the requirements of realist politics, he showed readiness to resume the old friendly intercourse with London where it was broken off. Hence when a little later France, taking him at his word, made advances with a view to joint action against England she met with an equivocal response. Judging the question in the cold light of facts, Bismarck declared (in Prince Hohenlohe's words) that " France was too uncertain an ally to risk losing England's friendship for her sake. Their policy would therefore be, not to reject the advances of France brusquely, but to act dilatorily." And with Bismarck to act " dilatorily " meant as a rule not to act at all.

Any record of the later events in Egypt and its dependencies, the Mahdi's insurrection, with the evacuation and later reconquest of the Soudan, the pacification of the vast Nile territories, which had not known for centuries the blessings of order and settled government, and the work of reform and reconstruction done under the direction of Sir Evelyn **Baring** (afterwards Lord Cromer),[1] belongs to a history of the British

---

[1] Sir Evelyn Baring, who had been prominent in the Egyptian administra-

and not of the German Empire. Yet not Egypt alone, but all
Europe, has shared in the fruits of the succeeding series of
ameliorative measures — the reorganization of finance in such
a manner that the country was enabled to pay its way and to
improve its credit in the money markets of Europe; the nar-
rowing down of the Capitulations with a view to restricting the
illegitimate privileges of Europeans; the abolition of what
Lord Cromer has called the three C's of past Egyptian demoralization, the courbash, the *corvée*, and corruption; the general cleansing of public administration; the development of national resources; the construction of irrigation works which
turned deserts into fertile places and banished famine from the
land; the victories of sanitation over plague and disease —
works which restored to an ancient country more than its ancient prosperity, adapted its civilization to modern conditions,
and redeemed in years the errors, follies, and crimes of generations. Germany's part and her credit lie in the fact that
in course of time, convinced by the force of reason and the
logic of events, she came to recognize that England had asserted her claim to remain in Egypt by a higher title than right
of arms or possession can bestow — the will and the power to
do for the native population greater and better things than it
had ever done or could do for itself.

The question of the British occupation continued to be regarded as a convenient subject for bargaining, but more and
more it ceased to have a practical and acquired merely a theo-
retical interest. France continued for many years to obstruct
a work of progress in which it was now too late for her to take
part, and her opposition was only withdrawn when open questions and sources of discord between the two countries in every
part of the world were closed as part of a comprehensive agreement. There never was a time when Germany formally conceded England's claim to continue alone in Egypt the work
which she had been compelled to begin alone, or struck out of
the list of her unrealized political assets the power to dispute
the British occupation, but as time passed it became increasingly clear that such acquiescence was unnecessary. There
are facts in political life which need no confirmation, since they

tion since March, 1877, became British Agent and Consul-General in September, 1883 (following Sir Edward Malet), and continued to hold that
office until May, 1907.

confirm themselves, and as such a fact the British tenure of Egypt, in virtue of duties undertaken in the first place unwillingly yet throughout disinterestedly discharged, was in course of time tacitly regarded in Germany as elsewhere.[1]

[1] In the fifth month of the Great War (December 19, 1914) the British Government declared a protectorate over Egypt.

CHAPTER XVII

(1880–1890)

THE COLONIAL ERA

The decade that saw Germany formally committed to a policy of Protection was notable for another political departure which modified her relations with the outside world even more profoundly. During the five years from 1880 to 1885 the pioneer work upon which two generations of explorers and merchant adventurers had been engaged in various parts of the African Continent and elsewhere culminated in the creation of a large oversea dominion which at once placed Germany, in extent of territory — over a million square miles — in the front rank of colonial Powers.

No misconception of modern German history is more common or less justifiable than the assumption that the German colonial movement dates only from the year 1884, when, apparently without warning, Bismarck proclaimed the first oversea protectorate. Throughout their history the Germans had been conspicuous as colonizing agents, and in the German lands themselves one race had repeatedly superimposed its civilization upon that of another. A thousand years ago North German tribes moved eastward into the regions inhabited by the Slavic races and, having once settled there, gradually extended their influence over large areas, either supplanting or overshadowing the original populations. The Wendish province of Brandenburg was so colonized and afterwards brought into the old German Empire as a part of what is now Prussia. In the South, Saxon and Swabian colonists in the twelfth century established themselves in Transylvania and other parts of Hungary, where the towns of Hermannstadt, Kronstadt, and Klausenburg still remain as examples of the early " peaceful penetration " of Germanism in that part of Europe. So, too, the Russian Baltic provinces of Livonia, Courland, and Esthonia were colonized by the Teutonic knightly orders in the thirteenth century, and in modern times German colonies were founded in many other parts of the Russian Empire.

The adventurous spirit of the North Germans was similarly shown in the formation in the thirteenth century of the great trading and maritime corporation known as the Hanseatic League, with depots not only in a large number of German towns but in many foreign countries. " Not Clive, but a Hamburg Senator," wrote the Würtemberg publicist Moser over a hundred years ago, voicing the German lament of even that distant day over neglected imperialistic opportunities, " would command the Ganges to-day, had the aims of the Hanseatic towns been supported instead of combated by the old Empire." The colonizing instinct was also illustrated in a striking way when the Augsburg commercial and banking house of Welser acquired the province of Caracas, in Venezuela, in virtue of a charter granted by Emperor Charles V, as security for a loan; whereupon the Fuggers, not to be outdone by their townsmen, immediately obtained permission from the same Emperor to search for and exploit minerals on part of the coast of Chile. The difficulty of keeping territories so far distant proved greater than the acquisition of them, and these adventures were soon abandoned.

The first serious attempts to create the beginnings of a German colonial empire were made in the last quarter of the seventeenth century by the Great Elector of Brandenburg. His objects in so doing were more commercial than political or imperialistic in the modern sense. The Brandenburg rulers have always been good men of business, and none had a clearer idea than the Great Elector of the value of trade for his country. " The surest sources of wealth and prosperity for a country come from *commercium*," he wrote to his Privy Councillor Fuchs; " navigation and trade are the most honourable pillars of a State." His first foreign venture was the foundation in 1647 of the Brandenburg East India Company, but towards the close of his long reign he conceived the idea of extending his rule to West Africa. After unsuccessfully trying to bargain with France for the establishment of a settlement in Guinea, he despatched to that region in 1680 two Dutch captains named Raulé and Blonk with several ships, flying the Brandenburg flag, in order " to carry on trade and industry there without injury to any one." Landing at Cape Three Points, on the Gold Coast, the explorers concluded treaties with native chiefs at Axim, by which the Elector was granted local territorial and trading rights. A year later he transferred these rights to the African Trading Company of Berlin (later of Emden), in which he was largely interested as a shareholder. Thus it was that there came into existence at Axim (1682–3) the fort Gross Friedrichsburg, the nucleus of the first Prusso-German colony to be established across the seas.

Nor was this the Great Elector's only imperialistic design. He also endeavoured to gain a footing in America, and he negotiated for the acquisition of one of the Antilles. His greatest ambition, however, was to have a share in the wealth of the East Indies, and it was with that end in view he formed his East India Company, but the project never prospered. He died in 1688, before his colonial schemes had matured or secured a lasting hold upon the imagination or faith of his subjects. His successor, Frederick III, the first King of Prussia, continued his interest in colonial undertakings. In the second year of his reign his fleet occupied Crab Island, between St. Thomas and Puerto Rico, and later he conceived the idea of acquiring the Isthmus of Panama, but the opposition of Spain prevented the realization of this bold design. Under the following ruler the African enterprise was abandoned. It had never prospered, and after he had subsidized it for a long time he sold it in 1717 to the Dutch West Indies Company for a sum which barely met the outstanding debts. In 1871 Great Britain acquired this strip of African territory and added it to Cape Coast Castle.

Thus the first Prussian experiment in colonial enterprise came to a premature and inglorious end. Brandenburg then possessed neither the ships, the money, nor the men needed to carry it to a successful issue. Now for two centuries Prussia and Germany remained without colonies, for what the largest of the German States had failed to accomplish no other had the power, the will, or the resource to attempt. The third King of Prussia, Frederick the Great, brought new maxims into Prussian statecraft, and one of these was expressed in the words, " All distant possessions are a burden to the State. A village on the frontier is worth a principality two hundred and fifty miles away." Hence when the famous Colberger Joachim Nettelbeck, after making expeditions to the West Indies and the Guinea Coast, proposed to the King in 1786 that Prussia should again secure an African colony and also one in Surinam he declined to be tempted.

Nevertheless, the formation of free German settlements in

various parts of the world continued. The first emigration of Germans to North America had been contemporaneous with the Great Elector's colonial adventures. William Penn visited Germany in 1677, and six years later the first body of settlers crossed the Atlantic. These emigrants were followed by others, and throughout the whole of the succeeding century the movement westward continued. With the beginning of the nineteenth century began emigration to South America, and principally to Brazil. In the meantime Russia continued to attract many settlers as before,[1] and agricultural colonies of Germans were formed in Turkey, Greece, Roumania, Palestine, and elsewhere. After the Napoleonic wars emigration to America in particular took large dimensions, though later there was a smaller stream to Brazil, Mexico, and certain of the British colonies, notably Canada, Australia, and Tasmania. From 1830 the outward flow of population became stronger, and it has been estimated that, after allowing for a large amount of repatriation, four and a half million Germans emigrated during the first eighty years of last century, all but half a million seeking new homes in the United States. From the middle of the century forward the movement was assisted by a host of emigration societies, the majority working on philanthropic, but some on purely commercial, lines.

An important part was played in the creation of a spirit of colonization by the German religious missions, of which the earliest, the Rhenish Mission of Barmen, and the work of the Bohemian Brethren, dated from 1729 and 1732 respectively, but a far greater influence was exerted by the enterprise and reports of the many indefatigable travellers and explorers who began to be active in various parts of the world from the beginning of last century. The objects of these men were for a long time purely scientific, but later imperialistic and commercial motives came into play. Following Alexander von Humboldt came, in the early decades of the century, Burckhardt and Hornemann (who both entered the service of an English exploration society), Rüppell, Ehrenberg, Rose, Prokesch, Hemprich, Schlimper, Kutte, and Kielmayer. In the middle of the century, in particular, exploration received a strong im-

---

[1] The number of German families settled in various parts of the Russian Empire — the Baltic Provinces excluded — was estimated in 1918 at 250,000, representing 1,700,000 individuals, and the extent of the land owned by them at 10,400,000 hectares. See article in *Die Hilfe* for May 2, 1918.

petus, and more than before Africa became the goal of endeavour. Leichardt, Rebmann, Overweg, Barth, Krapf, Vogel, Beurmann, Peters, Maltzan, the brothers Schlagentweit, Karl von der Decken, Gerhard Rohlfs, Karl Mauch, and others did notable work at that time; while explorers of later fame were Gustav Nachtigal, Robert Flegel, Pogge, Gustav and Clemens Denhardt, Güssfeld, Fritsch, Schweinfurth, Buchner, Hermann Wissmann, Junker, and Eduard Schnitzler, better known as Emin Pasha.

Gradually the colonial cause found advocacy in the literature of the day — in works of travel, political essays, and economical writings. One of the earliest writers to revive national interest in the question was Friedrich List, whose influence upon his country's material development was fruitful in so many directions. In proposing the acquisition of colonies while large portions of the world were still unappropriated, List sought rather to provide outlets for Germany's surplus population than to create markets for her trade. Wilhelm Roscher similarly pressed the claims of colonial policy. "The fruits of colonization," he wrote in one of his earliest works, " are usually reaped only in the second generation, and such long waiting is not to the mind of our time. Yet Germany must lose no time if the last suitable territories are not to be seized by other and more resolute nations."

Colonization was much discussed in political circles early in the 'forties. Charles Greville relates in his *Memoirs* how, when visiting Germany in 1843, he was surprised to hear people talking of the need for " colonies and a navy." [1] The idea of emulating his ancestor, the Great Elector of Brandenburg, occurred at that time to the fertile mind of the visionary Frederick William IV, who, encouraged by his envoy Bunsen in London, sanctioned the opening of negotiations for the purchase of California, then subject to Mexico, for the reception of the Germans who were at that time seeking their fortunes in America by the hundred thousand yearly. The Prussian envoy at Washington favoured the proposal, but Alexander von Humboldt appears to have dissuaded the King. Several years later California became independent, and in 1850 it joined the United States.

Fresh stimulus was given to the movement by several asso-

[1] *Memoirs,* Second Part, " Journal of the Reign of Queen Victoria," vol. ii., p. 180.

ciations of a politico-economical character which were formed
early in the second half of the century. The most important
of these was the " Central Association for Commercial Geog-
raphy and the Promotion of German Interests Abroad,"
founded in 1868 at the instigation of the traveller Otto Kersten, with its headquarters in Berlin. A branch of this society, the West German Association for Colonization and Export, of Düsseldorf, became later a powerful propagandist
agency in the cause, amalgamating in 1882 with the German
Colonial Association, then formed at Frankfort. Other societies which, though originally following purely scientific objects, did useful work for the colonial cause were the German
Society for the Scientific Exploration of Equatorial Africa,
dating from 1873, and the German African Society of 1876;
these societies were in 1878 merged in the German African Society of Berlin, which furnished many explorers of the Dark
Continent. Later the German Colonial Society was formed
(1881), and after it the Society for German Colonization
(1884), the forerunner of the German East Africa Company.

Most of the earlier colonial propagandists had in mind merely
the establishment on foreign soil of German settlements of the
old conventional kind, and only seldom was the occupation of
territory with political sovereignty contemplated. After the
middle of the century, however, the movement passed into this
more practical channel. Now travellers and explorers were no
longer content to bring back merely the scientific results of
their investigations, and their efforts took more and more a
distinctly acquisitive turn. Many of them returned home fired
with imperialistic ambitions, eager to see Germany emulate the
enterprise of the older colonial Powers, and these men soon
obtained a ready hearing. Von der Decken, who during the
years 1860 to 1865 explored the Kilimanjaro country and various parts of the East African coast between Cape Delgado and
the Juba river, where he lost his life, wrote home in August,
1864: " I am persuaded that in a short time a colony established here would be most successful, and after two or three
years would be self-supporting. It would become of special
importance after the opening of the Suez Canal.[1] It is unfortunate that we Germans allow such opportunities of acquiring colonies to slip by, especially at a time when it would be
of importance to the navy." He conceived the idea of buy-

[1] Opened in 1869.

ing Mombasa and making it the nucleus of a great trading settlement, and he predicted that " After two or three years' stay
at Chagga, on the eastern shore of the Victoria Nyanza, the
colonists would obtain better results than emigrants to America." He added: " I recommend to my country an enterprise as advantageous as it is glorious for individuals and for
the nation." Five years later Mauch, after exploring the Zambesi and visiting Mashonaland and the Transvaal, wrote of the
latter country: " Would to God that this fine country might
become a German colony! " Similarly, Gerhard Rohlfs, returning to Germany after exploration in the Cameroons country, addressed to his countrymen the appeal: " Is it not deplorable that we are obliged to assist, inactive and without
power to intervene, in the extension of England in Central
Africa? "

The movement now found warm supporters in the Hanseatic
merchants and planters who had long been active in many parts
of the world — wherever, in fact, trade was to be done under
peaceful conditions. In Africa these traders were settled in
Zanzibar, the South-west, and Liberia as early as the 'forties;
and during the two following decades they established themselves in Sierra Leone, Lagos, Togoland, and the Cameroons,
on the West Coast, and in Mozambique and Somaliland, on the
East Coast; while farther afield they became rivals of British
enterprise in Australasia and the South Seas. Not possessing
colonies of their own, Prussia and the North German Confederation, as later the Empire, concluded most-favoured-nation-
treatment treaties with European States and treaties of friendship and commerce with independent native rulers in respect
of such territories. Nevertheless, the German traders settled
in Africa grew increasingly impatient as they saw other countries add to their possessions while their own country still remained landless and inactive, though gradually the continent
was being partitioned. Amongst the countries recommended
half a century ago as fields for colonial enterprise were Madagascar, Formosa, Uruguay, North Borneo, Hainan, Timor, the
Philippines, New Guinea, Zululand, Tripoli, Tunis, and Morocco.

Attractive as some of these schemes must have appeared,
however, they failed to secure official encouragement. Since
1862 Bismarck had been the Minister-President and Foreign
Minister of Prussia, and since 1867 the Federal Chancellor and

Foreign Minister of the North German Confederation, and he was too much occupied with domestic and military questions, and above all with the question of Germany's consolidation, to give a thought to projects of colonial expansion. To him it was premature and incongruous to talk of a German empire abroad before the German Empire had been established at home, and, moreover, the Prusso-German navy was far too small to be the support of a policy of imperialism, and there was no money to spare for its increase. Nevertheless, the proposal to appropriate New Guinea, though entirely unofficial, created excitement in Australia at the time, and the British Government was urged to annex the island at once, before it was forestalled, a warning which was not heeded.

Bismarck's first important utterance on the colonial question is contained in a letter written on January 9, 1868, to Roon, then Minister of War and Marine.[1] In it he contended that the promotion of colonial undertakings was a matter for private enterprise, and not for the Government; he endorsed Roon's opinion that the navy was not strong enough to enable the Government to assume political responsibilities across the seas; he questioned whether from the material standpoint colonies were advantageous; convinced that they would be a cause of serious deficits, he held it to be " difficult to justify the imposition of heavy taxation upon the whole nation for the benefit of a few branches of trade and industry "; and finally, he feared that " the attempt to establish colonies in territories whose suzerainty is claimed by other States, whether rightly or wrongly, might lead to manifold and undesirable disputes."

Two years later the negotiations of terms of peace with France seemed to afford to Germany the opportunity of entering into a colonial house already swept and garnished. There were men in high position who would have made the cession of colonial territory an important part of the indemnity. Cochin China, Tahiti, Réunion, the Marquesas Islands, even Algeria and Madagascar were all mentioned; but, supported by his Liberal and individualistic colleague, Rudolf Delbrück, he turned a deaf ear to the voices of the colonial charmers. " I

---

[1] John (Lord) Morley relates that the Dutch Minister told the British ambassador in Vienna in 1865 how Bismarck had said to him that "without colonies Prussia could never become a great maritime nation: he coveted Holland less for its own sake than for her wealthy colonies " (*Life of William Ewart Gladstone*, vol. ii., p. 320).

want no colonies," he said at the time; " they are only good
for providing offices. For us colonial enterprises would be
just like the silk sable in Polish noble families, who, for the
rest, are without shirts." [1]   Three years later (1873) he said
to Mr. Odo Russell: " Colonies would be a source of weakness, because they could only be defended by powerful fleets,
and Germany's geographical position did not necessitate her
development into a first-class maritime Power." He said then
that he had been urged repeatedly to acquire colonies but had
refused: at the most he " wished for coaling stations acquired
by treaty with other nations." In holding this standpoint he
had the approval of an influential body of politicians and
economists, yet it cannot be questioned that he showed a great
lack of prevision, for vast territories were then still to be had
for the claiming, and the opportunities which were allowed to
slip by unimproved never returned.

Thus it was that during the first decade of the new Empire
the colonial movement continued as before to be almost altogether an unofficial movement; its adherents in political, scientific, and commercial circles were steadily growing, yet the
Foreign Office, and most of all its head, the Chancellor, looked
on in cautious inaction, apparently willing at the most to follow, but not willing in any circumstances to lead. Of the political parties represented in the Diet only the two Conservative groups and the National Liberals were as yet favourable
to the movement. The Radicals, true to their individualistic
principles, were conspicuously hostile; the Clericals individually were divided in sympathy, yet as a party they held back,
as much for diplomatic reasons as lack of conviction; while
the smaller groups were either unfriendly or sceptical. The
sentiment of the large uninformed section of the public outside
was in the main determined by the attitude of Prince Bismarck
himself.

When, therefore, in 1872, the ruler of the Fiji Islands, and
in 1874 the Sultan of Zanzibar, asked for the protection of the
Empire, Bismarck promptly declined to give it; and the Fiji
Islands went to Great Britain soon afterwards. When in
1874 the Sultan of the Sulu Archipelago sought protection for
Sulu and the portion of North Borneo over which he claimed
suzerainty it was likewise withheld. In that year also Bismarck refused to comply with the petition of Hamburg firms

[1] Poschinger, *Bismarck als Volkswirt,* vol. i., p. 63.

engaged in the Cameroons that he would establish at Fernando
Po a consulate-general for West Africa, and he seemed to welcome the action of the United States Government in proposing
to declare a protectorate over Samoa in 1875. On the occasion of a dispute with Spain in 1874 he avowed the renunciation of colonies as a deliberate act of German policy, while
at the same time insisting on the duty of other countries to
reciprocate by showing fair play to German trade in their
colonial territories. " If the Government of his Majesty "
(the German Emperor), he wrote to the Madrid Cabinet
(March 4th), " renounces the pursuance of a colonial policy
of its own, it is all the more bound to protect German trade
against unjustifiable interferences." When a German official
in the Chinese service proposed the establishment of German
settlements in China, to which end the Government was urged
to acquire a concession on the Yangtse-Kiang river, and Bismarck was asked by the Crown Prince to consider and report
on the idea, the answer given was that Germany had neither
money nor the right men for such an enterprise, and that to
undertake it would entail indefinite responsibilities which might
weaken her position abroad. About 1876 a representative
body of colonial politicians and African merchants laid before
him a formal scheme of colonization, to include the acquisition of Delagoa or St. Lucia Bay, but they received no encouragement.

So little jealous was Bismarck of the imperialistic aspirations of other Powers at that time that at the Berlin Congress
in 1878 he urged France to take Tunis, pressed Egypt upon
Great Britain, and pointed Italy to Tripoli. As late as February 22, 1880, Prince Hohenlohe, recording a conversation
with him, wrote: " Now, as before, he will not hear of colonies.
He says we have not an adequate fleet to protect them, and
our bureaucracy is not skilful enough to administer them. He
also spoke of my report on the French designs on Morocco,
and declared that we could only be pleased if France took
possession of the country." The refusal of the Diet in the
following April to approve the granting of a small subsidy, by
way of guarantee of interest, to a company which had been
formed to develop the commercial resources of Samoa in Germany's interest convinced Bismarck that public opinion was
yet far from being sympathetic to colonial enterprises and
risks. Later in the year (November) some Berlin bankers and

merchants placed before him an elaborate plan for the acquisition and development of New Guinea, but he declined to consider it, and the same fate attended a North Borneo scheme which was pressed upon his attention.

If, however, Bismarck was still holding back the colonial movement, it is impossible to resist the conclusion that had private enterprise from the first relied more upon itself, its own energy and resources, and followed its own counsels, instead of looking to the State for encouragement, patronage, and assistance, Germany might have won for herself far sooner than she did a prominent place amongst colonial Powers. Nevertheless, his lukewarmness failed to daunt the spirits of the men who were behind the movement. The more difficult it seemed to move him, the more their efforts and schemes multiplied. Patriotic feeling had revolted at the idea of German explorers continuing to open up undeveloped territories for other nations to appropriate at a later date and of German emigrants serving simply to populate alien countries and fill up the waste places of their colonial empires. "The question for us to consider," wrote the German colonial pioneer Moldenhauer in 1878, "is whether Germany is prepared to do anything else than send scientific missions to Africa and to strew the continent with the bones of her explorers." Active propagandism was again made at this time for the colonization of various parts of Africa, in the North-west, East, South-east, and South-west; and now Damaraland and Namaqualand received serious notice for the first time.

It was in 1880 that the movement came officially before the attention of the British Government. In November of the preceding year the traveller Ernst von Weber published in the *Geographische Nachrichten* of the Berlin Geographical Society a glowing panegyric upon South Africa, with an appeal to the Government to establish a new Germany there by the amalgamation under imperial influence of the Dutch republics and the territories lying to the north. It was Weber's idea to acquire Delagoa Bay and then, by means of a railway to Pretoria, to pass Germans into the Transvaal with a view "to secure the future dominion over the country and so to pave the way for the foundation of a German-African empire," for even the Transvaal was only to serve as a base from which to push forward German influence step by step to the Zambesi. The article does not appear to have attracted the attention of the British diplomatic representatives in Germany, but it was seen by Sir Bartle Frere, the Governor at the Cape, and he in alarm forwarded a translation to the Colonial Office, which in turn sent it to the Foreign Office. Submitted to him for his observations, Lord Odo Russell, in a despatch of September 18, 1880, pooh-poohed Weber's idea and that of German colonization in general with a too easy confidence. " Herr von Weber's plan," he replied, " will not meet with any support, either at the hands of the German Government or on the part of the German Parliament. . . . The German Parliament has marked its disinclination to acquire distant dependencies, however advantageous to German enterprise, by the rejection of the Samoa Bill. Under present circumstances the plan for a German colony in South Africa has no prospect of success." Thus assured, the Ministers concerned appear to have smiled at the phantom of colonial rivalry with Great Britain and to have dismissed the matter from their minds.

The historian Treitschke, too, at that time built expectations upon South Africa, where with the eye of desire he foresaw the decay of British power. " In the South of Africa," he wrote in 1878, " circumstances are decidedly favourable to us. English colonial policy, which has been successful everywhere else, has not succeeded at the Cape. The civilization which exists there is Teutonic, is Dutch. If our Empire has the courage to follow an independent colonial policy with determination, a collision between our interests and those of England is unavoidable." [1]

Bismarck's ultimate surrender on the question of colonization must be attributed to a chain of events the cumulative effect of which left him almost without choice in the matter. Perhaps most of all he was influenced by the feverish colonial activity which other nations — notably France, Portugal, and Belgium — were showing in Africa at the beginning of the 'eighties, since this gave rise to the apprehension that unless Germany bestirred herself without delay she would inevitably be excluded from what promised to be the final partition of Africa. In September, 1876, there had met at Brussels, at the invitation of the King of the Belgians, the memorable conference of geographers which led to the founding of the *Société Africaine internationale,* the forerunner of the strictly Belgian *Comité des études du Haut Congo,* and had given a

---

[1] *Zehn Jahre deutscher Kämpfe.*

powerful impetus to colonizing enterprise in the Dark Continent. H. M. Stanley and De Brazza were exploring Central Africa, the former on behalf of the King of the Belgians and the latter in the service of France. France, too, had just claimed Tunis (1881), and was about to appropriate Madagascar. Portugal was seeking to obtain international recognition for her ancient but obscure claim to suzerainty over the mouth of the Congo. Finally, Great Britain had taken the first steps towards abolishing dual control in Egypt and establishing herself — though this result was not discerned by the Government of the day — as mistress of the Nile and its territories.

He was also influenced by an untoward and still outstanding dispute with England over the status of German settlers in the Fiji Islands, which had led him to believe that German subjects in British colonies could not count upon the same consideration as of old. The dispute related to the land claims which had been acquired by these settlers from native Governments prior to the final declaration of British sovereignty over the islands in 1874. The colonial land commission had set the claims aside as invalid, while Bismarck had now for nearly ten years been vainly urging that they should at least be submitted to the adjudication of a joint tribunal. The grievance rankled, and the moral to which it pointed was plain; never again must German subjects be allowed to look to other countries for a protection which it was within the power of their own Government to give them.

It is to be noted also that emigration — implying a diminution of the Empire's military strength — was again ominously increasing. It had been large in the two years following the war with France, viz. 126,000 in 1872 and 104,000 in 1873, but during the succeeding years it had fallen to an insignificant figure. The high-water mark was reached only in the succeeding decade, when as many as 220,000 Germans sought new homes across the ocean in a single year. The loss which Germany thus suffered was also permanent, for these emigrants settled under alien flags, and seldom returned to their native country.

All these considerations stimulated colonial agitation in Germany in a high degree and forced the question upon the Government's attention with a greater urgency than before. Several new propagandist organizations were formed about this time, notably the German Colonial Association of 1882, which, backed by men of eminence in public life, at once exerted great influence both in Parliamentary and Ministerial circles.

Yielding to pressure from various sides, Bismarck now abandoned his past negative attitude towards colonial enterprise. If, however, to most onlookers in other countries the change appeared dramatic in its suddenness, the shock which it caused them was solely due to the fact that they had not sufficiently, if at all, distinguished in the past between official policy and private action — the one hitherto consistently hesitant, unsympathetic, and unwilling to countenance colonial enterprise in the absence of a clear national mandate, the other concentrated with unwearying zeal upon its objective and urging forward the Government with all the force and resource at its command. Nowhere were the surprise and the shock greater than in Great Britain, whose diplomatic representatives in Germany had clearly failed to allow for the strength of national sentiment and its importance as a motive force in political life.

The first definite appropriation of territory by Germany was due to the initiative of a Bremen merchant, F. A. L. Lüderitz, one of a small band of commercial imperialists who had long endeavoured to persuade Bismarck to declare himself openly for a policy of expansion in Africa. For some years he had aimed at the acquisition of the extensive territories of Namaqualand and Damaraland, lying between Cape Colony and the Portuguese protectorate of Angola. Since 1842 there had been a German Protestant mission at Bethany, the chief town of Namaqualand, and many German traders had settled in the land, but there had been no claim to occupation. Great Britain, the only European Power then interested in South Africa, had in 1878 appropriated the better of the two harbours of the region, Whale (Walfisch) Bay, later annexed to Cape Colony, lying midway on a coastline of over a thousand miles, but the rest of the territory was unclaimed.

The entire attitude of the British Government at that time was opposed to the extension of its responsibilities in that region. In sanctioning the annexation of the Orange River in 1850 the Privy Council had besought the Queen to let that be the last British annexation in South Africa, and had recommended " that all officers who represent or who may hereafter represent your Majesty in Southern Africa should be inter-

dicted in terms as explicit as can be employed, and under sanctions as grave as can be devised, from making any additions,
whether permanent or provisional, of any territory, however
small, to the existing dominions of your Majesty in the African
Continent." From that time successive British Colonial Ministers refused to assent to the annexation of further territory,
even when petitioned to do so by the German missionaries settled in Damaraland and by the native chiefs.

The rule then laid down was confirmed when in 1867 the
Governor of Cape Colony, Sir Philip Wodehouse, urged the
declaration of British sovereignty over the South-west Coast
as far as 22° of S. latitude, a bold stroke which would have
brought into the Empire the entire region between Cape Colony and Angola; for the answer of the Colonial Secretary of
that day, the Duke of Buckingham and Chandos (August
23rd), was a flat refusal. All that was done at the time was
to annex the small guano islands in the neighbourhood of Angra Pequena. Similarly, when in 1877 Sir Bartle Frere again
wrote to Lord Carnarvon, urging that British sovereignty
should be proclaimed over the same territory and also from
Natal to the frontiers of the Portuguese colony on the opposite
coast, his advice was rejected.

Nevertheless, when in the summer of 1880 war broke out
between the Namaquas and the Hereros (of Damaraland) and
the German settlers sought the Empire's protection, Bismarck's first step was to ask the Government in London if it
would be willing to afford to German subjects the same protection which was enjoyed by the British. On November 29th
Lord Granville, as Foreign Secretary, gave the desired undertaking, but with diplomatic caution added the reservation that
the British Government could not assume responsibility for
any events which occurred outside British territory, which was
said to be confined to " Whale Bay and a very small portion
of country immediately surrounding it." This answer was
clearly an implicit disavowal of any claim to other suzerain
rights in that part of Africa, and as such it was later interpreted by Germany. In that year all British officials were
withdrawn from Damaraland, and Whale Bay remained the
only point on the South-west Coast at which British influence
was represented. As late as December 30th Lord Kimberley
wrote to Sir Hercules Robinson, then Governor of the Cape
and High Commissioner for South Africa, that " It is the opin-

ion of her Majesty's Government that the Orange River is to
be regarded as the north-western frontier of Cape Colony, and
the Government will not give its support to plans for extending British jurisdiction over Great Namaqualand and Damaraland." The war in Damaraland continued through the year
1881, but it does not appear that any measures were taken by
the British Government to ensure the safety of the German
settlers and their property, though inquiry on the subject was
renewed in October.

For another year these territories continued to be no-man's-
land; the British did not claim them, and no one else wanted
them. Then in November, 1882, Lüderitz asked his Government if he might count on protection in the event of his acquiring territory on the Namaqualand coast. Bismarck gave
a promise, subject to the condition that the lands in question
were not claimed by any other Power. Having received the
assurance that the Empire would be behind him, the Bremen
merchant bought from the native chiefs their rights to a stretch
of coastal territory extending from the Orange River to the
bay of Angra Pequena, and duly claimed his country's protection. Other German traders concluded treaties with chiefs
in the remaining part of Namaqualand and also in Damaraland.

In the meantime Bismarck had instructed Count Münster,
the German ambassador in London (February 4, 1883), to inform the British Foreign Office of Lüderitz's plans, and to inquire whether it exercised rights of sovereignty over or was
in a position to give protection to the Angra Pequena region,
and to state that if this were not the case the German Government reserved the right to do so. Lord Granville replied that
before a definite answer could be given it would be necessary
to consult the Cape Government. Bismarck asserted later
that he only approached the British Foreign Office at all in
the matter for the purpose of allowing it to disclaim prior occupation and so to certify his action as regular, and that he
had no idea of inviting the Foreign Office to set up claims on
its own account. The minute of the verbal inquiries made at
the Foreign Office by the German embassy (February 7th)
certainly conveys the impression that if the British Government had been prepared to give protection to Lüderitz's properties Germany would then have been content to stand aside,
for it was said that she had not " the least design to establish

any footing in South Africa." Not only so, but Count Münster's despatch to Berlin (February 26th) reporting later conversations at the Foreign Office admits of no other conclusion that this was Bismarck's original standpoint, though it was soon abandoned for one less passive.

At the outset of the episode, therefore, Bismarck's action was as considerate as the response of the British Foreign Office was fitting and regular. He certainly did not act precipitately, and the presumption is that he was unwilling that Germany's first colonial venture should create friction. For precipitate action there was little opportunity. For nine months Bismarck's inquiries remained unanswered, and it was only after the British Foreign Office had twice been reminded that he was still waiting for an answer (September 10th and November 16th) that Lord Granville broke silence (November 21st). The reply was that although the British Government had claimed sovereignty at two points only of the southwest coast, viz. Whale Bay and the islands lying outside the harbour of Angra Pequena, it was of opinion " that any claim to sovereignty or jurisdiction by a foreign Power between the southern point of Portuguese jurisdiction at latitude 18 and the frontier of Cape Colony would infringe their legitimate rights." In other words, Great Britain did not even now claim prior rights, but only objected to another Power stepping in where she had hitherto not cared to tread. The German Government refused to understand how a country could have legitimate rights in regard to territory over which it simultaneously disclaimed sovereignty, and first in a verbal communication and then in a despatch of December 31st it asked for the production of proof of British title to the disputed territories. It was at this juncture that Bismarck decided to abandon the *rôle* of petitioner for British protection, and asked himself why Germany should not herself appropriate the country and take into her own care those of her subjects who might wish to settle there.

Now a further unfortunate delay of several months was allowed to occur before Berlin again heard from London. For the Foreign Office had handed the matter over to the Colonial Office, and the Colonial Secretary, Lord Derby, was sounding the Cape Ministry as to the propriety of an anticipatory annexation on its own account. During this time Bismarck, to all appearance, was still halting between two opinions on the general question of colonization. More than once he told the Diet that if it did not want colonies, and was not prepared to meet the contingent liabilities, he would certainly not force them upon it, and that it was for the nation and not the Government to give the necessary impetus to practical measures of the kind. " I can only advise you," he said in January, 1884, when asking for a vote for the establishment of mail steamship services to Africa and America, " to accept this Bill and therewith decide to retain and follow colonial policy in the sense in which the Hanseatic pioneers of our foreign trade began it, and in which the Government has taken it under its protection. If, however, you refuse this little vote, I shall accept the implication: you will have said ' No,' and responsibility for the consequences of so doing will rest with you and not with me."

Before he finally made up his mind to comply with Lüderitz's request he caused a memorandum on the whole question of the acquisition and administration of colonies to be prepared by the director of colonial affairs in the Foreign Office, Herr von Kusserow. In this important report, dated April 8, 1884, the view was taken that the Government should proceed by the method of Royal Charters, such as had been granted to British colonial companies — and so lately as in 1881 to the British North Borneo Company — leaving the administration of the territories to the companies and confining the Empire's responsibility to the stationing of ships of war in African waters and the establishment of a sufficient consular system. This view Bismarck adopted, and it became the keynote of his attitude towards all later colonial enterprises.

When the negotiations with Great Britain had lasted a year without reaching a definite issue, Bismarck determined to follow his own course. Herr von Kusserow has related how in April, 1884, he asked his chief whether he should again inquire in London when an answer to the Note of December 31st might be expected, whereupon Bismarck rejoined " Now we will act! " Accordingly he despatched (April 24th) to the German consul-general at Capetown a telegram proclaiming a protectorate over the entire coast between the Orange River and Angra Pequena, and in order that there might be no misunderstanding he simultaneously informed Lord Granville of what he had done.

Up to that time and for another month the Foreign Office

had not replied to Bismarck's letter of December 31st, inviting the production of proofs of the exercise of effective sovereignty. In the event proofs were not produced, because they did not exist. At last the Colonial Office received word from the Cape Government on May 29th that it proposed to undertake the control of the coastline from the Orange River to Whale Bay, including Angra Pequena, ignoring the fact that Germany had already proclaimed a protectorate over the latter region, whereupon the Colonial Office asked the Foreign Office to inform the German Government accordingly. This, however, was not done, for Lord Granville had the good sense to recognize that it was too late to set up claims for which there were not a shadow of justification, and which if advanced were sure to be contested by Germany on the ground of prior right. In a strong despatch of June 10th, marked by the " corporal tone " of which the Austrian Foreign Office had complained twenty years before, Bismarck reproached Lord Granville and Lord Derby with having interpreted his inquiries as an invitation to the British Government to annex the disputed territory, when all he had wished to know was whether Great Britain possessed " demonstrable legal claims or title to occupation in those regions," a question, he said, which might have been " exhaustively answered in a week without referring it to the Cape."

He had a feeling, he said, that Great Britain was not treating Germany as an equal, and he protested against the setting up of a Monroe Doctrine in Africa in the exclusive interest of Great Britain. He instructed Count Münster, therefore, that he must not encourage the idea that Germany was willing to sacrifice her vital interests to her wish for a good understanding with Great Britain, sincere though that wish was. Count Herbert Bismarck, the Chancellor's eldest son, then an official in the Foreign Office in Berlin, was sent to London with these instructions, nominally in order to communicate them with greater emphasis, but in reality to take charge of colonial affairs at the embassy, which was not credited with showing the requisite decision and strength.

The Angra Pequena episode, perplexing enough because of the conflicting claims involved and the fact that on the British side two Departments of State, whose interests, or at least sympathies, were not entirely identical, were concerned, was further complicated by extraneous issues. Cross-currents of a political character were flowing all the time, so that it soon became hopeless to expect that the question involved would be decided solely on its merits. It was in the summer of 1884 that the collective protest of the Powers against the Anglo-Portuguese Congo Treaty of the preceding February was organized, Germany here working cordially together with France. Moreover, Great Britain was at that time hampered by her uncertain position in Egypt, and it rested with Germany to cast a decisive influence either for or against her.

In a despatch of May 5th, forwarded to Count Münster for communication to the British Foreign Secretary, Bismarck gave expression to his favourite maxim " Do ut des," for he said frankly that while he was able and willing to co-operate with Great Britain on the Egyptian question there must be a *quid pro quo*, and it must be offered in the domain of colonial affairs. Later Bismarck complained in the Diet that he had received no reply to this despatch, which for better effect he produced to the affronted deputies. Lord Granville promptly rejoined that his Government had not answered it because it had not been received. Inquiry brought to light the fact that Bismarck had himself countermanded it.[1]

It was at this time that Germany first raised the question of the cession of Heligoland, the island commanding the Elbe estuary which Great Britain took from Denmark in 1807 as a prize of war and was secured by the Treaty of Kiel in 1814. On May 17th Count Münster informed Lord Granville that Bismarck was wishful to construct a canal connecting the North Sea with the Baltic, and hinted that as Heligoland would be the necessary key to such a plan its reversion to Germany was greatly to be desired. " It was a place of no importance to us in its present state, whereas it would be of im-

[1] Bismarck read the despatch to the succeeding British ambassador in Berlin, Sir Edward Malet, on January 24, 1885. "This despatch," the ambassador wrote to Lord Granville, "was a very remarkable one. It stated the great importance which the Prince attached to the colonial question, and also to the friendship of Germany and England. It pointed out that in the commencement of German colonial enterprise England might render signal service to Germany, and said that for such service Germany would use her best endeavours in England's behalf in questions affecting her interests nearer home. It pressed these considerations with arguments to show the mutual advantage which such understanding would produce, and it then proceeded to instruct Count Münster to say if it could not be effected the result would be that Germany would seek from France the assistance which she had failed to obtain from England, and would draw closer to her on the same lines on which she now endeavoured to meet England."

mense importance to Germany, to ourselves, and the whole world, if it was made into a good harbour of refuge. This would be an expensive work for us to undertake. We could not be expected to go to such expense, whereas Germany would be quite ready to undertake it. Prince Bismarck wished to cut a canal into the Baltic, which also would be a great advantage to us, as the most powerful maritime nation of the world. But Heligoland, which, of course, would be always open to our ships, would be a necessary key to such a plan." [1]

The idea that Heligoland might one day have to change hands had already occurred to Lord Granville himself. He relates that twelve years before he had consulted the War Office and the Admiralty as to the strategical value of the island for England, and that while the War Office was indifferent, the Admiralty was strongly convinced of its importance. Now he discreetly professed surprise at Bismarck's proposal, but did not commit himself to an opinion one way or the other, and it was understood that for the present the matter should be allowed to simmer. Nevertheless, an untoward question had been opened. [2]

In the complicated political situation then existing considerations of policy weighed at least equally with those of equity in deciding the attitude of the British Government. On June 17th the Colonial Office by telegraph forbade the Cape Government to adopt any further measure in regard to Angra Pequena, and on the 21st the German ambassador was informed that the British Cabinet had decided to acknowledge the German protectorate. Later, Germany extended her sovereignty to the frontier of Angola, with the exception of Whale Bay, and this further claim was likewise recognized. Even now,

[1] Memorandum of Lord Granville, quoted in *Life and Letters of the Second Lord Granville*, vol. ii., p. 351.

[2] In January, 1885, while a second colonial dispute, regarding New Guinea, was in course of adjustment, Bismarck, through his mouthpiece in London, raised the question again. He laid stress once more on the advantages to British shipping and commerce of the harbour to be constructed, but now no disguise was made of the intention to strongly fortify the island should it change hands. Once more Lord Granville treated the question, on Bismarck's well-known principle, "dilatorily." It was, however, his opinion at that time that "the cession would be unpopular in itself," and that Liberal Ministers would not be the best people to make it, but "it sometimes occurs to me whether it would not be a price worth paying if it would secure a perfectly satisfactory end to the Egyptian financial mess." (*Ibid.*, vol. ii., pp. 425 and 362.) It fell to another Foreign Secretary to give the final answer, for in June, 1885, the Gladstone Ministry fell and the first administration of Lord Salisbury succeeded.

however, when it had decided to give way, the Foreign Office succeeded in doing a wise thing in an unwise way. As Germany was already in possession of Angra Pequena, it would at least have been prudent to have made a virtue of necessity and accepted the situation gracefully. Instead of so doing, the Foreign Office on July 19th, with as little knowledge of Bismarck, as before, formally notified its willingness to acknowledge German sovereignty, subject to the condition that Germany would give an undertaking not to establish a penal settlement on the coast. Seeing that the transportation of law-breakers to the colonies was a British notion, though then for some years abandoned, the demand, to say the least, showed a singular want of tact.

Bismarck gave just the answer which the Foreign Office would presumably have given in the same circumstances. After recalling the fact that the German Government had already given verbal assurances that it had no intention to establish penal settlements, he described as " extraordinary " the proposal to impose upon Germany conditions as to how she should exercise her own rights. He refused to give the undertaking sought, since he did not recognize England's title to ask for it. On September 22nd the British Government finally accepted the German annexation unconditionally, and received no thanks for a surrender which might just as well have been made magnanimously more than a year before, with lasting benefit to the two countries concerned. Lord Granville had forgotten that wise maxim of his predecessor, Lord Clarendon, " When people dare not say ' No ' they had better say ' Yes ' with a good grace." At this time the Fiji question was also settled according to Germany's wish, for a mixed commission was at last appointed to consider the claims which Bismarck had been pressing for ten years.

Just before this (September 17th) the Cape Government had sent home a final protest that " no weight has been attached to the wishes of the colony with regard to the coast line from the Orange River northward, notwithstanding the offer of the colony to undertake all responsibility and cost in connection with the coast." It also urged the Government to annex the remaining unappropriated portions (i.e. the fertile interior) of Damaraland and Namaqualand, a suggestion to which Lord Derby discreetly replied (November 11th) that " it would not be in accordance with international comity to annex the territory immediately adjacent to the existing German limits."

In a letter of December 4th to Sir Hercules Robinson, Lord Derby did his utmost to pacify wounded colonial feeling, and now stated frankly that to have further pressed a claim to the South-west Coast and its hinterland would have been unjustifiable. He reminded the Governor that the dispute related to "a strip of territory to which the Queen of England had no sufficient legal title, and in which German trading and missionary interests were apparently more considerable than those of her own subjects. Great Britain, which already possesses large tracts of unoccupied territory, could not fairly grudge to a friendly Power a country difficult of development, with regard to which it might have been said that we had never thought it worth acquiring until it seemed to be wanted by our neighbour." Germany's first acquisition gave her an empire of over 300,000 square miles.

Deep and widespread resentment was caused in Germany by the attitude of the British Government, and the colonial movement immediately won hosts of ardent friends in circles which hitherto had been either indifferent or hostile to it. In a speech in the Diet Bismarck charged Great Britain with unparalleled egoism in claiming in Africa all territories which other Powers had not appropriated, again protested scornfully against the notion of England setting up a Monroe Doctrine in relation to that continent, and administered to the Foreign Office the severest reproach which could be made by one Government against another in the words: "We have not been fairly treated by England."

The unfavourable impression created by the behaviour of the Foreign Office — its unbusinesslike delays, its prevarications, and finally the belated counter-claim to a sovereignty which beforetime had been explicitly disavowed — was not confined to Germany. In England, too, there were those who felt that British diplomacy had not been shown at its best, and that the parliamentary head of the Foreign Office, himself the soul of honour, reasonableness, and suavity, had given way too much to the mute, invisible Palmerstons of his permanent staff, in comparison with whom all but the strongest and most independent-minded of Foreign Secretaries are as reeds shaken in the wind.

The events in South-west Africa were the signal for a general scramble for territory in a continent which was now ceasing, far too suddenly for its own good or for the peace of the world, to be a dark patch on the map, and to give scope merely for scientific expedition and missionary enterprise. German agents were already busy on all parts of the east coast and far in the interior, and now they began to extend their attentions to the north-west. The ambitious Lüderitz came near to repeating on the east coast the same success which he had achieved on the west. The project for the peaceful penetration and ultimate absorption of the Transvaal by Germany, which had been pressed upon Bismarck unsuccessfully in 1876, was now revived in another form. Negotiations of a more or less formal character were carried on between German agents and the Transvaal Government. They went so far, indeed, that a Boer deputation visited Berlin and was accorded an almost royal reception. The idea was seriously entertained that Germany should conclude a treaty with the Transvaal under which German emigration should be diverted to that country; closer relationships were to be left to settle themselves, and it was part of the design that a company should acquire Delagoa Bay or St. Lucia Bay, the one in Portuguese territory and the other in Zululand (as yet not under British protection), and build a railway from the coast direct to Pretoria. Lüderitz was also scheming to gain for Germany Pondoland, the neck of territory running inland between Cape Colony and Natal, and he had been prospecting in Mashonaland, in the interior.

At that time the future of British dominion in South Africa hung in the balance, and a turn of the scales might have changed the course of world-history. It was clearly the hope of Germany's agents to drive a wedge far inland from the east coast, so wrecking the dream of a composite Brito-Dutch empire. In regard to Delagoa Bay there was little danger, since Great Britain had obtained from Portugal a right of pre-emption in respect of it when in 1875 the territory was awarded to that Power as the result of arbitration. Zululand, however, was only lost to German influence by a miscarriage of plans. While Lüderitz was still negotiating with Dinizulu with a view to the establishment of a protectorate over the country, the British Government interposed, and on December 18, 1884, the British flag was hoisted at St. Lucia Bay. Almost simultaneously Sir Charles Warren detected the German-Boer plans in

Bechuanaland and frustated them. Early in 1885 he ejected the Boers who had trekked into the country and annexed the entire territory to the British Crown.

One result of the first class with British interests was that Bismarck's later colonial aims were not pursued so openly as in the case of Angra Pequena, and well-founded irritation was caused in England by the circumstances in which Germany acquired her next foothold in Africa. Here, again, the British Government was guilty of procrastination and want of foresight. On April 20, 1884, the Foreign Office was asked to give assistance to an expedition to West Africa which was to be undertaken on behalf of the German Government by Dr. Nachtigal. The communication made to Lord Granville was to the effect that Dr. Nachtigal had been instructed to " complete the information now in the possession of the Foreign Office in Berlin on the state of German commerce on that coast," and to " conduct on behalf of the Imperial Government negotiations connected with certain questions."

The latter words aroused no suspicion at the Foreign Office, and the desired courtesies were accordingly shown. When the British Government later told the story of the movements of the Nachtigal expedition, it claimed that it had for some time been preparing to annex the Cameroons. Nevertheless, official action to that end does not appear to have been expedited on the receipt of the German message: the Consul accredited to the Cameroons country was then absent on leave, and a month passed before he was directed to return to his post.

The instructions (dated May 19th) actually given to Dr. Nachtigal gave the first place to the acquisition in the name of the Empire of territory between the Niger delta and Gaboon, particularly the portions opposite the island of Fernando Po, in the Bay of Biafra, west from the mouth of the Cameroons River as far as Cape St. John; but Little Popo was also to be visited with the same aim in view. Nachtigal arrived off the west coast early in July, and promptly annexed Togoland and thereafter the Cameroons.

When later in the month the British Consul, Mr. Hewett — whose despatch to the scene had been delayed by haggling at the Treasury over his expenses — arrived on the Cameroons River the German flag had been hoisted for five days. Nevertheless, he was still in time to secure for Great Britain Victoria, in Ambos Bay (where the English Baptists had been settled since 1858), and other minor points, and later he proclaimed a protectorate over the still unclaimed coastline from the Rio del Rey to Lagos, including the Niger delta and the Oil Rivers. Bismarck had unquestionably engaged in sharp practice, and he admitted it, but pleaded in excuse that the Angra Pequena episode had taught him that his only chance of securing these desirable possessions lay in keeping his design secret until it had been executed. It was even made a grievance in Germany that the British Consul had prevented this colonial orchard, which had literally been planted and grown by English gardeners, from being further pilfered.

On the other hand, feeling in England was irate, and the Government was blamed at least as much as the astute German Chancellor. Lord Granville wrote at a later date (January 20, 1885) that if his Government had known that Dr. Nachtigal was bent on annexation it " would have exchanged opinions with the German Government, which must have prevented the present state of things ": in other words, had he suspected that a raid upon the stable was intended he would assuredly have locked the door. Public resentment was increased when the fact came to light that though the chiefs of the Cameroons had since 1879 been pressing for British protection their appeals had been disregarded. It was in vain that Lord Granville pleaded that the Government had intended to annex the country and would have done so had Germany only given it time; the only fact about which the public cared was that it had not done so, though there had been ample opportunity and justification. The boundaries of Togoland and the Cameroons as permanently fixed gave to these protectorates an area of 30,000 and 191,000 square miles respectively.

By this time Bismarck had formally accepted his new mission of colonial empire-builder, and for a man of his combative nature to meet with resistance meant to go forward all the more resolutely. Nevertheless, he still clung to the idea that Germany should colonize in her own way and not like the older nations. In a speech in the Diet on June 26, 1884, reviewing the progress already made, he had laid down clearly the aims which he had in view. He had no intention of colonizing with Germans; he conceived of protectorates given up to plantation and trading settlements worked with native labour, with German planters and merchants at the head, and with no more bureaucratic administration than could be avoided. He had in mind the early English merchant adventurers; the Empire was to secure for its traders suitable fields of operations, and then to leave them as far as possible to their own devices.

Before the year 1884 was out British susceptibilities were again excited by German activity in the Western Pacific. From the middle of the century, and in some cases from an earlier date, German firms had had trading stations and factories in all the important groups of islands in that region, and it has been stated that the acquisition of part of New Guinea was one of the projects put forward most persistently by the earlier imperialists in the course of their propagandism for the colonial movement. The Dutch had already obtained the western portion of this island, while British influence was represented by a land company to which its Government had granted a charter in November, 1881. Ever since the premature proposal of the Berlin bankers of 1880 the Governments of Australia had urgently implored the Colonial Office in London to annex without delay all that was still unappropriated of the island, and failing to move it, the Queensland Ministry in April, 1883, annexed the eastern part of the island on its own account, an act repudiated by the Imperial Government as both *ultra vires* and impolitic. Nevertheless, in December of the same year an intercolonial convention, meeting at Sydney, adopted resolutions in favour of the annexation by Great Britain of all New Guinea (except where the Dutch already had rights) and the adjacent islands, and also declaring that the further acquisition by any other Power of territory in the Western Pacific south of the Equator would be highly detrimental to the security and well-being of the British possessions in Australasia.

In Germany these resolutions were interpreted as tantamount to the declaration of another Monroe Doctrine in favour of Great Britain in the Pacific, and they led to protests both there and amongst Germans settled in the South Seas, who, remembering Fiji, promptly claimed the protection of their Government. At this juncture the financial *consortium* formed the New Guinea Company, and in May despatched an agent with a well-equipped expedition to the island with instructions to acquire such territories as were unappropriated

on the North-east Coast and in the New Britain Archipelago.
Simultaneously (June 27th) the German Government was requested to give to the prospective possessions of the Company
imperial protection, and this was promised.

The Colonial Cabinets were already in communication with
the home Government with a view to the annexation of the
south coast.   Now they wanted for Australia all that was left
beyond the Dutch territory.   Once more feeling ran high in
both countries, and the position became for a time critical owing to a division in the British Cabinet, one section, represented by the Prime Minister and the Foreign and Colonial
Secretaries, favouring a fair division between Great Britain
and Germany, another being opposed to compromise.

The New Guinea episode, following so closely upon the Angra Pequena and Cameroons disputes, marked the climax of a
crescendo of misunderstanding and ill-feeling between the two
nations.   Than Bismarck no modern statesman was readier
to fight for what he conceived to be his country's rights, or
had a keener appreciation of the principle of reciprocity; and
he was, no doubt, honestly persuaded at that time that Great
Britain intended to pursue a dog-in-the-manger policy in relation to German colonization and would carry that policy just
as far as she dare with impunity.   To a representative of the
British Colonial Office who had an interview with him on December 24, 1884, he confessed keen disappointment that Great
Britain should have sought to obstruct Germany in the Pacific
as she had done in Africa.   " He said that we had immense possessions in that part of the world, that we had already more
land than we could colonize for years to come, . . . and that
it was not worthy of us to grudge Germany a settlement on
the coast of New Guinea, separated from Australia by the islands and the south shore which we had taken."   He added
that " up to two years ago he had done everything he could to
facilitate British policy in Egypt and elsewhere, but for some
time past he has been treated in a different manner by England, whose actions do not accord with her professions."

Resentful at the obstructive spirit which he had to encounter,
he now for once put away all restraint, and the political Press,
taking its cue as ever from Ministerial hints, did its best to fan
the fires of national ire.   It was unfortunate for Great Britain that at that critical time she lost by death (August 25th)

the services in Berlin of Lord Ampthill (Lord Odo Russell), who had been ambassador to the German Court for thirteen years and had been on terms of exceptional friendship with the fastidious Chancellor. Russell was apt to hold too tenaciously to opinions once formed, yet if he failed, as he certainly did, to keep abreast of the march of the colonial movement in Germany or the change in the German Government's attitude towards it, he was able to exercise a moderating influence upon the official relations of the two countries at a time of special difficulty. Often Bismarck reposed in him confidences which did not fall to other members of the Diplomatic Corps, and if when the London Foreign Office showered upon him its interminable despatches he at times made the British ambassador the vent of his ill-humours, the cordial *rapport* between the two was advantageous for both countries.[1]

Towards the end of the year Bismarck published a collection of despatches — a new departure in German Foreign Office usage — telling the story of the colonial acquisitions and the accompanying disputes, whereupon the British Foreign Office, in self-justification, published a White Paper covering the same ground. Early in 1885 Bismarck followed with a series of inflammatory speeches in the Diet, in which he laid to the charge of the British Government an accumulation of wrongs sufficient, if true, to have justified any measure of reproach. Soreness over the colonial question was increased by grievances of a more personal kind, and because he spoke under aggravation he spoke neither wisely nor well. A charge that a certain despatch to the German Government had been published in a Blue-book before it reached his hands appears to have been true, and the rebuke which the indiscretion received may have been deserved. The worst of his grievances, however, were imaginary, and the worst of his accusations unfounded. He alleged that English consular officers, missionaries, and traders in the Cameroons had incited the natives to rebellion, yet failed to produce a particle of evidence to support the charge. He made it a grievance that an English corvette had omitted to salute the German flag in Cameroons waters, although its captain had had no notification of the new

[1] " At Berlin he was invaluable through his thorough understanding of Bismarck's character and methods, and through his tact in managing *the sensitive side* of the all-powerful Chancellor " (Lord Goschen, quoted in *Life of Lord Goschen,* by the Hon. A. D. Elliot, vol. i., p. 209).

protectorate. He went so far as to charge the Foreign Office with having neglected to reply to an important despatch — the despatch which, as subsequent inquiry showed, Bismarck at the last moment had countermanded.

Still more Bismarck took offence because Lord Granville had represented him as having advised the British Government to occupy Egypt. He denied having given any such advice — at least, he added, without reference to existing treaties. Lord Granville, with a restraint which was misunderstood in Germany, accepted the disavowal and explained that Bismarck's words must have been misunderstood. Nevertheless, that the advice had been given cannot be doubted, though it may not have been discreet to disclose the fact. But the crowning sin of the British Foreign Office was that it had sent him during the preceding summer no fewer than 128 despatches, containing between 700 and 800 pages. " During all the twenty-three years I have been a Minister," he said, " we have not received so many from all the other Governments together " (March 2, 1885).

Bismarck did not stop at ill-humour and hard words. His resentment against England coloured his relationships towards other countries, and particularly France and Russia. During 1884 Germany's attitude towards France improved just in the measure that her attitude towards England became strained, and France was all the readier to welcome Bismarck's advances since England had lost popularity in that quarter as well. For some years it had been his policy to support the Republic from a belief that the republican form of government would disqualify France from being the ally of monarchies. Now he took up the attitude of the disinterested and generous friend who sought only his neighbour's good. It was said that at that time he was the most popular man in Paris. He was able to tell the Diet on January 10, 1885 : " With France we have not for many years — I may truly say since the time before 1866 — been on so good a footing as now. This is due to the wise and moderate government in France, which values the blessings of peace as highly as we do." It was also due, in some degree at least, to the shadow which had been cast upon Anglo-French relationships by the Egyptian question, and to the susceptibility of the Ferry Ministry to German attentions.

Bismarck, as we have seen, had threatened that if England refused to assist his colonial schemes he would turn to France. This he did, and the first tangible result was the wrecking of the Anglo-Portuguese treaty relating to the Congo which had been concluded in the previous February and thereafter submitted to the judgment of the Powers. However tainted his motives in this episode may have been, the results were unquestionably of great advantage to Central Africa and to civilization. By this treaty Great Britain had agreed to recognize Portugal's claim to the mouth of the Congo, as defined, while Portugal in return undertook to give equal treatment to the subjects of all nations travelling or residing therein, to maintain the river as a free waterway, subject to strictly limited dues, to co-operate with Great Britain in suppressing the slave trade, and to grant to that country certain contingent territorial concessions. The British Government wished the river to be regulated by an international commission, but to this Portugal objected, and the treaty accordingly proposed to set up an Anglo-Portuguese commission to execute the provisions of the treaty.

It has been suggested that on the part of Lord Granville this agreement was, in spirit and purpose, a measure of retaliation upon Bismarck and Germany. Not only is the suggestion refuted by the fact that the negotiations leading to the treaty were opened before Germany had claimed territory in Africa or anywhere else, but it does not harmonize in the least with Lord Granville's straightforward character. The assumption that an agreement of such magnitude could be arbitrarily concluded by two Powers without any consultation with the rest of the world may surprise the present generation, but there is no justification whatever for doubting that Lord Granville acted in perfect good faith, while there is clear documentary evidence that he endeavoured so to frame the treaty as to justify the hope that the other Powers would be able to accept it without difficulty. During the negotiations he had never concealed from the Portuguese Government his view that the Governments were not engaged in a merely dual arrangement, and that if an agreement was to ensue it must be one which the other Powers would be willing to accept. " It is obvious," he wrote on March 15, 1883, " that there could be no advantage in concluding a treaty which would not be accepted by other

Powers whose acceptance would be indispensable before it could come into operation."

No sooner did the terms of the treaty become known than protests were raised on all sides, and Bismarck made himself the spokesman of the opposition, declaring roundly that arrangements so far-going, made over the heads of the other European Powers, could not be allowed to stand. It was in vain that Lord Granville pointed out (June 30th) that fourteen years before, during the Franco-Prussian War, Germany had already recognized Portugal's sovereign rights in the Lower Congo region, that but for Great Britain those rights would long ago have been asserted more positively, and that the proposed treaty subjected them to important limitations. Bismarck refused to recognize a transaction in which he had had no part, and the treaty was abandoned. Portugal had suggested an international conference, and he appropriated that idea.

Instead of consulting the British Government as to how the idea should be developed, he now approached the Ferry Cabinet and proposed that Germany and France should take the question in hand. During August, Baron de Courcel, the French ambassador, was with Bismarck at Varzin, and there the basis of the proposed conference was agreed upon. With scant courtesy, without prior consultation of any kind, Bismarck in October informed the British Foreign Office of the proposal of the German and French Governments to call the Powers together and asked whether it would be willing to cooperate. Only on request did he vouchsafe the information that the conference was intended to deliberate upon the questions of freedom of commerce in the Congo river territories, freedom of navigation on the Congo and the Niger, and the conditions under which new annexations on the coast of Africa were in future to be considered effective. An invitation given in these circumstances was mortifying, yet after satisfying himself by further inquiry that the Powers were not to be asked simply to ratify an agreement already drawn up, but that all would enter the conference free and unpledged, Lord Granville fell in with the proposal, upon which the conference was convened jointly by Germany and France.

In spite of its unpromising origin the Congo conference was a great success and its results were beneficial for the future of a large part of the African continent. Plenipotentiaries of thirteen European Powers (including the International Association of the Congo) and the United States met in Berlin from November 15th to February 26th following, and Bismarck both opened and closed the deliberations, but took no other direct part. The decisions of the conference were embodied in the General Act of February 26, 1885, which enacted freedom of trade in the Congo basin (as defined), prohibited the slave trade and the transit of slaves in the Congo territories, provided for the neutrality of these territories in case of war, introduced the principle of free navigation on the Congo and Niger, allowed the levying of river dues for administrative purposes only, laid down the conditions on which future annexations on the coasts of Africa should be deemed to be effective, and made provision for the territories coming under the Act remaining neutral in the event of any Power exercising sovereignty therein being at war.

France worked hand in hand with Germany throughout the proceedings, and for reward came out of the conference with an enlarged Congo territory; Portugal obtained some approximation to the frontiers at the mouth of the Congo which she had claimed; while the African International Association, King Leopold of Belgium's private enterprise, now became known as the Free Congo State, and as such received general recognition from the Powers of Europe, following Germany's lead. The Act thus left the Congo basin under the sovereignty of three States as before. From the conference Great Britain and Germany derived no territorial gain, nor yet special advantages of any kind. The former had, on the whole, no reason to be dissatisfied with the results, for the principle of the " open door " for which she had always contended was asserted and she was left with a now acknowledged supremacy in the Lower Niger. The principal gain to Germany, next to the security of equal treatment offered to her trade, was that the part played by her in this first great colonial conference of the Powers brought her into the full current of colonial politics.

At the closing session Bismarck used words which just thirty years later were to acquire a sombre significance.

" The special conditions in which you have opened up wide tracts of territory to commercial enterprise," he said, " have required special guarantees for the preservation of peace and public order. The evils of war would assume a specially fatal character if the natives were led to take sides in disputes between the civilized Powers. After careful consideration of the dangers which might attend such contingencies, in the interests of commerce and civilization you have sought to devise means to withdraw a large part of the African continent from the oscillations of general politics, and to confine the rivalry of nations therein to the peaceful pursuits of trade and industry."

The friction between Germany and Great Britain might have continued indefinitely had not an event occurred which abruptly disturbed Bismarck's calculations. The Ferry Cabinet, discredited by the disastrous Tonquin adventure, was tottering to its fall — the end came on March 30, 1885, owing to a hostile vote of the House of Deputies — and it was ever Bismarck's way to make sure of new friends before he cast off the old. The imminence of a reactionary Government in France, with the consequent uncertainty of his prospects there, sobered him and recalled him to the world of realities. Was France, after all, so certain a friend that he should desire to make England a certain enemy? On reflection he decided not, and the near event showed that his second thoughts were better than his first, for within a year came the Cabinet of M. Freycinet, bringing into prominence General Boulanger and new schemes of revenge.

Only a few days after the most violent of his parliamentary speeches on England's perfidy the political world heard with wonder that the Chancellor had again sent his son, Count Herbert, to London on a special mission, charged with power to adjust the outstanding causes of friction. The British Cabinet was still divided on the question of no surrender or compromise on the question of New Guinea, and it was due to Mr. Gladstone's dominating influence that resistance was offered to the pressure of Australian opinion, too far removed from the centre of disturbance to appreciate the danger which surrender to it might have involved. For him foreign politics mattered more than colonial, and the question of Egypt transcended in importance that of New Guinea. Assured, therefore, that Germany would make no trouble on the Nile if Great Britain was accommodating in the Pacific, he threw his influence strongly on the side of accommodation.[1] Writing to Lord

1 Replying to a letter from Lord Granville to the effect that "our Press

Granville on March 6th, the day after a talk on the absorbing question with Count Herbert Bismarck, who had told him that there could be no cause of quarrel between Germany and Great Britain "nearer home" (i.e. in Egypt) if the British Government were friendly on the colonial question, Mr. Gladstone said: "I do hope that you are pressing forward the Pauncefote settlement of the North Coast of New Guinea, which seems to me the main or only point remaining. It is really impossible to exaggerate the importance of getting out of the way the bar to the Egyptian settlement. These words, strong as they are, are in my opinion words of truth and soberness; as, if we cannot wind up at once these small colonial controversies, we shall before we are many weeks older find it to our cost." [1]

An understanding favourable to German claims was arrived at; Bismarck was appeased; and while he hastened to relieve the tension of public opinion in Germany, the British Premier and Foreign Secretary sealed the pact of peace by conciliatory speeches from their places in Parliament.

"There appears to be a suspicion in Germany," Lord Granville said (March 6th), "that we do not give full recognition of the present position of that great nation. I believe, on the contrary, that there is no country in which not only politicians but all classes of the population appreciate more and with greater pleasure the important position which Germany has taken in Europe since its unification."

Mr. Gladstone endorsed his colleague's utterances a few days later (March 12th) in the House of Commons in memorable words. After stating that if the countermanded despatch of May 5, 1884, had been communicated to his Government it would have received the friendly attention which it deserved, the orator added: "If Germany is to become a colonizing Power, all I say is, 'God speed her!' She becomes our ally and partner in the execution of the great purposes of Providence for the advantage of mankind." Germany at that moment was not thinking so much of the purposes of Providence and the advantage of mankind as of new markets for her mer-

has not been mollified by the *pièces justicatives* on Angra Pequena," Mr. Gladstone wrote: "As far as I can see there is a wild and irrational spirit abroad to which I, for one, do not feel at all disposed to give in" (December 26, 1884).

[1] *Life of the Second Earl Granville,* vol. ii., pp. 431-2.

chandise, yet the words evoked in that country a warm response.

In its final form the New Guinea agreement (April 25th–29th) gave to Germany a larger slice of the island than she had expected or perhaps could reasonably have claimed. She was assigned the northern portion between 141° of latitude east and 8° of longitude south, with half of the unexplored interior, and all the islands lying off the north coast, while the south of the island and the narrow eastern end went to Great Britain. German New Guinea was renamed Kaiser Wilhelms-Land. The New Britain islands — henceforth called Bismarck Archipelago — also remained with Germany. A further addition of some 90,000 square miles was thus made to her quickly acquired colonial empire.

Unquestionably the colonial rivalries of those days dislocated and disharmonized the relations between Germany and Great Britain for a long time. It is possible, and even probable, that they contained the germ of all later mistrust and misunderstanding. Germany never forgot that she obtained hardly one of her early protectorates without having first to overcome resistance from the British Government, and that in nearly every case this opposition was based, not upon any claim of prior occupation, but upon the tacit assumption that territories adjacent to British possessions, which had escaped appropriation, could not properly be claimed by any other country. A pretension of this kind may prove convenient for a great imperial Power so long as it passes undisputed, but when other countries challenge its equity, trouble cannot fail to arise. It is hardly too much to say that the strongest effective impulse to German colonization came from England. Bismarck had entered the field warily, haltingly, and against his will; it was only when he found himself face to face with opposition that his pugnacious spirit was aroused and he threw himself into the competition for territory, wherever it was to be found, with the joy of the combatant who loves the contest even more than the prize.

Is it possible to draw up a balance-sheet of rights and wrongs for that first unhappy period of Anglo-German colonial contention? An attempt is worth while, since the questions and issues which provoked the discords of 1884 and 1885 became the pivot upon which British policy towards Germany swung and swayed throughout the following generation. During all that time rivalry over imperial expansion continued in one form or another, and the early misunderstandings merely proved the precursors of far deeper and acuter antipathies. It is obvious that the question whether our balance-sheet will be a fair one or not will depend almost wholly upon what is allowed to figure on the two sides of the account. Thus England did not recognize as legitimate grievances which were very real to Germany, and Germany scouted as arrogant claims which to England were so well founded as to be entirely beyond dispute. There was a difference in equation also. Thus a tract of barren territory which in Germany's eyes possessed little intrinsic value was to England a vital link in the chain of Empire. It was plain to all impartial observers that the two nations — and not only their Governments — viewed the questions at issue from different and irreconcilable standpoints; the standpoint of England being that of the early prospector who had pegged out his rich claims and resented the presence of intruding neighbours, the standpoint of Germany that of the late arriver, determined to have a fair share of what had hitherto been no-man's-land. Hence when England projected further acquisitions Germany called it greed, and when Germany set eyes on unappropriated territories England accused her of intrigue. To discover a *modus vivendi* for nations which confronted each other in such a mood was at the best no easy task, and neither the stereotyped formulas of the British Foreign Office nor the brusque ways for which the German Foreign Office had made itself famous under Bismarck's strong and masterful guidance tended to resolve misunderstandings which were due to entirely new problems and situations.

Moreover, if it was difficult for Bismarck to appreciate the embarrassed position of British statesmen, called upon suddenly, owing to inacquaintance with the course which German colonial endeavours had been following for decades, to adapt themselves to the idea that Germany was just as free to take unappropriated territories as any other State, it was no less difficult for these statesmen to strike a fair and safe compromise between the claims of the colonies and the need of remaining on amicable working terms with a Great Power which at that time was able to make their path either rough or smooth in Egypt. Lord Granville in particular was severely handicapped, since while as Foreign Secretary he was compelled to view the political situation as a whole and to test every act of policy by its probable effect upon international relations, he was throughout the controversy pressed unduly by his colleague at the Colonial Office and by the Australian Governments, regardless of these wider and larger considerations. Bismarck himself admitted that " the sentiments towards us of Lord Granville are more benevolent than the policy of the English Colonial Office."

There were also personal differences of temperament, which were admirably reflected by the statesmen who bore the brunt of the diplomatic tourney on behalf of their countries; on the one hand, the plain blunt man Bismarck, able to give friendship or enmity as might be desired, in either case amply and heartily; on the other hand, the polished courtier Granville, typifying the dignity and restraint of the English ruling class, the guardian of the national ice-house, the Foreign Office, whose temperature might not be raised on any pretext, on pain of the melting of its frosty traditions.

In its parliamentary and public relations the history of the British Foreign Office, the most Conservative in the world, is a history of great statesmen and great gentlemen; but in the colonial controversies of 1884 and 1885 its proved and predominant traditions of strength and firmness, combined with equity and measure, were not conspicuous. Politics, and above all foreign politics, to be carried on successfully, can never be an affair of all taking on one side and no giving. The statesman who in any conflict of interest knows how long it is safe to resist and when it is wise to yield, who holds his hand when he has won enough for prudence, and is content for safety's sake to forgo the extreme advantage, is the one who invariably gains most, or at least most that is worth gaining, in the end. The golden rule of moderation in all things was not observed in the dealings of the Foreign Office with the young and rising Power which thirty years ago aspired for the first time to a place in the sun.

While, however, the major part of the blame for the disharmonies of those years must be attributed to his subordinates and to an obstinate official tradition, it must be added that Lord Granville's constitutional indisposition to face responsibility, and his propensity for letting difficulties be settled by proxy or ignoring them altogether, were also at fault. " I see every day," he told Lord Clarendon (January 5, 1852), just after he succeeded Lord Palmerston, " the proofs in the Foreign Office of the extraordinary ability and the little follies of my great predecessor." But at least Lord Palmerston never feared to face responsibility, of which, as a rule, he preferred to take upon himself too much rather than too little. It was not lack of moral force, but rather intellectual inertia, that caused Lord Granville to leave important decisions to others or, what was worse, to evade them altogether.[1] No one can study the diplomatic reports relating to these colonial disputes without coming to the conclusion that on each occasion the British case was prejudiced as much by irresolution, lack of clear purpose, and procrastination as by inherent weaknesses, though these were present.

But further, once again, as twenty years before, the British Government was not particularly well served by the watchmen on the observation towers abroad. Many years before Lord Odo Russell had formed the opinion, on information which at the time was no doubt well founded, that Bismarck did not want colonies and that the German Diet was indifferent to them, and to this opinion he clung long after circumstances had changed and the facts were entirely against him.[2] Altogether he appears to have taken the colonial movement too lightly and, ignoring the growing force of public opinion, to have treated as a caprice what was a genuine national aspiration. Lord Lyons, in Paris, who knew little about German politics that did not filter to him through the medium of his

[1] See on this subject the testimony of Lord Cromer in *Modern Egypt,* vol. i., pp. 392–3, note; also *Life of Lord Goschen,* vol. i., p. 225.

[2] Lord Odo Russell appears to have kept the Foreign Office in this belief long after the justification for it had disappeared. In a despatch of February 7, 1885, to the ambassador's successor, Sir Edward Malet, Lord Granville wrote: " Until the receipt of a report from Lord Ampthill (Lord Odo Russell) of the 14th June last (1884), of conversations he had had with Prince Bismarck, and up to the interviews which I had about the same time with Count Herbert Bismarck, I was under the belief that the Chancellor was personally opposed to German colonization. The reports of Lord Ampthill were continuously and strongly to that effect, and on the 15th March, 1884, his Excellency, referring to the agitation on the subject among the shipping and commercial classes in Germany, stated that it was well known that the Prince was absolutely opposed to their ardent desire for the acquisition of colonies by Germany, and was determined to combat and oppose their growing influence."

Berlin colleague, nevertheless volunteered to Lord Granville, in the midst of his painful grappling with the perplexities of a new and thorny problem (January 20, 1885), the opinion that Bismarck's colony schemes were " childish and founded as much on spite against England as on any real expectation of advantage to Germany "— an opinion wholly at variance with the facts, so far as relates to the genesis of the German colonial endeavours, and far below the mark of a mind so acute and usually so cautious and well balanced. It would have been more prudent to have assumed that the German Government understood its own business and was the best judge of its own policy, and Lord Granville in particular would have done well to have kept in mind his remark to Lord Odo Russell on November 27, 1873, that he did not feel " the slightest jealousy of the Germans acquiring colonial possessions." After all, it should not have needed great foresight to convince British statesmen that a country with a prolific population, a rapidly growing maritime trade, with incipient but very decided naval ambitions, a country also which, as we have seen, had taken an important part in African exploration, would not be willing to forgo for all time a share in the unappropriated parts of the earth.

In fairness to the British Foreign Office and its head, however, it must be added that they only represented, withal in a tempered way, the hostile sentiment of the British nation at large. In the heat of a controversy which offered peculiar scope for appeal to prejudice and passion one English statesman, indeed, distinguished himself by moderation, soberness, and sound common sense: it was the statesman who a few years later was destined to voice, as no other of his day, the true imperialistic spirit of his countrymen and race. " It would be humiliating indeed," Mr. Chamberlain said at Birmingham on January 1, 1885, " if England, the mistress of half the world, were to be driven to imitate the conduct of an angry scold, and indulge in a fit of hysterical passion because Germany had snapped up some unconsidered trifles of territory which we have hitherto not thought it worth while to acquire. If it be necessary, as I think it may be, to review our foreign and colonial policy in the light of recent events, let us face the altered circumstances of the problem in the spirit of full-grown men and not with the pettish outcry of frightened children."

Words of wisdom like these urgently needed saying at the time, yet they were rare. The more general attitude was that which statesmen and people had so commonly shown towards Germany for a generation. Germany's new prominence in the world was inconvenient, and it was still held to be expedient to say so frankly. It occurred to few people who held this sentiment to reflect upon its narrowness and impolicy, or to suspect the dangers which it held in store.

Virtue and vice in national as in personal characteristics tend to meet, like extremes of other kinds. Even in our later and less insular days there is always a danger of confusing imperialism with mere parochialism, the mark of which is to view the world from the standpoint of one's own opinions, feelings, and interests. There are facts and reasons enough in the history of the Anglo-Saxon race — the courage, steadfastness, strenuousness, and passion for action which have driven it in all ages to deeds of high emprise on land and sea, its inborn love of mastery and domination, its genius for government — which alone explain why so large a part of the globe has fallen, and was destined to fall, beneath British sway. The acceptance of such a view is consistent with a generous and unselfish patriotism. It is not truly imperialistic but truly parochial, however, to pretend that it was from all time written in the stars that other nations should be shut out from a share in the mission of civilization.

The attitude maintained towards German colonial endeavours by the British Government at that time was not, of course, that of conscious cupidity; indeed, its greatest danger lay in the fact that England was shown as making unreasonable demands without knowing that they were unreasonable, or suspecting that others could so regard them. Let it be said frankly that in the colonial controversies of 1884 and 1885 England put herself in the wrong, and that Bismarck's verdict, " It was a miscalculation on England's part to disapprove of our modest colonial endeavours " (March 2, 1885) was justified. Perhaps the severest condemnation upon the British Foreign Office was passed by Lord Granville himself in a note written on February 5, 1885, to Sir Edward Malet, who had reported to him on an interview with the German Chancellor. In this note he pleaded that " the misunderstandings referred to by Prince Bismarck in his conversation with your Excellency are due to the suddenness with which her Majesty's Government became acquainted with the departure by Germany from her traditional policy in regard to colonization." The words came perilously near to a claim that the Cabinet to which Lord Granville belonged could not be expected to know that Bismarck meant what he said.

On the other hand, Bismarck cannot be acquitted of a large share of responsibility for the discords of those days. His policy was straight at the beginning, but it soon went crooked and ended so. His behaviour also, after he had become convinced that he could only make headway in colonial matters by breaking down British opposition, was far from encouraging to a nation which may be led but can never be driven. Yet if he was provocative in the highest degree, it was because he had been provoked, and it was Bismarck's rule when his enemy smote him on the right cheek to smite back on both. We have seen that when the quarrel came to an end, so far as it did end, no warmer assurances of friendly intentions and of a desire to live peaceably with Germany were uttered on the English side than those which left the lips of the Prime Minister and the Foreign Secretary. The misfortune was that the desire for conciliation so handsomely avowed at the end of the episode was not discovered at the beginning. If Bismarck read Charles Reade one can imagine him, as he reflected on the professions of good-will which were so tardily wrung from British Ministers, asking himself, like the gentle heroine of *The Cloister and the Hearth,* why " those sweet words " had been withheld so long.

In the further extension of her oversea dominions at that time Germany had no readier auxiliary than the British Government, whose Foreign Secretary henceforth made generous amends, by ready co-operation and deferent concession, for past opposition. While a war of despatches was raging over the acquisitions in South-west and West Africa and New Guinea an empire destined to be larger and richer than any one of these was being built in East Africa. Here there was not the same danger of a collision with the older colonial Power, though British interests of long standing existed. The Sultan of Zanzibar had from time immemorial claimed sovereignty on the mainland from Warscheik in the north to Cape Delgado in the south, and far into the interior. Various countries had entered into treaty relations with him for commercial purposes — the United States in 1835, Great Britain in 1839, France in 1844, and in 1859 the German Hanseatic cities, Hamburg, Bremen and Lübeck (the treaty in this case being transferred later to the North German Confederation and the Empire), while in 1862 Great Britain and France had formally acknowledged the Sultan's independence. For many years British influence had been supreme in Zanzibar, and in 1878 the Sultan had been willing to place his East African dominion under British protection. Though Lord Beaconsfield declined to accept the liability, much was done by British enterprise for the development of the country.

Long before Germany began to regard East Africa from the standpoint of colonization German explorers had been active there. Rebmann, the missionary, discovered the Kilimanjaro in 1848, and some years later Baron Klaus von der Decken led a luckless expedition into the interior, where he was murdered. Later, two of von der Decken's companions, Dr. Richard Brenner and Dr. Otto Kersten, brought the country before the German public from the imperialistic standpoint, Brenner even persuading the Sultan of Witu in 1867 to ask through him the protection of the Prussian Government, which was refused.

The first practical steps towards obtaining a footing in East Africa were taken by the German Government in October, 1884, when a consul was appointed in Zanzibar in the person of Dr. Gerhard Rohlfs. This move alarmed the British Foreign Office, which invited an exchange of views, and there was relief in London when the assurance was given that Germany had no thought of establishing a protectorate there. In the meantime Dr. Karl Peters, a young and ambitious journalist and pseudo-scientist, who had become a colonial enthusiast during residence in England, had succeeded in establishing a new colonial propagandist organization, the Society for German Colonization, and from the first it devoted its attention to East Africa. Organizing an expedition, in spite of the refusal of official encouragement, Peters and his friends set foot in the country in November, and passing beyond the coast territory over which the Sultan of Zanzibar claimed suzerainty, they concluded treaties with native chiefs by which an area of 60,000 square miles came into their hands virtually as a free gift. Returning home, he formed the German East Africa Company for the exploitation of his dominion, and now the Government, which had refused to countenance Peters so long as he sought its patronage with empty hands, gave him the desired letter of protection in respect of it (February 27, 1885). Further expeditions undertaken by Peters and his friends gained for his Company still larger tracts of territory in Swaheliland, Somaliland, both the coast and the interior, and elsewhere. The sultanate of Witu was also placed under the Empire's protection.

Most of these acquisitions were obtained in clear infraction of the suzerain rights of the Sultan of Zanzibar, who protested in vain both to the German Emperor and the British Government. When, however, the Sultan sent troops into the interior to enforce his authority, a German squadron was sent to Zanzibar to overawe him, and in the end, on the advice of the British Government, he withdrew both his protests and his men, and acknowledged the German claims (August 14th). Sir John Kirk, who had been the British representative in Zanzibar for twenty years, earnestly remonstrated with his Government, but, having made peace with Bismarck, Lord Granville was in no mind for further difficulties.

In the meantime an English financial group, the British East Africa Association, had entered the field, and was interesting itself in projects for developing certain territories between the coast and the lakes. It became necessary, therefore, to delimit the adjacent spheres of influence, and this was ultimately done by a boundary agreement of October 29–November 1, 1886, which gave to Germany the coastline between the rivers Umba in the north and Rovuma in the south, and left her in possession of the Kilimanjaro region, Uganda, and Witu. The Sultan's authority was whittled down to a shadow of his ancient claims; but he was helpless, and accordingly he accepted the terms of his powerful neighbours without demur at the end of the year. The agreement was one of a series of colonial arrangements concluded with Germany by Lord Salisbury, who had in the meantime succeeded Lord Granville (June, 1885). Bismarck would have welcomed any change of Government which promised a new start, but the accession to power of Lord Salisbury, whom he knew from the time of the Berlin Congress, gave him special satisfaction. Throughout this, the first Salisbury administration and the second, which lasted from August, 1886, to August, 1892, the relations of the two countries were consistently cordial, and on the whole Germany secured the best of the subsequent territorial bargaining.

Nevertheless, East Africa was not yet to have settled peace. In 1888 the German protectorate was thrown into insurrection owing to the indiscretions of Peters and other agents of his Company, and the measures taken by Germany and Great Britain jointly for the suppression of the slave trade in their territories led to a widespread rising of the Arabs under the chief Bushiri, which lasted until the beginning of 1891. Meanwhile, Bismarck, who had become thoroughly distrustful of Peters, placed the colony more directly under the Empire's control, and from 1889 it was administered by an imperial commissioner. In the following year the Company surrendered its suzerain rights to the Empire for the sum of £1,350,000, and German influence in East Africa was consolidated by the purchase from the Sultan of Zanzibar for £200,000 of an extensive strip of territory on the coast. Peters was at this time engaged in another expedition, as a result of which he concluded with native chiefs many new treaties which, had they been valid and duly enforced, would have greatly circumscribed British influence in the interior, and diverted much of the trade of the Upper Nile into German territory. Unfortunately for his plans, however, in Peters's absence the German and British Governments had entered into new negotiations regarding their position and claims in East Africa, and when the traveller returned to civilization he heard, to his chagrin, that the resulting agreement, bearing date July 1, 1890, had made short work of his ambitious schemes. By it the spheres of interest of the contracting Powers were determined in such manner that Germany's empire was broadly confined within the limits imposed by Portuguese Mozambique in the south, the Lakes Nyassa, Tanganyika, and Victoria in the east, and the territory running from the river Wanga through (and including) the Kilimanjaro region to Lake Victoria in the north. A fairly compact empire of 384,000 square miles was thus formed. Great Britain secured Uganda, Witu, and also the protectorate of Zanzibar and Pemba. Territorial adjustments of a minor character were arranged in South-west and West Africa. As a crowning return for Germany's concessions Lord Salisbury ceded to her the island of Heligoland. The agreement gave general satisfaction in neither country. In Germany in particular the colonial party professed to regard the acquisition of Heligoland as insufficient to counterbalance the loss of German rights in Zanzibar and Witu, the truth being that at that time of short views on both sides Germany as little recognized how much she had potentially gained as Great Britain how much she had lost by the transfer of the Elbe island.

One other series of acquisitions, of minor extent and importance, fell to 1885, the red-letter year of German colonial history. They comprised several groups of small islands in the Western Pacific, and in relation to one of them Germany came into serious conflict with Spain. On August 6th of that year the Berlin Foreign Office informed the Government in Madrid that it intended to annex the Caroline and Pelew Islands, on the assumption that they were unappropriated. Spain protested on the ground of prior possession, and in a race of ships of war to the Carolines Germany succeeded in hoisting her flag first on the island of Jap. After angry recrimination on both sides the dispute was referred to the Pope for settlement, and he proposed (October 22nd) a compromise by which Spain was to exercise sovereignty over the islands, but Germany was to have a naval station and equal trading rights, an arrangement accepted by both countries in December. (In 1889 these islands were purchased from Spain for £800,-000.) In the same year the Marshall, Brown, and Providence islands, and some of the Solomon islands were annexed by Germany without protest. A little later began that persistent assertion of German influence in the Samoan islands which in 1899 brought Savaii and Upolu into her permanent possession in virtue of agreements with Great Britain and the United States, thus ending a long period of *condominium* which had lamentably failed to give to Samoa order and good government.

References to colonial developments of later date must be reserved for the chapters in which domestic affairs generally are surveyed.[1]

Although Bismarck's principal colonial difficulties were with Great Britain, his acquisitions of territory were not made without frequent struggles against parliamentary opposition at home. The practical culmination of the colonial movement

[1] See Chapters XIX., pp. 272-3, and XX., pp. 328-337.

had created a wave of enthusiasm in the country; a host of societies, old and new, were busily engaged in successful propagandism; German traders and financiers were investing large amounts of capital in the new ventures; only in the Diet was a hearty response wanting. There parties refused to judge the question on its merits, and insisted in confusing it with other issues. There was a strong group of ardent imperialists, but up to this point no party had completely identified itself with the colonial movement from settled conviction. The Conservatives voted for the acquisition of colonies rather out of loyalty to the Government than from any clear belief that Germany would be better for them. The Radicals and Socialists opposed them, not because they were on principle anti-Ministerialists, though that was the case, but on the ground of expense and risk. The National Liberals gave only a half-hearted support, while the rest of the parties were still rather unsympathetic than otherwise.

Thus it happened that three bills had to be introduced before Bismarck could obtain in 1885 a vote for subsidies to mail steamship companies, to ensure regular sailings to some of the outposts of Greater Germany. The first vote was for £250,000, an amount which was later doubled. Yet it was this outlay which made possible the commercial invasion of the British colonial empire by Germany and also the establishment of a penny post between that country and Australia twenty years before the mother country took the same step. It was made a condition that the ships to be so subsidized should have been built in German yards, and should both be quicker and charge lower fares and rates than existing vessels.

Bismarck resented the apathy of a Diet which was neither hot nor cold. He complained bitterly that it was unfair to expect him to carry out large schemes of colonial enterprise and at the same time to spend his time and energies in disputations with reluctant deputies on the question of finance. He held that any fair distribution of labour required that if he provided the colonies Parliament should at least provide the necessary funds, and do it willingly. Discouraged and depressed by the want of loyal support at a time when he was doing his best to build up the Empire at home and abroad, the ageing Chancellor, in one of the most moving of all his parliamentary speeches (March 2, 1885), lamented " the old, hereditary German enemy, the spirit of party strife, which finds sustenance in dynastic, confessional, and racial differences and in political struggles," and added: "The analogy of our German history with our German mythology is something that has troubled and disquieted me unceasingly during the last twenty years. There is in our national mythology a peculiar anticipation of the fact that as often as things go well with Germany the Loki is never missing who finds his Hödur, a weak-minded, stupid being, whom he artfully induces to blight the national springtime."

The constitutional position of the colonies was in the early years laid down by a law of 1886, since amended several times, which empowered the Emperor to exercise the executive power in the protected territories in the name of the Empire, of which the colonies were declared to be " oversea provinces." For a long time the affairs of the colonies were regulated in the main by Ministerial decrees and orders, greatly to the dissatisfaction of the political parties at home, which were jealous of their parliamentary powers. With the continual increase of the colonial estimates, however, it became year by year easier for the Diet to assert its wish for a more direct share in the government of Greater Germany in the way of legislation and free discussion. Several important questions, however, were from the first subject to imperial legislation, e.g. civil law, criminal law, judicial procedure, marriage law, the exercise of religious liberties, and finance.

It had been Bismarck's fixed intention that the protectorates should be administered by chartered companies formed on the British model, the Empire affording protection where necessary, but interfering as little as possible in the work of government and development. This system was, in fact, followed in the early years, but in course of time it broke down completely in the face of unforeseen contingencies. One of these was the financial difficulties with which the early colonial companies, with hardly a single exception, had to struggle from the beginning. These companies freely acquired large undeveloped territories, without considering the character and extent of the liabilities which their possession was likely to impose upon them. The consequence was that they had as a rule exhausted their funds before they had fairly faced their tasks. Companies so situated were ill fitted to take over the important function of administration. Viewing the colonies only or chiefly from the commercial side, the merchant adventurers, the " Hanseatics," and financiers, organized in their companies and syndicates, showed little desire and less aptitude for delicate work of that kind. Long before Bismarck gave place to a successor, therefore, it had become evident that the Empire would have to face the duty and cost of colonial government.

Nor did the record of imperial administration itself prove for a long time a successful one, for this was for Germany a voyage in uncharted waters. Perhaps failures were in the circumstances inevitable, yet they were made the more certain owing to insufficient care in the choice of the men sent out. Many of these were men of the wrong type — wrong in training and character, and often still more wrong in morals. Bismarck had once expressed the fear that to establish an imperial colonial bureaucracy might be to pack it with " questionable existences." Of doubtful characters the colonial service had far too many in the early years, and the result was wholesale misrule, abuse, corruption, and demoralization, which gave the colonial empire a bad name and for a long time seriously prejudiced the colonial movement altogether. Partly owing to the sudden change from the rude but familiar discipline of chieftain rule to the trammels of organized government on drastic and mechanical principles, yet also to systematic and often revolting ill-usage, serious native insurrections impeded the development of all the African colonies in the early years, and the retaliation which followed was always swift and severe. In particular, the explorer Peters, who later entered the colonial service, was said to have left a trail of blood wherever he went. Not a few administrators, even officials of the highest rank, were, like him, prosecuted for cruelty or immorality and dismissed the service.[1]

Gradually the chaff in the colonial service was sifted from

[1] Compare Hans Delbrück, in *Bismarcks Erbe* (p. 187); Dr. Alfred Zimmermann, in *Geschichte der Kolonialpolitik (passim)*; *Kolonien und Kolonialpolitik* (Staatsbürger-Bibliothek), pp. 27–29, etc. Delbrück writes: " The people who went out on their own account or were sent out proved themselves unsuitable, and understood neither politically, economically, nor socially what it was right to do nor how to control themselves properly; they quarrelled among themselves, were brutal to the natives and incited them to revolts. The colonial history of all nations is very often unedifying reading from the standpoint of humanity, but we should have hoped in Germany that a movement which was born in idealism would have remained untarnished by such cruelties."

the corn; greater circumspection was shown in the choice of men, and in time the service began to attract a higher type of official, free from the degrading tradition that codes of morality apply only in civilized countries, though his antithesis never entirely disappeared. During the early years the general administration of the colonies came directly under the Foreign Office as part of its routine work. In 1890 a special colonial department of that Ministry was created, with a Colonial Director at its head, subject to the Imperial Chancellor, and it is significant of the economical methods practised in the German civil service that the change was carried out at an extra cost of £1,200 a year. The new department was given the assistance of a colonial council, a sort of advisory committee composed of representatives of colonial undertakings and religious missions and experts on colonial questions.

CHAPTER XVIII

(1888–1890)

BISMARCK — THE LAST PHASE

In 1888 the throne of Imperial Germany was held by three occupants, of whom two passed away within the short space of a hundred days. The first Emperor had reached the ripe age of ninety-one years, thus exceeding by twenty-five and twenty-one years the age at which his immediate predecessors on the throne of Prussia, his brother and father, had died. His direct influence on practical affairs had long ceased, yet thanks to a life of simple ways and healthy work, and to a tenacious will, he still had strength and zest for the prescribed daily conferences with his Chancellor and Minister President. His tranquil end on March 9th was a fitting close to a life which, in its private aspects, had been one of singular harmony and placidity.

Three events of the preceding year had afforded him great satisfaction. One was the impressive demonstration of national devotion which was offered to him in March, on the occasion of his ninetieth birthday. The anniversary was observed as a festival of the Empire and of Germanism throughout the world, and the celebrations in Berlin were attended by nearly a hundred princely notables — federal Sovereigns, heirs-apparent, and members of reigning houses. The second event was the passing of a new Army Bill, making a further addition to the peace strength. The third event was a visit from the Czar in Berlin in November, a token to him that Germany and Russia, though no longer the close allies of old, continued in unbroken friendship. Bismarck believed that this meeting led to the removal of suspicions of his integrity which the Czar appears to have entertained for some time. In the course of conversation the Chancellor found him to be chafing under the grievance that Germany had been playing a double part on the Bulgarian question. Asked for the proofs he replied that he had documents which spoke for themselves. Bismarck was able to satisfy him that these documents were forgeries, and the interview gave satisfaction to both sides.

Beloved as no Prussian Sovereign was beloved before him, the idol of the whole German family, happy in the knowledge that the peace of the world was assured and his country strong and safe, William I had gained the things which to him were most worth striving for, and his death, while it left a large blank in the national life, created no immediate disturbance in the course of events. Within two years (January 7, 1890) the death of the Dowager Empress Augusta followed.

With him the last genuine representative of absolutism in Germany and thus in Western Europe may be said to have passed away. For if his first public interest was the army, his strongest instincts were centred on the preservation of every right retained by the Prussian Crown after the grant of the constitution of 1850. Sir Robert Morier regarded it as a weakness of the first Emperor that in politics he had no firm grasp of first principles. In regard to constitutional questions, the truth rather is that he grasped the wrong principles and grasped them too firmly. His opposition to every suggestion of parliamentary government was not merely uncompromising but unreasoning. For him the constitutional arrangements accepted by the nation under duress in the middle of the century were final, and he resolutely resisted all attempts at the further liberalizing of either the Prussian or the imperial system of government. Hence it was that he left the constitutional life both of the monarchy and the Empire just where he found it, for it had neither gone forward nor backward. Bismarck unquestionably spared no pains to poison his mind against democracy, and in so doing he sowed seed in fertile ground. In none of his known utterances will be found the slightest trace of sympathy with the political aspirations of the masses of the people.

Because the first Emperor was overshadowed as a statesman by his great Chancellor, the idea is commonly held that he was a man of small intellectual power, of little sagacity, and even only moderately intelligent. No estimate of his character could be wider of the truth. His comprehension of domestic politics may have been limited, because warped by political ideas and prejudices which made it impossible for him to enter into the mind and spirit of the modern world. His judgment of foreign affairs and relations, on the other hand, showed a clear comprehension of fundamental issues, an unerring instinct for the line of honour, and a sure perception of the true conditions of confidence between Sovereigns, Governments, and States.   No one can read his letters to Count Bernstorff on the Crimean War, the letters of a soldier who had had little training in public affairs, or his later correspondence on foreign politics with Bismarck, without being impressed by his quick, masterly, almost intuitive apprehension of complex issues and above all by his large fund of clear, direct, sane, downright common sense.   He came to many right decisions without knowing why they were right.   A more brilliant man would have been far more liable to mistakes.

Probably the disparagement from which he suffers is due to the fact that when serious difference of opinion occurred between Emperor and Chancellor it was the Emperor who almost invariably gave way.   What is now known of these conflicts, however, proves that his capitulations were often due to stratagems which he, in his simple truthfulness, could never have suspected, and that the victory in such cases was not one of argument or wisdom but of cunning and equivocation.   Not only so, but even when he gave way his own judgment was repeatedly justified by the event.

Bismarck himself has said, " William I was anything but an accommodating master.   He held tenaciously to his opinions, traditions and prejudices, and it was always difficult to persuade him to go a new way.   How often have I gone to him expecting that I should be able to take away his assent and signature, only to be disappointed.   More than once the long discussion ended with the words, ' At this moment I believe you are right, but give me another day or two to ponder the matter and sleep over it.   I do not want to run the risk of overhaste.' "   Never did he give his signature or assent to a document of State without first weighing it anxiously from all sides, and his correspondence with his chief Minister tells again and again of " sleepless nights " passed because of the too-ready endorsement of draft despatches which on further reflection he deemed to be indiscreetly worded and wished to recall.   Such a man may have been lacking in resolution, but he certainly had a mind of his own and more than once on large issues — as in the case of the wars of 1864 and 1866 — he resisted to the twelfth hour the importunate pressure of his overbearing Minister.

The Hohenzollern throne has been filled by greater and

stronger men than William I, but by none more conscientious, more honourable, or more devoted to the welfare of his State and people, as he understood it.   He was a pattern of private as of public virtue, and the example which he offered of personal probity, simplicity of character, and orderliness of life was not the least valuable of his services to the nation.

A double sorrow rested on the land in those days.   Germany had lost the old Sovereign, and knew that she must soon lose the new one.   For almost a year the Crown Prince, now Emperor Frederick, had been suffering from a throat malady, the malignant nature of which had been suspected but not definitely determined.   He no longer appeared in public, and he had ceased to use his voice even in private intercourse.   There had even been talk of a regency as soon as the old Emperor died. Meanwhile, skilful surgeons had operated upon and wrangled over him, and at last, after long denial on one side and perhaps over-hasty diagnosis on the other, it was admitted that the disease which had laid its malignant hand upon him was cancer and incurable.   All that could be done was to attempt to prolong his life until in the course of nature the call to the throne should come to him.   He was still wintering in the Riviera with his wife when the deathbed summons came to him from Berlin. Hastening north from sunny San Remo, he arrived home in blinding snow-storms, too ill to show himself to his people.

Seldom have a new ruler and a new reign given rise to more speculation, to wilder hopes on the one hand or wilder apprehensions on the other.   He was now fifty-seven years old, yet, owing to Bismarck's jealousy of any influence with the Emperor save his own, he had been excluded from participation in public affairs except when acting as regent during his father's incapacity.   A year before he had complained to Prince Hohenlohe: "I hear nothing; I learn everything through the newspapers.   And the Emperor is ninety years old."   Nevertheless, he had never concealed his opinions, which were uncompromisingly Liberal.   These had repeatedly brought him into conflict with his father and more openly with Bismarck, some of whose public acts he had vigorously denounced when they seemed to be contrary to the spirit of the constitution or to prejudice the Crown and dynasty in the eyes of the nation.   In politics he was said, with some justification, to be more English than German.   In a diary kept during the

French war, which was later to acquire an unfortunate fame, he had written, " Our principal thought is how the Liberal development of Germany may be carried out on the restoration of peace." That thought, which he had ever since kept before him, was in the spirit of the Court of Coburg, but not in that of Berlin.

The Conservatives attributed his progressive leanings to his marriage with the Princess Royal of England. Certainly he had been greatly influenced by the Liberal spirit and ideas which his wife brought with her as part of a rare intellectual dowry. Common tastes led to common friendships; both of them found pleasure in the society of men of enlightened opinions — politicians, scientists, and men of letters — and among the welcome and constant visitors to their home were Helmholtz, Virchow, Dubois-Reymond, Freytag, the Bunsens, Stockmar, and Geffcken. The idea of a woman consorting with learned men and, even worse, talking politics shocked the conventional Conservative of Prussia, and created against the Crown Princess great prejudice, from which her husband also suffered. Since by a perverted logic Liberalism to the feudalist mind was the negation of patriotism and loyalty, the deduction was drawn that to be a friend of the Crown Princess was to be an enemy of Prussia. Here Bismarck shared to the full the prejudices of his old political associates. With the Crown Princess he had little sympathy, though he probably distrusted her less than Empress Augusta, for whom he developed a positive dislike, unreasonably attributing to her influence every failure to win the Emperor for his own ideas and plans. If, however, the Crown Princess suffered from the distrust and bigotry of the barbarian section of the upper classes, cultivated people in all ranks of society appreciated her, and even the Philistines, without being able to enter into her mind, admired her in their torpid way.

Not only the German people but the old Emperor himself had been anxious as to the direction which events might take under the new reign. Bismarck, however, was never in doubt that though there might be changes the force of tradition and of his surroundings would prevent the Crown Prince from venturing upon any radical departure. " I have no information," he wrote in July, 1879, " on the question whether he will rule on fundamentally Liberal principles when he is called to assume the Government. Personally, I doubt this, and I certainly anticipate that if such a direction is really taken it will not be permanent." Now that the riddle was at last to be solved national expectation was strained to the utmost. Just as the Conservatives, conscience-stricken as they recalled the use which they had made of their long domination, assumed that their day was over, so the Radicals hoped that their turn had now come to wear purple and fine linen and sit in Kings' houses; the Clericals confidently counted at least on generous toleration; and the Socialists knew that their cause would henceforth be free from violent and unreasoning antagonism. To the surprise of most people and the chagrin of many matters went on just as before. The Emperor made a few changes in the Ministry and the administrative service, but the wholesale displacement of his father's counsellors which had been predicted did not take place. Above all, Bismarck continued at his post as if nothing had happened. Irresponsible people had predicted that the first and most certain act of the new reign would be his dismissal and the appointment of a Minister of truly Liberal ideas.

It was not yet known that three years before (1885) the Crown Prince, with the complete concurrence of the Crown Princess, had assured Bismarck of his wish that he would remain in office when the new reign began and had told him that he had neither intention nor desire to supplant him. Bismarck's hope had been that the old Emperor might outlast his own capacity for useful work, and that when the new reign came he would be justified in seeking retirement and so be able " like a pensioned court actor " to " exchange the stage for the stalls." Nevertheless, he gave his promise to stay, and now the promise and the conditions were faithfully fulfilled. There had been an understanding that there should be no violent changes, and such were not made.

The Emperor's illness threw a shadow upon the new reign and gloom upon the nation. He was unable to move amongst his people; all affairs of State had to be transacted in the sickroom, and communications with his Ministers and friends to be carried on in writing. With every week the inexorable disease which had seized him gained further hold, and before three months had passed (June 15th) the hopeless struggle with death came to an end.

During this short period affairs were more than ever in Bismarck's hands. He was at once Imperial Chancellor, President of the Federal Council, Foreign Minister, and Prussian Minister President, while his son Count Herbert worked in the Foreign Office under him as officer next in command. Happily few events of moment occurred either at home or abroad to trouble the stricken Sovereign. When the Imperial Diet and Federal Council adopted a bill prolonging the legislative period from three to five years he wished at first to withhold assent on the ground that it was a retrograde step. Bismarck had to remind him that in Imperial legislation the Emperor had neither veto nor voice, and the law was promptly promulgated. The same change was introduced simultaneously in relation to the Prussian Diet. The most notable domestic event of the short reign was the rigorous suppression of the system of election-manœuvring which has already been referred to. The Crown Prince Frederick had long watched with disapproval this trifling with the constitutional rights of Germans to exercise free choice in the election of their deputies, and though helpless to alter it he had condemned it unsparingly in letters to Bismarck. In assenting to quinquennial parliaments for Prussia he told the Minister of the Interior, Herr von Puttkamer, that the odious system of pressure of which he was the impersonation must cease, and that in general public opinion must henceforth be allowed freer expression. Puttkamer, however, was acting under the instructions of another master, and refused to take the warning. A little later the arbitrary Minister, for wholly insufficient reasons, prohibited at the last moment the performance in Berlin of a Luther drama, with the result that when the public assembled in the theatre it was to gaze at police constables instead of actors. The Emperor marked his displeasure at the occurrence by immediately cancelling the prohibition, and Puttkamer resigned, unregretted. A fortnight later the unpopular Minister died.

In foreign relations no change occurred. Bismarck was as insistent as ever upon the necessity for a good understanding with Russia, and here he found a willing ear. For a moment, but no more, there seemed danger of discord in consequence of the revival after several years of a project of marriage between Prince Alexander of Battenberg, now no longer Prince of Bulgaria, and the Emperor's daughter Princess Victoria. Bismarck pressed the old objection, the fear of offending Russia, and when that seemed insufficient he threatened to resign. Then Queen Victoria and the Grand Duke of Baden added their urgent influence to his own, and the Emperor and Empress gave way.

It is futile to speculate upon the direction which political and parliamentary life might have taken in Germany had there fallen to the Emperor Frederick a reign of normal duration. That important constitutional changes would have been introduced is very probable, yet they would have been gradual, and his moderation and marked sagacity would have eased the transition from the old order to the new even for the privileged parties which had hitherto claimed the German Emperor and his Government as exclusively their own. He never deviated from the principles laid down in a letter which he addressed to Bismarck in 1863, during the Prussian constitutional conflict, when protesting against the muzzling of the Press: " The principles which, in my opinion, must guide every (Prussian) Government in its treatment of the country are — loyal administration of the law and the constitution and esteem for and benevolence towards an easily guided, intelligent, and capable people." Whatever the Prussian monarchy and the German Empire might have become under his guidance, liberty would have flourished, the relations between the State and the citizen would have become less strained and suspicious, and above all the paralysing influence upon legislation of feudalist East Prussia would have been permanently neutralized. What he might have been expected to do for his country was to make it in reality what France was to have been under the later years of Louis Napoleon, a truly Liberal Empire.

There were not a few painful sequents to the tragic reign of three months — the callous treatment meted to the Empress Frederick by evil tongues and a pernicious Press, the public wrangling of the doctors and surgeons over points of professional etiquette, and particularly the episode of the Emperor's diary. In September the *Deutsche Rundschau* startled Germany by publishing what purported to be a diary kept by the Crown Prince during the war of 1870–1871. The contributor withheld his name, but it was stated that the diary had been placed at his disposal by the late Emperor himself. There were many passages which were not at all complimentary to

Bismarck, whose relations with the Crown Prince of that day were shown to be far from harmonious. The disclosures excited warm controversy, and the Liberals in particular extracted from them much material for political recrimination. Soon it became known that the diary had been published by Professor Geffcken, a Liberal publicist, who for years had enjoyed the late Emperor's friendship, whereupon Geffcken promptly offered to meet in due legal form any accusation to which his action might have exposed him.

In Bismarck's hasty judgment the occasion called for rigorous measures. He caused the professor to be summarily arrested as a preliminary to a prosecution of a charge of divulging secrets of State. In December he was tried before the Imperial High Court in Leipzig on a series of charges of which the most serious, yet in substance the most trivial, was high treason. Nobody seemed to know wherein the high treason consisted, and most people agreed that the true and greater cause of offence was injury to Bismarck's feelings. An allegation of falsification of documents had been made, but it had to be withdrawn, for when the copy of the diary came to be compared with the original it was proved that Geffcken had faithfully published extracts without additions or alterations. His conduct may or may not have been indiscreet, but it was legally correct, and he was acquitted upon all charges and set free. The only men who derived discredit from the ill-advised proceedings were the Chancellor and those who had egged him into a course of vindictive action which recalled the worst incidents of the Arnim episode.

If there was no mystery about Emperor Frederick's political opinions and inclinations, his son and successor William II was as a book sealed with seven seals. Born on January 27, 1859, he had had the all-round education of a Prussian Prince. From his seventh to his fourteenth year he was set on the pathway to knowledge by one of the discreetest of tutors, Dr. Hinzpeter. Then he passed several years at the gymnasium of Cassel, and for several terms he studied at Bonn. In February, 1881, he married Princess Augusta Victoria of Schleswig-Holstein-Sonderburg-Augustenburg, a union which was one of policy as well as of sympathy, for it closed for ever the personal feud between the Hohenzollerns and the claimants to the Elbe Duchies. Then Prince William had disappeared again into the background. Another life lay between him and the throne, and the Hohenzollerns were on the whole a strong race. No attempt was made, therefore, to hasten his introduction to public life, of which, indeed, his father himself was still little more than a passive spectator.

All that was known about his political opinions down to June, 1888, was that he oftener disagreed than agreed with his parents, that a sort of atavism had showed itself in his character, in which were already detected traces of the Great Elector and Frederick the Great, and that he was a devoted admirer of Bismarck. Ingenious attempts have been made to show that there never was any sympathy between Prince William and the Chancellor. It may be true, but all the evidence is against such a theory. Professor W. Maurenbrecher, with whom the Prince as a student read history at Bonn in 1877, tells a wonderful story of his pupil's immaturity when he came to him. The sober tutor was shocked " at the opinions which he avowed regarding the modern history and politics of Germany, and especially regarding Prince Bismarck." What the opinions were we are not told, but they appear to have been eradicated before the Prince had completed his university studies. " When the Prince took leave of Bonn and me," writes the Professor, " he was a fiery admirer of Prince Bismarck and the historical lifework of this statesman." That story, too, may be accepted or rejected at discretion.

A fact not to be doubted is that when he came to the throne he was as devoted and apt a pupil of the Chancellor as any statesman jealous of his reputation and power could have desired. Toasting Bismarck on April 6th, just a month after the death of his grandfather, Prince William said, in an outburst of generous warmth: " The Empire is like an army corps that has lost its commander-in-chief in the field, while the officer who stands next in rank lies severely wounded. The standard-bearer, however, is our illustrious Prince, our great Chancellor. Let him lead us; we will follow him!" For the rest, the only public interests which he seemed at that time to share were a socio-religious movement which had been started in Berlin several years before by Court Chaplain Stöcker, and above all the army. It was regarded as significant that his first proclamations on the day of his accession were not to the nation, but to the army and the navy: " so we belong together, born for each other, and so we will ceaselessly hold together, come peace or storm." The proclamation to " my people " was issued only three days later. Nevertheless, even in the army he had revealed no such spirit of *camaraderie* as had made his father equally popular amongst officers and men.

The son's reign, like the father's, began well, for the tragedy of the situation for a time imposed upon parties an unaccustomed restraint, and on all hands a desire was shown to speed the young ruler auspiciously on his way. His first public utterances created favourable expectations. In his proclamation to the nation he had promised " to be a just and clement Prince, to cultivate piety and the fear of God, to advance the welfare of the country, and to be to the army and navy a helper and a faithful guardian of justice." In opening the Imperial Diet on June 25th he endorsed the Social Reform Message of his grandfather, and promised to take into his care " the weak and crushed in the struggle for existence." " In foreign policy," he said, " I am determined to live in peace with every man so far as in me lies. My love to the army and my position towards it will never lead me into the temptation to deprive the country of the blessings of peace unless war becomes a necessity owing to the Empire or its allies being attacked." This was all in the spirit of Bismarck, and a reassuring intimation to the nation that the old steersman was to remain. Bismarck, convinced that he was needed, and moved by the pathos of the situation, had thrown himself enthusiastically into the service of a third Emperor, and William II for his part seems to have fulfilled for a time the Chancellor's highest expectations. Discussing him with members of the Prussian House of Lords in June, he is reported to have " spoken with great enthusiasm and with tears in his eyes " of the young Emperor's earnestness and devotion to his new duties.

After affairs had been settled at home the Emperor devoted some months to a round of calls upon foreign Courts. He first visited the Czar, travelling by sea, accompanied by his brother Prince Henry and Count Herbert Bismarck. A short time before Bismarck had excited political feeling in Russia by first allowing the youthful Crown Prince of Serbia to be forcibly taken from the custody of his mother while on German soil, on the demand of King Milan, and then expelling Queen Natalie herself. The Russian Press had broken out into a chorus of

bitter reproaches over these acts, and in other countries unconcerned with the political aspects of the question Bismarck's
treatment of the Serbian queen had been severely judged.　But
what was Hecuba to him or he to Hecuba that he should weep
for her?　Bismarck justified his conduct by reasons of State.
If Queen Natalie was Russia's *protégée*, so was King Milan the
favourite of Austria.　To offer her sanctuary were to take
sides; he therefore asserted Germany's neutrality in a curious
way by ordering her out of the country.　As by this high-
handed act Bismarck had sorely displeased the Pan-Slavists, he
was now the more concerned to please the Czar.　The two Sovereigns met at Cronstadt (July 19th) and several days of festivities followed at St. Petersburg.　Marked attention was
shown by the visitors to M. de Giers on the occasion, and when
later in the year the Russian Chancellor celebrated the fiftieth
anniversary of his official life the Emperor was amongst those
who most warmly congratulated him.　On the way home from
St. Petersburg visits were paid to the Swedish and Danish
Courts.　Later in the year (October) there were visits to Vienna and to Rome, where from the German embassy in the
Italian capital a call was made on the Pope.　Nor were the
Courts and chief cities at home forgotten; Munich, Leipzig,
Hamburg, Breslau, Bremen, Stuttgart, and Stettin were all
visited before the year was out.　The first year of the new
reign was thus a strenuous *Lehrjahr* of miscellaneous wander-
ings.

On the Emperor's return from the South the first inhar-
monious note was struck in the relationships between Sovereign
and people.　During his absence in Italy the popular newspapers of Berlin had freely and captiously discussed the earlier
tension between the Emperor and his father.　In receiving
from the Mayor and City Council a welcome home and the
present of a monumental fountain for the Castle Square, he
rebuked them for having neglected to discourage these tactless interferences in his family affairs, and gave them to understand that unless Berlin learned to behave itself better it
would cease to be a royal residence.

At the end of the year which spanned three reigns all seemed
to have gone well, and the Emperor had no reason to be dissatisfied with the outlook either at home or abroad.　Grateful
that in his difficult position the trusted adviser of his grand-

father was at hand with counsel and help, he wrote to his " dear
Prince " a cordial letter, assuring him that " the thought that
you stand faithfully by my side fills me with joy and comfort,"
and " hoping to God that it may be very long permitted to
me to work with you for the welfare and greatness of our
fatherland." The early months of the reign did not pass,
however, without important changes in the Government. New
men were placed at the head of the departments for Home
Affairs, Finance, Justice, and War; the hierarchy of the Prussian Court received new blood, and the diplomatic service was
severely sifted and screened. Above all the army command
was rejuvenated, and not a few old generals and other high
officers were weeded out somewhat ruthlessly. In August
Moltke himself, conscious of the weight of years, had sought
relief from his duties as Chief of the General Staff, and had
accepted instead the lighter responsibilities of President of the
Committee of National Defence. His successor was Count
Waldersee, already marked out as one of the Emperor's fa-
vourites.

So far the course of domestic policy had seemed to afford
a practical repudiation of the old tradition that the Crown
was in some sort an appendage of the reactionary parties, and
their ally against the rest of the people. Thoughtful men welcomed the detachment of a Sovereign who seemed to know no
classes but only a nation, but its effect upon the feudalists was
to provoke them to discontent and grumbling, and criticisms
of Government policy more vigorous than had ever been known
before in that quarter became common. Before six months had
passed pamphlets were being freely written upon the internal
politics of the new reign, a sign that the political armistice
was already at an end. The Emperor now began to shake
himself free from sundry importunate patrons who had ventured to magnify their influence with him. The Christian Socialist Court Chaplain Stöcker had publicly claimed him as a
friend of his party, and had made full use of his name in propagandism for social reform and less reputable political objects.
Now the Emperor publicly dissociated himself from the pushing
divine.

Bismarck at the same time suffered from a recurrence of the
Conservative animosity which had embittered him in the early
years of the Empire. He had many enemies, and some of the

most rancorous were men who in the past had been of his own household. Once again the *Kreuzzeitung*, which had already done him so much evil, associated itself with dark conspiracies against his reputation and influence. Politicians accustomed to look ahead had speculated, before the new reign began, as to how long the third Emperor and the first Chancellor would be able to work together. Prince Hohenlohe notes in his diary in March, 1888, while the old Emperor was still alive, " There are signs that when the Prince becomes Emperor he will not be able to live in permanent agreement with Bismarck." Bismarck likewise had come to the conclusion that " before he had long been Emperor William II would want to be Chancellor as well." To create mistrust and accelerate rupture became the congenial occupation of a band of intriguers, high in position and influence, of whom the *Kreuzzeitung* became the willing mouthpiece. Astutely playing off the Sovereign against his Minister, these men encouraged the idea that Bismarck aspired to rule the new Emperor as he had ruled the old one, and just as twenty years ago their newspaper had put forward Count Harry Arnim as a rival to the Junker who had dared to rise out of the ranks of the petty nobility and outshine the members of his class, so now they found in Count Waldersee the Chancellor whom the time and conditions needed. Waldersee himself, who was on terms of great intimacy with the Emperor, was said to lose no opportunity of urging him to throw off the tutelage of an old counsellor who was out of sympathy with the modern age, and take affairs into his own hands.

In February, 1889, the *Hamburger Nachrichten,* a newspaper which later became notorious for its attacks upon William II and his policy, startled the political world by publishing an article described as having been " specially contributed " from Berlin, in which Bismarck's position was discussed in language so ingeniously cryptic and ambiguous that at first reading few people could decide whether it came from the hand of a friend or a foe of the Chancellor. One passage puzzled the more it was read and studied ; in it the writer hazarded a doubt whether, if Bismarck were suddenly to be lost to the nation, there was any guarantee that his policy would continue unchanged, and hinted that the next Chancellor might be Count Waldersee, the favourite of the *Kreuzzeitung* cabal. Whencesoever the writer derived his inspiration, and whatever idea he wished to imply, his innuendoes confirmed the suspicion that active plotting was going on.

There was one circumstance, patent to all observers, which had large possibilities of misunderstanding and mischief. Bismarck had unquestionably long counted upon the reversion of his office, if not his influence, falling to his elder son. Hohenlohe, who had himself aspired to be the second Chancellor, had anxiously watched the development of this plan and had sorely chafed under it. " Bismarck thinks before everything," he wrote, " of planting his son firmly in the saddle. To this end he constantly works and schemes." Count Herbert Bismarck had risen in the diplomatic service by rapid strides, and every appointment abroad had been intended as part of his training for Ministerial office at home. At an age when the ordinary diplomat was content to be a Secretary of Legation he had become Under Secretary for Foreign Affairs and Secretary of the Imperial Chancellery, positions which made him his father's unofficial deputy and the recipient of his inmost confidences. Out of gratitude to the father the old Emperor had gone out of his way to help forward the son. Under the new reign men who believed their abilities to be equal to their claims became restive, and dared to protest against favouritism of the kind. There was even malicious talk of the " Bismarck dynasty " upon the establishment of which the Chancellor's ambitions were set. Subtle suggestions of this kind did Bismarck no good with a ruler strongly convinced of his own capacity and jealous of his position.

In the spring of 1889 the Emperor for the first time came face to face with the problem of Socialism, soon to mark a turning-point in German domestic policy. The occasion was a dispute with the Swiss Government relating to the execution of the reciprocal settlement treaty of 1876, under which subjects of each State resident in the territory of the other enjoyed equal civil, commercial, and industrial franchises with nationals. Bismarck complained that Switzerland did nothing to check the Socialistic and Communistic agitation which was conducted by Germans and their organizations and newspapers from the republic. To this accusation the Swiss Government replied that the German political police had set up a widespread system of espionage in Swiss towns, under which secret agents were bribed to worm their way into Socialist organizations and even to incite their members to illegal acts. It suggested, further, that before Germany could fairly complain of the hospitality shown in the republic to political refugees Germany should modernize her legislation in such a way that her subjects would not be driven into clandestine agitation abroad. Even Socialists, it was suggested, had to live somewhere, and a democratic country could not be expected to accommodate its laws to Germany's methods of government. The dispute reached a climax when in April, 1889, the Swiss authorities apprehended a German secret agent who had been proved guilty of incitements to illegality in Switzerland and after expulsion from Swiss soil had returned. The incident gave to Bismarck the justification for pressure for which he had been waiting, and he denounced the treaty of 1876 and prepared to adopt reprisals by closing the frontier of Germany to the canton in which the high-handed act had been committed. Rather than quarrel seriously with so strong a neighbour the Swiss Government discreetly made satisfactory amends and the dispute was thus adjusted amicably.

Early in that year also the Emperor had an opportunity for making good his promise, given when he opened his first Diet, that he would take into his care " the weak and crushed in the struggle for existence." A great strike of miners broke out in the Westphalian coalfield in May. In that area alone a hundred thousand men came out, and sympathetic strikes at once followed in Silesia, Saxony, and the Saar district. The demands of the men were for an eight hours day and for higher wages owing to the increased cost of living, and public opinion was warmly on their side. True to their traditional policy of hostility to the trade unions, the colliery owners refused to treat either with the men's organizations or their leaders, and it seemed likely that the struggle would have to be fought out to the bitter end. Then it occurred to the Christian labour unions to petition the Emperor to use his influence as a conciliator. The Emperor received first a deputation of the men and then one of the masters, and in consequence of his sympathetic attitude towards the former and of his plain speaking to the latter the dispute ended in a fortnight in perhaps the quickest and easiest victory on a large scale which has ever fallen to organized labour in Germany. Before this the Emperor had hoisted his colours as a social reformer in other directions.

He had interested himself in movements for improving the housing of the working classes, and had admonished the leaders of the Protestant State Church to direct their energies more actively into social reform channels. Already the impressionable masses of Berlin talked of a " Labour Emperor." In one of his first public utterances he had warmly endorsed the Social Message of his grandfather. In the same month the last of the triptych of social insurance laws promised in that document was passed — the law making provision for the workers in old age and permanent infirmity. Like the other insurance laws it relied for support chiefly on the Conservatives and the National Liberals; the parties supposed to be specially representative of the working classes, the Radicals and Social Democrats, voted against it.

By this time the return visits from foreign Sovereigns had begun. In May the Emperor received in Berlin the King of Italy, with the Crown Prince and the Minister President Crispi; in August the Emperor Francis Joseph; and in October the Czar. His own visits were also resumed; he was in England in August and later in the year in Greece, at the marriage of his sister Princess Sophie to the Crown Prince, in Italy, and — against his Chancellor's advice — in Constantinople, where he had a truly Byzantine reception.

So another year passed, and so far as the nation knew the relations between the Emperor and his Chancellor were still unclouded. " I pray God," the Emperor wrote to Bismarck on December 30th, " that He will continue to give me for many years your faithful and trusty counsel in my difficult and responsible task as a ruler." Those behind the scenes knew, however, that the halo with which the Sovereign had seemed to invest his Minister had already disappeared. The Grand Duke of Baden told Hohenlohe as early as April, 1889, that " the Emperor was beginning to notice that every now and then things were kept from him, and was becoming distrustful. There had already been a collision between the Emperor and the Chancellor, and the Grand Duke thought they must be prepared for the eventuality of the Chancellor's dismissal." Bismarck, for his part, confided to the same diarist the confession that " the sudden decisions of his Majesty " made his position difficult.

From May until the autumn Bismarck had remained for the

most part at Friedrichsruh, retired and almost inaccessible. A mood of melancholy, irritability, and bitterness appears to have fallen upon him at this time, as though he were under the influence of a depressing premonition. Stories were told of the ungovernable ill-humour from which he suffered; he was even said to be beyond the influence of the members of his own family. Hohenlohe in his diary refers to a conversation with him on January 24th which left upon him " the impression of a man not quite sound mentally," and in the same place he writes on June 24th: " Even Herbert Bismarck said he had ceased to understand his father, and many people were beginning to think that he was no longer quite sane." [1]

Whatever feeling of security Bismarck himself may have hitherto entertained, it was rudely shaken by a conversation with the Czar during the latter's visit to Berlin in October. To Bismarck's protestation of his determination to maintain the friendship between the two Governments at all costs the Czar had replied: " Yes, I believe you, and I place confidence in you, but are you sure that you will remain in office? " [2] Recalling this conversation later Bismarck wrote: " He (the Czar) was far better instructed than I when he put the question, whether I was quite sure of retaining my place under the new Emperor. I answered, as I then thought, that I was convinced that I possessed the confidence of Emperor William II, and did not believe that I should ever be dismissed against my will, because his Majesty, by reason of my prolonged experience in office, and the confidence which I had won for myself, not only in Germany but in foreign Courts, had in me a servant whom it was very difficult to replace. My assurance elicited from his Majesty an expression of great satisfaction, though he hardly seemed to share it unreservedly."

There seems to have been some justification for the suspi-

---

[1] *Memoirs,* vol. ii., pp. 399 and 404. It is interesting to recall a passage which appears in a letter written by Bismarck to the King of Prussia in February, 1869, when asking for permission to resign on account of physical and mental strain. " I have not the feeling," he said, " that a long life will be vouchsafed to me, and I fear that my organization promises to have a final development similar to that of the late King " (Frederick William IV, who died mentally deranged).

[2] The succeeding Chancellor, Caprivi, told Privy Councillor Otto Hamman, head of the Press Bureau of the Foreign Office (June, 1892), that the Czar said to him at Narva, when visited there by the Emperor in the summer of 1890, " I have never been able honestly to trust your predecessor " (Hamman, *Der neue Kurs,* p. 16).

cion which the Emperor had begun to entertain about this time that Bismarck contemplated a closer approach to Russia at the expense of the alliance with Austria. The Grand Duke of Baden told Hohenlohe in June that the Chancellor had set his Press agents to work "launching all kinds of articles against Austria," and that he was scheming that Austria "should attack Russia alone and of her own motion, so that no *casus fœderis* should be given and Germany could stand aside." Yet the direct cause of the breach, when it came, was disagreement not over foreign but home questions.

At the end of 1889 the time had come for prolonging the Socialist Law, failing which it would expire on September 30th of the following year. The Federal Council was of one accord on the question of necessity, and in October a bill had been laid before the Diet, embodying substantially the provisions of the existing law, though with certain amendments in the direction of greater severity. Dangerous agitators were to be driven from their localities, and were not to be allowed to return without the permission of the police authorities. In committee parties were principally divided over this proposal. The feudal Conservatives wanted expulsion from the Empire altogether; the Imperialists and National Liberals had no very decided scruples against expatriation, but feared that by creating martyrs it would help rather than check the Socialist peril; the Clerical and popular parties alone opposed the measure on the clear ground of political principle. The expulsion clause was rejected, but the majority adopted a proposal of the National Liberals that the bill as amended should now be a permanent instead of a temporary measure, and it went back to the Diet in January. Although the law had been promised in the speech from the throne, and was only awaiting a third reading, followed by formal confirmation by the Federal Council, the rumour now went abroad that the Emperor, acting upon one of those " sudden impulses " which Bismarck had already found disconcerting, had begun to doubt the wisdom of coercion. " Any one can govern with a state of siege, but I will govern them by liberty," said Cavour of the unruly Neapolitans in 1861. So thought the young Emperor of the Socialists; and remembering how Bismarck had for twelve years fought these adversaries with the weapon of repression, and had failed, the idea of demonstrating to the country and the world that he could fight and overcome them without resort to exceptional measures appealed to him irresistibly.

The result of the prevailing uncertainty was that when the time came for the third reading of the bill the Ministerial parties were left without a lead. As the expatriation paragraph had been excised the Conservatives had no great interest in the bill and voted against it, with the result that it was defeated by a large majority. Public opinion became mystified still more when the Government did nothing to retrieve its defeat; and the silence of the Chancellor strengthened the suspicion that the Emperor and he had quarrelled. The Diet was closed the same day with a speech from the throne in which the unhappy bill was not mentioned.

For once public surmise was altogether correct. The Emperor later gave his version of the disagreement to Prince Hohenlohe. Bismarck, he said, wanted to deal with the Socialists more rigorously, whereas he was for closing the chapter of force and beginning again on new lines. His grandfather had risked nothing in assenting to coercion, for he had behind him a long and glorious reign. " But he was in a different position, for he had as yet achieved nothing. He would be reproached with beginning his reign by slaughtering his subjects. He was ready enough to act if necessary, but he wished to be able to act with a clear conscience, and first to make an attempt to remove the legitimate grievances of the workmen and to do everything that was possible to satisfy their justifiable demands."

The Emperor's attitude became clearer when at the beginning of February he issued two rescripts on the labour question. One was addressed to the Chancellor and the other to the Prussian Ministers of Public Works and Commerce and Industry, yet neither of them bore Ministerial counter-signature. The Prussian rescript laid down certain principles for the guidance of the Government in its relations to employees in State works, while the rescript addressed to the Chancellor proposed an international conference on the subject of labour legislation. This idea had really originated with the Swiss Government, which had already approached the principal European States tentatively on the subject. The Emperor induced the authors of the proposal to retire in his favour and he developed it on larger lines.

Here, again, he had had to contend with determined opposition from his Chancellor. The Socialist Law had already been abandoned. To follow that capitulation with new measures of social reform seemed to Bismarck tantamount to a double admission that the Government had all along been in the wrong and the Socialists in the right. He fought the proposal by argument as long as he could, and unwisely did not stop there. Recalling many such disputes with the first Emperor in the past years, and his unfailing device for breaking down resistance, he at last threatened to resign if the conference project were pressed further. The effect of this threat was the reverse of that expected; a silence followed which was meant to imply that the Chancellor must act as he would. There was no more talk of resignation, but from that moment the idea of a change of Minister took definite form in the Emperor's mind. The Labour Conference duly met in Berlin during the second half of March and adopted a number of propositions, in the form of answers to a schedule of questions, committing the delegates — yet not in some cases, as it proved, the Governments they represented — to ameliorative measures in regard to the hours of labour that should be worked by women, juveniles, and children in factories. Laws were passed in various countries carrying out more or less faithfully the recommendations of the conference — by Great Britain in 1891, by France and Belgium in 1892, and Holland in 1895 — but in the principal industrial countries it cannot be said that the gain to labour was very considerable. The principal value of the conference was that it gave a wider recognition to the principle of international action in labour legislation.

A wide province of possible contention had been opened up by the inability of Emperor and Chancellor to see eye to eye on two questions so vital to a true understanding of the working classes and to the further progress of social legislation, and the fact that disagreement should have occurred over these questions revealed an incompatibility of outlook which was all the more remarkable since Bismarck was wont to claim as one of his greatest triumphs his success in winning the first Emperor to the cause of social reform. Nevertheless, it is not certain that differences over the Socialist Law and the Labour Conference proposal would alone have led to an open breach. More important was the increasing disposition shown by the

Emperor to restrict the large powers which Bismarck had been accustomed to exercise throughout his Ministerial career, and to take matters more into his own hand. By the exercise of a royal prerogative which, though altogether constitutional, had for a long time been in abeyance, he had already, against his Chancellor's protests, appointed a Minister of Liberal inclinations to the Home Office in the person of Herr Herrfurth. Now he wished to cancel an important right which had been secured to the Minister President of Prussia by Cabinet Orders of long standing, and since the establishment of the Empire — the King of Prussia being *ex officio* the German Emperor — extended to the Imperial Chancellor, viz., his right to be present at audiences given by the Sovereign to other Ministers. Regarding this arrangement as a restriction of his independence the Emperor challenged it, claiming for the future to confer with any of his Ministers when and as he pleased. Bismarck opposed the innovation as an invasion of his most valuable official prerogative and as undermining his authority.

The question was an old one in Prussian Ministerial life. Early in the century Hardenberg had had to assert the very right which Bismarck now defended. A Cabinet Order of January 11, 1819, gave to Ministers the right to report to the King upon the affairs of their own departments, but only in the presence of the Chancellor. Wilhelm von Humboldt tried to over-ride it, and before he agreed in that year to take office in Hardenberg's Cabinet he asked the King that his position might be that of an independent Minister, competent to report directly without the intervention of the head of the Government. The desired permission was not given, and the rule set up in 1819 continued undisputed, and was confirmed more explicitly by a Cabinet Order of Frederick William IV, of which the object was to secure the utmost unity of policy, and to make it possible for the head of the Cabinet to assume responsibility for all acts of government with full knowledge.

This Order dated September 8, 1852, imposed on the Minister President the duty of exercising " more than hitherto a general oversight over the various branches of internal administration, so that it may be possible for him to maintain intact the necessary unity therein and so give me information upon all important administrative measures on my demand." The Order, therefore, laid down the rules that upon all administrative measures of importance the departmental head must previously, either in writing or verbally, arrive at an agreement with the Minister President; should these measures require the King's assent a report upon them must be made to the Minister President beforehand, and this must be put before the King with his comments; should a departmental head wish to make a report to the King directly on matters relating to his portfolio he should previously inform the Minister President, so that he might, if he wished, be present at the interview.

Bismarck was thus not responsible for the right for which he was contending; it had been established in its existing form ten years before he became Minister, and all he now asked was that it might be faithfully observed in the future as in the past. Inasmuch as he was responsible, in the last resort, for the mistakes and failures as well as the successes of Ministerial policy, he contended that he must be allowed to hold his office on conditions which would enable him to exercise some effectual check upon the measures by which the reputation of the Government and his own credit would stand or fall. He had also a personal interest in protesting against any change at that time, for he knew that ambitious colleagues had gained the ear and the favour of the Emperor and were doing their utmost to undermine his position.

It is obvious that all the arguments which Bismarck was able to advance on his side were equally applicable to the other. What Bismarck understood by unity of policy was the unity of his own policy, and the Emperor wanted unity on just the same terms, for he was determined that Sovereign and Minister must once for all regain their rightful places in Germany, the one as entitled to originate, the other as bound to execute, national policy. When, too, Bismarck contended that the right to be present when the Emperor conferred with other Cabinet Ministers was necessary to his own liberty of action, the Emperor similarly contended that owing to his inability to hear and know anything at first hand his own liberty was crippled and made illusory. The real question between them was not, in truth, one of law or logic or precedent. They were contending over the far more fundamental issue: Which of the two was the real ruler of Germany? and both of them knew it. Bismarck was fighting for his old privileges, the Emperor for the right of the Crown to be free. Faced by the Cabinet Order of 1852, the Emperor called on his Chancellor to put it out of force. Bismarck answered that he could not do so if he was expected still to retain the position and responsibility of the first Minister of the Crown and the Empire.

There are few less gracious sights in the world than that of two obstinate wills conflicting for domination, but this was the spectacle now offered for Germany's and the world's edification. In the struggle which had come to a head there were all the elements of tragedy. No Minister in a constitutional State had ever exercised so much executive power as Bismarck. The large authority vested in him as the head of the Prussian Ministry by the disputed Cabinet Order has been mentioned, but under the constitution of the Empire his power was even greater and more arbitrary, for that constitution recognized only one Minister, the Chancellor, to whom all other agents of Government, however high their functions, were entirely subordinate. And as if his constitutional rights were not sufficient he had enlarged them by steady encroachment upon monarchical prerogative until his position was to all intents and purposes autocratic and supreme. Could this position still be maintained, or must it be relinquished? That was the issue of the struggle, and the tragedy of it lay in the fact that while for the Emperor surrender could only mean the continuance, for a time which in the course of nature could not be long, of an arrangement sanctioned by the assent of many years and justified by great results, for Bismarck surrender meant intolerable humiliation, the withdrawal of all power from a Minister who had been all-powerful, and virtually his degradation to the level of one of his own assistants. No definite decision had yet been arrived at, yet though the issue was left undetermined Bismarck was not for a moment in doubt that the Emperor would sooner or later insist on having his way, and that he himself would have either to give in, which he could not and would not do, or to go.

Soon the question became involved with another and less defensible attempt to restrict the Minister's independence. The elections to the Imperial Diet had taken place on February 20th, and they went against the Government and greatly weakened the Cartel formed in 1887. Now was seen one of the first effects of the Emperor's attitude towards Socialism and social reform. The Ministerial, law-abiding, Conservative parties, feeling the ground cut under their feet, fought half-heartedly. The Socialists, on the other hand, fought jubilantly and with a premonition of victory, for with the sophistry that broods in political controversy they pointed to the abandonment of the Socialist Law as a capitulation to their demands and as an indication that the Emperor could not be an enemy of their cause. The Ministerial majority, which had been made up in the main of Conservative and National Liberal votes, was reduced by about one-half, the Conservatives losing twenty-eight and the National Liberals fifty-seven seats, while the Radicals gained forty-four seats and therewith attained their maximum strength in the Diet, the Clericals gained eight seats, and the Social Democrats twenty-four, becoming now a party thirty-five strong. The displacement of votes was even more remarkable; the two Conservative fractions lost over half a million and the National Liberals the same, while the Radical groups gained a quarter of a million, and the Social Democrats nearly half a million. The breach between the Conservatives and the National Liberals had been widening for some time, and now Bismarck, seeing that his majority had disappeared, came to the conclusion that the time had come for a return to the old Conservative-Clerical coalition.

As soon as the elections were over (March 14th) he invited Dr. Windthorst, the Ultramontane leader, to meet him at his house in order to discuss the possibility of such an arrangement. In those days of hot passion and mutual distrust there were spies and eavesdroppers everywhere, and news of this meeting reached the ears of the Emperor, who immediately sent the chief of his Civil Cabinet, Herr von Lucanus, to the Chancellor with a verbal message to the effect that " before holding political conversations with deputies in future he must notify the Emperor." Such an intolerant order, given by an inexperienced young man of thirty to a statesman of seventy-five, was more than flesh and blood could stand. Bismarck sent back word that he could allow no such invasion of his home life. Not satisfied with the answer which his envoy had brought him, the Emperor himself called on the Chancellor early the following morning to demand an explanation of his dealings with Windthorst. He received the same answer, with the addition, " The commands of your Majesty stop short at

my wife's *salon*." Wrathful at the renewed affront and the
manner of it, Bismarck went further and reminded the Emperor that he occupied his position only that he might serve
him and his country, and that " if he was in the way he was
willing to make room for another." Once more the Emperor
answered with an ominous silence that meant more than many
words. It was evident that the old Chancellor was meant to
understand that a new will was now directing affairs and that
he was no longer indispensable. Once again, however, before
the fateful step was taken which for a time alienated Bismarck
from the Crown and the Crown from the nation, the old servitor
was brought back to the Cabinet Order of 1852 and given another chance of parting with it. Hard as ever the Iron Chancellor might be broken but he was not to be bent, and he still
refused to comply.

But the Moor had done his duty and he now might go.[1] On
March 17th Bismarck suffered the acute humiliation of receiving from the grandson of the man whom he had kept upon the
throne of Prussia in 1862 and placed upon the imperial throne
in 1871 a peremptory command, conveyed through an *aide-de-
camp*, that he would ask for " permission to resign." To that
order he refused obedience on the ground that he could not be
responsible for the consequences to the Empire. On the following day the command was repeated and was complied with.
It is not unlikely it had now come to Bismarck's knowledge
that the Emperor had for some weeks been looking out for a
successor, and had opened discussions with General von Caprivi.[2]

His resignation was formally tendered in a long letter, dated
March 18th, clearly reasoned and singularly moderate in tone
for a man whose soul must at the time have been as molten
metal. In this historical document of State he reviewed the
relationship of the Prussian Minister President to the Crown
and his place in the Ministerial system, explained the genesis
and purpose of the Cabinet Order of 1852, and argued that
unless the Minister President continued to occupy the status
and the power conferred on him by the Order he could not con-

[1] " Der Mohr hat seine Arbeit getan; der Mohr kann gehen " (Schiller's
Die Verschwörung des Fiesko, Act iii., scene 4).

[2] *Memoirs of Prince Chlodwig von Hohenlohe* (diary, under date March
21, 1890), vol. ii., p. 409. Bismarck is said to have recommended Caprivi to
the Emperor as his successor some time before.

scientiously or successfully undertake responsibility for the policy and acts of the Government whose head he was supposed to be. If, therefore, the King intended that the Cabinet Order should be repealed he could no longer hold his position as head of the Ministry of State. There was no formal mention of resigning the Chancellorship, for the abandonment of one office implied the relinquishment of the other.

The concluding part of the letter was not less reproachful because its irony was studiously restrained. " I should have sought from your Majesty release from my office a year ago," he wrote, " had I not had the impression that your Majesty would wish to use the experiences and capacities of a faithful servant of your fathers. Now that I am certain that your Majesty does not need them, I may withdraw from political life without fearing that my decision so to do will be judged by public opinion as premature."

The Emperor made an attempt to soothe the wounded feelings of the fallen Minister by the offer of a dukedom, to which he added a field marshal's staff and a full-length portrait of himself. Bismarck accepted the honour for his family's sake and because the title, Duke of Lauenburg (his estate of Friedrichsruh was in the old duchy of that name), recalled one of his earliest political triumphs, but to the last he continued to use the title given to him by the first Emperor. A few days later Count Herbert Bismarck resigned the office of Secretary of State for Foreign Affairs, and was succeeded by Baron Marschall von Bieberstein, a former Baden Minister. To the joy of the bureaucrats as well as the democratic parties the menace of a " Bismarck dynasty " now altogether disappeared.

No sooner was the Chancellor's resignation accepted than his ejection from the official palace — for it was nothing else — began. No time was left for preparations; he was put out, and his chattels were sent after him. Busch tells how within a few hours all his chief's papers were unceremoniously packed in chests and carted away after dark. Before a week had passed his successor was installed in the building which he had made famous. On March 29th, having first taken formal leave of the Emperor and Empress and visited the grave of his " old master " at Charlottenburg, Bismarck left Berlin amid frantic demonstrations of homage such as no emperor or king had received in Germany's capital before, either at his coming or going. On the other hand, there were many loyal subjects of the Crown who felt that the lament in which the Emperor voiced his feelings at that time, " My heart is as sad as though I had again lost my grandfather; but God has ordained it so, and I must bear it, even though I fall under the load," did not ring quite true.

The episode which thus reached its climax aroused throughout Germany and amongst Germans everywhere both pain and resentment, and foreign opinion was not slow to endorse the national verdict that by the humiliation of the foremost living statesman a great wrong and a great blunder had been committed. Most people recognized that a breach was unavoidable, but no one was found to excuse in the Emperor the impetuosity which had precipitated it. Bismarck himself was far from blameless. He had become unbearably autocratic, and no longer brooked opposition. One might say that it was his own system what had avenged itself upon him — that he had fallen upon his own sword. He had re-enthroned in a constitutional State a new absolutism almost more obnoxious than the old, for it was the absolutism of a Minister who exercised powers which he had usurped. That on the overthrow of this illicit despotism he should have been the first victim to be carried away on the tumbril was tragic, yet not altogether unjust. The Empress Frederick said of Bismarck to Hohenlohe in June, 1888, that " he had reigned for twenty years untrammelled, and now could not bear to meet a will in a monarch." Unquestionably he had hoped to manage the young Emperor as he had managed the old, and the Grand Duke of Baden probably did not exaggerate the issue when he said that " it had become a question whether the Bismarck dynasty or the Hohenzollern dynasty should rule," and that " if the Emperor had given way upon this occasion he would have lost all authority and all parties would have looked simply to Bismarck and obeyed him."

All such pleas, however, while they may properly be advanced in proof of the necessity of a change, cannot take away the reproach that clings to the manner in which the change was made. The man who does a good thing badly is almost more inexcusable than the one who, though doing a bad thing, takes care to do it well. The verdict passed by thoughtful people of all parties upon Bismarck's displacement was: " It was bound to come, but it should have come otherwise."

The most creditable act ever done by the German nation in modern times was its refusal to desert Bismarck in the hour of his humiliation and fall. The man whom the Emperor thought to erase became more than ever the people's hero. Universities embarrassed him with degrees of philosophy, law, and theology, and half a hundred cities and towns welcomed him into the ranks of their freemen. For a long time Friedrichsruh became a Mecca for grateful admirers and fervent patriots, but also unfortunately for impertinent busy-bodies and sordid mischief-makers. For Bismarck carried his grievances with him into private life. Cavour, who had also experienced the mortification of falling into the background, at least temporarily, wrote towards the close of his career (July 22, 1859): "There is nothing so ridiculous in the world as the sulking of a fallen Minister." Bismarck sulked, and like everything else done by him he did it well, not mutely but aloud, on a large scale, with a freedom which mocked discretion. As a consequence the first three years of retirement were productive of unedifying controversies and animosities which did good to no one concerned. They are not part of the history of Germany nor truly of a biography of Bismarck; they were aberrations, and having sunk into oblivion they are best left there.

Bismarck as the critic of Government policy was awkward and aggravating, yet European opinion was unpleasantly surprised when two months after his resignation Caprivi, the new Chancellor, acting on the Emperor's instructions, addressed a letter to the German embassies (May 23, 1890) instructing them to make it known wherever needful that " the opinions of Prince Bismarck were those of a private individual and no longer possessed practical value." Bismarck thought otherwise, and as the nation generally still preferred his opinions and judgments to those of the men who had succeeded him, he gave both with characteristic frankness. When in June, 1892, he travelled to Vienna — his journey to the South one unbroken triumphal progress — to attend the marriage of his eldest son, the head of the German embassy there received instructions from Berlin that neither he nor his staff might accept invitations to the marriage feast. Bismarck replied to the challenge with bitter words, while Germany's answer to this official boycott of her greatest son was to greet the dethroned

Chancellor on his homecoming with ovations even more tumultuous than before, and the Emperor knew that every cheer for Bismarck implied an unuttered groan for himself.

So it might have continued indefinitely had not Bismarck fallen dangerously ill in the autumn of 1893. Then the Emperor, making the first approaches, as was the privilege of youth, concluded peace with the old statesman, handsomely if not sincerely, and to the joy of the whole nation. Bismarck reciprocated with all the outward courtesy and deference of an old courtier, though it may be doubtful whether the time ever came when he either forgot or forgave the injuries which he suffered in March, 1890. To the last he believed, as a large part of the nation has believed ever since, that his dismissal was the chance effect of royal caprice and the intrigues of his enemies. Unquestionably royal caprice played a part in the episode, just as did the conspirators, base and less base, who lost no opportunity of helping the Colossus to his fall. But both caprice and intrigue were merely incidents in the play of larger forces. The fuller truth is that Bismarck's relinquishment of the reins of power was inevitable, because in the order of Germany's development; he had completed his special work, and his continuance in office obstructed the fulfilment of other tasks which did not fall within the range either of his sympathy or his vision.

It cannot be doubted also that to Europe in general the disappearance of Bismarck from the arena which he had dominated for over twenty years afforded genuine relief. It was not that European statesmen grudged to the great master of their craft his unique influence and apparent success in controlling the course of political events, but rather that they experienced a sense of liberation from dependence upon a man who to the political world at large had been an incalculable force, an inscrutable enigma, and for that reason an element of constant uncertainty and unrest. A strong belief — recalled at a later time with surprise — prevailed that with his passing, whatever might be the future of international politics, the elimination of the play of this powerful personality would make for greater quietude and stability, and that for a long time the history of Europe would be written in small letters.

Soon the death of his devoted wife, the pietist Johanna von Puttkamer (November 27, 1895), left him almost a stranger in the world. One by one his contemporaries of the older generation had predeceased him — the first Emperor, Roon, and last of all Moltke (April 24, 1891). He had made no new friends, for he had seldom admitted his official associates to intimate intercourse, and of the Ministers whom he had left behind some were busy making their peace with the new ruler and some were retaliating for past indignities by open hostility. The retirement for which he had often longed had not brought him the tranquillity which was to have been a fitting close to his strenuous and troubled career. Once, many years ago, before the allures of Ministerial office held him, he had gained solace in disappointment by the reflection that life is a passage and a show, and ambition and power, pain and sorrow, are mere figments of sense and brain. Perchance there came back to him in these hours of loneliness and disillusionment some words which he had written to his wife from St. Petersburg in July, 1859, before the fibre of his spirit had been hardened by rough labour and turmoil. They may be quoted here, as affording a revelation of an aspect of his character which is but little known. Anticipating the future of his country with anxiety, he wrote: —

" But God, who can hold up Prussia and the world or destroy them, knows why it must be so, and we will not be embittered against the land in which we were born and the authorities for whose enlightenment we pray. Thirty years hence, perhaps much sooner, it will be of little consequence how it fares with Prussia and Austria if only God's mercy and Christ's redeeming love remain in our souls. Yesterday evening I opened the Bible quite at random in order to forget politics, and my eyes fell at once upon the fifth verse of the 110th Psalm (' The Lord at my right hand shall strike through Kings in the day of His wrath '). As God will, it is only a question of time: nations and men, folly and wisdom, war and peace — they all come and go like waves, and the sea remains."

Weighed down by years, worn by toil, stricken by weakness, a prey to the demons of sleeplessness and depression, his once dazzling eyes dulled by age and sorrow, Bismarck at last became physically a mere wreck of his former self. He died on July 30, 1898, at Friedrichsruh, and there was buried quietly and simply as he had wished. With his eighty-three years he had done justice to the record of his long-lived family, though his two sons were cut off in middle age.[1]   It might seem that both physically and intellectually the strength of the Bismarck race had been exhausted in producing this unique figure, great in body and mind, in work and fame.

Bismarck once told Hohenlohe that when speculating in 1852 upon his career he had marked it out in decades; it was his wish in ten years' time to be a Prussian Minister, then to remain in office ten years, and finally to have ten years of rest in which to reflect upon his experiences. The speculation worked out with only partial accuracy; he became Minister in the year anticipated, almost a decade was left to him for retrospect, but his Ministerial career was prolonged far beyond either his expectations or his desire, for he was in office twenty-eight years without a break.

For all but five of these years the cares not only of the Prussian monarchy but of the Empire — first the half and then the whole — lay upon his shoulders, and it is upon his efforts and achievements in this larger sphere of German affairs that his reputation rests. His nation will never forget or seek to diminish the greatness of the services which he rendered to its unity. He did great things while other people were talking about them; schemes so bold that his fellow-mortals grasped them only as ideas, he held before their bewildered eyes as finished facts. The Empire had been in the making for half a century before he came to power; it was he who finally drew together the sundered peoples and welded their irresolute longings into a mighty will for union. For, as Ranke says, in the great turning-points of history " general tendencies do not alone decide: great personalities are always necessary to make them effective." He found Germany inarticulate and weak, almost a byword amongst the nations of Europe; he left her consolidated and strong, her unity no longer the figment of treaties but the foremost fact in Continental politics. By heredity and instinct a Prussian of the strict feudalist order, his patriotism gradually broadened as, under his masterful guidance, the Empire asserted a larger place in the world; more and more he became German in his political outlook, until Prussian particularism came to be even more obnoxious to him than the particularism of the petty States. For the greater

[1] Count William in 1901, at the age of forty-nine; Count Herbert in 1904, at the age of fifty-five.

part of his career as a Minister he may be said to have typified Germany and the German idea in a way that no statesman had done since the time of Stein.

Nevertheless, his Germanism was never narrow or intolerant. Mr. Odo Russell wrote from Berlin to his Paris colleague in March, 1873, that the two great objects of Bismarck's policy were " the supremacy of Germany in Europe and of the German race in the world, and the neutralization of the influence of the Latin races in France and elsewhere." There is a misconception here, and Bismarck's actions prove it. That he wished to neutralize the influence of the Latin peoples may be admitted, since he sought to neutralize the influence of all countries alike — Latin, Slavic, Anglo-Saxon — in the interest of German security; but the assertion of German supremacy in Europe and the world was never the conscious aim of his policy, nor was such a purpose in the order of his ideas. He wished to make Germany strong and great, but only in order that she might be able to realize herself, live her own life freely and do her own work in the world without menace, and not that she might assert an arbitrary superiority over other nations, still less impose her will upon them.

While, therefore, he was intensely proud of his nation, his nationalism was never vulgarly aggressive. Patriotism expresses itself in a great variety of ways, from the dervish dance of super-heated emotionalism to the frigid arrogance that divides mankind into one's own people and the others. Bismarck's patriotism may best be visualized by Englishmen as being of the Cromwellian order — strong, restrained, dignified, never given to boasting or to pompous words, but all the more prepared to resort to deeds at need. Nothing was more alien to his spirit than the Chauvinism which expresses itself in foamy passions and noisy objurgations; he was not above making use of such manifestations when they served his purposes, but he did not admire them. One can no more imagine him moving a hair at the singing of " Germany, Germany above everything in the world," than one can imagine a Palmerston or a Disraeli listening without *ennui* to the crude sentiment of " Rule, Britannia!" There was, indeed, a strong vein of cosmopolitanism in him, as there is in every man made in a large mould. The historian Delbrück has hazarded the theory that nationalism was to Bismarck only another form of doctrinar-

ianism, and a biographer who came into close official contact
with him during many years has asserted that he preferred at
heart to be regarded as a European.[1] It is certainly true that,
while he judged foreign questions from the standpoint of national interest, as every statesman must do, who is neither trai-
tor nor fool, he was able and ready in his dealings with other
countries to appreciate their standpoint, even when he could
not endorse it.[2]

In all his relations with foreign Powers he acted in the spirit
of the unabashed, unsentimental " real " politician. That attitude betrayed itself as early as 1857 in his dealings with
Louis Napoleon. Defending, against the reproaches of his
friend Gerlach, his readiness at that time to make advances
to or even conclude an alliance with France, he wrote (May 2,
1857) : " I do not borrow the standard for my conduct towards foreign Governments from stagnating antipathies, but
only from the harm or good that I judge them capable of doing to Prussia." As he did not hate other countries, so also
he did not love them. He confessed on one occasion that England was the only country to which he was ever strongly
drawn — social amenities rather than political conditions being here the source of attraction — yet if at times he was not
slow to show her friendship, he was also ready to do her ill
when Germany's interests seemed to make that course expedient. In all his political friendships it was a case of " Thus
far and no farther." When the reproach was thrown at him
that these friendships were " too platonic," he admitted the
limitation, as being a necessary consequence of his theory of
international relations. In his memoirs he has stated this theory in the words : " No great Power can place itself exclusively at the service of another. It will always have to keep
in view not only existing but future relations to the others, and
must, as far as possible, avoid lasting fundamental hostility
to any of them." [3]

Bismarck's unique position as a Minister of State and the

---

[1] C. von Tiedemann, *Persönliche Erinnerungen an den Fürsten Bismarck,*
p. 42.

[2] " What are in general the interests of France in regard to Germany? "
he asked in a speech in the Prussian Diet on December 20, 1866, defending
the provisions of the Treaty of Prague. " Let us view them entirely free
from German prejudices; let us try to adopt the French standpoint — for
that is the only way to judge foreign interests justly."

[3] *Reflections and Reminiscences,* vol. ii., p. 235.

peculiarity of his relationship to the Sovereign whom he served in various offices for nearly a generation can only be fairly appreciated in so far as we divest our minds of English ideas of parliamentary government.   The same historian, Delbrück, relates how Bismarck said on one occasion: " Many good qualities have been ascribed to me, but one has always been forgotten; that I am a good courtier."   In proof he declared that during the Prussian constitutional conflict of 1862–6 he would personally have been quite satisfied with two years of military service, and that he fought for three years only because the King wanted it, adding that for the same reason he would have been equally prepared to fight for ten.   Bismarck used to speak of *la relation sure* which existed between the Sovereign and himself and convinced him that his devotion would never be ill-requited.   This devotion was dynastic at root, the instinct of a man who had inherited loyalty from generations of soldiers and Kings' men, but with time it developed into a more intimate attachment, as the Emperor more and more yielded his will into his Minister's keeping.

That this subordination of the Crown to the subject was carried to a point at which it no longer served the best interests of the State must be at once admitted.   Yet it might have seemed inevitable.   Some men are fitted to rule and others are more fitted to serve.   Bismarck was a born ruler, and his relations with his Sovereign were not properly adjusted until it had been decided beyond possibility of cavil which of the two should be the master: until then both of them had many uncomfortable hours.   " I do not know how it is," he said to Roon once, " I do my best to please the King, but I succeed worse every day.   I have all the qualities that should enable me to please him and to do what he wishes.   I am a Junker and a soldier, and I wish to obey him."   " Oh, yes," Roon replied, " but you don't."   Obedience was a virtue which Bismarck appreciated only in others; it was not for the ruler but the ruled to obey.

The year after he became Minister President of Prussia he assured the King that he did not conceive of his position as " that of a constitutional Minister in the usual sense, but that of your Majesty's servant, to comply with your Majesty's commands in the last instance, even when they do not correspond with my personal views."   Such sentiments were excellent in theory, yet they did not prevent him from resisting opposition vigorously from the first, as a rule with success. The high language which he held in correspondence with the Crown Prince in 1863 on various aspects of the constitutional dispute then raging showed that he had already begun to take liberties with royalty, and that he felt so sure of his position that he could venture to take sides in the misunderstandings between father and son which occurred at that time, and which he certainly made no attempt to abate. Did he use the language of flattery when in 1866, fearing that his design of a war with Austria might be wrecked on the King's scruples, he wrote that even if his advice were disregarded he " would still think that God directs your Majesty's heart and would not therefore do my service less gladly "? Whatever may be the answer to this question, he overbore the King's objections on that as on most occasions, and had the war he desired, and the time soon came when his belief in his Sovereign's heart as a piece of clockwork divinely regulated and therefore sure to go right — if, indeed, such a belief was ever more than affectation — gave place to a less questioning reliance upon his own finite judgment. He had only been Minister a few years when he began to take the helm of affairs into his own hands and to threaten resignation when his will was thwarted. His line of action was first to convince the King that he was indispensable, and then, confident that the King would not allow him to go, to impose his own terms, which every year became more severe, as a condition of staying. " You know that the Ministerial crisis has been arranged," the King wrote to him on October 27, 1869, " and of course as you wanted." In that year he even dared, without asking the King's sanction, to remove from his post Count Usedom, the envoy at Turin, who had become displeasing to him. For a Minister of his overbearing will to take liberties with the King once with impunity meant to do it often. With every capitulation, however, the influence of the Sovereign in public life decreased and that of the Minister increased, until at last Bismarck became a power not merely behind but above the throne.

His resignations were for a long time deservedly regarded as amongst the most ingenious pieces of mechanism in his political workshop. Threats of retirement followed at almost regular intervals, and so long as they were genuine the desired effect promptly followed. But some were far from genuine, and he was candid enough to admit it. No man had a keener sense of humour than Bismarck, and one can imagine the glee with which in May, 1880, he wrote to the Emperor, who had protested against another resignation, as not yet due: " I have not since (1877) *seriously* requested to be relieved of my office, for my request of five weeks ago (April 6th) could not have been taken seriously." When, however, it was understood that his threats of resignation were of two kinds, the serious and the not-serious, they all alike came to be regarded as unreal, and henceforth ceased to disturb either the Emperor or the nation.

Lord Palmerston was rebuked by Queen Victoria for withholding from her at times important matters of State. Bismarck far more systematically kept his King and Emperor in the dark, and in the later years he probably consulted him upon few questions likely to provoke acute difference of opinion. Some of the most momentous decisions of his political career were arrived at before consultation with his " master ": such were the decision to press the Hohenzollern candidature for the Spanish crown in 1870, the decision taken after the receipt of the Ems telegram to force France by provocation into a declaration of war, and the decision to conclude the treaty of alliance with Austria in 1879; on all these occasions the Sovereign was ignored until the decisive action had been taken. But this did not prevent him from using the Emperor as a stalking horse in negotiations of a specially inconvenient kind, such as those with Louis Napoleon over the question of compensations, when it was expedient to give conditional pledges which he knew that the Emperor would never honour.

As time passed it came to be almost taken for granted that he was the real ruler of Germany and the Emperor merely the recorder of his decisions.[1] Long before the close of his reign the

[1] Writing of his negotiations with Bismarck in Berlin over the Turco-Greek frontier question in February, 1881, Mr. (later Lord) Goschen says: " What struck me especially was the degree of absolute independence with which he did his work. No obligation to communicate with a single colleague! No desire for a moment's quiet reflection! Nor did he suspend his decision, so far as I could see, for a formal reference to the Emperor. When he had brought matters to a point he turned to the Foreign Minister and Dr. Busch with the words, ' Now, gentlemen, you will write,' and in my presence he dictated *straight off* a circular to the German ambassadors at foreign Courts, giving them an abstract of our plans, with instruc-

Emperor had ceased to oppose him, and on occasions of serious disagreement used to send envoys, like Hohenlohe, to reason with him on his behalf. This was bad for the Emperor, for the country, and for Bismarck most of all. Possessing so much power, even more was ascribed to him, and if he was spoiled the fault was only half his own. In Germany crowned heads hung upon his word, sued for his favour, addressed him almost in the spirit of vassals, and lobbied in his official residence like railway directors in a House of Parliament. Bismarck's correspondence shows that, with all their notions of divine right, these fading relics of political mediævalism were conscious of a stronger title to power than their parchments and old descent, and were ready to accord it unbidden deference. A Prince of Reuss writes to implore that " no hostile attitude may be taken against me and my country," and the King of Saxony thanks him for deigning to offer his friendship to " one who, though only in the quality of an inferior workman, has been allowed to co-operate in the establishment of the Empire," and hopes that his apologetic letter will " not be taken amiss." Bismarck, whose estimate of human nature was never high, and became lower the longer he knew it, took all such suppliants at their own valuation. Speaking once to Hohenlohe of the kinglets and princelings who had settled upon Germany like a swarm of bees, he said they should be glad enough to have a roof above their heads. Probably that was the best he thought of them.

Such a man could not be crossed with impunity. Sir Robert Morier, who believed that Bismarck did his best to have him removed from Germany, once wrote: " He leaves no effort untried to crush those whom he cannot seduce, and nothing can exceed the virulence or persistence of his animosity." The severity of this judgment hardly admits of any softening. The cases of Arnim and Geffcken are, of course, the classical examples of his vindictiveness; but his correspondence with the King and Emperor throws light upon other equally unedifying illustrations of his despotic spirit — of the denunciation of men, who were doing their best, because they were not sufficiently servile, of reputations precious enough to their owners torn into rags and tatters by the man who had the power

tions to communicate it to the respective Governments to which they were accredited " (*Life of Lord Goschen,* by the Hon. A. E. Elliot, vol. i., p. 213).

of life and death over them.[1] He did not even scruple to put secret agents into the German embassies in order that they might spy upon men whom he wished to entrap and undo.

Early in his career he had wrung from the King a tacit understanding that he should be allowed to have about him just the men he wanted, and this right to choose and remove at will he exercised arbitrarily and without the slightest compunction. The highest Ministers of State who served at his side knew that they held their offices by the frailest tenure — the whim of a masterful dictator who had made them and could unmake them at will. Again and again men who had given their best strength to the service of their country suddenly found their way to the Tarpeian Rock for the only reason that they did not sufficiently obey or had ceased to please him. For courtesy's sake these victims of a harsh and rigorous discipline were said to have " resigned on account of ill-health," but all the world knew that the true cause of their disappearance from office and sight was that they were in Bismarck's way. Abeken wrote of his official chief : " His is a great nature but not a royal one." He overlooked no insult, forgot no injury, and forgave no debtor until he had paid the uttermost farthing. If an enemy smote him on the right cheek he promptly smote back on both. In all his personal relations he was a sheer, stark egoist, unmitigated, pitiless, and terrible. And yet — explain it who can — no man was more sensitive than Bismarck himself when wrong or unkindness was done to him. Some of his lamentations over the unfaithfulness of political associates who walked no more with him were obviously the utterance of acute spiritual suffering.

Nothing was allowed to frustrate the realization of his schemes, and if in politics he despised one thing more than another it was consistency. By every law of reason and statecraft he should have been a powerful pillar of legitimism, Conservatism, and tradition; yet he destroyed the Bund with violent hands, violated the constitution of Prussia for four years, overturned German dynasties and annexed German States, and

---

[1] Count Beust recalls in his *Memoirs* how, at his first meeting with Bismarck at the end of 1848, he chanced to speak of the execution of Blum as a political blunder, whereupon Bismarck retorted: "You are quite wrong; if I have an enemy in my power I must destroy him." Beust adds: "I have remembered this saying more than once" (*Memoirs,* English translation, vol. i., p. 57).

he was at one time ready to conclude an alliance with the usurping Louis Napoleon; he sent bishops of the Roman Church to prison and into exile, invaded the privileges of the Imperial Parliament, introduced the civil marriage contract, suspended the constitutional rights of free association and assembly, and over-rode the Press laws without a pretence of legality. Lord Augustus Loftus relates that Bismarck often said to him that " he gloried in having no principles, for he observed that when you wish to gain a certain object your principles cross your path and defeat your aim." [1]

Bismarck's statesmanship was of the great but it was not of the moral order. He said once that the maxims of diplomacy were summed up in the words, " Qui trompe-t-on ici? " and one who knew his official life as few others had to confess of him that in pursuing his political ends he adopted " oblique and often crooked ways." Not seldom men judge most severely in others their own special faults. Bismarck cordially hated the Jesuits who was himself the greatest of Jesuits. His confession of lack of principles has been quoted. The disclaimer is, of course, paradoxical, yet it veils a profound truth. It is a great tribute to the moral standards of our modern age, which conceited elderlies are apt to accuse of decadence, that most of the current notions of social relations and social order presume the tacit acceptance of a high ethical premise. Thus when people speak of principles they mean high principles, just as when they talk of maxims they mean wise maxims, and when they speak of law they mean good law. Of course, Bismarck was guided perhaps more consciously than most statesmen by principles, but they were those of an utterly deidealized worldly wisdom. Had he been questioned he might have said that in politics he followed not principles but a goal. There could be nothing discreditable in such an avowal so long as the goal was a right one, for the law of public and that of private conduct are not in all respects identical. In questions of private morality motive is everything; in questions of public morality motive is subordinate to the end pursued. Yet the ultimate test of motive and end is the same, since both are justified or condemned by the one ethical law. Such a test, however, had for Bismarck no meaning. If before his political decisions he was wont to consult an oracle it was to the temple at Delphi

[1] *Recollections,* vol. i., p. 316.

and not Jerusalem that he repaired, and the question which troubled him was not, Is it right? but Will it succeed? Not without reason did he lay down the doctrine that it is not the business of one Government to dictate moral behaviour to another, since with morality the State has nothing to do.

The compliment of utter truthfulness which was paid by the Duke of Wellington to Peel and by Lord Granville to Canning — the highest compliment that can fall to public or private man — cannot be claimed for Bismarck. He did not lie outright, but neither did he always tell the truth outright; his favourite compromise with veracity took the form of equivocation. Granted that his deceptions were chiefly over large issues and in the grand style, yet they were still deceptions, and no less flagitious because they were discovered or, as sometimes happened, frankly admitted only long after they had ceased to possess political significance. He practised deceit even in his dealings with his own colleagues. Upon many questions — and they were not the least important — he carried on two policies simultaneously: the official policy of his Sovereign and Government, and his own private policy, fostered clandestinely by such agents and measures as seemed to him most expedient in the given circumstances. If he did not wish the official policy to succeed, this subterranean intrigue gave him the means of obstructing it. In the Spanish succession episode in 1870 he instructed the German legations not to interfere on either side at the very time that he himself was secretly promoting the candidature of the Prince of Hohenzollern by all the means in his power. He undoubtedly connived at, even if he did not actually suggest, the denunciation by Russia, in November, 1870, of the Pontus clauses of the Treaty of Paris, yet he professed at the time to be shocked at the irregularity of the proceeding.

He never had any scruple about suppressing facts, tampering with documents, or making the worse appear the better reason. The motives to which he ascribed his public acts were sometimes wholly false and they were seldom wholly true, and it was never certain that the aims which he avowed were those which he was in fact following. So it came to pass that when he spoke the utter truth he was not always believed. Upon each of the three occasions when he wanted war he was shrewd enough to put his opponents as much in the wrong as possible, even by the use of strategy in which deceit played a prominent part. Perhaps no statesman — certainly no modern statesman — succeeded in an equal degree in attaining great ends by questionable means, so deliberately and systematically did evil in the hope that good would come of it, or was so skilled in establishing plausible justification for morally indefensible acts of policy.

One of his crooked ways was his systematic abuse of the Press. He reduced the manipulation of public opinion by the aid of venal newspapers to a consummate art, though an unclean one. He began the practice almost as soon as he became a Prussian Minister, and at first the King appears to have disapproved of it.[1] Complaining of an abusive article upon a reigning Prince which had appeared in the *Kreuzzeitung*, he writes to Bismarck in April, 1866: " You always told me that the Government has no influence on the *Kreuzzeitung*, but it seems to me that this is a case which proves the contrary." Caught in the act of newspaper intrigue Bismarck replied: " I would never dare to deceive your Majesty "— in point of fact he had just done it —" and openly confess that I myself suggested the substance of the article." In later years this perversion of the Press was carried on to an incredible extent by the use of public money. In his political bodyguard were skilled journalists chosen for their resource and their readiness to be his servile tools in an immoral propagandism which was not the less discreditable to them because they did his will with entire devotion. Even newspapers of the highest standing were willing to be duped and debauched by inspiration derived from these polluted sources. By their connivance public opinion was manufactured, obscured, or perverted at will, just as the interest of the moment required. From this pernicious system, which in its worst aspects ceased with Bismarck's resignation, the political journalism of Germany, free and bond

[1] Bismarck had begun to appreciate the value of a suborned Press even before he became Minister. In a letter to Schleinitz, President of the Prussian Ministry, written from St. Petersburg on May 12, 1859, he gave reasons for the greater cultivation of the newspapers, to which he attributed much of Austria's influence in the Diet at Frankfort. He was even then convinced that the Press could be easily bought: " Most of the correspondents write for their living, the chief object of most of the newspapers is to make a good profit, and an experienced reader, in reading some of our Berlin newspapers, can easily see whether they have recently received another subsidy from Austria, whether they are expecting one, or whether they are giving a threatening hint that they wish for one."

alike, has suffered permanently in influence and dignity. A Minister is known by the private secretaries he keeps. It is a question of sympathy, congruity, affinity. Something was assuredly amiss with the mind which could find satisfaction, and unburden itself so freely, in the company of the ex-journalist " Little Busch," faithfully as that capable intriguer repaid his patron's confidence.

By the spirit and methods which he introduced into political life Bismarck did much to pervert the moral sense of his countrymen and to lower the standard of public right in Europe. It cannot be said that in the whole course of his career he contributed to the world a single idea that could lift mankind to a higher level of ethical perfection. He spoke often, indeed, of the moral *imponderabilia* which he held it to be folly in a statesman, regardful of public opinion, to ignore, yet when he allowed for these impalpable forces he did so because of the importance attached to them by others and not from any esteem felt for them by himself. Count Caprivi, the second Chancellor, left a searching judgment of his great predecessor's influence in a letter written after his retirement and with no idea of publication.

" While entirely acknowledging the splendour of his person and of our heroic epoch," he wrote, " I thought, even before I became Chancellor, that I had perceived what serious blemishes were exhibited by the reverse of the splendid medal. What I thought ought to be the immediate aim of my endeavours, although it was an aim which could presumably only be achieved in the course of years, was to help the nation, without sacrificing any of its new national acquisitions, to return to an everyday existence in which it might again recover its old virtues. Prince Bismarck, as has often been said, had conducted domestic policy by the methods of foreign policy, *and the nation was in danger of seeing its moral standards lowered*." [1]

[1] The admission of such an obvious truism will be sought in vain in any of the German standard histories of modern Germany, or the earlier biographies of Bismarck. For that reason the frank criticisms of Bismarck's later biographer, Erich Marcks, greet, like a breath of fragrant air, the English student who is compelled to explore these works, and to brave their stifling atmosphere of perverted fact and indiscriminate flattery, and in sheer gratitude he is disposed to acclaim as superlative virtue a candour which is, after all, demanded by elementary honesty. The historian Hans Delbrück is another rare example of this new and healthy revolt against

And yet if, tried by the old moralities, Bismarck is found greatly wanting, it remains true that his very faults and transgressions were committed always for his country's sake, for its profit and not his own, and perhaps in judging the deserts of public men patriotism may cover the multitude of sins. He was made in a large mould, and though there were gross defects in the material his figure was nevertheless commanding and heroic.

If of the more intimate aspects of his character little is said here it is not because little is known or because there is anything to conceal. In personal dealings he was the soul of honour and his private life was blameless. His religious faith, too, of which in the early years of his official career he spoke and wrote with far less than the customary reticence of public men, was in its way genuine and profound. He might even be called a Christian in parts; though he did not believe, or at least ceased to " believe in soul "— it is questionable whether the word will be found in any of his countless speeches — he was " very sure of God." Once he spoke of himself as a bundle of prejudices; he was not less a bundle of inconsistencies. At a time when he was translating calories into exasperating despatches intended to provoke a rupture with Austria, he was penning to his wife edifying discourses upon the grace of God and the future state. It was after he had scarred the surface of Europe with three deliberately schemed wars that he set up the ideal of the Christian State and enacted a body of social reforms in the name of " practical Christianity." But the wars left his conscience untroubled; he said on one occasion that he had " settled that account with God." Not every statesman upon whose shoulders has lain the responsibility for bloodshed has been so fortunate.[1] There are obscurities

the past pernicious habit of falsifying biography from a misplaced concern for a reputation which is too great to need any such questionable aids.

[1] By way of contrast it is interesting to recall how his share of responsibility for the Crimean War haunted Lord Aberdeen to the end. Sir Arthur Gordon, his biographer, writes:

" The manse of Methlick was about this time (1857) rebuilt on a new site and in a better manner, but Lord Aberdeen declined to rebuild the parish church, though the structure was dilapidated, ugly, and inconvenient. ' I leave that for George,' he said. His reasons for this, in him, very unusual conduct, were never suspected, even by those most nearly in his confidence, until after his death, when the following text was found written by him more than once, and at different times on various scraps of paper: ' And David said to Solomon, My son, as for me, it was in my mind to build an house unto the name of the Lord my God; but the word of the Lord came and contradictions in every character and life, and only seldom is the clue discoverable.   Perhaps in Bismarck's case the clue may be found in the fact that in his policies and decisions he was pre-eminently governed by intuition and still more by instincts; had the instincts been finer the results would have been finer, too.

Speaking in his *Memoirs* of Bismarck's success as a statesman, Beust attributes it to " a conspicuous quality which is exactly described by the English word ' unscrupulousness,' " and to " the good fortune that always attended him." [1]   Yet to represent Bismarck's statecraft as an unbroken sequence of political triumphs would be to ignore the facts.   His career was so grandiose, he worked on so large a scale, and the immediate results of his plans were often so imposing, that it seldom occurs to the admiring and spellbound mind to ask whether, because he succeeded in carrying out so many of his policies, success could be claimed for the policies themselves.   His fame rests, for the most part, upon the unique part which he played in foreign affairs, including the events which contributed to the making of modern Germany.   His foreign policy, however, must be judged not merely by what it did for Germany, but by its influence upon and its effects for the world at large, and especially the European Continent which was the principal scene of his labours.   The life of any one nation is part of the life of all nations.   Hence foreign policy cannot be called successful at home if it fails abroad; if it fails at all it fails altogether, if it fails anywhere it fails everywhere.   The German nation saw, and sees, its Iron Chancellor only as the great unifier at home, never as the disuniter abroad; as the gainer of new territories, never as the spoliator of neighbouring States. It does not remember, in short, that much that he did for Germany was done at the expense of other countries, and that in settling the question of German unity he unsettled other questions, which have never since ceased to be a source of international disquiet and danger.[2]

to me, saying, Thou hast shed blood abundantly, and hast made great wars; thou shalt not build an house unto my name, because thou hast shed much blood upon the earth in my sight' (1 Chron. xxii., 7, 8)."

[1] *Memoirs*, vol. i., p. 241.

[2] There is at least a suggestion of the recognition of this truth in relation to Prussia's territorial appropriations in 1864 and 1866 in the words of the historian Hans Delbrück: "The annexation of Schleswig-Holstein, Hanover, Electoral Hesse, Nassau, and Frankfort was a violation of the

With all his dazzling triumphs of calculated statesmanship not a few feats of successful guesswork and even some brilliant failures must be laid to his account. Success has a way of creating its own conditions and so of repeating itself. When a halo had formed around Bismarck, and a Bismarck mythos had appeared, people began to look everywhere for signs and wonders, and because they expected they saw them. Acts and enterprises were successful simply because Bismarck was behind them; it seldom occurred to any one to ask for proofs. It is a safe surmise that some of his successes surprised himself most, and that some events which to his credulous countrymen appeared in the light of triumphs were to him the reverse. He saw far and deep, but even his keen sight could not penetrate stone walls. The judgment upon a few of his moves on the political chessboard must be that he failed entirely to discern the full significance, or to anticipate the outcome, of his own acts. It can hardly be pretended seriously that the choice which made Austria Germany's close ally and Russia her enemy was other than a blunder. That Bismarck came to recognize it as such is proved by the fact that long before he ceased to be Chancellor he rued it. Of course, he never intended that there should be an actual breach with Russia, and in fairness to his statecraft it should be remembered that none occurred so long as he continued in office; but the Vienna treaty of 1879 was fateful, and the Russo-French alliance which followed fourteen years later was the inevitable result. His mistake here was less in the choice than in the choosing. If a choice between Russia and Austria was really necessary he may have chosen wisely — and at least he could not at the time have chosen differently — but the deduction does not establish the premise.

Again, his encouragement of France in Tunis and of England in Egypt, though admittedly proceeding from a desire to see these countries embroiled in foreign complications, was from Germany's standpoint a misfortune, for Tunis led to Morocco and for England to go to Egypt meant that she would stay there. So, too, his shortsighted refusal to acquire colonies for Germany between 1867 and 1884, when pearls of great price were to be had for the picking up, was a stupen-

principle of legitimism, but it served the interests of Prussia " (*Bismarcks Erbe*, p. 38).

dous blunder, fortunate for other States. In his dealings with
the European Powers he would have succeeded more had he
not too visibly tried to play off one against another, all for
Germany's sake, forgetting that nations are not marionettes,
and that the ingenious policy of creating startling effects by
pulling strings may, after all, be only a foolish thing well
done. After breaking the peace of Europe three times he preserved it for twenty years, but it was by following the policy
of bribing every leading Power in turn with territory or the
promise of it — to each what it wanted — so long as Germany
was left in undisturbed possession of the spoils of 1870. Thus
he was wont to say during the later years of his Chancellorship: " In Serbia we are Austrian, in Bulgaria Russian, in
Egypt English," and he might have added in North-west Africa
French. Who dare maintain that an equal or a better result
might not have been attained by the pursuance of simpler and
less calculating means?

Similarly, some of his most conspicuous acts of domestic policy cannot by any exaggeration of charity be regarded as successful. He found Prussia emerging from a period of
political reaction, and he left her more hopelessly committed
to reaction than for half a century. Yet in fighting Liberalism he called into existence in its place a far more formidable
obstacle in the form of Social Democracy. This new political
force he strove to vanquish by the weapons of repression, only
to find that he had been sowing dragons' teeth, for every one
of which there sprang up a new and doughtier antagonist. He
tried conclusions with the Roman Catholic Church, and in the
end not only capitulated but incidentally raised up a powerful
anti-Ministerial party which he never ceased to regard as the
most dangerous factor in national politics. He lived to admit that his Polish policy had failed and to blame others
for the failure. His most dismal miscalculations in domestic
affairs, however, so far, at least, as the disappointment of his
expectations was concerned, were made in the sphere of social
reform. Late in life, haunted by the spectre of discontent, he
developed scruples on the social question and legislated on
original lines for the wrongs of the working classes. Unfortunately all his nostrums, effectual and ineffectual, were applied in the spirit and with the hand rather of the horse doctor
than the family physician; even in social politics coercion went

hand in hand with amelioration, and his touch was hard. Because he exasperated the working classes by repressive laws and edicts at the very time that he was offering them social reform, his great schemes of insurance were received by them sullenly and without gratitude, and altogether failed to accomplish the political purpose for which they were devised.

Here this unique personality, upon which it has been necessary to focus the reader's attention so long and so closely, passes into the background, though not out of sight. Now other men came upon the stage of national politics, bringing with them other ideas and other ways of realizing them. The first result of Bismarck's going was to afford his enemies in official and public life — and they were many — immense relief, and to set free a hundred imprisoned vanities and ambitions.[1] Hohenlohe, still Governor of Alsace-Lorraine, who had hung about the Court during the fateful weeks of March, hoping that his turn had come at last — he tells in his diary so early as March, 1877, how Bismarck's daughter had said that " her father had often thought of me when he was tired of vexations and wanted to resign "— was in Berlin again in June, and he wrote at that time, a little spitefully, but hardly without justification, that political reputations in the capital had become inflated; the old sense of being overshadowed by one masterful personality had disappeared, and now " each separate personality is conscious of his own value." On the whole the tendency was rather to excessive self-estimation. Small men were found climbing into large places, ambitious, though gifted with but a particle of Bismarck's talent and none of his genius, to emulate his fame and repeat his achievements. It was in vain. The strong bow could be drawn only by the strong man.

Once again it was Bismarck's system avenging itself, this time upon Germany. For so long as he was in power no other personality was allowed to assert itself. Strictly speaking, therefore, he left no disciples or followers. A later Chancellor spoke of Bismarck as " a postulate in himself," and said that it was " irrational to call for measures and enterprises for which this postulate is lacking." [2] That was true from the first,

---

[1] In his *Reflections and Reminiscences* Bismarck writes: " The majority of my official friends seemed to have felt as though relieved from pressure after my resignation " (vol. ii., p. 223), but so little was he aware of the compulsion of his dominating personality and will that the fact occasioned him surprise.

[2] Prince Bülow, *Imperial Germany*, p. 176.

though it was long before the German nation accustomed itself
to the fact that Bismarck's resignation marked the abrupt
close of a clearly-defined era in national history.

CHAPTER XIX

(1890–1900)

EMPEROR WILLIAM II. DOMESTIC AFFAIRS —
(i) THE NEW COURSE

THE position of the Minister who followed Prince Bismarck would have been difficult in the most favourable circumstances; the accidents of the first Chancellor's retirement made it also in a special degree unenviable. Count Waldersee, who had not come to the helm after all, had said that while he would not like to be Bismarck's successor he would gladly take a turn after that successor had eased the way. General von Caprivi had not wished for a distinction which, though a proud, was a painful one, and when in accepting it he asserted that he did so from a feeling of " imperious patriotic duty," his words were not those of empty convention. He succeeded at once in disarming his critics, however, when at his first official appearance in the Prussian Diet he confessed with creditable candour that he had hitherto been " strange to political affairs," yet promised that he would do his best. He had a high reputation as a capable administrator both in the army and the navy, for though a soldier he had once been head of the Admiralty, and all who knew him praised him as a man of perfect honour. Such qualities, added to soldierly simplicity and straightforwardness, more than counterbalanced for absence of brilliancy, and promised him success in the task of tiding over a critical transition.

Nevertheless, one of his first measures brought down upon him much shortsighted and undeserved censure. This was the conclusion in July, 1890, of the African convention whereby Germany ceded to Great Britain her rights in Witu and agreed to recognize a British protectorate over the dominions of the Sultan of Zanzibar, while she received in return the island of Heligoland and certain advantageous frontier rectifications in East Africa (giving access to the lakes), West Africa, and South-west Africa. The acquisition of the Elbe island realized a long-cherished German dream, but all political parties, and the colonial party in particular, contended that the price paid for it was excessive, since the renunciation of all claims in respect to Zanzibar and Witu made a great Central African empire impossible. For Great Britain the agreement had the advantage that there was henceforth no danger of British East Africa being hemmed in by German territory. On the other hand the cession of Heligoland was severely criticized, though the fact that it was made by a Conservative Ministry kept the militant imperialists under restraint.

To Germans in general the possession of Heligoland appealed at that time only on the ground of sentiment. The naval authorities, looking further, already recognized its importance for the completion of their plans and were prepared to buy it on any terms. Nothing was said in the agreement about the harbour of refuge for the benefit of British shipping which Bismarck had dangled before Lord Granville's eyes when at Caprivi's suggestion he first proposed the cession of Heligoland six years before, and it was understood that the only shipping which the island, when duly fortified, would protect would be the imperial navy.[1]

By this transaction Caprivi at once forfeited the confidence of the colonial party. He had never been a colonial enthusiast, however, and he plainly said so, maintaining that Germany had as many colonies as were good for her and that it was now her interest to consolidate rather than expand her oversea dominion. " The worst thing that could happen to us," he said a little later (November 27, 1891), " would be for some one to give us the whole of Africa, for we have quite enough as it is." He saw in the colonies a potential source of friction with other countries, and he refused to multiply the existing risks.

The early years of Caprivi's Chancellorship were for Germany a time of relaxation and liberation in many directions. Great as was the work which Bismarck had done for the Empire, and incalculable as was the nation's indebtedness to him, his disappearance from the chief seat of political influence unquestionably removed from official life an oppressive incubus, of which the full weight was only understood when the pressure was relaxed. The relief was felt particularly in the circles of the higher bureaucracy, but most of all in the Ministries. For

[1] See Chapter XVII., pp. 192–194.

the first time the colleagues of the Chancellor breathed freely, knowing that they had no longer to do with an arbitrary chief as of old, and the new consciousness of independence was naturally strongest just where the iron hand of restraint and discipline had rested most heavily. Prince Hohenlohe, writing from Berlin at that time, tells how a certain down-trodden Minister suddenly became as " gay as a snow king now that he can speak freely and the great man is no longer to be feared," adding, " This comfortable sentiment is obvious here on all sides." Each department of State began to develop a self-consciousness of its own, and in the hierarchy of the Empire Secretaries of State, though constitutionally subordinate to the Chancellor, deported themselves like members of the Prussian Ministry, in which all were equal. Hitherto one man only had wielded authority in the State; now minor men took courage, and looking no more with awe upon the tree of power began to nibble freely at its long-forbidden fruit.

Most free of all was the Sovereign himself, and more than any other he was in a position to appreciate the change. After sharing its authority with a despotic Minister for nearly thirty years the Prussian Crown was again independent; for the first time a German Emperor could claim to be his own master. Now the personality of the ruler began to make itself felt, to a degree unknown before, both in legislation and in the direction of public policy. In a speech made in April, 1890, immediately after Bismarck's resignation, the Emperor, in appealing for the nation's loyal co-operation, spoke suggestively of the " new course " which Germany was to follow under his guidance. For a time all the auguries seemed to justify the hope that this shifting of political influence would on the whole prove a change for the better. Generous impulses, buoyant hopes, and a passionate desire to achieve great things for his country's good were revealed alike by the Emperor's public utterances and his public acts. He showed active interest in all the varied life of the nation, in its moral and material welfare, in education and art, in religious and church activities, in trade, industry, and labour. Every indication pointed to his reign being identified in a special manner with social reform. All sorts of movements of an ameliorative character were set on foot at his instigation or with his encouragement — housing reform, endeavours to combat consumption and infant mortality, organized efforts for preventing accidents in factories, and the like. He tried to rouse the comfortable classes out of their torpid attitude towards social conditions, called for a closer sympathy between intellect and labour, and reminded the Protestant clergy, hitherto so concerned about religion that they had had no time to care for morality, of their civic responsibilities.

Seldom has a Prussian ruler thrown himself so completely upon the confidence of his people as William II appeared to do while still on the threshold of his reign. In his endeavours to improve social conditions he appealed for " the intelligent and joyous co-operation of all classes of the population, and especially of the working classes, whose interests are concerned, and of the employers who are prepared to make the necessary sacrifices." He tried to lift the social movement out of the atmosphere of party controversy: " all are heartily welcome," he said, " whoever they may be." In order to encourage his people in well-doing he established a new Order, called after his grandfather, in recognition of conspicuous social service.

Under these manifold impulses a new spirit seemed to come over the nation in relation to the many-sided problem of the condition of the people, and the social reform movement now took root in a way it had never done during the first reign. German writers on this subject often speak of contemporary Germany as distinctively the Social Empire. The foundation of the social legislation by which this title must be justified, if justified at all, had been laid before William II came to the throne, but it is certainly the merit of that ruler that for a time he gave greater definiteness and a clearer purpose to the vague humanitarian sentiment which had already become active and carried social policy forward on intelligent and sympathetic lines. From the first he found a valuable ally in the Clerical party, which, joining hands with the patriarchal Conservatives, now began to take a decided stand on social questions, so reviving a dormant tradition established many years before by earnest reformers of their faith like Bishop Ketteler, Canon Moufang, and Father Kolping. In convening the Labour Conference, the Emperor had invited the Pope to allow Prince Bishop Kopp, of Breslau, to take part, and the Roman Catholic Church had not been slow to reciprocate the compliment thus paid to it. Henceforth both the religious and the political leaders of Catholicism closely identified themselves with social reform, and all later measures for the amelioration of the people owed at least as much to Catholic as to Protestant support. In September, 1890, the Roman Catholics held an international labour conference of their own at Louvain, and in May of the following year Leo XIII published his memorable Encyclical on the labour question, *Rerum Novarum*, which for Roman Catholics everywhere became a rule of public conduct and policy.

The missing link in the system of social insurance had been added in 1889 by the enactment of the Old Age and Invalidity Insurance Law providing for the pensioning of the veterans and wreckages of the industrial army. Now the Labour Conference began to bear fruit. Laws for the amendment of the Industrial Code in the spirit of the resolutions adopted by the Conference and for the creation of Industrial Courts for the settlement of monetary disputes arising between workpeople and their employers were passed in 1890. Before this time the only imperial legislation relating to the hours of labour were provisions forbidding the employment of juveniles (i.e. youths under sixteen years) on Sundays and legal holidays and forbidding the employment on these days of workers generally against their will. In the absence of an express prohibition something had been done to encourage Sunday observance by police and administrative orders, but such measures were sporadic and partial, and in practice work on this day was still common in most parts of Germany. Now the weekday employment of women, juveniles, and children was restricted, though nothing was done for adult males, and Sunday rest was made obligatory instead of permissive for all workers. One immediate result of the new legislation was the virtual disappearance of children of school age from factories and workshops; in 1888 the number so employed was 23,000 in all Germany — nearly one-half being in Saxony alone — but by 1893 only 4,-000 remained. Factory inspection was also made more efficient. Bismarck, disliking every kind of interference between capital and labour, had opposed all efforts in this direction, and herein had found himself in rare accord with the individualist Radicals. The consequence was that in 1888 there were in all Germany only forty-eight factory inspectors with twenty-nine assistants, and that the factory legislation of the day, poor as it was, was enforced half-heartedly. The inspection of factories was still allowed to remain a function of the State Governments, but the Imperial Executive now required it to be done systematically. The workers were also given the right to form committees through which to negotiate with their employers regarding conditions of employment.

In 1892 a labour department was formed in the Imperial Statistical Office as a means of bringing the whole province of labour under more complete survey, and this example was soon followed in Great Britain and other countries. A weak attempt was made simultaneously to make severer the penalties for any abuse of the right of coalition, but the Diet, in its new enthusiasm for social reform, was unwilling to dilute conciliation by coercion in the old ungracious way, and it rejected this reactionary proposal, leaving the amendment of the Industrial Code a straightforward and sympathetic attempt to give to labour greater protection. All these measures marked an important advance in social legislation, yet to a large extent Germany was only bringing up to date arrears of work which had long been allowed to accumulate, and assimilating her laws to those of countries with an older industrial and a more advanced political system.

Milder measures were tried at this time in the treatment of the alien races in the East and West. So long as Bismarck remained in office the policy of hardness continued in the Polish provinces. The appointment of Caprivi was the signal for one of those fitful attempts to reconcile the Poles which for over a century have alternated with prolonged periods of rigorous government. The policy of land purchase and settlement was for a time suspended, but as there was no idea of its definite abandonment that half-measure proved unfortunate from the financial standpoint, for prices were exceptionally low in the early 'nineties, and the opportunities of buying on favourable terms which existed then never returned. For a time the Emperor-King went out of his way to win the good-will of his Polish subjects. Poles were admitted to positions of favour and eminence. A Pole, Florian von Stablewski, became archbishop of Posen in 1892; Polish nobles suddenly became welcome visitors at Court; and when the Polish group in the Imperial Diet voted for a new Army Bill in July, 1893, the Sovereign publicly applauded the act as one of exemplary patriotism by which other parties would do well to profit. This apparent favouring of the Poles created a violent outburst of indignation amongst the Germans of the Eastern Marks, and as Friedrichsruh then served as a Cave of Adullam to which the malcontents of all parties resorted a deputation promptly made pilgrimage to the ex-Chancellor and laid their grievances before him. As a result of this conference an organization, known as the Eastern Marches Association, was at once formed for the defence of Germanism in the Polish provinces. It was not long before this association changed its defensive for an aggressive character, and became a potent agency for fomenting ill-feeling between the two nationalities.

Yet friendly and indulgent as was the disposition of the new ruler towards the Poles at that time, his acts of personal goodwill were powerless to efface the consequences of the unsympathetic administration which was carried on in his name. In conferring upon Stablewski his see he had urgently charged him to endeavour to " reconcile antagonisms which have no right to exist between people of the same country." That was far more easily said than done. Try as he would, the Archbishop could not counteract the effect of the harsh policy which had gone before and the administrative shortsightedness which still continued, out of reach of royal influence. In a short time the new zeal for conciliation was exhausted, and it needed no effort to fall back into the old ways. Visiting the eastern districts of the monarchy in the autumn of 1894 the Sovereign foretold the end of his patience, and coming to Thorn he bade the Poles remember " I can be very disagreeable, and I shall be if necessary." Soon the necessity was held to have arisen. A new era of land purchase began, accompanied by the wholesale clearance of Polish and their replacement by German families. When the parliamentary grants were exhausted fresh funds were voted, first in 1898 and again in 1902.

The Government's experience in Alsace-Lorraine was even more discouraging. There Prince Hohenlohe continued to be the Stadholder, and he had become wedded to the idea that only resolute government could avail. Hohenlohe appears to have allowed the Ministers in Berlin a wider latitude than was needful, in view of the large powers secured to him by the constitution of the provinces, and Berlin, being convinced that the resistance of the Alsatians to German rule in the Prussian spirit was mere perversity, was but little disposed to pay further heed to the susceptibilities of the conquered population. Hohenlohe in March, 1891, relates a conversation with the Secretary of State von Marschall who had " spoken very contemptuously of Alsace-Lorraine, and said it was a matter of total indifference in Berlin whether the inhabitants were satisfied or not, and that in the event of war Alsace-Lorraine would become the principal battlefield." Even Caprivi seemed to regard the prospect of conciliation as hopeless. Convinced that the Alsatians could not be Germanized, he said that the only alternative was to " deepen the ditch " that divided them from France. Nevertheless, there was a sudden return to a milder *régime* in September, when it was decided to relax the passport regulations which had been issued in May, 1888, and to apply them for the future in the main to military persons. Other ameliorations followed, and if there was still little contentment in the provinces there was greater comfort. Never during the third reign was there any repetition of repression in the grosser forms which were common in the early years of the German occupation. Signor Crispi relates a conversation with Bismarck in May, 1889, in which he had suggested the old idea of neutralizing the provinces as a means of diminishing the risk of war with France. Bismarck disagreed and doubted whether Crispi's expectation would be realized. " The time for neutral States is past," he said. " The French Government will not agree to it, but not even that would suffice to ward off war. We should no longer be able to threaten France by land, while France would be able to attack us by sea."

The Emperor's first great disappointment came when he discovered that in spite of his efforts for their good the working classes refused to turn their backs upon Socialism. In 1887 the Socialist party had suffered a temporary reverse at the polls, for a war scare had seized hold upon the nation, with the result that the Conservative and National Liberal parties gained heavily at the expense of the parties of the Left. The Socialist deputies were reduced from twenty-four to eleven, in spite of a large increase in votes. Before the next elections took place, in February, 1890, the decisions to abandon the Socialist Law and to convene the Labour Conference had been taken, and the complete change in the Government's attitude towards labour thus indicated was represented by the Socialists as a vindication of their position and an endorsement of their claims. In these elections the party won its first great victory. Not only did it return to the Diet thirty-five strong, but the votes recorded for its candidates increased from three-quarters of a million to nearly a million and a half. The Socialist Law expired on September 30, 1890, amid the jubilation of the working classes, who celebrated the restoration of unfettered thought and speech by demonstrations in every part of the country. With the disappearance of coercion a flood of pent-up political energy was let loose and a powerful impetus given to agitation. The first congress of the party after its recovered freedom was held at Halle in October under the influence of this new elation, and there a triumphant story of progress could be told. At the Erfurt Congress of the following year the programme of the party was revised, its organization further strengthened, and its machinery of propagandism perfected. The result was that at the appeal to the country in June, 1893, the party again won a signal triumph. Having gained in three years over a third of a million votes, it was now a party of one and three-quarter millions, and its forty-four seats made it the fourth strongest group in the Diet.

All this was for the Emperor a disconcerting revelation. He had hazarded the belief, for which he had no justification other than a happy optimism which indisposed him to look facts fairly in the face, that Social Democracy was a " transient phenomenon which would be exhausted by its own violence," and while confident in the success of his social measures, he had declared that in passing them he looked for no thanks, but only for the approval of his own conscience. It proved difficult, however, to live up to such a high faith when ingratitude took the form of an ever-increasing army of malcontents, pledged to the destruction not only of the existing social order but of the institution of monarchy itself. In November, 1891, he had told the recruits at Potsdam: " If Socialist agitations continue as they are doing, I may have to order you to shoot down your relatives, your brothers, even your parents — which God forbid! — but even then you must obey my commands without murmuring." Later the Socialists became " a pack of men unworthy to bear the name of Germans " and " a treasonable horde," to combat which was the duty of every patriotic citizen. The avowal of sentiments like these only added fuel to the flames.

Soon disaffection ceased to be confined to the Socialists, and spread to political circles which had nothing in common with their extreme aims, even to those which the Crown had traditionally regarded as its special allies. In the meantime also the divisions created by the Emperor's quarrel with Bismarck, far from showing signs of healing, had been intensified by the defiant challenges which the ex-Chancellor constantly flung right and left. From his watch-tower at Friedrichsruh he followed with alarm the gradual abandonment of his own principles, and his censures spared neither his successor in office nor the Emperor himself. He had allowed himself to be elected to the Diet by National Liberal votes, but he did not take his seat; instead, he passed judgment upon the Government and its policy in incessant speeches to deputations and visitors, in letters to sympathetic inquirers, and in inspired articles in the Press of Germany and other countries. He claimed such right of criticism, since he had, as Metternich said after his retirement, " changed the stage for the stalls," and criticize he did freely and remorselessly. Many of his criticisms were intrinsically justifiable, and perhaps were necessary, though they might have come from another source with better grace and greater advantage to the public interest; others, on the contrary, were factious and mischievous, and often caused the Government acute embarrassment. It was the irritating influence of the ex-Chancellor's utterances and the knowledge that he had so large and sympathetic a hearing in the country that led the Emperor to remind the nation in a speech at Düsseldorf in May, 1891: " One only is master in the Empire, and it is I; I tolerate no other."

The Conservatives now forgot every reproach which they had ever made against the Junker Minister, in remembrance of the fact that on the whole his policy had been far more for than against them, while his successor refused to play the political game as the feudalists understood it. Even the middle-class parties, which had never been spoiled by privilege, were impatient that history was no longer being made on the grand scale of Bismarck's days. Their place then had, it is true, been in the background of the political stage, but at least they had had the consciousness of having witnessed upon that stage

the acting of a great national drama. Moreover, the Radicals
and democrats had viewed with growing misgiving and alarm
the Sovereign's constant intrusions in political controversy and
the frequent utterances in which he had made it clear that he entertained entirely new conceptions of the Crown's place in constitutional life. Already, in a much-discussed speech made at
Königsberg (May, 1890), where in 1861 William I had crowned
himself with his own hand, the Emperor had revived the doctrine of divine right, a doctrine disowned by his father and
discredited even by the official historiographer of Prussia,
Heinrich von Treitschke, as " Jacobite mysticism." Thoughtful men throughout Germany gravely disapproved when at a
visit to Munich (November, 1891) he wrote in the city's
Golden Book, " Suprema lex regis voluntas esto," and recalled
the truer and wiser maxim which the Chancellor Hardenberg
had dared to address to his forefather Frederick William III
seventy-five years before, " Salus publica suprema lex esto! "

The autocratic *régime* of Bismarck had been abolished, but
all the probabilities seemed now to point to the imminence of
another, even more insidious in character, under which parties
would have to deal, not as hitherto with a Minister whose political philosophy was summed up in the crude yet still argu-
able theory that might created right, but with a sovereign who
boldly claimed for his office divine sanction and for his acts
divine inspiration and guidance. Suspicion was even aroused
of his desire to return to the undiluted Cæsarism of the pre-
constitutional era. While still Chancellor, Bismarck had confessed to Hohenlohe that it was his belief that the Emperor
wished to be his own Chancellor. The anticipation was already
in course of realization.

Probably no modern Sovereign was so confident of his own
capacity in public affairs, or so ready to face responsibility
with so little justification, as Emperor William II in the early
years of his reign. No one could doubt his gifts or the earnestness of his desire to " exercise his office for the welfare of the
fatherland," according to the promise of his first proclamation
to the nation. Like many other men impatient for action,
however, he failed to recognize that the art of statecraft has
to be learned like other arts, and more laboriously than most,
and exalting intuition in the place of experience, he committed
many impatient and impetuous acts at which grave men shud-

dered. Bismarck, in all his policy, had been guided by a cold objectivity which respected only facts, and was sceptical even of them. The young Emperor allowed his judgment to be unduly swayed by subjective considerations, fugitive emotions, prejudices, and predilections, vehement likes and more vehement dislikes. He conceived himself to be the embodiment of a new spirit, and the representative of a new age, and with the credulity of the ardent discoverer he concluded that this age must be governed by forces different from those which had governed the old. Self-absorbed and introspective to an unhealthy degree, he was almost altogether closed to outside influences, and was thus without the master-key to the understanding of human nature and affairs. Fulsome adulation was showered upon him by professional courtiers and self-seeking worldlings without rebuke, and upon a man of his temperament its effect was fatal. All these incidents of his character and position conspired to encourage in him a disposition to judge events from a false perspective, and caused him to lose the right measure both for realities and abstractions.

It was obvious that the full significance of these influences and tendencies would be seen only in later years, but already there was much anxious foreboding, and his impatience of either opposition or criticism strengthened the doubts even of those whose loyalty to his person was beyond question. Addressing the Brandenburg Diet in February, 1892, he poured derision upon the whole tribe of critics and " naggers." While he worked, he said, all they could do was to find fault; very well, if conditions in Germany were really so unsatisfactory, " let them shake the dust from their feet and leave the country for its good and their own." His own confidence in himself and the future was unbounded. "We are passing," he added, " through moving and stimulating times, but unfortunately the great majority of men lack sound and impartial judgment. The stirring days will be followed by quiet ones if the people will do their duty, correct their ways, and, disregarding outside criticism, trust firmly in God and in the honest and solicitous labour of their ruler. . . . Brandenburgers, believe me, a great destiny awaits us. I lead you forward towards glorious days. Do not allow yourselves to become pessimistic in consequence of the fault-finding and criticism of party men. Direct your vision towards the future, and do not allow others to diminish your pleasure in co-operating with me. Sententious phrases prove nothing. To those who unceasingly allude with dissatisfaction to the new course and to those who steer it, I reply quietly but with determination: ' My course is the right one, and I shall continue to follow it.' " [1]

Early in the same year the fears of the Liberals seemed to be justified by the introduction in the Prussian Diet of an Education Bill so reactionary in character that it threw the whole country into consternation. The blow was as bold as it was unexpected. Two years before the Minister of Education, Dr. von Gossler, had produced a measure which, while retaining the old confessional principle, proposed to place the control over secular and religious instruction more definitely in the hands of the State. The bill was rejected, and its author in consequence resigned, his place being taken by Baron Zedlitz, a typical representative of the Conservative-feudalist party. To Baron Zedlitz and his friends the opportunity for a bold counter-stroke seemed too precious to be lost. The Conservatives and Clericals between them dominated the Diet, and a bargain between the two parties, which had so much in common in educational ideals, would make success certain. The Centre was, in fact, the predominant party in the Ministerial coalition. Through persecution and discredit it had at last come to triumph and repute; it had worn down the attack upon the Church and compelled Bismarck to own defeat; now it had secured a Government to its liking, and it exercised a decisive voice in parliamentary affairs.

The bargain having been concluded, Baron Zedlitz introduced early in 1892 an amended bill which would have deliberately handed over the elementary schools to the Churches as the legitimate spoils of party warfare, to be divided amongst them at leisure by friendly arrangement. Not only was the confessional basis of the schools recognized as before, but obstacles were placed in the way of any future deviation from it; dogmatic religious instruction was to be forced upon all children, regardless of parental scruples; clerical influence, both in the work of inspection and of general administration, was increased; the clergy were to be allowed to certify whether teachers were competent or not to give religious instruction, and

[1] Several Berlin newspapers which reprinted an article of the London *Times* commenting upon this speech were confiscated.

virtually to withhold the right to teach from any one objectionable to them. In short, the Church, Catholic and Protestant, was to be given complete control over the only part of public education in which it took serious interest.

The bill proved too much for the habitual complacency of the Prussian nation, which for once threw off its political apathy. The old leader of National Liberalism, Bennigsen, now emerged from retirement, raised again the flag of progress, and called upon all that had life and breath in the Liberalism of the monarchy to fight the measure to the death. The universities, so often silent in the past when violence had been done to intellectual interests of which they were the natural custodians, rained protests upon the Government. Lay Protestants everywhere, in public meeting and written petition, roundly condemned the bill as a complete capitulation to Clericalism and another and a more humiliating journey to Canossa. Even Bismarck accused his old party friends of having sold themselves into the service of their country's enemy. It was in vain that the Minister-President, Caprivi, who still knew less about politics than about the army, pleaded that the nation was engaged in a struggle between Christianity and atheism. The retort of the opponents of the bill, that if it was right now to place so much power in the hands of the Roman Church and clergy all the agitation against Clericalism in the last decade was either an imposture or a piece of intolerant persecution, was unanswerable.

It was obvious that Caprivi had allowed the bill to slip through his fingers unguardedly, and that he now defended it only out of loyalty to an unpopular colleague and regard for the unity of the Cabinet. Other Ministers were not so scrupulous, and as soon as it became evident that the bill was detested they hastened to disown it. When the storm had raged until March the Emperor intervened and called upon his Ministers to surrender. Reproached by his Sovereign for having shown so little regard for national sentiment, Baron Zedlitz could only resign, whereupon the bill was withdrawn. Caprivi likewise felt seriously compromised, and chivalrously offered to accompany the unlucky Minister of Education into retirement, but the crisis demanded no such sacrifice. He retired from the presidency of the Prussian Ministry, however, and Count Botha zu Eulenburg took his place.

The disrepute suffered by the Ministry and its head in Prussia was soon afterwards effaced by a notable success in imperial affairs. This was the episode of the commercial treaties of 1892 and succeeding years. When William II came to the throne the agricultural duties had just been increased, for the second time since 1879, by the customs tariff law of 1887. The revised tariff had been introduced by Bismarck in part by way of retaliation upon Austria and Russia for having increased their duties upon manufactured goods. As a weapon of offence it failed, for these countries now raised their tariffs still further. At that time some of the leading Continental States had adopted conventional tariffs on the principle of reciprocal concessions in every individual case. Germany had hitherto had a general tariff and had concluded commercial treaties only on the most-favoured-nation basis. These treaties all expired in the year 1892. Faced now by hostile tendencies in other countries, Caprivi had to choose between the alternatives of a retaliatory increase of the German duties according to need, leading almost inevitably to a series of tariff wars, or the acceptance and possible extension of the conventional tariff system, which meant some mitigation of the existing duties. He chose the latter course, and in doing so carried the Emperor with him.

Other considerations spoke in favour of the change. A strong reaction against the severe system of Protection which had been built up in the course of twelve years had already set in, and of late there had been serious manifestations of popular discontent. The year 1891 saw Germany in the throes of scarcity. The harvest had failed; the price of wheat and rye had risen to an alarming height; and hunger stalked through the streets of the industrial towns, gaunt and menacing. In August the exportation of corn was prohibited; the corn duties were suspended in the presence of an imminent famine; and so impressed were the leaders of the agrarian party in the Diet by the anomaly of their position, that they voted for the reversal of their own policy. It was the low corn prices of 1878 that made protective duties possible; the high prices of 1891 made them for the time being impossible. Nevertheless, the crisis did not pass over without violence. Not since the memorable " March days " of 1848 had Berlin been the scene of such alarming popular demonstrations and riots as took place

there in the closing days of February, 1892. Hunger and want
of work were the main causes of the outbreaks, and for several
days a reign of terror prevailed in certain quarters of the city.
Some of the streets fell into the hands of the mob; shops and
houses were looted; property was destroyed wholesale; obnoxious persons were victimized; the police were set at defiance;
and the wildest elements of the population for a time held sway.

On the industrial side also the tariff had proved no less irk-
some and unsatisfactory. Foreign trade had greatly increased, yet the retaliatory duties adopted by other countries
had done much injury. Russia and America had virtually
barred their doors to the outside world. The growth of the
Colonial Federation movement in England had also given rise
in German minds to the apprehension that almost the only remaining free markets might soon be closed. The uncertainty
of international trade, the perpetual unrest, and indefinite
fears as to the future conspired to make the Government, conscious of encouragement from the commercial classes, willing
to bargain with any country which was prepared to meet concession with concession.

It was the merit of Caprivi that he was the earliest of leading German statesmen to recognize that Germany had ceased
to be a purely agricultural State, and that her future prosperity and welfare were bound up with the development of her
industrial resources. He was no political economist, but it
was a true economic instinct that led him to the conclusion,
" With our increasing population we must export either goods
or men." Germany was, in fact, exporting men at that time
to the extent of 100,000 a year. Yet Caprivi was not hostile
to agriculture, but regarded its maintenance in an efficient and
prosperous condition as a paramount national interest, and
hence he favoured the continuance of moderate protection.
One of his forecasts received such a remarkable confirmation
many years later that it deserves to be recalled. " It is my
unshakable conviction," he told the Diet in December, 1891,
" that in a future war the feeding of the army and the country may play an absolutely decisive part. I am convinced
that we need to cultivate corn to such an extent that it will,
in case of need, be sufficient to feed the increasing population,
even if it be with restrictions, in the event of war." Nevertheless, he held that the existing duties were a needless hindrance

to industrial expansion, an oppressive burden on the working classes, and a menace to social harmony.

The discovery that industry and labour had a right to consideration equally with agriculture was the origin of the commercial treaties of 1892–4. Germany had had commercial treaties for a generation, but the treaties of the Caprivi *régime* marked a novel departure from past custom. The old treaties were based on fixed, invariable, autonomous tariffs, and most of them included the most-favoured-nation clause; the new ones, while containing this clause, were based on " conventional " tariffs, concluded as the result of special bargaining with the States concerned. He began negotiations with Austria, Italy, Switzerland, and Belgium. In regard to the first of these countries political considerations as well as economic influenced him, for Austria was an ally whose friendship it was desirable to strengthen. By the agreement concluded Germany was to reduce her agricultural duties and Austria her duties on industrial products. All these four treaties contained the most-favoured-nation clause, and by special tariffs fixed the duties on both sides until the end of 1903; that is, for a period of twelve years. The effect was to reduce the duties on wheat and rye from 50s. to 35s. a ton, on oats from 40s. to 28s., on barley from 22s. 6d. to 20s., and on flour from 105s. to 75s. The treaties were laid before the Diet in December, 1891, and in spite of vehement opposition from the Conservative agrarians they were ratified in the following month by 243 votes against only 48. The result was a great triumph for Caprivi, and industrial and commercial Germany was not slow or ungrudging in its gratitude. The Emperor's recognition of his achievement took the form of a title; the soldier-statesman became a Count.

In the course of the next two years treaties were concluded on the same principles with Spain, Roumania, Serbia and Russia, and with other countries later. France came into the arrangement automatically in virtue of the Treaty of Frankfort, under which the two States agreed to accord to each other most-favoured-nation treatment.

The treaty with Russia, which ended a tariff war between the two countries, was carried against the vehement opposition of the Conservatives and Anti-Semites, joined by most of the Imperialists, a minority of the Clericals, and a handful of National Liberals. It was an irony of Caprivi's position that though a Conservative by conviction and instincts he was, in the episode of the commercial treaties, thrown almost entirely upon the support of his political antagonists.

Bismarck, in his retreat at Friedrichsruh, spoke of the commercial treaties as a " leap in the dark." To the Free Trader they were a leap back into the light, and events seemed to support this view. By general consent the remarkable expansion of home industry and foreign trade which immediately followed was due in large measure to the policy of freer exchange which was introduced at this time. During the ten years from 1894 the value of Germany's trade with the treaty countries increased by nearly three-quarters. The benefit to agriculture took the form of a higher standard of life for the great mass of the working classes, with the result of a larger and more receptive home market for farm produce.

The year from which the first of the Caprivi commercial treaties dated (1892) witnessed the beginnings of a powerful organization of the agricultural interests of the country and of a new political movement destined to acquire a sinister influence and fame. The organization was the Farmers' League (*Bund der Landwirte*), and the movement for which it stood was agrarianism. Essentially representative of the large proprietors, and inspired and led by the corn-growers of Eastern Prussia, the Farmers' League captured the agricultural classes in all parts of the country, though in the North to a greater extent than in the South. It was Caprivi's declaration, in a speech in which he commended the commercial treaty policy to the Diet, that " Germany is no longer an agricultural but an industrial country," that for the first time opened the eyes of the agrarians to the economic revolution which had passed over the country. No sooner had the treaties been ratified than they began a vehement agitation against them in the rural constituencies. " We must tear up the treaties with Austria and Italy," said the time-honoured champion of law and order in the Press, the *Kreuzzeitung*, and later, when the treaty with Russia came into existence amid the Sovereign's felicitations, it asserted that " the German farmer will now be inclined to regard the Emperor as his political enemy."

From that time the agrarians closed their ranks for the strenuous defence of their threatened privileges, and the course of later domestic politics has been greatly influenced by their action. From the first the Agrarian League, as the Farmers' League is usually called out of Germany, was a signal success as a propagandist organization. The German Peasants' League uniting with it, a membership of 200,000 was soon gained, and having at command abundant funds, it was able to engage a large staff of lecturers, who perambulated the country, organizing the agricultural classes, enlightening them upon their grievances, and helping them to apply to the Government effective and continuous pressure, so supporting the hands of the party which existed to protect their special interests in Parliament.

From the beginning the organization was Conservative both in aims and in composition, and one immediate result was to create in the Conservative parliamentary party an unaccustomed spirit of independence. Hitherto the party had worked hand in hand with the Government in virtue of an alliance based on reciprocity of interest. So long as the reciprocity lasted, so long also did the alliance. When, however, both the Emperor and the Government showed a disposition to shrink from the agrarians' extreme demands, the traditional devotion of the Conservative party to throne, altar, and fatherland stood revealed in its true light as a very human yet very unamiable piece of egoism. Thereupon were developed a discrimination of judgment and a freedom of action which had never been seen before in the same quarter. For now the agrarians, too, chose to follow a new course, and by persevering in it they gained in the end all the preference lost in 1892, with much that they had never possessed or dared to hope for in the past.

Largely owing to the parliamentary pressure which they were able to employ, a number of important measures, some of a very partisan kind, were passed in the interest of agriculture during the next few years. Naturally most was done in Prussia, where the agrarian party entirely controlled the legislature. There laws were passed to facilitate the creation with the help of State credit of small holdings on a method which allowed the owner to redeem the purchase price by annual payments within a fixed period. Liberal State subsidies were made to encourage the construction of light railways and the improvement of the land by drainage, irrigation, and manurial works on scientific principles. Experimental farms were established for the encouragement of better methods of farming. State development boards were formed and large grants of public money made for the purpose of reclaiming marshes, moors, and other waste lands in various parts of the country. By a law of 1894 Chambers of Agriculture were formed as a connecting tie between the Government and the agricultural classes; in 1895 a State co-operative bank was created with a capital of a million pounds — afterwards increased to nearly four millions — for the encouragement of co-operative efforts; and by the reform of State taxation real estate was relieved of some of its ancient burdens. Something was done also to introduce a freer civic life in the rural districts of the backward eastern provinces by the Rural District Ordinance of 1891, which assimilated the system of local government in these districts to that prevailing in the western part of the monarchy. Nevertheless, there still remain in the East of Prussia many thousands of independent manorial districts, where the spirit of feudalism lingers in local administration, to the discomfort and injury of the whole population.

The legislative measures passed by the Imperial Government at that time, partly from love of but more from fear of the agrarians, included a Usury Law (1893) which restored the principles which were in force up to 1867; an extension of the sugar bounty system; and the abolition of the " identity certificates " in connection with rebates of duty in respect of re-imported corn. These " identity certificates " had originally entitled exporters of foreign corn which had already borne duty to a rebate of corresponding amount. Later, proof of identity was no longer required, and the rebate was made in respect of any corn, of whatever origin, sold abroad; and step by step the privilege was so abused until corn exporters were allowed to import to the value of their rebate certificates not merely corn, but rice, coffee, and petroleum. The result of this arrangement was that in times of good harvests the corngrower exported his surplus grain and imported in return marketable goods free of duty, receiving the duty as profit and at the same time reducing stocks at home and thus keeping up prices. To the most daring demand of the agrarians, however, the Government refused to yield. This was the proposal of Count Kanitz, an East Prussian landowner, that the State should purchase outright all the corn imported into the coun-

try, and retail it at a price based on the average of the past
forty years, the idea being that the price so fixed should regulate the sale of the home produce.   The vote of the Diet was
challenged on the proposal for the first time in 1894, but unsuccessfully, and later attempts had the same result, though a
hundred agrarians supported it in 1895.

The agrarian movement synchronized with another aberra-
tion of party life even more unhealthy, though, as it proved,
less permanent.   It began with a violent outbreak of anti-Semitism in 1890.   There had been an outbreak of the kind some
years before, yet, though widespread, its manifestations were
in the main of a crude and futile order.   In the meantime the
Berlin Court chaplain Dr. Stöcker had begun to mix anti-Semitism with religious and social reform work, and assisted by
an eloquent tongue he had gained a large and influential following, and prepared ground favourable to the growth of this
form of political intolerance.   Now an agitation of a more
serious kind took hold of the inflammable sections of the community, and for the first time led to the formation of a parliamentary group pledged to the advocacy of exceptional measures against the Jewish population.   In 1892, under the leadership of an elementary school teacher named Ahlwardt, who
carried the fiery cross of racial hatred through North and Central Germany, the anti-Semites formed a powerful organization for the defence of Germanism against Jewry.   Everywhere Ahlwardt was acclaimed as an emancipator whose mission it was to destroy the oppressive yoke of the Jewish money-
lender and trader.   His imprisonment at the instance of a man-
ufacturer of the alien race, who had objected to the use of
slander as a weapon against him, only served to increase his
reputation, and at last his following became so large that a separate political party, duly authenticated with programme
and electioneering organization, was formed, and in the elections of 1893 a large number of constituencies were fought by
Ahlwardt's friends on the alluring issue of Gentile *versus* Jew.
In the Diet five deputies had already sat as avowed anti-Semites, though they had not been returned by a compact anti-
Semite vote.   Now more than a quarter of a million electors
voted for anti-Semitic candidates, of whom sixteen were returned, Ahlwardt himself by two constituencies.   Most of these
successes were only possible because of the help given by the

Conservative party, which had meanwhile introduced in its revised programme of 1892 a paragraph declaring it to be one of its foremost objects to " combat the increasing and disintegrating Jewish influence in our national life," yet they were ominous of deep-seated prejudices, capable of being exploited for dangerous ends by sharp-witted agitators.

Ahlwardt's influence waned owing to the result of an inquiry made by a parliamentary committee into certain wild charges which he had brought against fellow-deputies. The charges were found to be unfounded, and Ahlwardt apologized and was censured. The party repeated its success at the polls in the three succeeding elections, yet in the Diet it never obtained serious influence, and more and more it lost reputation for everything except extravagance. When, however, it disappeared as a separate organization, the spirit which called it into existence still remained as vigorous as ever in the Conservative ranks. Before this Stöcker had fallen into disrepute. " Politics is good and religion is good, but they make a bad mixture," said Matthew Arnold, and this the Court chaplain found to his cost. During the short reign of the Emperor Frederick he had been required to choose between abandoning his political agitation and resigning his office as Court and cathedral preacher. He had promised to eschew politics, but had continued his old associations, though for a time parading his sympathies less openly than before. Constant quarrelling with the Jews brought him into many unpleasant situations, amongst them law-court episodes, which did not dignify his spiritual office, and this he was required to vacate in 1890. Henceforth he devoted himself exclusively to parliamentary life and a many-sided political agitation for which the metropolis served as an effective base. Perhaps of modern German political leaders none enjoyed to a fuller extent the attachment of his party associates or drew upon himself in greater measure the antipathy of his opponents than this eloquent divine, who for twenty years was pre-eminently a dividing force in the social life of Prussia.

The Emperor had not been long upon the throne before it became evident that military measures would retain the old prominence in domestic politics. In 1890 a momentous change in the foreign situation occurred, making it necessary that Germany should for the future rely upon her own strength even more than in the past. This was the abandonment of the reinsurance treaty with Russia, under which each Power had undertaken to be neutral in the event of the other being attacked.[1] Rebuffed and without an ally, Russia turned to France, who had long been waiting for this turn of events, and henceforth Germany had to reckon with the possibility of war on two fronts. The outlook was further darkened by the active military measures which were being taken at that time by France. A new law of 1891 had given to France a larger yearly addition to the army than Germany had made with her much greater population. In order to correct this inequality the German military authorities now proposed to enforce liability to serve more thoroughly than hitherto. It was estimated that in this way 70,000 more men would be added to the army yearly. The crux of the question, however, was the additional cost, for this would be three and a half million pounds a year, and the assent of the Diet to so large an additional expenditure was uncertain.

In 1890, midway in the new septennial period, Caprivi had obtained an increase of 18,000 to the peace strength. In November, 1892, a bill was introduced making a further addition of 70,000 for five and a half years, bringing the total to 479,-000, exclusive of non-commissioned officers, the number of whom was henceforth to be fixed in the army estimates each year. It was part of the scheme that service in the infantry was henceforth to be reduced to two years. The bill was rejected by the combined votes of the Clericals, who were still smarting under the affront which had been inflicted upon them by the abandonment of the Prussian School Bill, the Radicals, and the Social Democrats, whereupon the Government, rather than alter its programme, determined to take the verdict of the electorate. New elections took place in June, 1893, and were chiefly notable for the fact that the Agrarian League for the first time entered the political arena as a body of rough-riders in the service of extreme Conservatism. The result left the position of the larger party groups but little changed, though the Radicals suffered severely. To every new report of the defection and diminution of his followers the clever but unteachable leader of this party, Eugen Richter, only answered with James II's " Est-ce possible? " and continued on his un-

[1] See Chapter XXI., p. 390.

changing way, vainly hoping to capture the electors by an arid policy of obstruction and negation. Once again he brilliantly led the Radical party to defeat, for it emerged from the contest reduced by one-half and sorely chastened. The Government secured a majority, small but sufficient to save the bill, which was passed in July. By it the peace strength was fixed until March 31, 1899, at the figure originally proposed, exclusive of about 77,000 non-commissioned officers, and in spite of the opposition of the Conservatives the period of service was reduced by a year, a condition insisted on by the Clericals as the price of their support, which was still essential to the Government. Numerically the German army was now no larger than the French and considerably smaller than the Russian, but it was the fixed conviction and the boast of the military party that in efficiency, and particularly in quality of officers and non-commissioned officers, it excelled both of its rivals.

Nor was Caprivi immune from financial worries. The increase of the army threw the Empire still more upon matricular contributions, and in the financial year 1893–1894 these contributions exceeded by two million pounds the assignment made to the States from the revenue from the customs and excise duties. Hence new taxation was imposed with a view to raising an additional five million pounds a year. Before this, important reforms had been introduced in the taxation of sugar (1891), but not primarily for the sake of revenue. The old excise duty on raw materials was abolished, and the duty on the manufactured article was correspondingly increased. The revenue derived from sugar taxation had hitherto been diminished by drawbacks upon exports, which had developed into an elaborate system of bounties. The new law changed the basis of the export bounties, which henceforth were to be given openly as such, but to be reduced from August 1, 1895, and abolished two years later.

In the event this radical measure was found impracticable at the time prescribed, since bounties remained in force in competing countries. A law of 1895, therefore, repealed the provisions as to reduction and abolition, and in the following year the bounties were doubled, while simultaneously, with a view to checking over-production, all output beyond a specified amount was made subject to a special duty. With the conclusion of the Brussels Sugar Convention of March 5, 1902, the bounties were finally abolished and the duties were reduced.

The finances of Prussia were also successfully reorganized at this time by Dr. Miquel, one of the new men called to the Ministry by William II, and the first of two provincial mayors to hold the office of Prussian Minister of Finance during his reign. Miquel was an ex-republican who had taken part in the revolutionary movements of 1848. Later he became transformed into a useful parliamentarian, and as a member of the National Liberal party and a colleague of his fellow-Hanoverian Bennigsen he gave valuable help in the drafting of the Civil Code. When he became Minister in 1890 he found the finances of the country in desperate straits and the system of State and local taxation out of harmony with modern conditions. Between the years 1891 and 1895, by a series of masterly reforms, he succeeded in giving the Treasury a greatly increased revenue without exciting any violent antagonisms. This he did by shrewdly conciliating the agrarian majority in the Diet, for while he increased the income tax and made it progressive, he renounced the State land and building taxes, as well as the trade tax, and handed them over to the communes. The effect of the transformation of the land tax was to relieve the large landed proprietors, who saved far more by the abolition of the State tax than they had henceforth to pay in the form of a new local rate. Equally valuable in its way was his reform of municipal taxation, the effect of which was to place within the reach of local authorities novel and remunerative sources of revenue.

So long as he kept to finance Dr. Miquel was a great success, but as a colleague he was not beloved by the rest of the Cabinet. Like many politicians who, after sowing wild oats, have sobered with years, he became a reactionary, and he was never tired of giving proof of his repentance, forgetting that his rush to the other extreme, far from covering up the sins of his youth, only brought them more to remembrance. As a Minister he earned a fatal reputation for disloyalty and self-seeking. He encouraged the agrarians in resisting the Caprivi commercial treaties and in throwing out a Prussian Canal Bill introduced at a later date. No one doubted his great abilities, though no one rated them so highly as himself. The impression which he made upon his contemporaries was that of a pushing egoist, fighting for his own hand; he thrilled for recognition, and was so convinced of his cleverness that he aspired to supplant two successive Chancellors, and did not hesitate to intrigue to that end. His ambition was in the end his undoing.

The Army Law of 1893 was the last important achievement of Caprivi's Government. He had not desired office, and the longer he held it the less it attracted him. Moreover, he had made enemies in many quarters. The Clericals had not forgiven him for failing to carry the Prussian School Bill; the East African treaty of 1890 and his general attitude towards imperialism had embittered the colonial party against him; ever since the conclusion of the commercial treaties he had been marked out for the vindictive attacks of the agrarians; and the military party, which had intrigued against him for some time, made his concession of two years' service a pretext for open hostility.

On the other hand, Caprivi had a genuine grievance against the Emperor which had for a long time been growing more acute. He had spent most of his life in services in which loyalty is proverbial and obedience almost an instinct, yet before two years passed he had begun to resent the Emperor's habit of talking too freely, of saying one thing in his official capacity and another in private intercourse, so that misunderstandings occurred. He had even had to complain that he was at times entirely ignored in important matters of State. Bismarck was wont to commit the first Emperor to important acts and tell him afterwards, and it was the constant complaint of William I, so long as complaining availed, that he was kept in the dark. The third Emperor reversed this practice; he formed the habit of adopting decisions and acting upon them on his own initiative and without conferring with his Chancellor.

Incidents of the kind constantly came to public knowledge, and the effect was to weaken the Government, discredit its head, and to create strong prejudice against the Emperor in widening circles, which deplored his activity in politics as bad for the country and contrary to the spirit of the constitution. More emphatically than the old Emperor he made it clear that the policy of the Government was his policy, and that failure to support it implied want of loyalty to his person. " Dishonoured be the man who deserts his King," were the words in which, at Königsberg, he rallied the nobles and gentry of East

Prussia in September, 1894, when some of their number had united to defeat a Canal Bill which was intended to join the Rhine and Elbe and thus make it possible to convey corn by inland waterway from the extreme West to the extreme East of the kingdom. When the Prussian Lower House refused to increase the salary of the Chief of the Royal Cabinet, the Emperor-King, in sign of disapprobation, promptly conferred upon that official a high order, an act of which so staunch a Conservative statesman as Herr von Kardorff, the leader of the Imperialist party, spoke as "a demonstration against the constitution."

Never since the Prussian "Conflict time" of thirty years before had political passions been so stirred as now over the Emperor's attempt to reduce his constitutional Ministers to ciphers and to take the government both of the monarchy and the Empire into his own hands. It was in vain that he besought the nation not to place party considerations above the welfare of the community, so long as he himself pursued a policy which played directly into the hands of one party, and could only succeed by its acquiescence — the party that hated constitutional government and had no more ardent wish than to see it discredited and destroyed. Writing of the first years of the reign of Frederick William IV, Treitschke says that they were "a long chain of misunderstandings, and for this mutual misjudgment the King was as much to blame as the fermentative tendency of the time." The words faithfully describe the strained relations between ruler and people which began shortly after Bismarck's fall and never again entirely disappeared. For the first time it became impossible to keep the Emperor's name out of parliamentary debates, and the dignity of the Crown was not increased by the plain speaking of democratic deputies to whom the only sacred things in political life were the constitution and the rights which it conferred upon the nation. Outside the Diet the criticism took forms even less discriminating, and there occurred a contagion of prosecutions for *lèse-majesté* such as had never been known before. And yet no ruler was ever more desirous of standing well with his people. He craved for popularity, and resented every indication of flagging attachment as a personal wrong.

For a time the strain was relieved by the Emperor's reconciliation with Bismarck, who in token of the happy event visited Berlin at the beginning of 1894 (January 26th) for the first time since his banishment nearly four years before, and there paid his respects at the royal castle. The reconciliation was not sincere on either side; on the Emperor's it was a pure act of policy, a concession to political necessity, and an attempt to restore a popularity which had been severely tried. Talking with Hohenlohe in the evening of the reconciliation day, which for the nation was one of universal rejoicing, he said: "Now they can erect triumphal arches for him in Vienna and Munich, for I am always a horse's length ahead of him." When told that the "rabid Bismarckians" thought that it was his duty to go to Friedrichsruh, he rejoined: "I know, but they would have had to wait long enough for that. It was for him to come here."

Caprivi had done his best to bring about an understanding, and he was deeply mortified that the Emperor had made the first approaches to Bismarck without consulting him. He told Hohenlohe of the affront, and that diarist comments: "He bears it resignedly; I should not like to be Chancellor under such conditions." Caprivi bore his humiliations until October of that year, and then was allowed at his own wish to pass quietly into retirement, Count Eulenburg simultaneously resigning the Presidency of the Prussian Ministry. He had served his country efficiently and devotedly, and he took back into private life an unblemished reputation, with the good-will of all men capable of appreciating unselfish public service. History affords examples of statesmen to whose public words and acts the only safe clue has been a presumption of ambiguous or unscrupulous motive, yet also of statesmen who have always seemed to do the right thing by instinct and whose very probity and sincerity have exposed them to misjudgment by the unthinking crowd. To this smaller band of rare spirits Caprivi belonged. He died on February 24, 1899, at the age of sixty-eight.

With Caprivi's resignation Prince Hohenlohe's turn came at last, and he accepted the Chancellorship, and with it the Presidency of the Prussian Ministry, without demur (October 27th), though he would have done it with far greater satisfaction four years before. In the management of foreign affairs he had the assistance of Baron Marschall von Bieberstein, still

Secretary of State at the Foreign Office, with Herr von Bülow, but lately installed in the diplomatic service, as his lieu-
tenant.

Hohenlohe's appointment was a reward of long-proved fidelity in the service of the State, as well as of patience and per-
severance. It was also a compliment to kinship, for he was
the Emperor's uncle. He had special qualifications for the
great office of Imperial Prime Minister, an office requiring far
less than in democratically governed countries that its occupant shall be all things to all men. He was emphatically and
in the best sense a diplomatist, with a proper appreciation of
the cardinal virtues of diplomacy — faith, hope, and silence.
His training in high politics had given him the statesman's
judgment and breadth of view, while his residence abroad had
added a valuable acquaintance with the life, ways, and political thought of other nations which is more desirable than
usual in Ministers who have to conduct foreign relationships.
Moreover, he had already in 1880 acted as head of the Foreign Office under Bismarck, and no man was more in the confidence of that statesman. Finally, his scholarship and bent
for philosophy added greatly to his reputation with a Diet
whose erudition recalled the British House of Commons of the
pre-Reform era, and whose greatest weakness as a legislative
body was that its ponderous wisdom smacked too much of the
study and of midnight oil.

To all but the East Prussian phalanx it was a further merit
in him that he was a South German, with all the South German's flexibility of mind and none of his exaggerated devotion
to the " narrow fatherland." His political views were those
of a Liberal conscious that in a country of vigorous monarchies the limits of Liberal policy are very narrowly defined.
In personal relationships he represented the high traditions
of race and breeding: however he might differ from his opponents or they from him, he could always be relied on to
carry the etiquette of private into public life, for as were his
instincts so were his manners — those of a chivalrous gentleman.

It was a fine tribute to the character of Hohenlohe, in a
time when even men of honour found it difficult to follow the
path of courage, that he had not allowed Bismarck's fall to
interfere with their old friendship, and that though in 1890

Caprivi had taken the place which he thought should have been his own, he gave to that " dignified, honourable and loyal man," as he called him, all the assistance within his power. His long co-operation with the first Chancellor now proved a valuable recommendation with the Conservatives, for it encouraged in them the hope that he would divert national policy back into the old course. Hohenlohe's principal drawback was his age, for with his seventy-five years he had reached a time of life when men, and pre-eminently statesmen, are apt to look backward rather than forward, to value tranquillity more than action. Moderate in judgment and equable in temper, he made an earnest attempt to work harmoniously with the two Diets, and for a time he succeeded. His diplomatic training had taught him patience. When he failed to obtain his way he did not threaten dissolution, but accepted failure with the same equanimity as success; if a bill was rejected, he simply waited and tried again another day.

Hohenlohe took with him to Berlin, to be the Prussian Minister of the Interior, a dashing official of the Strassburg corps in whom he had great confidence, Herr E. M. von Köller. A reactionary bureaucrat who sailed under progressive colours, it was this adviser who caused him to commit two inexplicably rash acts at the very outset of his career as Chancellor. At the close of the ceremony connected with the opening of the new Imperial Diet buildings on December 6th cheers were called for the Emperor in the usual way. To the disgust of the loyal parties, the Socialists remained silent and seated. Forgetting that the Diet was governed only by its own laws, Hohenlohe a few days later asked it for permission to prosecute the more prominent offenders for *lèse-majesté*, and received a prompt and indignant refusal.

Later in the same month he made a still more inexcusable mistake. Ever since the Socialist Law had fallen the North German Conservatives had worked, in season and out of season, for the renewal of its coercive provisions in some new form. As another law directly aimed at Socialism seemed for the present out of the question, they endeavoured to reach the same end by amending the Penal Law of the Empire. So long as Caprivi remained they met with no encouragement. Hohenlohe, as Stadholder of Alsace-Lorraine, had for ten years lived in an atmosphere of exceptional legislation, and one of his first Ministerial acts was to capitulate to the reactionaries, perhaps more from habit than from conviction. The Anti-revolution Bill (*Umsturzvorlage*) was accordingly introduced in the Diet in December, 1894. Without mentioning Social-ism, it was intended in the good old-fashioned way to penalize all endeavours to " subvert the existing social order." In the hope of capturing the support of the Clerical party, which had suffered too much from exceptional laws to be willing to coerce others because of their political convictions, a clause was introduced making illegal all attacks upon religion, mar-riage, and the family tie. The bill reached the committee stage, but it never had a chance of success, and when it came back to the full House in the following May it was summarily rejected.

It was the new Chancellor's first and last experiment in coercing political opinion upon an imperial scale. When by constant contact he came to understand the Prussian reaction-aries more thoroughly, he refused either to assist their designs or to throw himself unduly upon their support. Their suc-cess in compassing Caprivi's downfall, however, had fired the Conservatives at this time with new and bolder ambitions, and during 1895 a well-organized agitation against the imperial franchise was carried on by the party Press, which openly ad-vocated a *coup d'état*. The Emperor and Government were bidden to give the Diet the opportunity of annulling this em-blem of popular government voluntarily if so minded, but in default of its so doing they were to abolish both the franchise and the Diet together, and a dictatorship was to be established until further notice. Against such indiscreet counsels even Bismarck, in his seclusion, warmly protested, urging his coun-trymen to hold fast by the old ways.

During Hohenlohe's Chancellorship there was a lull in do-mestic legislation, for much of the ardour which had been thrown into social reform had been diverted to unfruitful po-litical controversy. The agrarians were as persistent as ever, but, strive as they would, they were impotent to undo the com-mercial treaties, which blocked any interference with the cus-toms tariff until 1904. Nevertheless, a few useful laws of a minor kind were passed for their benefit, including the Stock Exchange Law of 1896 prohibiting dealings in futures, in corn and flour, supplemented in Prussia by a law which empowered the Chambers of Agriculture to co-operate in the management of the produce exchanges, and a drastic law relating to the sale of margarine (1897). In Prussia large Government subsidies were granted in 1896 and 1897 towards the erection of elevators in the corn-growing districts; while by the reform of State taxation already mentioned real estate was relieved of some of its ancient burdens. The small tradesmen benefited by imperial laws against unfair competition and regulating the practice of selling goods on the payment-by-instalment principle; while housing reform was encouraged by the grant in 1895 of the first of a series of large votes of money for the provision of cheap dwellings for workmen in State employment.

In 1896 there was completed the *magnum opus* of German jurisprudence since the establishment of the Empire, the Civil Code, upon which the cleverest lawyers of the land had worked for twenty years. The union of Germany in 1871 disclosed the existence of a hopeless medley of legal systems. The Prussian Common Law of 1794 was in force only in the old provinces of the monarchy; in the Western provinces and in the Western and Southern States generally the Code Napoléon applied; Saxony had a Code of its own; the Austrian Code of 1811 applied to portions of Bavaria; and in Prussian Pomerania there were still relics of Swedish Law. Moreover, many of the minor territories, and even the City Republics, had legal and judicial systems of their own marked by important variations and peculiarities. One of the first acts of the Imperial Government in 1871 was to appoint a commission to draw up rules of civil and criminal procedure and a scheme for the organization of the law-courts. The recommendations of this commission were published in the following year, but it was 1879 before agreement was arrived at between the North and South and the necessary laws could be passed. Meanwhile, the larger question of the codification of the civil law had been taken in hand. A commission of experts worked upon this great task from 1874 to 1890, when a new commission was appointed to revise its recommendations. Not until August, 1896, was the Civil Code of the Empire enacted, with full force as from January 1, 1900. This great law expressed the unity of the nation as nothing else had done — neither armies, nor railways, nor posts — and with its consummation the last traces of the old disruption may be said to have been obliterated.

An attempt was made by the Socialist and Liberal parties to obtain the introduction into the Civil Code of provisions enlarging the existing very limited right of association and public meeting, and so protecting the working classes against the arbitrary action of the State Governments. Although the Socialist Law was no more, the omnipotence of the police authorities left but little liberty of political agitation, and the old laws were sufficiently stringent, when narrowly interpreted, to make even trade union activity difficult and ineffectual. In the summer of 1895 a private bill, which would have empowered labour organizations to federate, given to men and women full right of coalition and assembly, and greatly reduced the controlling powers of the police, passed through committee; but it had to be abandoned in the final stages owing to the resolute opposition of the Conservative groups. When a year later a large majority of the Diet agreed upon a bill of a single paragraph, legalizing the federation of national associations and repealing all State laws in a contrary sense, the Federal Governments in turn refused assent.

The only hope remaining was that the same provision might be added to the Civil Code, now nearing completion. A majority of the Diet was in favour of this course, but now Prince Hohenlohe objected. He regarded the provision itself as reasonable and necessary, but contended that it related to private and not to public right, and hence would be out of place in the Civil Code. Moreover, he was able to assure the Diet that the Governments of the States were themselves about to abolish the prohibition of federation between political associations where it still existed, and he promised that Prussia should lead the way. The pledge thus given by the Chancellor was not fulfilled. A bill was duly produced in the Prussian Diet early in the following year, but it was wrecked by the reactionaries. The question, therefore, came back to the Imperial Diet once more, and finally Hohenlohe secured the passing in December, 1899, of a law permitting the federation of societies of all kinds throughout the Empire, whether the laws of the States allowed it or not.

The Diet showed more freedom than usual in opposing retrogressive measures about that time. In the same year it rejected a bill, pilloried by popular opprobrium as the Penal Servitude Bill, intended to protect free labour against intimidation. A year later the friends of the Anti-revolution Bill of 1895 reintroduced this measure in an even more aggressive form. For practical purposes it was a Socialist Law without the name, though it contained the old provisions intended to protect religion and its institutions and symbols against ill-mannered attack. For the Clericals, however, the bill was not extreme enough, and in their clumsy but honest championship of public morals they proposed amendments which would have established a rigorous police censorship of literature and art. Against this attempt of a narrow religious philistinism to subordinate the æsthetic tastes of Germany to the tutelage of the Vatican the nation protested with no uncertain voice, though it was the special merit of the Socialist party to have brought about the discredit and eventual abandonment of the bill.

No such breakwater against reactionary legislation existed in the Prussian Parliament, and an encroachment upon the language rights of the Polish population of the Eastern provinces in 1900 added to the prevailing discontent there. A Government regulation dating from 1842 stipulated that instruction in the elementary schools should be given in the language spoken by the majority of the children. The result was that in many localities German made no headway, and in order to remedy this the regulation was repealed in 1872, from which time it was required that instruction in all subjects except religion should be in German. In 1900 even this reservation was cancelled in some districts which had been conspicuous for anti-Prussian agitation, with the result that Polish was excluded from the schools altogether. Polish parents answered by unteaching at home the German taught to their children at school and by insisting more and more upon the use of the proscribed language in intercourse amongst themselves and their German neighbours.

To Hohenlohe's Chancellorship fell a great measure of naval expansion, for which the preceding thirty years had been a slow preparation. Prince Bülow has paid Emperor William II a doubtful compliment by the suggestion that he embraced the idea of a large navy as an antidote to the national depression which was caused by his quarrel with the first Chancellor. " The pressure which rested on the German spirit," he writes, " could only be thrown off if the Emperor placed before the nation, which at the time lacked common hopes and wishes, a new goal, and showed it the place in the sun to which it had a right and which it ought to endeavour to attain." [1] This is not quite accurate or just. The Emperor had taken a warm interest in the navy long before he came to the throne, and after his accession it was only preoccupation with other tasks — and not least the strengthening of the army — that prevented him from making the navy question at once a capital question of policy. Nevertheless, progress was not delayed. He became Emperor in June, 1888, and by August his naval advisers were working upon a new plan of shipbuilding, to take effect the following year; four large armoured vessels were to be asked for as the nucleus of an efficient battle fleet, and four cruisers were to be built for special use on colonial stations. The Diet was in no mood to thwart the wishes of the new ruler, and the modest scheme was sanctioned. A further indication of a forward movement at the Admiralty was the reorganization of naval administration early in the following year. Hitherto this had been concentrated in the hands of the Chief of the Admiralty, who was also the First Sea Lord. Now the functions of supreme command and administration were separated, the former being vested in a naval officer and the latter in the Imperial Marine Board, the head of which (corresponding to the First Lord of the Admiralty) was henceforth a Secretary of State, while a Naval Cabinet was formed as a nexus between the naval administration and the First Sea Lord and between these and the Emperor. The First Sea Lord under the new *régime* was Admiral von der Goltz and the First Secretary of State for the Navy Rear-Admiral Häusner, soon succeeded by Rear-Admiral von Hollmann.

Before, however, parliamentary sanction could be obtained for a policy of shipbuilding on a large scale, public opinion needed to be educated, and this task the Emperor took upon himself and discharged with unwearying persistence and great resource. At naval launches, harbour openings, regatta junketings, on any and every occasion which furnished him with a text, he preached to the nation the need for a great sea

[1] *Imperial Germany* (edition 1914), p. 20.

change which was to make of Germany the strongest naval as she had already become the strongest military Power. In the meantime he devoted his attention to the improvement of the fleet he had. He sought to create in the navy new traditions, a new code of discipline, a new *esprit de corps* and *moral*, and ever his eyes were upon England, from whom he learned his most important naval lessons. The administration of the navy was revolutionized; the conditions of service were revised, and training was adapted to modern conditions. Hitherto training had been confined to home waters and to the summer months, and during winter the ships were put out of commission and laid up. Now the fleet was turned out into the open sea, and evolutions and manœuvring on a large scale, with sham fights, became part of the regular routine all the year round. All past comparisons of the German with other navies had been limited to France, Russia, and Italy; the superiority of the British navy had been assumed as self-evident. From 1890 forward the comparison became one with England; all other navies had become for Germany of secondary importance.

The year which thus marked a new era in German naval policy saw Germany also committed to untried ways in high politics, for Bismarck now ceased to be Chancellor, and the young Emperor, taking the helm in his own hand, ordered the ship of State to go " full steam ahead " upon a " new course." It was in July of the same year that Great Britain ceded Heligoland to Germany, on whose behalf the Emperor hailed the Elbe island as " a bulwark by sea, a protection for German fishermen, a base for my ships of war, and a shield and shelter for the German Ocean against every enemy who may venture to show himself upon it." Five years later the Kiel Canal was completed and opened (June, 1895). Both of these events were of vital importance for the creation of a navy that was to be of real value as a fighting force. From the beginning of the reign the expenditure upon the navy had gradually increased until it had grown from two and a half to five million pounds a year. The amount was thus still moderate, for Hollmann had resisted the strong pressure brought upon him in favour of shipbuilding on bold lines.

In 1897 reports began to circulate that Hollmann's position was uncertain. In the previous autumn it had been rumoured that one Herr Tirpitz, then a rear-admiral on service in East

Africa, had laid before the Emperor a large shipbuilding project, but the *Official Gazette* denied this rumour, and even added that a rear-admiral was not in a position to make any such representations direct to his Sovereign. Early in that year Hollmann laid before the Diet a modest plan of ship-construction, to be completed in three years, yet with no suggestion that naval expenditure should be voted otherwise than for a year at once as hitherto. Both the chief of the Admiralty and the Imperial Chancellor then gave assurances that there was no ambitious scheme in the background.

Nevertheless, the idea of a large navy was already in the air. In three public utterances during 1897 the Emperor had hinted that the time had come for a further extension of naval power. When in April he deputed his brother Prince Henry, admiral of the fleet, to attend the celebrations in connection with the jubilee of Queen Victoria's reign, he publicly deplored the fact that " while other nations will shine with their proud war vessels," Germany would be represented by an old hulk. Drawing the moral, he added: " This is the sad result of the attitude of the unpatriotic people who succeed in preventing the building of the necessary ships. But I shall not rest until my navy has been brought to the same standard as that of the army." On another occasion he used the suggestive and often-cited words, " The trident belongs in our hand." Still more urgently he declared in the speech from the throne with which he opened the Diet in November: " The development of our fleet is not equal to the tasks which Germany is compelled to impose on it. . . . While it cannot be our duty to rank with naval Powers of the first rank, Germany must be put in a position to maintain her prestige among the other nations of the world by her naval armaments. To this end it is necessary to strengthen the home fleet and to increase the number of ships needed for foreign service in time of peace."

In this speech the Government's intention to lay down a comprehensive programme of shipbuilding, with a time limit for its execution, was admitted for the first time. By this time Rear-Admiral Tirpitz had returned to Germany, and public opinion was not surprised to learn at the end of November that Hollmann had left the Admiralty and the unknown naval expert had taken his place as the Emperor's fleet-planner. Thus was formed a partnership in naval enterprise which lasted for nearly twenty years. The idea of a strong navy, which should at need be able to give the army effective support and prove powerful in offensive as well as defensive warfare, was the Emperor's. It fell to Tirpitz to put this idea into concrete form, reorganize the navy in accordance with it, and carry through the Diet, at first in the face of much hostility, but later with ever-increasing facility, a succession of measures in which it was translated into a fact.

A bill introduced at the end of the year became the first Navy Law of April, 1898, which laid down a large programme of shipbuilding, to be completed in seven years, and provided the Government with the necessary vote, in the aggregate nearly fifty million pounds. The bill was cordially supported by the Conservatives and National Liberals; the Clericals accepted rather than welcomed it; while the Radicals and Socialists, though forming a small minority, fought it tenaciously. The attitude of Hohenlohe towards this impetuous departure was not enthusiastic. He defended the bill loyally, but he did not conceal his opinion that the admirals were moving much too fast for safety. It was in reference to the Emperor's action in the matter that he wrote in his Diary at that time (November 7th): " It is not desirable that the Emperor should disturb things by his impulsive nature. It is to be wished that he were more phlegmatic." The opponents of the bill complained that the Diet should have been asked to give away its control over the naval estimates for so long a time, and pointed out that the imperial debt had increased by seventy million pounds since the commencement of the reign, for the most part owing to expenditure on the army and navy, and that the bill would further add to the Emperor's indebtedness. Neither financial scruples nor the objection that by passing the bill the Diet would bind its hand for seven years availed against the appeal to patriotic spirit, and the bill duly became law.

The case for a larger navy was greatly assisted by events which were happening at the time in China. In the autumn of 1897 two German missionaries had been murdered and the German mission stations wrecked in the province of Shantung, and the German warships in East Africa waters received instructions to exact prompt expiation. Troops were accordingly landed in November, and before they re-embarked they had secured from China the bay and coast of Kiauchau, to

serve as a permanent pledge of remorse and incidentally as a
German naval station.

The Navy Act of 1898 was represented as marking the limit
of Germany's naval ambitions for at least seven years. The
ships to be built in this time were twelve battleships, eight
armoured vessels for coast defence, and ten large and twenty-
three small cruisers, so that, independently of cannon boats,
torpedo boats, and training ships, the navy would be increased
to nineteen battleships, eight armoured coast vessels, and forty
cruisers (twelve large and twenty-eight small), thirteen of
these intended for foreign service. The life of armoured vessels, large cruisers, and small cruisers was fixed at twenty-five,
twenty, and fifteen years respectively.

In March, 1899, a further reorganization of the naval administration was introduced. The chief command of the navy
was abolished, and the Emperor became the head of the navy
as of the army; but the Imperial Marine Board, directed by a
Secretary of State, and the Naval Cabinet remained. Later
in the year the navy which had been planned as sufficient for
all purposes was already found to be inadequate. Now events
again occurred which seemed to strengthen the Emperor's contention that Germany would never be able to assert her rightful influence abroad until she was in a position to support
her arguments by ships as well as bayonets. The Jameson
raid of December 31, 1895, had created a strong feeling of
hostility against England, particularly amongst the political
and commercial members of the colonial party, who still recalled with resentment how fifteen years before timely British
action had thwarted the German design of gaining a foothold
in the Transvaal. This hostility was redoubled when in October, 1899, President Krüger's declaration of war precipitated the long-deferred and lamentable struggle between Briton
and Boer. The attitude of the German Government during
that struggle was outwardly correct, but the succeeding Chancellor, Bülow, admitted later that only the want of a strong
navy prevented Germany from intervening in a way hostile to
England early in the war, when for a critical moment it seemed
as though she had been committed to a task beyond her power.

Instead of running risks, therefore, the Government determined to prepare for the future. Not only was the army
again increased in that year, bringing its peace strength to

495,500, but a new Navy Bill was introduced. There was now no concealment of the fact that it was desired to strike a first blow, to be followed in due time by others, at England's naval supremacy. "Germany," the *exposé des motifs* said, "must have so strong a battle fleet that war, even for our most powerful naval opponent, will be attended by such dangers that its supremacy will be at stake." That these words referred to England was admitted by Admiral von der Goltz, who told the Diet: "Let us consider the idea of war with England. There is nothing improbable in it, having regard to the animosity which Germany bears towards England and to the attitude of the British nation towards all Continental Powers, and especially Germany." The entire theory of the purpose of the fleet was now changed. Hitherto it had been intended to be merely defensive; now it was to be organized avowedly for offence. "Let us continue without relaxation," the Emperor said in one of his public utterances, while the bill was under discussion, " and end quickly the work begun; so shall we impose peace on the sea also " (May, 1900). In the existing state of public feeling, the Government might have had all the ships and money it wanted, and in June the second Navy Law was passed by 201 votes against 103. Only the Radicals and Socialists now kept up a futile resistance, and they knew that the country was against them. Prince Bülow relates how Richter, the leader of the Radical party, who had fought the colonial movement and was now fighting the naval movement, came to him one day in 1900 and said: "You will get your ships, though I should never have thought it. You may be right, but I am too old to go new ways."

Under the new law the battle fleet was to be increased in the course of sixteen years to thirty-eight ships of the line, in four squadrons, two active and two reserve; the coast vessels provided by the first law were to be dropped, and instead of them fourteen large cruisers instead of ten and thirty-eight small cruisers instead of twenty-three were to be built; and there was also to be a fleet of eighty torpedo boats.

A large-navy agitation flooded Germany from north to south at this time, and it powerfully strengthened the hands of the Government. A Navy League had been founded under high patronage in 1898, and it soon covered the country with a network of branches, which carried the crusade into factory and

workshop, school and home. By means of persistent propagandism of all kinds, by stirring appeals to patriotism, interest, and even fear, the national imagination was impressed,
and the conviction brought home to the minds of the taxpayers
that Germany needed all the ships the Government asked for,
and that it was their duty to supply them. The Emperor
could say with perfect truth in 1900: " The German nation
is at one with its Princes and Emperor in the determination to
mark further our powerful development by the creation of a
great navy. A little later (June, 1901) he gave to the large-
navy party and the nation a rallying cry in words which the
poet Herwegh had used just half a century before: " Our
future lies on the water."

Hardly had the second Navy Law been passed than Admiral
(now von) Tirpitz prepared the country for new demands, and
it responded with a readiness never excelled even in meeting
the demands of the army. By this time the idea that the Government was building according to a programme and a time-
limit had become a pretence. If that fiction was still continued, it was only for the purpose of obtaining money more
easily and of diverting the attention of foreign Governments
from the capital fact, which was that Tirpitz intended to
build just as much and as fast as the Diet would allow him.
Foreign critics, venturing to recall the earlier professions with
which their anxiety had been allayed, were now told that what
Germany did was no business of theirs. " The German nation," the Emperor said in 1904, " has a right to maintain
just such an army and navy as the protection of its interests
requires, and no one will venture to prevent it developing these
two forces according to its own wish and will." The words
gave definiteness to the suspicion which had for some time been
forming in many minds in Great Britain that the German naval
rivalry was a deliberate challenge to British sea power.

It has been convenient to follow the course of the large-navy
movement into its later stages, so anticipating developments
which did not belong to Hohenlohe's Chancellorship. Although Hohenlohe, as the first Minister of the Empire, was
officially responsible for the early naval schemes out of which
the larger ones grew, and although he came to the conviction
that " without a fleet a powerful empire is inconceivable "
(June, 1900), he never allowed his patriotic feelings to de-

stroy his sense of proportion. To the last he feared that the admirals were bent on committing the country to naval ambitions and expenditure beyond the limits of reason and safety, and his suspected lukewarmness turned against him the whole naval party and its influence with the Emperor, which was great. The generals and the military party likewise disliked him because he was not one of themselves.

More serious, however, was the hostility of the agrarian Conservatives. To make them his enemies was not difficult, for all that was necessary was to go counter to their demands. This he had done from the first on the question of Protection. The East Prussian corn-growers wanted higher duties and the abandonment of the Caprivi treaties; — how the treaties were to be denounced before the proper time was a question which did not trouble them. Like his predecessor, however, Hohenlohe recognized frankly that Germany had, for good or ill, become an industrial country, and that in any adjustment of her customs relationships the needs of the working classes, and preeminently the need of cheap food, must be carefully weighed. "We cannot admit the excessive demands of the agrarians," he said in 1896, and therewith he sealed his doom, though as yet he knew not the day nor the hour. Before he had been Chancellor a year he had been aware that " a number of politicians and highly placed busybodies are doing their best to discredit me with his Majesty." A year later he had had reason to believe that his resignation was desired. " My relations with his Majesty are peculiar," he then wrote. " Sometimes owing to his little acts of thoughtlessness and want of consideration I come to the conclusion that he purposely avoids me and that it cannot go on. Then I see him again and I think I was mistaken." So it continued until 1900, his relations with the Emperor being " now friendly, now reserved," though always uncertain, while the hostility directed against him from many sides increased. On October 16th of that year he resigned, judging from various signs that the step would not be unacceptable. Like Caprivi, he had ceased to be the confidant of the Emperor's inner counsels. " How can one bear the responsibilities of office," he said to a friend just before his resignation, " if one is not admitted into the secrets of policy? " It was a curious situation, only to be resolved in one way. He has put it on record that the Emperor had been waiting for his resignation, and had already chosen his successor.

Hohenlohe's tenure of the Chancellorship left German politics but little changed from Caprivi's time. His enemies complained that he did not give the country an example of " resolute action." For that he was too old, nor did he believe that it was the country's need. The longer he remained in office the more convinced he became that the greatest service within his power to render to Germany was to hold back the reaction, whose main strength was now derived from feudal Conservatism in the North and Clericalism in the South, and whose pressure, though from time to time relaxed, was still the most constant force in national politics. As a South German he was never thoroughly acclimatized in Prussia. He distrusted the Prussian nobles, and accused them of prostituting loyalty and patriotism to the advancement of their own interests. They were " too numerous, too powerful, and have the kingdom and the army too much on their side," he wrote in December, 1898, and he suspected that they would have been willing to sacrifice the Empire's unity if they could thereby have served their own ends. " As I laboured from 1866 to 1870," he wrote, " for the union of South and North, so I must strive now to keep Prussia attached to the Empire. For all these gentlemen do not care a rap for the Empire, and would rather give it up to-day than to-morrow."

It was good for Germany to have had at that time a Chancellor so acutely conscious of these subtle influences and of the need of holding them in check. Yet partly wrangling was not in keeping with Hohenlohe's temperament. His tastes predisposed him far more to high politics than to controversies over customs tariffs, naval programmes, and army laws; and the never-ending frictions and jars with a parliamentary majority, whose support had in every emergency to be bought at the market price of the moment, were repulsive to his fine spirit and love of probity and decorum. He was not a strong man, if tested by the characteristics to which Bismarck's pre-eminence was chiefly due, and his quiet nature constantly exposed him to a temptation to defer to the pushing men around him, and even to fall too much into the spirit of his *milieu*. There was a pathetic incongruity in the idea of this benign old gentleman, with the serene eye and pensive brow of the scholar, the incarnation of the civic virtues, pleading with Bismarck, while yet Stadholder of Alsace-Lorraine, that he would do his duty and maintain his dignity more successfully if only he might be given the rank of general.

Nevertheless, with all the limitations which, conjoined with his age, prevented him from becoming a really great imperial administrator, Hohenlohe filled a difficult office at a difficult time with more than passable success, and his high repute and authority in foreign affairs were to the last an asset which Germany could ill afford to lose. As his coming had been received with but a passive interest, so his going created no surprise, for all it meant was that another phantom had ceased to flit across the stage of political life; the real Chancellor still remained. He died, at the age of eighty-two, on July 6, 1901, thus surviving his retirement for an even shorter time than either of his predecessors.

CHAPTER XX

EMPEROR WILLIAM II. DOMESTIC AFFAIRS —
(ii) THE REACTION

DURING the remaining years covered by this survey of domestic affairs the spirit which rested upon German political life was in the main a spirit of reaction, notwithstanding that the elections to the Imperial Diet in the middle of the period produced one of those recurrent revulsions of national feeling which, impressive though they may appear to outsiders, merely emphasize the impotence of the democratic parties in an undemocratic parliamentary system. The new Chancellor was Count Bernhard von Bülow, who since June 28, 1897, had been Foreign Secretary in succession to Baron Marschall von Bieberstein, on his appointment to the embassy at Constantinople. With the choice of Bülow a new type of Minister entered German parliamentary life. Both Bismarck and Hohenlohe had graduated in the diplomatic service, but of neither of them could it be said as of Bülow that he was a diplomat pure and simple. Gifted in a rare degree with the courtier's temperament, a polished man of the world of brilliant intellectual parts and fascinating address, and an accomplished orator, whose fluent periods hypnotized rather than persuaded, his strength lay less in force of conviction or will than in a large fund of astuteness, a thorough knowledge of human nature, and, above all, an incomparable acquaintance with every device and resource of the craft of politics. His defects are perhaps best indicated when it is said that, while he had none of Bismarck's rough, downright strength of character, he lacked also Caprivi's moral earnestness and Hohenlohe's grave outlook upon life and the world.

Bülow was in no doubt as to the influences which had precipitated his predecessor's retirement. The strongest of these was agrarianism, and against that rock he was determined not to break himself. The first domestic problem with which he was faced compelled him to choose whether he would have the agrarians as friends or as enemies, and as became a practised diplomat, he decided for peace. The Caprivi commercial treaties were to expire at the end of 1903. What was then to take their place? The question was one of immense importance for agriculture, and ever since the beginning of 1893 the Agrarian League had been preparing for the inevitable renewal of the fight between country and town. The question of prolonging these treaties was discussed in the Diet as early as 1897, at which time the Government set on foot the preparatory inquiries. For the conduct of these an Economic Committee was appointed, consisting of thirty persons, fifteen nominated by the Executive and five each by the Central Association of German Industrialists, the German Agricultural Council, and the German Commercial Diet. This revisory committee, of whose members the great majority were avowed Protectionists, elaborated the tariff with a view to a greater differentiation as between various classes of goods belonging to the same group. Hence it came about that when the tariff was issued in draft form it particularized nearly a thousand classes of goods. Upon the basis of this now highly specialized " autonomous " tariff, fixing maximum rates, negotiation was to take place with each country individually. Maximum rates were well enough. But now the agrarians raised the cry for minimum rates as well. What was the good, they asked, of enacting maximum duties when it was known that they would not be maintained against a single State? It was cold comfort to talk to the farmer of a protection which was beyond his reach; he would much prefer to know the protection of which he could be quite certain.

This demand of minimum duties the Government eventually conceded in principle in the case of agriculture, and henceforth it became the purpose of agrarian agitation to fix the irreducible duties as high as possible. In this the landed party was aided by a formal *concordat* with the Central Association of German Industrialists, a Protectionist organization representing especially the large iron and textile trades, the terms of which were that the agrarians should support higher industrial duties, in return for which the Association would not be found averse to an increase of the agricultural duties. The pressure which assailed the Government was thus pressure from two sides.

Early in January, 1901, the agrarians gave the Government

to understand that when the commercial treaties came to be revised they would expect a substantial increase of the duties on corn, live stock, and all agricultural produce, and later in that month Bülow formally gave the desired assurances on the point. When the bill was produced in July it proved to be almost as highly protective to industry as it was to agriculture. About two hundred classes of goods were allowed to remain free of duty; in a number of others — notably raw materials and partially manufactured articles — the existing duties were reduced, but in the great majority of cases there was an increase. The duties on corn, live stock, and meat were raised all round, and the agrarians were relieved of duties on certain articles of importance for agriculture.

The new tariff obviously marked a clear departure from the policy pursued with so much success by Caprivi. It was the object of that policy to do equal justice to agriculture and industry, while making due allowance for the fact that Germany was becoming more and more an industrial country, and that the vital condition of that transition was cheap food for the working classes. Bülow professed that it was likewise his desire to show fair play to both of these great factors in the productive life of the nation — in his words, to " strike the balance between interests that are in many instances opposed to each other "— but with him agriculture had prior consideration. The proceeds of the old duties as a whole averaged in 1902 19 per cent. of the aggregate value of the imports taxed. It was estimated that the new duties would add a further 17 per cent. to the taxation of agricultural produce and 6 per cent. to that of industrial goods.

A long and bitter struggle over the tariff took place in committee, a struggle in which all sorts of antagonisms came to light — town against country, landowner against tenant, large cultivator against small, industry against industry, and capital of all kinds against labour. So long did the proceedings drag on, that no time remained for a full consideration of the tariff bill in the full House if it was to be passed before the end of the session. Hence came the irritating mimic *coup d'état* of December 13th, when, in accordance with prior agreement, a majority consisting of the Clerical, Conservative, and National Liberal parties passed the bill *en bloc* as revised by committee, directly the schedule of agricultural duties had been disposed of. The effect was to prevent discussion of any one of the seven hundred duties affecting industry and manufacture.

The new tariff was a triumph for the agrarians, and particularly the large corn-growers of the East of Prussia. They did not get all they wanted, but they got more than they expected, and on the whole they were well satisfied, for the corn duties, reduced in 1892, were now raised beyond the earlier level; those on wheat ranged from £2 15s. to £3 5s. a ton, those on rye and oats from £2 10s. to £3, those on barley from £2 10s. to £4, and the duty on flour was fixed at £9 7s. 6d. By way of concession to the working classes, whose staple food articles were again to become dearer, the Government agreed to add to the new Tariff Law a clause (the " Trimborn clause "), proposed by the Clericals, providing that any increase in the revenue from the duties on corn, flour, and meat in excess of the average amount yielded during the years 1898 to 1903 (as calculated per head of the population) should be passed to a fund which should be used at some future time for the benefit of the survivors of persons coming under the Industrial Insurance Laws.

The man who reaped least credit for the tariff was its author which could not be said of Caprivi in 1892. Bülow's case was a hard one. Clinging to the Ministerial superstition that in Germany in general, but in Prussia in particular, Junkerdom was the foundation of monarchy and the bulwark of law and order, and therefore that political interest required that the State should do for Junkerdom what it was prepared to do for no other section of the community, he had exerted himself, at no small sacrifice of popularity elsewhere, to satisfy the demands of the agrarian classes, yet he received only ingratitude and reproach that he had not done more. " It will be a long time," he lamented, " before an Imperial Chancellor will do again for agriculture what I have done."

In the later negotiations over the new commercial treaties Germany enforced the minimum rates for corn, while corn-exporting States, like Russia, Austria-Hungary, and Roumania, in return increased their duties on industrial articles. Most of the new treaties came into force in March, 1906, with duration until the end of 1917. Higher corn duties were not, however, the only concession required by the agricultural party in return for its support in the Diets of Prussia and the Empire.

In the early years of Bülow's Government a drastic law regulating the inspection of imported cattle and meat was also passed, the effect of which was to restrict greatly supplies from abroad. On the other hand, the Sugar Taxation and Sugar Convention Bills, under which export bounties were abolished, were carried in 1902 in the face of resolute agrarian opposition.

The revision of the customs tariff in the interest of agriculture had an important sequel in the Prussian Diet when several years later the Government brought forward a large scheme of canal construction. The first effect of the railways upon river and canal traffic in Germany had been injurious, and there was a disposition in the middle of the century to assume that the canal had become obsolete. For many years there was little new canal building, the rivers were neglected, and it was only in the last quarter of the century, when it became recognized that the two systems of transport were complementary and not antagonistic, and that there was room and need for both, that active interest in inland navigation was revived. A new era in canal construction opened during the later years of William I's reign. The Dortmund-Ems Canal was begun in 1886 and completed in 1899, and with it the development of a large industrial district, with immense natural resources, received a new impetus. A year later a canal connecting the Elbe and the Trave was opened, bringing the North and Baltic Seas into communication before the Kiel Canal, opened in June, 1895, accomplished the same end on a bolder scale. In 1899 a bill was introduced in the Diet to empower the Government to construct a series of canals connecting the Rhine with the Elbe, a deep canal navigable for large vessels from Berlin to Stettin, with smaller connecting waterways, and extensive works of rectification on some of the shallower streams. Fearing that the extension of inland waterways, by cheapening the carriage of imported corn, would lower the price of this commodity to the industrial districts in the west and centre of the kingdom, and so to some extent neutralize the new tariff, the agrarians rejected the bill.

The project was one in which the Emperor-King was specially interested, and the rebellion of the great landowners drew from him a severe rebuke and led to the removal from office of certain Landrats who were among the ringleaders. It was 1905 before a compromise was reached and the bill was passed in a somewhat curtailed form, the waterway from Hanover to the Elbe being omitted, and the condition being introduced that before the canals were opened to traffic the Government should take steps to impose dues upon the navigable rivers of the monarchy, a transparent device for increasing the cost of waterborne imported grain. This proposal likewise roused bitter controversy, this time in the Imperial Diet, since it involved an amendment of the constitution, and when some years later (1911) opposition was withdrawn, it was subject to stipulations which defeated the hopes of the agrarians.

Most of the canal works authorized by the law of 1905 have since been completed, in some cases on a larger scale than was originally contemplated. While spending money thus lavishly upon canal construction the Prussian Government usually leaves the working of the canals, together with the cost of their maintenance, to the provincial authorities. In the case of some of the later canals, however, the towing service has been monopolized by the State, and the same arrangement has been introduced by the Imperial Government on the Kiel Canal. This is not the only peculiarity of State canal enterprise as carried out in Germany in modern times. In the old days the landowners only allowed railways and canals to be built by sufferance and on the payment of heavy tribute. Now the tables have been turned. It is a feature of recent canal projects that the adjacent owners have been required to contribute towards the cost. In some cases the contributions have been paid partly in land and partly in money. In other cases the State has expropriated the adjacent proprietors altogether, with a view to securing to the community all future increase in land values. Thus the Canal Law of 1905 empowered the State to expropriate owners of land within one kilometre (five-eighths of a mile) of the Rhine-Weser Canal, such power to be exercised in favour of the provinces of Westphalia, Rhineland, and Hanover, and the State of Bremen, with a view to securing to them the increased value which might accrue to the land owing to the works carried out.

All the large German canals intersect the great northern plain; owing to the configuration of the land the artificial waterways of the south and centre of the country are of minor importance. On the other hand, the navigation of the rivers and their tributaries has been greatly improved in all parts of the country. Counting the cost of the Kiel Canal,[1] the expenditure incurred by the States in canal construction and extension and the deepening and regulation of rivers during the reign of the present Emperor has been estimated at over forty million pounds, while schemes are still in course of execution or contemplated which will cost an equal sum.

While the States have as a rule undertaken the cost of river improvements, the riparian towns have emulated each other in the construction of harbour and docks, and to-day the Rhine from its entrance into Germany at the Swiss frontier is lined by an imposing succession of busy harbours, docks, and quays, upon the construction and equipment of which many millions of pounds have been expended during the past twenty years. On the seaboard ports like Hamburg, Bremen, and Lübeck have renewed their ancient fame, and outdistanced their olden prosperity, while other ports, like Emden, have come to the front and given hostages to a prosperous future. In consequence of the constant endeavour to keep the canals and rivers in an efficient condition from one-fifth to one-fourth of the inland goods traffic of the country has for several decades been regularly carried by water.

There has been a large simultaneous increase in the mercantile marine. The total tonnage of German sea-going ships had been doubled during the twenty years 1850 to 1870 (from half a million to a million tons) and it doubled again during the following three decades. The same period also witnessed a large concentration of shipping in a few powerful companies of Hamburg and Bremen, which, having unlimited capital at command, came to dominate the German shipping trade. Another notable transformation has been the gradual transfer of shipping to the North Sea from the Baltic, some of whose ports as a consequence have lost much of their ancient commercial importance.

In 1909 a successful attempt was made to abolish the chaos in railway rates and tariffs which had increased since Bismarck's premature endeavour thirty years before to acquire the railways for the Empire. Something was also done at the same time to reorganize traffic management in the direction of uniformity and to overcome the particularist spirit which had

[1] The Kiel Canal was deepened at a cost of eleven million pounds, and so improved was reopened for traffic in June, 1914. A British squadron was present at the ceremony.

hitherto led the railway-owning States to work their lines with a too exclusive regard for their own interests.

All these developments in transport and the mechanism of distribution generally reflected a corresponding expansion of industry and commerce. Germany had become one of the most important workshops of the world; her products invaded every market and her argosies were found on every sea. In few of the staple industries of the great commercial countries did she lag behind, while in some she overtook, and even outdistanced, far older competitors. Like England before her, yet without England's wealth of mineral resources, Germany has to a large extent built up her industrial prosperity and reputation upon coal and iron. Still following far behind her principal European rival in the production of coal, she surpassed the United Kingdom in the production of pig-iron in 1903, and with every succeeding year increased her advantage, though the United States continued to maintain the lead which they obtained in the first year of the century. More significant than the mere volume of production, however, was the fact that the home consumption of this metal had increased by two-thirds during the twenty years 1890–1910, an increase due in large measure to the great demand for steel caused by the unexampled expansion of the engineering and shipbuilding industries. In the production of steel Germany had likewise outdistanced all competitors except one. Up to 1892 the United Kingdom still held the second place, though at a great distance behind the United States. In the following year Germany replaced her, and the position thus gained has been held and strengthened ever since.

In the first half of the nineteenth century Germany's most important contributions to civilization were in the domain of philosophy and letters. In the second half of the century her principal achievements were won in the realm of science and material values. To a profound belief in science and to its systematic and unremitting application in the service of industry, more than to any other causes, is due the prominent position which has been gained in the world markets by not a few of her great staple trades, and particularly the chemical and electrical trades, whose present stage of development is a standing testimony to the value and necessity for modern industry of intelligently directed research. A passionate devotion to material pursuits, not without danger for her intellectual life and the high national ideals of the past, led her to dispute the pre-eminence of the older industrial countries in the markets of the world. Here the system of protection introduced in 1879 undoubtedly proved for a long time of great indirect assistance. The home trade having been reserved to home production by high tariffs, it provided at once a foundation upon which to build prosperous industries and a base from which to conduct operations in foreign markets. For, enjoying a quasi-statutory guarantee of remunerative prices for the goods sold at home, her manufacturers were able to sell more cheaply abroad, and thus supplant their rivals in some branches of production in which exceptional technical skill and more efficient methods of distribution already placed them at a natural advantage. These efforts to capture foreign trade were supplemented by other measures, such as the formation of syndicates and other industrial combinations, to be mentioned later, the co-operation of the large banks, preferential railway rates for exported goods, and, not least, the encouragement given to German enterprise abroad by the Empire's diplomatic representatives.

Although the protective system had been carried to such excess that it pressed heavily upon the salaried classes and the poor, organized labour in general shared in the country's increasing prosperity, to which its higher standard of life in turn contributed. One important consequence of Germany's development on industrial lines was the almost entire cessation of emigration. Ten years after the Franco-German War the number of emigrants exceeded 200,000 a year, but a gradual decline during the succeeding twenty years brought the number to one-tenth of that figure. In later years, indeed, Germany has imported instead of exported labour, and for a long time the alien element in her industrial and agricultural army of workers — chiefly Russians, Poles, Italians, and Austrians — has been estimated at little short of a million.

When inaugurating the era of social legislation Bismarck predicted that it would survive his generation, and a series of laws passed in the early years of the century confirmed this prophecy. Following the amendment in 1899 of the Old Age and Invalidity Insurance Law, greatly to the benefit of the workers who came under it, the Accident Insurance legislation was applied to new groups of occupations in 1900, and in 1903 the Sickness Insurance Law was amended so as to afford longer

(twenty-six instead of thirteen weeks) and more generous help
to those cast aside by ill-health.

In 1903 also an important law was passed for the protection
of children against exploitation by their parents and guardians.
As a result of a Government investigation it had been found
that more than half a million children of school age were in
regular employment, 307,000 in industry (for the most part as
outworkers), 172,000 as messengers, errand boys, and the like,
22,000 in public-houses, and 18,000 in shops. A large number
of these little bread-winners were employed before and after
school hours, and often employment lasted far into the night.
Five years later an important law was passed restricting the
hours of labour of young people and women engaged in factories and workshops. While children under thirteen years
might not be so employed at all, a maximum work-day of six
hours was fixed for those between thirteen and fourteen years
and one of ten hours for young persons between fourteen and
sixteen years. In the case of women the maximum work-day
was fixed at ten hours, with eight hours on Saturdays; their
employment during night hours was prohibited; and the close
time already prescribed for women at child-birth was prolonged
to eight weeks. The effect of the various laws relating to
child labour passed during these years was that children of
school age were now entirely excluded from factories and workshops. Meanwhile, Merchants' Courts, analogous to the Industrial Courts, had been introduced in 1904 for the summary settlement of disputes arising between tradesmen and their employees.

Prussia in 1900 set an example in legislation to check the
increasing prevalence of hooliganism by a law which empowered
local authorities to remove from their homes young persons
(under eighteen years) held to be in danger of demoralization
and bring them under healthy influences in institutions or other
suitable surroundings. The law was much criticized at the
time as an excessive invasion of parental right, but on the *a
posteriori* principle its need was held to be proved by a crime
which occurred a little later, recalling tragic experiences in
the lives of William I and his Chancellor. On March 6, 1901,
on the occasion of a visit to Bremen, the Emperor was attacked
by a young rough, who violently flung at him a piece of iron
as he drove through the streets after an evening banquet in

the town hall, inflicting a severe wound in the face. There was no suggestion of political malice — it was proved later that the youth was not responsible for his actions — but in replying to addresses of sympathy from the Presidents of the Imperial and Prussian Diets, the Emperor said that although the attack had left him " neither elegiac nor melancholy," he attributed it to " the confusion which reigns in the immature heads of our young people " and to the fact that " respect for the Crown, the Government and authority have in recent decades more and more diminished." He urged, therefore, that it was the duty of the schools to provide the remedy, and of the legislatures of the land to do their part by showing greater moderation in controversy and criticism. Addressing the Emperor Alexander Regiment at the opening of new barracks in Berlin later in the month (March 28th), he took a more serious view of the outlook and told the assembled troops that if ever again, as in 1848, the populace of that city broke bounds they would be relied on to " repel unruliness and misbehaviour towards its royal master."

The incident encouraged the friends of denominational education in Prussia to make renewed efforts to place the elementary schools beyond reach of secularizing tendencies. The result was that in 1904 these schools were definitely given a confessional basis; only children of the same faith might be educated together, and instruction was to be given by teachers of their own creed, while management committees, upon which Protestants and Roman Catholics were to be represented, were to work side by side with the ordained education authorities. In the same year there was formed under powerful influence an Imperial League for the Combating of Social Democracy. Financed liberally by the Conservative party and the large employers of the West, the League from the first carried on an unremitting struggle with the " internal enemy," but in the main its influence was confined to people, who were already convinced, and the only obvious effect of its efforts was to rouse the Socialists to greater exertions.

A long-standing grievance of the Imperial Diet was removed in 1906 by the Government's surrender on the subject of payment of members. Members of the Prussian Diet had since 1876 received an allowance of 15s. a day, which might not be refused, while members of the Diet of the Empire had never had more than free railway passes, available over all lines, and since 1884 only passes between their homes and Berlin. The proposal to grant money allowances had been debated and quarrelled over ever since the Empire was established, but Bismarck, apprehensive that an assembly of paid deputies would be dangerously democratic, had to the last resisted it. More than once since his retirement the Diet had affirmed the principle, but as the Federal Council still withheld assent, nothing had been done. Now, influenced chiefly by the increasing difficulty of forming a quorum, the Government came round to the Diet's view, and henceforth allowances became payable at the rate of £150 a year. Even now, however, the boon was not conceded unconditionally; members were required to earn their salaries by regular attendance, for a rota of attendance was to be kept, and there was to be a deduction of £1 for every sitting or important division missed.

Another open question was discreetly settled for a time in April, 1908, by an imperial law on the subject of association and public meeting. The law fell far short of the demands of the labour party, but it greatly extended popular rights in regard to both matters, and by curtailing the power of the police it put an end to much petty persecution and chicanery. Upon the language question the Government would not give way; only German might be used in public meetings (other than those held during political elections) except in districts more than 60 per cent. of whose inhabitants spoke a different language, and even this concession was made only until 1928. The provision proved a new source of aggravation in the disaffected borderland districts, the Polish provinces of Prussia, North Schleswig, and Alsace-Lorraine.

The comparative advance made by social legislation during the early years of the new century was largely due to the impetus given by Count von Posadowsky, the Imperial Secretary of State for the Interior (emulating the example already set by Baron von Berlepsch), who faithfully acted up to his promise: "So long as I hold office I shall be a Minister for and not against social reform." He retired in June, 1907, to the cordial regret of the Socialists as of the orthodox parties, and was succeeded by the Prussian Minister for the Interior, Herr von Bethmann-Hollweg, a friend both of the Emperor, with whom he had studied at Bonn, and of the Chancellor.

Bülow boasted that he never allowed himself to be irritated, but followed the maxim of that hard old soldier Wrangel, who used to say: " I seldom worry — I prefer to worry others." Nevertheless, man of peace though he was, he was not destined to have a tranquil Ministerial career. He had quieted the Conservative agrarians for a time by agreeing to their demands. He had also to pacify the Clericals. For in the Diet elected in 1903 it was the attitude of these two parties, and particularly the Centre, which in the main determined the fate of the Government. The Ministerial Conservative groups controlled less than a hundred votes, and even with the opportunist National Liberals thrown in they formed little more than a third of the House, and the parties in permanent opposition, the Radicals, Social Democrats (now a stately phalanx of eighty-one), and the nationalist groups, outnumbered them. It followed that the Clericals, numbering a hundred without the Poles, held the casting vote, and for the Government it was unfortunate that they were able at will to use this vote in one of two ways, either in alliance with the Ministerialists, which was the normal course, or, if their interests lay in that direction, in conjunction with the Social Democrats and the Radicals. Encouraged by a knowledge of its power, the party, true to its principle of doing nothing for nothing, succeeded in obtaining amongst other concessions the reversal of one of the most obnoxious laws passed during the *Kulturkampf*. In March, 1904, the restrictions upon the movements of the Jesuit order and congregations, which had been introduced in 1872, were greatly modified. The order itself and kindred organizations continued to be excluded from the Empire, but their members might no longer be required, or refused permission, to live in special districts as hitherto. Later, Bavaria introduced further ameliorations on her own account.[1]

In the winter session of 1904–5 the Government was further thrown upon the support of the Centre for the success of a new Army Bill, which was intended to fix the peace strength, again for five years, at 506,000, exclusive of officers and one-year re-

[1] In the summer of 1917, a year observed by Protestants as the four hundredth anniversary of the German Reformation, the last memento of the *Kulturkampf,* the anti-Jesuit Law, was quietly repealed. In the Federal Council some of the States, especially of Central Germany, warmly opposed the measure, but the importance of being on good terms with the Vatican at a time critical in German history was held to outweigh all other considerations.

cruits. Germany was suffering at the time from a fit of nervousness, for Great Britain and France had concluded a series
of agreements closing open questions in various parts of the
world, and in this pacific measure apprehensive minds persisted
in seeing a veiled threat. Without the Roman Catholic vote a
coalition able to carry the bill was impossible, and Count von
Bülow had no choice but to accept it and with it the obligations that were to come after. Now the Clericals began to use
their power without restraint or scruple. By pressure here
and interference there, by open suggestion and covert threat,
the Government was left in no doubt that without the support
of the Centre its life was not worth a day's purchase.

In one direction the influence of the Clericals would have
been entirely beneficial had it not exceeded due limits. This
was in relation to colonial policy. The colonial movement of
1884–5 aroused at the time no enthusiasm in that quarter of
the Diet. When, however, Cardinal Lavigerie took up the
question of the slave trade and the Government in 1888 began
to give him cordial support, the Clericals abandoned their passive attitude and henceforth made the welfare of the natives
their special concern, with beneficial results, of which the full
fruits were to be enjoyed only in later years. During and since
Caprivi's Chancellorship the colonial movement had perceptibly
slackened. The reason for this lay only in a secondary degree
in the cooler attitude of the Government. The ardour of the
colonial propagandists, indeed, continued unabated, but the nation at large had been discouraged by a series of gross administrative failures and by the growing cost of its imperialistic
adventures. For a long time the colonies were governed by a
special department of the Foreign Office, to which later a council of experts was added, and for local administration a colonial civil service had to be created. No doubt the central Executive did its best in the choice of men, but in many cases the
choice was unfortunate, and the results were disastrous. The
colonies had been acquired suddenly and without deliberation,
and it soon became clear that the country had embarked upon a
momentous enterprise with no clear ideas as to what colonization meant, how it was to be carried out, or the exertions, sacrifices, and responsibilities which it would entail. Now it
learned that the acquisition of territories was merely a preparatory step, and that the real task came later. If the task was

not faced in the right spirit, it was perhaps less from ill intent
than from ignorance and inexperience.

Bismarck's first idea of colonial empire, as we have seen, was
a purely commercial idea ; the object of colonies was to be trade,
and not territorial expansion for its own sake.   Accordingly
he gave prominence to the merchant and planter, and sought
to keep the official in the background, confining the function of
the Government, as far as possible, to guaranteeing protection
to the whites in the exercise of their acquired rights.   That
plan did not long succeed, if it can be said to have succeeded at
all.   The traders, left to themselves, made free and often unscrupulous use of their opportunities of advantage; and the
growth of native discontent compelled the Government against
its will to assume administrative responsibilities of a far larger
kind than it had originally contemplated.   Now it went to the
other extreme, and stringent bureaucratic control was installed
in place of the crude *régime* of the " Hanseatics."   The natives liked the new system as little as they had liked the old,
and disaffection and disorder continued.   In 1891 and 1892
repeated risings occurred in East Africa ; they were suppressed
without menace to German authority, but not without heavy expenditure of life and treasure.   When this colony had been pac-
ified, the Cameroons took up the tale, and the disorder which
occurred there continued without intermission for some years.
Every outbreak of the kind helped to shatter the early dream
of colonial enterprise as an affair of cheaply won prestige and
glory, and thus it was that much of the nation's earlier enthusiasm for empire gave place to apathy.

Endemic insurrection in the colonies continued, and in Bülow's time disaffection reached a climax.   During the three
years 1904 to 1906 no fewer than seventeen separate expeditions and campaigns, of greater or smaller extent, were necessary in the Cameroons alone.   German East Africa was also in
constant rebellion.   Worst of all, however, was the rising of
the Hereros in South-west Africa which occurred in 1903, a
movement which took the form of a determined attempt to eject
the German intruders root and branch.   Unsympathetic administration and excesses by the German traders were the principal causes of this lamentable episode.   The German judge lo-
cated at Windhoek, the centre of administration in the colony,
admitted that the rebellion there was due to outrages by Ger-

man traders, who, pretending to be Government officials, seized the natives' land and cattle in the discharge of debts already paid, and it was significant that while the Hereros attacked the Germans wherever found — women and children alone being spared — no Englishmen or Boers were harmed.

More than any other party except the Social Democrats the Clericals showed an earnest desire to probe the causes of the recurrent disorders and insurrections in the African colonies. They were unsparing in their exposure of the wrongs done by the white traders and settlers, and unwearied in their championship of the natives.   The zeal with which at this time they endeavoured to create a cleaner and more efficient colonial administration had also material results of no small importance, for they were able to unearth certain objectionable colonial contracts for transport and supplies the cancelling of which saved the Empire large sums of money.   Had they stopped at disclosure and criticism, all would have been well.   They began, however, to obtrude their influence in administration in illicit ways, claiming special favours for the Roman Catholic missions, setting up black lists of officials displeasing to them and pressing for the acceptance of nominees of their own. This interference reached such limits that it became at last a question whether the Government or the Centre was in charge of colonial affairs.

A crisis came in December, 1906, when, after having succeeded in defeating a bill for the reorganization of the Colonial Office, they refused the Government's demand for a vote of a million and a half pounds required for the military operations against the Hereros.   They offered, indeed, to vote a million pounds, but even so only on the condition that the German troops in the colony should be at once reduced, a demand which virtually challenged the Emperor's hitherto undisputed right to fix the number of troops needed for warlike purposes. Upon a two-fold issue of such importance no compromise was possible, and the question went in due course to a division. Then the Social Democrats joined hands with the Clericals, with the result that the Government was defeated by 177 votes against 168.   The Diet was promptly dissolved, and with its dissolution the Conservative-Clerical coalition came to an end.

The immediate need was to secure such a favourable grouping of parties as would relieve the political situation and bring the war in South-west Africa to a speedy and successful close. Bülow determined, however, to fight the elections upon a larger issue. A situation had arisen which he had long and anxiously foreseen. For nearly seventeen years, ever since the defeat of the Cartel in the elections of February, 1890, the Clericals had virtually given to the Government its marching orders, yet while working with the Conservatives there had been a constant fear that they would one day cast off those associates and, in the pursuit of some special interest of their own, make common cause with any party or group of parties strong enough to create with them an anti-Ministerial majority. For a long time the Government had deferred this danger by following a course of sheer bribery, buying their support for one measure and buying off their opposition to another, regardless of the fact that with every capitulation the Clericals became more conscious of their power and increased their terms accordingly.

Confident that his cause was popular and the hour favourable, Bülow, now Prince von Bülow, appealed to the nation to vote against the Centre. He was not forgetful of the valuable assistance which the party had given to the Government during recent years in connection with the Customs Tariff, the Navy Bills, and social policy, nor was he wishful to see it reduced to a position of insignificance and sterility, even were that possible. He wanted a majority which, without necessarily excluding the Clericals altogether, would yet be independent of them; they were to be at liberty to help the Government, if so disposed, but on the Government's terms and no longer on their own. The best arrangement would have been a return to the old Cartel of Conservatives and National Liberals, but from such a coalition there could now be no hope of victory. Rather than risk defeat by forcing the Radicals to regard themselves as a disparaged and unneeded party, he decided to work for a combination which would bring into the Ministerial fold all parties which pursued national aims. In a well-considered electioneering manifesto Bülow placed before the country the grave issues upon which it had to decide, appealed for the subordination for once of party to national interests, and called upon Conservatives, National Liberals, and Radicals to join forces for a vigorous campaign against Clericalism and Social Democracy. The Conservatives were willing but not eager converts to this new idea of public duty. The Radicals, on the other hand, were flattered by the compliment paid to them in being recognized in so handsome a way as constituting one of the pillars of the State, and for the first and last time in their history they sank political differences without splitting and co-operated with their ancient enemies. Thus was formed the memorable parliamentary *bloc*, a Wallenstein's Camp of ill-assorted combatants, which lasted but little longer than the crisis which called it into existence.

The composition of the new Diet fulfilled the Chancellor's expectations. The Clerical party returned in somewhat greater strength, but the Social Democrats lost nearly one-half of their eighty-one seats to the Conservative and Liberal groups in almost equal proportions. A *bloc* majority was the result, and it put the Government out of immediate danger. The Southwest African war vote was promptly granted, and the military operations in the disturbed colony were continued with redoubled energy. Nevertheless, the struggle was still a severe one, and when tranquillity was at last restored the Hereros had been reduced by the sword and exile from a tribe of 200,000 to a remnant of 50,000, while their stock was extinguished and their land appropriated. The war cost Germany two thousand men in killed and wounded and an expenditure of over twenty-two million pounds, a sum largely increased by the cost of subsequent works of reparation. After 1907 the Clericals did not again refuse Army, Navy, or Colonial Bills.

The colonial controversies of that time had later results of great importance for Germany's foreign empire in general. As colonial questions had precipitated the elections, the return of a Ministerial majority was held to indicate the nation's desire for a forward policy. Dr. Bernhard Dernburg, then a bank director, had in 1906 been called to the head of the colonial department of the Foreign Office, and to his duties he brought the aptitudes and instinct for practical affairs of a successful business man. He saw at once that the first condition of successful colonization must be the study of administrative methods in the best school. With that idea in mind he visited British colonies in Africa, after first being given a free run of the Colonial Office in London, and fortified by the observations and experiences which he gained in this way, he was able to revolutionize the too bureaucratic methods of his own officials and to correct many of their narrow conceptions of colonial policy.

In particular he took to heart one fundamental difference between English and German methods of colonial administration,
viz. that while in the treatment of native populations and the
organization of their life England had followed the wise guidance of experience and instinct, the growth of centuries, German action had been determined far too much by mechanical
principles, borrowed from the Prussian bureaucratic system.

His first task, however, was to rehabilitate the colonial movement at home, to rescue it from the disrepute into which it had
fallen, and to re-create, if possible, a strong colonial sentiment.
To this end he undertook an evangelizing tour through Germany, and, aided by Princes, Ministers, and other men of authority in the States visited, he succeeded in renewing something like the old ardour and faith which twenty years before
had sent the colonial movement on its way so propitiously.
Receiving in this way a sort of national mandate, he was able
to go to the Diet with confidence and, convincing it that the colonies were still a sound business proposition, ask for liberal grants for the purpose of works of development which had
long been neglected. Amongst these railways took the first
place.

The administration of the colonies was at this time detached
from the Foreign Office and entrusted to a more or less independent Colonial Office, with separate departments for administration, finance, military questions, and the civil service, and
Dr. Dernburg became the first Colonial Secretary. The old
Colonial Council was abolished and its place taken by agricultural and economic sections, composed of permanent officials,
one of whose principal functions was the study of the resources
and needs of the colonies from the standpoint of agriculture
and commerce. Further, the colonial service was reconstituted,
the finances of the colonies were reorganized, new principles
were applied to the dealings of the local administrations with
the native populations, military and police services were established, and the legal and judicial arrangements in the colonies were reformed. Henceforth local administration in the
colonies was made less bureaucratic. Already there had been
attached to some of the colonial governments (1903) councils
composed, on the principle of the legislative councils of British Crown colonies, of officials and citizens, and this system was
extended. In several colonies also administration was to some

extent decentralized by the introduction of local self-government in so far as it was practicable in regions in which the whites still formed an insignificant part of the population, and were seldom concentrated in large numbers. Here the German system of local government was applied with necessary modifications, the commune being treated as the unit of local government.

Many blunders which had been committed by colonial governors were rectified. In their eagerness and haste to see the colonies opened up and their resources developed some of the governors had granted railway, mining, land, and trading concessions and monopolies both to German and foreign adventurers far too freely and sometimes for an altogether inadequate consideration. Some of these privileges were good neither for the colonies nor the mother country, and where possible they were cancelled or bought back.

Above all, the interests and rights of the natives were for the first time frankly recognized, and the arbitrary and often cruel conduct of the white settlers, which in some colonies had long been a crying scandal, was sternly repressed. Dr. Dernburg had found on visiting East Africa that in his treatment of the natives the German trader systematically used the lash. He reported to the scandalized Diet that no German trader went about the streets of Dar-es-Salaam without a whip, and that he even found one on the table of the chief tax office in the town. Brutality of the kind, in East Africa and other colonies, was rigorously prohibited and known offenders were brought to book. Colonial governors had been dismissed and punished before for misconduct, conspicuously the notorious Dr. Karl Peters, who was found guilty in 1897 of murdering a native who had dared to compete with him in profligacy, as well as of other revolting cruelties, and was deprived of office and pension. In 1907 two other governors, Horn and von Puttkamer, were degraded and cashiered, the first for torturing to death a native who had been guilty of peculation. Improved measures were adopted for combating epidemics and ameliorating insanitary conditions generally; hospitals were established more freely, a proper medical service was instituted, and the work of the Red Cross Association was transported to the colonies. Schools and agricultural training for the natives were also provided.

From that time may be dated a new era in colonial development. In the tropical colonies of Africa the German and other white planters have since greatly increased the area under rubber, tea, coffee, cocoa, cotton, fruits, and other produce in constant demand in European markets, while the native populations have been trained to industry by the establishment of experimental farms and schools. Nevertheless, valuable as the colonies have since proved for commercial purposes, as sources of tropical produce and raw materials needed for industry, and as markets for home merchandize, they have offered no solution of the emigration question. This qualification applies still more to the latest colonial acquisition, the large slice of the Congo rubber region ceded by France to Germany under the Morocco agreement of 1911,[1] and added to the Cameroons, which was thus carried to the boundaries of the Congo State. The one colony which is suitable for settlement by whites is South-west Africa, and here, in spite of the discovery of mineral wealth, only agriculture on a large scale would appear to be possible. One of the later governors, Herr von Lindequist, has estimated that the colony will not support more than 10,-000 ranchers, the labour being done by blacks.

The protectorate for which most has been done is Kiauchau,[2] which is a naval station and an outpost of the Empire rather than a colony, and has been developed from that standpoint. Considering that the place is nominally held only on lease, Germany has sunk an enormous amount of money in Kiauchau. The port itself has been converted into a first-class harbour; a railway has been built 250 miles into the interior of China, with lines to Tientsin and other large centres of population; schools, a university, and hospitals have been established for the benefit of the native population, but chiefly as centres of German influence; industries have been established, roads built, and European methods of agriculture and forestry introduced. By these and other measures the way had been prepared for a bold policy of pacific penetration in China proper when war broke out in Europe in the summer of 1914 and the protectorate passed into other hands.[3]

[1] See Chapter XXIII., p. 470.   [2] Chapter XXI., p. 406.
[3] With the exception of a small part of German East Africa the whole of Germany's colonies were captured by Great Britain, the Dominions, and the Allies during the World-War which began in August, 1914. Their fate had not been decided at the time of the publication of this book.

Dr. Dernburg did not remain in office long enough to see the full fruition of his work, for in June, 1910, he resigned, rather than continue to resist a conspiracy of the Conservatives, who, tolerating middle-class men in Ministerial office only when they were prepared to disown, as Miquel did, their middle-class sympathies and interests, had resented his appointment from the first and had worked unceasingly for his downfall. Nevertheless, he will always be held in honour as the man who for the first time put the colonies and their administration on a sound basis and sought to mete even-handed justice to the native races.

Bülow's Chancellorship lasted nearly ten years, and the second half of the period was for the Empire a time of growing anxiety both at home and abroad. To the foreign affairs of the period detailed reference will be made in the following chapters, and it is only necessary to record at this point several facts of outstanding importance. There now took definite shape a new combination of Great Powers which, though it seemed to Germany a direct menace to her individually, was yet a natural result of and a counterpoise to the system of alliances by which she herself had divided the Continent for a generation. Simultaneously, French influence in North Africa was consolidated by the pursuance in Morocco of a policy of political penetration, a policy which was destined to bring the rivals of 1870 once more into pronounced antagonism, yet in circumstances which placed Germany at a great disadvantage. Meanwhile, Russia and Austria had become seriously alienated over the Balkan question. Above all, the political situation was strongly coloured by an increasing tension between Germany and Great Britain, with the gradual growth on both sides of a premonition, fatalistic in the oppressive sense of imminence which it created, that a dangerous crisis in the relations of the two nations was approaching.

At home a deep-seated spirit of unrest and discontent had laid hold of large sections of the people. There had been amazing strides in national prosperity and in the accumulation of wealth, yet taxation had become every year heavier under the pressure of the ever-increasing armaments — first the army and of late years, in rapid acceleration, the navy as well — and now, to aggravate the evil, a time of rising prices set in. Food riots occurred again in 1907 in some of the large towns, just as on the eve of the Caprivi commercial treaty departure, but the agrarian party, then taken unawares, was now so powerful that any attack upon its positions, even had the Government dared to make it, would have had little chance of success. The people suffered, therefore, and complained all the more.

The Socialist movement also had grown to still more threatening dimensions. Although in the elections of January, 1907, the parliamentary party lost ground, little comfort could be derived from the fact, except by those who wished to be deceived, seeing that a quarter of a million electors more than before voted the red ticket and that with proportional representation the party, instead of having 43 seats, would have had 120, or nearly one-third of the House. The remarkable growth of Socialism as a force in imperial politics further increased the dissatisfaction of the working classes with the electoral arrangements which denied to them a corresponding influence in the Diet of Prussia. The electoral areas and their numerical representation remained as originally fixed both in the Empire and the monarchy, in spite of the great changes in the distribution of population; but while in the imperial elections, owing to a democratic franchise, the Socialists were able to assert predominance in many of the large towns and industrial districts, in the Prussian elections the antiquated three-class system of voting virtually excluded them from the Lower House, which remained, as before, essentially a house of landowners and farmers, State officials, rich industrialists, and professional men.

Some moderate concession to popular aspirations might at this juncture have conciliated the Socialists, while at the same time pleasing the Radicals, but the Government would not hear of it. For Bülow was at heart a reactionary, and from the moment that he became Minister the restraints which Hohenlohe had tried to impose upon the feudalist party were removed. He was entirely out of sympathy with Liberal movements of all kinds, and in parliamentary life his one determination was to resist any tendency to shift the centre of political gravity from Right to Left. Hence he opposed every attempt to enlarge the nation's constitutional powers, or to alter the basis of election in the direction of a more democratic representation. All his sympathies predisposed him to the aristocratic system of government, and he never disguised his low opinion of the middle classes. The German nation, he was wont to say, was intellectually and temperamentally unfit for self-government, and needed the control and guidance of a strong centralized Executive — the argument by which German reactionaries have at all times defended the existing system of pseudo-constitutionalism. Occasionally he threw to the popular parties a patronizing phrase or a philosophical platitude, which seemed to suggest broad-mindedness and appreciation of progressive political thought, but his acts belied all such pretences; this smiling courtier, who never quarrelled and never worried, shared to the full all Bismarck's hostility to democratic aspirations, though he was less open in his manner of showing it.

No factor in political life contributed more powerfully to produce unrest and disharmony than the renewal in a still more emphatic form of that system of " personal government " which had begun to excite alarm in Caprivi's time, had already seriously undermined the constitutional position of the Ministers, and had been largely responsible for the retirement of all the first three Chancellors. During the Bülow *régime* this reassertion by the Crown of powers and functions which belonged to the pre-constitutional era reached a climax. From the moment that Bismarck went the power which had been concentrated in his hands became dissipated: the domination of one great personality had given place to the rivalries of many small ones, yet all the combined capacities and activities of the men who had divided amongst them the Empire-builder's mantle did not compensate for the absence of a single mind conscious of a definite and resolute purpose and of the will to accomplish it. Prince Hohenlohe had seen from the first how matters were bound to tend. Visiting Berlin in the early months of Caprivi's Chancellorship, he formed these dominant impressions:

" Two things have struck me in these last three days: one, that no one has any time, and that every one is in a greater hurry than before; and secondly, that individualities have expanded. Every individual is conscious of himself, while before, under the predominating influence of Prince Bismarck, individualities shrank and were kept down. Now they are swollen like sponges in water. That has its advantages, but also its dangers. The single-minded will is lacking." [1]

[1] *Memoirs*, vol. ii., p. 416.

No words could better describe the effect of Bismarck's disappearance. It was his good luck that he had been able to have a constitution made to his liking and virtually to his order. The office of Imperial Chancellor was created for him, and he was careful to protect it against any such division or limitation as was theoretically possible in the Prussian Cabinet. This he did by making the Chancellor the sole Minister of State, so that all his necessary colleagues became subordinates and, at his will, supernumeraries. His constitutional power, considerable as it was, he had increased by the usurpation of functions which were not his at all, but the Crown's, and gradually he made his position autocratic by allowing no interference either by the Secretaries of State or the Emperor himself. He had, indeed, on one occasion induced the Sovereign to issue a declaration bidding the nation know that all acts of his Government were acts of his imperial person, but the vital question was, Who was in effect the Government? and the Government was Bismarck.

It was impossible that the large powers which the first Chancellor had exercised could be handed down to his successors, seeing that the new Emperor had been determined from the first to rule in deed as well as word. Bismarck once said: " A good Minister should not trouble about his Sovereign's favour, but speak his mind freely," and he sacrificed himself to his own philosophy. Had he not tried to follow with the third Emperor the policy which had succeeded with the first, he might have remained in office to the end of his days. He ventured to press his independence too far, however, and he had to go. In later life he reflected not without bitterness: " Former rulers looked to their advisers for capacity more than obedience. If obedience alone is to be the criterion, then demands will be made on the general genius of the monarch which even Frederick the Great would not have satisfied, though politics, both in war and peace, were less difficult in his time than in our own." The later Chancellors successively took office with a full consciousness that in proportion as they endeavoured to follow the path commended by their own judgment they risked the disfavour either of the Emperor or his Conservative bodyguard or both.

Bismarck was right when he said that William II intended to be his own Chancellor. Caprivi was quick to recognize this, and chafed as he saw his office gradually belittled and his responsibilities reduced to a show. Under Hohenlohe the usurpation by the Sovereign of his Chief Minister's functions made further progress. At that time the Bismarck party hankered more than ever for a " resolute Minister." But for resolute Ministers there was now no place or need, and such men would only have been in the way. More and more the Emperor had taken the reins of government into his own hands, with the result that the Chancellor had fallen into the background. Since there was no longer a powerful central personality, around which the whole machinery of government revolved, the minor men, thirsting for distinction, began to take liberties, each in his own sphere, and that, too, meant the disparagement of the Chancellor's office.

The same tendency continued in the early years of Bülow's successor in office, between whom and Admiral von Tirpitz there was waged a continual struggle, the Chancellor holding to the constitutional doctrine that he alone was the responsible Minister, and the head of the Admiralty endeavouring to magnify his office and thereby to increase naval expenditure in every possible way. Bismarck was Chancellor for twenty years. During the ten years following his resignation three men held that office, while Imperial Secretaries of State and Prussian Ministers came and went with the seasons, welcomed always with smiles, often dismissed in disregard as soon as they were weary of the puppet play in which they were called to take part, or ceased to act their parts satisfactorily.

So it was that there grew up in the room of the old Bismarckian autocracy a far more mischievous personal *régime* of the Emperor, expressing itself in forms and measures which were contrary both to the spirit and the letter of the constitution. All initiative was taken from the Government; everywhere the Sovereign stood forth as the real director of public policy, even identifying himself openly with official acts and attitudes regarding which the nation was hopelessly divided, and resenting opposition to any policy approved by him as opposition offered to his own person. The result was to increase the hostility of the Government's opponents, and more and more to moderate or alienate altogether the sympathy of those who had been amongst its truest friends. The more the Emperor declared that all was right, the more the nation disbelieved him. Now nothing was taken on faith, and the old German disposition to criticize and cavil belittled successes and magnified failures. The eager quest for unity which had fired the national imagination for two generations had been gratified, but, having gained unity, the nation no longer seemed to have delight in it. People coined weird phrases like " empire-weariness " and " empire-dejection " to express the political lassitude which had fallen upon them. It was in vain that the Emperor begged his people (as at Breslau in September, 1906) to " look with clear gaze upon the future," and declared that he " would not tolerate pessimists." He was told that his own policy more than anything else had obscured the outlook, and that if all the pessimists were to be disowned he would have few subjects left.

It was not only in Prussia that this depression prevailed. In the secondary States a painful impression was caused by acts and words of the Emperor which seemed to show that he entirely misunderstood his position amongst the federal Princes, and forgot that the German Emperor was not the Emperor of Germany. His repeated declarations, made with no pretence of equivocation, that he alone was lord and master in Germany, that there was only one will in public affairs, his own, and that his policy alone should be carried out, were warmly resented in the South, and gave fresh life to the old particularism which Bismarck, whose official dealings with Prussia's federal allies, whatever his secret sentiments regarding them may have been, had generally been marked by the greatest tact, had succeeded in appeasing. The Bavarian Crown Prince found it necessary to protest publicly (May, 1900): " I do not see why, because we belong to the German Empire, we should not have just the same rights and privileges as North Germany. Above all, I protest against the idea that it is a favour to belong to the Empire, for the Empire has been welded together quite as much by Bavarian blood as by the blood of any other German tribe, and for that reason we will not be regarded as inferiors but as equals."

The smaller States were no less concerned about their position and rights. When a dispute over the regency of Lippe, an internal matter affecting that State and no other, had been settled to the satisfaction of the people of the principality, the Emperor, whose brother-in-law had failed in his claim to the succession, telegraphed that he would neither acknowledge the new ruler nor allow the troops to take the oath to him. With a dignity worthy of the occasion the Government of Lippe answered that no outside interference could be allowed in the affairs of the little country. Other interferences of the kind were the result rather of thoughtlessness than aggressive intentions.

Thus when in 1903 the Lower House of the Bavarian Diet, for reasons of its own, rejected a vote for the purposes of art, the Emperor telegraphed to the Prince Regent his " deepest indignation at its contemptible attitude," and offered the money out of his own purse. The Bavarian people protested against the slight both in Parliament and the Press.

Bülow, like the good courtier that he was, defended the sending of the telegram on the ground that it was not a State but a personal act, and laid down the doctrine, which later was to prove embarrassing to him, that " the idea that all the monarch's expressions of opinion should be endorsed with the signature of the Chancellor is wholly foreign to the constitution." His argument rested on the plea that inasmuch as the Emperor had not acted in his capacity as head of the State, his action could not be wrong, but the plea ignored the really pertinent fact that quite as binding upon Sovereigns as the written letter of the constitution is the unwritten law of discretion.

It would have been well for Bülow if he had worried, if only a little, over the Empire's increasing difficulties. With great talent he had little courage, however, and for the sake of a quiet life he would have compromised many a theory dear to even the soberest of constitutionalists. It was chiefly due to his easy toleration of the Emperor's impetuous interventions in public affairs that there grew up a system of co-government under which the Sovereign and the Chancellor worked at cross-purposes; for while the chief Minister of the Empire carried on politics officially in one way, the Emperor by his compromising utterances, in the form of speech, letter, and conversation, did the same thing on his own account.

Undoubtedly political parties were to blame for much of the impotence and futility of parliamentary life both at that time and later. Most of them had ceased to represent clear, decided principles, and some had become identified with the advocacy of class interests in the crassest form. If the Conservatives saw in politics merely a means of benefiting agriculture at the expense of the rest of the community, the National Liberals in a less effective way had become the special advocates of the great industrialists. Both the Clericals and the Social Democrats were no doubt inspired by a genuine solicitude for the less fortunate members of society, but while the former viewed all political questions from the standpoint of the Church, the latter viewed them solely from the standpoint of labour, and neither saw them truly and as a whole. Least excusable of all were the Radicals, who had ceased to follow a consistent course and had more and more become opportunists and time-servers. This want of clarity and principle in political life meant loss of vigour, influence, and authority. Never were the custodians of public life themselves so greatly in need of vigilant watching.

Moreover, the old days of rigid party discipline were past; in the higher councils of every fraction there was a host of men every one just too small to lead and just too large to be a willing follower. Even the Clerical party lacked the cohesion of Windthorst's time. When that consummate leader died no legitimate successor existed, and the consequence was that rival pretenders strove for his mantle and in so doing tore it into fragments. A unanimous vote was invariably certain on capital issues; but there was much loose manœuvring by ambitious sharpshooters, whose unofficial escapades did no credit to the party or its cause. In the ranks of Social Democracy also the spirit of discord, premonitory to many outside observers of disintegration, seemed to have set in, for a " revisionist " wing had begun to challenge the authority of the old leaders, and to throw doubt upon some of the party's most cherished doctrines.

The publication in 1906 of the diaries which Prince Hohenlohe had diligently kept throughout his official life added to the prevailing discomfort. The memoirs drew aside the veil which had partially obscured many critical incidents of the reign, including some of quite recent years, and afforded to contemporaries the material for judging sundry heated controversies which is usually reserved until the interest in the actors has evaporated or the controversies themselves have become ancient history. Many of the opinions and conclusions which the nation had formed regarding the Emperor, his strong will and intolerance of opposition, his determination to go his own way, and his readiness to part with three of his Chancellors, received unexpected confirmation from his own utterances and those of near friends, here prematurely made known. The disclosure of confidences of so intimate a character was unusual, and the generally accepted opinion, that it was prompted by the desire of the late Chancellor's relatives to avenge his grievances, as well as to justify his public life, was probably not far from the truth.

In the same year the public mind was further disquieted

by certain disagreeable revelations made by a popular censor of the private life of public men, the journalist Maximilian Harden, showing that near to the Emperor's person and enjoying his confidence were men of evil disposition — notably the ex-ambassador Prince Philip zu Eulenburg — whose proper place was in gaol. The fact that the Emperor, against whose private life slander never raised its voice, was unacquainted with the character of these associates was held to be a tribute rather to his personal virtue than to his discretion. It was his eldest son, the Crown Prince, better versed in the ways of the world, who had warned his father of the questionable company he was keeping.

The climax of this accumulation of untoward occurrences came in 1908, when two embarrassing incidents led to a storm of public censure before which not only the Chancellor but the Emperor himself was compelled to bow. Early in the year (March 6th) the London *Times* published the fact that in the preceding month the First Lord of the Admiralty had received from the Emperor a letter (February 17th) suggesting the reduction of the British shipbuilding programme and stating reasons why the excitement caused in England by German naval expansion was unjustifiable. It has been shown that Germany's naval preparations had created great uneasiness in England.[1] A new Navy Bill of 1908 finally exhausted English patience, and a cry was now raised for a navy so large that Germany, when she had done her utmost, would still be left hopelessly behind. It was in the hope of allaying apprehension and moderating the agitation for shipbuilding on this large scale that the letter to Lord Tweedmouth was written. Perhaps more was made of the letter than the circumstances justified. Its contents were admitted to have been harmless and its spirit was friendly. As a letter from Sovereign to Sovereign it would have been free from objection; what was, of course, irregular was the apparent attempt to influence English policy through a Minister of State, though against this criticism it could be urged that the letter was intended to be a perfectly private communication. Had the Emperor spoken his mind in conversation, no one would have taken his frankness amiss: his indiscretion lay in the fact that he had put his thoughts into writing.

Both in the British House of Commons and the Imperial Diet

[1] See Chapter XIX., pp. 306–13, and pp. 379–84, *infra*.

the unfortunate communication gave rise to interpellation and debate, in each case without loss of temper. Prince Bülow, speaking of the letter as one which " any sincere friend of good relations between Germany and England " might have written, still harped unconvincingly upon the difference between the Emperor's private and public acts, declaring that " the letter of the Sovereign does not, from the fact that it deals with political questions, become thereby an act of State." The distinction was perfectly true and just, though confusing to ordinary people, who cared nothing about fine points of constitutional law and were concerned only with the indisputable fact that owing to lack of reticence the Emperor had again compromised himself and his country. To them the letter was merely another illustration of the dangers of the " personal *régime.*"

No sooner had the controversy aroused by the navy letter died down than another and a more serious newspaper disclosure, again in England, brought the Emperor once more into violent conflict with his people. On October 28th the London *Daily Telegraph* published a report of an alleged interview with the Emperor on current political questions, and vouching for its unimpeachable authority the journal commended it as a message of good-will from that Sovereign to the British people. As such the report was unquestionably intended, whatever its actual effect may have been. While the authenticity of the statements contained in the reputed interview has never been disputed, it became known later that the report was not the record of a single continuous duologue, but rather a mosaic of isolated *Logia,* made at sundry times and in divers manners, so skilfully put together as to give the impression of a single unpremeditated utterance.

Briefly the Emperor was represented to have said that he was cordially friendly to England, contrary to England's belief; that for years he had kept German policy free from Anglophobist tendencies and had incurred the distrust and hostility of his own people in so doing; that during the Boer War he was England's only friend in Germany, and that it was he who wrecked the Boer delegates' hopes of European intervention; and that he likewise prevented France and Russia from rushing in when they wished both to save the Boer Republics and humiliate England to the dust. There were also vague suggestions of a plan of campaign which he had caused to be drawn up by his generals and had despatched to Queen Victoria in " black December," when everything seemed to be going wrong in the war and all the world feared for the future of the British Empire except the Empire itself. Intermingled with these professions of friendship for England were references to France, Russia, and Japan which were not likely to please those countries.

The publication of the interview created consternation in Germany, while the rest of the world wondered. Interpellations rained upon the Government, and now it was found that the manner of the Emperor's pronouncement was hardly less remarkable than the contents. It appeared that the report had first been submitted to the Emperor and then sent by him to the Chancellor for approval, but that, without reading it, Bülow had passed it on to the Foreign Office, which in turn had returned it to the Emperor for publication without remark. Probably never before did an important State document run the ordeal of official scrutiny and reach the outside world more easily. Aghast at his own lack of prudence, and recognizing his responsibility for the consequences, Bülow at once honourably tendered his resignation, but without any desire to press it, for his duty was obviously to endeavour to undo the mischief which he had helped to create. There was no more talk of the subtle distinction between the Emperor's public and private utterances and acts. Whether the awkward interview was or was not an act of State, Bülow was at last shaken out of his complacent theory that the Sovereign had as much right as any private individual to hold his own opinions and to utter them. Now the Diet and the nation looked to him for resolute action, and for once he did not fail them.

The question was debated by the Federal Council, which agreed with the Chancellor that this greatest of the Emperor's indiscretions must be the last, and that he must be required to pledge his word to that effect. Addressing the Diet on November 10th — a day described by a lachrymose Ministerial journal as " a day of mourning for the German nation "— Bülow said: " The opinion that the publication of these utterances has created in Germany profound excitement and painful regret will — this conviction I have firmly formed in these sorrowful days — cause his Majesty the Emperor in future to impose on himself, even in his private conversations, the reserve which is indispensable to unity of policy and the authority of the Crown. Were it otherwise neither I nor my successor would bear the responsibility of office."

The manliest thing — perhaps the only manly one — ever done by Bülow was when on November 17, 1908, he went to Potsdam to read the Emperor probably the first serious lesson he had ever heard upon the position and duties of a constitutional Sovereign. Yet the task was not, in truth, a difficult one, for the Chancellor carried the mandate and spoke with the united voice of the federal Princes, the Government, the Diet, and the nation. The Emperor, though protesting that his action had been misunderstood and its importance exaggerated, gave the undertaking required of him, and the same evening the *Official Gazette* reported the audience and its result as follows:

" The Emperor received the representations and explanations of the Imperial Chancellor in a highly serious spirit, and announced his will as follows: ' Undeterred by the exaggerations of public criticism, which he regards as unjust, he regards it as his highest imperial duty to safeguard the stability of the policy of the Empire, with due regard for his constitutional responsibilities. He accordingly approved of the statement made by the Imperial Chancellor in the Diet and assured Prince Bülow of his continued confidence.' "

Thus fortified, the Chancellor had now to pacify the Diet, which was waiting impatiently the result of the Potsdam conversation. Never before had that body been so unanimous and so unsparing in its criticism of the Crown as in the vehement debates which occurred over this incident, when the first Minister of the Empire led the attack and staunch Conservatives, loyal to the marrow, vied with uncompromising democrats in their denunciation of the " personal *régime* " as the fount and origin of Germany's humiliation in the eyes of the world. In spite of Bülow's complete surrender to his critics, the Diet refused on this occasion to be satisfied with apologies: it wanted a victim, and as this could not be the Emperor it vented its ire upon the Chancellor by passing a vote of censure upon him by an emphatic majority, yet was none the less greatly relieved when it knew next day that the censured Minister did not intend to resign.

It might have seemed at that time that a decisive crisis had occurred in the relations between Crown and Parliament and that the future of the constitutional cause was bright with promise. Eloquent deputies talked confidently of the coming new order of responsible Ministers, and indulged in visions of parliamentary government on the English model. But in Germany, where reaction is never far from progress, the only safe rule in political life is that the past always repeats itself, and of this rule the nation before long received a rude reminder. For visiting Königsberg in August, 1910, the Emperor recalled the time when in that city his grandfather placed the Prussian Crown on his head with his own hand in sign that " it was conferred upon him by God's grace alone and not by Parliaments, national assemblies, and popular resolutions," adding the moral, " Regarding myself likewise as an instrument of the Lord, I go my way, which is devoted only and solely to the welfare and peaceable development of our fatherland, indifferent to the views and opinions of the day." The words may not have been intended as a direct answer to the Diet's action of two years before, yet they were no less a significant evidence, which could not be explained away, of the political mediævalism which divided the Emperor from the majority of his people and alienated Germany herself from the modern world.

Bülow remained in office in 1908, but he did so as a matter of duty, and when the opportunity of laying down his responsibilities returned he seized it. He had not long to wait, for in the following year another adverse vote, due to a different combination of parties, convinced him that further delay was inadvisable. Once again the Conservative landowners wanted a new Chancellor, since from this one no more was to be expected. A taxation bill was made the pretext for a quarrel. More money was wanted — more money was always wanted — for the army and navy and the colonies, and the difficulty of raising it increased every year, as expenditure multiplied and the possible sources of revenue were one by one exhausted. The service of the imperial debt alone represented a serious and growing liability which could only be evaded, as it was for a time evaded, by paying interest out of new loans. The practice of borrowing began only midway in Bismarck's Chancellorship, and when he resigned the total debt of the Empire fell below fifty million pounds. During the ensuing ten years it had more than doubled, and most of the additional indebtedness had been caused by expenditure which should have been covered by current taxation, chiefly expenditure on the army and shipbuilding, and by deficits otherwise unprovided for. In consequence financial reform was a theme which seldom disappeared for long from the proceedings of the Diet, and the sessions were rare in which no changes in taxation were made or at least proposed.

Bismarck's last reform gave to the Empire four million pounds more revenue from brandy, and this increase, together with the normal growth of revenue from other sources, made it independent of the matricular contributions for several years, and even enabled it to distribute to the States, under the terms of the Franckenstein provision, already explained, a considerable sum from the proceeds of the customs and excise duties earmarked for that purpose in 1879. The next important reform of taxation was that of 1900, which became necessary owing to the passing of the second Navy Law. On that occasion some of the existing excise and stamp duties were increased and new stamp duties were imposed on bills of lading. Hitherto wine had been exempt from excise duty, but now a duty on champagne was introduced.

The revision of the customs tariff which took place in December, 1902, as has been said, was not undertaken primarily with the object of raising more revenue, but as this effect was bound to follow, the Government accepted the " Trimborn clause " of the new law, already mentioned (see p. 319). Then the calls upon the States became again so regular that in 1904 the matricular contributions were made permanent by a law which repealed the condition which had hitherto limited their continuance, viz. " so long as imperial taxes are not introduced." This law also abolished the Franckenstein proviso; yet while as a consequence the Empire henceforth retained the entire proceeds of the customs duties and the tobacco excise duty, it was still required to pay over to the States " assignments " (*Überweisungen*) consisting of the net proceeds of the brandy duties, as well as of certain stamp duties. Henceforth all surpluses were to go normally towards meeting extraordinary expenditure, in the hope of diminishing the need for borrowing.

In 1906 the larger expenditure on armaments and the accumulating deficits made necessary further additions to taxation. Baron von Stengel, the Secretary to the Treasury, needed at that time twelve and a half million pounds of additional revenue in order to put the Empire's finances in a healthy condition and to meet the imminent needs of the defensive services. A direct increase of the tobacco duty was refused, but revenue was obtained from tobacco by a duty on cigarettes. The beer duty was increased by the introduction of the South German principle of progressive taxation. At that time Bavarians, with their higher taxation and larger consumption of beer, were being taxed on this commodity to the extent of 5s. 3d. a head, while North Germans paid only 8d. a head. New duties were also imposed on railway tickets, motor-cars, and company directors' fees. Most important of all, a series of imperial probate (legacy) duties were introduced for the first time. These duties already existed and yielded a large revenue in some of the States. All existing duties were now abolished; but the States were to receive one-third of the proceeds of the imperial duties, and they were also to be empowered to levy for their own purposes a further percentage of these duties and to apply the duties to lineal relatives, who were exempted by the imperial law. The reform was carried in the teeth of strenuous resistance from the landowning classes, whose loyalty to the Government was strained to the utmost. Another attempt was made by the Liberal friends of direct taxation to gain acceptance for their old proposal of an imperial income tax; but this, like proposals for the taxation of capital, failed owing to the opposition of the State Governments, which protested against any further invasion of their staple sources of revenue.

As so much was required from the States at that time, an important concession was made to them in return in the proviso that when the matricular contributions exceeded the assignments by more than 40 pfennige (5d.) per head of the population the excess should not be levied until July of the third following budget year, the hope being entertained that by that time it might not be necessary at all. The result was that by 1909 the unpaid contributions exceeded fourteen million pounds.

By a further reform of that year the Empire took over this liability, but was empowered for the future to levy matricular contributions to the amount of 80 instead of 40 pfennige a head of the population. This increase of the matricular contributions was part of a larger scheme of taxation reform. Not only had the taxes introduced in 1906 proved disappointing, but expenditure had further increased. There had been a general increase of Civil Service salaries, due to the higher cost of living; larger subsidies were needed under the social insurance laws; there had been the costly military expeditions to the colonies; and above all the insatiable demands of the army and navy continued. It was estimated that the revenue in 1908 only exceeded by ten million pounds that of 1904, while the expenditure was twenty-two millions more; and the imperial debt had further increased, and now stood at two hundred million pounds. As no new large source of taxation appeared to be available, it was necessary to develop the existing ones and to fall back upon a series of petty fancy taxes, which yielded little except annoyance. Beer, brandy, and tobacco, which were still lightly taxed, might easily have supplied all the revenue needed, had not the vested interests been so powerful. The taxation of these articles was, indeed, increased, but only moderately, and for the rest an unearned increment tax was introduced, with duties on electric light and gas mantles, matches, dividend coupons, cheques, and acetic acid. Taxes on unearned increment had been introduced already by a large number of towns in all parts of the country, and had proved very remunerative. Now the Government appropriated this form of taxation, and, making it universal and placing it on a new basis, retained one-half of the proceeds for imperial purposes and assigned 40 per cent. to the communes or communal unions and 10 per cent. to the States to cover the costs of collection.

The Government also favoured the introduction of death duties, and the proposals made on the subject would have saved the situation. Against such an attempt to restrict further the immunities of real estate, however, the Conservative landowners at once raised violent protest, and, the Clericals joining them, in resentment at Bülow's attitude in the last elections, the proposal was rejected by the narrow majority of eight votes on June 24th.

Early in the year Bülow had given the Conservative leader to understand that if his party refused to vote the succession duties and he were compelled in consequence to choose between dependence upon a majority which was unacceptable to him and resignation he would resign. A compromise was patched up, to ease the difficulties of the moment, for money had to be found somehow, and then Bülow retired (July 14, 1909), glad to lay down an office of which he was weary and in which he had done the hardest work of his life. Perhaps already he had a premonition that there were in store for the ship of State heavy seas that would baffle the seamanship of a fair-weather steersman. Considering the difficulties with which he had to deal, his long term of office was a remarkable tribute to his astuteness and *savoir vivre*. A political wit, parodying one of Bismarck's memorable *dicta*, once said that " Bülow fears the Junkers, and nothing else in the world." That he was able to keep the Junkers at bay so long was due to the fact that he was the only Chancellor who really succeeded in winning the Emperor's complete approval. Of the four Chancellors who had now served William II he was the only one who quitted office with flying colours, bearing with him the regrets as well as the gratitude of a ruler who was not easy to please. His resignation was a " resignation with brilliants "; the Order of the Black Eagle, the highest distinction of the kind in the gift of the Sovereign, was the memento which fell to him at parting.

It cannot be said that his retirement excited great regret or created any serious gap in political life, for parliamentary parties took Bülow no more seriously than he took them. Easy-going, *débonnaire*, accommodating, he was but little suited to the strenuous ways of modern statecraft. No fighter, he preferred always to gain little by gentle ways than much by violent, and while success gave him no elation, failure never depressed him. As a dialectician he excelled, and German parliamentary life has known no more consummate master of rhetorical artifice. He had appropriated to excellent purpose Mephistopheles' injunction, " Mind, above all, you keep to words!" He kept to words always, and they never failed him, even in the most difficult situations. Most political orators who, like Socrates, wait for the inner light to tell them what they shall say blurt out at the critical moment only follies and ineptitudes. Bülow's ready wit shone equally in extemporized or prepared speech; always he had at command the happy phrase that soothed and satisfied all but the most exacting of his hearers, whether they understood him or not. In truth he was only understood when he wished to be, for no man had greater skill in darkening counsel. Subtlety and sophistry are as brother and sister; the same blood runs in both. Bülow's keen intellect disposed him to resort in his parliamentary oratory to mystifications of language which at times bordered on flippancy. Even when, as often happened, he trod safer ground by retailing Bismarck's phrases or clothing that statesman's shrewd maxims in his own language, his reputation for elegant shallowness compromised his influence; never did he succeed in giving the impression of weight, force, or compelling

conviction. No modern statesman took public life less tragically, and it is probable that on the whole none derived from
politics more entertainment than he.

The pressure of the agrarian party upon legislation, which
reached a climax in its obstinate resistance to all proposals to
tax real estate, led in this year to the organization of the commercial and trading classes in the Hansa League, a body claiming a non-political basis, yet in fact representing views on commercial and fiscal questions directly opposed to those of the
" German Conservative " and kindred parties. Within two
years branches of the League covered the whole country and
its members numbered 300,000. While not setting up parliamentary candidates of its own, the aims of the League have
since been embraced by a considerable group of deputies in
both the Imperial and Prussian Diets, nearly all of them members of the National Liberal and Radical parties, which have
consistently represented the interests of industry and commerce.

An economic development of greater importance, and in its
way the counterpart of the agrarian movement, was the organization of industry in the form of cartels and syndicates
which was in progress at this time. Encouraged by the protective tariff introduced in 1879, though of earlier origin, this
movement made rapid strides during the 'eighties, and in course
of time powerful combinations were formed in all the important
industries, more particularly those engaged in the production
of raw materials or the earlier processes of manufacture. The
largest organizations of the kind were established in the coal,
iron, and steel industries, though other industries passed so
completely under the control of the syndicates that they almost
came to have a monopolist character. While the syndicates
undoubtedly represented a higher form of industrial organization, the immediate effect, and usually the purpose, of their
formation was to curtail competition and to increase prices.
The syndicate movement is, however, only one phase of a general tendency towards the concentration of industry and capital in large undertakings. During the past two decades this
tendency has been specially marked in relation to the colliery,
iron and steel, engineering, chemical, shipbuilding, and shipping
industries. In all of these branches of enterprise the small
capitalist has more and more been supplanted by gigantic combinations, usually capitalized on a joint-stock basis, and not

infrequently controlled by or working in close association with powerful banks.

The revelation of much abuse of their power by the syndicates led the Imperial Government to institute an inquiry into the extent, management, and influence of these organizations. Several volumes of evidence were published as a consequence from 1903 forward, but no restrictive legislation was proposed, nor has any been foreshadowed since. On the other hand, something was done in Prussia to check the tendency of the syndicated colliery companies to abandon the less remunerative pits, a practice resulting in a serious displacement of population, by the passing of the Mining Law of 1905, which made such action dependent, in certain circumstances, upon Government assent. Later the Prussian Government itself, in the hope of exerting a moderating influence upon prices, joined the powerful Westphalian coal syndicate in virtue of the State collieries in the Westphalian and Saar coalfields, but its membership did not long continue. More important from the standpoint of labour policy was the action of the same Government in 1910 in taking control of the potash mining industry, in which it had large proprietary interests, and converting the potash syndicate, which had existed since 1884, into a statutory organization. The law which effected this change introduced a principle new in the relationships between a monopolist corporation and its workpeople, for it provided that whenever the wages of labour fell below the average of the years 1908 and 1909 (later the standard years were altered to 1912 and 1913) the share of output falling to the mine concerned should be curtailed.[1]

One of Bülow's last acts as Prussian Minister-President was to apply to the Polish districts a still severer measure of coercion. Easy-going and easily convinced, Bülow had at once accepted the inevitableness of resolute methods. His attitude was expressed in the words: "In a struggle between nationalities a nation is either hammer or anvil, either conqueror or conquered." As, however, the Land Commission had hitherto failed to use the hammer with effect, and the Poles still stubbornly refused to accept the position of anvil, another measure for the forcible Germanization of the Eastern Marches was

[1] An amending law of 1916 required the mine-owners to bear the costs incidental to the removal of workpeople and their families from one part of the potash mining field to another when transference became necessary in the interests of more efficient exploitation.

resorted to. This was the law of 1909 empowering the Government to expropriate landowners whose estates were held to be suitable for settlement by Germans. Formally the law made no distinction between German and Pole, but its purpose was obvious. The country at large regarded the proposal as one of desperation and as a frank confession of failure. Bülow, however, described expropriation as " the logical consequence of the policy of settlement," and because it was logical it was adopted, yet only after a bitter struggle, in which the usual party distinctions were strangely confused. For some time the Conservative landowners resisted the proposal as strongly as the Radicals, fearing that by assenting to it they would forge a weapon which might one day be used against themselves, but in the end it was their votes which saved the bill. In the Lower House there was a minority of 119 Clericals and Radicals against the bill, while in the Upper House the minority was 143. The measure was sped on its way by a further grant of several million pounds for land purchase and by a vigorous German propagandism organized by the Eastern Marches Association.

The Expropriation Law has not as yet been used with the freedom which was expected, since the Land Commission has since been able to obtain by voluntary arrangement as much land as it has been able to deal with, especially as a further vote of eleven and a half million pounds was granted for the purpose in 1913; yet it remains in reserve, an *ultima ratio* of force to which, when applied, there can be no reply. Short of the actual expatriation of the Poles, the Government has now reached the utmost limit of coercion. What, however, have been the results of this coercive scheme of colonization, of which a German historian has spoken as " perhaps the worst mistake of Prusso-German policy in recent decades? " [1] The answer to this question is that although great results have certainly been achieved they have not been the results aimed at or desired. As to the political aspects of the question, it cannot be doubted that the effect upon the Poles of prolonged coercion has been to strengthen their national spirit and their aspiration for racial unity. As if that were not failure enough, it has been found that the effect of driving the Poles from the land has been their concentration in the towns of the East and West,

[1] Hans Delbrück, *Bismarcks Erbe,* p. 154.

where they have become an easy prey to Socialist agitation and have joined the army of the discontented.

The economic results of the struggle have been more obvious and also more unexpected. Far from injuring the Polish rural population or diminishing its influence, the policy of Germanization has conferred upon it great benefits and renewed its prosperity. It is true that since 1886 over a million acres of land have been acquired by the Land Commission on behalf of the State and parcelled out into holdings at a cost of roughly thirty-five million pounds, and that 21,000 German families, representing in the aggregate, with dependents and labourers, about 200,000 individuals, have been settled in the Polish districts.[1] But of the land so acquired little more than one-fourth was previously in Polish hands, and of this minority a third was bought during the first three years. Moreover, by the Government's competition as a buyer the value of land has greatly increased to the advantage of the Poles even more than of the Germans, for they have been enabled to sell, where willing, at their own prices.

The Poles have shared equally in the prosperity which has come to the eastern provinces generally owing to the Government's action. Hundreds of thriving communes have been created; poverty has been banished from whole districts which formerly were hopelessly stagnant; modern methods of agriculture have been introduced; by the improvement of roads and railways and the use of co-operative methods the farmers everywhere have been enabled to dispose of their produce more advantageously; and while the owners and cultivators have chiefly benefited, the labourers also have found steadier employment under better conditions and at higher wages. All these benefits have been shared by the Poles equally with the German inhabitants, so that in many ways measures which were intended to be merely repressive have proved ameliorative in the highest degree, and so far as the Poles are concerned have produced results just the reverse of those desired.

[1] In an address made to a deputation of German visitors from the province of Posen on September 16, 1894, Bismarck asserted that the Polish colonization plan had not followed his ideas. He had no intention, he said, of ejecting the small Polish owners and holders, whom he did not regard as dangerous to Germanism, nor yet of setting up a large system of peasant properties. This, he explained, was a proposal imposed by the National Liberals as a condition of their support, and he had to accept it because he was unable to dispense with their support at the time.

Even in the towns the Polish traders and handicraftsmen have thriven as never before in consequence of the larger purchasing power of the agricultural districts. Where there has been an increase in the German relatively to the Polish population, it has chiefly been caused by the migration of Poles to the wealthier industrial districts of the West, and only in a minor degree can it be claimed as a result of the settlement policy. Nor can it be said that the creation in the West of a race problem which did not exist before is any compensation for the small degree of relief which may have been gained in the East. In a word, the policy of repression, pursued so long, persistently, and rigorously, has merely proved, in Goethe's words, " a part of that great power that ever does the good while seeking ill." [1]

Towards the end of Bülow's Chancellorship a tardy act of conciliation eased the long-standing difficulty of the optants' children in North Schleswig, in number about twelve thousand. The optants themselves were Danish subjects; but, since under the Danish law nationalization is conferred only by birth in Denmark, their children were aliens. At the same time they were not Prussians, since in Prussia nationality follows the rights of the father. The consequence was that these children had no fatherland and no national status. Their equivocal position was now regularized by their admission to Prussian citizenship as an act of special grace. The question might have been settled by legal regulation as a domestic matter; by the wish of Denmark it formed the subject of a treaty between the two States (January 11, 1907) which incidentally made it clear beyond further doubt that Denmark no longer claimed the *plébiscite* of the North Schleswig population on the annexation question which was provided for by the Treaty of Prague and never granted. For Prussia the agreement was in so far advantageous that it removed a cause of grievance and irritation, and brought a large number of future citizens under the civil and military laws of Prussia and the Empire.[2]

---

[1] " In the province of Posen," writes Privy Councillor Paul Koch in *Zeitschrift für Politik*, parts ii.–iii., 1911, " Germanism faces on the battlefield a fanatical enemy whose arms it has forged for him, whom it has trained for the struggle, and whom it has provided with the means necessary for waging it. At present there is no promise that the German will emerge as a victor from the economic and political struggle with the Poles."

[2] In agreement with the German Government a complementary law was passed in Denmark in November, 1916, in the interest of the children of optants: it effected the naturalization in Denmark of persons without nationality in Schleswig.

Bülow's successor was Herr von Bethmann-Hollweg, in whom a typical Prussian bureaucrat of the best type rose to the highest office in the State. Bethmann-Hollweg at the time held the portfolio of Home Affairs both in Prussia and the Empire, and in this capacity he had won a high reputation as a plodding worker of great industry, rather solid than original, and safe than brilliant. It was his misfortune to have inherited a heavy load of domestic difficulties which his predecessor, without exactly creating, had aggravated by his constitutional unwillingness to face disagreeable facts, and in foreign affairs to have fallen into evil traditions which it was too late to disown yet none the less dangerous to perpetuate.

As little provocative as Bülow himself, he was far more concerned to remove the causes of mischief by timely action, and he accordingly first devoted himself to the task of conciliation at home. He increased his reputation at the outset of his career as Chancellor by the promptitude with which he succeeded in preventing threatened friction with the Vatican. Although the *Kulturkampf* ended with the complete capitulation of the secular power, the religious bitterness which it had excited had never subsided; smouldering embers of passion were left which provocation on either side easily fanned into flame. Protestant sentiment was outraged in 1910 by the publication of the Borromeo encyclical *Editio sæpe* of May 26th, directed against free-thought. In this letter Pope Pius X spoke of the Reformation as " a vicious corruption and a perversion of discipline," and referred in unflattering terms to the association of some of the German Princes with the movement. Prussian Protestantism in particular felt acutely aggrieved, and a vehement outcry arose against the foreign Pontiff who had thus dared to revile the memory of Dr. Martin Luther and the faith of his followers. Yielding to the clamour, the Prussian Government sent a tactful remonstrance to Rome, whereupon the Pope disowned any intention of hurting the feelings either of the Protestant Princes or their subjects, and a council of cardinals resolved that the encyclical should not be circulated in Germany.

About the same time a still more serious misunderstanding with Rome threatened to reopen the very issues over which the *Kulturkampf* had been fought. A papal encyclical of September 8, 1907, *De pascendi dominici gregis*, directed against the heresies of the Modernist School, as represented by Loisy and Tyrrell, had required the priests and teachers of the Church to take the oath against this innovation, so disruptive of Catholic dogma and tradition. The prospect of a second invasion by the Papacy of the State's province in public education created alarm in Germany, and there was premature talk of abolishing the Roman Catholic faculties at the universities. Controversy raged violently for a long time, and peace was only restored when the Pope gave an undertaking, which was notified in a letter to the German prelacy on February 1, 1910, that the taking of the oath would be restricted to priest-professors and would not be required of professors engaged in purely lay functions. Nevertheless, the Prussian Government let it be known that if teachers of the higher schools were asked to take the oath against their convictions they would be protected against the consequences of refusal. An attempt made a little later by certain over-zealous Clericals to discredit the Christian trade union movement of the Rhineland and prevent any future co-operation between Roman Catholic and Protestant workmen in labour organizations was suppressed owing to the timely intervention of several princes of the Church, acting on instructions from Rome.

One of Bethmann-Hollweg's earliest acts as Prussian Minister-President was a feeble attempt to abate a long-standing political grievance of the working classes, who were almost deprived of representation in the State Diet owing to the inequitable franchise on which the Lower House was elected. There had of late been electoral reform in Saxony, Baden, and Bavaria, and even Mecklenburg had responded to the call of progress; but in Prussia, in spite of repeated efforts to move the Government, the system of election and the distribution of seats continued just as when the Diet was created over half a century before. In 1908 these efforts had been resumed, and the friends of labour were able to point to the flagrant fact that in the elections of that year the two Conservative parties secured 212 seats with 16 per cent. of the primary electors, while the Socialists with 23 per cent. of the electors secured only seven seats. The speech from the throne with which the Diet was opened in October promised a reform of the electoral law in the form of " an organic development, in accordance with economic evolution, the spread of knowledge and political intelligence, and the growth of the sense of responsibility to the State."

Not satisfied with these impressive phrases, however, and calling to mind the declaration of Prince Bülow some months before, that when the time came for broadening the franchise plural voting, based on age, property, or educational qualifications, would be introduced as a check, the Socialists rashly concluded that popular demonstrations might accelerate progress. Accordingly, early in 1909 they organized in Berlin and other large towns street processions, followed by mass meetings at which inflammatory speeches were made. Whatever the Government might have been willing to do had it been left alone, the pressure of the populace was regarded as an attempt to intimidate the Crown, and Bülow refused to yield to it. When in July he resigned nothing had been done.

In the following February the new Minister-President produced the long-deferred Electoral Reform Bill, and to the disappointment of all friends of honest parliamentary representation it left the principal inequalities untouched. No attempt was made to adjust representation to the existing distribution of population; all the constituencies, whether under-represented or over-represented, were to continue as before; voting was still to be open; and even the three-class system of grouping the electors was to remain. The only changes proposed were the abolition of indirect or mediate voting — i.e. the electors were no longer to exercise their suffrage through middlemen — the reclassification of the electors with a view to less numerical disparity in the three groups, and the addition of an educational to the existing income qualification in the case of the first group with a view to its enlargement. Nevertheless, moderate as it was, the Conservatives and Clericals refused the bill as a dangerous surrender to democratic tendencies. The fight was therefore between these two groups on the one hand and the National Liberals, Radicals, and Social Democrats on the other, and as the reactionaries were in a large majority, they were able to alter the bill to their mind. After they had restored the indirect method of election the measure was no longer worth passing, and at the end of May it was withdrawn. Since then no further attempt has been made to modernize Prussia's political arrangements. The Government's last word on the subject was the warning to the Prussian Lower House on January 13, 1914, that it would never accept an electoral law of the Diet's framing.[1]

[1] The foregoing paragraph and the paragraphs on pages 373–78 must be

Before this a minor concession to the humaner spirit of the time was made by the Imperial Government when a law was passed (1909) abolishing the disqualification for the exercise of the franchise in elections to the Imperial Diet which had hitherto been entailed by the receipt of public assistance of several kinds, e.g. care in sickness, institutional care in case of tuberculosis, casual relief given in emergencies and refunded, etc. It was left to the States to adopt this principle at will. An attempt was made to this effect by the Radical party in the Prussian Lower House, but the Government opposed it.

Bethmann-Hollweg was more successful with the reform of the constitution of Alsace-Lorraine, for there he had to deal with the Imperial Diet, with its strong leaven of Liberal sentiment. The autonomist party of Alsace had never ceased to agitate for a constitution which would give to the Imperial Province the status of a federal State; and in this endeavour it had gained powerful allies in the immigrants who, to the number of some hundreds of thousands, had come from other parts of the Empire, and particularly the Southern States, bringing with them traditions of independent sovereignties and more or less free government. However greatly they might differ upon other questions, the autonomist programme offered to the old French and new German populations a platform upon which they could work together. So strengthened, the demand for self-government came to be regarded in Berlin as one to be welcomed rather than any longer feared. Bethmann-Hollweg confessed, indeed, a little later that he had already come to the conclusion that " we shall not go forward in Alsace-Lorraine until we abandon the fruitless attempt to make out of the South German Imperial Province a North German Prussia."

The only question now to be decided was, how far self-government should go. The dictatorship paragraph had been abandoned in 1902; but that was merely a concession to sentiment, for the powers which were conferred upon the Stadholder by this paragraph existed only in name and had no practical importance. By the constitution given to Alsace-Lorraine in 1911 the Province became for most practical purposes an autonomous federal State, though without political independence. The constitution substantially reproduced in a modified form

understood as representing political conditions as they existed at the outbreak of the war. At the time of correcting proofs of the later chapters of this volume (October and November, 1918) fundamental constitutional changes seemed imminent.

the political arrangements of Prussia or any of the other German monarchies, the principal difference being that the Emperor, in the name of the Empire, took the place of an independent Sovereign. The chief executive power continued to reside, as before, in the Emperor, acting through a Stadholder, appointed by him; the powers hitherto exercised by the Federal Council were abolished; and the Province was given a Diet consisting of two Chambers, whose independent assent, followed by that of the Emperor, is necessary to all legislation. Just as by the imperial constitution all ordinances and decrees of the Emperor require to be countersigned by the Imperial Chancellor, so by the constitution of Alsace-Lorraine these acts of government need the counter-signature of the Stadholder, who in the same way is held to accept responsibility for them to the Diet. The Stadholder may thus be regarded as in some sort the Chancellor of the Imperial Province. On the other hand, all decrees issued by the Stadholder require to be countersigned by the Secretary of State.

The Upper House of the Diet consists as to one half (twenty-three) of its members of nominees of the Emperor — being citizens of the Empire and inhabitants of Alsace-Lorraine — proposed by the Federal Council; and as to the other half of (a) five ex-officio members, viz. the Roman Catholic bishops of Strassburg and Metz, the President of the Chief Consistory, and the President of the Synodal Executive of the Augsburg and Reformed Protestant Churches respectively, and the President of the Supreme Court of the Province; and (b) eighteen elected representatives of various corporations, viz. four for the large towns, Strassburg, Metz, Colmar, and Mülhausen, chosen by their Municipal Councils, one for Strassburg University, one for the Jewish Consistories, four for the Chambers of Commerce of the above towns, six for the Council of Agriculture of the Province, and one for the Chamber of Handicrafts. The Lower House consists of sixty deputies, elected for single-member districts on a democratic franchise modelled on that of the Imperial Diet. Members were to be paid at the rate of 20s. for each day's presence at Strassburg on legislative work, together with travelling expenses. Three representatives were assigned to the Province in the Federal Council; they were to be appointed by the Stadholder, and inasmuch as he was the nominee of the Emperor-King, it was assumed that he would choose only persons whose sympathy with Prussia could be relied on. For that reason it was stipulated that the votes of the Alsace-Lorraine delegates might not be counted when they would give to Prussia a majority or when the questions under consideration related to alterations of the imperial constitution.

During both the Committee stage of the bill and its later readings in the full Diet a determined attempt had been made by the popular parties to give to the constitution a truly Liberal character, in the hope of satisfying the desire of the Imperial Province for complete self-government. Amendments were accordingly adopted by large majorities, the effect of which would have been to deprive the Federal Council and the Diet of the power to interfere further in its internal administration, and to transfer from the Emperor to the Federal Council the appointment of the Stadholder, the former having henceforth only an empty right of confirmation. To all these amendments, however, the Government offered uncompromising resistance.

The constitution as enacted marked, indeed, a great advance in the political independence of the Imperial Province, yet because it came short of the expectations of a democratic population it was received without enthusiasm. There was still, in fact, to be government from Berlin, though in another form, for the Emperor-King continued to be the sole repository of executive power; and not only was he entitled to nominate one half of the members of the Upper Chamber, but his right to an equal voice with the Diet in legislation — a right denied him by the imperial constitution — gave him in effect a veto upon the decisions of that body.

Nor did the constitution bring peace. The first elections to the Lower House of the Diet were sufficiently premonitory, for they resulted in the return of twenty-six Clericals, ten members of the Lorraine *bloc*, twelve Liberal-Democrats, and eleven Social-Democrats. Limited though its powers were, the Lower House from the first showed a determination to assert them to the full, and conflicts between the two Chambers soon became common. Matters were not improved when in May, 1912, following one of these exhibitions of independence, the Emperor, then a visitor to Strassburg, threatened that unless the Diet proved more tractable he might have to repeal the constitution and even incorporate the Province in Prussia. The Emperor's powerlessness to do either of these things rather increased than diminished the significance of the threat, as an indication of the spirit of ascendancy which in the North still fought for mastery with the spirit of conciliation.

In November, 1913, the cause of pacification was again thrown back owing to the tactless folly of a young officer attached to the garrison of the little Alsatian town of Zabern (Saverne). Street demonstrations against the mischief-maker and the soldiery under his command followed, resulting in an outburst of military ferocity which outraged the whole nation. Martial law was illegally proclaimed over the heads of the civil authorities; a large number of citizens were imprisoned in a cellar; machine guns were set up for use in the streets; indiscriminate bayonet charges were made upon crowds whose worst crime was that they jeered at the offending officers, and in these charges many innocent and defenceless people were injured. It was in vain that Herr von Bethmann-Hollweg attempted to assuage the passions of the Diet and promised amends for every fault that had been committed by the military authorities. A vote of no confidence in the Chancellor was passed on December 4th by 293 votes to 54, the latter given by Conservatives, who alone defended the officers and soldiery. The vote had no effect upon the course of events, but it was welcomed by the nation as an expression of its own indignation. The Zabern garrison was removed in deference to public opinion, but an uneasy feeling was created later by the Emperor's action in decorating the officer in command. A year later it was possible for a German statesman to say that " the Germans living in Alsace-Lorraine are in an enemy's country."

The Zabern incident was the more disturbing since it followed immediately after a series of unpleasant law-court disclosures relating to the methods adopted by the great Essen armament firm of Krupp in obtaining orders for munitions. It was shown that the firm maintained agents in Government departments, that they practised the systematic bribery of Government officials, and that naval and military officers and civil servants had vied in divulging official secrets to them. As a result of the proceedings the principal defendants were sentenced to terms of imprisonment. The episode led later to an inquiry by a committee of the Diet, but its usefulness was diminished owing to the fact that the Government refused to appoint as a member the Socialist deputy Dr. Liebknecht, who had unearthed the scandal. The consequence was that the Socialist party, the largest and most independent in the House, declined to take part in the proceedings.

Several useful measures of social reform were enacted about this time. One such measure passed in 1911 gave tardy recognition to the grievances of the home workers. These workers, who formed and still form one of the largest, hardest-worked, and worst-paid groups of manual labourers in Germany, had hitherto been ignored by labour legislation. Now the Industrial Code was amended so as to secure for them healthier conditions of employment, reasonable hours of labour, and some guarantee of better remuneration. A more important social law was the monumental Imperial Insurance Code of the same year, consolidating all the workmen's insurance laws of the preceding thirty years, extending and amending their provisions, and introducing State-aided provision for the dependents of insured persons by a system of survivors' pensions. Simultaneously an independent law was passed for the insurance of clerks and *employés* against sickness and old age, with provision here also for their survivors. A law of 1913 introduced an important change in the legal status of persons of German birth domiciled abroad. Under the old Nationality Law (June 1, 1870) German citizenship was forfeited by any German who lived for ten years continuously in another country. A law of July 22, 1913, superseding the principle of *jus loci* (right of domicile) by that of *jus sanguinis* (right of blood), abolished the absolute forfeiture of national rights, and allowed Germans henceforth to be nationalized abroad without loss of their old nationality. In the same year the law of relief settlement was made uniform for the whole Empire. When the law of the North German Confederation was taken over by the Empire in 1871 Bavaria was allowed to retain her special legislation, which was intimately bound up with her Poor Law and local burgess rights. There had been an amendment of the law in 1908, when in Alsace-Lorraine the French law of public assistance was assimilated to the German system, i.e. relief by the communes of settlement, and domicile was henceforth acquired throughout Germany by persons of sixteen years after one year's residence. Now Bavaria surrendered her particularist customs, and the law of relief settlement, and with it the provision for poor relief, became uniform for the entire Empire.

Memories of Bismarck's State monopoly projects were revived by a novel legislative measure proposed in 1912. Although these projects were originally received with distrust and vehement opposition, insomuch that their author was never tempted to reopen the question, public opinion in Germany had undergone a great change since the syndicate movement began, the conviction growing that if the nation had to choose between monopolies in the form of the *régie* and monopolies created and manipulated by private corporations, its interests would be safer in the hands of the State. This was shown by the favourable reception given to an imperial law by which the Government, with a view to defeating the attempts of a powerful foreign trust to dominate the German market, proposed to create a State monopoly in the import and sale of petroleum, without engaging directly in the retail trade. The scheme was ultimately withdrawn owing to technical difficulties.

The greatest of social problems continued as before, however, to be the steady progress of Social Democracy. The setback which was supposed to have been suffered by the movement in 1907 soon proved to be more apparent than real. Political grievances, increasing taxation, and the serious rise in the cost of food which, beginning in 1905, continued steadily for some years, furnished the Socialists with powerful arguments against the Government, and there were repeated outbreaks of popular discontent in various parts of the country. The climax was reached in the autumn of 1910, when a dearth of meat, accompanied by exorbitant prices, aroused protests so widespread and threatening that the Governments were compelled to bow before them. As in 1891, the cry was again for open frontiers and the abolition of the food duties. Without interfering with the tariff, however, the Imperial Government agreed to the relaxation of the veterinary regulations relating to imported meat, which had been virtually prohibitive in effect, each State being allowed to decide how far it would go. Successful action to relieve the dearth on these lines was taken in all the larger States except Prussia, in which agrarian influence once more proved too strong for the Executive.

The rising resentment of the working classes took effect in the elections of 1912, when the Junker party experienced the worst defeat which it had suffered during the existence of the Imperial Diet; for the two Conservative groups together only won 57 seats, against 84 in the *bloc* elections of 1907, reaching the lowest ebb since 1874. The Centre, the National Liberals, and Radicals also lost ground. The great feature of the elections was the resurgence of Social Democracy. Whereas in 1907 the increase in Socialist votes had only been a quarter of a million, it was now a million; and in the aggregate four and a quarter million electors, or more than one in every three, voted the red ticket. The result was that the parliamentary party not only recovered the ground lost five years before but excelled all previous records, becoming with its 110 seats the strongest group in the Diet; thus for the first time in its history Social Democracy obtained a representation fairly proportionate to its voting strength. A party so strong had a claim to a share in the presidential offices of the Diet, and it was the unique experience of a Socialist member, an ex-printer of great ability, to be elected senior vice-president. As his colleagues promptly resigned office in protest, it fell to him to conduct the proceedings of the Diet until new elections could take place. In the end the Clericals secured the presidency for their nominee, with 196 votes against 175 given for the Socialist leader Bebel, and the first and second vice-presidencies also went to the loyal parties.

The cohesion and vitality of the Socialist movement were never shown more conspicuously than at this time, which was one of transition and grave inner conflict. Not only were the Revisionist tendencies making steady progress, but successive congresses revealed with increasing clearness the deep-seated antagonism between the North and the South upon the old question of the attitude of Socialist deputies towards parliamentary budgets. Ever since 1905 the Revisionist movement, led by energetic men like Frank, Bernstein, Südekum, Vollmar, and Heine, had been steadily extending its influence. Originating in the impatience of the younger leaders of the party with the extreme doctrinarianism of the fathers of Social Democracy, the movement was in essence a demand that the party should honestly recognize facts and accommodate itself to them. Under the old leaders, who clung tenaciously, without doubt or question, to the Marxian faith as delivered to the first pioneers, Marxism had petrified into a Ptolemaic system whose basic assumption was that the laws of society had been laid down once for all in " Das Kapital " and were therefore unalterable. The Revisionists pointed out, first tentatively, yet with growing courage the more they were bidden to hold their peace, that the world had not progressed according to the Marxian formulas: that poverty was not progressive, that the doctrine of surplus-value contained only half a truth, and that the economic system which Marx was supposed to have discredited for ever showed no signs whatever of disintegration.

Above all, they insisted on the importance of pursuing practical politics, contending that Socialists would do better to trouble themselves less about the organization of an ideal society which existed only in their dreams, and to concentrate their efforts upon the immediate duty of reforming the social order and system of government which still held the field, and so of making the best of the world as they found it. With that end in view they invited their colleagues not to be too fastidious as to the means they employed, but to work openly and cordially with other parties pursuing corresponding aims. Dr. Frank, one of the leaders of the Revisionist wing, shocked his older colleagues when in the Imperial Diet in February, 1912, he frankly offered to co-operate with the Radical and Liberal groups in contending for such objects as the reform of the Prussian franchise, redistribution of seats both in Prussia and the Empire, and the introduction of a real system of Ministerial responsibility. It is probable that at that time a substantial majority could have been obtained for these measures if all the progressive groups had been willing to act together.

The attitude of the Socialist parties towards the budgets of the various parliaments had for years been a subject of acute controversy. Discussed at successive congresses, and particularly at those of Dresden (1903) and Nuremberg (1908), it came again into prominence at the Magdeburg congress of September, 1910. By a subtle process of reasoning peculiar to themselves the North German Social Democrats had always held that, while it was perfectly proper for parliamentary deputies to take an active and even a leading part in the discussion of budgets, new taxes, and expenditure of every kind, even to the extent of voting for or against taxation bills and bills authorizing expenditure, they could not, consistently with their opposition to the principle of monarchical institutions, vote for a budget as a whole, even though it realized some of their most cherished theories and wishes. The more practical South Germans argued that to refuse to pass a budget after co-operating in its preparation and amendment was not merely inconsistent and a waste of time and energy, but was playing into the hands of the enemy, and on various occasions they had distressed their Prussian comrades by transgressing the party law on the subject.

In 1909 this offence was repeated by the Socialists in the Baden Diet, and their action formed the principal theme of discussion at the congress of the following year. Bebel led the attack against the rebels in a speech of three hours' duration; he was answered by Dr. Frank, one of the incriminated deputies; and the congress debated the question for several days. The fact that by voting for the budget the Baden deputies had helped a good financial scheme to success and had kept in office a sound progressive Minister, whom the Clericals had wished to overthrow, carried no weight with zealots jealous only for the sanctity of the law and the covenant, and in the end the duty of abstaining from budget divisions was restated and the offending deputies were censured by large majorities. Nevertheless, the refusal of the South German delegates to give any undertaking for the future made it clear that the difficulty had only been deferred and not settled. The practical effect of the controversy was to consolidate the Revisionist wing and convince its members that they were far stronger than they knew.

The party's congress of 1912 was the last which Bebel attended. He died in the following year (August 12, 1913), at the age of seventy-three, to the last militant, uncompromising, and confident in the ultimate triumph of the principles for which he had fought for more than half a century. Like many a party politician before him, Bebel received from his parliamentary opponents far more praise at his death than in his life. It is a singular proof of the charity or shallowness of political controversy that with the disappearance of this doughty champion of a movement which they had been wont to execrate as treason to the State some of the harshest opponents of Socialism tardily discovered in its veteran leader merits, virtues, and accomplishments which they had never recognized before. His death may be said to have marked the close of an epoch in the history of the cause with which his name will ever be identified. He was the last of the great leaders who won the German working classes for Socialism and Socialism for the German working classes. All the older men with whom he had been associated in the storm and stress period of So-

cialistic agitation had predeceased him. The last of these died
in the preceding year — Paul Singer, a retired tradesman of
ample means, Jewish like so many Socialist leaders, almost
superstitious in his Marxian faith, yet otherwise a man of well-
balanced judgment, who did much to assuage party antagonisms,
and was a consummate organizer. Bebel was now the last notable survivor of the local efforts of Lassalle out of which a vast
national movement had sprung. As in years, so in ideas, he
belonged to the older generation. He had forgotten nothing
of the Marxian doctrine and had added nothing to it, but held
with undiminished enthusiasm to his first devotion to a Socialism that knew no compromise, no half-way house, no easy by-
ways, but only the one clear, final goal of a thoroughly democ-
ratized society, in which private capital and private enterprise
should have no place. In the ardour of his allegiance to the
undiluted doctrine of Marxism Bebel was frankly intransigent;
yet if Marx was his oracle he was himself no less an oracle to
the mass of Socialists, and to the last he ruled the party con-
claves with a will of iron. True to the wise principle of using
the big man only for the big tasks, the Executive seldom put
him forward except on questions of critical moment; but when
these occurred Bebel's word was paramount. There might be
resistance, but it was almost sure to be that of a hopeless minority, which was discredited by the mere fact of opposing him,
and as rule ended by apologizing for and then effacing itself.

So long as Bebel overruled the party the Revisionists had
no chance of coming to the top, chiefly owing to the fact that
the authority of the veteran leader was against them, but also
owing to their own unwillingness to exaggerate fundamental
differences on points of doctrine and policy during his lifetime.
The effect of his disappearance and of the greater freedom to
which it gave rise was seen at the party congress at Jena in
September, 1913, of which it was said that no congress had
been so reasonable and none so dull. More than ever before
moderate counsels were in the ascendant. Even the proposal
to resort to a general strike as a means of securing franchise
reform in Prussia was rejected on the recommendation of the
Executive by 335 votes against 142. The general spirit of
the proceedings created the impression that the doctrinaire
members of the party were losing ground and that the Revisionists, no less convinced if more discriminating in their Socialism, and far more temperate in their methods, were surely

winning recognition and influence. These men had for years warned the party of the impossibility of any short cuts to the Socialist millennium, and had called for the concentration of its thought and effort upon a practical programme realizable in the present, leaving the future to take care of itself. The Jena congress made it clear that the extremists had abandoned all hope of further dominating the Socialist movement and that the future lay with the right wing of the party.[1]

Nevertheless, in spite of the growing ferment caused in its midst by new ideas, there was no trace of disruption; still, as ever, the Socialists remained a united party, offering to all its adversaries an unbroken front. Prince Bülow has written: "Only in a State whose citizens are accustomed to discipline, who have learned in the army unconditional obedience, who feel daily and hourly the stern pressure of the apparatus of administration, could a party organization so large and coherent as German Social Democracy originate." Whether this explanation of the strength of Social Democracy is to the praise or blame of the German politico-military system is a question which must be left unanswered here, but the fact itself is indisputable. It may be, however, that the sociologist, taking a comprehensive view of modern social phenomena, will be disinclined to regard Social Democracy as a development altogether apart from the general tendency towards economic combination on a large scale which has fallen to recent decades. The co-operative movement, which has attained such large proportions both amongst the working classes and in agriculture, the industrial syndicates, and the powerful defensive organizations of labour and capital which wield so great an influence in Germany are other notable illustrations of this tendency which have gained prominence during the past generation.

No such striking record of steady progress, and above all no such proof of unshakable unity of aim, can be claimed by

[1] *Inter arma silent leges.* In consequence of the war the Erfurt programme of the Social Democratic party, which since 1891 had enjoyed the authority of a Median law, was modified in several important points as a result of a party conference held at Würzburg in 1918. In particular the old attitude of opposition to any sort of co-operation with the so-called *bourgeois* parties was abandoned, and the demand for a republican system of government gave place to proposals for strengthening the existing monarchical system in the direction of a more democratic parliamentary *régime*. These and other changes denote a further marked advance on Revisionist lines.

any of the other political parties. Taking these in their
sequence from the extreme Left to the extreme Right, the Radical (*Freisinnige*) or Progressist party has now for many years
escaped the violent oscillations to which it was exposed during
the Bismarck *régime*, though if now apparently a fixed star in
the political firmament, it is one of minor magnitude. For if
the party has in the main remained true to its first faith, it has
purchased consistency by the periodical ejection of the waverers who have blocked the way. More pedantic and doctrinaire
than any other group of German politicians, with the single
exception of the Socialists, the acute divisions which have occurred in its ranks on critical occasions have almost invariably
resulted in formal splits of varying importance. The last of
these was caused by an Army Bill of 1893, on which occasion
the party divided into two groups, one calling itself the Radical Union and the other — the remnant of the old stock, still
clinging to the veteran leader, Eugen Richter — the Radical
People's Party. Only in 1908, after the *bloc* formed by Prince
Bülow had exhausted its usefulness for the purpose in view, and
proved itself a union of incompatibles, did these groups make
peace and reorganize themselves, together with the hitherto independent South German People's Party, as the Progressive
People's Party. One of the best known parliamentary representatives of the party, Dr. Friedrich Naumann, has complained that German Radicalism suffers from " anæmia of spiritual force," and has traced this weakness to the absence of a
sincere conviction that it is its duty " to devote itself absolutely to the cause of the people, humanity, and progress." It
is true that the party as a whole is distinguished for attachment to abstract political principles rather than enthusiasm
for humanitarian endeavours; and so long as this characteristic, which dates from its first beginnings, continues, so long will
the party fail to attract to itself the large and ardent body
of middle-class social reformers who, in default of a more congenial home elsewhere, now ally, without exactly identifying,
themselves with Social Democracy. Dr. Naumann's ideal of a
formal coalition of Radicals and Socialists, with the view to
the formation of a " great united Left," has hitherto proved
impracticable, but since 1914 its prospects might seem to be no
longer hopeless.

It is usual to speak of the Clericals as the Centre party.
There are, in fact, two Centre parties in German parliamen-

tary life, the second consisting of the National Liberals, who occupy a position between the Radicals and the Conservatives, with, for many years, a decided leaning towards the latter. For ever since the first decade of the Empire the National Liberals have belied their earlier record of progressive sympathies. To be just to them, they have been progressive and reactionary in turn; but owing to the lack of definite principles, and of consistent fidelity to such principles as they professed, they have more and more become a nondescript and invertebrate party, never certain to give to genuine Liberalism a helping hand in an emergency, and, as is the common and just meed of opportunist politicians, despised as enemies and distrusted as friends. Upon most political questions the party finds itself in agreement with Conservatism, from which it differs chiefly in the fact that it approaches these questions from another angle of vision — that of the great industrialists. Nothing has made this cooperation more easy or advantageous for both sides than their common interest in protective legislation, and so long as this bond of union continues National Liberalism will never be able to reassert itself as a true and powerful progressive force in political life. It juggles, as ever, with the arrogant word "National," but it is neither more nor less nationalist in sympathies and aims than the other middle-class parties; and in practice its nationalism merely connotes a readiness to support Ministerial policy with a lack of discrimination which was unknown during the time of its first and only great leader, Rudolf von Bennigsen.

While on the Left there have been repeated transformations and readjustments of party relationships, the Conservatives, and with them all the ideals and views for which Conservatism stands in Germany, have undergone little perceptible change. There is, it is true, now as ever, a difference between the Conservatism of the North and North-east, nurtured upon feudalist soil and imbued with strong military traditions, and that of the South, which has never been entirely inaccessible to vitalizing influences. The only Conservatism that counts in practical politics, however, is the agrarian " die-hard " Conservatism of Prussia and the adjacent backward agricultural States; and its antagonism to political progress in any form is almost as strong and unbending as seventy years ago, when it endeavoured to prevent Prussia from becoming even a constitutional State. In this respect the Imperialist party, which also belongs to the extreme Right, is hardly to be distinguished from the Conservative party formally so called, and even were it disposed, it is numerically too weak to act as an effective check upon the extravagant tendencies of its allies, as shown particularly in their aggressive agrarianism.

The Clerical party or Centrum continues, as from the first, to maintain its sectarian basis and to represent primarily the interests of Ultramontanism and the Ultramontane view of things. Only the powerful confessional tie could have succeeded in preserving so long unbroken and undivided a party otherwise so heterogeneous in composition, for no other is in an equal degree an amalgam of the entire social life of the nation. The backbone of the party, however, are the peasantry of the South and the manual workers of the industrial States. The continued adherence of the former is hardly open to doubt. How far the party will succeed in retaining the active sympathies of the Roman Catholic working classes, for whom the ideal of a great national labour party and the *ignis fatuus* of the Socialist State are not without attraction, will largely depend upon the continued strength of the religious tie and upon the ability of the leaders of the party, priestly even more than lay, to appreciate the social signs of the times and the courage and success with which they adapt themselves to new conditions. A strenuous effort has been made to organize the Roman Catholic workers as a separate order, segregated from the rest of the labour world, and it has so far appeared to succeed. Nevertheless, it is notorious that in the larger towns these workers show an increasing disposition either to identify themselves openly with the Socialist trade unions, as the only really combatant labour organizations, or to combine surreptitious membership of these unions with adhesion to their confessional societies, as a supplementary form of insurance against capitalistic aggression.

The description of the various political groups as " fractions " is peculiarly applicable to a parliamentary system in which room is found for no fewer than eighteen parties, large and small. Of the particularist or territorial parties the most important are the Poles and the Alsatians and Lorrainers. The Poles, while asserting party independence, can always be trusted, as a solidly Roman Catholic body, to vote with the Centre, and for the same reason most of the deputies from Alsace-Lorraine support that party on general questions. Of the other minor fractions, several — like the Guelphs, Danes, and Hessians — exist to keep alive old protests against absorption by Prussia, while the remainder for the most part represent more or less factious differentiations in social reform conceptions which have their root in the German passion for controversy.

It would be injudicious, at a time when, owing to an abnormal situation, political conditions and to some extent party relationships are in a state of transition, to attempt to anticipate the transformations which German parliamentary life may undergo in the near future. Nevertheless, it may be useful to state certain facts and considerations which must have a bearing upon any speculations of the kind. The battle royal between the Right and the Left, as representing respectively ultra-Conservative and progressive tendencies, and more concretely the alternatives of constitutional stagnation and advance towards parliamentary government as understood in Western countries, remains still to be fought. The multiplicity of parties which is the misfortune of German political life, and is not the least potent cause of the inability of the progressive forces to assert themselves effectively, has hitherto prevented any clear and direct conflict upon this fundamental issue. If at one extreme are the feudalists, who would abandon constitutionalism altogether, and with it the Empire itself, rather than countenance any further concession to the principle of popular sovereignty, at the other extreme are the Social Democrats — for many years by far the strongest party in the country and now the strongest party in the Imperial Diet — whose aim is the replacement of the monarchical by the republican system.

Not only has the adoption by the Socialists, with the uncompromising austerity of zealots to whom party programmes are sacrosanct and glittering abstractions more important than sober realities, of this unpractical standpoint prejudiced the cause of constitutional reform in the eyes not merely of its enemies but of moderate men, not on principle unfriendly to it, but it has made impossible that " great united Left " to which the Radical leader looks as the presupposition of any genuine political advance. Meanwhile, the party of reaction has been the *tertius gaudens*, only too well pleased to see the constitutional cause blocked owing to lack of unity of aim on the part of two progressive forces which have every interest in working together.

How the two middle parties, the National Liberals and the Clericals, would range themselves in any contest upon the clear-cut issue of constitutional reform must be a matter of speculation. The National Liberals as a party have never taken up a merely negative, *non possumus* attitude on this question. In their early and more ardent days, when their Liberalism was thoroughgoing and vital, they did their best to give to the constitution such a democratic form as would have secured to the nation the substance of self-government without reducing the Crown to a cipher. Even during recent years a considerable section of the party has more than once given practical proof of its adhesion to the constitutional principle of Ministerial accountability, implying the subordination of the Government to the Diet. It is possible that the searching and chastening experience through which Germany, with the rest of the world, is passing may reinvigorate the Liberalism of this party and win its support for a bold forward movement in constitutional reform.

Still more uncertain is the attitude of the Clerical party, whose opportunism has ever been one of the *imponderabilia* of party politics. Prince Bülow truly said of the Centrum on one occasion that it has " always been an incalculable party, representing aristocratic and democratic, reactionary and Liberal, Ultramontane and National, and all other tendencies except one — the Social-Democratic." A party so constituted is, in its nature, capable to a large degree of adaptation, and it would be unsafe to assume that the Centre, whose strength lies in the main in its popular sympathies and whose following in the country is made up predominantly of the working classes and the little people in town and country, would league itself with the parties of the Right in the event of a serious struggle for the extension of constitutional liberties. At present all that can safely be said is that the leaders of the Roman Catholic party have not fully made up their minds upon this subject. There are strong forces pulling both ways, but it is easy to see the grave risks that would attend a formal and official determination to identify the party with the reactionary elements in political life. In illustration of a divided attitude in the ranks of the hierachy the fact may be mentioned that in

1918 Cardinal Hartmann removed from office the diocesan lay president of the Roman Catholic trade unions of West Prussia because of his active advocacy of franchise reform. The leading West Prussian Roman Catholic labour journal thereupon threatened that if that was to be the policy of the powers above, Roman Catholic workmen would have to consider the question of seceding from the confessional trade unions.

Whatever changes in party grouping the near future may bring with it, however, the fact should be remembered that the present impotency of the popular parties as a parliamentary force is due in no small measure to their under-representation under an electoral law which has never been amended since it was originally enacted nearly fifty years ago. The distribution of seats as fixed when the population of the Empire was forty millions, and the great migration from the country to the towns had not begun, continues to-day when the population is seventy millions and the proportion of the inhabitants resident in towns of twenty thousand and upwards has increased from one in eight to one in three. Even now, with proportional representation, the Radicals and Social Democrats alone, without counting the progressive members of the smaller fractions, certain to act with them on critical issues, could almost count on a clear majority in the Diet.

It remains to be added that all hopes and expectations of coming constitutional changes are subject to an important proviso — the fact that it rests with the Sovereigns, as represented by the Federal Council, to determine in the last resort, as co-equal with the Diet in legislative power, whether such changes shall take place and how far they shall go. It is that fact which more than any other creates the obscurity of the outlook of the democratic cause in Germany and gives to speculation a merely academic interest.

Essentially a man of peace though he was, the years of Herr von Bethmann-Hollweg's Government were marked by feverish activity in military and naval preparations. In the early years of the Empire it was difficult to pass Army Bills, even when Bismarck was their advocate, with Moltke always in reserve, while to naval programmes the Diet would not listen at all. Latterly bills of both kinds were to be had almost for the asking, and since 1907 neither the Clericals nor the Radicals dared to raise a voice in serious protest. Repeated additions

had brought the peace strength of the army in 1912 to 544,-
000, exclusive of one-year volunteers.   All past Army Bills,
however, were insignificant in comparison with the special Defence Law of 1913, by which the Diet sanctioned the addition
to the army at once of 4,000 officers, 15,000 non-commissioned
officers, and 117,000 rank and file, as part of a scheme which
would eventually give the army on a peace footing a strength
of 870,000 men of all ranks.   The Socialists were the only
party of importance which offered to this new and unexampled
demand flat resistance.   They attributed the project to the in-
satiate imperialistic ambitions of the militarists and the Pan-
Germans; yet while these parties had unquestionably done the
pioneer work which made the project possible, there was no
denying the fact that, from whatever motive — vigilance, fear,
or love of conquest — the nation at large, with the exception
of the working classes, accepted almost without question the
assurance that the bill was necessary.

Two events of national interest helped to make its passage
easier.   One was the marriage in May of the Emperor's only
daughter, Princess Victoria Louise, to Prince Ernst August
of Cumberland, a union which closed the old feud between the
Hohenzollern and Guelph families and gave back at least the
throne of Brunswick to the dispossessed heir to the Hanoverian
crown.   The other was the twenty-fifth anniversary of the
Emperor's accession, which occurred in June and evoked a cordial outburst of loyalty, of which the climax was reached when
the rulers of all the States brought to Berlin their united congratulations.   When the third reading of the bill was taken at
the end of June only the Socialists, Poles, and Alsatians voted
against it.   The first cost of so large an addition to the army,
together with the necessary barracks and a liberal provision
for new frontier fortifications and for a large air fleet, was estimated at fifty million pounds.

The Defence Law created a very uneasy feeling abroad, and
nowhere so much as in France.   During the same summer the
French Parliament replied to the challenge by voting forty
million pounds, to be raised by loan, for the further increase of
the army by the rigid enforcement of the three years' service
system, as well as a progressive income tax, estimated to yield
two and three-quarter million pounds a year, to meet recurrent expenditure.   Russia also accelerated the re-equipment of

her army which had been in progress ever since she began to recover from the impoverishment caused by the war with Japan.

Similarly, the increase of the navy continued as before, though no longer unheeded by neighbouring countries. Great Britain in particular had ceased to be a passive spectator of German naval expansion, and was becoming seriously alarmed. Now many of the Emperor's unguarded disclosures of the working of his mind were recalled, like the phrases: " The trident belongs to our hands," " Sea power is world power," " Our future lies on the water," " The Admiral of the Atlantic salutes the Admiral of the Pacific," his declaration that he " would not rest until he had brought the navy up to the same standard as the army," and his claim that it was Germany's mission to " impose peace on the sea " as well as on the land. These utterances had fallen to a time — from 1897 to 1901 — when the German navy was small and its growth was still slow, because obstructed by parliamentary division, and for that reason they had excited in most English minds rather curiosity and uncertainty than positive unrest and apprehension. In proof of this it is only necessary to recall the fact that in basing the British Naval Defence Act of 1889 on a two-Power standard the Government of the day had in mind France and Russia. They acquired a new significance when a German policy of world-wide intervention had been avowed by a ruler who had behind him not only the strongest and best equipped army in the world, but a sea force of formidable proportions. With whatever premeditation and purpose these and similar winged phrases may originally have been coined, they now began to create grave alarm in a country whose food supply, commerce, prosperity, empire, and very existence were altogether dependent upon its naval supremacy.[1]

[1] As another illustration of how history repeats itself, the earlier Anglo-French naval rivalry of the same kind may be recalled. Many of the speeches made in the German Diet, and the British House of Commons during the naval discussions of the last decade of the nineteenth and the first decade of the twentieth century sounded like echoes of the forgotten controversies of fifty and sixty years before. Thus M. Thiers said in the French Chamber of Deputies in 1846: "We pay England the compliment of thinking only of her when determining our naval force. We never heed the ships which sally forth from Trieste or Venice; we care only for those which leave Portsmouth or Plymouth." Conversely, Lord Palmerston, advocating a strong navy, said in the House of Commons on July 23, 1860: "The Committee, of course, knows that in the main I am speaking of our immediate neighbours across the Channel, and there is no use in disguising

The British nation was divided into two parties, of which one demanded the concentration of all efforts, both technical and financial, upon the single object of making England's naval position as regards Germany not only absolutely but relatively stronger than before, the other wishful for an amicable agreement, based on reciprocal concessions, hoping by this means to avert the threat of a wild and insensate competition in naval expenditure which might eventually exhaust the resources of both countries and make impossible the realization of great domestic reforms. The latter view was embraced almost generally by the Liberal party, which came into power in December, 1905, after being in Opposition uninterruptedly for over eleven years. The new Cabinet and House of Commons were emphatically bent on pursuing a pacific policy, and the only war of which the majority in either case would hear was a war against the Army and Navy Estimates. Faithfully interpreting the will of its parliamentary supporters and the mind of the nation, the Government decided to renew the efforts at disarmament which had been made without success by its predecessors several times before. In nearly every European country the burden of national defence had reached a crushing weight, yet the unreasoning rivalry in the production of instruments of war continued unabated. If there was to be relief, it could only come by concerted action, and to sanguine minds it seemed that there would be the greater hope of this if the initiative were taken by a country which could fairly claim ability to hold out longest in the competition, if competition it was still to be. The fact that a second International Peace Conference was near seemed to make the time specially appropriate for a serious attempt to lift the question of disarmament out of the arena of merely academic discussion.

The first time a British Government had held out the olive-branch on this question was in March of 1899, the year of the first Peace Conference. Mr. Goschen, the First Lord of the Admiralty in Lord Salisbury's last Cabinet, had then declared in the House of Commons that England would be prepared to reduce her programme of shipbuilding if the other great naval

it." Again, in March, 1861, in the same place: "The French make no secret of their preparations, but when some well-intentioned gentleman asks them if they really mean to invade this country, if they really have any hostile intentions towards us, of course they say: 'Not the least in the world'; that their feeling is one of perfect sympathy and friendship with us, and that all their preparations are for their own self-advancement,"

Powers would do the same, but there had been no response. The consequence was that while the conference held at The Hague in the following May established a tribunal of conciliation and arbitration for the adjustment of international disputes, all it was able to do for the cause of disarmament was to commend it to the sympathetic consideration of the Powers. Now in further practical proof of his country's good faith the Cabinet of Sir Henry Campbell-Bannerman announced (July, 1906) a large reduction in the naval estimates, hoping that its example would bear immediate fruit.

In the eyes of the Opposition parties this step seemed all the bolder, or more fatuous, by reason of the fact that Germany had just made another addition to her shipbuilding programme. That measure had been justified, according to custom, by the demands of the foreign situation. Not only had the Russo-Japanese war, which broke out in February, 1904, revealed the rising Eastern island Empire as a new and formidable naval Power, but recent events of still greater importance for Germany were the conclusion in 1904 of the *entente* between Great Britain and France and the Morocco controversy of 1905, leading in the following year to the conference of the Powers at Algeciras, in which Germany found herself almost isolated. The super-battleship had also been launched from an English dockyard in the shape of the *Dreadnought* (February, 1906), and with this fateful innovation naval shipbuilding for all countries promised to enter a new phase marked by still more lavish expenditure, yet offering less prospect of finality than before. The third German Naval Law (June, 1906) had added six cruisers, but no new battleships, to the programme in hand; its principal significance lay in the importance attached to the building of larger vessels, to which end the expenditure already authorized was increased by one-third.

In view of all these circumstances the time was but little favourable to the consideration of disarmament proposals, and it can hardly have surprised the British Cabinet that Germany's reply to its pacific overtures was that she was determined to go her own way, and that she would have no reason for complaint if other countries did the same thing. Not only so, but the Emperor and his Government refused to take part in any discussion of the general question of disarmament at The Hague, and gave warning that Germany would stay away if the question was to be raised. The German objections to the reduction of the army were those advanced as long ago as 1869 and 1870, when, at the request of the French Government, Lord Clarendon unsuccessfully pressed disarmament proposals upon Bismarck — on the one hand, the country's military and geographical position, exposing it to special risks, and on the other hand, the fact that the size of the army was determined by the constitution, i.e. a given ratio to population. As to the navy, it was objected that inasmuch as it was being built in accordance with special laws, each binding for a period of years, any modification of the prescribed programme would be inconvenient and might meet with parliamentary resistance.

Accordingly, when the Peace Conference met in September, 1907, all it could do was to adopt a resolution commending the question of disarmament to the sympathy of the Powers, though the British delegate, in the name of his Government, offered to exchange naval estimates in advance with any other Power that might be willing, in the hope of paving the way for more practical measures later.

In the following year a new Navy Law was passed (April, 1908). It accelerated the speed of shipbuilding by reducing the age of battleships and armoured cruisers by five years, and provided that by 1917 Germany should have fifteen large fighting ships more than were contemplated by the programme of 1900. Between 1901 and 1908 the naval estimates had increased from nine and a half to sixteen and a half million pounds, and now an average expenditure of nearly twenty-one million pounds was planned for the years 1909 to 1917.

Early in 1909 unrest was caused in England by reports that the German Government was pre-dating its statutory programme of shipbuilding, and it was concluded that the intention was to produce a further Navy Bill before the due expiration of the one in force. This unrest led to discussions in the House of Commons and also to inquiries in Berlin resulting in assurances that the apprehensions on the subject were baseless. In order, however, to provide against future misunderstandings, and possible unpleasant surprises, the British Cabinet suggested that the two Admiralties should keep each other acquainted, through their respective naval *attachés*, with the progress of the larger vessels, but the idea did not find favour in Berlin. Nevertheless, the British Government now deemed that the time for resolute counter-action had arrived, and from that year forward it adopted larger programmes of construction, which made it impossible that Germany could hope, at least for many years, to be more than a good second in the race for supremacy. At the same time well-meaning but inconclusive endeavours to arrive at a *modus vivendi* continued as before. Their sequel must be told in later pages.[1]

Amongst the other legacies inherited by Herr von Bethmann-Hollweg was a legacy of debt, and this could only be liquidated by new taxation. The revenue derived from the various fiscal reforms introduced in 1909 fell far short of expectations, and in view of the larger expenditure entailed by the Army and Navy Laws of 1912 a favour hitherto shown to the brandy distillers, by the taxation of a certain quota of production at a lower rate than the rest, was withdrawn. For the rest a larger revenue from existing taxes, larger receipts from the remunerative services, and economies in various directions were relied on. The Conservatives were ready enough to vote additions to the army and navy, but they were not equally willing to pay the bill. The Secretary to the Treasury at that time, Herr Wermuth, one of the soundest men who ever had charge of imperial finance, insisted upon the common-sense principle " No expenditure without provision to meet it "— provision in the form, not of loans, but new revenue — and recognizing how severely existing sources of taxation had been drained, he wanted to revive the death-duty proposals of 1909. Confronted by the opposition of the agrarians and the Clericals, and the Government declining to support him, he resigned in March, 1912.

The passing of the Defence Act of 1913 threw imperial finance once more into confusion. Fifty million pounds were needed to cover the first cost of this great measure, and it was estimated that the cost of maintenance would be two and three-quarter millions in the first year, rising to a maximum of nine and a quarter millions in three years. How were these large sums to be raised? The discussion of this question reopened the old controversy over direct *versus* indirect taxes. The Radicals and Social Democrats called for the taxation of income, capital, and real estate; the Conservatives and Clericals, ever with the dread of death duties before their eyes, advocated the increase of the customs duties as a simpler and more effec-

[1] Chapter XXIII., pp. 486–497,

tual method. The Government, however, refused point-blank
to impose any new taxes which would make the cost of living
still dearer to the working classes, and as its own proposal to
levy high matricular contributions was unpopular, choice was
ultimately narrowed down to the alternatives of an imperial
income tax or a tax on real and personal estate. The compromise ultimately agreed to was a substantial victory for the
principle of direct taxation.

By the Finance Law of 1913 a special national defence tax
(*Wehrsteuer*) was imposed to meet the first costs of the
equipment of the new army. It was to be levied once only
on all properties, real and personal, of a value of £2,500 and
upwards and on incomes of £500 and upwards, and was to be
paid in three yearly instalments, the rate in the former case
ranging from 0.15 to 1.5 per cent. and in the latter from 1 to
8 per cent. The recurring expenditure was to be met by a tax
on increment in the value of real property, graduated from
0.75 to 2.5 per cent., properties not exceeding £1,000 and increment not exceeding £500 being exempted. At the same time
the Government renounced the Empire's share in the proceeds
of the existing unearned increment tax, which was given back
to the States for the benefit of the communes as from 1915.
The imperial probate duties were also raised, and the Empire's
share in the proceeds was increased from two-thirds to four-
fifths. As drafted, the measure made no provision for the taxation of reigning Princes, but the Socialists soon discovered
the omission. In Committee the Conservatives and National
Liberals still voted for their exemption, but the majority, and
later a majority of the Diet, decided otherwise.

The way of every Minister of Finance is hard, and the periods in which the strain upon the German Imperial Treasury
has relaxed and its custodian has been free from anxiety for
the morrow have been rare and short indeed. Nevertheless,
it would be fallacious to conclude that the cause of their constant failure to make both sides of the budget agree has been
due to the absence of taxable sources of wealth. The explanation must be sought rather in the fact that on questions of
finance the Empire and the States pull against each other,
since the former is compelled by its growing liabilities to make
ever larger demands upon the resources to which the States
have likewise to look for their own needs. Thus every deputy
is called upon to legislate in two capacities, as a subject of the

Empire and as a subject of his "narrower fatherland," and the more he is identified with the political life of the State to which he belongs the less willing is he as a rule to assist the Imperial Government to restrict the financial rights of that State. So grudgingly have successive Diets granted new taxes that all the taxes introduced during the forty years 1873 to 1913 were represented in the budget for the latter year by the relatively small sum of sixteen million pounds out of a total revenue from taxes of all kinds of eighty-three millions.

Several further outstanding facts of the problem of imperial finance deserve notice. One is the large and growing proportion of imperial expenditure which is covered by customs duties. When the Empire was established only five million pounds a year were raised by these duties; the revenue from the same source had in 1913 increased sevenfold. Nevertheless, the opinion has long been general amongst thoughtful people that the system of indirect taxes has been developed to the extreme limits of prudence, if not of safety, and even beyond the limits of equity, and that the taxation of food and the other necessities of life in particular bears with disproportionate weight upon the incomes and homes of people of small means. At the same time many of the subsidiary taxes which were warmly opposed in the early years of the Empire have since been introduced under pressure of growing expenditure caused by the insatiable demands of the army and, during the present reign, of the navy. These taxes include in particular the probate duties and the tax on capital. The Liberals still continue to demand an imperial income tax — to be fixed annually, as in the United Kingdom — not from a greater love of taxation than other people of normal minds, but because such a method of taxation would in their belief give to the Diet greater control over the purse and therefore over the Government. A further notable fact is the overwhelming proportion of the expenditure which falls to the army and navy and incidental services, like that of the debt, which has to a large degree been created by handing forward liabilities incurred on behalf of national defence. If outlay upon remunerative undertakings, like the imperial railways, post and telegraph, be disregarded, almost two-thirds of the annual expenditure are due directly or indirectly to these services.

The amount of the imperial debt in 1913, viz. 245 million pounds, seemed heavy in view of the fact that up to that time it had been incurred in times of peace, but when regarded as part of the public debts of Germany as a whole it ceased to be alarming. For while the debts of the Empire and States together exceeded in that year a thousand million pounds, only that of the Empire represented in the main non-productive expenditure. The debts of the States were as a rule represented by at least equal assets in the form of profit-yielding undertakings, like railways, canals, coal-mines, ironworks, and other industrial enterprises, the value of which in some States then exceeded the entire amount of the national debt.

CHAPTER XXI

(1890-1904)

FOREIGN RELATIONS —(i) *WELTPOLITIK*

IN order to obtain the right point of view from which to judge
the foreign policy of Germany under the third Emperor it is
necessary to recall the ends which were constantly pursued by
Prince Bismarck and the means by which he endeavoured to
attain them. His steadfast aim was the maintenance at all
costs of the peace of Europe, since peace was Germany's first
interest and greatest asset, the condition of her prosperous
development, and the pledge of her retention of the spoils of
victorious war as harvested from 1864 to 1871. Never once
did he swerve from this aim, and towards the end of his career
he emphasized it with growing concern. In conversation with
Signor Crispi on October 2, 1887, he said: "I labour for the
maintenance of peace; I live for it alone. We have done
enough for war; now let us work, and work together, for
peace." [1] But, further, since Germany's possible enemies were
the Powers to the East and the West, it was necessary to render these Powers, if possible, harmless — Russia by conciliation, France by isolation.

In the policy which he built upon these leading ideas he
seemed to succeed completely until the Berlin Congress of 1878
and the conclusion in the following year of the close union with
Austria which in 1882 became, by the adhesion of Italy, the
Triple Alliance. After these events trouble began. France
was politically isolated as before, but so now, though in a less
direct way, was Russia.

Although Bismarck increased his efforts to maintain, now,
necessarily, in a more passive form, the old cordial relationship
with St. Petersburg, he never doubted that Russia would sooner
or later cease to be satisfied with a position which left her
without active allies. The knowledge of the Czar's restive-
ness, as well as his own desire to obtain for Germany a double
sense of security, was the explanation of the supplementary
treaty which he concluded at Skiernievice in 1884, in virtue of

[1] *Memoirs of Francesco Crispi*, vol. ii., p. 221.

which Germany and Russia gave reciprocal undertakings to observe benevolent neutrality in the event of either of them being attacked. That treaty, while it left the Triple Alliance in full force, brought Russia again to some extent within the ambit of German influence: as Bismarck said, the wire to St. Petersburg still remained uncut. For both sides the treaty seemed to be one of substantial value; on the one hand, Germany secured the continued advantage of the practical isolation of France, while, on the other hand, Russia benefited in that her pseudo-ally became in some sort responsible for Austria's good behaviour. Later (as Caprivi told Hohenlohe in December, 1891) the treaty did even more for Russia, for under it Bismarck agreed to give her a free hand in relation to Bulgaria and, in certain eventualities, to Constantinople.

This was all in keeping with Bismarck's fixed maxim in Oriental policy, that Germany would best serve her own interests by holding her hand, whenever complications threatened, until events made it clear how she might bargain to the best effect for herself, as being " the Power which has least interest in Oriental questions and will gain the more the longer it holds up its stake." Already he had begun to count on Russia's occupation of Constantinople as a possible development, and he was even prepared to welcome it on terms. " We must not seek to prevent Russia from going to Constantinople," he said to Crispi several years later (May, 1889): " situated as she is, it is impossible to attack her. On the Bosphorus she would be weaker and might easily be overpowered. . . . As for the Sultan, we need not trouble ourselves about him. The Russians once established at Constantinople, the Sultan will accept their protectorate. If they leave him his harem, he will be quite satisfied." [1] In any case he was resolved not to oppose Russian aspirations in that quarter unless compelled by the operation of the treaty of alliance with Austria. That was why he had objected to the Emperor's visit of friendship to the Sultan in November, 1889, as being contrary to the spirit of his policy, which was the maintenance primarily, not of the Ottoman, but of the German Empire. To the last he continued firmly convinced that no justifiable ground existed for a rupture with Russia, and that timely concessions on Germany's part, always at the expense of other States, would tide over any conceivable difficulty.

[1] *Memoirs of Francesco Crispi*, vol. iii., p. 251.

When Caprivi succeeded to the Chancellorship in 1890 the Russo-German reinsurance treaty was still unknown to the outer world. In that year the treaty had to be either prolonged or abandoned. Bismarck had been wishful for its renewal, and Russia was of the same mind, but at the time of his dismissal in March the transaction was not completed. According to Busch, the negotiations had actually reached the point of signature when a change of Chancellors compelled their postponement. Caprivi's straightforward way of facing facts convinced him that the treaty was wrong. He believed that even in politics no man can serve two masters faithfully, and hence contended that the alliance with Austria lacked complete sincerity so long as it was countervailed by this equivocal arrangement. Double agreements were well enough for political prestidigitateurs, but he had no mind or capacity for sleight of hand; he confessed that the whole arrangement was " too complicated " for him. He won the Emperor over to his view, and the treaty was allowed to lapse on the ground that it was incompatible with Germany's liabilities towards her ally, as, on a fine appreciation of the facts, it undoubtedly was. Caprivi told Prince Hohenlohe, his successor, that he had not prolonged the treaty, since, " had it become known," the Triple Alliance would have inevitably come to grief.

Several other important considerations may have helped to determine the action of the new Government in the matter. It was believed in Berlin in the spring of 1890 that Russia wished to undertake at once the military occupation of Bulgaria, and that this was why the prompt prolongation of the treaty was desired. Had Bismarck still been in power, this prospect might have created no alarm. Only a short time before (February 6, 1888) he had told the Diet that Bulgaria was " assuredly not an object of sufficient magnitude " for Europe to fight about. So the Emperor and the new Chancellor may likewise have thought, but they were not prepared to run risks, and it seemed morally certain that to reopen the Balkan question in that way would bring Russia and Austria into the old antagonism. But, further, the abandonment of the treaty was deemed to be necessary in order to quiet once for all the persistent apprehensions which had been entertained for some time in Vienna that official Germany was in two minds about the Triple Alliance, and would not be indisposed to exchange Russia for Austria as an ally. Even Crispi, at his meeting with Bismarck in 1889, already referred to, noted " a certain coldness towards Austria in his conversation." Bismarck, for his part, suspected that there was running in France a strong current of feeling favourable to Austria, and he feared lest this feeling should be reciprocated.

Whatever change, if any, Bismarck might have given to Germany's relations with the neighbouring Empires, had he continued in office and in full control of foreign affairs, there seems ground for the belief that he had ceased to attach to the alliance with Austria the same importance as in 1879. He had entered into the alliance, as he entered into some other important commitments, impetuously, and against the judgment of the old Emperor, whose predilections drew him powerfully to Russia, and who, had he been able to have his way, would still have been contented with the more flexible *entente*. That he was no longer satisfied with his own handiwork may be concluded from the fact that he had attempted to improve it by inviting into the partnership Great Britain, whose traditional sympathy with Austria was still unimpaired. In a private letter written to Lord Salisbury on November 22, 1887, with a view to allaying English official apprehensions of the reported strong Russian sympathies of the young Prince William of Prussia, and published only after many years,[1] he had spoken of Great Britain and Austria-Hungary as belonging, like Germany, to the " saturated States " and consequently her natural allies, and had assured the British Premier that no German Emperor would ever assist Russia in weakening the Habsburg Empire. While down to the time of his retirement that assurance still held good, his faith in Austria as an ally had been rudely shaken with the growth of the Pan-Slavic movement, the effect of which was to force that country and Russia more and more apart. It is probable, if not certain, that if Bismarck had been compelled to make again in 1889 the choice which he made ten years before he would have reversed his decision. The truth is that upon this question, wary and resourceful master of political strategy though he was, Bismarck had landed himself between the Caudine Forks, and he knew it. To have abandoned Austria might have meant throwing her into the arms of France; to hold fast to her meant to risk the greater danger of a Russian alliance with the same

---

[1] It was published for the first time in the London *Daily Telegraph* of May 13, 1912.

Power. It was a great mistake of his foreign policy — the greatest, for this miscalculation was not the only one of his career. Never, however, would he have made the danger of counter-alliances more real by weakening the tie with St. Petersburg, since that tie, prudently fostered, enabled Germany to exert a restraining influence upon both of her neighbours.

In estimating the influences which determined Caprivi's Government to make this critical departure it is to be remembered also that the year in which the reinsurance treaty was allowed to lapse was also the year of the Anglo-German treaty, effecting the exchange of Heligoland for East African concessions, and apparently preparing the way for that more cordial co-operation with Great Britain for which the Emperor had seemed to work ever since he came to the throne. Russia, however, was still the bugbear of the British Conservatives, who at that time were in power. Five years before (1885), in succeeding to the legacy of unpopularity which its early attitude towards Germany on the colonial question had brought upon the British Government, Lord Salisbury had recognized that, in the uncertain temper of France, a good understanding with Berlin was a vital necessity. Six years more were to pass before his formal repudiation of the idea of a " permanent and necessary antagonism " between Great Britain and Russia as " the superstition of an antiquated diplomacy." [1]

For the present, however, the tradition which had been confirmed so emphatically by the Treaty of Berlin in 1878 was unbroken. The slighting of Russia was part of the price which the Emperor was prepared to pay in 1890 for British friendship. The step thus taken was not the less fateful because at the time it became known only to a limited circle. Bismarck, who later complained that by it " the most important part of his foreign policy " had been sacrificed and undone, waited six years before he disclosed the fact that the treaty of 1884 had existed at all.

Meanwhile, the Emperor tried to make good the loss of Bismarck's influence in foreign affairs by feverish exertions of his own. In the second half of 1890 he visited Queen Victoria, the Czar, and Emperor Francis Joseph. His reception in Vienna was enthusiastic, that in St. Petersburg correct but

[1] Guildhall speech, November 9, 1896.

not cordial. In the following June the Triple Alliance was renewed for twelve years. At home the Emperor's continued attempts at this time to strengthen the ties with England were as unpopular as ever with the official and military classes, partly because of their traditional dislike of a country under free government, but also because they justly feared that in the existing tension of Anglo-Russian relationships friendly overtures in London would prejudice Germany in St. Petersburg. This opposition to his plans, of which he was fully aware, did not prevent the Emperor from visiting England again in July, 1891, and declaring in a speech in the Mansion House: " So far as it lies in my power I shall always maintain the historical friendship between our two nations, who have so often stood together in the protection of liberty and justice."

Now the abandonment of the reinsurance treaty, of which both the German and Austrian peoples as yet knew nothing, began to bear fruit. Bismarck could have told the Emperor and his new and untried Chancellor what would be the first result of their daring departure from the policy which had been followed by himself so long and so scrupulously. The chance for which France had for years been waiting now came. Vexed at the renewal of the Triple Alliance, which still kept Italy in alien surroundings, and at the Emperor's effusive friendship for England, the Government of M. de Freycinet made formal overtures to St. Petersburg, and they were promptly reciprocated. In July, 1891, a French fleet under Admiral Gervais called at Cronstadt as part of a pre-arranged plan, and was there visited by the Czar. The festivities begun at Cronstadt were continued in the capital. The effect in Germany was to create a feeling of consternation, and nowhere more than in the imperial palace, and the feeling was intensified when in September the Czar passed through Berlin without stopping to greet and be greeted by the Emperor. Asked by Hohenlohe a little later how his relationships with the Czar stood, the Emperor replied: " I have none," and added: " I only write ceremonious letters to him now." [1]

[1] Reporting on a conversation with M. de Giers on November 21, 1891, M. Ribot refers to this incident in the words, " L'Empereur (i.e. the Czar) n'a pas voulu s'arrêter à Berlin parce qu'il lui est impossible de prendre ' un visage composé.' Il était trop irrité contre l'Allemagne pour pouvoir faire des politesses à l'Empereur. Il a préféré ne pas laisser d'équivoque sur ses dispositions " (French Yellow Book on " L'Alliance Franco-Russe," published 1918).

For a long time prior to his dismissal Bismarck had maintained that the only tie that had kept Russia attached to Germany was the Czar's confidence in himself. In conflict with this belief was the remark attributed to the Czar by the Emperor, and repeated by him to Hohenlohe in August, 1892: " Whenever Bismarck had said anything to him he always had the conviction *qu'il me tricherait*." The probability is that the Czar had ceased to count on the fidelity of a country whose ruler and leading Minister could not be trusted to see eye to eye. There was no suggestion of a formal estrangement, but the old feeling of confidence had gone.

The year 1893 brought the return visit of a Russian fleet to Toulon, and the conclusion of a formal military convention between the new friends dated from December, though the fact and its full import were for some time concealed as carefully as the Russo-German reinsurance treaty had been concealed before.[1] In 1895 M. Ribot, the French Premier, for the first time publicly spoke of Russia as " our ally," and when in June squadrons of French and Russian vessels attended the opening of the North-Baltic Sea Canal they ostentatiously entered the harbour of Kiel together. Nevertheless, it was only when, two years later (August, 1897), on the occasion of President Faure's visit to St. Petersburg, the Czar, Nicholas II, referred to " les deux nations amies et alliées," that the world knew for a certainty that the republic and the autocracy were joined in a formal union as associates in peace and, if need be, as comrades in war.

Bismarck had long ceased to believe that differences of government would stand in the way of a Franco-Russian alliance if political interest could be served thereby. He held always that " for Russian policy there is a limit beyond which the importance of France in Europe must not be decreased," and he believed that the limit was reached by the Treaty of Frankfort. France does not readily forgive an injury, especially when the injury is done to her pride, but she also never forgets a kindness, and conscious of the gratitude of the French nation for the friendly intervention of the Czar and Gortchakoff when war threatened in 1875, Bismarck had from that moment counted upon a more cordial understanding between the two Governments and nations as one of the serious possibilities of the future. His private utterances as well as his public acts

[1] See Appendix A, p. 525.

proved that to the last he was deeply sensible of the danger of a breach with either of these Powers, knowing that a war with one would in all probability mean a war with both. He confessed that " the idea of coalitions gave him nightmares," and the worst of these nightmares arose from the thought of an alliance of Russia and France against Germany. Always this possibility haunted him, and with it the fear that if such a trial of strength occurred things might not go as well with Germany as in 1866 and 1870. Busch, the recorder of so much of his table-talk, relates a conversation of 1888 in which he said: " It is not yet certain that Russia would take up arms against us, if we were again attacked by the French; but if the Russians were to declare war upon us the French would certainly join them at once, and in such a war we should not be so very certain to win, while it would be a great misfortune even if we were victorious." Only three months before his dismissal he said to Hohenlohe (December 15, 1889), when discussing the same contingency: " As far as we are concerned we shall begin no war with Russia or with France," adding that " at any rate the war would break out with both countries at once, and then it would be doubtful whether we should be victorious enough to be able to dictate terms to Russia."

The Franco-Russian alliance was a justification of Bismarck's policy, and by inference a condemnation of the policy which had replaced it; it also brought to light the fact, which the Emperor, in his desire to be at peace with all men, had either never understood or had forgotten, that the day of purely dynastic attachments is past, and that in modern times a political union which does not rest upon the solid basis of national sympathy or community of interest must lack the elements of reality and permanence.

It was while under the influence of a quite honest resentment at the results of the abandonment of his policy towards Russia that Bismarck made known to the world for the first time, in the *Hamburger Nachrichten* of October 24, 1896, the existence of the reinsurance treaty of 1884.[1]   The disclosure, which served as the occasion for a violent attack upon the foreign policy which had supplanted his own, created a painful impression upon public opinion both in Germany and Austria, which hitherto had been kept in the dark, and while the skilful manœuvring to which he confessed proved that Bismarck's as-

[1] See Appendix B, p. 527.

tuteness had not been exaggerated, it cannot be said that it added to his reputation. Called upon by the Diet a month later (November 16th) to take it into confidence and make a clean breast of all the circumstances of the episode, the Chancellor, now Prince Hohenlohe, refused to draw aside the veil of secrecy, and only claimed that " the clouds of distrust which at first appeared in certain sections of the population of this country have again vanished." The Foreign Secretary, Baron Marschall, was equally reticent as to the inner history and the implications of the treaty, yet he " energetically repudiated the idea that any agreement was ever made by Germany that was incompatible with other international obligations; neither in spirit nor in letter was this done." At the same time he confessed that the existence of the two treaties placed Germany potentially in a position of great difficulty.

" According to paragraph 1 of our treaty with Austria-Hungary," he said, " we were bound to aid that country with our whole fighting strength in the event of its being attacked by Russia. A war between Austria and Russia would have raised the question whether we ought to remain benevolently neutral or go to the aid of Austria, and we should have been obliged to decide which of the two parties was the aggressor and which the attacked." In other words, while Bismarck had not done wrong in concluding the reinsurance treaty, his successor had done right in abandoning it.

The break with Russia was not the only proof that there had entered into the foreign policy of the " new course " a spirit and a tendency altogether opposed to those which had been sanctioned by the usage and the successes of twenty years. With the disappearance of the old Chancellor, Germany found herself committed to a succession of foreign adventures and entanglements. Early in the 'nineties a phrase of ominous meaning, which will probably be searched for in vain in Bismarck's parliamentary speeches — until his retirement the only ones which he ever made — gained currency in German political life; it was the phrase *Weltpolitik* or world-politics. In the early years of the Empire it occurred to no serious German statesman that the destiny of his country would not be fulfilled unless it played a prominent part in world-affairs. " The pacific disposition of Germany," said Lasker, one of the ablest parliamentarians of his day, on April 27, 1877, " lies in the fact that she does not arrogate to herself world-jurisdiction, but confines herself to the preservation of her own interests." That was pre-eminently the attitude of Bismarck himself. While no statesman of his generation played so prominent a part in Continental politics, his interferences had always the clearly defined aim of maintaining such a " constellation " of the Powers as would keep mischief-making countries in order and safeguard the general peace. Never did he interfere for the sake of mere prestige; and regarding Germany as, in Metternich's phrase, an " *état saturé*," there was not a rod of Continental soil which he envied for her sake. All he asked of Germany's neighbours was that they would leave her to develop her resources in peace and tranquillity. In later years he even acquired colonies against his will, and to the last, after ceasing to be Chancellor, he declared that he was " no colony man." [1] There is no reason to doubt Bismarck's good faith when he wrote in 1891:

" Germany is perhaps the single Great Power in Europe which is not tempted by any object which can only be obtained by a successful war. It is our interest to maintain peace, while without exception our Continental neighbours have wishes, either secret or officially avowed, which cannot be fulfilled except by war. We must direct our policy in accordance with these facts; that is, we must do our best to prevent war or to limit it."

The new Sovereign was no less pacific in intention, but a lack of constancy and discrimination frequently betrayed him into acts which were utterly at variance with his professions. His rejection of Bismarck's guidance threw upon him the obligation to justify himself in the eyes of the world, and he proceeded to do this by reversing the old safe policy of restraint. No sooner was he free than he made it clear that as the first reign had witnessed the assertion of Germany's influence in Europe, the mark of his own reign was to be the assertion of that influence across the seas. Emperor William II appropriated not a few of the maxims of his ancestor, Frederick the Great, but one of the most sagacious he altogether disregarded: " All distant acquisitions are a burden to the State. A village on the frontier is worth more than a prin-

[1] Signor Crispi relates a conversation with Bismarck in May, 1889, wherein the German Chancellor asked him in jest: " Will you buy our German colonies? " to which Crispi replied: " Your Highness, I am quite prepared to sell you ours " (*Memoirs of Francesco Crispi*, vol. iii., p. 258).

cipality two hundred and fifty miles away." Many of his speeches in the first few years following Bismarck's dismissal were open appeals for support in the pursuance of a spirited foreign policy. In these speeches will be found many sentiments like the following:

" Nothing must henceforth be settled in the world without the intervention of Germany and the German Emperor."

" Present events invite us to forget internal discord; let us be united in case we should be compelled to intervene in the politics of the world."

" The ocean proves that upon it and far away beyond it no great decision can any longer be taken without Germany. I do not agree that our German nation has for thirty years conquered and bled under its Princes in order to be pushed on one side in foreign affairs. To prevent this by suitable and, if necessary, severe measures is my duty and my highest privilege."

It is true that emphatic protestations of peaceful intentions often accompanied utterances of this kind, but rightly or wrongly, it was the explosive and aggressive spirit of the Emperor's oratory that most impressed Europe, and this, together with the constant increases in the army, and later in the navy, created widespread unrest and apprehension. The weakness of German foreign policy at that time lay in an instability and uncertainty of purpose, a lack of clear foresight, and above all in a conflict of tendencies, for again and again the quiet work of the Chancellery was thwarted and stultified by the Emperor's exuberant speeches and impetuous acts. How far Germany here departed from the traditions of Bismarck may be judged by comparing *dicta* like the foregoing with the cautious words of Bismarck, spoken on February 8, 1888, when the first Emperor was still under his guidance:

" Every Great Power which seeks to exert pressure on the politics of other countries and to direct affairs outside the sphere of interest which God has assigned to it carries on politics of power and not of interest; it works for prestige."

Yet the audience to which the Emperor addressed himself was not unresponsive. The military and colonial parties applauded him, and he became the idol of the *All-Deutscher Verband* or Pan-German League. This imperialistic organization grew out of a less influential society which had been formed in 1891, with the name " General German League " (*Allgemeiner*

Deutscher Verband), for the encouragement of Germanism abroad. Under the direction of a Leipzig publicist, Professor Ernst Hasse, the aims of this society had gradually taken a more aggressive and Chauvinistic form, and in 1902 its name and constitution were changed in sympathy with its larger scheme of propagandism. Covering the whole country with a network of branches, each one a powerful centre of organization and agitation, the reconstructed League appealed to the nation with a programme of territorial aggrandizement which sought to give concrete expression to the vague aspirations of the more idealistic forerunners of the Pan-German movement — the poets and philosophers of a century before. Its object now became the creation of a Greater Germany, which should comprise all the Germanic peoples, irrespective of geographical areas. Hence it was contended that to the larger fatherland must belong the German parts of Austria and of Switzerland, Holland, Luxemburg, and even part of Belgium. None of the non-Germanic races were to be put out of the Empire, but the Germans outside were to come in. Serious politicians smiled at the idea as irresponsible and fatuous: it was both, yet it nevertheless took root and made quick growth, with the result of creating in the countries whose integrity was threatened great unrest and deep and justifiable resentment. Perhaps no body of political propaganda has on the whole exercised a more sinister or more immoral influence upon a nation's mind than that of this powerful organization, whose predatory doctrines implied the practical repudiation of international faith and the negation of public right.[1]

It was one of the ironies of German foreign policy in the early 'nineties that the new doctrine of foreign intervention was first applied practically in relation to the affairs of the country with which the Emperor had seemed specially desirous to be on good terms. One of the first effects of the " cutting off of the wire " between Berlin and St. Petersburg had been to strengthen his resolve to win England if she were willing to be won. For several years he paid regular visits to Osborne, and on these occasions he lost no opportunity of meeting British Ministers and statesmen. In spite of large reservations

---

[1] A recent German writer says of the Pan-German League: "Well as it may have acted as a national leaven amongst the Germans at home and abroad, it has greatly injured the reputation of Germany abroad by its fulsome boasting of the power of the Empire and its naïve depreciation of foreign nationalities" (Otto Hamman, *Der neue Kurs* (1918), p. 104).

on both sides, there existed at that time a widespread mutual desire for a *rapprochement*, though it is probable that this desire proceeded less from conscious inner sympathy than from considerations of prudence and caution, for which the political situation afforded abundant justification. Unfortunately for the later relationships of the two nations the movement received a serious check before it had had time to gather strength and become a real force in the public life of either country.

That the Emperor was ever quite clear about either the strength of his intentions or the depth of his sympathies might appear to be an assumption difficult to reconcile with his early action on the Transvaal question. Until the time of the irresponsible Jameson raid of December 31, 1895, nothing had occurred to mar the effect of the African colonial convention of 1890. In 1895 the Emperor was in England as usual, and in June a British fleet took part in the festivities at the opening of the Kiel Canal. Then came the telegram to President Krüger of January 3, 1896 (following the receipt in Berlin the night before of news from London of the defeat of Jameson's troops at Krügersdorp), wherein the Emperor said:

" I sincerely congratulate you that, without making any appeal for the help of foreign Powers, you have succeeded with your people and your own strength in repulsing the armed bands which have troubled the peace of your land, in re-establishing order, and in defending the independence of your people against attacks from without."

The famous telegram has since been a subject of profuse controversy. Considering the treaty relations between the Transvaal and Great Britain,[1] the suggestion that foreign Powers — with Germany at their head — would have intervened had they been asked, was in the highest degree provocative, whether intended to be so or not. Nor can it be claimed in extenuation of the Emperor's act that these treaty relations were unknown to his Government, since the German commercial treaty with the republic, concluded in 1885, had been submitted to the British Government for approval before signature. It was understood later that before the despatch of the telegram the Foreign Secretary, Baron Marschall, invited the French

[1] By article 4 of the Transvaal Convention of 1884 the Transvaal Government was prohibited from concluding alliances or treaties with foreign Powers (the Orange Free State excepted) unless with the assent of Great Britain.

ambassador in Berlin, M. Herbette, to say whether his Government would join with the Government of the Emperor in inviting diplomatic intervention by the European Powers on behalf of the independence of the Transvaal, that he was asked in return whether Germany would be prepared to support France in pressing England in Egypt, and that as an undertaking on the latter point could not be given, France declined to be implicated.

While the Emperor has ever since borne the onus of this fateful intrusion into South African politics, the telegram was, as Prince Bülow later admitted (March, 1909), " an act of State " and " the result of official consultations," and was " in nowise an act of personal initiative " on his part.[1] It was, in fact, supported at the time by an official declaration by the Government that it regarded the continuance of the independence of the Transvaal Republic and the **Orange Free** State as for Germany an important political and commercial interest. In fairness both to the ruler and his Government it should also be said that they faithfully voiced the feeling of the nation, which now again, after long intermission, gave the Sovereign enthusiastic assurances of its complete support. The British Government answered the challenge by promptly commissioning a flying squadron and calling attention to the existence of the London Convention of 1884.

It is probable that the man who suffered the bitterest disappointment as a result of this episode was President Krüger. Krüger, who came to power in 1883, had ever since astutely traded upon German sympathies. He visited Berlin in 1884, and was cordially received by the Government and the population. That he seriously entertained the design, which has often been attributed to him, of placing the Transvaal Republic under direct German protection may fairly be questioned. He was in his way a skilful intriguer, however, and there can be little doubt that he would have welcomed — he may have even encouraged — the intervention of Germany in South African politics, as a countervailing force hostile to complete British hegemony, hoping that the Transvaal would

[1] Count Reventlow states that the telegram was drawn up by the Foreign Secretary, Baron Marschall, in the presence and with the concurrence of the Naval Minister and other heads of the Admiralty (*Deutschlands auswärtige Politik,* 1888–1914, p. 75). Hamman, in *Der neue Kurs* (p. 120), says the Emperor and the Chancellor were present at the council, and that it took place in the latter's official residence.

benefit by the complications which would inevitably result. From the beginning of the 'eighties German attention had been directed in an increasing degree to the South-east African coast, and particularly to Delagoa Bay. A project much discussed both before and after Krüger's visit to Berlin was the construction of a German railway from the Bay to Pretoria with a view to flooding the Transvaal with German emigrants. Nothing more was heard of that scheme after 1896.

The immediate effect of the Krüger telegram and the controversy to which it gave rise was the creation both in Great Britain and Germany of resentful feelings, which never entirely disappeared. Nevertheless, the Government of Berlin clearly drew from the events of that time the conclusion that South Africa could never safely be made the pivot of its foreign policy in relation to Great Britain. Later, when the Boer war broke out, it did its best to atone for an unaccountable miscalculation, but without receiving in England the thanks which were expected. In the meantime it had given other signs of a desire to see the episode assigned to oblivion. When in 1896 the British Government sought approval for its proposal to charge the Egyptian Treasury with the cost of an expedition against the marauding dervishes Germany at once assented, while France and Russia both refused. In April, 1898, the Emperor congratulated Queen Victoria on Kitchener's victory over the dervishes at Atbara. In that year also the two Powers concluded a treaty (September) defining their attitude towards the Portuguese colonies. It seemed likely at that time that Portugal, in order to ease her financial position, might find it necessary to sell her colonial possessions, or some of them. It was therefore agreed that if the opportunity offered Germany was to be free to acquire the southern part of Angola (adjacent to German South-west Africa) and the northern part of Mozambique (adjacent to German East Africa), while Great Britain was to be able to acquire northern Angola, the southern part of Mozambique, as well as Madeira, the Azores, and the Cape Verde Islands. It is probable that the treaty soon came to the knowledge of the Portuguese Government, for in the following year the old Anglo-Portuguese alliance, dating from the reign of Charles II, was renewed by the Treaty of Windsor. In 1899 the British Government gave even more marked evidence of its desire to live in amity with Germany by the conclusion of the Samoan Conventions of November and December, by which Great Britain withdrew altogether from the Samoan archipelago, whose civilization owed so much to English missionary enterprise, and Germany was established in the islands of Sawaii and Upolu, and the United States received the island of Tutuila.

In October of the following year came the Boar war. In March Mr. Cecil Rhodes, visiting Berlin for the purpose of seeking help for his railway and telegraph projects, had met the Emperor and enlightened him upon aspects of the Krüger *régime* which had hitherto been ignored or insufficiently regarded by his Ministers. Long before hostilities began the Boer President had received from Berlin the advice to agree with his enemy while he was in the way, and the subsequent endeavours made by the Transvaal Executive to win the support of Continental Governments received no official encouragement in that quarter. In pursuing this policy of non-intervention, so unlike the attitude adopted four years before, the Government was entirely alienated from the Diet and the nation, with which the South African war was intensely unpopular. Political parties, indeed, justified their hostility to Great Britain by much talk about humanitarianism, though in reality far more concerned at the prospect of a further extension of British dominion than for the fate of the Dutch republics.

It was due to the refusal of the German Government to cooperate that a proposal of mediation, made by Russia with the encouragement of France, was abandoned. The proposal was not in itself unnatural in the circumstances, for the idea of international arbitration had just before been brought down from the clouds to earth in a striking way. Europe had for a long time been an armed camp. Not only had the Great Powers taxed their resources to the utmost in the creation of huge armies, which every year became greater, but the minor States, even to the little principalities of the Balkans, had followed the example of their strong neighbours. Appalled by this spectacle of prodigal waste, and foreseeing that unless it were checked the end would be catastrophe, the Czar of Russia, in an impressive rescript of August 24, 1898, invited the Powers to confer upon ways and means of escaping from the thraldom to armaments beneath which they had allowed themselves to fall.

The result of his action was the summoning of the Peace Conference which met at The Hague in May, 1899. There the

British delegates had supported the principle of international arbitration more cordially than those of most of the Powers which had taken part. Count Muravieff, the Russian Foreign Minister, who had been closely identified with the Czar's ideas, now proposed that England should be allowed to prove her words by acts, and he invited France and Germany to join Russia in offering mediation. Prince von Bülow told the Diet later (November, 1908) that " in no quarter and at no time was the idea of any kind of mediation except peaceful mediation, with the assent of England, entertained." Nevertheless, Germany refused to take part, and, visiting London in November, the Emperor and his Chancellor gave the impression that the reason for her refusal was the discovery that the peace overtures were intended to be a hostile demonstration against England. Encouraged by the cordiality of their reception and the gratitude shown for their timely sympathy, the German visitors went so far as to suggest that as England now knew who her real friends were it would be a suitable opportunity for joining the Triple Alliance. The invitation was declined; but that a change had come over the official British attitude towards Germany at that time was shown by a speech made at Leicester in December by Mr. Chamberlain, then Colonial Secretary, in which he advocated a new alliance between Germany, America, and Great Britain, who together were to be the arbiters of the world's peace, and a little later by a more or less informal suggestion, made by the same statesman, that Germany should be an active participant in the partition of Morocco.

A second invitation to Germany to join Russia and France in mediation, made in the following March, had the same result, and when at the end of the year the Boer delegates were welcomed and fêted in France and other countries they were refused an official welcome in Berlin. The Chancellor would have been willing to advise their reception by the Emperor provided they were introduced by the British ambassador and undertook not to raise an anti-British agitation. As, however, compliance with these conditions was refused, the desired audience did not take place. To all the public appeals which were raised on behalf of the stormy petrels of South Africa Bülow turned a deaf ear. He even spoke slightingly of the " Boer hubbub," told the Diet (December 13, 1900) that he could not " conduct foreign policy from the standpoint of pure ethics," and while disclaiming any idea of being influenced by love of England, refused point-blank to " play the part of a Don Quixote and tilt at English windmills " at the dictation of politicians who allowed their reason to be overruled by sentiment. It was again, as so often in Bismarck's time, a case of irresponsible agitators breaking windows and leaving the Government to repair the damage.[1]

The effect of the Transvaal war, and of the bitter controversies which it created in both countries, was to leave Anglo-German relations worse than before. Nevertheless, the Emperor still seemed firmly resolved to seek the reconciliation of the two nations. His visit to Queen Victoria in her last illness and his presence at her funeral in January, 1901, met with a very warm response in England. In the following year the Prince of Wales was his guest at Potsdam in January; he invited Lord Roberts and several British generals to the autumn manœuvres, and bestowed upon them many marks of distinction; and in November he visited King Edward at Sandringham. These, however, were all personal courtesies, and while they gave satisfaction to peace-lovers in both countries, they left untouched the deeper currents of national feeling.

In the meantime Germany had been busy in the Far East, where she now, for the first time, obtained a foothold. Her interests in China were of a commercial order, and her political relations with the country had been confined to her co-operation with Russia and France in compelling Japan to give back the Liao-Tung peninsula, including Port Arthur, which China had ceded, together with Formosa, to the rising island empire under the Treaty of Shimonoseki at the close of the war of 1894–5. For that service to China France obtained her next loan, while Germany received only the assurance from the Czar that he would have no objection if she were to acquire a piece of Chinese territory for use as a coaling station.[2] Two

---

[1] The foregoing are the motives of German policy in relation to South Africa as openly avowed by the German Government at the time. It is necessary to add that Prince von Bülow, writing some years later, said that the consideration which most influenced Germany in her determination not to intervene in the Boer war was her lack of a sufficiently strong navy (*Imperial Germany*, English translation, p. 31). The Emperor is reported to have made the same admission in private. " For Germany to have thrown herself in the way of Great Britain," he said, " would have been like trying to stop a runaway bull by waving a handkerchief." Whatever their real motives may have been, the action of the Sovereign and his Chancellor for a time completely estranged them from national sympathy.

[2] Hohenlohe, *Memoirs*, vol. ii., p. 463.

years later this suggestion was acted upon. In the autumn of 1897 two German Roman Catholic missionaries were murdered in the Chinese province of Shantung. In expiation Germany demanded and obtained the lease for ninety-nine years of the part of Kiauchau in that province, to be used as a naval station. It was only a small acquisition, but suspecting that a hankering for " prestige politics " was behind the transaction, Bismarck said of it at the time that it was " large enough for all sorts of foolishness." A little later China granted to her new neighbour important railway and mining privileges in the same region, and early in the new year the Emperor's brother, Prince Henry, took over the protectorate amid due state. In a parting address to his envoy at Kiel (December 15th) the Emperor said: " The task which you have to fulfil denotes nothing new; it is the logical consequence of what my grandfather and his great Chancellor began . . . it is the first participation by the newly established German Empire in its duties across the seas." The then Foreign Secretary, Bülow, stated a few weeks later (February 8, 1898) that " the despatch of our squadron was the result, not of sudden impulse, but of mature deliberation and the expression of a policy calm and sure of its end." [1]

Deliberate and calculated though this bold stroke of *Weltpolitik* may have been, it led to results which could not have been anticipated. Germany's example proved the signal for a scramble for Chinese territory by the leading European Powers. Russia promptly obtained Port Arthur, from which she had ejected Japan three years before; England stipulated for Wei-Hai-Wei; and France for Hainan and Kwang-Chow-Wan. All these territories were for decency's sake acquired on lease, though with little idea of again parting with them. When finally Italy put in a claim for Sanmen Bay, the Chinese Government thought it time to cease her forced benefactions.

Encouraged, no doubt, from above, the traditional prejudices of the Chinese against foreigners deepened into hatred, and in the summer of 1898 the Boxer rising broke out, leading to wholesale massacres of the white population and of native

[1] Bülow, who claims in his book *Imperial Germany* (p. 123) that *Weltpolitik* dates from 1897, when he became Foreign Secretary, speaks in the same place of the Treaty of Shantung as " one of the most significant actions in modern German history," since it " secured for us a ' place in the sun ' in the Far East, on the shores of the Pacific Ocean, which have a great future before them " (pp. 96–7).

Christians. The English and American victims, for the most part members of the religious missions, alone numbered two hundred, and reliable estimates placed the number of native Christians murdered as high as thirty thousand. Amongst the victims of Boxer excesses were the German Minister, Baron von Ketteler, and the Japanese Minister, Baron Sugiyama. No allowance was made for Chinese provocation in the prompt reprisals which followed. While Japan hurried a large number of troops to the scene, the principal European Powers and the United States all sent expeditionary corps, and the joint forces were placed under the German general, Count Waldersee. A large combined fleet also assembled in Chinese waters. The Emperor's address to his officers and troops prior to their departure from Bremerhaven on July 27, 1900, in which he charged them " in the name of their oath " to give no quarter to the enemy, and " so to use their weapons that for a thousand years no Chinaman would dare to look sideways at a German," was often recalled to his prejudice in later years. Pekin, which had long been in the hands of the rebels, was relieved in the late summer of 1900, only to suffer more from the rescuers than the Boxers, for it was ruthlessly looted. The Chinese Government had no other choice than to accept the terms imposed by the allies, these including the payment of an indemnity of sixty-six million pounds and the despatch of expiatory missions to the German and Japanese Courts. The mission to Germany was headed by Prince Chun, a member of the reigning family, and it discharged its task in September, 1901.

Having done their best to break up the Chinese Empire, the European Powers now discovered that their interest lay in strengthening it again. Germany and England, during Lord Salisbury's Government, concluded a convention of October, 1900, pledging them to respect the integrity of China and to maintain the policy of the " open door." Later the two Powers were disagreed as to the extent of this agreement, England contending that it bound them to resist Russian advance in Manchuria, which had already begun, Germany that it applied only to China proper. Upon this question the policies of the two Powers soon went apart, for Japan again entered the field as a brake to Russian aggression, and by a treaty of January 30, 1902, she became Great Britain's ally. By this treaty the two Powers undertook to recognize the territorial integrity of the empires of China and Korea, to abstain from acts of aggression therein, to maintain a strict neutrality in the event of either of them becoming involved in war in defence of its interests in these countries, to endeavour to secure the neutrality of other Powers, and to conduct war in common in the event of any other Power or Powers joining in such hostilities.[1]

The importance of this alliance was seen when two years later Russia and Japan found themselves at war. The Treaty of Shimonoseki of 1895 had inflicted upon Japan a humiliation which rankled deeply, and when Russia followed the annexation of Port Arthur by the occupation of Manchuria (1900) and the other Powers, which had been so jealous for the integrity of the Chinese Empire, similarly appropriated portions of Chinese territory, it was evident that Japan had a score for which she would sooner or later require a reckoning. Step by step Russia now advanced from Manchuria into Korea, and, as diplomatic protests led to no result, Japan declared war in February, 1904.

Again, as in 1895, Germany sided with Russia, this time more actively than before. German shipping companies were allowed to sell four large merchant cruisers to the Russian Government; German war material was freely supplied; the Russian fleet shipped German coal in the Baltic before its despatch to East Asia; and so marked was the Emperor's goodwill that Russia was able to denude her western frontier of troops, as Prussia had been able to do in 1866 owing to the benevolent neutrality of France. Although numerically far superior to her rival in military and naval resources, Russia was beaten both on land and sea after a struggle in which desperate endurance and superb courage were shown on both sides. Japan's crowning victories were the capture of Port Arthur after a siege of three months (August 14, 1904), the sanguinary battle of Mukden (March 10, 1905), and the sea-fight of Tsushima (May 27th), in which the entire Russian fleet engaged was either sunk or captured. The war dragged on for two months longer, but in the meantime the combatants

[1] The treaty was first concluded for five years; but in 1905 it was superseded by one larger in scope, inasmuch as it bound each of the allies to help the other in the event of its being attacked by a single Power, and it was henceforth to apply to India. The revised treaty, which was concluded for ten years, was in turn revised in 1911, a supplementary clause now exempting the contracting Powers from the obligation to go to war with any States with which they had concluded treaties of general arbitration so long as such treaties continued in force.

had accepted an offer of mediation made by the President of the United States, and peace was concluded in August and ratified by the Treaty of Portsmouth, U.S.A. (September 5th). Russia ceded to Japan half of the island of Saghalien, which she had annexed in 1875, and Port Arthur, with the Kwangtung peninsula, which she had occupied since 1900, and undertook to hand back Manchuria to China and to recognize Japan's right to a controlling influence in Korea, which that country later annexed.

Germany, by her encouragement, was believed to have helped Russia into the war with Japan; England, by her sympathy, helped her out of it. It was largely due to the influence of that Power with its ally that Japan showed great moderation in the hour of victory, setting greater store on future good relations with Europe than on present advantage. Nevertheless, she gained what for her was vital — a foothold on the mainland and a promising sphere of influence for the abounding activities of her people. Nor was the war altogether a misfortune for Russia, for the internal disorders to which it gave rise led by devious and thorny ways to constitutional government and the institution of a Duma, or national parliament. The German Emperor had decorated both the attacking and defending generals (Nogi and Stoessel) of Port Arthur fame, yet he made no secret of his belief that Japan's victory was a misfortune for Europe and civilization. In March, 1905, he told his recruits at Wilhelmshaven that the victorious Japanese were for Russia " a scourge of God, like Attila and Napoleon in their day," and bade them take heed " lest the Almighty should send a similar trial to Germany "; while in a speech to his officers at Strassburg in the following May he spoke of the " yellow peril," and warned them that as Russia had been unable to withstand it the duty might one day fall to Germany. A speech from the throne, opening the Diet in November, contained a passage in which Japan was welcomed into the ranks of the Great Powers, but the compliment did not alter the fact that Japan had won her position in the face of Germany's active opposition.

Another of Germany's excursions into *Weltpolitik* was more chivalrous than successful. During the Spanish-American war over Cuba in 1898 she took the side of the European Power, and at one time during the blockade of Manila Admiral Dewey had to threaten to turn his guns upon the too officious German vessels of war which were then lying off the coast. After the war Spain showed her gratitude to Germany by agreeing to sell her the Caroline Islands. Germany had claimed the islands as no-man's-land in 1885, but on Spain's protest, on the ground of prior possession, the question of title was referred to Pope Leo XIII, who decided against Germany, but awarded her certain trading rights. Now Germany acquired the islands, and with them the Marianne and Pelew islands, for the sum of £800,000.

The Manila incident had created coolness between Germany and America, and as soon as peace was restored the Emperor, whose proneness to do the wrong thing was conjoined with a singular readiness to recognize his mistakes and rectify them, made the task of reconciliation his own. Pleasing attentions of many kinds were now showered upon the republic in sign that its good-will would be valued. In February, 1902, he sent his brother Prince Henry on a special mission of friendship to President Roosevelt and the American people; but the genial visitor lamented later that while he had seen much of the German-Americans, he had been allowed to see little of the true Americans. In May he presented to the American nation, for erection in Washington, a statue of Frederick the Great. To Harvard University he gave a unique collection of casts of the finest examples of mediæval German sculpture and architecture, taken from cities and towns of the West and South. He also waived in favour of America the rule, which had been laid down in Bismarck's time, that German diplomatic representatives should not marry foreigners. Momentary apprehensions were occasioned when in the succeeding winter arbitrary action by Venezuela led to reprisals, in which Germany took part. The Venezuelan Government had refused to recognize liability for loans and stores forcibly requisitioned from German and other foreign merchants during the civil war of 1898 to 1900, and as all representations made by the States concerned were disregarded, a combined German, British, and Italian fleet blockaded the Venezuelan coast in December, replying to land fire at several points, yet not landing troops. In the United States the naval demonstration was unnecessarily interpreted by a nervous public opinion as a challenge of the Monroe Doctrine, but few reasonable public men took that view. Eventually the dispute was referred to the Court of Arbitration at The Hague, which decided against the Venezuelan Government.

In the summer of 1903 the friendly relationship with the United States was so far restored that an American squadron visited Kiel, where a cordial official welcome awaited it.

To the friendship which sprang up between the Emperor and President Roosevelt at that time was due the inauguration of a plan for a yearly exchange between the two countries of representative professors, one on each side, the American professor lecturing at Berlin and the German at Harvard. The idea originated with Dr. Althoff, perhaps the most enlightened but also the most dictatorial Minister of Education Prussia has ever had, and it took effect in 1905. The original " exchange " professors, as they were called, visited for a single term; but this official system was supplemented by another, due to the formation in America of a fund in connection with Columbia University, whereby, in addition, professors of American universities were enabled to exchange places with professors of any German universities for two successive terms.

In his search for new spheres of influence abroad the Emperor in his own person made overtures to Turkey in 1898. The way had already been prepared by the appointment as ambassador to Constantinople of the strongest man in the diplomatic service, Baron Marschall, who left the Foreign Office the year before in order to undertake that important post. Marschall at once introduced a new departure in diplomatic usage. While other ambassadors, notably the British, had clung to the idea that diplomats were concerned only with high politics, their German colleague, overflowing with energy, began to cultivate diplomacy from the neglected commercial side. The British way may have been the more dignified, but the German way secured the material and subsequently the political rewards. Now German adventurers — engineers, railway contractors, banking agents — poured into Constantinople, bringing with them attractive projects warranted to confer prosperity upon the Sultan's territories and to replete his impecunious coffers. For these projects a ready hearing was obtained at the German embassy, and with its support at Yildiz Kiosk. Fortified by this material argument, German influence waxed, while British influence waned.[1]

[1] Lord Lyons relates that when British ambassador at Constantinople in the years 1865 to 1867 he refused on principle to assist pushing British contractors with their schemes on the ground that " There is often much dirty work connected with the management of such matters at the Porte, and I wish to be clear of them " (*Lord Lyons: a Record of British Diplomacy*, by Lord Newton, vol. i., p. 176).

The prestige of Germany in Turkey was further increased, both politically and economically, by a visit paid to the Sultan, Abdul Hamid II, by the Emperor while on his way to Palestine, in October, 1898. Toasting the Sultan at Damascus before his return home (November 8th), the Emperor used the cryptic words, " May the Sultan and the three hundred million Mussulmans scattered over the earth be assured that the German Emperor will always be their friend." Only two years before the name of Abdul Hamid had been execrated throughout Christendom by reason of the renewed massacres of Armenians which had been perpetrated with his direct connivance. It was regarded as a curious testimony to the tolerant spirit of modern statecraft that a Power which had immemorially claimed to be the bulwark of Protestantism on the Continent now stood forth as the Sultan's special friend. England had in the past cultivated ties with Turkey more intimate than the nation as a whole approved, but she had as the price of friendship gained important concessions for the benefit of the Christian populations under Ottoman rule — for some independence and for all greater security for religion, liberty, and life. About Germany's relations with Turkey there was no sentiment whatever, and the contrary was never pretended. As a later Chancellor (Bülow) said, they were based altogether on political expediency and commercial interest, and in that light both sides viewed them. Not only was Germany at that time engaged in commercial enterprises in the Turkish Empire, but chosen officers of her General Staff were reorganizing the Turkish army and her armament firms were supplying it with cannon.

The Emperor's visit to the East was a political and commercial tour on an imposing scale, intended to *viser* the efforts of the diplomatic agents who had for some time been busily preparing the way. From that time the German Foreign Office and its representatives in Turkey pressed more energetically than ever for trade concessions, and were more successful in obtaining them.[1]

A year later the Sultan handsomely repaid the attentions which had been showered upon him by granting to a German banking combination, calling itself the Imperial Ottoman Railway Company, a railway concession of very elastic propor-

[1] The result was soon seen in a remarkable increase in Germany's trade with Turkey; her share in Turkish imports increased from 2½ per cent. of the whole in the year 1900–1 to 6 per cent. in 1908–9.

tions. This company was an offshoot of the German Anatolian Railway Company, which had already built a line from Haidar Pasha (opposite Constantinople on the Asiatic side of the Straits) to Angora and Konia. Now it was proposed to carry this line through the valley of the Tigris to Bagdad and beyond. Not only was this new evidence of German enterprise a blow to British pride, but there was a peculiar irony in the fact that the Anatolian railway was built by an English company, which afterwards handed it over to a far-seeing syndicate of German banks.

The Bagdad Railway project, which was for many years to provide occasion for mild friction between the four leading European Governments, illustrated in a remarkable way the conjunction of economic pursuits with political aims which from the first characterized German policy in Turkey and the Middle East. Incidentally it also threw a flood of light upon the foresight, energy, and resource by which the modern German industrialist and financier were revolutionizing the old commercial methods. In Asia Minor, as in some other parts of the world, British enterprise had been first to enter the field, only to slacken effort prematurely and so to tempt younger rivals to reap the rewards of its exertions. The earliest railways there had been built and financed by British companies at a time, in the middle of last century, when the influence of Lord Stratford de Redcliffe was still supreme at the Golden Horn. In 1857, with the assistance of that ambassador, a concession was even obtained for a British company authorizing the construction of a line from the coast opposite Cyprus the entire length of the Euphrates valley. It was estimated that the cost would be from eight to ten million pounds, and in view of the inadequate subsidies offered by the Turkish Government and of the fact that the British Government promised no financial help at all the project was not proceeded with. Nevertheless, as late as 1871 a Select Committee of the House of Commons reported favourably upon the construction of a line from a port in the Levant to the Persian Gulf, though holding out no hope of its financial success in the absence of a Government guarantee. It has been suggested that in securing Cyprus for Great Britain in 1878 Lord Beaconsfield had in mind the execution of such a project.[1] From that time forward

[1] See the article on "The Bagdad Railway" in the *Quarterly Review* for October, 1917.

British interest in the commercial development of Asia Minor was no longer maintained at the old level of energy and tenacity, and it was not difficult for the Germans to secure a footing there.

For this eastward pressure of German ambitions and endeavours, however, there had been much diligent preparation. More than half a century before the idea of the future assertion of German influence in Turkey and across the Sea of Marmora had exercised Friedrich List, Wilhelm Roscher, Karl von Rodbertus, and other economists and publicists of great authority in their day. Even the soldier Helmuth von Moltke, later the great strategist, in whom there was a strong vein of imagination, in spite of his hard calling, when visiting Turkey officially in 1841 had speculated upon the creation of a German principality in Palestine. Since then much had been done to establish German influence in Syria and Asia Minor generally, by the introduction of schools, hospitals, and other civilizing agencies, as well as by the more practical enterprise of the engineer, the banker, and the trader. There were also small agricultural colonies of Germans in several parts of the country.

German enterprise was first seriously directed to railway development in Asia Minor in 1888, when the group of financiers named succeeded in obtaining control of the Haidar Pasha-Ismidt line, and also secured a concession for its immediate extension to Angora, a distance of 300 miles, with a conditional right to make further extensions later; and with this concession was given a Government guarantee of interest on a kilometric basis. The responsible promoters of the scheme were the Deutsche Bank and the Württembergische Vereinsbank of Stuttgart, though the concession was assigned to an intermediary. This bold transaction was a direct blow to British diplomatic and commercial prestige at Constantinople; but the full weight of this blow was only felt later, when, owing to various causes, not the least effective of which was want of foresight and prompt decision on the part of Great Britain, the entire project fell into German hands and was financed by German capitalists. In 1893 a concession was given to the German group for the continuation of the railway to Konia. The British ambassador endeavoured to delay the grant of the concession and have the whole question reopened, upon which the German Government let it be understood that British obstruction in Asia Minor meant German obstruction in Egypt, though German support there had been bought by colonial concessions some years before. With the Konia concession was given a new Government guarantee of interest, to be met somehow by an already impoverished and bankrupt treasury. The extension was completed by 1896, and now the scheme of the Bagdad Railway proper took more definite shape.

In a series of new agreements, culminating in the important convention of March, 1903, the German financial group obtained from the Turkish Government a ninety-nine years' concession for the extension of the existing line from Konia to Bagdad by way of Adana and Mosul, and from Bagdad to Basra, on the Shatt-el-Arab, north of the Persian Gulf, with tributary lines to the Syrian coast at Aleppo and elsewhere, to the Persian frontier at Khanikin, north-east of Bagdad, and to the Gulf at a point to be decided later. The concession also comprised the right to establish ports on the Tigris, at Bagdad, on the Shatt-el-Arab at Basra, and at the Gulf terminus, to navigate the inland waterways, and to work minerals within an area of fifteen miles on either side of the line.

Exploited to its full extent, the concession would have given to Germany unquestioned economic supremacy throughout the most important part of Asiatic Turkey. In obtaining it the railway group unquestionably owed much of its success to boldness, resource, persistence, and readiness to face risks; but it was also greatly assisted by the influence which the Government in Berlin and its diplomatic agents in Constantinople were able and ready to employ in its service, and which was all the more effective owing to the fact that Germany's relations with the Porte had never been clouded by animus against the rigours of Ottoman rule and constant interference in the interests of its victims. Here Great Britain was at a great disadvantage, for it was the time of her political isolation in Europe. In Egypt she was still struggling against opposition both from Turkey and France; the Boer war had turned almost the entire Continent against her; and there seemed then no promise of the series of international accords which were before long to restore her shaken friendships and rehabilitate her prestige.

When the earlier concessions were obtained, in 1888 and again in 1893, the Governments of Great Britain and of France, though well aware of what was going on, appear to have viewed the Bagdad project with cheerful indifference. Even when in 1903 the promoters of the railway, needing money, invited these two Powers to come in and each subscribe one quarter of the capital, while Germany and the Anatolian Railway Company were together to provide the remainder, they still held back. Now the Russian Government also opposed the scheme, as foreboding aggression in Persia, where she claimed a special position. Public opinion in the three countries whose Governments thus stood aloof seemed to be agreed in the conclusion that the hostility offered to the Bagdad Railway project at that time was either very wise or very foolish, but was unable to decide which. For the present, however, obstruction succeeded, to the annoyance of the German Government, which had been behind the promoters, as it was behind other large industrial and commercial enterprises in which German capital was now being freely invested in the Near East.

It was from the beginning inevitable that Germany's endeavour to assert an economic grip upon Asia Minor would sooner or later bring her into antagonism with Great Britain, which had immemorial interests of an imperial as well as a commercial character in that region. Her earlier railway enterprise there has already been mentioned. Apart from that large stake, however, she had enjoyed special navigation privileges on the Tigris and the Euphrates since the reign of Charles I, while her influence in the Persian Gulf had been paramount for more than a hundred years, insomuch that the buoying and policing of that water had been recognized as her exclusive right. It is not too much to say that the very security of the Gulf and its shores and the prosperity of Lower Mesopotamia had been established under British influence.

Hitherto the British Government in holding aloof from the Bagdad Railway project had believed itself to be sufficiently protected by its traditional rights and by the knowledge that the increase of the Turkish customs dues, which was believed to be necessary if the guarantee of interest was to be met, could not take effect without its assent. Now, however, that there was no uncertainty as to the character and extent of the power which threatened to pass into the hands of a country which had only recently appeared upon the scene, an attitude of complete inaction was no longer safe or possible. It is evident from words used by the Prime Minister of the day (Mr. Balfour) in the House of Commons (April 8, 1903) that the Government had ceased to attach the old importance to its right of veto upon the customs dues, and that it now entertained no doubt that, whether with or without British co-operation, the great engineering scheme was practicable and would sooner or later be carried out in its full extent. It would also appear that the British Government was now disposed to join in the project, subject to the condition that the entire line from Haidar Pasha to the Gulf should be under some form of international control, securing to Great Britain an equal voice with Germany or any other Power in its administration, and that there should be no interference with the existing political status on the Gulf. If this, however, was the official British opinion, the view still held in political and financial circles generally was that Germany was more dependent upon outside co-operation and good-will than she was willing to admit, and that against British opposition the execution of the scheme in its entirety would prove impracticable.

In the event the conversations on the subject of British participation failed to lead to a definite result, and the German *concessionnaires*, drawing upon their own resources, continued to build the line, though progress was for a long time slow owing to engineering obstacles, financial difficulties both at home and in Turkey, and later the political convulsions incidental to the Young Turkish movement, leading to a merely temporary decline of German influence in Constantinople.

While thus Germany was gradually superseding Great Britain in the esteem of Turkey, that apparent gain was counterbalanced by less doubtful loss elsewhere, for gaining influence with the Sultan meant corresponding estrangement from Russia. Great Britain, too, was not without compensations. For Germany's " new course " in Oriental politics and her constant concern to identify herself with Austrian interests in the Balkans were, more than any other causes, responsible for that reorientation in the relations of the Powers which changed the position of Great Britain from one of isolation to one of commanding influence.

There is no more remarkable chapter in the history of modern European politics than that which records how at the beginning of the twentieth century Great Britain took the place in the Concert of the Powers which Germany, under Bismarck's guidance, had held for twenty years. The years from 1890 to 1900 may be regarded as the propagandist period of German world-politics, as carried on by the third Emperor, and at the end of that period Germany had unquestionably fewer friends in Europe than at the beginning. Throughout the greater part of that decade England, too, from various causes, suffered from obstinate unpopularity, which during the Boer war took the form in some quarters of unmeasured dislike, yet the end saw most of her enemies willing and waiting to be conciliated, while she herself, having taken stock of her old antipathies, had learned in the school of adversity to place a higher value upon foreign friendships.

It was customary at that time to speak of England's position as, in Lord Salisbury's phrase, one of " splendid isolation." Stolid and impassionate both in its likes and dislikes, taking the joys and bearing the sorrows of its world-wide responsibilities " neither with too great concern," never greatly desiring to have friends, if to have them involved an effort, and in general caring little what the rest of mankind thought or said about it, the British nation almost seemed to have settled down to the belief that its permanent destiny was the loneliness of the great and the misunderstood. The Gladstone and Rosebery Cabinets of 1892–1895 had endeavoured to approach both France and Russia, and it was the knowledge of these advances that caused the German Government to hail with lively satisfaction the return of Lord Salisbury to power in July of the latter year. Great was the surprise felt in Berlin when the new Government showed a disposition to continue in the same path of conciliation.

More than any other British statesman it was Lord Lansdowne, Foreign Secretary during the later years of the Conservative Government of 1895 and again in that of 1902, who succeeded in persuading his countrymen that it was no virtue in a nation to be without friends, if friends were to be had on acceptable terms, and who directed British policy into new channels. Perhaps prudential considerations more than any serious moral stirring on the subject of the comity of nations convinced the British Government of that day of the unwisdom of an excessive detachment from the rest of Europe. Isolation might be safe for a nation sufficiently strong on land and sea to defy any hostile combination; but England's land forces were hopelessly insufficient, and were never designed, for a struggle with Continental Powers, while her naval power, though still supreme, was being threatened.

In abandoning its old attitude of cold aloofness the British Foreign Office had an invaluable helper in King Edward VII, who from the moment of his accession in January, 1901, devoted himself heart and soul to the cause of international conciliation. The new Sovereign may not have been a man of conspicuous intellectual parts, and books and book-knowledge may have bored him as much as some of his biographers have said; but he had other gifts of greater value in the occupant of a throne — ripe experience and judgment, wide knowledge of the world and of human nature, unfailing tact, and consummate common sense. No man was better fitted to act as his country's unofficial envoy in the service of good-will and peace. The leader of the German National Liberal party, comparing his methods and influence in European politics with those of his nephew, said: " The King of England travels, too, but without talking." That was not quite correct: it was nevertheless true that King Edward spoke in whispers. He visited the more important European Courts, and wherever he went he established new or strengthened old ties, for here the genius for friendship which distinguished him in private life found a perfectly congenial sphere. It would be untrue to say that he initiated the policy of international accords which is commonly associated with his name, but he contributed largely to its success.

But at reciprocal professions of good-will this new spirit in British diplomacy did not stay. The Foreign Office adopted a new *leit-motif* in the idea that a statesmanship worth the name could not be content with the negative duty of warding off the menace of war, but should endeavour to remove the conditions which made such a danger possible. This idea took practical shape in a series of five agreements concluded with France in 1904, during the Government of Mr. A. J. Balfour, settling points of disagreement between the two countries in various parts of the world. For a long time Great Britain and France had fratched and bickered at each other without having the heart for a downright quarrel. The principal subject of discord was Egypt. In spite of the pacification of that country, England's withdrawal from it had proved impracticable, owing to the magnitude of the task of reconstruction and the hopelessness of raising up a native administration capable of meeting it. On the other hand, France, thrust out of Egypt, was not disposed to abandon the hope of establishing herself higher up the Nile; and it was with this aim in view that M. Hanotaux, while Foreign Minister, sent Colonel Marchand to that region as an "emissary of civilization" on a roving expedition in 1896, though the year before the deliberate warning had been uttered in the British House of Commons (March 28, 1895) that the despatch of a French expedition into the Nile valley would be regarded as an "unfriendly act." On July 10, 1898, a month after the British and French Governments had concluded a general delimitation treaty (June 14th) defining the spheres of influence of the two countries in North Africa, greatly to the advantage of France, who now had a priceless opportunity of consolidating her interests, actual and anticipated, in the North-west, Marchand reached Fashoda, capital of Bar-el-Ghazal, on the Upper Nile, and hoisted the tricolour. Arriving there two months later (September 19th) fresh from the subdual of the Mahdist rebellion at Omdurman and the fall of Khartoum, General Kitchener disputed possession in the name of Great Britain and Egypt.[1] The incident gave rise to strong feeling in France, though danger of actual rupture existed only in the imagination of a frenzied Press. As the result of an exchange of Notes the French Government formally withdrew all claims to territorial advantage in the Soudan, while in March, 1899, a further convention was concluded in amplification of that of the preceding year. Later the name Fashoda was blotted from the map as one of unhappy memories, and the place was henceforth known as Kodok.

M. Delcassé had in the meantime succeeded M. Hanotaux as Foreign Minister, and he retained the confidence of the Chamber in that capacity for the long period of seven years. While M. Hanotaux had leaned towards Germany, M. Delcassé was a warm friend of England. He is reported to have said in November, 1898, just after his appointment, that he " wished

[1] " In order to give an outward and visible sign that in the eyes of the British Government the political status of the Soudan differed from that of Egypt, Lord Kitchener was instructed, on the capture of Khartoum, to hoist both the British and Egyptian flags side by side. These orders were duly executed. . . . That meant that the Soudan was to be governed by a partnership of two, of which England was the predominant member." (The Earl of Cromer, *Modern Egypt*, vol. ii., p. 115.)

not to leave the Chamber or lay down office until he had established a good understanding (*la bonne entente*) with England." That was undoubtedly one of the leading objects of his foreign policy, and he realized it completely. It was largely owing to his untiring efforts that the long-standing Anglo-French frictions were overcome and the relations between the two countries placed on a cordial footing. Here the tact and affability of King Edward proved invaluable. While still Prince of Wales he had helped to smooth not a few rough places in Anglo-French relationships. Now his first official visit abroad as King was made to the French President, M. Loubet. Delayed by the illness which deferred his coronation more than a year and a half, the visit took place in May, 1903. As a private individual the King had often visited and had greatly endeared himself to Paris. Visiting the city now as a Sovereign, he was enthusiastically welcomed, and all France shared in the satisfaction of the Parisians when once again, for the first time since the fall of the Second Empire, the British Sovereign came to them as an official guest. Two months later the President visited London in return, and there had a flattering reception, while in October the ground for more practical measures of reconciliation was laid by the conclusion of the Anglo-French treaty of arbitration, providing for the submission of disputes of certain kinds to adjudication by the tribunal at The Hague.

Already the two Governments, in the persons of their Foreign Secretaries, Lord Lansdowne and M. Delcassé, had agreed in conferences in London upon the necessity of a comprehensive settlement of all open questions, and active negotiations were now pursued to this end. On April 8th of the following year (1904) agreements were signed in London by Lord Lansdowne and M. Paul Cambon, the French ambassador, settling long-standing disputes regarding the Newfoundland fisheries, Siam, Senegambia, Madagascar, and the New Hebrides, but above all closing the question of Egypt, where France gave England an entirely free hand, while England in return undertook to efface herself in Morocco in the interest of France.

CHAPTER XXII

(1904–1906)

FOREIGN RELATIONS — (ii) MOROCCO

BETWEEN the Berlin Congress and the beginning of the new century no more disturbing question appeared upon the political horizon of Europe than that of the settlement of Morocco, a country of which Lord Salisbury, with notable prescience, said in 1891, while Prime Minister, that it was destined to be "as great a trouble to Europe" and to "carry with it as great a menace to the peace of Europe as the other Mohammedan countries further to the East twenty or thirty years ago." [1] It seems desirable to detach this question, made acute by the Anglo-French convention of April, 1904, from the general survey of foreign politics at this point, since to view it merely as one episode amongst others, with most of which it had little direct connection, might involve the danger of a wrong perspective, leading either to the exaggeration or, more probably, the minimizing of its true proportions.

The full significance of the provisions of the convention relating to Morocco cannot be appreciated unless antecedent facts are borne in mind. For half a century the policy of Great Britain in regard to that country had followed the principles laid down by Lord Palmerston. "How could we," wrote that statesman to Lord Clarendon on March 1, 1857, "combine to be unprovoked aggressors — to imitate in Africa the partition of Poland by *the conquest of Morocco for France*, of Tunis or some other State for Sardinia, and of Egypt for England? And more especially, how could England and France, who have guaranteed the integrity of the Turkish Empire, turn round and wrest Egypt from the Sultan? A coalition for such a purpose would revolt the moral feelings of mankind, and would certainly be fatal to any English Government that was a party to it. Then as to the balance of power to be maintained by giving us Egypt. In the first place we don't want Egypt . . . and its possession would not, as a political,

[1] Speech at Glasgow, March 10, 1891.

military and naval question, be considered in this country as a set-off against the possession of Morocco by France. Let us try to improve all these countries by the general influence of our commerce, but let us all abstain from a crusade of conquest which would call down upon us the condemnation of all the other civilized countries."

These characteristically dogmatic utterances were strictly in keeping with British policy ever since Nelson's declaration that Tangier must either remain in the hands of Morocco or pass into those of England. Two years after Palmerston thus wrote the British Government refused to allow Spain to occupy that greatly coveted port. During the succeeding four decades the main objects of British diplomacy in Morocco had been to confirm its independence and particularly to ward off menace from France. In the meantime not only Great Britain but the European Powers generally had ceased to be squeamish on the subject of territorial rights where undeveloped countries were deemed to obstruct the path of progress, and above all the free advance of trade. Nevertheless, as late as 1889, Lord Salisbury, as British Prime Minister, had formulated the attitude of his Government touching the status in the Mediterranean in the words:

"Our treaty obligations are matters of public property. . . . Our policy with respect to Europe and the shores of the Mediterranean has been avowed again and again to be a policy of peace, of maintaining things as they are. . . . If there is any particular change which I might indicate as, in our judgment, more pernicious than another, it is a change which would increase the territories of any of the Great Powers of Europe, because such a change would have the infallible effect of raising dread and apprehension and jealousy in other Powers, and of precipitating us into a catastrophe which we are all anxious to avoid." [1]

Morocco had for a long time been a source of growing anxiety and contention to European diplomacy, but its independence had never hitherto been seriously threatened. When in 1880 eleven States, including the United States, concluded with the Moorish Government the Convention of Madrid (July 3rd), conferring upon all the signatory Powers increased trading facilities and the right of most-favoured-nation treatment,

[1] Speech in the London Guildhall, November 9, 1889.

and so made the affairs of Morocco for the first time an international concern, they negotiated with it as the Government of a sovereign State. Later commercial treaties with the country, like the earlier ones, similarly proceeded from that presupposition. Moreover, if any Powers were more than others under a moral pledge to respect the *status quo*, those Powers were France, Great Britain, and Spain. On the other hand, the Power which next to Great Britain had in the past shown the greatest desire to work harmoniously with the rest of Europe in all dealings with an empire whose ruler responded unwillingly to outside influences was Germany. Ten years after the Madrid Convention had paved the way for freer mercantile relations with Morocco, Germany concluded a special commercial treaty with the Sultan (June 1, 1890), but before allowing it to be ratified she submitted it to the judgment of the other Powers.

The same attitude, cautious towards Morocco and considerate towards the Powers, was held by the British Government when two years later it despatched to the Moorish Court a special mission, under Colonel Sir Charles Euan-Smith, with a view to the conclusion of an improved commercial treaty. Special care was taken on that occasion to prevent any suspicion that the mission had a political purpose. The instructions issued to the envoy extraordinary set forth that " it has been the constant aim of her Majesty's Government and of your predecessors at Tangier to preserve the independence and territorial integrity of the empire of Morocco, while neglecting no opportunity of impressing upon the Sultan and his Ministers the importance and advantage of improving the government and administration of the country," and he was bidden to act faithfully in the spirit of that tradition.

When later the military head of the mission was eager to be authorized, in the event of difficulties arising with the Sultan, to " hold language to his Majesty of a character more vigorous than that of mere remonstrance and disappointment," such permission was promptly refused, Lord Salisbury directing him to abstain from any action which might give colour to the idea that Great Britain wished to employ menace or to assume the protection of the country. Before the draft treaty was presented to the Sultan it was submitted to the principal Powers, in proof that Great Britain sought for herself no special privileges. The Governments of Austria-Hungary, Germany, Italy, and Spain approved of its provisions; only the Government of France withheld assent.

The mission set out amid imposing circumstance, and after remaining three months in the country obtained the acceptance of a treaty which fell far short of the proposals at first put forward. When, however, it came to the signing of the agreement the Sultan drew back. The treaty had been pressed upon him as the most efficacious means of protecting himself against territorial aggrandizement by covetous Powers, and there was no concealment of the fact that French hostility prevented its ratification and no doubt as to the reason for this hostility.

For some years after this French influence was pressed on Morocco with growing insistence, and in the same degree British efforts to maintain the Sultan's authority and independence increased, with the result that at the beginning of the new century Great Britain, and not France, was in special favour at the Shereefian Court. A clear suggestion of how France intended that events should be shaped was conveyed in a letter written on July 27, 1901, by the French Foreign Minister, M. Delcassé, to the French envoy at Tangier, wherein he said that France could be, in Bismarckian phrase, either " a good friend or a good enemy," just as the Moorish Government wished, yet still instructing him to assure the Sultan that it was her wish to uphold his independence and to preserve him from danger.[1] Asked in June, 1901, by the German ambassador in Paris whether there was any truth in the report that France designed a protectorate, M. Delcassé replied: " If by the word ' protectorate ' it is implied that France, as the mistress of Algeria and Tunis, has and should preserve in Morocco an entirely special position, it seems to me self-evident." Of a protectorate so innocently defined the ambassador remarked that " nothing could be more proper."

Nevertheless, in the same year the French Government made proposals to Spain, the Sagasta Cabinet being in power, for the partition of the country, of which Spain was to have the Mediterranean littoral with a stretch of *hinterland*, compris-

[1] French Yellow Book on Morocco, published on December 14, 1915, which contains a full account of the diplomatic relations of France with the Moorish Government and of the French communications with Germany on the subject of the agreement of April, 1904. The published British and German official sources should also be consulted.

ing Fez and Tuza, and France the remainder. After the negotiations had dragged on until the end of the following year, without reaching an issue, Sagasta resigned, and his successor, Señor Silvela, declined to proceed further along a path which he perceived to be beset with manifold dangers. His avowed reason for renouncing the agreement was that in it and all the negotiations relating to it Great Britain had been entirely ignored. Little more than a year passed before the negotiations which had broken down in Madrid were reopened in London, leading to the agreement of April 4, 1904.

In so far as it related to Morocco this agreement was divided into a public and a secret section. The public agreement, which was called by the less suggestive name " Declaration," affirmed that the French Government had no intention of altering the political status of Morocco, though it contained no definite undertaking that an alteration should not take place, and certain of the provisions clearly anticipated that contingency. The British Government, on the other hand, recognized that " it appertains to France, particularly as a Power whose dominions are coterminous for a great distance with those of Morocco, to preserve order in that country and to provide assistance for the purpose of all administrative, economic, financial, and military reforms which it may require," and declared that it would " not obstruct the action taken by France for this purpose, provided that such action shall leave intact the rights which Great Britain, in virtue of treaties, conventions, and usage, enjoys in Morocco."

The two Governments also agreed to maintain in Morocco and Egypt respectively, at first for a period of thirty years, the principles of commercial equality and equal taxation as between the different nationals. In order to secure " the free passage of the Straits of Gibraltar " they undertook " not to permit the erection of any fortifications or strategic works on that portion of the coast of Morocco comprised between, but not including, Melilla and the heights which command the right bank of the river Sebou "; but this condition was not to apply to the places already in the occupation of Spain on the Moorish coast of the Mediterranean, of which Melilla was one.

Nothing was said specifically as to the rights of other countries, except in the case of Spain, whose special interests the signatory Powers recognized, on which account the agreement provided that France and Spain should come to an understanding on the subject, duly communicating its terms to the British Government.

Finally — a momentous provision, as it was to prove — the contracting Governments agreed to " afford to one another their diplomatic support in order to obtain the execution " of the agreement.

More important than the Declaration, however, were the five secret articles which were attached to it and which were not made public until November, 1911, and then, in the first instance, by a Paris newspaper.   One of these secret articles was intended to safeguard the engagements specified in the general agreement in the event of the French Government finding itself constrained, by the force of circumstances, to modify its policy in respect to Morocco.   Another stipulated that the Mediterranean coastline of Morocco, with a tract of the *hinterland*, should come within the Spanish sphere of influence " whenever the Sultan ceases to exercise authority over it " ; that Spain should not alienate the whole or any part of such territory to another Power ; and that her acquisition of the territory should be conditional upon her acceptance of the articles of the Declaration relating to the maintenance in Morocco of economic parity and the prohibition of new coastal fortifications.

In the following October the French and Spanish Governments supplemented these agreements by a public Declaration and an accompanying secret convention of sixteen articles. The Declaration affirmed their attachment to " the integrity of the Moorish empire under the sovereignty of the Sultan," while the secret convention contained elaborate provisions for the future partition of that empire and the conditions under which such partition should take effect.   A special sphere of influence was assigned to Spain, and within it she was freely to exercise her right of action " in case the continuance of the political status of Morocco and of the Shereefian Government should become impossible, or if, owing to the weakness of that Government and to its continued inability to uphold law and order, or to any other cause, the existence of which is acknowledged by both parties, the *status quo* can no longer be maintained."   These secret engagements likewise came to full light only seven years later, and in the same circumstances as those of earlier date.

The two agreements formed in effect a single comprehensive transaction. Stripped of their merely formal reservations, they amounted to a claim by Great Britain and France to dispose of Morocco without regard to any other States save one, though most of the European Powers and also the United States possessed treaty rights in the country. Great Britain, it is true, did not expressly hand over to France the sovereignty of Morocco, for to do that was not within her power, but she put France in the way of obtaining it and undertook to give to her diplomatic support in any measures which she might take to that end. France thus came appreciably nearer to the realization of a project of which nearly half a century before (1857) Lord Palmerston wrote as " the secret aim of Louis Philippe," and as " one of the plans deposited for use, as occasion may offer, in the archives of the French Government."

For Great Britain the agreement of April, 1904, was, of course, an entire and abrupt reversal of the policy regarding Morocco which had been enunciated by Palmerston, hitherto accepted by all succeeding British Governments and statesmen, and loyally supported by the British diplomatic representatives accredited to the Moorish Court, and notably by Sir John Drummond Hay. By the agreement Morocco was still to remain independent; *de facto* it was to pass under the control of France on conditions which provided for that control leading eventually to occupation and annexation. Yet the essential fact to be emphasized at this stage, and to be remembered at all later stages by those who impartially seek the truth of this sorely entangled episode, is that neither Great Britain nor France had any proprietary rights whatever, actual or contingent, in Morocco, and strictly speaking had no business to discuss, still less to dispose of, the future of the sultanate at all.

A quarter-century before Lord Salisbury, when British Foreign Secretary, had refused to do for France in regard to Tunis what Great Britain now proposed to do for her in regard to Morocco. " If France occupied Tunis to-morrow we should not even remonstrate," he wrote to Lord Lyons on July 20, 1878, parrying inopportune pressure from the French Government on the point; yet he took care to add, " but to promise that publicly would be a little difficult, because we must avoid giving away other people's property without their consent, and also because it is no business of ours to pronounce beforehand on the considerations which Italy would probably advance upon that subject." Great Britain, in fact, opposed French claims to Tunis to the end, and when they were pressed to the point of annexation offered the only resistance still possible in the circumstances — a vigorous and honest protest.

Let Morocco be substituted for Tunis and Germany for Italy, and the position was the same in 1904 as in 1878, except that where twenty-six years before Great Britain asserted, and for some time succeeded in preserving, the rights of an independent North African State menaced by France, she was now prepared to help France to acquire rights of a precisely similar kind in return for corresponding advantages. Many things had, of course, changed in the relations of these and other Powers in the interval, and it would be absurd to pretend that in foreign politics the precept and practice of one Government can be binding upon succeeding Governments for all time. Inasmuch, however, as Germany later reproached Great Britain for having abandoned her traditional attitude towards Morocco, in holding which Germany had been her warmest supporter, it is the more important to visualize the question as it appeared to the Government and public opinion of that country.

Nevertheless, it cannot be said that the agreement, so far as it was divulged at the time, created great surprise, for the conditions in Morocco had for some time been intolerable. Growing friction with France had resulted from the inability of the Sultan, Abdul Aziz, to preserve order in his own household. There were local rebellions, frequent raids by Moorish tribes on the Algerian frontier, and occasionally French convoys were attacked and captured. Events of this kind kept large parts of the country in unrest, and acted in restraint of legitimate commercial intercourse. France had repeatedly co-operated in suppressing frontier disturbances, but in May, 1903, the position was so unsatisfactory that Abdul Aziz formally appealed to her for help in the establishment of his authority, and this help was duly given. In this way France had steadily increased her influence and strengthened her claim to a special position in the country. If a spirit of aggression drove her forward, as it undoubtedly did, it must be frankly admitted that she was also urged into action by circumstances which were only in a partial degree within her control.

Before 1904, therefore, the diplomatic world of Europe knew how events were moving, and it is not likely that to this world the Anglo-French agreements came as a shock. In Germany, more than in any other country, recent French action in Morocco had been followed with suspicion. In March, 1904, the French ambassador in Berlin, M. Bihourd, reported to Paris that the Pan-Germans were restive and, at a congress held in Würtemberg, had called on the Government to claim for Germany a special sphere of influence in West Morocco, to comprise the ports of Qualidia and Agadir, in case the *status quo* should be disturbed. Later in the same month Prince Radolin, the German ambassador in Paris, privately asked the French Foreign Minister whether it was true that an agreement with Great Britain had been, or was on the point of being, signed, whereupon M. Delcassé replied that while there had been negotiations for a long time and a positive understanding was probable, " nothing had been signed or was on the point of being signed." The Anglo-French Declaration was, in fact, signed and sealed only eleven days later.

The reception of the agreement in Great Britain was a mixed one; but perhaps in the minds of most people the complete reconciliation with France, of which it was held to be a token, overshadowed for the moment all other considerations. In so far as the agreement purported to be a business transaction, there was a disposition to judge it unfavourably and to conclude that the Government had been outwitted. An earlier Foreign Secretary, Lord Rosebery, asserted at the time that " no more one-sided agreement was ever concluded between two Powers at peace with each other." Viewing this agreement alone, and independently of the other territorial settlements to which it belonged, this was strictly true; for while France merely recognized a British tenure in Egypt which existed *de facto* already, and could no longer be shaken, Great Britain conceded to France a status in Morocco which she had not hitherto held or claimed. This was the view generally taken in France, where the *Journal des Débats* claimed that " France has only conceded rights which were without value save for the purpose of hindering and annoying the British; while the latter

Power has granted most important concessions of real and practical value."

France had, in fact, received far more than she had ever hoped for. Long as her eyes had been turned to Morocco, her responsible statesmen had recognized that if ever French influence were to be established in the country it must be subject to important limitations, of which those most readily accepted were the integrity of the sultanate, the maintenance of the sovereignty of the Shereefs, the guarantee of complete commercial freedom, and, not least, the neutralization of Tangier. Not only so, but there is reason to believe that France, remembering the bad blood which had been created by the Tunis episode, would only have been too glad to receive permission to enter Morocco at the hands of the Powers collectively, as their mandatary, which would have meant on their conditions.

If, however, the Morocco convention appeared to show France as the better bargainer, the series of Anglo-French territorial agreements as a whole conferred upon Great Britain very substantial advantages. Irritating disputes of long standing in other parts of the world, not least embarrassing that relating to the Newfoundland fisheries, were finally adjusted, and — a political gain of the utmost value — the wound to French national pride which had been caused by the Fashoda episode was now healed. Even in Morocco Great Britain induced France to forgo claim to any part of the Mediterranean littoral, so renouncing the hope of obtaining an outlook upon the Straits of Gibraltar, though she was to be cut off from the Atlantic only in the extreme north.

Lord Rosebery called attention to a more serious aspect of the Morocco agreement when he said that it committed Great Britain to " the unwritten liabilities of the Continental system," therein speaking more truly than he knew at the time. Many other leaders of political opinion in Great Britain, almost exclusively on the Liberal side, entertained the same misgiving, and already detected in the agreement an implied pledge of obligations of indefinite extent. Nevertheless, whether opposed or not to the apparent reversal of England's traditional policy, described by Canning as " revolving in her own orbit," all parties were alike relieved that an *entente* with France had been established. One of the immediate results of this *entente* was that France, relying upon British friendship for the se-

curity of her northern coast, transferred her Channel fleet to
the Mediterranean, while Great Britain was able to release vessels in the Mediterranean for future service in the North Sea
and Scandinavian waters.

While the British Government communicated to the Powers
directly concerned that part of the agreement which related to
Egypt, the Morocco stipulations were not similarly communicated either by that Government or the French, though a general statement on the subject was made to the German ambassador in Paris and, through the French ambassador in
Berlin, to the German Foreign Secretary.[1] Relying upon
French pledges, the German Government appears to have anticipated the conclusion of the agreement without anxiety.
The Ministerial journal, the *North German Gazette*, reflected
this attitude when it stated (March 26th): "In view of the
repeated assurances officially given by France that she has no
thought of conquest or occupation, but simply aims at opening
North-west Africa to European civilization, there is no reason
to believe that German commercial interests in Morocco are
in danger." At the end of the month M. Delcassé again assured the German ambassador in Paris that France wished to
"uphold in Morocco the existing political and territorial
status," adding that "that status, if it is to last, must obviously be reinforced (*soutenu*) and improved"—a reservation far more likely to remove than to arouse suspicion.
While, however, it seems clear that in the various communications which were made by the French Government to the German Foreign Office through the recognized diplomatic media in
Paris and Berlin only the purport of the public Declaration
was disclosed, it is probable that the existence and even the
general terms of the secret articles soon became known in that
quarter.[2]

[1] When at a later date the German Chancellor, then Count von Bülow,
denied that the Morocco provisions of the Declaration of April, 1904, were
communicated to his Government either by the British or the French
Foreign Office, M. Delcassé pleaded in excuse that as the treaty was concluded in London he had not thought such communication necessary. It is
obvious, however, that if it was not the duty of the French Government to
make known the full terms of the Morocco arrangement, that duty could
not reasonably be attributed to the British Government.

[2] Defending himself, on April 13, 1904, against the reproach that the
agreement, when signed, had not been formally communicated to the German ambassador for transmission to his Government, M. Delcassé suggested
to Prince Radolin that the explanations which had been given before the

In a letter addressed to the French diplomatic representatives abroad (April 12th), notifying the conclusion of the five Anglo-French agreements, M. Delcassé said in regard to Morocco that it was " necessary to know whose influence should preponderate " in the country, and he again used the words, " The present state of things can only last on condition of its being reinforced and improved." He added that it was the duty of France to show herself " the best friend of Morocco because most interested in her prosperity," and that her civilizing mission there could be carried out " *sans léser les droits acquis de personne.*" This letter likewise contained no reference to the secret articles.

It follows that in the spring of 1904 not only Europe at large but the nations directly affected were compelled to judge of the significance of the Anglo-French *entente* upon incomplete evidence.

The secret articles of both treaties have been defended on the plea that to have affirmed the integrity of the Sultan's empire and at the same time made known the arrangements for dividing it, in the event of its government proving incapable of reform, would simply have precipitated the end of Moorish rule. On the contrary, unless ultimate annexation was deliberately contemplated — a question which only France was in a position to answer — it would have been at least a negative merit to have made these provisions public, for to have done so would have given to the Sultan and his unruly people a fair warning in advance that the watchful eyes of the two neighbouring Powers were upon them, and that unless they mended their ways these Powers were prepared and determined to give to their country order and good government in spite of themselves. To hold in reserve, in the dark, the weapon of partition and annexation may have been considerate to the Sul-

agreement was signed left nothing to be added. " I even revealed to you," he said, " the principal stipulations of the arrangements affecting Morocco, that is to say, assistance by France to the Sultan for the establishment of security, which would encourage commercial operations, absolute and strict respect for freedom of trade, and recognition of the situation and interests of Spain." There is no suggestion here of the vital articles providing for the contingent partition of the country. Nevertheless, such and so many are the opportunities for the leakage of diplomatic confidences in modern times, that there can be little doubt that at least the purport of these articles quickly came to the knowledge of the Continental Chancelleries. Before the later Franco-Spanish agreement had been concluded the fact that it contained secret provisions was published generally in the Press.

tan's feelings, but it was distinctly menacing to his independence. Nowhere was the resentment caused by the later disclosure of the secret commitments greater than in France.[1]

Although knowing as yet but little of the meaning of the Anglo-French agreement, German opinion nevertheless at once became nervous over the sudden reconciliation of two Powers whose hostility had been regarded as part of the ordained order of things; but it is important to note, in view of later events, that the Chancellor, Count von Bülow, professed to welcome it as " natural and inoffensive." He regarded it as a sensible attempt on the part of the two Powers to settle their colonial disputes amicably, as Germany and England had done already, and of the treaty he said in the Diet (April 14, 1904) : " From the standpoint of German interests we have no objection to raise to it. For a strained relationship between the two nations would be a menace to the peace of the world, the maintenance of which we sincerely desire." He added: " As to Morocco, which constitutes the essential part of the agreement, we are interested in that country, as elsewhere in the Mediterranean, principally from the economic standpoint. Our interests there are, above all, commercial, so that we have an important interest in the maintenance of tranquillity and order. It is our duty to protect our mercantile interests in Morocco, and we shall protect them, but we have no reason to fear that they will be ignored or injured by any Power whatsoever."

Bülow had told a representative of the Paris *Figaro* in May, 1902: " Our (German) interests in Morocco are less than in China. To speak frankly, I do not look upon this question as one likely so very soon to occupy our diplomacy. We have no bay-window frontage on the Mediterranean. In Morocco, as in China, we want peace as the sole condition of our economic expansion." He appears to have been still of the same

[1] Baron d'Estournelles de Constant asked in the French Senate on February 6, 1912: " Why was the French Parliament told only half the truth when it was asked to pass its opinion upon our arrangement with England? . . . It was a treaty of friendship with England, recognizing the freedom of our political action in Morocco, and also proclaiming our will to respect the integrity of that country; that was what the public knew and approved. But the public was ignorant that at the same time, by other treaties and by contradictory clauses hidden from it, the partition of Morocco between Spain and France was prepared — that Morocco of which we guaranteed the integrity."

mind. Rejecting a suggestion that Germany should at once protest against the agreement, he said:

"It has been stated that this agreement, and particularly that part referring to Morocco, has been received in Germany with shame and dejection. The (previous) speaker maintained that we suffer other Powers to assume for themselves a greater influence in Morocco than we have. That could only have one meaning, namely, that we demanded a portion of Morocco for ourselves. But if a great Empire like the German Empire makes a demand, it must carry it through, *coûte que coûte*. Now, what would he advise if such a demand were to meet with opposition? Should I have to draw the sword? I believe that just at present, the moment when a war is raging in the Far East, the consequences of which are still incalculable, and when much is still unsettled in the Near East, a policy of sobriety, calmness, and reserve is most useful for us in the interests of the Empire, and I will not allow any foreign or any malicious or impatient home criticism to dictate to me the moment when we shall abandon our present reserve."

This declaration, in spite of the cryptic and presumably well-considered words with which it closed, was generally received in Germany as an explicit renunciation of direct political interest in Morocco, and was a rude shock to the party which represented *Weltpolitik* in the Diet.

Meanwhile, the British Government was careful to explain, in perfect good faith, that friendship with France did not mean hostility to any other country. It was not the fault of British statesmen, therefore, that in France the *entente* was immediately and widely regarded as formally identifying Great Britain with the French attitude towards Germany, and as a second valuable policy of insurance against isolation in the West in the event of the antagonists of 1870 again coming to blows. In spite of Ministerial assurances, however, a large section of thoughtful English opinion feared even then that this might sooner or later be the effect of the indefinite liability which their country had undertaken.

Official relations between Berlin and London continued for the present unchanged. In the following June King Edward visited the Emperor at Kiel, and a month later a treaty of arbitration, of more value than many official protestations of good-will, was signed by the two Governments. Germans in general, however, had become restless and irritable, and in the winter months of 1904 one of those unaccountable scares to which emotional nations are liable took possession of them. It was caused by the circulation of wild reports to the effect that England contemplated a sudden naval descent upon Germany's coasts and the destruction, if not of her seaports, at least of her fleet. An English naval newspaper had just before published an article urging the Government to lay down a limit beyond which the German navy should not be allowed to increase on pain of challenge, and this article, to which official authority was ignorantly attributed, was quoted by the agents of the Navy League throughout Germany as a proof of nefarious design. The action of the British Admiralty in assigning part of the Channel fleet for service in the North Sea had also had a disquieting effect. The scare died a natural death, though it filled the coffers of the German Navy League and gave Chauvinist politicians and newspapers an excuse for much acrimonious polemic.

Immediately after the publication of the first Morocco agreement the French Minister at Tangier reported (April 24th) that its objects were being exaggerated at the Sultan's Court, and that attempts were being made to stir up feeling against France because of it. M. Delcassé thereupon instructed him to assure the Moorish Government that " far from diminishing the Sultan's authority, we are engaged in reviving his prestige "; but the assurance did not dispel alarm. Great Britain having forsaken her traditional *rôle* as warden of the Moorish kingdom, and disclaimed further responsibility for its independence, and France having ostentatiously proclaimed the policy of political penetration, with a scheme of partition hidden in the background, Morocco now turned to Germany for protection, and that protection Germany was only too ready to offer.

The French ambassador in Berlin had already warned his Government (April 21st) that while the German Chancellor seemed satisfied with the terms of the agreement, as far as they were known, the Emperor was likely on his return from abroad to favour intervention with a view to placing Germany on the same footing as Great Britain in regard to future commercial dealings with Morocco. With a fuller knowledge of the facts, Bülow also began to change his ground. The reconciliation of

Great Britain and France was one thing, but the agreement which affirmed it was another, and he began to distinguish between the two. Now he came to the conclusion that in proposing to plan out the future of Morocco the two Powers had gone beyond their rights, and that in any event Germany should have been consulted before they sealed their friendship by an agreement to dispose of the affairs of a neutral country in which she had old treaty interests. The more the agreement was studied, the plainer it appeared that the scouting of Germany had been deliberate. Spain, who already occupied a number of positions on the Moroccan coast, had been bought off by a provision to the effect that if at some future time the country should be partitioned she should have a further share. The assent of Italy had been secured by assurances, independent of the agreement, of French support in the event of her appropriating Tripoli. Thus of the Powers specially interested in the trade of Morocco, Germany, whose share in that trade exceeded the shares of Spain and Italy combined, though it fell far below that of either Great Britain or France, was the only one to be ignored.

For Germans this reflection was the more galling when it was recalled how loyally their Government had supported successive British Governments in their opposition to the endeavours of France to assert a predominant influence in the country, and how only a few years before a British Colonial Secretary, Mr. Chamberlain, had vaguely suggested the partition of Morocco on a method which would have given to Germany a seaport and a sphere of influence on the Atlantic coast. Both before and after that proposal the colonial party had confidently counted on Germany receiving a share of the sultanate in the event of France forcing its dissolution, and much Pan-Germanist literature had been devoted to the subject. England, it is true, now stood aside, but she could well afford to do so, since she had renounced her interest in Morocco in return for valuable considerations elsewhere.

All the jealousies and rancours created by the first colonial disputes of 1884 and 1885 were suddenly revived in Germany. Great Britain was represented as resuming her old *rôle* as the determined obstructor of German imperialistic ambitions. Thirty years before she had set up the doctrine that territory which she had not occupied Germany could not be allowed to claim; now the same doctrine was advanced, but in the interest of Germany's enemy, France.

Looking back upon events which have now entered into other relations, and have no longer a separate significance, the fact which stands out most prominently in the story of the first settlement of Morocco is that a grave mistake was committed by the French and British Governments in ignoring Germany so deliberately in a matter in which she had a legitimate claim, in virtue of treaty rights and commercial interests, to be consulted. There are probably few people familiar with the history of the Morocco dispute who do not now agree that a perfectly straightforward arrangement open to the whole world, concluded either by France, Spain, Great Britain, and Germany, or by the whole of the States interested in the Madrid Convention, might have prevented much misunderstanding and aggravation, while securing to France the preferential position in the country which she claimed. If nothing else should have put the British Government in particular on its guard, before lending itself to a clandestine and one-sided arrangement of the kind, it was the recollection of the untoward fate of the Anglo-Portuguese treaty of February, 1884, which was similarly concluded in the dark and with the same disregard for German and other collateral interests, and was no sooner made known than it had to be repudiated.

The importance of Germany's material stake in Morocco was indisputable. German travellers had taken a large and creditable part in the earlier exploration of the country; there were two German Residents, at Fez and Tangier, one established since 1873, and a Moorish envoy was accredited to the German Imperial Court; there were German consuls at the more important seaports; much German capital had been sunk in engineering, industrial, and mining enterprises, and German traders were to be found wherever trade was to be done; there were German banks in several centres; and German steamship lines plied regularly between the two countries. France, at least, could not plead ignorance of these facts. Only a short time before M. Méline, an ex-Premier, had written of Germany's relations to Morocco: "Her commerce is always increasing; there are nearly fifty German firms on the coast, German medical men at Mogador and Casablanca, German consuls everywhere, and even meteorological stations have been established on the coast, supported by the German Government." [1] To have ignored the claims of so sensitive a rival was in the circumstances an inexcusable miscalculation. It is highly probable, of course, that Germany, if brought into the agreement, would have demanded compensation, but so had the other Powers concerned, and moreover the compensation which was not offered to her in the beginning had to be given under pressure at a later date, when it earned no more gratitude than it deserved.

What was now plain to Germany was that France, with British assistance, was bent upon asserting in Morocco as complete an influence as in Tunis, with a view to the one country like the other eventually going the way of Algeria and becoming a French province, with the result, sooner or later, of that embargo upon foreign trade which was a feature of French colonial policy. Already there were indications in Paris of a desire to accelerate that process. In June, 1904, a Committee for Morocco, consisting of influential parliamentarians and colonial politicians, among them Prince A. d'Arenberg, MM. Étienne, Chaillez Bert, Charles Roux, de Vogué, and René Millet, was formed for promoting the " peaceful absorption " of the sultanate. The programme of the Committee proposed that the French Government should offer to Morocco its influence with a view to the preservation of order and good government, and should lend the money needed for internal development; but it was not yet to resort to active interference, and no French officials were to be sent to the country. On the other hand, a separate group in the Chamber of Deputies was even then working for the proclamation of a formal protectorate.[2]

It may be said that the force of Germany's objections was weakened by the fact that under Bismarck's influence the German delegates at the Madrid conference of 1880 had been foremost to support French pretensions, holding that, as was

[1] *République française,* March 28, 1904.

[2] Paris correspondent of *The Times,* June 16, 1904 (reported in that journal the following day). Writing of the later treaty with Spain on October 5th and 6th of that year, the same correspondent said: " When once this Franco-Spanish treaty has been signed France will no longer have any pretext for deferring active *pourparlers* at the Court of Fez. . . . There are reasons for believing that French plans are fully matured for the application of her methods of peaceful penetration of Moroccan territory " (*The Times,* October 7, 1904).

stated by the Foreign Secretary in the Diet later (November 17, 1911), " it could only be desirable for Germany were France to establish herself as firmly as possible " in Morocco. Such moral support of France, however, was not equivalent to a formal act of State, but was rather analogous to the advice to take Tunis which was given by Bismarck and Lord Salisbury to France in 1878; and it had never been translated into an agreement of any kind. Moreover, in changing her ground Germany had only followed the example of Great Britain: of the three Powers chiefly interested France alone had from the first followed a consistent, undeviating course. On the other hand, Germany was able to appeal to rights secured to her by two treaties, the Treaty of Madrid of 1880, securing to all the signatory Powers most-favoured-nation treatment, and her own treaty of 1890 with Morocco, which, among other things, confirmed this right to her. Weighing all these considerations, the German Government now determined that if existing treaties were to be put aside and France allowed to assume a dominant position in the sultanate, it must be by the common assent of all the Powers with which the Moorish Government was in treaty relationship. There is no evidence to show that in deciding upon a policy of intervention at this time official Germany desired to obtain a territorial foothold in Morocco, though this was the aim of the Pan-Germanists.

Before the end of the year 1904 the German Minister at Tangier warned his Government that events were marching fast there, and that if Germany had any intention to make a practical protest against French aggression there was no time to lose. Early in the new year (February 21st) the French Minister served on the Sultan at Fez a scheme of reforms, relating to administration, justice, police, customs, and the construction of roads and other public works, with the offer of financial and administrative assistance. It was now that the first official notification was sent from Berlin to Paris that the German Government could not regard itself as bound by agreements to which it was in no way a party. Nevertheless, Bülow informed the Diet on March 29th that all Germany still asked and all she wanted was " the maintenance of the open door," and " the equal treatment of all trading nations." " So far as an attempt is being made to alter the international status of Morocco, or to restrict the economic development of the country," he said, " we must see more closely than before that our economic interests are not endangered. Our first step, therefore, is to put ourselves into communication with the Sultan."

On Bülow's recommendation, as was later admitted, the Emperor himself undertook to be the medium of this communication — a task peculiarly sympathetic to a histrionic temperament, and on the last day of the month he landed in Tangier. Welcomed there by the German merchants, he spoke to them of the importance of Germany's commercial interests in the country, and promised to protect them and to secure for all the Powers complete equality of treatment, an object which was " only possible on condition of the sovereignty of the Sultan and the independence of the country, both of which are for Germany open to no question at all. I am therefore ready to answer for that at all times." " I believe," he added, " that my visit to Tangier proclaims this explicitly and clearly, and will call forth the conviction that what Germany does in Morocco will be arranged exclusively with the Sultan." Receiving later the representatives of the Sultan, the Emperor assured them that he regarded the Sultan as an independent ruler and looked forward to the maintenance of Morocco as a free land open to the peaceful competition of all nations without monopolies or preferences. Two months later a diplomatic mission was sent to Fez in order further to assure the Sultan that Germany was on his side.

Whether the visit to Tangier was deliberately designed as a rebuff for the *entente* Powers or not, it was obviously intended to serve as a reminder that the imperial envoy's warning of July 3, 1900, that " Neither on the ocean nor across it can any great decision be taken without Germany and the German Emperor," still held good. In thus tardily taking up an attitude of obstruction, Germany did not up to this point claim rights in Morocco superior or antecedent to those possessed by the other treaty States, but demanded the observance of the *status quo* simply as one State acting, though without mandate, in the interest of all. Bülow had still not departed from the position which he held in April, 1904, when urged by the colonial party to make Germany's assent to the Anglo-French treaty dependent upon a cession of Moroccan territory. He claimed that the Emperor had only encouraged the Sultan to insist upon remaining, as the treaty of 1904 declared that he was intended to remain, the independent ruler of an independent country. The worst to be said against Germany's intervention so late in the day is that it was inconvenient, inopportune, and irritating to France, though perhaps not more so than it was intended to be. Yet of this the treaty Powers of 1904 had no right to complain. They had not consulted Germany when they disposed of Morocco; and if it would have been more candid had her Government objected to the agreement at an earlier date, it could at least contend that no candour had been shown on the other side. A year before Bülow had said, when reproached by his critics for quiescence, that there was a time for action and a time for reserve. On that occasion he saw no reason for committing himself to a definite decision, but now he no longer saw any reason for deferring it.

In a despatch addressed to the German embassies abroad on April 12th, Bülow formally justified his Government's changed attitude. Recalling the Anglo-French Declaration of a year before, he said:

"The German Government took no action, seeing that the Anglo-French arrangement postulates the *status quo*, and that consequently we thought ourselves entitled to suppose that the Powers interested in the Madrid Convention (of 1880) would be consulted by France in case she had in view in Morocco innovations tending to circumscribe the rights and liberties of the other signatory Powers of the convention in their extent or in their duration. We perceived, however, that that opinion was erroneous, and that the time had come to think of the protection of German interests, when the Morocco Government inquired if it were true that the Minister of France at Fez was, as he professed, the mandatary of the European Powers, and it became known that different features in the French alleged programme of reforms were inconsistent with the maintenance of the *status quo*."

In the meantime the Emperor had attempted a daring stroke of secret diplomacy on his own account in another quarter. During the early months of the Russo-Japanese war, which began in February, 1904, the British Government had raised objections to the coaling of Russian ships of war in the Baltic by Germany as being a breach of neutrality, which, if persisted in, might bring that country into the war, and therewith Great Britain as Japan's ally. Russia resented this protest, and the relations between London and St. Petersburg became for a short time further strained when on the night of October 21st some vessels in Admiral Rozhdestvensky's fleet, in crossing the Dogger Bank, fired upon some Hull fishing smacks, honestly, though irrationally, mistaking them for enemy torpedo boats. The Emperor deemed the moment propitious for pressing upon the Czar a treaty the object of which was to detach France from the *entente* with Great Britain and confront the latter Power by a new Triple Alliance.[1] " In this way," he wrote (October 27, 1904), " a powerful combination of the three strongest Continental Powers would be formed, to attack which the Anglo-Saxon group would think twice before acting." The Czar at first welcomed the proposal, and accordingly a draft was drawn up and sent to him. Then he hesitated to affix his signature until the French Government had been informed. The Emperor, however, insisted upon secrecy. " It is my firm conviction," he telegraphed to the Czar on November 26th, " that it would be absolutely dangerous to inform France before we have both signed the treaty. It would have an effect diametrically opposed to our wishes."

Whatever may have been the exact purport of the treaty, it is admitted to have been directly aimed against Great Britain and to have been duly signed by the two Sovereigns, in the form proposed by the Emperor, at Björkö on July 24th following. It is also clear that the Czar, realizing on reflection that he had committed himself to an engagement which France, as the informal ally of Great Britain and the unconciliated rival of Germany, would be bound to repudiate, later endeavoured to retract his word. That act explains the Emperor's warm reminder of September 29th: " We joined hands and signed before God, who heard our vows. I therefore think that the treaty can well come into existence. What is signed is signed. God is our testator." [2] The treaty, nevertheless, remained a dead letter.

[1] Secret correspondence between the German Emperor and the Czar, extracted from the Russian Imperial archives and first published in the *New York Herald* in September, 1917. Authenticity was promptly admitted by the German Government.

[2] The Russian ex-Premier, Count de Witte, who died on March 12, 1915, claimed that the Russo-German treaty of Björkö (which, on the demand of the German Emperor, had been countersigned by a Russian admiral, in the absence of a Minister of State) was annulled at his instigation as soon as he returned from the peace negotiations at Portsmouth, United States.

That knowledge of these surreptitious German overtures to Russia reached the British Foreign Office through Paris need not be doubted, and it cannot have been without an important and justifiable influence upon its action in deciding to give to France vigorous and undivided support in the later developments of the Moroccan controversy.

Fortified by the Emperor's assurances, the Sultan of Morocco rejected overtures from France which would have given to that Power a practical ascendancy in a country in which hitherto she had neither possessed nor claimed peculiar rights; and at Germany's instigation he proposed that a conference of the Powers which were represented at Madrid in 1880 should be convened to consider certain reforms which he wished to introduce and the manner of doing it. So long as he had the Cabinet behind him Delcassé resolutely stood out against this proposal, apprehensive that by taking part France would find herself opposed by Germany on every point. Germany, with equal tenacity, supported the Sultan, and warned the French Government (June 10th): "The alternative is the *status quo*, and it is necessary that you should know that we are behind Morocco." That was a clear hint that for France the choice was between compliance and war, for Germany was committed too far to the conference proposal for withdrawal without abject humiliation.

In addition to the pledges given to the Sultan, however, there was behind the German Government another driving force — the memory of the Emperor's promise, made at Damascus seven years before (1898) in a moment of religio-political elation, that the "three hundred millions of Mohammedans might always regard him as their friend." To forsake the five million subjects of the Sultan of Morocco, the "Prince of True Believers"— a descendant of the Prophet — would not be reassuring to the rest of the Moslem world; and Baron Marschall, still the ambassador in Constantinople, is reported to have warned the Chancellor that if Germany abandoned Morocco after raising the expectation that her help was to be counted on, she would, "at one stroke forfeit her position in Turkey and therewith the advantage and prospects which we have acquired by years of laborious work." [1]

The hot breath of war was in the air at that time, and while

[1] Count Reventlow, *Deutschlands auswärtige Politik*, p. 271.

there were in Germany strong forces working for a catastrophe, it is improbable that M. Delcassé, for his part, would have hesitated to accept a decision of arms as an alternative to a conference had the choice rested with him. The Cabinet refused to support him, but at the meeting at which he was outvoted he spoke of the certainty of British support in the event of a German attack. Here M. Delcassé would appear to have spoken without authority. It is true, however — and nine years later the fact was officially affirmed — that during the ensuing winter the British Foreign Secretary gave to France, on her inquiry, assurances sufficient to justify her in counting on British co-operation in the event of an unprovoked attack upon her by Germany.[1] M. Delcassé resigned after the adverse vote (June 7th), not, indeed, as was represented, on the direct demand of Berlin, yet no less in sign that the influence of Berlin had overpowered his colleagues.

For France, however, the time for a firm stand was singularly unpropitious, for Russia had just emerged from the war with Japan bruised, sore, and for the time disabled, and the treaty of alliance with her seemed to have become all at once a mere documentary record, representing on Russia's side liabilities which she was unable to meet. Even from the German standpoint Delcassé's retirement was none the less a blunder, for it strengthened his ardour in the cause of Anglo-French friendship and his desire to see Great Britain drawn into a triple accord. Some years later he found a congenial sphere of work as the ambassador of his country at St. Petersburg.

In the critical emergency created by M. Delcassé's resignation M. Rouvier, the Premier, took over the management of foreign affairs, and in his hands negotiations soon returned to a cooler temperature. Rouvier made his acceptance of the conference conditional upon a prior understanding between France and Germany on general questions, on the analogy of Russia and Great Britain in 1878, and to this Berlin assented.

By the agreement which followed Germany undertook that she would not at the forthcoming conference pursue any aims which might conflict with the rights of France resulting from treaties or other arrangements so far as they were in harmony with the following principles: the sovereignty and independence of the Sultan, the integrity of his empire, economic lib-

---

[1] See Chapter XXIII., p. 475.

erty subject to no inequality whatever, the introduction of police and financial reforms regulated by international agreement, the recognition of the special position of France in Morocco as created by the contiguity of Algeria and the Shereefian Empire and the intimate relations of these two countries. Justifying the attitude of his Government to the Diet later, the Emperor said, in a speech from the throne (November 28th), that the difficulties which had arisen at that time between the two countries " had no other origin than an inclination to settle without our co-operation affairs in which the German Empire had also interests to maintain," and in the following year he told Lord Haldane in Berlin, in reference to the Morocco treaty: " If you (the British Government) had only told me early, there would have been no misunderstanding," adding that " what he wanted was, not territory, but trade expansion." France made it a grievance that during the few months of her ascendancy at the Moorish Court Germany had secured commercial privileges of considerable value. Her banks had succeeded in negotiating with the Sultan a loan of large amount, and her diplomatic representative at Tangier, Count Tattenbach, had obtained several important contracts for public works.

The Morocco conference met at Algeciras, in Spain. In demanding it Germany had wished, for her own greater assurance, to supersede a dual bargain between France and Great Britain by an agreed convention of all the Powers, and this was the result. The Powers represented were those which had drawn up the Madrid convention, with Russia in addition, and their delegates conferred from January 16 to April 7, 1906. At the first sitting the president, Duc d'Almodovar. proposed that three postulates should be accepted as a basis of all discussions, viz. the sovereignty of the Sultan, the integrity of his empire, and equality of treatment in commercial matters, i.e. the " open door," and all the delegates agreed.

In the further proceedings the six principals concerned ranged themselves into two camps — France, Spain, Great Britain, and Russia on one side, Germany and Austria on the other. Later (April 12th) Emperor William thanked the Austrian Foreign Minister, Count Goluchowski, for the loyal support given to Germany in the proceedings. " You showed yourself," he said, " a brilliant second on the fencing floor, and you can count on a like service from me on a similar occasion." Italy oftener than not gave her vote in favour of France and not of her ally of the Triple Alliance. Subsequently explaining and condoning this apparent inconsistency, Bülow attributed it to the delicate situation in which Italy found herself, compelled as she was to choose between a new political union and old historical ties, and above all to the fact that, with Germany's full knowledge, she had already entered into obligations towards France on the Moroccan question which she was not able to ignore. The only Great Power which entered the conference quite unbound was America, and her influence was on the whole favourable to the independence of the sultanate, in so far as the reasonable claims of France and Spain could be satisfied.

The General Act of Algeciras which resulted from the conference bore the date April 7th. The Sultan ratified it on June 18th in a letter reciting the pledge of the Powers that his sovereignty and independence and the integrity of his realm remained inviolate. In seeking his assent on behalf of the Powers, the King of Italy assured him in their name that the treaty would bring " much honour to your Majesty and incalculable good to your Majesty's empire." The Act affirmed the principle of economic equality for all States in relation to Morocco, but recognized that internal reforms were necessary to the country's welfare and security. It therefore contained provisions regarding the organization of the police, the prevention of smuggling and the illicit trade in arms, the execution of public works, the institution of a State bank, the raising of new revenues, the collection of taxes, and the better regulation of the customs and administrative services. French and Spanish officials were to be employed in the police under a Swiss inspector-general, and France and Spain were to co-operate with the Moorish Government in suppressing the illicit trade in arms on the frontiers of their respective possessions; but no preference was given to any of the Powers in connection with trade, industry, or contracts for public works. Upon the fundamental issue raised by Germany for the decision of the Powers the Act was perfectly explicit, for it recognized Morocco as still politically an independent State. France had secured certain rights of interference in minor matters of internal government, and to that extent her preferential position was recognized; but the Act contained no admission whatever, actual or implicit, of any claim on her part to exercise special political influence in the country, still less to territorial rights of any kind.

The German Chancellor professed to regard the results of the conference as satisfactory —" we did not achieve all we desired," he said, " but we achieved the essential things "— and the Ministerial Press, taking its cue from him, declared that " the name of the little Spanish town of Algeciras will be named in the history of the world with greater and more lasting fame than many a vaunted battle." Bülow was, indeed, much more reasonable and much more easily satisfied than either the Diet or the nation. The Colonial party and the Pan-Germans in particular were incensed by his public confession, " Germany has not, like Spain, been associated with Morocco for several centuries, nor has she, like France, a common frontier of several hundred miles with Morocco; she has not historical rights acquired by all sorts of sacrifices, like those two civilizing nations," crowned as it was by the declaration, " We have no direct political interests and no political aspirations in Morocco." The Pan-Germans had, in fact, wanted a share of Morocco — their eyes were fixed particularly upon Agadir and the region of which it is the vestibule — and to this end they had vehemently agitated to the last day of the conference. This hope foiled, their resentment was unbounded.

While, therefore, the Act of Algeciras did not install France in the sultanate, Germany signed and accepted it as token that she herself looked for no territorial expansion in that part of Africa. For his share in the proceedings at Algeciras Bülow received the title of prince.

Germany's action in calling for a conference of the Powers in 1905 has often been represented as a calculated attempt to weaken the Anglo-French accord, and perhaps force the new friends apart, her assumed reasoning being that if the Morocco dispute led to extreme measures Great Britain would in the end withdraw, from motives of prudence. If that was her aim, it was not realized; on the contrary, the immediate and most visible effect of her action was to place the accord upon a surer and also a more practical basis. To that result the exchange of military confidences to which reference has been made powerfully contributed. Originally the *entente cordiale* had been intended by England to imply no more than a friendly *rapport*, like the informal tie which bound the three Continental empires prior to 1879; but from the first France either understood it as something more or, what is likelier, was determined that it should become such. An amiable courtesy shown by a naturally cold and diffident gentleman was accepted as a declaration of passion by a fascinating lady of ardent temperament, quite ready to be won by the right suitor. And that suitor was the stolid, substantial John Bull. Well as John Bull may have liked the ensuing courtship, he was unquestionably drawn into it, and for some time most of the wooing and nearly all the tenderness were on the side of France, until the time came when he recognized that what on his part was originally meant to be merely a cordial *camaraderie*, or at most an innocent flirtation, must by all the rules of chivalry end in a formal marriage. But the union was one between equals, and it proved happier than most unions in which chance or design has played a determining part.

After the critical days of 1905 no further doubt existed that the two Powers were determined, and destined, to work together in foreign politics. In the following January the British Foreign Secretary publicly stated that the Liberal Government then newly formed would do its utmost to improve British relations with Germany, but he added that a genuine *rapprochement* must be dependent upon the existence of a good understanding between Germany and France. As for the Morocco agreement in particular, for Great Britain, who had gone with France so far, there remained now no choice but to see it through to the end, at whatever cost.

CHAPTER XXIII
(1906–1913)

FOREIGN RELATIONS —(iii) THE TRIPLE ENTENTE

For Great Britain the *entente* with France proved the fore-runner of a series of understandings which greatly eased her foreign relations all round, and put an end to the isolation which she had seemed to accept so long as the penalty of fame. By far the most important of the supplementary agreements was that concluded with Russia, greatly to the benefit and satisfaction of her ally. M. Delcassé had described the 1904 agreement from the first as " a means towards the arrangement of a definite understanding between England and Russia." Towards that further accord it had proved at once, if not an intentional, at least a helpful stage.

The unreasoning prejudice against Russia which Disraeli had so successfully fostered, owing in no small measure to resentment at the persecutions experienced by his race under Muscovite rule, continued to infect a large part of the British nation long after he had passed away, and disenabled it to judge the aims of Russian policy candidly and on their merits, or to weigh justly Great Britain's true interests whenever the two countries came in contact. The conversion of British public opinion advanced quickly after Lord Salisbury, influenced by the readiness with which Turkey, from the early 'nineties of last century forward, had responded to the overtures of Germany, a country which hitherto had shown but little interest in her welfare, had declared his belief that England had been " putting her money on the wrong horse." The settlement of the Afghan frontier question in 1893 had removed one source of constant danger, but the relations of the two Powers with Persia still presented serious possibilities of friction. Perhaps nothing contributed more to the lessening of Russian distrust than the attitude held by the British Government after the Russo-Japanese war. Before hostilities broke out the British Foreign Office did its best to prevent a rupture, warning St. Petersburg repeatedly of its imminence and grave consequences. The warnings were not heeded, but at least their sincerity was recognized when they proved to have been only too well founded. Later the influence of Great Britain with Japan was able to mitigate to the beaten Power the penalties of defeat.

A new era in Anglo-Russian relationships was opened by the conclusion, on August 31, 1907, after long and delicate negotiations, of an agreement by which the two Powers adjusted all outstanding questions between them in Central Asia. As to Afghanistan, the ancient centre of contention, Russia declared that she had no interest therein, while Great Britain affirmed her intention to respect the existing political status, not to appropriate any part of the country, and not to interfere in its internal affairs. Further, the two Powers divided Persia into spheres of influence, while recognizing its integrity and independence: a north-central zone was marked off for Russia's special activity, the southern zone, including the Gulf, was similarly assigned to Great Britain, and between these zones was left a neutral territory. The agreement also provided for the construction of a railway through Persia connecting with Central Europe through Batoum and with India through Charbur. Special care was taken on this occasion to avoid wounding German sensibilities. "During the course of the negotiations," the German Foreign Secretary, Herr von Schön, told the Diet (March 24, 1908), "both Powers had spontaneously offered to Germany the assurance that her interests would be in nowise infringed."

Describing later (February 16, 1911) the purpose of the agreement, the British Foreign Secretary said: "The object of the agreement was this: two great nations who had frequently been at diplomatic tension and friction with each other came to the conclusion that if they were to live together peaceably in Asia they must not work against each other's interests." It should be added, however, that the interests of the signatory Powers were advanced more visibly than were those of Persia, which, in spite of the guarantee of its independence, became henceforth subject to interferences, particularly from Russia, of a character difficult to reconcile with its right to be regarded as a suzerain State.[1]

[1] After the outbreak of the war of August, 1914, the Persian agreement was suspended, and whatever its ultimate fate may be, it is unlikely that the spheres of influence will be reaffirmed.

The effect of the Anglo-Russian understanding was to dispel
for Great Britain the spectre of a Russian menace in Far Asia
which, with little intermission, had disturbed her peace for a
century and ever since the Crimean War had proved a recurrent source of division and estrangement in her domestic politics.   For Russia, and therefore for Germany, the importance
of the understanding lay in the fact that as she now renounced
further advance in the East she was all the freer to turn her
glances to the West.   The reorientation of the Great Powers
which had been the aim of the German Emperor when he
opened the era of *Weltpolitik* had thus made further progress,
but on lines little contemplated by that Sovereign at the time.

Great Britain did not, in consequence of the agreement of
1907, join the Franco-Russian alliance, but she counted henceforth as the good friend of both of the allies.   The Triple Alliance, described by Bülow as " a mighty fortification dividing
the Continent into two," had now received its counterpart in
the Triple Entente.   The British Foreign Secretary spoke of
the enlarged accord as merely a " diplomatic group."   It was,
however, from the first more than that, and as time passed it
became very much more.   In June of the following year (1908)
the reconciliation of Great Britain and Russia was cemented
by the meeting of King Edward and the Czar at Reval.
Meanwhile, both France and Russia, who had jointly opposed
Japan's aspirations in 1895, concluded agreements with that
Power (June and July, 1907, respectively) guaranteeing their
reciprocal rights in China and the integrity of that empire.

If the Franco-Russian alliance had proved a critical moment in the foreign relations of Russia, the Anglo-Russian
entente marked a new step in the emancipation of her political
life from German influence.   Owing to the domination of feudal
Conservatism in German politics that influence had always been
in the direction of reaction, not merely because for Prussia an
autocracy in the East was an admirable counterpoise to a democracy in the West, but because it was recognized that
the longer a national awakening could be delayed in Russia the
more time would Germany have in which to prepare for the
inevitable clash between Teutonism and Slavism.   Gortchakoff
once said that " Russia might be dumb but she was not deaf."
Silently and wistfully Russia had long listened to the stirrings
of the Western spirit, unable to make response.   Now sud-

denly, yet amid appalling convulsions, utterance came, and the last and greatest of Europe's despotisms passed into the fellowship of constitutional States. The revolution of 1905 and the succeeding introduction of parliamentary government (March, 1906) marked a turning-point in Russia's political relationships with her Western neighbour. From the first Liberal Russia turned away from Germany to England, as to the mother of free institutions, and the Duma based its rules, precedents, and analogies almost wholly on English experience.

When, however, Russia, casting her gaze above and beyond the central barrier to political progress which extended from the Vistula to the Rhine, began thus to respond more and more to the liberating influences of Western civilization, Germany betrayed a deepening consciousness of the " Slavic peril," and began to anticipate with anxiety the destiny of the adjacent empire. There was one compensation, for Turkey, knowing no longer where to turn, now placed herself more completely than before under German protection.

The British treaties with France and Russia were supplemented by other agreements of a minor yet important character, the effect of which was to strengthen the Triple Entente. In the summer of 1907 Notes were exchanged between the Governments of Great Britain and Spain, and between those of France and Spain, and later communicated to the other Powers, setting forth their intention to maintain the *status quo* in the Mediterranean. Between Great Britain and Italy there had always existed a strong bond of sympathy, and it seemed as though events were fast fulfilling Bismarck's prediction that whenever the time came, as come it would, for Italy to choose between the Powers, she would inevitably side with England and her allies, whoever these might be.

Italy's attitude both towards France and Germany had also been profoundly modified since 1882, when under Bismarck's influence she became a member of the Triple Alliance. In attaching her to that alliance, as he did by so astutely making Tunis a bone of contention, Bismarck had only one aim in view, to prevent her reconciliation with France. For a long time, however, the question of Tunis was alone sufficient to make such a reconciliation impossible, while, on the other hand, France let it be known, on every fitting occasion, that an ally of Germany could never be a true friend of hers. When Signor Crispi, following Depretis, came to power in August, 1887, the relations between the Latin Powers soon became further strained owing to the suspicion entertained in France that Italy, under the new Premier, was allowing herself to be swayed in her foreign politics by excessive consideration for Germany's good-will. Crispi had visited Bismarck for several days in October, and from that time forward he remained under the spell of that statesman, ready to follow him wherever he should be pleased to lead.

Six years had passed since France took the first step that was to bring Tunis altogether under her control, yet Crispi still resolutely refused to surrender the rights which Italy claimed under the Capitulations without equivalent advantages elsewhere. Equity was on his side, but hardly prudence, since in maintaining this stubborn attitude he was exposing his country to the risk of further disappointments in North Africa, for the movements of France gave rise to the suspicion that she intended to appropriate the *hinterland* of Tripoli and thus to cut off communication between that Turkish province, long coveted by Italy, but as yet not occupied by her, and the interior. When in July, 1890, there were rumours of the impending conclusion of a treaty between France and the Bey of Tunis, by which French influence in that country was to be placed on a permanent footing, Crispi urgently appealed to the German Government, on the strength of its obligations under the Triple Alliance, for assistance in securing a settlement that should pay due regard to Italian interests. Bismarck was now no longer in office, but that fact did not make less difficult the position of his successor, whose hands were bound by Germany's action in encouraging France in her Tunisian enterprises from 1878 forward. "Desirous and eager" as he was to help Italy, therefore, all that Caprivi could do was to urge that pressure should be put upon the Governments of Vienna and particularly of London. To Great Britain Crispi accordingly appealed on the ground that her position in Egypt would be threatened if France were allowed to extend her influence further in Northern Africa. Let Italy have Tripoli and she would be satisfied. "As Tunis cannot be rendered independent and the Protectorate prevented from becoming one day or another a sovereignty," he wrote to Lord Salisbury (July 23, 1890), "it is of great importance that we provide against the future occupation of Tripoli by France by forestalling her. If we held Tripoli, Biserta would cease to be a menace either to Italy or Great Britain. We are your necessary allies and our union guarantees your dominion in Malta and Egypt."

Great Britain was already pledged to the recognition of the new status in Tunis, and was also at that time negotiating a convention — which was actually signed the following month — under which France was to recognize the new British protectorate over Zanzibar and Great Britain to recognize the French protectorate over Madagascar, and to agree to the appointment of a joint commission to delimit the territories under French influence in Africa. Nevertheless, Lord Salisbury gave Crispi the reassuring reply that he was " convinced that on the day that the *status quo* in the Mediterranean shall suffer any alteration whatever, Italy's occupation of Tripoli will become an absolute necessity." " The interests of Europe," he said, " demand this occupation, that the Mediterranean may be prevented from becoming a French lake "; and he added that Italy should have Tripoli whether Great Britain remained permanently in Egypt or not. He was of opinion, however, that the time for action had not yet come. In August, M. Ribot, the French Foreign Secretary, added his assurance to the Italian ambassador in Paris that France likewise would not be indisposed to see Italy established in Tripoli, provided she would cease to cry over the spilt milk of Tunis, and would withdraw from the Triple Alliance.

When four years later Germany, by an agreement of February 4, 1894, recognized the *hinterland* of Tripoli as falling within the sphere of French influence, Crispi, who had just returned to power, after three years of retirement, was himself constrained to admit that the Triple Alliance had ceased to be for Italy a source of security or strength, since it only excited French hostility, while guaranteeing to her no effective support from her treaty friends. He dated the decline of its efficacy from the fall of its author from power. Later, during the Chancellorship of Hohenlohe, he told Herr von Bülow, when German ambassador in Rome: " I had perceived the advantages of the alliance in Bismarck's day, but not afterwards with his successors. Previous to the year 1890 whenever a question arose I had only to notify Bismarck, who would immediately make his voice heard in London or Paris, and the matter would be settled." More despondently he said on another occasion: " It is said that the Triple Alliance was established for the maintenance of peace. For us it has had the opposite effect. For us the Triple Alliance means war." [1]

Italy knew, of course, that if France were to attack her, or force her into a position in which the alternatives would be war or intolerable humiliation, Germany would be certain to intervene. But the assurance that relief would be at hand in case of extremity did not prevent the existence of a condition of perpetual tension and harassment, and this Germany did and could do little to abate. So it continued for some time longer, until, to the alarm of Germany and the satisfaction of France, Crispi fell in March, 1896, discredited by the disastrous issue of the last of the Erythrean campaigns. Depressed by the thought that the Triple Alliance was bringing Italy increasing responsibilities with decreasing advantages, he had written to the Italian ambassador in Berlin just a month before: "Berlin cannot be ignorant of the strength which diplomatic compacts derive in our day from the support of the masses, especially when those compacts imply a brotherhood in arms and in the shedding of blood. The Italian people are not yet disillusioned with regard to the alliance with Germany, but who can guarantee that they may not be so to-morrow if things continue as they are?" [2] These representations were by Crispi's wish brought to the knowledge of the Emperor, upon whom they made such an impression that he determined at once to visit the Italian King. Before the intention could be put into effect Crispi had resigned on a vote of no confidence.

Italy's enthusiasm for foreign adventures had for some time been cooling down, since the most tangible results so far had been prodigal sacrifice of life and treasure, a heavy burden of taxation and debt, and a serious loss of military prestige. It was not unnatural, therefore, that the immediate effect of Crispi's fall should be the reversal by the succeeding Government of Rudini of his philo-German policy and its decision to put an end to the eternal bickerings with France. M. Bourgeois, the French Minister-President, had told the Italian ambassador in Paris early in the year: "In this country all eyes are fixed upon the lost provinces, and all are aware that Italy's alliance with Germany is an obstacle in the way of their return to the mother country. You must accept the fact that so long

[1] Conversations of January and February, 1896, quoted in *Memoirs of Francesco Crispi*, vol. iii., pp. 335, 337.
[2] *Memoirs of Francesco Crispi*, vol. iii., p. 347.

as you belong to the Triple Alliance no understanding with us is possible." [1] Italy could give no promise to forsake her allies, but by an agreement concluded with France on September 28, 1896, the first step was taken towards ending the long-standing estrangement. By this agreement Italy withdrew all special claims to Tunis, while France undertook to give to Italy a free hand in Tripoli. Two years later a commercial peace was also concluded between the two countries by a convention of November 21, 1898, and thereafter French money began to flow again freely into the peninsula. By a further convention of 1900 Italy recognized the preferential position of France in Morocco, while France now formally recognized Italy's special claims in Tripoli and Cyrenaica. For a time nothing further was done towards extending Italian influence in that region; it was sufficient to know that the danger of being forestalled, as had happened in Tunis, had now entirely disappeared. When two years later the Triple Alliance came to be renewed (again, it was understood, for twelve years), the Italian Foreign Minister stated publicly (May 23, 1902) that the Italian treaty had been adjusted to the new relationships with France, and that from the Italian standpoint the Alliance had now no aggressive character as regards that Power.

Her vigorous, patriotic, but costly empire-builder, Crispi, having left the arena which he had dominated in one capacity or another for nearly twenty years, and the differences with France having been passably adjusted, Italy regained full independence of action, and with it a decided bias towards the *entente* Powers speedily showed itself. More and more the conviction was forced upon her that the Triple Alliance existed only for the good of the two Empires, and that she herself was merely the superfluous third who spoils good company. Even now her defection from the Alliance seemed to be only a question of time and occasion. While there was still no reason in political conditions why Germany and Italy at least should cease to be friends, there was every reason why Italy and Austria should continue to be enemies so long as the Irredentist districts, with their million of Italians, remained under Habsburg rule. If, however, Italy's attachment to the alliance became weaker, all the closer and stronger became the basic union between Germany and Austria, Italy's adhesion to which was posterior and subsidiary.

[1] *Memoirs of Francesco Crispi,* vol. iii., p. 336.

A little incident which occurred in 1907 was as the proverbial straw telling how the wind blew. That year was appointed for the holding of the second Peace Conference at The Hague. Before it met the British Cabinet, as has been stated, sought support amongst the Powers for a discussion of the general subject of disarmament. While Germany and Austria replied that no practical proposal on the subject was possible, and declined to consider it, their ally, Italy, groaning under the burden of the military and naval expenditure which the Triple Alliance had imposed on her, declined to take in advance a negative attitude. In April King Edward and Victor Emmanuel met at Gaeta, and in referring to the meeting in the Chamber on May 15th the Italian Foreign Minister, Tittoni, affirmed Italy's unchanging friendship for England and declared the Government's readiness to discuss the limitation of armaments. Although in the ensuing conference Germany's principal delegate, Baron Marschall von Bieberstein, succeeded in thwarting the pacifist movement, even wrecking the British proposal for compulsory arbitration, it was significant that Italy's influence was not thrown on the side of her allies.

These several accords and understandings, together with her ancient alliances with Portugal, as renewed by the Windsor Treaty of 1899, and that with Japan, dating from 1902, made England early in the century the centre of a constellation of warm friendships almost unique in her history. Now it was the turn of Germany, whose foreign policy had for over a generation been built up on military alliances and political combinations, to face the prospect of growing isolation. After she had endeavoured to draw every European Power in turn into her orbit, Germany herself seemed in the way of becoming the eccentric comet of the political firmament, pursuing no fixed course, but driven hither and thither by conflicting forces.

This remarkable change in the positions of the two Powers not merely synchronized with, but was in no small degree a result of, the growing uneasiness to which Germany's activity in foreign politics had given rise. It would be unjustifiable to regard the measures adopted at that time in the name of *Weltpolitik* as deliberately intended to be a provocative challenge to other countries. From the standpoint of prudence alone rulers and statesmen prone to rashness of the kind would first need to satisfy themselves that behind them was a military power vastly superior to any combination likely to be opposed to it.

But, notwithstanding their continuous growth, the defensive resources of the Empire had never been so paramount as to justify any such assumption. This became more than ever the case after the formation of the Franco-Russian alliance. Apologizing to Crispi in 1896, when the current of *Weltpolitik* was in full flux, for his inability to espouse Italy's grievances against France with the vigour which that statesman desired, Baron Marschall, the Foreign Secretary, pleaded, with good reason, the fact that Germany could no longer " tenir le verbe haut " as in the old days, when France was weak and Russia had not become her ally. Now, he said, she had to be prepared to back up every word with acts if necessary; hence arose the need for circumspection and restraint.[1]

If, however, German statesmen were conscious of this need, as in the abstract they doubtless were, so much the more remarkable was their omission to pay heed to it in practice. To acquit them of deliberate design to disturb the tranquillity of Europe is not to condone the policy which had that effect. At home as well as abroad this policy was freely criticized as one of indiscriminate imperialism, and the prejudice which it created was magnified by the singular faculty of its authors for choosing the wrong means for attaining their ends. Germany was eager for power and prestige abroad, yet troubled little to consider how these might be most wisely obtained; she sought empire, and in seeking it gave the impression that she expected to enrich herself at the expense of other nations; in both of these quests her ruler and statesmen were wanting as much in discrimination as in patience. The policy was also vitiated by want of foresight, definiteness, and consistency. Never did the Emperor and his advisers seem to have a clear perception of the aims which they were following, or to hold for long to the pursuit of any given objective. The " new course," direct enough at first, so long as it concerned itself with domestic affairs, became in foreign policy under the lethargic Hohenlohe, and still more under the compliant and supple Bülow, a " zig-zag course." Friendships were sought and sundered with an indifference to the consequences which bewildered old-fashioned statesmen; and endeavours, more daring than astute, were constantly made to play off one Power against another, a species of diplomacy in which Bismarck excelled, but hopelessly beyond the capacity of his successors. In these haz-

[1] *Memoirs of Francesco Crispi*, vol. iii., p. 344.

ardous enterprises, as the Björkö Treaty of 1905 showed, candour was not always conspicuous.

While Bismarck continued at the helm, German foreign policy was directed towards the one aim of making secure the imperial structure which he had erected; never did he intervene, except under compulsion, in international politics, and even then the part which he played was that of the mediator and conciliator; while of " prestige politics " he had an honest detestation. From the closing years of the century forward this attitude of prudent restraint was abandoned, and Germany embarked upon a succession of aggressive enterprises and interferences in all parts of the world, obviously undertaken without definite plan and sometimes, it seemed, without any other purpose except to remind other Powers that nothing might be done, within the sphere of international politics, without her active co-operation. A foreign policy dictated by that motive was bound to prove a source of widespread unrest, distrust and irritation, and in fact it left Germany's relations with the rest of Europe less friendly than ever before. It is true that the Triple Alliance continued and that Turkey had been gained, but the old union was already marked for disruption, while the new one was from the first a source of weakness rather than strength.

But a further result of this policy of foreign adventure was that in the end it undermined at home the old sense of national security. " What to-day complicates and makes difficult our position," said the Imperial Chancellor (Bülow) in the Diet on February 19, 1907, " are our oversea endeavours and interests. If we were not involved in this direction, we should not be so susceptible on the Continent, and it would be easier than it is to avoid friction with England." To this avowal Dr. Riemer, the spokesman of the Radical party, replied: " That is what we have always said — that Germany's European position, which for us is the principal concern, would not be made easier, but more difficult, by engagements of the kind. This holds good of our unfruitful colonial policy, but still more of what is called *Weltpolitik*." It has been shown how a vigorous policy of naval and military expansion was entered upon as a necessary counterpart of the Emperor's foreign enterprises. Other countries were compelled in turn to increase their armaments in self-defence, and the irony of the resulting situation was that in the end Germany, after setting in mo-

tion this disastrous competition, came to regard it as a justification for her own determination to outdistance her rivals in
warlike preparations.

As they contrasted Great Britain's multiplying friendships
with the growing isolation of their own country, German politicians saw something uncanny and malign in the formation
of alliances and accords without noisy protestation and clatter
of sabres. There was talk of deep designs against Germany's
position and security. It was assumed that to be friendly to
France and Russia necessarily meant to be hostile to their
neighbour. The theory was now set up that the British Government, inspired by the least designing of men, King Edward,
was deliberately endeavouring to compass the political " encirclement " of Germany in the hope of reducing her to impotence. Bülow, who took politics far too lightly ever to lose
his head in the midst of the ensuing irrational alarm, told his
countrymen that " the alleged ' encirclement ' of Germany is
no more than a phrase: German policy has not hitherto been
obstructed by the *ententes* concluded around us, and it will
not be obstructed." He even confessed that England had often
" had a soothing and sobering effect on France, and has done
valuable work for the preservation of peace in Europe." All
such assurances failed to carry conviction or to afford relief;
the fear of " encirclement " became to the German nation,
what the fear of coalitions had been to Bismarck, a nightmare;
and to the Chauvinists the measure of England's popularity
was the measure of her perfidy.

Much — undoubtedly too much — of the credit for the English policy of accords and the success which attended it has
been awarded to King Edward. Be his claims as they may,
no Sovereign of modern times deserved better of his country
than the affable gentleman who, without a trace of *double en-
tendre* in his nature, succeeded by personal charm, unfailing
tact, a flexibility of mind far more French than English, and
above all by consummate common sense, in winning friends on
every hand for his country and for peace. Not without reason did he earn in France the title of *roi pacificateur*.

Throughout these early " encirclement " scares and controversies the two rulers continued on the best of terms. Following a visit by the King to the Emperor at Cassel in August, 1907, the Emperor (accompanied by the Empress) visited
Windsor in the following November and in London was re-

ceived with marked cordiality. He was banqueted at the Guildhall, where he made a speech reiterating his attachment to England and used the words " Blood is thicker than water "; he was made a freeman of the City; and the University of Oxford conferred on him the degree of doctor of laws. A visit to Berlin made by King Edward and Queen Alexandra in February, 1909, though it was generally welcomed, failed to destroy the " encirclement " myth, which still lingered after the King's death in May of the following year. Germany's alarm was that of the nervous night-watcher who has " seen something." To her the apparition was unmistakably real, and nothing ever convinced her that it was merely the figment of a disturbed imagination.

In the meantime Germany had joined the other maritime Powers of the North in concluding two notable treaties of friendship (April 23, 1908), one the North Sea Convention, by which Germany, Great Britain, France, Denmark, the Netherlands, and Sweden undertook to be good neighbours, to respect each other's sovereign rights, and to maintain the *status quo* in those waters and the adjacent territories, and the other the Baltic Sea Convention, by which Germany, Russia, Denmark, and Sweden pledged themselves to the same objects.

Before this time the question of Morocco had passed through several stages. If Germany had resented the attitude of France on this question during the controversies of 1904 to 1906, much more did she resent it in the course of the later developments. The year after the Algeciras Conference Prince von Bülow authorized a French journalist to assure his countrymen (July, 1907): " You may be sure that we are not going to place obstacles in your way in Morocco. The Algeciras convention will be loyally observed by us. You, on your part, must carry on the economic policy of the ' open door ' sincerely and without *arrière pensée*: Germany will ask no more of you." Events soon showed that too many cooks had been engaged on the Morocco dish, with the proverbial result: the country did not settle down under the restraints of a police system imposed from the outside.

From the standpoint of Europe at large one of the most important articles of the Act of Algeciras was the last (No. 123) which declared: " All existing treaties, conventions and arrangements between the signatory Powers and Morocco remain in force. It is agreed, however, that in case their provisions be found to conflict with those of the present General Act the stipulations of the latter shall prevail." It might have seemed that if this provision meant anything at all, it meant that the secret articles of the two French conventions were annulled, and that any attempt to enforce them would be an act of bad faith towards the other treaty Powers.

Such, however, was not the view adopted officially in France, who had bargained away her rights in Egypt and expected to receive the covenanted *quid pro quo*. From June, 1906, forward France was drawn into repeated interventions, both diplomatic and military, in the affairs of Morocco of a kind not authorized by the Act of Algeciras, justifying them by the prevalent disorders — the conflict of rival claimants to the throne and tribal disturbances on the Algerian frontier — but also by disputes over railway concessions in which French subjects were concerned, and by the interest in the country's tranquillity which was created by the ever-increasing amount of the French loans. The inability of the Sultan to maintain order and guarantee security in his own dominion became more evident from day to day. Nevertheless, for several years after the conclusion of the Act of Algeciras the French Chamber periodically and consistently affirmed its adhesion to the fundamental basis of the treaty — the independence of Morocco and the integrity of the Sultan's sovereignty.

The outlook became more serious after the murder of French, Spanish, and Italian subjects in 1907 and 1908. A strong French force occupied Udja in March, 1907, and when in July Casablanca was given up to anarchy, following native riots arising out of the execution of certain French engineering contracts, French and Spanish warships bombarded the town and then landed troops to occupy it. The two Powers had communicated their intentions beforehand to the German Government, which formally acquiesced in their action. In the midst of the disorders Mulai Abdul Aziz was deposed, and his brother Mulai Hafid succeeded him (January, 1908). Germany hastened to acknowledge the new Sultan, and on his promise to observe faithfully the Act of Algeciras, the French, Spanish, and British Governments followed suit. It had become abundantly clear, however, that no native ruler of Morocco was capable, single-handed, of keeping the peace which was so necessary to his neighbours, and forced by the logic of events, as the German Government later admitted, France showed a disposition to exaggerate the scope of the special position in the country which the Powers had accorded to her in 1906. In the autumn of 1908 strong diplomatic representations were made by the German Government to Paris owing to violence done to a German consul at Casablanca, who had helped German, Austrian, and Russian deserters from the Foreign Legion to escape. The dispute was eventually referred to the tribunal of The Hague.

Early in 1909, Great Britain standing aside, the French and German Governments concluded a separate agreement (February 8th), very favourable to France, which it was hoped would solve all difficulties. By it the two Powers declared themselves " equally anxious to facilitate the execution of the Act of Algeciras," and undertook not to procure any economic privilege either in their own favour or in that of any other country. While, further, France repeated her firm attachment to " the maintenance of the independence and integrity of the Shereefian Empire " and promised not to obstruct German commercial and industrial interests in particular, Germany again affirmed that her concern in Morocco was purely economic, and now recognized that France had special political interests there. In this further act of abstention the German Government had again to resist powerful influences at home, where the colonial party and more particularly the Pan-Germans were still clamouring for a policy of open aggression and the appropriation of a part of Morocco before France obtained the whole.

The time came, however, when Germany felt compelled to protest, justifiably or not, that in spite of good-will and concessions on her part France was not showing an equal spirit of reasonableness. Disputes arose out of the attempt by French *entrepreneurs* to assert an exclusive position in regard to certain mining and railway undertakings, in which German capitalists wished to participate. French military operations also multiplied, and Germany feared that aggressive designs were behind them. " Our action at Udja is not a step towards Fez," M. Pichon, the French Foreign Minister, had written to the *chargé d'affaires* at the Moorish capital on March 30, 1907. It was for the present only a step towards Casablanca, but the further step to Fez was soon to follow. When early in 1911 a new rebellion broke out and his own military force proved insufficient to quell it, the Sultan called in the help of France, and in May a large French force under General Moinier occupied the capital on the plea that the lives of Europeans were in danger. The French Government assured the signatory Powers that as soon as peace and security had been established the troops would be withdrawn. The British Government promptly signified its approval of the measure taken. The German Government raised no formal objection, but taking note of the purpose of the expedition and the pledge of withdrawal, informed the French Foreign Minister that "should the expedition go beyond its alleged object, even should such action be merely the result of circumstances arising out of the expedition," it would regard the Act of Algeciras as no longer binding and would reserve to itself full liberty of action. The French occupation of Fez led to the Spanish occupation of Laraish and El-Kasr, on the North Atlantic coast, and in each case the force of occupation remained.

Contending that the latest armed intervention of France was a direct infraction of the Act of Algeciras, and believing that unless a firm stand were now taken all the treaties and agreements regulating the affairs of Morocco might as well be torn up, the German Government called upon France either to abide by the strict letter of her obligations or, if these were to be ignored, to offer to Germany compensation. The proposal that Germany might withdraw all claims in Morocco save those of an economic character, provided France were prepared to cede territory elsewhere, had been made with the acquiescence and even the encouragement of the French Foreign Minister shortly after the Emperor's visit to Tangier. Part of the French Congo had been suggested as a suitable equivalent, but formal negotiations had not yet been opened.

Now, as before, the French Government did not reject the idea of compensation, but neither was it in a hurry to make definite proposals on the subject. Failing to obtain satisfaction, the German Government at the end of June sent a gunboat to the closed port of Agadir in West Morocco. Whether the proceeding was urgently necessary or not, there was at least no secrecy about it, for the Powers privy to the Algeciras treaty simultaneously received a verbal notification (June 30th) in which the insecurity of German subjects was pleaded in justification and the promise was given that " as soon as the state of affairs in Morocco has resumed the former tranquil aspect the vessel charged with this protective mission will leave the port of Agadir." The communication made to the British Government set forth various acts done by France in alleged contravention of the treaty of 1906. Just before this the Emperor had made one of his politico-domestic visits to England.

At the beginning of July Europe was startled by the news that the *Panther* had arrived in Moroccan waters, and the conclusion was widely drawn that Germany, after long professing disinterested motives, had now changed her mind and was determined to obtain a footing in the sultanate. It was also recalled that Agadir was the port which the Pan-German League had for years been urging the Government to appropriate as a naval station and the vestibule to an eligible *hinterland*. At a later date (November 17th) the Foreign Secretary, Herr von Kiderlen-Wächter, told the Diet that the intention to set foot in Morocco was never entertained, such a step being " impossible after the agreement of 1906, which has since been the directing principle of our action." Nevertheless, German writers have frankly admitted that if the suspicion of an acquisitive design prevailed abroad, as it did, the action of the Pan-Germans and imperialists at the time amply justified it.[1] In the assistance which it gave to France in the critical conjuncture the British Government faithfully observed the bond of April, 1904. From the first it even seemed to attach to the Agadir incident an exaggerated importance, and one which was not, on the whole, attributed to it in France.[2]

After the French Government had despatched the expedition to Fez " for the succour of Europeans," the British Foreign Secretary had publicly stated (May 2nd) that his Government " could not see why any objection should be taken to it." Germany now retorted that she could not understand why objection should be offered to a passive demonstration designed to ensure the safety of her own subjects. Confronted by the charge that the Agadir incident was an intimation that it was determined to reopen the Morocco question, the German For-

[1] Count Reventlow, *Deutschlands auswärtige Politik*, 1888–1914, p. 401.
[2] The deputy M. Marcel Sembat stated in the Chamber (December, 1911) that " the despatch of the German boat to Agadir was regarded by a large part of the French Press as the manifestation, not of a hostile desire or feeling, but simply of a wish to discuss matters."

eign Office replied that the question had already been reopened by France when she intervened in the affairs of the sultanate in a manner neither sanctioned nor contemplated by the Act of Algeciras. Undoubtedly a new situation had arisen in Morocco, but it was only one of a series of new situations which had been created during the past seven years, first by France and Great Britain jointly in concluding the bipartite convention of April, 1904, and later by the action of France in going beyond the strict letter of the treaties to which she was a party.

In the meantime the German and French Governments, in the persons of Herr von Kiderlen-Wächter and M. Jules Cambon respectively, were negotiating in Berlin on the subject of compensation. By prearrangement the negotiations were carried on in secret, but such facts as came to light indicated that Germany was making excessive demands. Her Foreign Minister had deemed the occasion opportune for consolidating and greatly extending the German dominion in Central Africa, and it was understood that while offering to cede to France her little colony of Togoland, he had asked for the greater part of the French Congo region in return. For a time a deadlock threatened. Then Great Britain intervened in circumstances which recalled the Palmerstonian thrills of half a century before. In an interview with the German ambassador, Count Wolff Metternich, on July 21st, the Foreign Secretary referred to " news which appeared the day before as to the demands which the German Government had made on the French Government — demands which were in effect, not a rectification of the frontier, but a cession of the French Congo — and which it was obviously impossible for the French Government to concede," and being in the dark, he asked for precise information concerning Germany's intentions in regard to Morocco and her territorial claims elsewhere. Unable to reply in detail, the ambassador promised to communicate with his Government, meanwhile giving the assurance that Germany had no intention of acquiring territory in Morocco, and that nothing would be done by her which could injure British interests, yet adding that if France wished to proclaim a protectorate over the country, Germany would require an equivalent elsewhere, just as Great Britain had done already.

The same evening Sir Edward Grey, after consultation with the Prime Minister, caused a public warning to be issued to

Germany, reminding her that in treating with France she was also treating with France's Western ally. The sensation caused by the movements of the *Panther* was insignificant in comparison with that created by a considered statement made on July 21st at the Mansion House by the Chancellor of the Exchequer, Mr. Lloyd George, who, in referring to the dual negotiations, said:

" If a situation were to be forced on us in which peace could only be preserved by the surrender of the great and beneficent position Britain has won by centuries of heroism and achievement, by allowing Britain to be treated, where her interests are vitally affected, as if she were of no account in the Cabinet of nations, then I say emphatically that peace at that price would be a humiliation intolerable for a great country like ours to endure."

The effect of the speech was explosive, for the outside world had had no apprehension of any danger to peace, and public opinion, in England and elsewhere, approved or disapproved according as it favoured France or Germany in the Moroccan controversy. The claim that England should not be overlooked was in the circumstances perfectly justifiable, but it gave to the anti-British Press in Germany a peg upon which to hang anew its complaint that in the initial agreement for the settlement of Morocco Germany had been altogether ignored. Recalling the incident at a later date (December 5, 1911), when the Morocco question had been settled in a manner acceptable to the three Governments, the German Chancellor stated:

" Sir Edward Grey said that the Chancellor of the Exchequer by his speech wished to make it clear, without provocation, that where English interests were affected England could not be treated as if she did not count. I claim the same right for Germany. When, however, I look back, I find that the Moroccan complications arose because this right had not always been accorded to Germany. The year 1904, in which England and France disposed of Morocco without consideration for the interests which Germany had in the settlement of the Moroccan problem, was the *proton pseudos* (fundamental error). From this proceeded the necessity for us to go to Algeciras, and then to Agadir; in other words, the necessity for us to safeguard our economic interests ourselves and to show the world that we are firmly resolved not to suffer ourselves to be pushed on one side."

The Mansion House speech was not allowed, however, to disturb the pacific course of events; referring to these at a later date, Sir Edward Grey claimed (November 27, 1911): " Everything we did or said in our communications with the French Government was in the direction of helping and not impeding the negotiations." The German Government protested against the speech at the time, both through its ambassador in London and in the Diet, as incendiary, but the idea of either defiance or offence having been at once disclaimed by the British Foreign Secretary, the incident was regarded as closed. None the less, Europe was greatly relieved when it was announced that an agreement had been concluded on November 4th by which Germany gave to France a perfectly free hand in regard to future political developments in Morocco, even to the extent of acquiescing in a protectorate should that be deemed necessary. On the other hand, the treaty contained stipulations of great value to the Powers generally, for the economic equality which France in 1904 had guaranteed to maintain in Morocco for thirty years was now made permanent; trading monopolies which she had hoped to secure for herself were renounced; in a word, the principle of the " open door," with equal opportunity for every one who passed in, was explicitly affirmed, and a guarantee was given that in Morocco the exclusive methods which were a tradition of French colonial administration, and which inflicted as much harm upon the colonies themselves as upon the countries wishful to trade with them, should not be applied. In these respects Germany rendered to Europe in connection with Morocco the same service which she had rendered in connection with the Congo in 1884 and 1885.

Nor was territorial compensation overlooked. Three years before, indeed, the German Foreign Secretary had assured M. Jules Cambon: " We cannot barter Morocco's right for territory or indeed for anything else: honour obliges us to respect the independence and maintain the integrity of the Sultan's dominions, and we are fully determined to obey the dictates of honour." Under stress of temptation that virtuous resolve was forgotten. Germany's material consideration consisted of a slice (about one-third) of the French Congo, adjacent to her colony of the Cameroons, in extent over 100,000 square miles, without prejudice to the mining and other rights held by French adventurers. France also waived in Germany's favour her right of pre-emption in regard to Spanish Guinea, Corisco Island, and the Elobey Islands, belonging to Spain, and, more important still, she abandoned the right of pre-emption in relation to the Congo State which she had obtained from King Leopold of Belgium in 1884, and agreed that any proposed change in the status of that State should be submitted to the Powers which were parties to the Congo Act of 1885, and thus become a matter of international arrangement.

For Germany the Morocco agreement thus concluded was, in all its aspects, an advantageous one. Not only had she reaped solid territorial gains elsewhere, but by concluding a bargain with France alone and recognizing French influence in the whole of Morocco, she had left the other Powers interested in the country to settle as they would whatever misunderstandings, arising out of their secret arrangements, the future might bring forth. While henceforth, from the territorial standpoint, Germany's interest in this sorely tried country ceased, the commitments and obligations of Great Britain remained in full force. Simultaneously with the conclusion of this agreement it was gravely announced that all danger to the lives and property of German subjects had passed away at Agadir, and by the end of November the *Panther* and the other vessels which had been sent to support it steamed away.

"You are now masters in Morocco," were the words with which the German Chancellor — since the middle of 1909 Herr von Bethmann-Hollweg [1]— described to M. Jules Cambon (who had signed the treaty on behalf of France) the effect of the final Morocco settlement. That was also the impression formed in Germany as soon as its terms were known. The consequence was a renewed outburst of indignation on the part of the Chauvinists, who clamoured for the dismissal of the Minister who, in their view, had brought upon his country an unexampled humiliation. The Pan-Germans in particular, knowing well that this was Germany's last opportunity of gaining a foothold in Morocco, had made extraordinary attempts to stir up national feeling on behalf of a strong forward policy, and as soon as it was found that the Government had left France in full possession of all she had asked for they raised the cry that the country had been betrayed. In the course of

[1] See Chapter XX., p. 359.

fiery debates in the Diet, Herr von Bethmann-Hollweg protested (November 9th and 10th) that Morocco was not worth a European war, and maintained that Germany had reason to be satisfied with the settlement, since it had relieved the tension all round.

" Morocco," he said, " was like a continually festering wound in our relations not only with France, but also with England. The French expedition to Fez led to an acute stage and rendered an operation necessary. We have performed the operation in order to heal the wound. We should never have reached the result now before you if both Governments had not steered for the same goal. I consider it a great gain that it should have been possible for Germany and France to arrive at a peaceful understanding on such a delicate question as that of Morocco, involving as it did so many dangers, open and concealed. . . . In virtue of treaty stipulations England stood on the side of France, at least diplomatically, in all differences between us and France respecting Morocco. Our understanding with France accordingly also cleans the slate in respect to our relations with England."

All such pleas, however, were wasted upon the imperialists, for they seemed only to confirm their accusation that Germany had made an ignominious surrender. It was in vain that the Chancellor warned the war party that " To raise national passions to boiling-point for the sake of Utopian schemes of conquest, and for party ends, is to compromise the patriotism which is our most valuable possession." So far did passion supplant judgment that the remarkable spectacle was witnessed of the Crown Prince applauding from his seat in the imperial box hostile criticisms passed by Conservative speakers upon the policy of his father's advisers. When two days later the Prince attended one of the large entertainment halls of Berlin he received from the audience of ten thousand people a turbulent ovation which showed how strongly the Chauvinistic spirit had infected the unthinking populace, and proved that by his action in the Diet, wholly irregular as it was, he had not unfaithfully reflected the inflammatory public opinion of the moment.

France, on the other hand, was well content with the settlement, and the cession of Congo territory in consideration of a consolidated North-west African empire caused in that country no serious heart-burning. It was evident, indeed, that throughout the negotiations the British Government, perhaps not knowing the full extent of the French commitments to Germany on the subject of compensation from 1905 forward, had taken the question far more tragically than the French themselves. The equity of the agreement was frankly admitted by leading French statesmen at the time. M. de Selves, the Foreign Minister, stated in the Chamber (December 14, 1911):

"Germany said to us, ' All right, we agree — take Morocco, and establish your protectorate there. But as you have bargained with England, with Italy, and with Spain, on what other basis will you treat with us? German public opinion will not tolerate that we should not obtain elsewhere compensation for the renunciation which we are about to make in your favour and our promise to assist you by our diplomacy in obtaining the ratification by the Powers of the agreement we have concluded.' "

"Could we affect to ignore the efforts of Germany in Morocco for half a century," said M. Deschanel, Chairman of the Foreign Affairs Committee, " the travels of her explorers, the activity of her colonists, her agricultural and mining enterprises, her steamship lines, her post offices, and especially that movement of ideas which gravitated towards the Shereefian Empire? "

The confession of that standpoint by France completed Germany's case for compensation, but inferentially it carried condemnation of the policy pursued in 1904. It will be the task of later historians to attempt, with fuller knowledge of the facts, to decide whether the settlement which was concluded under compulsion in 1911 would not have been practicable, on the same or an equivalent basis, seven years before, and to determine to what extent the international discords of the intervening and later years might have been averted or mitigated had the authors of the convention of 1904, so excellent in intention, shown greater prescience.

With the signature of the Franco-German agreement of 1911 the Morocco question was regarded, from the diplomatic standpoint, as closed. Outside the world of Cabinets and Chancelleries, however, little satisfaction or assurance was derived from an arrangement which had originated in the heated atmosphere created by national jealousies and resentments.

The part taken in the transaction by Great Britain increased her unpopularity in Germany, since it was held to confirm the suspicion of hostile motives which had long been attributed to her by the Colonial and Pan-Germanist parties, who in justification of their attitude pointed to the fact that on the whole no Continental Power had so little obstructed, or shown a desire to obstruct, British expansion and British foreign interests generally as Germany. There had been a progressive estrangement between the two countries since 1910. During the summer of that year the rumour was again circulated in Germany that the British navy meditated an attack, and baseless and ludicrous though it was, there was a revival of it in the autumn. The prevailing nervousness was increased by a speech made by the Emperor at Hamburg in August, in which he appealed again for national sacrifice in the interest of a larger navy, so that " we may be sure that no one can dispute the place in the sun which is our right."

The end of the Morocco episode left Anglo-German relations worse than at the beginning, worse, indeed, than they had been since the colonial disputes of 1884 and 1885, and substantially the friction was due to the same cause. While British Ministers were conscious only of having done a good turn to a friendly Power, Germany reproached them with having deliberately connived at the violation of the Treaty of Algeciras, and even their own agreement of 1904, by which France explicitly undertook not to disturb the political independence of Morocco, and with having baulked a justifiable attempt to assert that sanctity of international obligations upon which British statesmen were never weary of insisting. It was difficult to rebut these accusations altogether, for there was in them just sufficient truth to make not a few moderate people in England feel uncomfortable under the criticism. These were ready to admit that Morocco was bound to come to France sooner or later, and that there was no reason in the world why Great Britain should not have assisted in that reasonable solution of a century-old problem. What they chiefly criticized was their Government's failure seven years before to make allowance for German sentiment and claims. If, it was argued, the British Government and its advisers were satisfied that Germany had no designs on Moroccan territory, there could have been no objection to bringing her into the agreements of 1904. If, on the other hand, they suspected such designs, the case for inviting her co-operation was doubly strong, since to ignore her was deliberately to seek misunderstandings and hand to the future an inevitable legacy of difficulty and danger.

In one respect, however, German strictures upon Great Britain were singularly out of place. For the country which was held to have endeavoured to throw obstacles in the way of Germany's economic advancement had been the first to proclaim the doctrine of commercial equality in all parts of the world. It was forgotten at the time that whenever Germany had knocked at the doors of British colonies these doors had been opened to her on equal terms with the mother country, and that if many countries were now guarding their markets more jealously then heretofore, it was Germany which had set the example by the pursuance of a policy of extreme protection.[1]

The support which had been given to France so openly and ungrudgingly by the British Government in the course of the final negotiations over Morocco led to renewed discussions in both countries as to the precise character of the *entente cordiale*. Was it merely a friendly understanding, as had always been maintained, or an alliance *sans phrase?* Was the support promised by England to France merely moral and not at all material, merely diplomatic and not military? Or were there behind the agreement mutual obligations of a graver and more engrossing nature? It was not the first time that questions of this kind had been asked. Two years after the conclusion of the agreement the French Government had been challenged in the Chamber of Deputies to say frankly whether it had a military significance or not. Asked on November 20th,

[1] The traditional British policy of the "open door" had been followed not long before in the settlement of another part of Africa. When in January, 1899, after the reoccupation of Khartoum and the pacification of the Soudan, an agreement was concluded between the British and Egyptian Governments, regulating the political status of this territory, it was laid down that no special trading privileges should be accorded to the subjects of any single Power. "In other words," writes Lord Cromer, "the German, the Frenchman, the Italian, and others were placed on a precisely similar commercial footing to that enjoyed by a subject of the Queen of England. Even the most militant Anglophobe could not fail to be struck by the contrast between this liberal attitude and the exclusive commercial policy adopted by other colonizing European Powers" (*Modern Egypt,* vol. ii., p. 119).

1906, to state " Yes " or " No " to the question whether a military convention with England existed, M. Clemenceau, then new to office, replied: " I should be the most embarrassed man in the world if I had to reply to you ' Yes ' or ' No.' All I can say is that I do not think that any such convention exists." Formally, perhaps, there was none, yet the responsibility undertaken by Great Britain as an obligation of honour for the security of the northern coast of France and her own withdrawal of ships of war from the Mediterranean, where France was now acting as guardian of the interests of both Powers, were regarded as indications that behind the *entente* was an understanding, not less definite because implied only and not as yet put into writing, that the two Powers had for practical purposes pooled their military and naval resources. Early in 1911 (February 2nd) the question was raised again in the French Senate in a more direct manner. The statement then made by M. Pichon, Foreign Minister, was not explicit, but the impression which it conveyed was unmistakable.[1]

The fact was disclosed later that during the British general election of December, 1905–January, 1906, when the Algeciras conference was meeting, the French Government, alarmed by the development of the Morocco question and by the possibility of further German pressure, asked the British Foreign Secretary whether, in the event of France being attacked by Germany, Great Britain would be prepared to give her not only naval but military assistance, the idea being that British troops should co-operate in resisting a German invasion across the Belgian frontier. On that occasion Sir Edward Grey gave both the French and German ambassadors to understand that it was his belief that, in view of the cordial relations which had sprung up under the Anglo-French *entente*, the British nation

---

[1] Answering a Conservative critic who had asked what results the *entente* with England could show for itself, the Minister said: " It is singular that it should be asserted that the *entente cordiale* with Great Britain is so unreal that it produces no results, and that for the last two or three years there has never been any conversation of a military character with England. What do you (to the Senator) know about it? Is the Minister of Foreign Affairs in the habit of acquainting newspaper editors with his diplomatic or military conversations? Do you think that diplomacy is carried on in public places? You have too much experience of these things for me to have to press the point. I declare that the *entente cordiale* was never more complete and more intimate than to-day. I declare this not only in my name and in that of the Government, but on the strength of assurances given to me in the name of the British Government."

would not wish to stand aside if France, owing to no fault of her own, were to be threatened by her neighbour.[1] Thereupon the French Government pressed for a more definite and substantial pledge of assistance in the contingency named, and suggested formal conversations on the subject. The members of the Cabinet were at the time scattered about the country, and a collective reply to this proposal was impossible. The Foreign Secretary conferred, however, with the Premier (Sir Henry Campbell-Bannerman), the Secretary for War (Mr. Haldane), and the Chancellor of the Exchequer (Mr. Asquith), and with their concurrence the desired conversations were authorized, subject to the condition that the Government and Parliament retained complete liberty of action. From that time forward systematic conferences between military and naval experts on both sides were held, in which the contingency of armed co-operation was discussed and planned for.

After the Agadir crisis and the resulting second Franco-German agreement, the two Governments concluded that the time had come for putting into definite and documentary form the understanding which hitherto has rested upon more or less informal negotiations. In a letter addressed to M. Paul Cambon on November 22, 1912, Sir Edward Grey recalled how the French ambassador had once remarked that " if either Government had grave reason to expect an unprovoked attack by a third Power, it might become essential to know whether it could in that event depend on the armed assistance of the other." Developing this thought, the British Foreign Secretary " agreed that such a contingency would call for discussion as to whether the two Governments should act together to prevent aggression and to preserve peace, and if so, what measures they would be prepared to take in common." " If these measures involved action," he added, " the plans of the General Staffs would at once be taken into consideration and the Governments would then decide what effect should be given to them." M. Cambon confirmed the arrangement suggested in this letter, and so the matter appears to have rested.[2]

[1] See the full explanatory statement made in the House of Commons by Sir Edward Grey on August 3, 1914.

[2] Answering a question in the House of Commons on November 27, 1911, the Under-Secretary for Foreign Affairs accurately stated the technical position of his Government in the words, " An agreement to afford diplomatic support does not impose on any Power an obligation either to give or to withhold military or naval support."

While no formal military convention was even then concluded, it is none the less clear that, unknown to the world at large, or even to the Parliaments concerned, the *entente* had already become in substance a defensive alliance, needing only the occurrence of certain well-understood conditions in order to become at once effective. No one was more energetic in directing the *entente* into this practical, and perhaps inevitable, channel than M. Paul Cambon while acting as French ambassador in London. He received ready sympathy and response from the permanent Ministers-without-portfolio of the Foreign Office, but it was his own unwearying persistence and clear consciousness of aim that chiefly succeeded in making the Anglo-French accord what he, and M. Delcassé before him, always intended that it should be, a union of arms as well as of hearts.

German opinion, official as well as public, had already arrived at that conclusion in the early days of the *entente*, whose developments on the military and naval sides, from 1905 onwards, were no secret to the Berlin Foreign Office. From the outset the nation, and later the Government, persisted in viewing the cordial concert first of two and then of three Powers as a measure deliberately aimed against Germany. To English people this suspicion appeared irrational and unjustifiable. From the moment that the Anglo-French agreement of 1904 was concluded British statesmen had spoken of it as a step on the way to a wider European understanding. Lord Lansdowne, the co-author of the agreement, made this object clear at the time, when he said that " friendship with one Power did not mean hostility to others." Recalling the genesis of the *entente* at a later date (1911), he stated that " If the Government of that time (1904) had any one aspiration which they cherished particularly, it was that the agreement with France should be the precursor of other agreements with other Powers," and that " the whole policy of the late Government was quite inconsistent with the idea of coming to an agreement with France which should exclude the possibility of agreements with other Powers or which should divide other European Powers into hostile camps."

Amongst British Liberals in particular the hope was entertained that an agreement with Germany on the same lines would be one of the earliest results of the new diplomatic departure. It was in this spirit that Sir Henry Campbell-Bannerman, the

Liberal leader, said (November 16, 1905), just before the formation of his first and only Government: " Our stock of good feeling and international good-will is not exhausted by France. Let us hope that this wise policy may be extended. There is the great empire of Russia, and again there is Germany." Under Lord Lansdowne's successor at the Foreign Office the Anglo-French accord, owing to the pressure of events for which Germany herself was not free from responsibility, gradually assumed a character more intimate and less exclusively diplomatic than may have been originally intended. Nevertheless, the policy of the four consecutive Liberal Governments which dated from December, 1905, was a consistent attempt to adhere to the maxim of Sir Edward Grey, who had charge of foreign affairs in each Cabinet: " Separate diplomatic groups need not necessarily be opposing diplomatic groups." Not less than his predecessor he endeavoured to the last to prevent the Powers of the Triple Entente and of the Triple Alliance from falling into a relationship of hopeless antagonism.

However obvious this view of the case might be to English minds, however, the German nation, judging it from its own standpoint, with other preconceptions, and a fixed bias towards suspicion, came to a different conclusion, and it may perhaps be claimed that, considered quite subjectively, one interpretation of the facts, so far as they were known, was as tenable as the other. Against all the assurances of the Entente Powers that their association was entirely free from an unfriendly, still less an aggressive, purpose Germany set the fact that throughout the Morocco controversy from 1905 forward the British Foreign Office had made it clear that its influence must be regarded as wholly pledged to the support of France and French interests.

Moreover, on the part of France at least these assurances were at best formal and diplomatic, and they could not possibly have been otherwise. To her the *entente* had first been welcome because of the sense of relief and confidence which it gave her. France wanted peace, but it would be doing an injustice to the spirit of that proud nation, still as unreconciled as ever to the loss of her eastern frontier territories, to suppose that she any longer thought of war with the former reluctance and dread.

Shortly after the visit of a British squadron to Brest in the summer of 1905 M. Delcassé, when in a position of less responsibility and greater freedom, for he had ceased to be Foreign Minister, spoke openly of the defensive significance and value of the *entente*. " Of what importance," he asked, " would the young navy of Germany be in the event of war, in which England, let me tell you, would assuredly be with us against Germany? What would become of Germany's ports, of her trade, of her mercantile marine? It would be annihilation for them. That is what will be the significance of the visit, *préparée et calculée*, of the British squadron at Brest, while the return visit of the French squadron to Portsmouth will complete the demonstration." [1] To that utterance, since it came from one of the authors of the *entente*, an importance was attributed which was probably not justified, yet the alarm which it excited in Germany was genuine and natural. It was a French Senator, Baron d'Estournelles de Constant, who, speaking for his own country, said at a later date: " That the *entente* was perverted by being made to appear anti-German is beyond question "; and men so dissimilar in political views as M. Ribot and M. Jaurès publicly endorsed that opinion.[2] Reports from Belgian diplomatic representatives to their Government, published since the war, show that the same idea was entertained in quarters friendly to the *entente* Powers.

For a time, indeed, Great Britain's more intimate relations with France undoubtedly exercised a steadying influence in Paris, just as Russia's close alliance had done already. As the Morocco misunderstanding increased, however, passions on both sides of the Rhine rose to a temperature never reached since the climax of the Boulanger episode more than twenty years before. For if in France the idea of *revanche*, which all the world believed to have been abandoned, was again discussed with the old freedom and vehemence, there were not wanting in Germany corresponding currents of feeling which did not stop short at mere vituperation. To the Chauvinists there the thought of having suffered diplomatic humiliation at the hands of a nation which once had been compelled to ask mercy of the German sword was intolerable. With a crude virulence that

---

[1] Statement in the Paris *Gaulois* of July 12, 1905.
[2] Speaking in the Senate as late as February 6, 1912, Baron d'Estournelles de Constant referred to " the puerile character of our policy of the isolation of Germany," and contrasted it with the earlier " irreproachable policy of equilibrium."

wounded to the quick the pride and honour of a singularly sensitive people, these men did their utmost to stimulate national hatred of France and to inflame the desire to meet and abase her again on the battlefield.

To regard as phantoms, therefore, Germany's suspicion of a plot for her political isolation and her belief that the *entente* was a direct challenge to the Triple Alliance, and to her in particular, does not imply that her apprehensions, if groundless, altogether lacked justification. In political life it is not intentions, but facts and effects, that count, and upon these alone history has to pass judgment. " Never mind what were your intentions," Mr. Disraeli told the Government of Lord Palmerston as he probed the causes which led the Hindoos into mutiny, " the question is what were *their* thoughts, what were *their* inferences? " [1] Nothing that is known of the inner history of the Triple Entente and of the events in which it played a part down to the summer of 1914 can be held to justify even the assumption that its purpose was to harass, thwart, and ultimately to isolate Germany. This, however, was the belief entertained almost universally in that country, and it cannot reasonably be denied that there were facts and appearances which must have made the belief easy for a suspicious Government and a nervous nation. It is not likely that further light upon the subject will weaken this conclusion.

Just before the closing of the Morocco question Germany came to an understanding with Russia concerning the Bagdad Railway project. In November, 1910, the Czar visited the Emperor at Potsdam, and as a result there was concluded in the following year an agreement which, without prejudice to existing alliances and obligations, brought the two countries into line in regard both to this project and to their future relations in Asia Minor and Persia generally. Russia withdrew objection to the railway and agreed to its being linked on to the lines which she proposed to build in North Persia, while Germany undertook to recognize Russia's special position in that region subject to the concession of equal trading facilities. Speaking in the Diet of the result of the meeting (December 10th), the Chancellor said that the two Powers had exchanged assurances that they would enter into no combinations of an aggressive character, and would maintain the *status quo* in the

[1] Speech in the House of Commons, July 27, 1857, on British annexation policy prior to the Indian Mutiny.

Balkans and the Near East generally, while the Emperor in private conversation hazarded the opinion that the Franco-Russian alliance was by no means so secure as it had been represented. Out of Germany, however, no great expectations were built upon the Potsdam agreement so far as the European relationships of the two Powers were concerned. Soberly considered, all it proved was that they were willing to come to terms in regard to external questions involving on neither side vital interests; the main lines of their foreign policies were unaffected.

The year 1912 will be remembered as a year fateful for the relations of Germany to Great Britain. The violence of the anti-British and anti-French outbreak just before was a signal of danger not to be lightly disregarded, for it was symptomatic of the existence of pent-up forces hostile to peace, which were capable at any time of passing beyond control. For a long time systematic endeavours had been made by the military and naval leagues, by means of countless meetings, the free use of the Press, and a large inflammatory literature, to indoctrinate in the public mind the theory of so-called " preventive warfare." The idea that the State, if it believed war to be inevitable, was justified in anticipating the purpose and preparations of its enemies, and taking the initiative as soon as circumstances seemed propitious, was not new in Prussian history. Moltke was the most conspicuous modern representative of the doctrine, and on two notable occasions he had been willing to apply it.

The first occasion was in 1867 during the Luxemburg dispute, when, believing that a collision between Prussia and France must come sooner or later, he wished to precipitate it on that issue while the military situation was still altogether in Prussia's favour. Bismarck refused to incur responsibility for so direct a challenge to fate. " The personal conviction of a ruler or a statesman, however well founded," he wrote at the time, " that war would eventually occur could not justify its promotion. Unforeseen events might alter the situation and avert what seemed inevitable." [1]

[1] *Essays, Speeches, and Memoirs of Count Helmuth von Moltke*, vol. ii., pp., 204–5. Bismarck writes in his *Reflections and Reminiscences* (vol. ii., p. 102): " That at the time of the Luxemburg question, during the crisis manufactured by Gortchakoff and France (*sic*) in 1875, and even until recent times, the General Staff and its heads have allowed themselves to be betrayed into acts menacing to peace lies in the necessary spirit of the

The second occasion was in 1875, when, as has been shown, the great strategist so seriously considered the expediency of forcing a new war upon the same nation before it had fully recovered from the defeat of 1870–1. With this design the Imperial Chancellor was supposed to sympathize; it is more probable that his apparent toleration of it up to a certain point was intended as a warning to the French Government that it would do well to steady the firebrands who were at work to the west, no less than the east, of the Rhine at that time.

In later years Bismarck condemned the policy of " preventive warfare " in uncompromising terms, defining it on one occasion as a policy of " suicide in apprehension of death." [1] More accurately it might be defined as one of murder in apprehension of assault. From the first decade of the new century this policy had been preached with fervour by the militarist party, particularly of Prussia, and in a country in which public opinion looks so much for guidance to the Government the danger of such propagandism for war was all the more insidious owing to the fact that it seldom received official rebuke. Open incitements to war for the purpose of territorial conquest, disparagements of peace as debasing for a great nation, confident assurances that the French and British were effeminate and decadent peoples, whose conquest was in the order of nature and history, with much ugly talk of " trials of strength " (*Machtproben*), a phrase of evil omen for industrial as well as political relations, were the usual substance of this agitation. The entire episode forms a remarkable passage in the modern cultural life of Germany for which a parallel will be vainly sought in earlier times.[2]

institution (the army), a spirit which I should not wish to disappear, yet which can only become dangerous under a monarch whose policy lacks a sense of proportion and power to resist one-sided and constitutionally unjustifiable influences." See also his opinions on the same subject in vol. i., pp. 441–2.

[1] Thus he said in the course of a speech in the Imperial Diet on February 6, 1888: " If I were to come before you and say : ' We are seriously menaced by France and by Russia; it is to be foreseen that we shall be attacked; that is my conviction as a diplomatist, based also on military information; for our defence it is better to employ the anticipatory thrust of the attack and open hostilities at once; accordingly I ask the Imperial Diet for a credit of a milliard of marks, in order to start the war against both our neighbours — well, gentlemen, I do not know whether you have sufficient confidence in me to vote such a grant, but I hope not.' "

[2] A mass of evidence on the subject is contained in the book *Der deutsche Chauvinismus*, by Dr. O. Nippold (Stuttgart, 1913).

Nevertheless, the idea that the people of Germany as a whole, or even in large part, were at that time bent on war is a legend of later origin, and as such may be dismissed. On the one hand, only a few responsible leaders of public opinion or men of political and social influence took seriously the intemperate oratory of the military party, still less of the Pan-Germanists. On the other hand, among the active and vocal friends of peace were many influential statesmen and diplomatists, prominent spokesmen of the Protestant Church, and representatives of scholarship and science of international reputation. The foremost leaders of industry, commerce, and finance in general had no stronger wish than for continued tranquillity, well aware that war, even if waged successfully, would check and throw back indefinitely the pacific conquest of the world's markets which Germany had been pursuing with unwearying zest and growing success for a generation. The democratic parties were unanimous and emphatic in their zeal for international concord in every direction; and behind the peace movement was a large and powerful Press, comprising many newspapers and reviews, both metropolitan and provincial, which ranked amongst the most influential in Germany.

So far as the attitude towards Great Britain in particular was concerned, while the idea of war with that country was undoubtedly abhorrent to the mass of the German people, there was yet a distinct and deepening consciousness of alienation, and — so faithful is human nature to itself — this alienation followed, in the main, the same social and political line of cleavage which divided the British nation in its attitude towards Germany. For suspicion and ill-feeling existed by no means on one side only; if in Germany there was a strong Anglophobist party, represented by the soldiers and the higher bureaucrats, with a sprinkling of intellectuals and industrialists, and in political life by the Conservatives generally, there was also in England an anti-German party, no less strong or irreconcilable, recruited predominantly, yet with many distinguished exceptions, from the same elements in the population. In England at least — in Germany never — the old colonial quarrels were well-nigh forgotten, and even the grudge against Germany as a too successful commercial rival was dying down as her manufacturers and merchants, rousing themselves to more earnest efforts, were finding that while much trade might have been lost there was still far more to be gained. Yet suspicion and distrust was widespread; if in Germany there was a settled belief that England was thwarting her legitimate desires for expansion, in England there was a growing apprehension as to the purpose and issue of her rival's naval projects.

A desire to open the way for friendlier relations was shown by the Emperor early in the year, when he invited the British Cabinet to send to Berlin a special envoy of authoritative position to discuss with his Ministers questions of common interest. The invitation was accepted with good-will, and the delicate mission was entrusted to Lord Haldane, the only British statesman of his generation who can be said to have seriously studied Germany and to have brought to his study the sympathy without which it is impossible to enter into the mind and understand the point of view of another nation.

Lord Haldane had already visited Berlin officially as Secretary for War in September, 1906, and had on that occasion been afforded the opportunity of examining the organization of the German army and particularly the War Office and General Staff, an exceptional privilege which he used with great and lasting advantage to his own country. His second official visit was made early in February, 1912. In the course of his three days' sojourn he met the Emperor and his principal Ministers, as well as the heads of the army and navy, and the frank exchange of views which took place on that occasion was reported at the time to have cleared up much obscurity and suspicion and eased the prevailing tension all round. Herr von Bethmann-Hollweg told the Diet just afterwards (February 15th): " The exchange of views, which was heartily welcomed on our side, took place in numerous conversations of an exhaustive and frank character and will be continued "; while Mr. Asquith said in the House of Commons (February 14th): " The anticipation that good would result from a free exchange of views has been realized. It has dispelled the suspicion that either Government contemplates aggressive designs against the other."

If the immediate practical results were not as substantial as Lord Haldane desired, it was not due to lack of either clear aims or effort on his part. He was able to satisfy the German Chancellor of the pacific disposition of the British Government, and his assurance that it had no agreements with France and

Russia except those that were in writing and published to the world at once cleared the ground for the discussion of the possible basis of an accord which should supplement, and perhaps comprehend, the existing Anglo-French and Anglo-Russian *ententes,* to the advantage of all the four Powers. The objects of the negotiations were not precisely defined, nor was it contemplated that binding understandings or pledges should then be given or asked on either side. The visit of the British envoy was, in effect, a voyage of discovery, an endeavour to survey the ground, take stock of the political situation in Berlin, estimate the genuineness of the conciliatory advances which had been made there, and ascertain in what directions, and within what limits, cordial co-operation between the two countries might be possible.

The sincerity of the German Chancellor's desire for a friendly understanding was not open to question, and his assertion that reconciliation with Great Britain had been " the dream of his official life " was consistent with all his known actions on that occasion. He first put forward as the basis of an agreement a formula which recalled the rejected unconditional neutrality proposal of 1909. On examination this formula broke down before Lord Haldane's objection that an unconditional promise that neither of the two Powers would enter into a combination directed against the other might prove unworkable in certain possible, though in practice hardly conceivable, circumstances. Thus Germany, for example, would presumably feel herself bound to intervene in the event of British attack upon some Power whose independence was to her vital interest, just as Great Britain would wish to have complete freedom of action in the same circumstances. Moreover, the formula proposed would have allowed Germany to fulfil to the fullest extent her existing liabilities to her allies, while it would have prevented Great Britain, because unbound by formal alliances, from giving help to her friends of the *entente.*

Recognizing that any pledge of neutrality must be consistent with fidelity to all existing obligations towards third Powers, Lord Haldane suggested reciprocal undertakings against aggressive or unprovoked attacks and hostile combinations, military or naval agreements and plans, as giving to Germany every reasonable guarantee, while at the same time respecting Great Britain's engagements, which were declared to be en-

tirely free from hostile purpose against Germany or any other
Power. A formula was accordingly elaborated on these lines.
In its final form it would have bound the two Powers to declare
that neither of them would make any unprovoked attack upon
the other or join in any combination or design against the
other for purposes of aggression, or become party to any plan
or naval or military combination, alone or in conjunction with
any other Power, directed to such an end; that if either of the
contracting parties became involved in a war in which it could
not be said to be the aggressor, the other was at least to observe a benevolent neutrality towards it and endeavour to
localize the conflict; yet that such duty of neutrality should
not apply in so far as it might not be reconcilable with existing agreements with other Powers, and in conformity with this
provision the making of new agreements which might render it
impossible for either of the contracting Powers to observe neutrality towards the other beyond the limitations above stated
was to be excluded.

All these undertakings, however, were of a negative order,
and directed to the statement of the conditions upon which the
two Powers should or should not be entitled to wage war in
given contingencies rather than to positive measures for the
preservation of peace. Perhaps the most statesmanlike feature of the proposed agreement was the provision that the two
Powers should undertake for the future to exchange views upon
all questions which might arise between them with a view to
bringing about a solution conformable with their respective interests, and that each Power should make use of its good relations to third Powers in order to influence the relations of the
other Power to such third Powers in a friendly sense. It was
suggested that the agreement should be concluded first for ten
years, and thereafter continue automatically by mutual consent.

The adoption of a conditional neutrality formula, however,
was only a step — though an important step — on the way to
an agreement. All that had been done so far was to prepare
a design for the desired temple of peace, but before the actual
work of building could begin the foundations had still to be
laid. It was here that the first and real difficulties in the way
of an understanding were encountered. Now, as three years
ago, Germany was eager to have a political agreement, but

failed to appreciate sufficiently the importance from the British standpoint of a concurrent naval agreement. The political *ententes* between Great Britain and France and Russia were not based upon formal professions of good-will, but had resulted naturally from the removal of certain outstanding causes of friction; the contracting Powers had been reconciled because there was no longer any reason for their estrangement. It was Lord Haldane's hope to establish the new *entente* on the same basis, and for him the question upon which the relaxation of the existing tension was most urgently desired was obviously that of naval rivalry.

In order to understand how this question stood at the time, it is necessary to take up the threads of the story of the naval overtures at the point at which it was left in an earlier chapter (pp. 380–4). Prince von Bülow resigned the Chancellorship in July, 1909, and with the appointment of Herr von Bethmann-Hollweg as his successor a better future seemed to open for the official relations of the two countries. Judged by his actions, Bülow must be regarded as having been at best a lukewarm friend of Anglo-German concord. He was no doubt unwilling that the growing coolness between the two countries should be allowed to develop into a formal alienation; but while he was profuse in fair speeches, he made no serious attempt to avert such a misfortune. In particular he was not prepared to make any concession which could abate the increasing naval rivalry, while to general disarmament proposals he would not listen. His written confessions as given to the world in 1913, and with greater frankness three years later, throw an unfavourable light upon his attitude in regard to more than one episode which brought the two nations into conflict, and suggest doubt whether his concern for international conciliation went deeper than his political convictions generally.[1]

The new Chancellor took an early opportunity of affirming his desire for a better understanding, and his advances were cordially reciprocated in London. Pressed by the Diet in December, 1910, to disclose his views on the subject, he admitted that the idea of limiting naval armaments had repeatedly been suggested by England, but added that before such a thing could

[1] The book published in England with the title *Imperial Germany,* being a small portion of a large collective work reviewing German affairs during the first twenty-five years of the Emperor William II's reign, and published as a *Festschrift* in 1913.

be considered the nations would need to be friendlier disposed towards each other. Renewed advances led Herr von Bethmann-Hollweg to make a definite offer of a more or less speculative character. It was that Germany, without curtailing, would agree to retard her naval programme, provided Great Britain would enter into an undertaking that neither of them should attack or take part in acts of aggression against each other, while in the event of either of them being involved in a war with a third Power or a group of Powers the other would remain neutral. For the British Government such a pledge of absolute neutrality was an arrangement so one-sided and so inconsistent with the spirit of the *entente* with France and Russia, the character of which Germany well knew, that it never had the slightest prospect of acceptance.

Nevertheless, intermittent discussions on the naval question continued for some time, though without reaching a basis that promised real success. A temporary retardation of the German shipbuilding programme was again suggested in Berlin, but while still under consideration this proposal was abruptly withdrawn in 1911 on the plea that its adoption would prove injurious to the shipbuilding industry. Once more also the international situation afforded little encouragement to the friends of conciliation on either side. The relations between Germany and France were becoming more strained, for the Morocco dispute was entering its last and acutest phase. It was in July, 1911, that the climax of this dispute came with the incident of Agadir. Thus the hope of an understanding seemed to become more remote. There had been no lack of effort on the British side and no lack of friendly assurances on the German; what had been wanting was the determination to sweep difficulties out of the way and face the hard realities of the situation.

So the *impasse* on the naval question remained at the time of the Berlin conversations of February, 1912. Recognizing that this question was the essential cause of estrangement between the two countries, and that unless agreement could be reached here there could be little or no hope of agreement in other directions, Lord Haldane endeavoured to bring home to the German Chancellor the futility of a policy of naval rivalry which promised to involve both countries in illimitable expenditure, without changing their relative strength. His work was made the more difficult by the fact that at the very moment a new Navy Bill was about to be introduced in the Diet, though when he went to Berlin he knew about its contents only as much as the world in general, viz. that more battleships and cruisers were to be added to the programme of construction and important changes in the organization of the navy introduced. For whereas the active battle fleet had hitherto consisted of two squadrons, leaving two squadrons in reserve, a third active squadron was now to be formed, with a view to the greater part of the navy being henceforth maintained in permanent commission, ready at any moment for war.

There was a transparent inconsistency in the two Powers making mutual protestations of a desire for concord, and giving undertakings against aggressive designs, while at the same time Germany was increasing her navy and by implication inviting Great Britain to do the same thing. Lord Haldane, therefore, suggested that if the German shipbuilding programme could not be curtailed it might at least be spread over a longer period — say twelve years or more, instead of six years as was intended. The Chancellor was convinced and ready to come to terms. It soon became clear, however, that the only Minister known to the imperial constitution was not master in his own house, but that above him on this question was the Emperor, and above the Emperor was the Naval Secretary of State.

Not the least important result of Lord Haldane's visit to Berlin was the confirmation which it afforded of the fact — suspected long before — that, alike in military and naval matters, two parties were contending for influence with the Emperor, one a party of moderation and peace, represented by the Chancellor and some at least of his civilian colleagues, wishful and even eager for the friendship of Great Britain, and ready to pay a fair price for it, the other unconciliatory, disposed to let matters go their own way, and indifferent, to say the least, whether the end were open rupture or not. To the latter party belonged Admiral von Tirpitz, who already was believed to cherish the hope of changing the Admiralty for the Chancellery.

In the further discussion of this question the Emperor and his chief naval adviser took the lead out of the Chancellor's hands. The Emperor urgently wanted a peace agreement, but he wanted just as urgently a large navy, and one inclination neutralized the other. To Tirpitz a large navy was the supreme consideration,— he had worked and lived for twenty years for the realization of this ambition — and in comparison with it peace formulas were of little consequence. He even challenged the British two-Power standard of naval supremacy as one which Germany could not accept, only to be told that Germany had never been asked to accept it, yet that it none the less represented for Great Britain a principle of self-preservation as automatic and inexorable as any that Germany might claim to apply to her own military strength. The fact that Tirpitz was the real stumbling-block in the way of an agreement on the naval question was not disguised by the Chancellor.

Nevertheless, the idea of retardation seemed to find favour, and it was ultimately understood that while any agreement that might result would not define a standard ratio of naval power, or indeed refer specifically to shipbuilding, if a political agreement were concluded the German Government would modify its naval programme according to the altered conditions, spreading construction over a longer period. It was stated later by a German publicist, to whom the confidences of the February conversations were revealed from the German side, that as a result of Lord Haldane's persuasions four battleships were dropped from the new shipbuilding programme.[1]

In relation to another open problem, that of the still unfinished Bagdad Railway, practical progress was made, and only developments in the international situation, entirely unforeseen in 1912, prevented a later solution as part of a formal territorial agreement which would have been at least as important and far-reaching in its way as the Anglo-French and Anglo-Russian agreements of 1904 and 1907 respectively. Here, again, regard for the sequence of events makes necessary a brief retrospect. During the earlier phases of the Bagdad Railway controversy the question had not been viewed on either side as an occasion of legitimate grievance, but had been treated purely as an affair of business bargaining. As has been shown, Germany had the concessions, and Great Britain believed herself to have in reserve a power of veto which might in case of need make the concessions, if not inoperative, at least of far

[1] Count Reventlow, in *Deutschlands auswärtige Politik*, 1888–1914 (third edition), p. 428.

less value than they seemed to be. The long protraction of
the dead-lock, however, had in the end, as was inevitable, provoked untoward consequences. Concurrently with the refusal
of Great Britain to accept the project without such modifications as seemed necessary in order to safeguard her special and
ancient interests in Asia Minor and the Persian Gulf, the German promoters began to give a disquieting prominence to its
political and military aspects, and even to the hostile and aggressive possibilities which it held in store. Gradually a large
Bagdad Railway literature sprang up as part of the active
propagandism of Pan-Germanism, and a host of publicists and
politicians, putting the economic aspects of the question in the
background, now based its chief claims to support upon its
value as a menace to British rule in Egypt and eventually in
India.[1]

Five years before (November, 1907) the first serious advance towards an agreement was made on the occasion of the
German Emperor's visit to England. Meeting the Emperor
at Windsor, Lord Haldane, then Secretary of State for War,
had at his invitation stated plainly what the British Government wanted — it was, he said, a " gate " to protect India
from troops coming down the new railway to the Gulf, and he
explained that only the complete control of the terminal section
of the railway would afford this protection. " I will give you
the gate," the Emperor had then said. He went further, for
with the acquiescence of his Foreign Minister (Herr von
Schön) and his War Minister (General von Einem), who were
with him in England, he agreed to the further condition, proposed by the British Foreign Office, that France and Russia
should both be brought into the agreement. Nevertheless, the
hope of a satisfactory settlement which had thus been created
so suddenly was just as abruptly shattered. Prince Bülow,
the Chancellor, had not been consulted, and no sooner did the
imperial negotiators return to Berlin than it was discovered
that the idea of including two other Powers in an Anglo-German convention was impracticable. It is not clear that, even

---

[1] Count Reventlow chides his countrymen for having avowed their hostile
designs too openly. " That it would be possible," he writes, " after the development of the railway system, to make of Turkey a dangerous menace to
Egypt and India was quite correct, but it should not have been said so long
as Great Britain had the power to obstruct and delay the building of the
line " (*Deutschlands auswärtige Politik*, 1888–1914, p. 340).

from the British standpoint, their inclusion was essential. There could be no question of either country sharing with Great Britain the special position which was to be secured to her in respect of the Bagdad section of the railway and the Gulf. Russia, indeed, by the Anglo-Russian convention of the preceding August, had already agreed to recognize her controlling position in the Gulf, and the vital interests of France lay in other parts of Asia Minor. Whether the quadruple arrangement was necessary or not, Bülow's reason for objecting to it can only be conjectured. He may have been opposed to the basis of the compromise itself and have made the proposal to associate with it both France and Russia an excuse for thwarting it. It is at least as probable, however, that he was suspicious of the idea of negotiating with the three Entente Powers together owing to unwillingness to give to the *entente* the formal recognition which such action would involve and hence to create a precedent which might prove inconvenient on later occasions. Whether cause or only pretext, however, the attempt of the Triple Entente to negotiate as a sort of diplomatic *consortium* upon a question which had become one of international politics had the effect of delaying a settlement which was highly desirable in the interest of all parties concerned and became the more urgent the nearer the railway approached Bagdad.

Early in 1911 the promoters of the project made a new agreement with the Ottoman Government under which they secured a further financial guarantee, to meet the continuation of the line to Bagdad, while, on the other hand, they agreed to renounce their concession in respect of the section from that town to the Gulf on condition that in the capital of the new company to be formed for its construction they should be allowed to participate to at least the same extent as any other foreign group. Whatever the disadvantage for Germany of this new agreement, the condition attached to it did not seem to increase the chances that Great Britain would succeed in securing the " gate " at the Gulf end of the line which had been promised to her in 1907. Nor was the British position improved by the fact that just before this Russia, for whose sake (with that of France) Great Britain had risked the " gate " arrangement, had concluded an agreement of her own with Germany — the Potsdam Agreement of November, 1910 — under which she undertook not to put further obstacles in the way of the construction of the railway, though it is true that the two Powers disagreed later as to the precise extent of this commitment, Russia contending that it was limited to the line as far as Bagdad, Germany that it related to the complete project.

On the other hand, it was a gain from the British standpoint that Turkey had been released from the original concession and was now again to some extent a free agent. Accordingly, the London Foreign Office made renewed efforts to obtain from the Porte some practical recognition of Great Britain's claim to control of the Bagdad-Gulf section of the line and to supreme influence on the Gulf itself, even considering as an alternative the building of a second railway from Bagdad forward. Neither with Turkey nor Germany, however, had an arrangement been reached upon this question in February, 1912.

Now Lord Haldane succeeded in restoring the Bagdad Railway negotiations to the position which they had reached after the *pourparlers* at Windsor in 1907. Subject to the withdrawal of British opposition to the completion of the line (e.g. by withholding sanction to the raising of the Turkish customs duties), and to an undertaking that Germany should participate in any railway schemes projected within the British sphere of influence in Persia, Germany was to renounce in favour of Great Britain her claim to build the Bagdad-Basra (Bassowrah) section of the line and to give full recognition to British interests in the Persian Gulf and South Persia. In proof of such recognition Germany was to assist Great Britain to obtain from Turkey an extensive concession for the Bagdad-Basra section and also a concession for a harbour at Koweit, similar to the concession obtained for a German company at Haidar Pasha. The adjustment of certain colonial questions, including the rounding-off of several territories on both sides, was to have been part of this agreement, Germany receiving concessions in Africa, while giving them in the Pacific. The agreement, in fact, was to have been on Great Britain's part a positive and practical disproof of Germany's suspicion of her desire to " encircle " an inconvenient rival and thwart its rightful imperialistic aspirations.

What, then, were the immediate results of the notable departure in Anglo-German diplomacy which was made in February, 1912? It would appear to be undisputed that the British peace envoy took away with him from Berlin the assurance that the men who were still in power in Germany cherished no designs against the peace of Europe, yet at the same time that he discovered around the Emperor the play of sinister influences which, though as yet held in check, were sedulously striving for the mastery. The German Empire still was peace in 1912, as the Second French Empire had been until the summer of 1870: it remained to be seen whether the maintenance of peace would prove more certain in the later case than it had proved in the earlier. It followed from his reading of the runes that Great Britain's true policy was to continue to do her utmost to encourage the party of conciliation in Germany, while at the same time strengthening her own military and naval position in view of unforeseen contingencies.

Meanwhile, a new and more intimate *rapport* had been established between two Governments which had for a long time been going more and more apart; their relations had been translated into a warmer and more genial atmosphere; sundry grounds of unrest and friction had been removed, and it seemed as though Germany and Great Britain, like France and Great Britain eight years before, were about to make a new start. It was a happy omen that the conciliatory utterances with which, as has been stated, the British Prime Minister greeted the result of Lord Haldane's visit were warmly re-echoed by the leaders of the Opposition. " If," said Lord Lansdowne, the co-author of the *entente* with France, in the House of Lords on February 14th, " he has come back with anything in the nature of an olive-branch, we shall congratulate him on this side as warmly as he will be congratulated by his friends on the other side of the House." Similarly in the House of Commons Mr. Bonar Law said on the same day : " No man in this House is more anxious for a good understanding with Germany than I am, and no one would regard with more horror a war between this country and Germany."

The " new orientation " was observed with approval by other countries, and to Russia in particular it appeared to afford unalloyed satisfaction. Even in France, whose ruling statesmen were at first apprehensive, and not a little jealous lest negotiations which begun by aiming merely at a *détente* should end with a too cordial *entente*, all anxiety disappeared as soon as it was understood that there had never been a question of Great Britain's unconditional neutrality and that no agreement had been proposed or contemplated by her or on her behalf which would in the slightest degree weaken the accord of 1904 or diminish the obligations which had grown up under it.

From the German nation likewise the peace movement in that year won a notable endorsement in the issue of the general elections to the Imperial Diet. Morocco and imperialism played a prominent part at the hustings and the polling booths. While, on the one hand, the Pan-Germanists, with the Conservative parties in collaboration, made a strong attempt to arouse in the nation an aggressive and warlike temper, the popular parties, and particularly the Social Democrats, comprehending the great mass of the working classes, directly challenged the Chauvinism which had so recently brought the country to the verge of war and appealed to the nation chiefly upon this issue. The results of the elections, as shown by the voting strength of parties, indicated that the nation endorsed rather than resented the Government's refusal to play with fire, for while the Conservatives lost a little ground, the Progressives gained over a quarter of a million votes and the Social Democrats nearly twice that number.

After Lord Haldane's return to London the negotiations which he had begun passed into the hands of the Foreign Office, between which and the German ambassador, Count Metternich, friendly conversations took place for some time. The formula for a political agreement which had been drawn up tentatively in Berlin seemed to afford complete satisfaction to neither side. After new proposals had been considered without result, the British Foreign Secretary suggested an agreement by which Great Britain was to declare that she would neither make nor join in any unprovoked attacks upon Germany, that aggression upon Germany was not the subject and formed no part of any treaty, understanding, or convention to which she was a party, and that she would not participate in any action which had that object in view. Germany, however, once more fell back upon her old demand for unconditional neutrality, and as she was unwilling to depart from this standpoint, agreement proved impossible.

Nor did further progress towards a naval understanding

prove feasible. If during the British envoy's presence in Berlin the large-navy party seemed for a moment to have been overruled, with his departure it recovered courage and influence. Tirpitz had from the first been hostile to the suggestion that his shipbuilding programme should be cut down, and as he had the Emperor's ear, there was never any doubt as to which view would prevail in the end. When Great Britain abandoned the formal application of the two-Power standard in favour of a ratio as regards Germany of sixteen ships to ten, Tirpitz professed to accept the concession as a basis for negotiation, and there seemed again a hope of agreement; but this hope disappeared when the German Naval Minister made it clear that such an arrangement could only be considered as temporary and would not imply any cessation of building, and, further, contended that ships built by the Colonies should be included in the British quota. As the German view of the sixteen to ten formula virtually meant that the two countries should be free to continue building against each other so long as they adhered to an accepted ratio, little was to be gained by it. No greater success attended the suggestion made by the British First Lord of the Admiralty, when introducing the Naval Estimates for 1913, that the two countries should take a " naval holiday "; in other words, should agree to defer for twelve months the new building planned for the coming budget year — in the case of England four ships, in the case of Germany two. At that time the naval expenditure of Germany had already become half as large as that of Great Britain; twenty years before it was not one-quarter.

On the German side Herr von Bethmann-Hollweg, unlike his predecessor, was profoundly impressed by the apparent hopelessness of the outlook, and had he had the Emperor's support in his resistance to the Naval Minister's importunacy it is probable that an agreement would have been concluded. But to the Emperor the desire to possess the strongest navy as well as the strongest army in the world had become an absorbing ambition, and however disposed to make concessions he may have been in February, 1912, he changed his mind a year later — a sign that in his counsels a new spirit and temper were in the ascendant. Against the combined opposition to any concession offered, therefore, by two men — the real makers of the German navy — all efforts at accommodation were shattered. As time passed, bringing the rival naval Powers no nearer to an understanding, it became increasingly clear that the effect of the dead-lock would be that each country would go its own way, and already in 1913 this was tacitly assumed on both sides to be the position. It was not a question of right or wrong, but merely of different views of national interest, which divided them. Where such was the issue neither was entitled to force its views upon the other, and in fact neither made the attempt. Yet in each country the naval controversy to the last left a large party unconvinced that the difficulty was insoluble, and immeasurably distressed that the combined statesmanship of two great nations, which otherwise had so many interests in common, had failed to discover the golden middle way of moderation and reason.

The result of Germany's final refusal to consider a reciprocal restriction in the growth of navies was that Great Britain immediately made an unprecedented increase in her naval estimates. No disquieting pronouncements were made from the housetops, but to preserve an attitude of vigilant preparedness became more than ever before the settled policy of the British Admiralty, and the nation readily accepted the additional burden imposed upon it in consequence without knowing all the facts which were held to justify it. It was in November, 1912, also that the British and French Governments put into definite and documentary form the plans for military and naval co-operation, in the event of an unprovoked attack upon France by Germany, which had been discussed by their experts since 1906.

Inability to agree upon these questions of capital importance did not, however, check at once the movement towards conciliation. In May, 1912, the German Government had reciprocated Lord Haldane's efforts by appointing to the London embassy the ablest man in the German diplomatic service, Baron Marschall von Bieberstein, who for the purpose left the scene of his successful labours at Constantinople. Baron Marschall's sudden death, after he had been but a few months in his new home, and the death in the ensuing December of Herr von Kiderlen-Wächter, who had been Foreign Secretary since 1909, and had never belonged to the large-navy party, deprived the cause of reconciliation of two good friends; but their places were taken by Prince Lichnowsky and Herr von

Jagow respectively, both men of the same pacific spirit. In a memorandum,[1] reviewing the diplomatic relations of the two countries at that time and during the remaining period of his work in London, Prince Lichnowsky has paid a warm tribute to the conciliatory attitude of the Government to which he was accredited.   Of the British Foreign Secretary he says: " His intention was not to isolate us, but to make us, so far as possible, partners in a working concern.   Just as he had succeeded in bridging Franco-British [2] and Russo-British difficulties, so he wished as far as possible to remove causes of friction between Germany and Great Britain, and by a network of treaties — which would finally include an agreement on the unfortunate naval question — to secure the peace of the world." A beginning was made with the revision of the treaty of 1898 relating to the Portuguese colonies in Africa.   That agreement had been concluded on the supposition that Portugal might soon be disposed to sell her African possessions, and as that contingency had not arisen, their provisions had remained inoperative.   While affirming their intention to respect and protect the sovereign rights of Portugal, the two Powers now proposed simply to divide these large and only partially developed territories into spheres of influence for trading purposes.   All Angola as far as the 20th degree of longitude and the northern portion of Mozambique were assigned to Germany, whose wishes and interests, on the testimony of her ambassador, received generous consideration, so that the treaty as concluded entirely met her views.   Though eventually initialled by the negotiators in August, 1913, the treaty was never signed, for the reason that the German Government declined to agree to its publication and the British Foreign Secretary would not sign except on that condition.[3]

In the course of a speech made in the Diet at the end of the year (December 9th) the Chancellor cordially reciprocated

[1] Prepared as a confidential document in May, 1916, and published, it was stated, in breach of faith, in March, 1918.

[2] The Agreements of 1904 with France were, of course, concluded by Lord Lansdowne.

[3] Memorandum of Prince Lichnowsky. " Sir Edward Grey," he says, " was willing to sign only if the treaty was published, together with the two treaties of 1898 and 1899. England has no other secret treaties, and it is contrary to her existing principles that she should conceal binding agreements. He said, however, that he was ready to take account of our wishes concerning the time and manner of publication, provided that publication took place within one year, at latest, after the signature."

the friendly attitude of Great Britain, and uttered the hope
" that the confidence which at present characterizes our relations with the British Government will extend itself to those
circles in both countries which still contemplate with a certain
scepticism a *rapprochement* of the two kindred nations," adding: "Let the past be the past; let us continue to work in
confidence on the basis which the present offers us!"

It was in this spirit that the two Governments applied themselves anew to the solution of the Bagdad Railway question.
If it was to Germany's interest to close this awkward question,
not less was it to the interest of Great Britain, whose supposed
veto upon the completion of the scheme had hitherto proved
a harmless weapon of defence. In considering the concessions
to be offered elsewhere to Germany, therefore, the British Government had to reckon with the fact that the German position
in regard to the Bagdad Railway was impregnable. Sir Edward Grey had told the House of Commons (March, 1911):
" The time to oppose the Bagdad Railway, if it was to be opposed in British interests, was before the concession was
granted." Germany was now in possession of the ground, however, and was able to make good her claims just in the way and
to the extent that interest and expediency might dictate.

As the result of long and complicated negotiations an arrangement was eventually arrived at which amounted to the
division of Asia Minor into politico-economic spheres of influence, separate areas being assigned to Great Britain, Germany, France, and Russia. The question of sovereignty was
not explicitly raised in the resulting treaty. As to the Bagdad Railway in particular, Great Britain now withdrew her
claim to participate in the Gulf section of the railway, and it
was agreed that her assent to the increase of the Turkish customs dues should be given, subject to conditions intended to
secure the continued predominance of British influence on the
Gulf. Thus Basra was now to be the terminus of the line, and
there was to be no continuation to the open water except with
British consent, which meant on British conditions; the ancient
British rights of navigation on the rivers of Mesopotamia were
to be protected; representation was to be given to Great Britain on the board of the Bagdad Railway Company; and the
construction and exploitation of ports at Bagdad and Basra
were to be carried out by a separate company, in which Great

Britain was to be interested to the extent of 40 per cent. On the other hand, Great Britain undertook not to give support to any railway offering direct competition to the Bagdad line, though this stipulation was not to apply to a railway from Egypt to the Gulf. The Smyrna-Aidin railway zone was also regarded as falling within the British sphere of influence. As a part of this comprehensive bargain German wishes in regard to certain colonial adjustments which had been discussed two years before were to have received considerate treatment, and German writers have since spoken of the British concessions offered in this connection as meeting all reasonable expectations.

Negotiations with France and Russia having led to a satisfactory agreement — Syria being reserved as the special sphere of French influence and Armenia as that of Russian — all that remained in June, 1914, in order to the completion of the final and crowning Bagdad Railway convention was the settlement of certain points in which Turkey was specially interested. In that month, however, events occurred which changed the entire European situation, and the convention was not signed. Prince Lichnowsky says of the two uncompleted territorial treaties that had they only " been concluded and published an agreement would have been reached with England which would have finally ended all doubt of the possibility of an Anglo-German co-operation." That means that the conciliatory efforts which began in 1912 must be counted among the tragic " too lates " of international diplomacy.

CHAPTER XXIV

(1913–1914)

FOREIGN RELATIONS — (iv) THE LATTER DAYS

An attempt to review the history of the last dolorous days, wherein the whole world has seen evil, is attended by disadvantages arising from the fact that some of the capital events of the time either appear in the twilight obscurity in which figures and movements are seen vaguely and uncertainly or are still veiled in total darkness. In such circumstances the completeness which is to be desired in historical narrative is impossible, and upon some questions judgment must be passed with reserve or be altogether suspended.

Before the time reached ominous shadows had fallen upon the European horizon in several directions. Political meteorologists, in accordance with the empirical nature of their science, for the most part turned their gaze to the West. The chronic tension in Germany's relations to France had been increased by the passing of the special Defence Law of 1913, already described, under which fifty million pounds were to be spent at once in the increase of the army and of armaments, a measure to which France and Russia immediately replied with corresponding expenditure on a large though not an equal scale. The situation was also to some extent complicated by uncertainty regarding Italy's future relationship to the Triple Alliance, the prolongation of which had already been discussed by the Governments of Vienna and Rome. It was understood that Italy wished for important modifications, with a view to safeguarding still more securely the *status quo* in the Balkans and the Mediterranean, but that the choice offered to her was the treaty unchanged or no treaty at all. No one believed that her acceptance of the alliance on what would virtually be forced terms would denote a whole-hearted attachment to the two Empires. On the other hand, the relations between Germany and Austria were never before so cordial and intimate.

Nevertheless, all this time it was in the East that the storm portents were most threatening. Clouds had begun to gather

501

in that quarter before the Morocco difficulties had been adjusted. From the moment that the alliance of the Central Powers was counterbalanced by the Triple Entente it behoved restless statesmen to walk more warily than before, not because the new combination of Powers was intended any more than the old to be one of defiance, but because the equilibrium of political forces had been brought to so fine a point that the slightest disturbance was fraught with danger. All the more inexplicable, therefore, were the motives of Austria when in 1908 she reopened the Balkan question by a sudden yet carefully premeditated act of aggression, and so openly challenged Russia. In order to appreciate fully the significance of this episode, which marked a turning-point in the development of the Near Eastern question, certain anterior facts must be called to mind.

The association of Serbs, Croats, and Slovenes in a powerful Jugo-Slavic State, which should revive the power and splendour of the olden days, had long been the dream of the Serbian race. It was plain, however, that the realization of that design would profoundly modify the political situation in the Balkans to Austria's prejudice, and it was in the hope of thwarting it that Austria obtained at the Congress of Berlin the assent of the Powers — given, indeed, from mixed motives — to her occupation and administration, but not annexation, of Bosnia and Herzegovina, and also to her maintenance, in the interest of public order and security, of garrisons and military roads in the region dividing Serbia and Montenegro known as the Sanjak of Novi-Bazar, all three territories remaining under Turkish suzerainty as before. The military occupation of Novi-Bazar was to carry no administrative powers and was to be effected later in agreement with Turkey. Accordingly, in the following year Austria exercised her option in relation thereto. In this way she was able not only to drive a wedge between Serbia and Montenegro and the Adriatic seaboard, but to keep open for herself an avenue to Salonica and the Ægean, the ultimate goal of Habsburg ambitions. These arrangements gave to Austria a larger stake in the Balkans, but they also brought her into more direct conflict with Russia, which the Congress Powers had allowed only to extend a friendly patronage to the new principality of Bulgaria.

Contrary to the intentions of its authors, the Treaty of Berlin, owing to the political and territorial adjustments which it introduced, gave a powerful stimulus to nationalism both amongst the races now freed from and those still subject to Ottoman rule. More apprehensive than ever for the continued cohesion and stability of her own polyethnic empire, Austria henceforth endeavoured to prevent the growth in the Balkans of any powerful concentration of Slavic influence. In particular it was part of her policy to keep Serbia weak, to thwart her political aspirations, and to prevent her from playing the part of a Piedmont in the inflammable South-east of Europe.

The abandonment in 1890 of Bismarck's reinsurance treaty with Russia was not followed by any immediate change in the relations of that Power with Austria. For a few years longer these appeared outwardly to be friendly, and in proof of good intentions the two Emperors in 1897 adopted what was known as the St. Petersburg Agreement binding their Governments to observe the *status quo* in the Balkans. Austria had long wished to annex Bosnia and Herzegovina outright, and sought to obtain Russia's assent as part of that compact, but in view of the Czar's opposition the proposal was withdrawn. In the meantime Alexander III had been succeeded by his son Nicholas II (November, 1894), under whose Foreign Minister, Prince Lobanoff, Russian influence in the Balkans was, after a time of decline, powerfully reasserted. Notably Bulgaria made peace with the Empire to whose care the Powers had committed her in 1878, and in sign of this Prince Ferdinand's eldest son went over to the Orthodox Church in February, 1896, an event which was followed immediately afterwards by the formal recognition of the Prince by the Powers and the Sultan as ruler of Bulgaria and Eastern Roumelia.

For some time longer both Austria and Russia continued to abstain from aggressive intervention in Balkan affairs, and their repeated injunctions to Serbia and Bulgaria not to disturb the peace proved successful. Count Goluchowski, the Austrian Foreign Minister, was not slow to give the same advice at home. Addressing the Delegations as late as May 7, 1902, when the negotiations for the renewal of the Triple Alliance were in progress, he uttered a grave warning against the " danger of reviving prestige policy in the Balkans." In October of the following year he entered into an arrangement known as the Mürzsteg Programme, whereby the same Powers again agreed to renounce aggressive designs in the Balkans and also pledged support to various measures of reform needful to the tranquillity of the races still subject to Turkish rule. The accession of a new dynasty, that of the Karageorgevitches, following the assassination in June, 1903, of King Alexander and Queen Draga, led to no marked change in the relations of the two Emperors with Serbia, whose new ruler, King Peter, though the nominee of the regicides, was promptly recognized both at St. Petersburg and Vienna.

The first rift in the lute occurred in 1905, when Serbia and Bulgaria concluded a customs union. That measure, signalizing the end of Serbia's economic dependence upon her powerful neighbour, gave great offence in Vienna, and Goluchowski rashly answered it by tariff reprisals against Serbia, who vigorously responded, with the result of the memorable " Pig War," in which Austria bore the brunt of the incidental inconvenience and injury. The consequence was that Serbia turned more than before to Russia and also formed stronger commercial ties with France, from whom she both borrowed money and bought armaments.

In the following year (October, 1906) Goluchowski was succeeded at the Ballplatz by Baron von Aehrenthal, a man of greater force of character, more ambitious, but both less cautious and less scrupulous. Goluchowski had left Austria's relations with Russia fairly harmonious, and for a time it seemed to be the policy of the new Minister, who had been called to his post from the St. Petersburg embassy, to strengthen, if possible, the ties with that Power. The prospect of an Anglo-Russian reconciliation was already sufficiently serious to alarm him, and the idea occurred to his fertile mind of wrecking the plan which he knew to be maturing by drawing Russia and France together into an understanding with Germany and Austria — Bülow in Berlin was credited with entertaining the same notion — thus effectually isolating Great Britain, a manœuvre to be accounted brilliant if it proved successful, ill-considered and clumsy if it failed. He was even confident enough to hope to re-create a union of the three Empires on the lines of that which was supplanted by the Dual Alliance of 1879 but revived for a time by the Skiernievice conference of 1884, with the difference that Austria instead of Germany was henceforth to take the leading place, and the tables of the law were to be proclaimed no longer from Berlin but from Vienna.

Aehrenthal was clear-sighted enough to perceive that if anything was to be done in that direction it must be done at once. Austria and Russia had, in fact, been acting together in close accord for some time on the question of Macedonian reforms, and had Aehrenthal, a subtle as well as a strong man, been earlier in the field, it is conceivable that he might have succeeded in converting this accord into a firm attachment based on mutual advantage. The statesmen of a new and Liberal Russia were now, however, unwilling to undo the good work of reconciliation with Great Britain which had advanced so far, and behind the forces which were drawing these two countries together was the steady pressure of France. On the last day of August, 1907, the Anglo-Russian convention was signed, and therewith the Triple Entente was complete.

His schemes frustrated, Aehrenthal showed his disappointment by a deliberate and almost ostentatious disregard of Russian sensibilities in the further development of Austrian policy in the Balkans. Early in January, 1908, he entered into an agreement with Turkey by which Austria, in consideration of a concession for the construction of a railway through the Sanjak of Novi-Bazar from Bosnia to Mitrovitza, the northern terminus of the existing Salonica railway, withdrew from the Macedonian reform movement, in which all the Powers were now interesting themselves. By this act of defection Austria not only wrecked the work of amelioration in a part of the Ottoman Empire where it was most urgently needed, but broke up the European Concert and, above all, betrayed Russia's confidence. Germany alone upheld the action of her ally.

But worse was soon to follow. An understanding already existed between Aehrenthal and the Russian Foreign Minister, M. Isvolsky, that Russia would not stand in the way of Austria's formal annexation of Bosnia and Herzegovina if carried out after due notice and in a form that should as little as possible excite the disfavour of Europe. On July 24, 1908, the Young Turkish revolution broke out, and for a time it promised to be the prelude to a new era of reform from which not only Turkey but her tributary territories in Europe would benefit. It even seemed possible that a strong Government might now arise capable of pulling the tottering empire together, and defying its enemies. Regarding Bosnia and Herzegovina as still belonging to Turkey, the reformers proposed, indeed, to embrace these provinces in the parliamentary system which was part of their scheme of national regeneration.

With a view to frustrating this design, and at the same time ending Serbo-Croatian agitation in these territories, Aehrenthal determined to convert Austria's legal occupation into formal possession. For territories hitherto under Turkish rule any change of government could not fail to be an improvement and it must be said for the Austrian occupation of the provinces that it had brought about steady political and material progress; administration, if inclined to be rigid, was fairly efficient, and if the Serbian population at least never recognized finality in the new order of things it would have been reluctant to go back to the old.

Now, without prior communication with the signatories of the Treaty of Berlin, Aehrenthal persuaded the Emperor to issue a decree on October 3rd proclaiming the annexation of the two provinces as an " accomplished fact." At the same time Austria retroceded to the Sultan her rights in respect of the Sanjak of Novi-Bazar, giving him the flattering assurance of her confidence that the Sultan was now strong enough to maintain order and good government in that region without outside help. In connivance with Vienna, Prince Ferdinand of Bulgaria two days later threw off the Turkish suzerainty and proclaimed his realm as henceforth an independent kingdom.

In Austria-Hungary the decree of annexation was hailed as a masterpiece of policy, a proof of strong statecraft, and an earnest of reviving prestige. Elsewhere, except in Germany, the feelings which it created were those of irritation and resentment. Although the Russian Government had not been taken into confidence as to the moment of the daring stroke, M. Isvolsky had little cause for complaint, for he was an accomplice before the fact; but the nation warmly condemned it. Russia, however, was still weakened by her war with Japan, and was neither willing nor able at that time to face another and perhaps a more hazardous struggle, even for the sake of Serbia and the Slavic cause. Italy also had reason for annoyance, inasmuch as by the treaty with Austria by which she joined the Triple Alliance each Power bound itself to adopt no measure that would disturb the *status quo* in the Balkans without prior agreement with the other. Great Britain and France protested, but without great vigour or urgency, for raiding Turkey had for half a century been regarded as no less venial than robbing an orchard, and all the Powers had at one time or another either committed the offence or condoned it in others. When, therefore, the German Government, while denying prior knowledge of Austria's intentions, promptly asserted the doctrine, " My ally, right or wrong! " and gave Russia to understand that if a quarrel arose she would have to be reckoned with as an antagonist, no other choice remained except to tolerate the act of illegality and allow the geographers to recolour the map of South-east Europe accordingly.

Even Russia's proposal, which the British Government accepted, that the proceeding should for the sake of appearances be regularized by a conference of the Powers had to be abandoned on the refusal of Germany and Austria to take part. So far was Prince Bülow from disclaiming Germany's connivance, that he admitted that in taking Austria's side she had not acted merely from motives of fidelity, but " above all things and in the first line " from a desire to assert " German prestige and Germany's international position." Still more did the Emperor seal his complicity in this act of aggression when on visiting Vienna in September, 1910, he reminded the City Council, in replying to its address of welcome, how he had " taken his stand in shining armour at a grave moment by the side of your most gracious Sovereign." Prince Bülow contended later that the acceptance by the Powers of Austria's action as an " accomplished fact," consequent upon Germany's resolute determination to support it, if necessary, by war, proved that the policy of " encirclement," which for him had never had any terror, lacked substantive value.[1]

The Government of Vienna pleaded at the time that annexation was necessary in order to defeat a conspiracy of Serbo-Croat with Serbian politicians for the subversion of Habsburg power in the provinces, and in order to give colour to this contention it instituted the notorious Agram high treason trial, of which the intended victims were some fifty Croatian Serbs. The trial had a sequel in which the Austro-Hungarian Foreign Office, its diplomatic agents in Serbia, and the historian Dr. Heinrich Friedjung played an unenviable part. Primed with

[1] *Imperial Germany*, p. 53.

Foreign Office documents, Dr. Friedjung, in an article published in a Vienna Ministerial journal in March, 1909, had professed to demonstrate the existence of this conspiracy and had even accused a number of well-known Serbo-Croatian politicians by name. Prosecuting the historian for slander, the accused men were able to prove that the documents on which he had based his accusations were fictitious and had been concocted in the Austro-Hungarian legation in Belgrade. Although the judge had been chosen as a safe man and the jury had been carefully picked, the evidence of forgery and subornation was irresistible, and the Foreign Office and its chief witness emerged from the trial humiliated; whereupon Aehrenthal disclaimed belief in the existence of the conspiracy which his too credulous Press agent had been instructed to lay bare.

In Serbia and Montenegro, which now saw their hopes of union destroyed, the annexations created a violent outcry against Austrian duplicity and treachery, and had Serbia been allowed she would at once have made war single-handed upon the powerful aggressor. Restrained by the Powers, she protested for a long time, until it was seen that Russia was not disposed to risk war by raising objection, whereupon the incident was discreetly regarded as closed. In March, 1909, the Serbian Government, on the pressure of the Powers, formally withdrew all claims against Bosnia, and Austria, on the other hand, gave a written assurance of her friendly disposition and her intention to respect Serbian independence. In the meantime, recognizing the wisdom of regularizing her action as far as was possible, Austria had concluded a convention with Turkey under which she agreed to pay to her the sum of two million pounds, to respect the religious rights of the Mussulman population in the annexed provinces, and to renounce all rights in relation to the Sanjak of Novi-Bazar, with the result that Serbia and Montenegro were now able to join hands and the former gained access to the sea, though without obtaining a port of her own. Nevertheless, the annexations remained a flagrant violation of international law and a dangerous precedent for Sovereigns and Governments attracted by the dictum that " Might is right." Aehrenthal's reward was his elevation to the rank of count, an honour which he did not long enjoy, for he died in February, 1912, and was succeeded by Count Berchtold.

Meanwhile, the revolutionary movement had won another triumph in Turkey. After a temporary reverse the Young Turks came to power again at the end of April, 1909, and deposed Abdul Hamid.[1] Originally welcomed by the Western States as a portent of brighter days for the Turkish Empire, the Young Turk movement nevertheless ended by disappointing Liberal expectations. Under the new order there was as much despotism as under the old; anarchy continued in Macedonia, the cockpit of Turkish misrule; and in 1910 Albania, failing to secure the redress of her grievances, rose in revolt.

Austria's act of aggression set in train a series of larger events which further threatened the integrity of the Turkish Empire. Now Italy argued that if one party to the Triple Alliance had a right to set at naught Germany's ally, the same right could not well be refused to another, and deeming the time opportune for enforcing the long-deferred claim to Tripoli, her Government in September, 1911, served on the Porte a demand for the voluntary cession of the province. As the demand was not conceded, war was at once declared, and as Italy was well prepared she was at a great advantage. Early in November Italy declared the annexation of the Tripolitana and Cyrenaica, but hostilities continued on land and sea for the greater part of a year in the form of a succession of indecisive engagements, in which large forces were on no occasion employed.

Turkey would have continued the struggle longer but for the fact that more serious trouble had arisen in her European dominion. A definitive treaty of peace was concluded at Lausanne on October 18, 1912, Turkey agreeing to withdraw from the Tripolitana and Cyrenaica, though not formally ceding these territories, and Italy to withdraw from the islands of the Ægean which she had occupied during the war. Italy also undertook to pay annually to the Treasury of the Ottoman Public Debt a sum corresponding to the average of the sums which in the three years preceding the war had been allocated for the use of the Public Debt from the revenue of the provinces, provision being made for the commutation of this charge by arrangement.

The Tripoli episode placed Germany, as Turkey's protector, in a difficult position, and her unwillingness to give to

[1] Abdul Hamid died in Constantinople on February 10, 1917.

Italy the ready support which she had offered to Austria in her aggressive adventure three years before convinced the Southern Power still further that the union of the three allies was not one of equals.

Turkey was in urgent need of a peace, however, since in the Balkans she had suddenly been assailed by a powerful combination of enemies who had long been impatient to strike a blow together for freedom. Austria's action in 1908 had convinced the Balkan States that none of them was any longer safe from aggression so long as they trusted to outside help. In their uncertainty they therefore united, and the Balkan League, composed of Bulgaria, Serbia, Montenegro, and Greece, was formed in the winter of 1911–12 as a bulwark against hostile pressure either from North or South, but also with the object of expelling Turkey from Macedonia and Thrace. Roumania remained outside, but without concealing the fact that her sympathies were with the allies. In October, 1912, the States of the League rose against their ancient oppressor, and within two months Turkey was beaten and at their mercy. Throughout the war Germany had openly espoused the Turkish cause, and had only been restrained from more active measures by the influence of the Entente Powers, whose sole concern was to localize the conflict. For some months also the Austro-Hungarian army was mobilized in readiness for intervention, until the removal of diplomacy to a cooler temperature eased the tension.

At the invitation of the British Government, a series of Conferences of ambassadors met in London in December, 1912, and as a result of a friendly exchange of views it was agreed to press the Porte to make such cessions of territory as the fortunes of war seemed to justify, and the proposals on the subject were embodied in the Treaty of London of May 13th. This treaty was never ratified. Before a final settlement was arrived at, Bulgaria, greedy for a larger share of the spoils, challenged Serbia and Greece, and all efforts to prevent a second conflict proved futile. " The Balkan States," said Count Tisza, the Hungarian Minister-President, " can decide for war; we shall, of course, regret it, but the decision is within their right." Grave doubts were entertained about this regret: Austria was believed, with good reason, to have provoked the second appeal to arms.

In the London Conferences Germany and England had worked cordially together and their association in the common cause of peace seemed to create a new bond of sympathy between the Governments and to bridge over many outstanding points of difference. No one was more enthusiastic in praise of the conciliatory part played at that time by the British Foreign Secretary than the German Chancellor, who said in the Imperial Diet (April 7, 1913): "Europe will know how to thank the British Secretary for Foreign Affairs for the extraordinary devotion and spirit of conciliation with which he has conducted the discussions in the Ambassadors' Conferences in London, and has already succeeded in adjusting differences of opinion. Germany shares in these thanks all the more willingly since we know that we are at one with the aims of British policy, and, while remaining faithful to our allies, have worked with her on the same lines." He added: "It seems to me that the mutual confidence which has for so long been absent, to the detriment of both countries and the world, is beginning to return. Mr. Asquith and Sir Edward Grey have affirmed that Anglo-German relations are good at the present time. I can confirm and joyfully welcome this."

There can be no doubt that these words faithfully reflected Herr von Bethmann-Hollweg's attitude to Great Britain at that juncture and the spirit which he was still determined to cultivate in his official dealings with that country.

Hostilities having been resumed in circumstances no longer unfavourable to her, Turkey was now able to retrieve some of the concessions which the Powers, in their abortive conferences, had wrested from her on behalf of the victorious League. Gallantly though Bulgaria had fought against Turkey, she was now outmatched, and she came out of the struggle gaining little save humiliation and a huge debt. To the surprise of Europe, Roumania, who had hitherto kept aloof from the League, sided with Serbia and Greece against Bulgaria in the second war, and so gave a decisive turn to the final struggle, though in so doing she placed herself in direct opposition to Austria.

The sequel to the two Balkan wars was the Treaty of Bucharest (August 10, 1913), which was likewise the work of the European Concert. In the enforcement of this treaty upon such of the Balkan States as were unwilling to be at peace and disarm the German Emperor played an important part. By it Roumania obtained Silistria and a strip of Bulgarian territory on the Dobrudja frontier, while Macedonia was divided between Serbia, who received a large region in the interior, and Greece, to which fell Salonica and Kavalla. During the first war Serbia had occupied Durazzo, in Albania, but now Austrian jealousy of her ambition for a place on the Adriatic led to her withdrawal within her old eastern frontier. Out of regard for Austria the Powers, against their better judgment, elevated Albania into an independent principality, thereby adding to the political oddities for which the East of Europe had so long been famous. As Kavalla had likewise been taken from her, Serbia equally lost her outlook upon the Ægean, though the final territorial adjustment left her with an addition of 15,-240 square miles to her former area: Montenegro gained 2,130 square miles, Bulgaria (on balance) 6,860 square miles, Greece 16,920 square miles, and Roumania 2,970 square miles.

Next to Turkey, at whose expense the rectification of frontiers was made, the treaty of Bucharest gave least satisfaction to Austria, whose Foreign Secretary professed to regard the settlement as " highly artificial " and provisional. Austria had, indeed, gained the attachment of Bulgaria, but she had lost the confidence of the rest of the Balkan States and increased the antagonism of Russia.

To the superficial observer the two outstanding facts in German politics at the beginning of 1914 were, as regards France, a widening breach, creating everywhere the apprehension that the conflict which both countries had anticipated so long was at hand, but as regards England a distinct movement, if not towards a positive friendship, at least towards a tolerant understanding. The belief still prevailed almost generally in Germany that the real, if not the only, centre of danger was the West. The Morocco question had been settled to the satisfaction of France, yet without abating the friction to which it had given rise, for while France was convinced that she had only received her due, and accordingly felt under no obligation to be grateful, the treaty of 1911 was regarded by most Germans as for their country a humiliating surrender. The exceptional military measures adopted by both countries in 1913 may also have emphasized the fact, as old as 1870, that the question of Alsace-Lorraine was an insuperable obstacle to a genuine and permanent reconciliation.

Nevertheless, although the strain upon the relations with France seemed to be tending to a rupture, it was clear to all who looked below the surface of events that an even greater, if not more immediate, source of anxiety for Germany and for Europe at large was to be found on the Eastern frontier, where Russia had long been chafing more and more under Austrian provocation.   Never since the fall of the first Chancellor did German statesmanship show itself so short-sighted as in its attitude towards Austria's Balkan policy from the opening of the new century forward.   The fact that Germany claimed for herself no special interests in the Balkans might appear to have obscured the minds of the Emperor and his Ministers to the fact that Russia did claim there interests of vital and overwhelming importance, and to have caused them to forget that the more Germany identified herself with Austrian aims the greater became her responsibility and also her risks as the major partner in the Triple Alliance.

For inasmuch as Germany never tried to conceal the fact that she was behind her ally in her aggressive designs in the Balkans and in her evident determination to challenge Russia's right to be regarded as the natural protector of the Slavic States there, it followed necessarily that the antagonism over the Balkan question was viewed by Russia as merely another form of the old antagonism between Teutonism and Slavism. Bismarck, in general one of the least nervous of men, had from the beginning of the 'eighties been haunted by anxiety as to the possible development of the Pan-Slavic movement in Russia, and by a conviction that the more the movement spread and deepened the less it would be possible for Germany and Russia to work together harmoniously.   In the end German statesmen deliberately went out of their way to precipitate this long-feared and long-threatened conflict.

The course and issue of Germany's Austro-Balkan policy during the reign of the third Emperor have afforded a remarkable confirmation alike of the foresight and the fears of her greatest Chancellor.   It is the fashion to regard Austria as having been the mere tool of German diplomacy throughout the whole duration of the Triple Alliance.   So long as Bismarck remained in office it is true that Germany exacted full obedience to the laws of the alliance as laid down by himself, and it was well for her and for the peace of Europe that this was so. One of these laws required that Austria should do nothing that might disturb the political equilibrium in the Near East and so set Russia by the ears. But the strength of an alliance and its effectiveness for the purpose in view depend only in a minor degree upon formal pledges, and for the rest altogether upon the existence on the part of the allies of unity of aim, or, if that be absent, upon the purpose and will that happen to predominate. Before Bismarck went complete unity of aim had ceased to exist as between Germany and Austria, and when he disappeared there was no longer a strong hand capable of directing Germany's ally in the ways of prudence and safety. Freed from control, Austria began to think less of the alliance and more of her own interests. The positions of piper and dancer were reversed: now Austria began to set the tune and it was Germany who performed the *pas seul*, while Italy stood by, an impatient and irritated observer. It was a situation which Bismarck, in his later years, had anticipated with growing anxiety. "We should not forsake Austria," he wrote at the end of his Memoirs, "but we should not, on the other hand, lose sight of the fact that the policy of Vienna with or without intention, may forsake us." [1] There was no danger of that defection of Austrian policy so long as Germany remained in such a relation to Austria and Russia as enabled her to exert a direct influence on both. This relation continued until 1890. No sooner, however, had Bismarck ceased to be Chancellor than the old *rapport* with Russia was broken, and his earliest and most urgent warnings, when he exchanged the *rôle* of actor upon the stage for that of critic in the stalls, related to this departure from the tried tradition which he regarded as his most valuable legacy to his successors. For he saw clearly that the freer from Germany's influence Russia was allowed to become, the freer would Austria likewise become from Germany's restraint, until the time arrived when she would break loose from control.

The abandonment of the reinsurance treaty may have proceeded, as was claimed at the time, from the laudable motive of integrity — the desire to evade a possible conflict of loyalty and

[1] *Reflections and Reminiscences,* vol. ii., p. 278–9. Chapters xxix. and xxx. of this work are occupied with a minute examination of German relations, actual (at the time Bismarck wrote) and hypothetical, to Austria and Russia, and the whole of his judgments and speculations on the subject therein contained have a profound interest for the present time.

to be quite open with Austria — yet the effect was to impose on German statesmanship a new and heavy responsibility. Bismarck clearly indicated the risk which was being run when he wrote in 1891: " From the moment that the conviction is established in Vienna that the bridge between Germany and Russia is broken down Austria will assume a different attitude towards the German Empire, and Germany will run the risk of becoming in a sense dependent on Austria." [1]

When at a later date he disclosed to the unsuspecting world the existence of the treaty of 1884,[2] he again warned the Government of the danger of one day " being dragged at the wheels of the Austrian chariot," instead of remaining itself in charge, and suggested that already " in consequence of the estrangement between Germany and Russia Austria has been enabled to exercise considerable pressure upon Germany." " Apparently," he added, " German statesmanship no longer observes a disinterested attitude in Eastern affairs. By following the path upon which she has entered, Germany is in danger of gradually becoming dependent upon Austria, and in the end she may have to pay with her blood and treasure for Austria's Balkan policy." [3]

The contingency which Bismarck had feared arrived early in the new century. In championing Austria in a policy of provocation against Russia, Germany ran an incalculably grave risk, yet this risk seemed to cause her no anxiety or misgiving. The Imperial Chancellor, indeed, in a speech made in the Diet as late as April, 1913, spoke impressively on the subject of the " Slavic peril " and of the folly of doing anything that could hasten its entrance into the sphere of immediate speculation.

[1] Article in the *Hamburger Nachrichten,* January 28, 1891, as certified by the conductor of that journal. See Hofmann, *Fürst Bismarck,* 1890–1898, vol. i., p. 314.

[2] *Hamburger Nachrichten* of October 24, 1896.

[3] Bismarck develops the same line of argument in his Memoirs. Thus, " If the breach or alienation between us and Russia should seem irremediable then Vienna would believe itself entitled to make great claims upon the services of its German ally; first, in the extension of the *casus fœderis,* which hitherto, according to the published text, goes no further than the repulse of a Russian attack upon Austria; secondly, in the demand that for the *casus fœderis,* as above defined, there should be substituted the representation of Austrian interests in the Balkans and in the East. . . . It is not, however, the duty of the German Empire to sacrifice the lives and treasure of its subjects in the realization of its neighbour's aspirations " (*Reflections and Reminiscences,* vol. ii., pp. 273–4).

He even discouraged the use of the very phrase itself as likely to " act suggestively and irrigate the soil upon which popular passions thrive." Even he, however, failed to recognize that the real irritant of the situation was his own Government's short-sightedness in allowing Austria to use Germany in support of an aggressive Balkan policy. It seemed as though Austria was at last avenging herself for the contumely inflicted upon her by Prussia half a century before. Now the positions of the two Powers as established by Bismarck in his diplomatic encounters with Rechberg and Mensdorff, and confirmed more definitely by Sadowa in 1866, were reversed. Not since the time when Schwarzenberg directed Prussian policy with an iron hand had Vienna asserted so complete a control over the statesmen of Berlin as during the years of Aehrenthal's and still more of Berchtold's astute and masterful management of foreign affairs.

To outside observers the growing disposition of the Berlin Foreign Office to defer to Austria and go her way was the more incomprehensible since it was just as unnecessary from the standpoint of policy as it was injudicious from that of safety. For from the military standpoint Austria was still no less dependent upon Germany than in Bismarck's time. Russia being impossible as an ally, and her alliance with Italy being unreal and liable to rupture at any moment, the withdrawal of German support would at once have made her position precarious. Because Germany had Austria still in her power, therefore, she might, had she been so minded, have continued to control Austrian policy in the interests of peace without in the slightest degree endangering the political ties uniting the two countries. Justifying her support of Austria by the obligations imposed upon her by the Triple Alliance, Germany in fact went counter both to the spirit and the letter of the treaties upon which that compact was based. Bismarck had often pointed to the impropriety and danger of allowing the Alliance to be used as a cover for aggressive action in the Near East or elsewhere. The Alliance was not, indeed, expressly designed to maintain in perpetuity the status established by the Congress of Berlin, of which it was not merely a sequel but a direct effect, but it was no less a vital interest of all the allies that there should be no arbitrary disturbance of the Balkan equilibrium, and Italy had required formal stipulations on the point. In inviting

Austria to exercise a free hand in the Balkans, therefore, Germany exceeded her liabilities to one ally and came short of her duty to another, whilst challenging Russia's resentment into the bargain. This perversion of an alliance, whose strongest justification was that it was originally pacific in purpose, involved the obvious risk that at any time local questions of Balkan politics might become European questions and small causes of disagreement and friction give rise to grave international crises, since if Germany was behind Austria, so also was France behind Russia.

Since 1908 the gulf between Austria and Russia had been steadily widening. In that year Russia had tolerated Austria's absorption of Bosnia and Herzegovina, in contravention of the Treaty of Berlin, because in her then enfeebled state and in face of Germany's menace she could not have made resistance effective. On the other hand, the diplomatic reverse thus inflicted upon her had been somewhat retrieved when with her help Serbia came out of the Balkans wars of 1912–13 with largely extended territory, and with at least a telescopic outlook, over a friendly neighbour's domain, upon the sea. The fact that Serbian ambition had to this extent been gratified roused Austria's jealousy, and it became a fixed aim of her Balkan policy to prevent any further Slavic concentration so near her own frontiers. Signor Gioletti, Italian Foreign Secretary at the time, is responsible for the disclosure that immediately after the signing of the Treaty of Bucharest in August, 1913, the Austrian Government sounded Italy as to the propriety of a joint attack upon Serbia.

Serbia was by no means free from reproach. She repaid hostility in kind, and her success in the Balkan campaigns revived in her people the hope that Bosnia and Herzegovina might yet be won back from Austrian hands. This hope gave motive power to a renewed Greater Serbian agitation, which, spreading beyond the frontiers of the kingdom, was actively carried on in the coveted provinces and even in the other Slavic territories under Austro-Hungarian rule. Unhappily these Serbian endeavours did not stop at agitation. On June 28, 1914, while visiting the Bosnian town of Serajevo, the administrative centre of Austria's new provinces, the Archduke Francis Ferdinand, the heir apparent to the Habsburg throne, and his wife, the Duchess of Hohenberg, were assassinated in broad daylight in the public street. Investigations made by the Austrian Government made it clear that the murders were political. It was even maintained that the crime had been arranged in Belgrade and assisted by Serbian military officers and Government officials. These, it was alleged, had supplied the murderers with arms, had facilitated their entry into Bosnia, and had, in fact, co-operated in the foul conspiracy in every detail of its execution. Without giving the Serbian Government an opportunity of meeting the charge of official complicity, the Austro-Hungarian Government on July 23rd served on it an ultimatum — it was later declared euphemistically to be only a *démarche* — requiring a public condemnation of and a declaration of dissociation from anti-Austrian propagandism, and compliance within forty-eight hours with a series of demands, some of a very arbitrary kind, intended to secure the prompt punishment of the assassins and their fellow-conspirators, the suppression of all movements in Serbia hostile to Austria-Hungary, the removal from office of persons who could be shown to be connected with such movements, and the co-operation of Austrian agents with the Serbian authorities which should be charged with the future watching of Slavic propagandism. The ultimatum was in its entire tenor so peremptory and in its purpose so humiliating that out of Austria few people believed that it could be accepted, and in Austria few wished that it would be.

How far the Serbian Government was implicated in or had knowledge of the agitations which led up to the murders of Serajevo may never be known, but there can be little doubt that these agitations, if not directly encouraged by the Government, were at least not discouraged, and that minor Serbian officers and officials were directly or indirectly involved. At the same time, Austria's indictment was to some extent discounted by the fact, now recalled, that in 1909, as the Friedjung trial had proved, her Government had not hesitated to resort to the use of forged documents in its endeavour to discredit Serbia and the Serbian cause. Confronted, however, by Austria's threatening attitude, and unwilling to enter into a quarrel in which Serbia might find herself without friends, the incriminated Government appears to have been more concerned to make amends and to give reasonable guarantees for the future than to quibble over the precise degree of its legal or moral responsibility. Accordingly it immediately notified its willingness to accept the major part of the Austrian demands, while offering to accept the adjudication of the International Tribunal of The Hague upon the others, several of which involved an unjustifiable interference with the internal affairs of Serbia as a sovereign State. Austria had served upon the Great Powers on July 24th, a copy of the Note to Serbia, and the German Government, untroubled by its own passive attitude towards the Pan-German movement, for years so menacing and obnoxious, not to one but several neighbouring States, promptly signified its full approval of Austria's demands.[1]

Meanwhile, Serbia had sought the advice of Russia, and that Power had let it be known in Vienna that, as the protector of the Slavic races, it must not be regarded as indifferent to the interests of its Balkan *protégé*. To Germany at least this action by Russia could not have given surprise. In a statement subsequently published by the Foreign Office in Berlin it was stated: "We were perfectly aware that a possible warlike attitude of Austria-Hungary against Serbia might bring Russia upon the field, and that it might, therefore, involve us in a war in accordance with our duties as allies."

During the next few days there was a busy exchange of Notes between the Great Powers, with constant diplomatic conversations in their capitals, Serbia in the meantime withdrawing into the background, since the dispute had now been taken up by more important contestants over larger issues. Great Britain's position hitherto had been that of the mediator and conciliator, eager to ease the way of negotiation and to find a basis of reasonable compromise. With this idea in view the British Foreign Secretary proposed that the whole question

---

[1] At that time, and for three succeeding years, the Berlin Foreign Office maintained that it had had no cognizance of the text of the Austrian Note to Serbia prior to its delivery. On the other hand, the Bavarian Minister-President admitted to the French envoy at Munich on July 23rd that he knew even then of its contents. The British ambassador in Vienna also wrote to his Government that his German colleague there "knew the text of the Austrian ultimatum to Serbia before it was despatched, and telegraphed it to the Emperor." The explanation of this apparent contradiction was afforded by the disclosures of Dr. Mühlon in March, 1918, from which it appears that while the German Emperor and Government may not have seen the actual document prior to its despatch, they both knew of and approved its contents before it was put into final form, since the Vienna Government had conferred with the Emperor personally on the subject in the middle of July.

should be referred to the ambassadors accredited to London by the four disinterested Powers, Germany, France, Italy, and Great Britain. To this course only Germany objected, and the suggestion that Germany should propose a formula of reference acceptable to herself and her ally was likewise rejected in Berlin. The German Government contended that Austria and Serbia must be allowed to settle the dispute alone, without the intervention of third parties; but the implication conveyed by this contention, that she was and wished to remain a neutral spectator, was inconsistent with the important facts that as Austria's ally she had, on her own admission, " permitted Austria a completely free hand in her action against Serbia," that even if she had not collaborated in the preparation of the Austrian Note to Serbia, she had, as was later established, been cognizant of its terms prior to its issue, and that she had on the day of its communication to the Powers informed the latter that it had her complete approval. Even when Austria had signified her willingness to accept mediation Germany still adhered to the view that such mediation should not extend to the dispute with Serbia " but merely to the relations between Austria-Hungary and Russia." By this time (July 28th) Austria had declared war on Serbia, though St. Petersburg and Vienna continued in diplomatic communication.

While thus the Governments of the three Empires were contending over points of form and order, to Europe at large trivial and negligible, their rulers were simultaneously mobilizing their vast military forces. If there was to be war, it was obviously for Germany and Russia equally a matter of vital importance which should be first in the field. Apprehension and suspicion on both sides as to the precise character of the precautionary measures which were being taken may have helped in no small degree to precipitate the ensuing catastrophe. Nevertheless, it is impossible to doubt that, had it been allowed to meet, the Ambassadors' Conference, which had conduced so signally to harmony amongst the Powers in 1912–13, and by so doing had created an invaluable precedent, would have adjusted the dispute which the fates or human perversity willed should be decided by appeal to arms. A sort of fatalism appears to have forced events forward to the disastrous climax. The obsession of the " Slavic peril " had worked so long upon the imagination of Germany that because the long-dreaded clash between the two races now seriously threatened it was assumed to be inevitable; the hour had come for Germanism to assert its supremacy or be overthrown.[1]

Austria was committed to war with Russia from the moment that she invaded Serbian territory, and both she and Germany knew it. Behind her, however, was the Triple Alliance, or at least, with certainty, the major partner, her close ally for weal or woe since 1879. Russia having mobilized, while giving the undertaking that no hostile step should be taken so long as negotiations continued, Germany promptly did the same, but for her mobilization was meant to be an act of war, and such it proved. The entrance of Germany into the quarrel necessarily brought in France, whose aid was pledged to Russia under the terms of the dual alliance.[2]

There remained still to be defined the attitude of Great Britain towards the Powers of the Triple Entente and that of Italy towards her allies of the Triple Alliance. There was at no time real uncertainty as to what Great Britain would do.

[1] A singular parallel with the war of 1870 may be recalled. It will be remembered how that year opened with the promise of continued peace for Europe, insomuch that in the Prussian Parliament there was a debate on disarmament. In the early months of 1914 likewise the visible portents seemed equally pacific: as late as June a largely attended conference of German and French legislators met at Basle in token of good-will, a British commercial mission visited Germany and was there cordially welcomed, a British squadron took part in the reopening of the enlarged Kiel Canal, and the British Chancellor of the Exchequer, in conversation with a French publicist, hazarded the belief that for twenty years there had been no such favourable time for reducing expenditure upon the implements of war.

[2] Prince Lichnowsky, in his Memorandum of May, 1916, mentioned above, sums up Germany's share in the fateful events of the last week of July in the following words:

"We encouraged Count Berchtold (the Austrian Foreign Minister) to attack Serbia, although no German interest was involved, and the danger of a world-war must have been known to us. . . . In the days between July 23 and July 30, 1914, when M. Sazonoff (the Russian Foreign Minister) emphatically declared that Russia could not tolerate an attack upon Serbia, we rejected the British proposals of mediation, although Serbia, under Russian and British pressure, had accepted almost the whole ultimatum, and although an agreement about the two points in question could easily have been reached, and Count Berchtold was even ready to satisfy himself with the Serbian reply. On July 30th, when Count Berchtold wanted to give way, we, without Austria having been attacked, replied to Russia's mere mobilization by sending an ultimatum to St. Petersburg, and on July 31st we declared war on the Russians, although the Czar had pledged his word that as long as negotiations continued not a man should march, so that we deliberately destroyed the possibility of a peaceful settlement. In view of these indisputable facts it is not surprising that the whole civilized world outside Germany attributes to us the sole guilt for the world-war."

The German Government knew well the importance attached by her to the maintenance of the integrity of French territory, for if any obscurity had existed before 1912, Lord Haldane's mission in that year had removed it.   Moreover, during the ten days which intervened between the serving of the Austrian Note upon Serbia and the actual opening of hostilities in that country the British Foreign Secretary, in his conversations with the German ambassador in London, had emphasized the danger of supposing that if France were drawn into the quarrel England would or could remain neutral.   When war seemed no longer avoidable the German Government tried to win England over to a passive position by the promise that in the event of a German victory no French territory should be annexed.   Asked if a similar undertaking would be given in regard to the French colonies, the German Chancellor, with undiplomatic candour, replied that he was unable to give a pledge.

Whatever may have been the possibility of England's abstention — and it was never strong, even if it existed at all — all doubt was removed when, in response to an invitation to France and Germany to declare whether they would respect the neutrality of Belgium, an obligation resting upon all three Powers in virtue of the treaty of 1839, France replied affirmatively and Germany refused to give any undertaking: before this time, indeed, the German Chancellor had plainly hinted that it was intended to use Belgium as a military road to France. On August 2nd German troops invaded Luxemburg, whose integrity Germany had likewise guaranteed by treaty, and also France, and two days later they invaded Belgium.   Simultaneously hostilities broke out on the distant eastern frontier, which was crossed by Russian troops on August 1st.   Great Britain formally declared war upon Germany on August 4th, but only eight days later upon Austria-Hungary.   Her entrance into the war was endorsed by the entire British Empire, every portion of which contributed voluntarily but unstintingly both of manhood and treasure.

Italy's attitude turned upon the question whether for her a *casus fœderis* had arisen under the terms of the treaty of alliance of 1882.   Her Government decided that it had not, contending that Austria and Germany had been the aggressors, whereas the alliance was intended to be of a purely defensive character.   Defining the liabilities created by the Triple Alliance, Bismarck wrote in 1890 in his Hamburg organ (April 26th) that it covered " only the *damnum emergens*, not the *lucrum cessans*, of the Power concerned," adding, " least of all is it Germany's affair to promote the ambitious plans of Austria in the Balkans." To the last he maintained also that it was never contemplated that Germany should accept responsibility for Austria's Oriental policy against Russia or for its consequences. For Italy, however, it could be claimed that her liability was still more narrowly circumscribed, since Austria was under a pledge to her to resort to no measure disturbing to the existing status in the Balkans. The Italian Foreign Secretary stated later that his Government had been kept completely in the dark as to the measures contemplated against Serbia until action had been taken: " we were not consulted," he said; " we were told nothing."

Bismarck was accustomed to say that the stability of all treaties depended upon two tacit conditions — *rebus sic stantibus* and *ultra posse obligatur nemo*, and of the Triple Alliance he once said that although it had been repeatedly renewed " it would be unwise to regard it as a permanent security against all possible eventualities altering the political, material, and moral conditions under which it was created." The alliance which had been formed only for protection and defence broke down in the most critical moment of its history because it was invoked on behalf of a policy of aggression; formed in order to meet a specific contingency, it broke down because a new set of circumstances had arisen to which it was not intended to apply; Italy withdrew because she was no longer willing to be used as a tool for Austria's restless ambitions.

At a later date Italy, and after her Japan and Portugal, in virtue of their special obligations to Great Britain, entered the field as combatants on the side of the Entente Powers, while Turkey and Bulgaria joined the two Empires. Not only the greater part of Europe, however, but the Asiatic dominions of Turkey, and Germany's African empire, were gradually drawn into active hostilities. After the war had raged more than two years, Roumania took sides. From the beginning she had declined to support her allies of the Triple Alliance for the same reason as Italy — that the war was aggressive and that she had not been consulted before the decision of Austria and Germany to chastise Serbia was taken. When in September,

1916, Roumania entered the struggle it was in pursuance of national aspirations hitherto obstructed by her traditional enemy, Austria: for her, as for Italy, the war became one for the liberation of countrymen long held under alien Habsburg rule. Finally, early in 1917, the United States owing to repeated invasions by Germany of her rights as a neutral State, made common cause with the rest of the Anglo-Saxon family and its allies in a struggle which had in the meantime been recognized throughout the world as involving issues of the deepest moment for the welfare of mankind.

Out of a Balkan dispute had thus grown a world-war, but of this unparalleled catastrophe the Balkan dispute was not the cause but only the occasion.

This History leaves Germany, as it found her at the opening of the narrative, in the throes of internal convulsion. A hundred years ago her peoples, freed from foreign thraldom, were striving for unity and political liberty. Unity came after another half-century of struggle, but the oligarchic forms of government still persisted. To-day the nation's age-long political aspirations are nearing fulfilment, but the unity which was so hardly won appears to be jeopardized. It is inevitable that the crisis through which Germany is passing at the time these closing words are written (December, 1918) will entail far-reaching departures and transformations, both political and social. Nevertheless, it is justifiable to believe that, under whatever form of government the nation may choose to live henceforth (for the choice, for the first time in its history, is in its own power), the Empire will continue; nay, more, that it will be strengthened in the end rather than weakened, by renovation and adaptation to the imperious demands of a new and, let us hope, a brighter era of European and world civilization.

APPENDIX A

(To p. 394)

THE FRANCO–RUSSIAN ALLIANCE

THE story of the origin of the Franco-Russian alliance and the text of the military and naval conventions upon which it was based is told by the French Government for the first time in a Yellow Book published late in 1918, while this volume was in the press. Serious negotiations with a view to a formal *entente* were begun in 1891, and it is interesting to note that Russia was influenced not only by the cutting of the Berlin–St. Petersburg wire, but by the apprehension that Great Britain contemplated overtures to the Triple Alliance. On August 10th of that year M. Laboulaye, the French ambassador in St. Petersburg, was able to report the Czar's assurance, " Le principe d'une entente cordiale avec la France est arrêté, mais la forme à donner à cette entente est à examiner." Later in the month the formula for an " *entente cordiale* " was adopted: the two Powers were to act together in the interest of peace and devise concerted measures should peace be threatened by the aggressive acts of other Powers. A year later (August, 1892) an undated *projet de convention militaire* was signed by General de Boisdeffre for France and General Obroutcheff for Russia.

Contemplating the eventuality of either of the Powers being attacked by the forces of the Triple Alliance, this *projet* provided that if France were attacked by Germany or by Italy with Germany's support Russia would employ all her available forces against Germany, and that if Russia were attacked by Germany or by Austria with Germany's support, France would employ all her available forces against the same enemy; in the event of the forces of the Triple Alliance, or one of the Powers thereof, being mobilized, France and Russia were to mobilize immediately all their forces and transport them as near to their frontiers as possible; the two allies were not to conclude peace separately; the convention was to have the same duration as the Triple Alliance; and all the clauses of the convention were to be " kept strictly secret."

Although France was pressing the matter forward all the time, it was only on December 15th, 1893, that M. de Giers reported the formal adoption of the convention by the Czar.   In July, 1912, the military convention was supplemented by a naval convention.

APPENDIX B

(To p. 395)

THE RUSSO–GERMAN REINSURANCE TREATY OF 1884–90

BISMARCK's disclosure of the existence of this treaty was made in the *Hamburger Nachrichten* of October 24, 1896, and further articles bearing on the subject appeared in issues of that journal for October 31st and November 12th. The substance of the revelations was published in *The Times* of October 26th, and supplementary statements from Berlin, Vienna, and other Continental capitals appeared in many succeeding issues of that journal.[1]

A large amount of controversy has arisen regarding the treaty, and the chief difficulties involved have been well stated in a discussion printed as an appendix to Mr. C. Grant Robertson's excellent political study, *Bismarck*, published after the present volume was in print.

The terms of the treaty have never been published, but, whatever its character, the arrangement concluded lasted until just before or after Bismarck's retirement in March, 1890. Was the treaty first concluded for three years only, as is widely believed, or was it of six years' duration? If the former, was the treaty of 1884 simply renewed in 1887, or was an altogether new treaty concluded in that year? It is true that in the debate which took place in the Imperial Diet on November 16, 1896, following Bismarck's disclosures, Prince Hohenlohe, the Chancellor, spoke of " the negotiations which took place between Russia and the German Empire from the year 1887 to 1890." It is quite possible, however, that these negotiations, the date of which is so vaguely stated, may have referred to the form which the treaty would have taken had it been renewed in 1890. There is reason to believe that Russia was desirous of having a freer hand in relation to problems

[1] I take this opportunity of acknowledging the courtesy of the Publishers of *The Times* in allowing me to consult many volumes of that journal — some going back three-quarters of a century — for the purpose of verifying facts and dates.

of the Near East.   It is more to the point that the Bismarck articles in the *Hamburger Nachrichten,* as well as the speakers who took part in the Diet debate referred to above, assumed that the treaty abandoned in 1890 was the one concluded in 1884.

A delicate point relates to the date of the treaty of 1884. Was the treaty concluded, as a French writer, M. André Mévil, says, on February 24, 1884, and merely ratified verbally at Skiernievice?

INDEX

Abdul Aziz (Turkey), 126, (Morocco) 429, 463; Murad V, 126; Hamid II, 126, 412, 509.
Abeken, 261.
Aberdeen, Lord, 119, 266 (note).
Achenbach, 15.
Adalbert of Prussia, Prince, 64.
Aehrenthal, Count von, 505–7.
Afghanistan, Great Britain and, 152, 153, 451.
Agadir incident, 465, 488.
Alexander II, Czar, 103–7, 127–31, 135, 140, 149; III, 149, 223, 234, 240, 392–4, 503.
Alexander of Serbia, King, 504.
Alexandra, Queen, 462.
Alfonso, Don, 99.
Algeciras, Conference and Act of, 446–8, 463–4, 473.
Almodovar (d'), Duc, 446.
Alsace-Lorraine, Government of, 48–55, 278–9, 362–5.
Althoff, Dr., 411.
Ampthill, Lord, 201.
Andrassy, Count, 86, 122, 132, 134, 143, 144.
Antonelli, Cardinal, 117.
Arabi, Ahmed, 159.
Arenberg (d'), Prince A., 439.
Arnim, Count Harry von, 91–97, 121, 236.
Arnold, Matthew, 293.
Asquith, Mr., 476, 484, 511.
Augusta, Empress, 224, 227.
Augusta Victoria, Princess (Empress), 231.
Austria and Bosnia and Herzegovina, 120, 129, 134, 485–7, 495; Dual Alliance (1879), 142–6; Triple Alliance (1882), 146, 503, 513, 523; war of 1914, 517–23.

Baden, Grand Duke, 230, 239, 241, 250.
Bagdad Railway, 413–17, 490–5, 499–502.
Balfour, Mr., 416, 419.
Balkan League wars, 510–12.

Balkan question, the, 119–39, 503–23.
Baltic Sea Convention, 462.
Bamberger, Dr. Ludwig, 7, 25, 44.
Baring, Sir Evelyn, 170.
Barth, 177.
Battenberg, Prince Alexander of, 153–6; 229.
Beaconsfield, Lord. See Disraeli.
Bebel, August, 368–71.
Belgians, King of the (Leopold II), 184, 206, 450.
Bennigsen, Rudolf von, 13, 14, 23, 24, 61, 76–8, 285, 296, 374.
Berlepsch, Baron von, 327.
Berlin Congress, 111, 132–41, 388; Memorandum, 122, 126; Treaty of (1878), 133, 502.
Bernstein, Ed., 368.
Bernstorff, Count, 225.
Berchtold, Count, 508, 516, 522 (note).
Bert, M. Chaillez,, 439.
Bethmann-Hollweg, Herr von, as Chancellor, 327–87; electoral reform proposals, 359–62; gives constitution to Alsace-Lorraine, 362–5; Morocco, 468–71; attitude towards Great Britain, 485–97, 510–11; naval agreement negotiations, 487–90, 496–7; Balkan Wars, 511.
Beuermann, 177.
Beust, Count, 85, 86, 261 (note), 267.
Bey, Sadoullah, 133.
Bihourd, M., 430.
Bismarck, Count (Prince) Herbert, 137 (note), 166, 191, 212 (note), 229, 233, 237, 240, 254 (note); Count Wilhelm, 254 (note).
Bismarck, Prince, Fiscal reform and Protection, 1–34; views on labour questions and social reform, 39, 40; attitude towards Alsace-Lorraine, 48–55; Army Bill, 60–64, 100, 114–17; threats of resignation 12, 62, 108; naval measures, 66; monopoly projects, 70–2; attitude towards France, 90–118,

202–6; policy of consolidation, 83, 84, 388, 396–98, 459; Russian policy, 84–8, 121, 141, 388–91; policy towards Austria, 84–6, 513–17; Italian policy, 85, 88–90, 455; " Is war in sight? " scare, 102–8; influence on William I, 101, 225, 226, 256–61; quarrel with Gortchakoff, 104, 105; Triple Alliance, 117, 146, 455, 513–16; Eastern question, 119–70; at the Berlin Congress, 132–42; alliance with Austria, 142–6; reinsurance treaty with Russia, 294, 389–90 395–6, 514, 525; Egyptian question, 157–69; attitude towards England, 164, 165 (note); colonial era, 173–222, 397; and William II, 231–51; quarrel and resignation, 235–50; estimate of character, 253–71; and Morocco, 440; on stability of treaties, 523.

Björkö, Russo-German secret treaty of, 443.

Blonk, 174.

Böhmert, Victor, 4.

Boisdeffre, General de, 525.

Bosnia and Herzegovina, Austria and, 120, 129, 133, 506–8, 517.

Bötticher, Herr von, 53.

Boulanger, General, 114–18.

Bourbon, Don Juan de, 99.

Bourgeois, M., 456.

Brazza, De, 185.

Bremen, enters the Customs Union, 30.

Brenner, Dr. R., 215.

Brentano, Lujo, 38.

Brisson, 114.

Broglie, Duc de, 94.

Bromme, Karl, 64.

Buchanan, Sir Andrew, 152 (note).

Bucharest, Treaty of, 511.

Buchner, 177.

Buckingham and Chandos, Duke of, 187.

Bulgaria, after the Berlin Congress, 133, 154–6; wars with Serbia, 154, 512; later relations with Russia, 503.

Bülow, Prince, 300, 401, 452, 455, 507; as Chancellor, 316, 359, 487; bows to the agrarians, 317–19; attitude on the Polish question, 355–58; characteristics, 316; on Social-Democracy, 372; the Boer War, 403–4; and *Weltpolitik,* 406

(note); Morocco, 432 (note), 434–5, 440–8, 462–3.

Bunsen, 177, 227.

Burckhardt, 176.

Busch, 249, 265.

Cambon, Paul, 421, 476–7; Jules, 467, 469, 470.

Campbell-Bannerman, Sir H., 476–8.

Camphausen, Otto von, 6, 13, 14.

Canning, Sir Stratford, 122 (note), 137; Mr., 122, 263.

Caprivi, Count von, Chief of the Admiralty, 67; opinion of Bismarck, 265; as Chancellor, 240 (note), 248, 272–99; commercial treaties, 285–9; friction with the Emperor, 297; resignation, 299; character, 300.

Carlos, Don, 99.

Carnarvon, Lord, 130, 187.

Cavour, 87, 251.

Chamberlain, Mr., 212, 404, 437.

Chambord, Comte de, 109.

Chanzy, General, 109.

Charles II, King of England, 402.

Charles V. Emperor, 174.

Clarendon, Lord, 66, 152, 194, 211, 422.

Clemenceau, M., 161, 475.

Clive, 174.

Coburg, Prince Ferdinand of, 156, 503, 506.

Conrad, 38.

Constant, Baron d'Estournelles de, 434 (note), 479.

Corti, Count, 132, 133.

Courcel, Baron de, 204.

Crispi, Signor, 134, 135, 147, 239, 388 (note), 397, 453–7.

Cromer, Earl of, 170, 171, 211 (note), 420 (note), 474 (note).

Customs Union, 2, 3.

Cyprus, British occupation of, 132, 134, 139 (note), 414.

Décazes, Duc, 95, 104.

Decken, K. von der, 177, 178, 215.

Delbrück, Rudolf, 6, 11, 12, 29; Hans, 255–7, 265 (note), 267 (note).

Delcassé, M., 421, 425, 430, 432 (note), 433, 436, 444–5, 450, 477–9.

Denhardt, Gustav, 177; Clemens, 177.

Depretis, Signor, 147.

Derby, Lord, 83 (note), 122, 124, 131, 132, 157, 162, 189, 191, 194.

Dernburg, Dr., 333–7.
Deschanel, M., 472.
Dewey, Admiral, 409.
Disraeli, B. (Lord Beaconsfield), 123–38, 152, 167, 255, 414, 480.
Döllinger, Dr., 96.
Donnersmarck, Count H. von, 108.
Draga of Serbia, Queen, 504.
Dubois-Reymond, 227.
Duclerc, M., 161.
Dufaure, M., 108.
Dufferin, Lord, 138.

Edward, King, 405, 419, 421, 435, 452, 458, 461–2.
Egypt, the Powers and, 156–62; British occupation, 162–72, 269, 402.
Ehrenberg, 177.
Einem, General von, 491.
Elector, the Great, 174–7, 232.
Étienne, M., 439.
Eugénie, Empress, 86.
Eulenburg, Count Friedrich, 13–15; Count Botha, 15, 285, 299; Prince Philip, 345.

Falk, Dr., 95.
Faucher, Julius, 3.
Ferdinand, Prince (King) of Bulgaria, 503, 506
Ferry, M., 161–7, 170, 206.
Flegel, Robert, 177.
Flottwell, E. H., 55, 57.
Forckenbeck, 13, 25, 27.
France, recovery after war of 1870–1, 91, 110; resignation of M. Thiers, 93; Clerical agitation, 94; army reforms and expenditure, 91, 99, 379; the "Is war in sight?" scare, 101–8; colonial schemes, 111, 113; Boulangism, 114–18; and Russia, 156; and Egypt, 158–65; and Tunis, 98, 111–13, 135, 147, 185, 269, 434, 454–6; Russian alliance, 394–5, 525; Morocco agreement, 421–49.
Francis Ferdinand, Archduke, 517.
Francis Joseph, Emperor, 85, 144, 147, 239, 392.
Franckenstein, Baron von, 24–5, 117.
Frank, Dr., 369–70.
Frankfort, Parliament, 3; Peace of, 50; Diet of, 84.
Frederick Charles, Prince, 85, 89.
Frederick, Crown Prince, 53, 98, 149, 151, 182, 228, 229; Emperor, 226–

31, 293; Crown Princess (Empress), 227, 228.
Frederick III, 175.
Frederick the Great, 1, 55, 142, 175, 231, 397.
Frederick William II, 2, 55; III, 55, 282; IV, 177, 240 (note), 244, 298.
Frere, Sir Bartle, 184, 187.
Freycinet, M., 109, 112, 114, 158, 160, 161, 206, 393.
Freytag, G., 227.
Friedjung, Dr. H., 507.
Fritsch, 177.
Fuchs, 174.
Fugger family, the, 174.

Gambetta, 105 (note), 108, 137, 159.
Garibaldi, 89.
Geffcken, 227, 231.
George, Mr. Lloyd, 468.
German Empire, Fiscal policy, 5, 10–32; the bubble company era, 7, 8; measures of taxation, 15, 26, 68–73, 349–52, 384–6; political parties, 17, 45, 63, 64, 77, 78, 117, 118, 246–7, 279–80, 327–33, 371–8; railway system, 32, 33; economic progress after 1870, 36, 37; social reforms, 40, 47, 243, 275–7, 302; industrial insurance laws, 42–45, 324; Army Bills, 60, 63, 100, 114, 294–5, 378–9, 384–5; Navy schemes, 64–7, 306–13, 380–3, 482, 490, 496, 497; the Drei-Kaiser-Bund, 87; the "Is war in sight?" scare, 102–8; Eastern question, 119–71; alliance with Austria (1879), 109, 142–6; Triple Alliance, 117, 147, 456, 513–17; colonial era and colonies, 173–222, 272, 309, 329–37, 405, 410, 470; Social Democracy, 279–80, 326, 338, 368–73; syndicates, 355–6; Zabern incident, 365; Agrarian League and movement, 289–92, 317–19; anti-Semitism, 292–3; recent commercial progress, 322–5; recent labour reforms, 324–5; Pan-German League, 398–9, 448, 470; Morocco, 424–5, 428–49, 462–80; Triple Entente, 450–500; Lord Haldane's visit to Berlin, 484–95; Bagdad Railway, 490–93, 499–500; support of Austria's Balkan policy, 506–523; war of 1914, 517–23.
Giers, M. de, 107, 144, 148, 150, 234, 525.

Gladstone, Mr., 122, 123, 126, 134, 138, 162, 164, 193 (note), 206, 207.
Goblet, M., 118.
Goltz, General von der, 140; Admiral, 306.
Goluchowski, Count, 446, 503–4.
Gortchakoff, 84, 105–7, 111, 121, 125, 132, 135, 141, 148, 149, 394, 452, 482.
Goschen, Mr. (Lord), 112, 139 (note), 201 (note), 211 (note), 260 (note), 381.
Gossler, Dr. von, 284.
Gramont, Duc de, 88.
Granville, Lord, 112, 139 (note), 159, 161–9, 187–213, 216, 263, 273.
Great Britain, and Eastern question, 122–41, 152–3; Egypt, 156–61, 268, 402; Cyprus, 132, 134 139 (note), 414; Afghanistan, 152–3, 450–1; cession of Heligoland, 192–3, 273; the Navy, 380–3, 487–90; Bagdad Railway, 413–16, 488–93, 499–500; Morocco agreement, 421–49, 465–80; *entente cordiale* with France, 475–80; *entente* with Russia, 450–52, 505; Triple Entente, 450–500; Lord Haldane's visit to Berlin, 484–95; war of 1914, 522–3.
Greville, Charles, 177.
Grévy, M., 109, 117.
Grey, Sir Edward (Lord), 451, 467–68, 475–6, 499–500, 511.
Grolmann, General von, 55.
Güssfeldt, 177.

Hafid, Mulai, 464.
Haldane, Lord, 446, 476, 484–95, 522.
Hamburg, enters the Customs Union, 30.
Hanotaux, M., 420.
Harden, Maximilian, 345.
Hardenberg, 2, 244, 282.
Hartington, Lord, 129.
Hartmann, Cardinal, 378.
Hasse, Ernst, 399.
Häuser, Rear-Admiral, 306.
Hay, Sir J. D., 428.
Haymerlé, Baron, 132.
Hefele, Bishop, 96.
Heine (deputy), 368.
Heligoland, 67, 193, 194, 273, 307.
Helmholtz, 227.
Hemprich, 176.
Henry of Prussia, Prince, 233, 308, 406, 410.
Herrforth, Herr, 244.

Herwegh, Georg, 312.
Heydt, August von der, 8.
Hinzpeter, Dr., 231.
Hindenburg, 2, 244, 282.
Hobrecht, Arthur, 15.
Hohenberg, Duchess of, 517.
Hohenlohe, Prince C. von, 11, 101, 126, 132, 146, 151, 226, 236, 274, 278, 281, 339–40, 390, 393, 395, 455, 459; Stadholder of Alsace-Lorraine, 52–5; ambassador in Paris, 95–8, 111, 121; and Dual Alliance, 142, 145; and colonies, 182; as Chancellor, 299–314, 396; characteristics, 300–1, 313–14; his Diaries, 344; Triple Alliance, 525.
Hohenzollern, Prince Charles of, 119.
Hollmann, Rear-Admiral von, 306, 308.
Holstein, Herr von, 137 (note).
Hornemann, 176.
Humbert, Crown Prince of Italy, 89.
Humboldt, Alexander von, 176, 177; Wilhelm von, 244.

Imperial, Prince, of France, 110.
Isabel II of Spain, 99.
Ismail Pasha, 157–8.
Isvolsky, M., 505–6.
Italy, Germany's relations with, 85, 88–90; and Tripoli, 113, 437, 451–55, 510; Triple Alliance, 117, 146, 453–7, 501, 506, 522–3.

James II, 294.
Jameson raid, 400.
Japan, war with Russia, 408–9, 442.
Jaurès, M., 479.
Junker, 177.

Kalnoky, 151.
Kardorff, Herr von, 298.
Karolyi, Count, 132.
Kersten, Otto, 179, 215.
Ketteler, Bishop, 275; Baron von, 407.
Kiderlen-Wächter, Herr von, 466–7, 497.
Kiel Canal, 65, 67, 192, 307, 321, 394, 400.
Kiel, Treaty of, 192.
Kielmayer, 176.
Kitchener, Lord, 402, 420.
Kimberley, Lord, 187.
Köller, Herr von, 59.
Kolping, Father, 275.
Kopp, Prince-Bishop, 275.

INDEX 533

Krapf, 177.
Krüger, President, 310, 400, 401.
Kusserow, Herr von, 190.
Kutte, 176.

Laboulaye, M., 525.
Lansdowne, Lord, 421, 477, 494.
Lasker, 24, 25, 28, 33, 79, 396.
Launay, Count de, 132.
Lavigerie, Cardinal, 329.
Law, Mr. Bonar, 494.
Layard, Sir Henry, 135 (note).
Leflô, General, 104.
Leichardt, 177.
Leo XIII, Pope, 116, 218, 276.
Leopold of Belgium, King, 205, 470.
Lette, W. A., 3, 4.
Lichnowsky, Prince, 497, 498 (note),
   521 (note).
Liebknecht, Dr., 365.
Lindequist, Herr von, 336.
List, Friedrich, 177, 415.
Lobanoff, Prince, 503.
Loftus, Lord Augustus, 127.
Loisy, 359.
London, world exhibition (1851), 4.
Lotz, Professor W., 9.
Loubet, President, 421.
Lucanus, Herr von, 247.
Lüderitz, F. A. L., 186–8, 196, 196.
Luther, Martin, 359.
Lyons, Lord, 83 (note), 112, 211, 412
   (note), 428.

MacMahon, Marshal, 93, 94, 107–9.
Madrid, Convention of, 423–4, 438.
Malet, Sir Edward, 192 (note), 312
   (note), 213.
Malmesbury, Lord 124 (note).
Maltzan, 177.
Manteuffel, Field-Marshal von, 52,
   141.
Marchand, Colonel, 420.
Marcks, Erich, 265 (note).
Marquardsen, 78.
Marschall von Bieberstein, Baron,
   249, 279, 299, 315, 396, 401 (note),
   411, 444, 458, 497.
Marx, Karl, 368–71.
Mauch, Karl, 177.
Maurenbrecher, 232.
Méline, M., 438.
Mensdorff, 516.
Metternich (Prince), 281, 397; Count
   Wolff, 467, 495.
Michaelis, Otto, 3.

Mijatovich, Count Chedomille, 154
   (note).
Milan of Serbia, Prince, 120, 154
   (note), 234.
Millet, M. Réné, 439.
Minghetti, 89.
Miquel, 78, 296.
Mohamed Tewfik, 158.
Moldenhauer, 183.
Möller, Eduard von, 49.
Moltke, 60–3, 85, 90, 101, 104, 115,
   118, 235, 253, 415, 481.
Morier, Sir Robert, 98, 103, 126, 224,
   260.
Morley, John (Lord), 181.
Morocco question, the, 422–49, 462–
   80.
Moser, 174.
Moufang, Canon, 275.
Münster, Count, 104, 128, 188, 192.
Mühlon, Dr., 519 (note).
Muravieff, Count, 404.
Mürzsteg, Programme, the, 504.

Nachtigal, Gustav, 177, 197, 198.
Napoleon I, 409; Louis (Napoleon
   III), 58, 82, 86, 93, 110, 230.
Natalie of Serbia, Queen, 233.
Naumann, Dr. F., 41, 373.
Nelson and Tangier, 423.
Nettelbeck, Joachim, 175.
Nicholas, Grand Duke, 130; Czar
   Nicholas II, 394, 404, 480, 443,
   452, 503, 521 (note).
North Sea Convention, 462.

Obroutcheff, General, 525.
Overweg, 177.

Palmerston, Lord, 127, 162, 255,
   259, 380 (note), 422–3, 480.
Paris, Comte de, 114.
Paris, world exhibition (1855), 4;
   Treaty of (1856), 133.
Peel, Sir Robert, 263.
Persia, Anglo-Russian Convention,
   451.
Peter of Serbia, King, 504.
Peter the Great, 127.
Peters, Karl, 177, 215, 217, 335.
Pichon, M., 464, 475.
Pickford, 4.
Pittié, General, 147.
Pius X, Pope, 359.
Platen, August von, 97.
Pogge, 177.
Poland, partition of, 55, 56.

Portugal, treaties affecting, 402, 498; British alliance with, 458.
Posadowsky, Count von, 327.
Potsdam agreement, the, 480.
Prague, Treaty of, 58, 358.
Prokesch, 176.
Prussia, fiscal traditions, 1–5; railways, 32, 33; patriarchal traditions, 40; Polish provinces and question, 55–7, 277–8, 355–8; agrarian legislation, 302; canal construction, 320–1.
Puttkamer, Herr von, 76, 229; Johanna von, 252.

Radolin, Prince, 430.
Ranke, 254.
Raulé, 174.
Rebmann ,177.
Rechberg, 516.
Redcliffe, Lord Stratford de, 414.
Reventlow, Count, 401 (note), 491 (note).
Rhodes, Cecil, 403.
Ribot, M., 394, 455, 479.
Richter, Eugen, 28, 78, 294, 373.
Rickert, 25.
Riemer, Dr., 460.
Robinson, Sir Hercules, 187, 195.
Rodbertus, K. von, 415.
Rohlfs, Gerhard, 177, 179, 215.
Roon, 66, 180, 253, 257.
Roosevelt, President, 411.
Roscher, W., 38, 177, 415.
Rose, 176.
Rosebery, Lord, 430–1.
Rouvier, M., 445.
Roux, M. Charles, 439.
Rozhdestvensky, Admiral, 443.
Rüppell, 176.
Russell, Earl, 65; Lord Odo, 83 (note), 104, 107, 128, 132, 165–6, 184, 201, 211, 255.
Russia, Czar Alexander II of, 103–7, 127–30, 138, 140, 149; Alexander III, 149, 223, 233, 240, 392–4, 503; Nicholas II, 394, 403, 443, 452, 480, 503.
Russia, German relations with, 84–8; French alliance, 394–5; war with Turkey, 130, 131; and Bulgaria, 133, 154–6; relations and alliance with France, 156, 394–5, 525; reinsurance treaty with Germany, 294, 389–90, 395–6, 515, 525; war with Japan, 407–8, 442; *entente*

with Great Britain, 451, 505; war of 1914, 518–23.
Rustow, Pasha, 140.

Sabouroff, M., 146, 151.
Sagasta, 425.
St. Petersburg Agreement, 503.
Salisbury, Lord, 111, 112, 129, 131–5, 193 (note), 216, 381, 391–2, 407, 418, 422–4, 428, 440, 450, 454–5.
Schlagentweit, 177.
Schleinitz, 264 (note).
Schleswig question, the, 58–60, 142, 358–9.
Schlimper, 176.
Schmidt, murder of Captain, 99.
Schmoller, Gustav, 38.
Schnaebele incident, the, 117.
Schön, Herr von, 451, 491.
Schönberg, G., 38.
Schouvaloff, Count, 131, 132, 141.
Schwarzenberg, 516.
Schnitzler, Eduard, 177.
Schweinfurth, 177.
Schulze-Delitzsch, 3.
Selves, M. de., 472.
Sembat, Marcel, 466 (note).
Serajevo murders, the, 518.
Serbia, wars with Bulgaria, 154, 512.
Serrano, Marshal, 99.
Silvela, Señor, 426.
Singer, Paul, 371.
Skiernievice, meeting of three Emperors, and treaty, 150–1, 388, 504.
Skobeleff, General, 149.
Smith, J. P., 3; Sir C. Euan-, 424.
Sombart, Werner, 4 (note).
Sophie, Princess (Prussia), 239.
Spain and Morocco, 423, 425–7, 439, 446.
Stablewski, Florian von (Archbishop), 277.
Stanley, H. M., 185.
Stauffenberg, 13.
Stein, 2, 255.
Stöcker, Court Chaplain, 232, 235, 292.
Stockmar, 227.
Stolberg, Count, 15.
Stosch, General von, 66.
Strassburg, university, 49.
Südekum, 368.
Suez Canal, 124, 169.
Sugiyama, Baron, 407.
Sybel, H. von, 61.

Thiers, M., 82, 91–4, 126, 150, 380 (note).
Tirpitz, Admiral, 308, 312, 341, 490, 496.
Tisza, Count, 510.
Tittoni, 458.
Treitschke, H. von, 184, 282, 298.
Triple Alliance, 117, 146, 455, 501–2, 506, 513–23.
Tripoli, Italy and, 113, 437, 454–6, 509.
Tunis, France and, 98, 111–13, 135, 147, 185, 268, 428, 453–5.
Turkey, war with Russia, 129, 130; war with Italy, 509; Balkan wars, 510–11.
Tyrrell, 360.

Usedom, Count, 88, 258.

Victor Emmanuel, 88–90, 147 (grandson), 458.
Victoria, Queen, 103, 125, 127, 128, 229, 259, 308, 392, 402, 405; Princess (Prussia), 229.
Vienna, Congress of, 55; Treaty of (1864), 59.
Virchow, Dr., 29, 227.
Visconti-Venosta, 89.
Vogel, 177.
Vogué, M., 439.
Vollmar, 368.

Waddington, M., 108, 109, 111, 132, 169.
Wagener, Councillor of State, 8.
Wagner, Adolf, 38.
Waldersee, Count, 235, 236, 270, 407.
Wales, Prince of, 109, 405, 421.

Warren, Sir. C., 196.
Weber, Ernst von, 183.
Wellington, Duke of, 263.
Welser family, the, 174.
Wermuth, Herr, 384.
William I, Emperor, Social Reform Message, 43; visits St. Petersburg, 88; visits Italy, 90; fear of Bismarck, 101; meets Alexander II at Alexandrovno, 141; meets Alexander III in Berlin, 223; death, 223; character, 224–5.
William II, early years, 231; quarrel with Bismarck, 240–9; and Socialism, 241–2; social reform, 243, 275–7; characteristics, 282–3; navy schemes, 305–12, 345, 490, 496–7; personal government, 339–49; Daily Telegraph interview, 346–9; Krüger telegram, 400–1; attitude in Boer War, 346; Weltpolitik, 388–421; approaches to Great Britain, 392–3, 399, 483; visit to Constantinople and Palestine, 411; visit to Morocco, 441–42; relations with Austria, 506–24.
William of Prussia, Prince, 391.
Windthorst, Dr. L., 24, 26, 28, 117, 247.
Wirth, Max, 3, 4.
Wissmann, Hermann, 177.
Witte, Count de, 443 (note).
Wodehouse, Sir Philip, 187.
Wolff, Sir H. D., 136 (note), 138 (note).
Wolseley, General, 162.
Wrangel, General, 328.

Zedlitz, Baron, 284–5.

THE following pages contain advertisements of Macmillan books on kindred subjects.

National Governments and the World War

By FREDERIC A. OGG
Professor of Political Science in the University of Wisconsin

AND

CHARLES A. BEARD
Director of the Bureau of Municipal Research, New York City

Cloth, 8°, $2.50

In this new volume Professors Ogg and Beard give us a fuller realization of the bearings of governmental organization and practice upon public well-being, a better knowledge of the political experience and problems of other peoples, and a new enthusiasm for national and international reconstruction on lines such as will conserve the dearly bought gains of the recent conflict. In dealing, as it does, mainly with a comparative exposition of political institutions, ideals and practices — national and international — this work will enable us to trace their power in contributing to or detracting from human welfare.

A good part of the book undertakes to show what the heritage and genius of the principal peoples lately engaged in the World War have meant in the shaping of contemporary political institutions and ideas. The great changes wrought in governmental organization and procedure during the war are carefully described, beside pointing out clearly the major political problems that remain for settlement during the early years of peace.

THE MACMILLAN COMPANY
Publishers   64–66 Fifth Avenue   New York

The History of Europe from 1862 to 1914

FROM THE ACCESSION OF BISMARCK TO THE OUTBREAK OF THE GREAT WAR

By LUCIUS HUDSON HOLT, Ph.D.

(Yale), Lieutenant-Colonel, U. S. A., Professor of English and History, U. S. Military Academy,

AND

ALEXANDER WHEELER CHILTON

Captain of Infantry, U. S. A., Assistant Professor of History, U. S. Military Academy

With Maps, 8°, $2.60

"Lieut.-Col. Holt and Captain Chilton have written a very useful volume, one that no one can afford to ignore who wishes to understand clearly the causes and meaning of the great war, and they have done it in a manner so admirable and have invested their survey of events with so much interest that their successive chapters are like the unfolding of a mighty panorama."— *New York Times.*

"The plan of the volume is admirable. The mass of historical data is presented clearly and with fine coördination. Military campaigns are not given undue space, that side of the course being left to other departments, but excellent condensed accounts of the successive European wars are included. The chief stress is laid upon the elucidation of international relations and considerable attention is paid to internal affairs in each of the great powers."— *Argonaut.*

A Political and Social History of Modern Europe

By CARLTON J. H. HAYES

Associate Professor of History in Columbia University

Volume I: 1500–1815 8vo $2.25
Volume II: 1815–1915 8vo $2.60

"Here is a history of European affairs that will satisfy the reader whose time cannot be devoted entirely to the subject; a history that the busy man or woman will appreciate as setting before them in not too brief a form the social and political progress of transatlantic nations since the beginning of the sixteenth century."— *N. Y. Times.*

"It gives succinctly the necessary basis of fact for a thorough and intelligent understanding of modern politics and of the great underlying causes of the great war."— *The Nation.*

THE MACMILLAN COMPANY

Publishers   64–66 Fifth Avenue   New York